# What's New in This Edition

- **Hardware**: Evolution and systematic comparison of all bus architectures up to PCI; also SCSI adapters, LAN technology. See Chapter 2.

- **Microprocessors**: Evolution of architecture from the 8088 to the Pentium, local bus and cache technology, internal clock multiplying, RISC/CISC difference and confluence, multiprocessor systems, the future, and more. See Chapter 3.

- **Clock Doubling and Beyond:** Technical details and real-life implications. See Chapter 4.

- **Disks**: Enhanced IDE (mode 3), SCSI-3, PCMCIA, recordable CD-ROM, and super-dense optical storage. See Chapters 5, 9, and 10.

- **On-Screen Video**: Latest standards, display adapter components, whither monitor technology, merging video and PC graphics, video on the PC, 3-D graphics, measuring PC graphics' performance and more. See Chapter 11.

- **PC Character Set**: International characters and double-byte character sets, new Unicode standard. See Chapter 12.

- **Communications**: State-of-the-art in modem standards and specifications, data compression and error correction, synchronous and asynchronous transmission, cable and fiber optic connection to the Super Highway, and more. See Chapter 21.

- **Windows 95**: Evolution and systematic comparison with Windows 3.*xx*, Windows and DOS partnership, 32-bit access, multitasking, Windows 95 interface and architecture, Windows memory models compared, event-driven philosophy, and the programmer's view of Windows. See Chapter 23.

- **Plug and Play**: Underlying philosophy, ISA port address, IRQ level, DMA channel and memory address contention, levels of PnP support, user strategy, impact on system costs, other related standards, and much more. See Chapter 24.

- **Multimedia**: Audio compression/decompression techniques, True Speech, special effects and DSPs, audio synthesis, MIDI, games, CD-ROM, speech recognition and synthesis, Windows sound system, native signal processing, wave guide technology, video capture, video processors, video compression/decompression standards, real-time 3-D, WinG, DCI, multimedia on the LAN and on the digital network, shopping tips, and more. See Chapter 25.

- **PC History:** An inside account of the factors and decisions that shaped the original IBM PC and that determine the architecture of the latest Pentium systems. See Appendix A.

# Peter Norton's Inside the PC,

## Premier Edition

Peter Norton

**SAMS**
PUBLISHING

201 West 103rd Street
Indianapolis, Indiana 46290

**Publisher**
Richard K. Swadley

**Acquisitions Manager**
Greg Wiegand

**Development Manager**
Dean Miller

**Managing Editor**
Cindy Morrow

**Acquisitions and Development Editor**
Sunthar Visuvalingham

**Production Editor**
Carolyn Linn

**Copy Editor**
Keith Davenport

**Editorial Coordinator**
Bill Whitmer

**Editorial Assistants**
Carol Ackerman
Sharon Cox
Lynette Quinn

**Technical Reviewers**
Jerry Cox
Lewis C. Eggebrecht
Nick Stam

**Marketing Manager**
Gregg Bushyeager

**Assistant Marketing Manager**
Michelle Milner

**Cover Designer**
Tim Amrhein

**Book Designer**
Alyssa Yesh

**Vice President of Manufacturing and Production**
Jeff Valler

**Manufacturing Coordinator**
Paul Gilchrist

**Imprint Manager**
Kelly Dobbs

**Team Supervisor**
Katy Bodenmiller

**Support Services Manager**
Juli Cook

**Support Services Supervisor**
Mary Beth Wakefield

**Production Analysts**
Angela Bannon
Dennis Clay Hager
Bobbi Satterfield

**Graphics Image Specialists**
Becky Beheler
Steve Carlin
Brad Dixon
Jason Hand
Clint Lahnen
Cheri Laughner
Mike Reynolds
Laura Robbins
Dennis Sheehan
Craig Small
Jeff Yesh

**Production**
Carol Bowers
Mona Brown
Michael Brumitt
Charlotte Clapp
Mary Ann Cosby
Terrie Deemer
Terrie Edwards
Donna Harbin
Ayanna Lacey
Kevin Laseau
Paula Lowell
Donna Martin
Brian-Kent Proffitt
SA Springer
Susan Van Ness
Mark Walche
Dennis Wesner
Michelle Worthington

**Indexer**
Bront Davis

# Overview

# Contents

# Acknowledgments

My thanks to Scott Clark, Lewis Eggebrecht, and John Mueller, whose efforts and creativity have brought this new Premier Edition to fruition.

I would also like to thank my agent Bill Gladstone, of Waterside Productions, for all of his efforts on my behalf.

Finally, I would like to thank acquisitions and development editor Sunthar Visuvalingham, production editor Carolyn Linn, copy editor Keith Davenport, and technical editors Jerry Cox and Nick Stam for their hard work and dedication to the production of a book of highest quality.

# Introduction

You're about to embark on an amazing voyage of discovery, understanding, and productivity. Welcome!

From the day it first appeared, the IBM PC stirred excitement and fascination: The PC marked the coming of age of "personal" computing, a drastic change from the days when all computers were managed by other people who doled out computer power to users on an as-needed, as-available basis. Today, the PC is the tool without equal for helping business and professional people improve their personal performance and the quality of their work. Students of almost all ages and other home-based users have successfully expanded personal computing into near ubiquity. The exploding home-PC market has accelerated the development of an ever-growing range of applications from word processors for homework, to technologies that allow people to actually work *at* home, to recipes, games, education, and research.

The original IBM PC also spawned a great many other computers—some from IBM, but most from the makers of IBM-compatible computers—that make up the PC family. In fact, when I first wrote this book, it was actually called *Inside the IBM PC*, but the strong influence that companies other than IBM now exert on the PC industry inspired me to change the title a few years ago. "PC" is now universally used in the computer industry to refer to any IBM-compatible computer, and that's exactly how I use the term in this book.

I am excited and enthusiastic about the PC family; I want you to be too. I want to lead you into understanding the workings of this marvelous machine and to share with you the excitement of knowing what it is, how it works, and what it can do. Armed with that knowledge, you'll be positioned to make intelligent decisions about computers for yourself, your family, or your company.

# My Approach

If you know anything about me or the first edition of this book, you know that I made my reputation by explaining the technical wizardry of the PC. In the early days of the PC, that was what PC users needed most—an inside technical explanation of how the PC worked. The world of the PC has matured and changed since then, and so have the needs of mainstream PC users. But I haven't changed my approach, and it occurs to me that you might want to know how *I* look at what I do.

From my perspective, the most useful approach to a subject such as this one has always been to assume that you, my reader, are an intelligent, curious, and productive person. That means that you'll never find me endlessly repeating elementary stuff, as though my books were "for dummies," and you're spared from all the dysfunctional over-simplification and condescension that such writing makes inevitable.

I like to write in the same way that I talk, and you may already know that my conversational approach was something of a novelty back when this book was first published. I don't mind saying that I'm proud to see my basic belief—that people *can* talk about technology like people, not like machines—has been adopted by hundreds of other writers, including my competitors. I think you'll intuitively agree that you'll learn more about your computer from "talking" with me about it than you would if just I handed you pages of technical lists and hieroglyphic diagrams and told you that the test will be on Wednesday. But, when this book premiered, that's exactly what most computer documentation was like.

I would never, of course, suggest that computer professionals have maintained their personal job security by keeping computers as mystical and unfathomable as possible. But I will observe that many companies have experienced notable jumps in productivity at all levels when certain types of technology management people are made obsolete. These companies have taken steps to empower everyday computer users to make many of their own decisions, to solve their own problems. You may not be employed by a large multilevel company, or you may be a student and not employed yet at all, but this book will lead you to the same power and enable you to make the same sorts of productivity jumps by giving you a personal, direct, and complete understanding of your PC.

# About This Book

This isn't a book for people who are having trouble finding the on/off switch on their computers. Instead, it's for people who have enough experience and curiosity to begin examining in greater depth these wonderful machines. My goal is to make understanding the PC easy as well as fun.

This is, more than anything else, a book written to help you learn what you really need to know about the PC. You can successfully use a PC without really understanding it. However, the better you understand your PC, the better equipped you are to realize the potential in the machine and—don't forget this—to deal with emergencies that can arise when working with a PC. After all, when something goes wrong, the better you understand the machine, the more likely you are to make the right moves to fix the problem and reduce its impact on you and your business.

There are many reasons you might want to understand the inner workings of your PC. One reason, a really good one, is simply for the intellectual satisfaction and sense of mastery that comes with understanding the tools with which you work. Another is to open up new realms for yourself. After all, there is plenty of demand these days for people who have PC savvy. But perhaps the most practical reason is the one that I suggested above. By analogy, think back to the early days of the automobile when you had to be an amateur mechanic to safely set out on a journey by car. It doesn't take the skills of a mechanic to drive a car today because cars have been tamed for everyday use. I'd like it to be that way with computers, but, frankly, computing hasn't progressed that far. Today, to safely and successfully use a personal computer, you need some degree of expertise, and the more expertise you have, the better you can deal with the crises that sometimes arise.

Vitally important, too, in today's economy, is the realization that by understanding what goes on inside your PC, you'll be much better equipped to make intelligent decisions when it comes time to pull out your—or your company's—wallet. You won't end up paying for what you won't use, and you'll really minimize your risk of "driving home with an Edsel," when you can look at technological trends and understand where things are and where they're likely headed. With high technology, more than anything else, advances tend to antiquate much of what came before. Last year's innovation will probably be this year's low-end model, and in the grand scheme of things, we wouldn't want it any other way. For you and me personally, however, this type of evolution-by-replacement can make buying equipment extremely stressful. By the time we're finished here, you'll be in a very strong position when it comes time to analyze all of your purchase options and make a purchase choice that will give you the most for your buck—the greatest longevity.

If you're looking for interesting and useful technical information about the PC from the inside out, you won't be disappointed. I am dedicated to making this book a guide to what makes the PC tick. But, just as the hardware has changed drastically over the past couple of years, so has the focus of the user. And, I address both the technology's and the users' changes.

To that end, I divide the material covered in this book into two types: first, the basic principles of theory and operation that I think PC users want and need to know; and second, the more detailed technical information for readers who really want to dig deeper into the underlying processes that get things done inside the PC.

It's easy for you to differentiate between these areas in this book. The sections that contain the heavier, technical stuff are marked with this mechanical pencil icon.

These advanced sections are for anyone who wants *more* than a practical understanding of the PC, or whose practical applications—and therefore, the requirements of their practical understanding—go beyond those of most users. (You know who you are.) When you see this symbol, you either can explore the technical details or skip those sections.

And, while this is primarily a book about PC hardware, you can't completely separate the machine from the software that makes it do what it does. Thus, you'll also find a few sample programs that you can use to show off some of the PC's capabilities, demonstrate and exercise features of the machine, or just have some fun. Most of these programs are written in the BASIC programming language, so it should be relatively easy for you to try out what they have to show you by simply keying them in from the listings that appear.

I also talk a little about the operating systems that perform the housekeeping functions of running the machine and talking to the application software (spreadsheets, word processors, database managers, and so on). I show you some of the most important features of user interface programs, such as Microsoft Windows, that help isolate you from the nuts-and-bolts of hardware operation.

You'll also find, at the end of many chapters, some exercises that you can use to test your understanding or to develop your PC skills. You can try these exercises as you read each chapter or use them for review after you have finished major sections. Simply read through them for additional information or step through them for some hands-on experience or enlightenment.

Some of these exercises involve BASIC programming, but don't let the concept of writing computer programs intimidate you. In the early days of PCs, users relied heavily on BASIC to make their computers perform because there weren't many commercial programs available. And, in the beginning, many of the programs used for business and personal applications were written in BASIC. By writing some of your own simple programs, you can develop a deeper understanding of how the hardware does what it does and can gain an appreciation for the complex, user-friendly, and capable software applications that are so much a part of today's PC.

There have been many different versions of the BASIC language; it even came built in to the *hardware* of the first IBM-brand PCs. A lot of changes and evolution have taken place since then. The version of BASIC that is becoming a wide-spread standard today is called Visual Basic. It's sold by Microsoft, and it lets you to write your own programs with a true graphical interface, just like all of the Windows applications you use every day. A much simpler version of BASIC, QBasic, is still included free with DOS (the Disk Operating System), however, and that's what I use in this book, because everyone with a PC already has it.

# A Maze to Think About

For the fun of it, I wrote a little program in BASIC that illustrates what a lot of life can be like, including learning about PCs. (You can find the listing for this program, called MAZE, in Appendix B, along with all of the longer programming examples.) Figure I.1 shows the program in progress. This program draws two boxes, START and FINISH, and works a path from one to the other. The program doesn't know where it's going, so it winds a random path until it stumbles onto the goal; however, when it gets there, it rewards you with some fanfare (as you can see if you run the full program).

*Figure I.1.*
*The start-to-finish*
*maze in progress.*

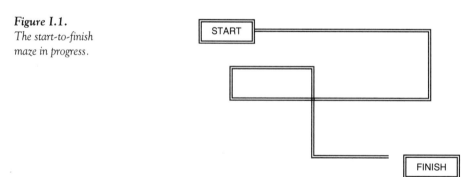

Fortunately, this book isn't like that. I help you work your way in a purposeful fashion toward the goal of understanding the PC. I offer this toy program for two reasons. The first is that you actually may find a use for it—for example, if you ever have to convince someone just how circuitous the path to success can be. The second reason is to provide a little food for thought.

One of the most important and valuable things to learn about your computer is just how complex a task it is to add polish and refinement to the programs it uses. If you understand that, then you're better prepared to understand the realities of the programs with which you work (or any programs you may want to design and build).

# Some Things to Try

Here are some questions to ponder about the maze program before you plunge into Chapter 1 and explore the basic ideas of computers.

1. If you haven't already taken a peek at the maze program listing in Appendix B, ask yourself how complex a task it is to write a program that draws a random path from a box called START to one called FINISH and recognizes when it gets there. Write an outline—in English or in any programming language with which you're familiar—of a program to do this. How can you make sure that the lines don't run off the edge of the screen? How can you know when the program reaches its goal?

2. Take a look at the maze program listing. Is it longer and more complex (or shorter and simpler) than you thought it would be? If you know how to read a BASIC program, or if you can puzzle your way through it, check to see if this version includes any important steps that your outline didn't and vice versa.

3. As the maze program draws its path, it writes over any lines that already have been drawn. What if you want to recognize when you cross an old line or avoid retracing an existing line? Without getting into the programming specifics, try to work out the logical details that would have to be added to the program. What details are most important? Which details might be called icing on the cake? Does adding a feature like this make the program much more complex? What does that suggest to you about the overall character of computer programs?

4. Remember that the basic PC hardware can do almost nothing by itself. Aside from checking itself for proper operation and loading the first information from a disk during the start-up process, the hardware—even though it is extremely powerful—can't do very much without sophisticated instructions. These instructions must be excruciatingly detailed, must account for every conceivable contingency, and must be flexible enough to accommodate a wide variety of end-user needs.

The maze program can become rather complex, as evidenced by the questions I posed above. However, it is functioning at a very high level. The actual instructions that control your PC hardware function at a much lower level.

Suppose that a person whom you do not know is sitting in a chair in the middle of the room. That is all you know about the situation. Now, think about what kind of instructions at the lowest possible level are required to instruct that person to stand, walk across the room, open the door, and exit.

You may be tempted to say something like "Stand up." But wait. I said at the lowest possible level, so you have to go behind the English language (or whatever language this unknown person may speak) to provide more basic instructions.

For example, you need to specify how much electrical energy must be sent along the thousands of nerve paths—and which nerve paths, for that matter—from the brain to parts of the body to cause a specified amount of force to be applied at specific angles to specific muscles to cause the body to stand up. That's one level of instruction. Also going on in the background, however, are many layers of simultaneous instructions, including:

- Interpreting impulses from the semicircular canals to feedback information to the original muscle instructions to maintain balance
- Processing visual information from the eyes to help with balance and direction and to provide modifying instructions to the original muscle movement orders
- Noting and interpreting aural data to turn your spoken instructions into movement data
- Heart rate, breathing, and other basic life process instructions

You get the idea. While your PC is in no way as complex as your body, many of the same programming functions are required. There are low-level, background instructions that keep the machine functioning, there are environmental sampling functions that help it know what is happening (for example, has a key been pressed, is the mouse moving), output processing (for example, updating the display screen, sending information to a printer), and more.

Thankfully, most people don't have to interact with the machine at this level (although designers and programmers do). But, by understanding at least part of what is going on inside the PC, you can have a better understanding of how it works, what it is capable of, what is wrong when it malfunctions, and what to do about it.

Ready to look at basic PC components and hardware types? If so, move on to Chapter 1.

**Note:** The programming information in this book is based on information for developing applications for Windows 95 made public by Microsoft as of March 1995. Since this information was made public before the final release of the product, there may have been changes to some of the programming interfaces by the time the product is finally released. We encourage you to check the updated development information that should be part of your development system for resolving issues that might arise.

The end-user information in this book is based on information on Windows 95 made public by Microsoft as of March 1995. Since this information was made public before the release of the product, we encourage you to visit your local bookstore at that time for updated books on Windows 95.

If you have a modem or access to the Internet, you can always get up-to-the-minute information on Windows 95 direct from Microsoft on WinNews:

On CompuServe: `GO WINNEWS`

On the Internet:

```
ftp://ftp.microsoft.com/PerOpSys/Win_News/Chicago
http://www.microsoft.com
```

On AOL: keyword `WINNEWS`

On Prodigy: jumpword `WINNEWS`

On Genie: `WINNEWS` file area on Windows RTC

You can also subscribe to Microsoft's WinNews electronic newsletter by sending Internet e-mail to `news@microsoft.nwnet.com` and putting the words `SUBSCRIBE WINNEWS` in the text of the e-mail.

# 1

# Inside the PC

When I first started using personal computers, they weren't very common. A few intrepid types had them in their workshops or studies and a few really adventurous people were using them for business applications. For the most part, however, if people were aware of personal computers at all, they viewed them as something that somebody else needed. Moreover, the people who were computer savvy, who really understood the power and functionality computers offered, usually didn't believe the PC or anything like it was up to the job. The experienced believed that only minicomputers or even mainframes from giants such as Digital Equipment Corporation, Hewlett-Packard, Wang, IBM, and others could be trusted with real work.

That's not true today, of course. Personal computers—I'll just call them "computers" from here on— are truly everywhere and are capably handling jobs of all types. Even the most inflexible holdout has had to accept the fact that ubiquitous, powerful desktop computers are many times more powerful than the megabuck marvels of only a few years ago and easy enough for anybody to use.

Still, it's not always obvious just what is inside the box you're using or how these components work together, or even which components you need to own to get *your* job done. In this chapter, I show you how the basic personal computer is designed, introduce you to its major components, and help you find some specifics about the machine you're using. In Chapter 2, "Hardware: The Parts of the PC," I revisit some of these components to offer additional detail on what they are and how they function.

# Computer Components

There are five key parts to a computer. These include the processor (sometimes called the central processing unit, or CPU), the memory (of which there are several types), the Input/Output circuitry (I/O, as it usually is called), disk storage, and programs. There also are other components that form part of the packaging and support for these basics, such as the power supply, the motherboard, the bus (really part of the I/O circuitry), and the peripheral cards. Figure 1.1 shows these basic components and how they fit together.

I take a quick look at each of these key parts here. Later in this chapter, I provide an overview of the basic computer types in common use today. The rest of the book is devoted to delving into the fascinating details of these topics and more.

The motherboard concept was a new one when personal computers started gaining popularity. Before the miniaturization brought on by highly integrated circuits, individual portions of computers were housed on separate boards or even in separate units made up of many boards. Today, however, the majority of the components that make up the computer proper are housed on a single printed circuit board called the system board or motherboard.

**Figure 1.1.**
*The major components
of a PC.*

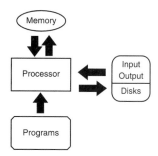

The usual components on the motherboard include the main processor chip and its support circuits, memory, I/O interface (serial port, parallel port, keyboard interface, disk interface, and so on), and bus (which enables the CPU to talk to other components that are not integrated with the motherboard). Figure 1.2 shows a typical motherboard with the major components labeled. I talk a little about each of the major components to give you an overview of their functions.

The processor is the brain of the computer. It is the engine, the working heart, of this marvelous machine. The processor carries out instructions to the computer at a very low level (see the discussion of computer function later in this chapter); in other words, the processor executes programs. The processor is also the part that knows how to add and subtract and carry out simple logical (true/false) operations. In a mainframe computer, the processor often is called a central processing unit, or CPU. In a microcomputer, like a PC, the processor is sometimes called a microprocessor, or just "the processor." This is the term I use almost exclusively in this book. Although early PCs all used a single, uniform type of processor, today's systems use a wide variety of processors.

As I write this, we're standing on the brink of a new era of computing. In fact, the definition of what "PC-compatible" means is being muddied-up again. "PC-compatible" originally meant a computer system that was guaranteed to run the same software and hardware add-ons that an IBM-brand model of personal computer would run. Today, the term is most commonly used to designate the personal computers based on the Intel 86 family as opposed to the Apple Macintosh, with its Motorola-brand processor. "PC-compatible" really means "Intel-compatible" these days. But Motorola, IBM, and Apple Computer have recently worked together to introduce a new family of processors, the PowerPC RISC (Reduced Instruction Set Computer) processors. (You find out more about this new family of processors in Chapter 3, "Brains: The Processors.") These new chips themselves are not inherently compatible with Intel processors, but they can be made to emulate an Intel chip. There has even been discussion in the industry of producing a PowerPC chip that will have a clone of an Intel processor built into it!

Because of how they are designed, these new RISC chips, when they are used with software written especially for them, can provide a tremendous power advantage over the Intel-compatible chips, at the same (or a lower) price. (Actually, most of the software for them will be rewritten, not written: Most of the applications you use every day will very likely be revised into RISC-compatible versions.) It's very likely, therefore, that someday you will own a single computer that works not only with products that are compatible with Intel chips but also with those that are incompatible with them. Whether we'll end up calling these new machines "PC-compatible" remains to be seen. The term is sufficiently generic, however—like "aspirin"—that I expect it will continue to be used in perpetuity.

I talk much more about all of the different types of PC processors and what they can do—both Intel-compatible and the PowerPC—in Chapter 3, "Brains: The Processors."

**Figure 1.2.**
*A typical PC motherboard. (Drawing courtesy of Gateway 2000.)*

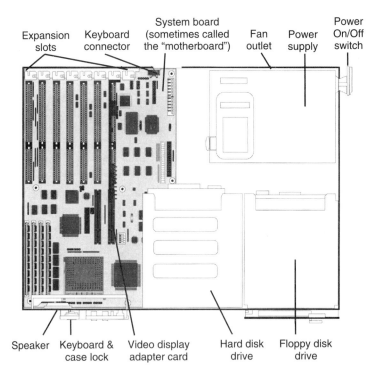

A computer's memory is nothing like a person's memory, so the term can be misleading until you understand what a computer's memory is and what it's used for. Memory is the computer's workplace, the place where all activity happens. It's analogous to the desktop of an office worker, the workbench of a carpenter, or the playing field of a sports team. The analogy to a workbench is particularly good because it helps you understand when the amount of memory is important and when it's not.

Like the size of a workbench, the size of a computer's memory sets a practical limit on the kinds of work that can be undertaken. The number and variety of tools that can be used or made available at any one time is also largely determined by the size of a carpenter's workbench, and the same is true for the computer. That's one reason why you often see computers rated by the amount of memory they have, usually in megabytes (MB)—millions of bytes. (You learn more about measuring memory and other data factors in Chapter 15, "The Memory Workbench.") For example, when the IBM PS/2 model 75 computer was announced, it came with a minimum of 8MB of memory, which today is about the very minimum reasonable configuration. When I first started working with computers, on the other hand, the basic models had as little as 64KB (kilobytes—thousands of bytes) of memory. Things have certainly changed!

Input/Output, or I/O, is how the computer takes in and sends out data. It includes what you type on the keyboard and what the computer shows on the video display screen or prints on the printer. Every time the computer is taking in or sending out data, it is "doing I/O," using I/O devices, which also are called peripheral devices. Among the many kinds of I/O devices is one that's so important to the operation of the computer that I single it out as the next of the five key parts of a computer, disk storage.

Disk storage is a very important kind of I/O. It's the computer's reference library, filing cabinet, and toolbox all rolled into one. Disk storage is where the computer keeps data when it's not in use in the computer's memory. Data can be stored in other ways, but disks are the most practical and important medium for getting the job done.

Programs are the last of the five key parts of a computer. They are what bring the computer to life, make it go, and turn it from a heap of fancy parts into a powerful working tool. Programs are the instructions that tell the computer what to do.

With that simple summary out of the way, let me give you a slightly more detailed look at each of these key parts. Bear in mind that the real details come in the following chapters.

# The Processor

The whole point of the computer is to carry out a series of steps called a program; the processor is the part of the hardware that's designed to do that job. Thus, both the purpose and the internal organization of the computer come together in this key component. To perform this miracle, the processor must have particular capabilities. The first is the capability to read and write information in the computer's memory. This is critical because both the program instructions that the processor carries out and the data on which the processor works are stored temporarily in that memory. The next capability is to recognize and execute a series of commands or instructions provided by the programs. The last is the capability to tell the other parts of the computer what to do so that the processor can orchestrate the operation of the computer. As you might imagine, the way the processor carries out its assigned tasks and the way it acquires these varied skills are complex matters. Chapters 3 and 4 tell you how the processor performs its magic.

Throughout this book, I talk about programs and data. To the processor, the distinction between programs and data is vital. The program tells the processor what to do, and the data is what the program acts on. Most parts of the computer don't make this distinction, as you'll see shortly.

# Memory

Memory is where the computer's processor finds programs and data when it is doing its assigned task. As I have mentioned, the memory is the activity center, the place where everything is kept when it's being used. For you to understand your computer, you must understand that the computer's memory is just a temporary space (like a scratch pad or chalkboard) where the computer scribbles while work is being done. Unlike our memories, the computer's memory is not a permanent repository. Instead, the computer's memory simply provides a place where computing can happen. It is the playing field where the game of computing is played. After each game, the memory playing field is relinquished to the next team and the next game.

While the computer's processor makes a vital distinction between programs and data, the computer's main memory does not. To the computer's memory (and to many other parts of the computer) there is no difference between programs and data—both are information to be recorded temporarily. A piece of paper neither knows nor cares what you write on it—a love poem, your bank balance, or your plans to run for president. It is the same with the computer's memory. Only the processor recognizes the difference between programs and data. To the computer's memory and also to the I/O devices and disk storage, a program is just more data, more "stuff" that can be stored, moved, or manipulated.

**Technical Note:** Most of today's systems come with dedicated processor cache memory (see Chapter 2) which, for reasons of speed optimization, does distinguish between data that is program code and data that is the user's content. However, your computer's main RAM, which is what I mean when I talk about "memory" in general, doesn't know an assembly language command from your Great-Aunt Ada's phone number.

The computer's memory is more like a chalkboard than a piece of paper in that nothing is permanently recorded on it. Anything can be written on any part of the memory, and the writing can be changed in a wink by writing over it. Unlike a chalkboard, the computer's memory doesn't have to be erased before something new can be written to it; the mere act of writing information to the computer's memory automatically erases what was there before. Reading information from the memory is as simple and as straightforward as reading anything written on paper or a chalkboard.

Both the processor and the I/O devices have the capability to read (and write) data from and to the memory.

## Main Memory

Just for the sake of accuracy in the wake of analogies, I should mention that neither the piece of paper nor the chalkboard gives you a very accurate picture of memory. With the exception of a specific type of memory called "static" memory, your system must use power, and dedicated circuitry must dedicate time constantly rewriting (or refreshing) every piece of data that is stored in memory. Many times each second, your system must remind the memory chips, if you will, what data belongs in them. If this refreshing did not occur, the data in memory would simply fade away, unlike the writing on paper or a chalkboard, which remains after you stop writing. In static memory, specially designed chips are able to hold data without being refreshed. However, if power to the computer is turned off, even the data in static memory disappears just as it would from regular, or "dynamic," memory. This susceptibility to lose data in a power loss (or even a power drop, such as a brownout) is called "volatility."

You may also be aware that memory exists—and you'll find it available for portable computers, particularly—which is permanent, for all practical purposes. This "nonvolatile memory" doesn't change or disappear when the power goes off. The processor can write to it and read from it at will, but nonvolatile memory will keep whatever data is stored in it for months, or even longer, without any external power whatever. You'll find a lot more information about these variants of memory in Chapter 15.

The processor and the memory by themselves make up a closed world. I/O devices open that world and enable it to communicate with us. An I/O device is anything, other than memory, with which the computer communicates. As I've mentioned, these devices include the keyboard, the display screen, the mouse, the printer, a telephone line connected to the computer, and any other channel of communication into or out of the computer. It also includes the circuitry that manages the video images on your monitor, even if that circuitry is built onto the motherboard. Taken together, I/O is the computer's window on the world—the thing that keeps the processor and memory from being a closed and useless circle. I give you an in-depth look at I/O devices in the later chapters of this book.

# I/O Devices

In general, I can say that the I/O devices with which the computer works have the user as their real target; they are a bridge between the user and the computer. The computer sees what the user types on the keyboard, the user sees what the computer writes on the printer or displays on the screen, and so on.

However, there is one special category of I/O that is intended only for the computer's private use: the disk storage devices. Information on disk can't be read or written by users and is not for users; it can be read and written only by the computer.

# Programs

Finally, you have to consider software programs. Programs tell the computer what to do. As it turns out, there are two very different kinds of programs, and you'll want to know the difference. There are systems programs, and there are applications programs. All programs accomplish some kind of work. Systems programs help operate the computer itself; in fact, the inner systems of a computer are so complex that you can't get them to work without the help of systems programs. An applications program carries out a task that you, the user, want done, whether it's adding up a column of numbers or checking the spelling of something you've written. In summary, applications programs get our work done, and systems programs help the computer manage itself (and carry out the work).

A few of the systems programs that the PC needs to manage its operations are permanently built into it. These can be called the ROM programs or firmware because they are permanently stored in read-only memory (unlike the rewritable kind of main memory that I've been discussing). These kinds of systems programs do the most fundamental kind of supervisory and support work, such as providing essential services that all the application programs use. These service programs are called the Basic Input/Output System, often referred to as the BIOS or ROM-BIOS.

Other systems programs build on the foundation created by the ROM-BIOS program and provide a higher level of support services. Operating systems, such as the PC's familiar DOS and the new Windows 95, from Microsoft, are examples of these higher-level systems programs that aren't built into the computer. Systems programs are among the major topics discussed in the rest of this book, because my goal is to help you understand the workings and the potential of the PC, both of which are tied closely to the PC's systems programs.

This brief outline of your computer hardware gives you a good starting background. However, there are some additional components that also are important. These are discussed in the next sections. Finally, at the end of this chapter, I explain what it is that the computer—particularly the computer's processor—can and can't do for you.

# Power Supply

The computer is an electrical device. It needs power for all of its components to function properly. And, while you plug the computer into the wall to connect it to 110-volt alternating current, this is not the kind of power the machine uses. Instead, the cord from the wall plug attaches to a power supply, an electronic device that converts the standard household current that runs your vacuum cleaner and microwave oven into a form the computer can use. If you look inside your computer's case, you'll find the power cord plugs into a metal box—usually silver or black—and that the box is quite warm. This is normal, and it happens because the conversion of electricity from what comes out of your wall sockets into the kind of power the computer uses is a process that produces a lot of residual heat. The power supply has always been one of the primary reasons why your desktop computer needs that obnoxiously noisy fan inside it. (There are other reasons, too, which I'll mention later.)

This power supply takes in a nominal 110-volt alternating current (AC) and puts out a 5+, 5–, 12+, and 12– volt direct current (DC). Some newer power supplies output +/– 3.3 volts for components that are designed to maximally conserve power. Direct current does not change directions from negative to positive like alternating current does. Instead, DC provides a constant voltage at a fixed polarity, either positive or negative. Direct current is the type of current supplied by your car battery and is the type of power your computer needs.

Power supplies are marketed in several ways. However, as a consumer of computers, you probably will deal with the power rating of the supply, expressed in watts. A watt is a measure of the capacity of a power device and is the multiplicative product of the voltage and the current supplied by the device. Even though today's devices offer more features and capabilities than ever before, a 150- to 200-watt power supply can operate most personal computers today because of the low power requirements of very-large-scale integration (VLSI) components and other built-in power saving measures.

# Peripheral Cards

As I mentioned earlier in this chapter, the majority of the components that make up the computer proper are located on a single printed circuit board called the motherboard. However, there are times when you need to attach other devices to the motherboard so that they can work with the processor and other computer components. This frequently is done by plugging an expansion card into one of the bus (I/O) connectors on the motherboard.

As you can see in Figure 1.3, traditionally, cards plugged into bus slots have stood perpendicular to the motherboard, but in several new, compact designs a special, single card, called a "riser," is the only card that is plugged into the motherboard perpendicularly. All other peripheral cards plug in to the riser card, perpendicular to it and parallel to the motherboard.

The motherboard on the left in Figure 1.3 is a standard desktop motherboard with room for a total of seven expansion cards. On the right is the newer "riser" card design. In this configuration, the motherboard only has a single slot, into which is placed a riser card. This riser card has three slots on it so that they fit into the smaller case.

**Figure 1.3.**
*Comparison of traditional motherboard to riser card type. (Illustration courtesy of Gateway 2000.)*

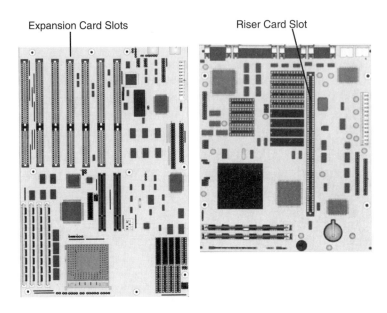

A card (or cards) attached to the main computer in this way resides in a card frame, or cage, that helps protect it, provides physical stability, and helps maintain proper spacing between cards to maximize air circulation (which keeps the cards cool). Early computer designs contained elaborate card cages; today, the card cage may consist of merely a card guide on one end and a screw terminal on the other to hold the card in place.

# Computer Types

Desktop and desk-side computers come in a wide variety of designs. All of them, strictly speaking, are "personal" computers in that they are relatively small, relatively inexpensive, and are designed primarily for use by one person at a time. (There are significant exceptions to this, such as powerful personal computers that are used as data- or application-servers in a networking environment.)

As I mentioned earlier, the "PC" moniker generally contrasts computers based on the Intel 86 family of microprocessors and compatibles with Apple Computer's Macintosh, and other non-Intel systems. This started with IBM's original Personal Computer, which was based on the Intel 8088 processor and quickly labeled "the PC" when it reached the market in the early 1980s. (For more information on IBM's early machines and some general PC history, see Appendix A, "How IBM Developed the Personal Computer.") Even with this limitation, there are many PC designs. In this section, I provide an overview of these basic designs to set the stage for conventions and terms used in the rest of this book.

# IBM PCs, PS/1s, and PS/2s

IBM is the company that started it all. There were many other personal computers on the market before IBM released its version, but these computers lacked the backing of a big company, suffered from shaky or nonexistent standards, or failed to develop a dedicated business following. All of this changed when IBM released its first machine with open architecture, which means that IBM publicly released all specifications for the computer, in the hope of encouraging other companies to produce add-on peripherals.

For a while, only IBM manufactured and sold the PC design. Before long, however, a number of other companies released compatible designs of their own. Today the tables have practically turned; instead of assessing a non-IBM computer on the basis of its compatibility with the original IBM design, many users are concerned with how well these machines match one or more of the industry wide standards. The questions asked today to judge PC compatibility include the following:

- Which bus does it use?
- Which processor does it use?
- What operating system does it use?
- What type of display adapter and monitor does it use?

A few years ago users could have asked simply, "Is it PC compatible?" meaning will it accept expansion cards designed for IBM personal computers and run software written for IBM personal computers.

Then, for a time, it was IBM with its PS/1 and PS/2 designs that stepped slightly away from the original design to produce a machine uniquely its own. Those IBM machines ran software designed for other PCs, but there were some hardware issues—such as display adapter compatibility and bus design—that set off those IBM offerings from other designs generally available in the computer marketplace.

For example, the majority of PCs sold to date have used the ISA (Industry Standard Architecture) expansion and I/O bus. This is sometimes referred to as the AT bus because it is the bus design around which the original IBM PC/AT was built. Those different IBM machines, however, used a proprietary design called the MCA (Micro Channel Architecture) bus, which was not compatible with the more common ISA bus. Because IBM kept the MCA design proprietary, other companies had to pay a royalty to produce MCA cards. Because of the royalty, MCA cards were uncompetitively expensive, and because of that, few people bought them. MCA still exists on the highest end of IBM's personal computer and server offerings, but IBM's PC line has, in the main, either reverted back to the ISA bus or else is moving to the new PCI bus. (Chapter 2 explains much more about bus technologies.)

# PC Clones

The fact, of course, is that most of the personal computers sold today don't come from IBM at all. Most are designed, built, and sold by one of the dozens of high-profile manufacturers who offer a wide range of PCs for business, education, and home use. These machines used to be called "clones" because they were made to look, feel, and work like an IBM PC although they weren't built by IBM. And the clone name seems destined to stay with these machines, even though different manufacturers have moved in their own directions.

This section offers a broad overview of these clones. You'll find more detail in later chapters.

## 386s, 486s, and Pentiums

While IBM's machines have commonly been given names reminiscent of minicomputer designations of a few years ago (for example, PS-2 M57 or PS/2 model 90), most clone manufacturers base their machine names on the type of processor inside. Thus, a Gateway 2000 (the company name) machine designated as a 486DX2-66VLB is interpreted easily: It's an 80486 processor using a DX2 speed doubling design, running at 66MHz, and using the VESA standard of local bus. (More on local bus designs in Chapter 2.)

Another manufacturer might offer a model called simply a 486-33 to show that the machine uses an 80486 processor rated at 33MHz. You don't know what other design features it may have, but you know, at least, what processor it uses.

In fact, the majority of today's PCs are 386-based machines (there are fewer and fewer of these), 486-based machines, or Pentium-based machines. The 486 designs use an 80486 processor, and "Pentium" is the actual name that Intel gave to the successor to the 80486. I give you a lot more information on these processors later in this book, so don't worry if all these numbers are rattling around inside your head. The point is to show you general conventions within the industry so that you can begin to interpret the advertising you read, understand a little better the specifications of your machine, and have some common ground for discussion in the rest of this book.

**Note:** You may be wondering why Intel made such a radical change in naming its most recent chip. Like so many things today, the answer comes down to...lawyers. A few years ago, Intel was growing frustrated with the increasing number of non-Intel clone processors on the market. Most of these were called "386"-something or "486"-something, to better market their compatibility with true Intel chips (which generally cost more). Intel was further frustrated by its inability to trademark the numbers "80386" and "80486." Wanting to avoid giving their competitors any further marketing assistance, Intel decided to name what *would* have been the 80586 with a proper name that *was* protectable under trademark law. So, it came up with "Pentium," which vaguely keeps the sense of the number five (as in PENTagram), and which can legally bear the friendly little ™ symbol next to it.

# Servers and Disk Arrays

Servers and disk arrays can be network configurations of personal computers. Networks enable multiple computers and their users to share processing power, disk storage, printers, and other peripheral devices.

Most of the computers I've already mentioned can function as a server or as the controller for a disk array. In fact, personal computers increasingly are evolving peer-to-peer relationships where the differentiation between clients or workstations and servers that operate as a network repository is diminishing. A server is usually a high-end PC (one with a lot of memory and, very likely, several large disks for storage) dedicated to managing network traffic, storing common programs or data used by many people across the network, or directing communications data via telephone lines or dedicated links outside of the local network.

The server concept evolved because traditional networking required considerable processor power and above-average storage to manage the many requests for processing and data from attached users. Many popular networks today require fewer computer resources than before and, at the same time, individual users' machines have gotten more powerful. The result is that, for many network installations, one machine is pretty much like another, each functioning as a server when it is handling requests from other network machines and acting as a client when it asks another machine for information or processing.

A disk array is a special kind of server that uses a large portion of its processor power simply to manage I/O for a large collection of disk drives. Whereas a regular PC may contain one or two hard drives with a total of 500-1000MB of storage, a disk array may contain many times this much room for programs and data.

# But How Does It Work?

Computers are based on the simple idea of modeling, or imitation. Radios and compact disc players work that way too, and if you pause to think about them, you can understand your computers more easily.

When you play a compact disc, you hear music even though there are no musicians inside the CD player. Instead, the disc contains an electronic model of the sound. Radios and CD players exist because someone discovered a way to capture a mechanical or electronic imitation of sound and build machines that can reproduce the sounds. The same sort of thing goes on with the visual images provided by television and motion pictures.

Computers do essentially the same thing, but they do it with numbers and arithmetic. (Audio CDs, which are digital, do it with numbers, too.) The most fundamental thing that goes on within a computer is that the computer imitates and creates an electronic working model of numbers and arithmetic.

If you set out to invent a machine that can do arithmetic, you must find a way to match what machines can do with whatever the essence of arithmetic is. Needless to say, accomplishing this calls for a great deal of intellectual creativity and some heavy-duty mathematical theory. Essentially, a meeting ground had to be found where math and machines could merge. This meeting ground is binary arithmetic.

The numbers that you and I work with are based on the number 10. The decimal number system works with 10 symbols—0, 1, 2, 3, 4, 5, 6, 7, 8, and 9—and builds larger numbers using these ten symbols. However, there is nothing primordial about the decimal system; you can base numbers on any quantity of symbols. Math theory and some simple exercises demonstrate that you can write the same numbers and do the same arithmetic operations in any number system. However, in order to have enough building blocks—that is, symbols—to work with, you cannot use a number system smaller than 2; the binary, or base 2, number system can capture the smallest essence of what mathematics is.

This is important for hardware designers. It is very easy to make a machine, particularly an electronic machine, that models binary numbers. A binary number is written with two symbols, 0 and 1—just as decimal numbers are written with ten symbols. Electric parts, such as switches, naturally have two states: on or off. It's easy to see that an on/off switch can represent a binary 0 or 1. In fact, it's such an obvious connection that you see the power switches on many appliances and machines, including computers, labeled 0 and 1 for off and on, respectively.

Of course, it's a giant step between seeing that a switch or an electric current can represent a 1 or a 0 and having a computer that can perform complex calculations. However, it shouldn't be too hard to see how this electronic model of a simple binary number can be elaborated upon and built into something much larger. It's like knowing that, after children have learned to write simple sentences, they can grow up to write essays, term papers, and books. A lot of work is required, and many complicated steps are involved, but the basic idea is clear enough.

That's the foundation on which computers were built. Information, including numbers and text and even music, can be represented in a binary form; electronic parts, such as switches that are turned on and off, are binary at heart. Using switches and other parts, an electronic machine can model numbers and all other forms of information.

You can probably imagine that at this level, a computer would be very difficult to use. As it happens, this is how early computer users *did* interact with their machines. They flipped switches on a front panel to set the on and off state of specific memory locations that in turn had to be specified by setting another series of switches in binary format. Imagine preparing your income tax return with that method!

Today, using a computer is much easier because the hardware and firmware (the software stored in the BIOS) are more sophisticated and because you have the benefit of high-level operating system software that enables you to interact with the hardware at a very different level.

# Your Computer: Exploring What You've Got

What kind of computer do you have? Now may be a good time to conduct a little inventory of your system. If you already know about your computer—if you know what kind of processor, how much memory, the type of display, and so on, that it has—you can skip this section. If, on the other hand, you are interested in the things I have discussed so far but don't have a clue about how your computer fits into it all, read this section to know more than the average user.

First, you might discover down the road that you will want to have easy access to the information you're about to uncover. If you like, use a piece of paper to design a simple chart, such as the one in Figure 1.4, to help you keep track of the various features of your machine. The sample shown here includes more detail than I cover in this section, but you can fill in the other blanks as you read through other sections of this book.

*Figure 1.4.*
*A sample personal computer*
*inventory sheet.*

Personal Computer Inventory

| | |
|---|---|
| Manufacturer | |
| Model | |
| Case Design | |
| CPU | |
| System Speed | |
| BIOS | |
| Base Memory | |
| Upper Memory | |
| Floppy A: | |
| Floppy B: | |
| Hard Disk | |
| Network | |
| Mouse | |
| Display Adapter | |
| Monitor | |
| Other adapters | |
| Operating System Version | |

Let's start by issuing a few DOS commands to see what you can learn about your system. Turn on the computer and wait until the DOS prompt is displayed. This should be something like:

C:\>

If your computer is configured to start Windows or another user interface automatically, use the appropriate command to return to DOS. In Microsoft Windows you click on the File menu, choose Exit, and then press Enter when Windows asks for confirmation that you want to leave Windows.

Type the following:

```
VER
```

When you type a command in DOS, you need to press Enter or Return after typing the command. That tells DOS you have entered all of the letters that make up the command. When you press Enter, DOS starts processing the command.

You should see a display similar to this:

```
MS-DOS Version 6.22
```

Your version number may be different from this, but this command tells DOS to display its version number. Write down the results in the appropriate column of your computer inventory chart. This gives you some insight to the machine you are using. If your DOS is earlier than 6.0, it probably has been a long time since your system was updated. Your computer may contain a lot of relatively old software, and it is time for a general housecleaning and updating.

If the version is 6.0 or later, your system has been updated fairly recently (particularly if it says 6.22). This means the rest of the software you are running probably is current as well. DOS 6.22 is the latest version of DOS available as this book goes to press.

What else can you learn about your system? Do you know how large a hard drive you are using or how much memory you have? Use the CHKDSK command at the DOS prompt to find out. You should get a display similar to this:

```
Volume SHC created 10-11-1994 12:08p
Volume Serial Number is 2950-15EB

340746240 bytes total disk space
48758784 bytes in 8 hidden files
1409024 bytes in 170 directories
281346048 bytes in 3330 user files
9232384 bytes available on disk

8192 bytes in each allocation unit
41595 total allocation units on disk
1127 available allocation units on disk
655360 total bytes memory
615264 bytes free
```

It means one of two things if you receive an error message, such as Bad Command or File Name, when you issue a DOS command. Either the files required by the command are not on your system, or (more likely) they reside in a subdirectory that is not part of your current path. If you receive an error message, locate the directory that contains your DOS files (normally C:\DOS) and use the CD command—for example, CD C:\DOS <enter>—to make that directory the default. Then try the command again.

The CHKDSK (Check Disk) command, a part of DOS, examines your hard drive for error conditions (although it is no substitute for a really thorough disk utility) and reports the total size of the disk, how many files are stored there, and the space remaining. Additionally, CHKDSK reports on the total amount of conventional memory in your system and tells you how much is still available. In the example, a total of 655,360 bytes of conventional memory exists and 615,264 of it is available for use. (This test machine also contains another 16MB of extended RAM, but CHKDSK doesn't report that.)

**Note:** If you are using a DOS Version greater than 6.0, you will likely see a message at the bottom of your screen that recommends you use the SCANDISK command if you want to search your disk for errors. This is good advice, and SCANDISK is a utility program that was added to DOS when Version 6.0 was released. It still doesn't perform the kinds of advanced error-elimination that a utility like Norton Disk Doctor can do, but SCANDISK is, at least, a more powerful problem-solver than the older CHKDSK command.

You can also find out something about the way your system is using its upper memory, with the MEM command, also a part of DOS. In its simplest form, MEM reports on available conventional and upper memory. Type the following:

```
MEM
```

You should get a display similar to this:

```
Memory Type        Total  =  Used  +   Free
---------------    -------   -------   -------
Conventional        640K      147K     493K
Upper               131K      131K       0K
Reserved            384K      384K       0K
Extended (XMS)   15,229K   14,205K   1,024K
---------------    -------   -------   -------
Total memory     16,384K   14,867K   1,517K

Total under 1 MB    771K      278K     493K

Largest executable program size      493K (504,320 bytes)
Largest free upper memory block        0K      (0 bytes)
MS-DOS is resident in the high memory area.
```

Now you know a little more about the internal workings of this particular machine. You know the largest executable program size, for one thing. Notice that when CHKDSK was run, a larger amount of available RAM was reported. This is probably because the available RAM is broken up into more than one segment and programs running under DOS need contiguous memory to execute. In this case, 504,320 bytes is the largest program you can run.

With MEM you also get a report on memory above 640KB. This machine has a total memory of 16MB, as you can see from the MEM report. Some of the conventional memory (between 0 and

640KB) is in use, but there is some available memory in this area. However, all of the memory above 640KB is in use on this machine. That's because this report was generated inside a DOS partition within Microsoft Windows. When you start Windows, all available memory is taken over so that Windows can manage it for you.

Your MEM report may not look exactly like this, but it should be similar. This sample report was done in DOS 6.2; if you are using an earlier version the format is different. The report varies with the amount of memory in your machine, what software is running, and so on.

The MEM command has a number of switches you can use to get different information. For example, to find out what programs are running where, use this version of the command:

MEM /C

Try it on your machine and see what happens. It is an interesting way to look into your computer's memory and find out what is running there. Notice that you have discovered a fair amount of information about your computer without really looking at the physical computer. You have used built-in features of the machine to tell you what you want to know. Isn't that what computers are supposed to do anyway, relieve you of redundant, menial tasks?

**Note:** Incidentally, if you find that your MEM /C command results in more information than will fit on your screen, the information at the top will scroll out of view. Type the command

MEM /C /P

and when the first screen of information is full, your computer will display the "Press any key to continue..." message at the bottom of the screen and wait. Press any key, and the remainder of the information will be displayed.

Now, let's go a step further. If you are running Windows 3.1 or DOS 6.0 or later, you have another built-in utility that can tell you a lot more about your machine. Type the following command at the DOS prompt and see what happens:

MSD

This is the Microsoft System Diagnostics, a utility that scans your system hardware and software and displays a summary screen like the one in Figure 1.5.

This is an extremely valuable report, and you can click on any of the topic buttons to open windows with additional information. You can see from Figure 1.5 that the computer is a Gateway 2000 with an 80486 processor. You also can see the amount of memory, the type of video display, the operating system version, and more. Again, if you are running a version of Windows before 3.1 or DOS prior to 6.0, you do not have access to MSD. If you have it, it is an easy way to learn some interesting information about your computer; if you don't have it, you still can get a lot of this information in other ways. I show you how a little later. (Incidentally, you may have more than one copy of MSD on your hard disk, because it can be installed with DOS and with Windows. Check to make certain that you are using the latest version you have. If you have Windows 3.11 or later and DOS 6.0, the version in your Windows directory will be the newest. If you have a version of DOS later than 6.0, and you only have Windows 3.1, the DOS version will be the newest.)

**Figure 1.5.**
*An MSD screen.*

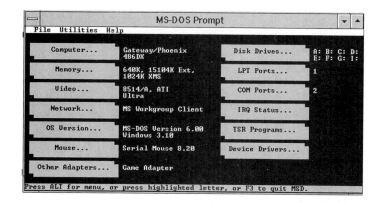

What else do you need to know about your system? You might be interested in the type of keyboard you have. There are two basic types with an almost unlimited number of variations on each. The original PCs used a keyboard with about 83 keys, similar to the one in Figure 1.6.

**Figure 1.6.**
*An 83-key PC keyboard.*

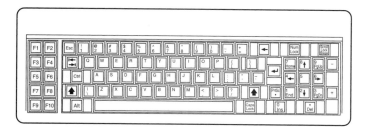

Some keyboard manufacturers still produce a keyboard similar to this one for people who simply don't want to take up a lot of desktop space. The enhanced keyboard (see Figure 1.7) is almost universally found on newer machines. This keyboard is larger and has about 101 keys. When you see computer advertisements that say a system comes with a "101-Keyboard," you'll know that you'll be getting the larger variety.

**Figure 1.7.**
*An enhanced 101-key PC keyboard. (Drawing courtesy of Gateway 2000.)*

What type of keyboard does your computer have? How does it differ from the samples shown here? Write down a description or model number in the space available on your computer inventory sheet. (You'll likely find the model name and number on the bottom of the keyboard itself.)

Later in this book, I'll guide you through taking the cover off your machine for some real "inside" information. For now, let's focus on what you can learn from the outside.

When you look at a desktop PC, you see three main physical parts. First, there is the box, called the system unit, which holds most of the computer. Next is the keyboard. Finally, there's the display. All PCs are relatively small, but the smallest ones sit right on your desk, with the display on top of the system unit. (The portables, of course, have their displays built into the system unit, as have one or two rather odd-looking desktop models from Compaq and other manufacturers.) Larger computers stand upright on the floor, in what is called a "tower" configuration.

Take a look at the system unit case of your PC. There are five general types of nonportables, which I talk about at length in Chapter 2: desktop, mini-desktop, slimline desktop, tower, and mini-tower.

If your machine is designed to sit on the floor, like the one in Figure 1.8, it is a tower.

**Figure 1.8.**
*A desk-side tower PC.*

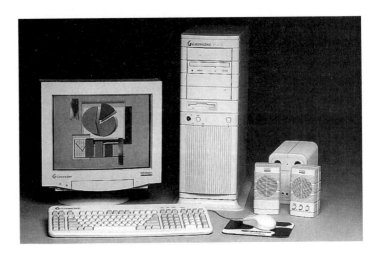

Notice that a lot of users place desktop machines on the floor instead of on top of the desk. If you are using a tower, the disk drives are oriented so that the floppies are inserted horizontally, parallel to the floor. If yours is really a desktop machine sitting on its side on the floor, it's a good bet that the floppies are inserted vertically, perpendicular to the floor. What kind do you have?

**Note:** In fact, when you see the word "desktop" in a computer system advertisement, it's referring to the fact that the case is designed to be positioned horizontally, as opposed to the vertical "tower" position. However, many desktop units can be set vertically on the floor. Before doing so, ask your manufacturer if a special stand is needed to allow proper air-flow beneath the unit. Also be aware that if your system has a CD-ROM drive that does not use a tray to hold the CD , a vertical orientation will contribute to unnecessary wear.

The advantage to the tower design is obvious if you want to place the system unit on the floor. The tower is oriented so that the disk drives are easy to access. And, when you place the main system unit on the floor, you clear up a lot of desktop space. Tower designs always have more potential for expandability than desktop units. This means additional bays for internal storage devices like hard drives and tape drives, as well as a larger power-supply to guarantee adequate power is available to support a fully utilized tower.

The disadvantages to the tower case include its size, if you have limited room around your desk or if you sometimes move your office computer from desk to desk, and its cost. Most manufacturers extract an additional fee to package the computer components in a tower instead of one of the desktop designs. This is usually minor, in the neighborhood of $100.

A full-size desktop machine looks like the one in Figure 1.9. It has room for three or four disk drives that you can access from the front panel and one or two internal bays to hold a hard drive. There also is probably room for as many as eight expansion cards.

This is more or less the "standard" PC case, and it can take on several styles, depending on the manufacturer. The advantage to this case design is it is big enough to hold a reasonable number of expansion cards and disk drives, yet small enough to sit on your desk with the monitor on top and the keyboard in front. As the standard PC case, the full-size desktop enclosure usually is included in the price of the basic machine; you don't pay extra for this case design.

The disadvantage to this design is also its size. For many users, it is too tall to sit on the desk with the monitor on top; for many people, the size of this case places the monitor too high for comfortable viewing. And, because it is designed to sit on the desk, it isn't always convenient to put it on the floor. As I mentioned, you can do it, but the disk drives are oriented the wrong way when you do this. Furthermore, when you purchase a complete system designed around the standard, full-size case, the monitor and power cables may be too short to reach the system case if you place it on the floor.

**Figure 1.9.**
A *full-size desktop computer*.

There also is a compact desktop case that is popular today. These look similar to the one in Figure 1.10.

**Figure 1.10.**
A *compact desktop computer*.

The advantage to this design is that the computer takes up a minimal amount of desk space, and it also isn't very tall, so it's easy to sit a monitor on top without having to stretch your neck to view it. The disadvantage is that there may be as few as two drive bays accessible from the front. There may be only one or two drive slots inside also, and you may have room for only two or three expansion cards. However, motherboards designed for these compact cases frequently have more built onto them, so you may not miss the additional expansion slots available in the bigger cases.

That's enough for now. If you've stepped through this series of investigations, you probably know a lot more about your computer than you did when you started. Keep your personal inventory sheet handy. You'll use it later to refer to what you already know and add to it in future hardware discussions.

Following are a few additional exercises for you to try if you want to play some mental games and test your understanding of computer theory. In the next chapter, I delve a little deeper into computer hardware theory and help you take a closer look at your machine.

# Some Things to Think About and Try

1. I've said that computers model arithmetic just as radios and compact disc systems model sound. Are there other machines that work by modeling? You could say that television models both sight and sound. Do our computers model more than numbers?

2. Suppose that electrical switches were somehow completely different than they are. Instead of having two settings or states (on and off), they always had three states. Would it still be possible to make a calculating machine out of them? Would anything be fundamentally different or would the details just change while the principles stayed the same?

3. List any computer programs with which you're familiar. Which ones would you categorize as systems programs and which as applications programs? Is there a strict dividing line between the two groups? Are there programs that have characteristics of both?

# 2

# Hardware: The Parts of the PC

In the previous chapter you learned about the major components of a PC system as a set of input/output devices and the main system unit. The most common input/output devices are the keyboard, mouse, display monitor, and printer, which all attach to the main system unit. The main system unit is the heart of any PC system. It contains the microprocessor, high-speed memory, low-speed memory devices, input and output adapters, and expansion slots and ports that permit the system to attach to the other system components and be expanded. This chapter concentrates on the system unit's hardware, especially its adapters and ports, and the enhancement features that can be installed inside the main system unit.

# Hardware Components of a Computer System

One way to look at a PC system's hardware components is to ignore the physical packaging and look at it from a hardware functional block point of view. This results in a slightly different view of the PC than presented in Chapter 1, where the functional blocks were processor, memory, I/O devices, disk storage, and programs. Here I add the concept of busses, adapters, ports, and expansion slots. In general, these components are the hardware "glue" that supports the building of the functional blocks described in Chapter 1. A basic PC system has eight major hardware elements:

1. A processor. In most PCs today this is an Intel 486 or Pentium microprocessor, or one of the Intel-compatible processors now available from several companies.

2. A set of input and output devices, including devices such as a keyboard, mouse, scanners, CD-ROM drives, and bar-code readers. The most common output devices are printers and display monitors. These devices attach to the microprocessor through ports or adapters that attach to the system unit's microprocessor busses.

3. A set of high-speed memory and slower storage devices to save and retrieve programs and data. Later you will learn there is a hierarchy of storage in a computer and its access speed, location, and use is dependent on the speed at which the microprocessor needs the data or program.

4. A bus or set of busses that connect the microprocessor to its memory and to the adapters that enable connection to other devices through their ports or expansion slots. The busses can be thought of as the electronic highway that interconnects the hardware components of the PC. Often a system has multiple bus types in a single system design and has devices that "bridge" between the bus types. The system's busses are a very important feature, defining system performance and adapter compatibility, and are covered in much greater detail later in this chapter.

5. A set of adapters that enables the microprocessor to communicate with and control I/O or storage devices. These adapters are a set of hardware circuitry that attach to the system's busses and convert each bus to an interface port supporting the attachment of specific I/O

The next few sections provide an overview of the various standard devices that connect to your computer. First, I talk about external devices, such as the display, keyboard, and mouse. Next, I cover internal devices, such as disk drives and processors. Again, these sections just provide an overview— most of the devices covered here have complete chapters devoted to them later in the book.

# Display

The primary output device for the PC system is the display device. In most desktop or tower PCs, the display device is a Cathode Ray Tube (CRT) monitor. In notebooks, it is often a flat panel device called a Liquid Crystal Display (LCD). The term *monitor* is used to describe the CRT display because it is similar to a TV monitor that is used to monitor a TV signal without using a TV channel tuner. This display monitor device is very similar to your TV, but is designed to be viewed at a much closer distance and has a much higher resolution. In addition, the screen data is displayed at much higher rates, typically more than 72 frames per second. Your TV displays images at only 30 frames per second. Like TVs, the PC display monitor's size is specified by the diagonal measurement of the viewing surface. Typical PC systems today use 14-, 15-, and 17-inch diagonal displays. Larger displays are available but are very costly. High resolution and high refresh rates are needed to display computer-generated text and images that do not flicker and appear realistic when viewed at close range. Most modern PC displays are able to display images with pixel resolutions in the 1024×768 range. This means 768 horizontal lines where each line contains 1,024 picture elements. A pixel is defined as the smallest single picture element that can be created and displayed by the system and display monitor.

The display monitor is attached to the computer through a short cable attached to the system unit's display adapter port. Inside the system unit, a display adapter attaches to the system bus. The display adapter is either integrated on the system's motherboard with the processor or installed as a separate adapter board in one of the motherboard's expansion bus slots. More on displays and display adapters in Chapter 11, "On-Screen Video."

# Keyboards

Keyboards attach to the system unit through a special keyboard port. Two types of keyboard ports exist on PCs: PS/2 keyboard ports and PC AT keyboard ports. The primary difference between the two ports is the actual port connector used. IBM redefined the connector to a micro DIN type as compared to the Mini-DIN connector on the PC AT. DIN connectors are small circular connectors designed to accept the keyboard's cable. The older DIN connector is large, approximately .5 inches in diameter, and the Micro DIN is approximately .25 inches in diameter. Often keyboards are sold with adapter plugs that can adapt the keyboard to either type of keyboard port. Inside the keyboard is an 8-bit microprocessor that is programmed to continuously scan the keyboard and report key presses and releases to the PC's keyboard adapter, which is integrated on the system unit's main board (some-

devices. For example, a PC serial port adapter attaches to a PC bus and creates a COM (Communications) port where a modem can be attached. The adapter is thus the bridge between the PC's bus and the device that needs to be attached to the PC. Adapters may "integrated" (on the PC's motherboard) or on adapter boards that plug into expansion slots.

6. Ports are hardware interfaces (physical connectors) created by the adapters supporting t attachment of I/O devices.

7. Expansion slots are physical connectors where adapters can attach to the PC's busses so that the PC can be configured with a variety of adapters during manufacturing or later the user/owner. Expansion slots permit easy expansion or upgrading of a PC system with new I/O devices and/or memory.

8. Low-speed storage devices where data and programs are stored long-term. This includes nonvolatile magnetic media and optical media storage such as hard drives, CD-ROMs, floppy disks.

The simplified block diagram in Figure 2.1 illustrates the basic elements in a typical PC system. dotted-line box contains those elements that are inside the PC's system unit.

**Figure 2.1.**
*A simplified block diagram of a PC system.*

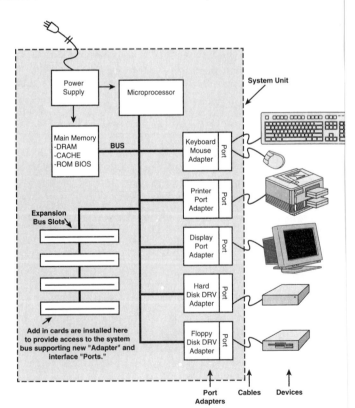

times called the motherboard). This keyboard adapter is actually another 8-bit microprocessor that communicates with the keyboard's microprocessor and sends the received keystrokes to the main processor over the system unit's bus. Keyboards are covered in greater detail in Chapter 13, "Keyboarding."

# Printers

Printers attach to the system unit through a parallel port, sometimes called the printer port. The term *parallel port* is derived from the fact that data is transferred 8 bits at a time in a parallel fashion to the printer, as compared to the keyboard port where data is transferred in a serial mode, one bit at a time. The printer or parallel port is sometimes referred to by a third name, Centronics printer port. Early printers manufactured by a company called Centronics defined a parallel port interface for their printers and this interface was selected by IBM on the original PC. Since the interface is a generalized parallel port, it is often used to attach other devices. Most PCs come with parallel or printer ports as standard; sometimes the parallel port adapter is integrated on the main system unit's main board, and sometimes it is on an adapter board installed in one of the expansion bus slots. Often—to save expansion slots—the printer port function is included on a multi-I/O port adapter board supporting several commonly used ports and adapters.

Three basic types of printers dominate the PC market: wire matrix impact printers (often called wire dot-matrix impact printers), laser printers, and ink jet printers. There are other technologies, but they have relatively limited applications and markets.

# Mouse

With the advent of graphical-user interfaces, such as Microsoft's Windows, the mouse has become the preferred input device for user navigation through an application. The mouse pointing device can attach to the system unit in one of three different ways. When IBM introduced the PS/2 systems, it defined a special mouse port using a micro DIN connector on the main board. The adapter was the same 8-bit microprocessor that supported the system's keyboard. On most PC AT systems, the mouse is attached using one of the two PC asynchronous communications ports, or COM ports. The mouse can also be installed in one of the PC expansion bus slots using a "bus" mouse adapter board. The mouse operates by detecting motion on a surface and sending tracking information to the mouse port or serial port.

# Other Ports and Adapters

Most PC systems today come with two serial communication (COM) ports and a game port. As mentioned earlier, often one of the serial communications ports is used to attach the mouse pointing device. These serial ports support data rates up to 115 kilobits/second using an asynchronous start/stop serial protocol. This protocol frames the serial data that is transmitted over the interfaces so that it can be recovered at the receiving end. The electrical interface is called an RS-232-C standard interface. The two COM ports are accessible at the rear of the system unit as either 9-pin or 25-pin D shell connectors. The COM ports are typically created using a 16550 UART (Universal Asynchronous Receiver Transmitter) chip attached to the processor's bus. Older systems and some low-cost designs still use an older devices called the 8250 and 16450 UARTs. Sometimes the 16550 chip is integrated on the system unit's main board, but most often it is installed on an adapter board in one of the bus expansion slots. Often it is combined with other adapters on a single board called a multi-I/O adapter board. The game port connector is often on the same multi-I/O adapter board. The PC's game port supports two resistive sensing potentiometer joysticks, each with two fire buttons. The joystick's position is determined by sensing the position of the variable resistance potentiometers built in to the joysticks. The joysticks are attached via a cable connecting to a 15-pin D shell connector at the rear of the system. Some systems do not come with joystick ports or require that an internal cable and connector be added inside the system unit to gain access to the joystick ports. The COM ports and game ports are covered in more detail later in this chapter.

# The PC System Unit

It's probably obvious now that most of the intelligence and functioning of a PC system resides in the system unit. All external input/output devices attach to the system unit; upgrade and expansion features are installed in the system unit. The system unit is the heart of the PC system. Figure 2.2 is a detailed view of the insides of a desktop PC system unit. In the upper-right corner is the system power supply and, in front of it, several drive bays. The drive bays are designed to accept hard disk drives, floppy disk drives, and CD-ROM drives of various physical sizes. The motherboard is installed on the base of the system unit, with its processor, cache memory, system DRAM, core logic chip set, integrated adapters and ports, BIOS ROM, and expansion slots. Figure 2.2 illustrates three adapters/ports installed in the expansion slots: a display adapter, a multi-I/O port adapter, and a local bus IDE or hard disk/CD-ROM drive adapter. What is actually in a PC system unit depends on the PC's packaging style and its bus architecture. For the moment I'll leave the issue of bus architecture and concentrate on the major elements in the system unit. These elements are independent of the packaging style of a PC system unit. The list follows:

- A power supply that converts standard wall outlet Alternating Current (AC) voltage to the Direct Current (DC) power voltage levels required to run the system unit.
- Drive expansion bays for
  a. one or more floppy disk drives (either 3.5-inch or 5.25-inch devices)
  b. one or more hard drives (either 3.5-inch or 5.25-inch devices)
  c. one or more CD-ROM drives (5.25-inch devices)
- Most importantly, a motherboard containing a microprocessor, system memory, and integrated adapters and ports. In Figure 2.2 the motherboard shows the keyboard and mouse ports as integrated adapters.

- Adapter boards are installed in the motherboard's expansion slots. In Figure 2.2, three adapter boards are installed. One is a multi-I/O adapter board supporting two serial COM ports, a parallel port, a floppy disk port, and a game port. A second adapter board is the display adapter and the third adapter board is a local bus IDE port used to connect the hard drive and CD-ROMs to the system. Basically, all PC package styles contain these same basic functional elements. In some designs, one or more of the three expansion bus slot adapters may be integrated on the main motherboard. Multi-I/O board designees are most common in "clone systems," whereas some PC suppliers such as Compaq and IBM have integrated the I/O functions on the motherboard.

*Figure 2.2.*
*Inside a typical PC desktop system unit.*

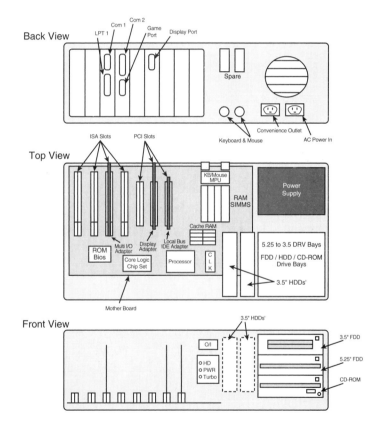

# PC System Unit Packaging Styles

Before we get into the details of the hardware elements of the system unit, I would like to briefly cover the most basic packaging styles used by PC systems. PC system units have evolved to a number of PC system unit packaging styles, primarily to support different levels of expansion capability and specific ergonomic needs of the users.

For desktop designs, the packaging of the PC has changed very little over its 14-year life. As illustrated in Figures 2.3, 2.4, and 2.5, the PC XT, PC AT, and Baby AT desktop systems' styles have changed very little over time. System developers have maintained the basic design and simply dress up the systems with unique front bezel designs and custom colors and logos. The basic layout and partitioning of function usually remains intact. Over time, other mechanical packages have evolved to meet specific needs not addressed by the basic desktop design. The tower package illustrated in Figure 2.6 moved the PC system unit from the desktop to the floor and added significant expansion capacity. This included space for additional disk drives and hard drives and in some designs, additional bus expansion slots. Tower designs often had larger power supplies and additional cooling fans to support these expansion features. Tower package designs are often used as servers in network environments, due to their ability to support large numbers of hard disk drives.

**Figure 2.3.**
*PC XT packaging style.*

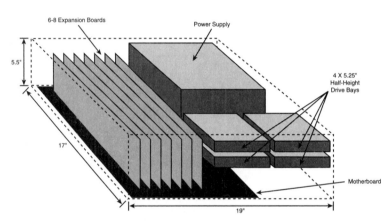

**Figure 2.4.**
*Full-sized "original" PC AT packaging style.*

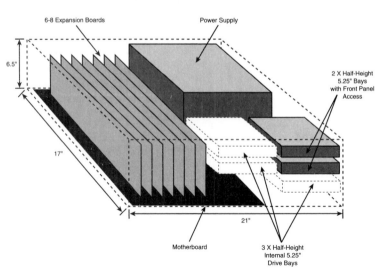

**Figure 2.5.**
*Baby PC AT packaging style.*

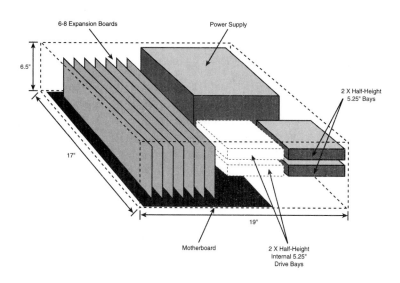

Mini Baby AT Style PC AT Case

6-8 Expansion Boards

Power Supply

6.5"

17"

19"

2 X Half-Height 5.25" Bays

Motherboard

2 X Half-Height Internal 5.25" Drive Bays

**Figure 2.6.**
*PC Tower packaging style.*

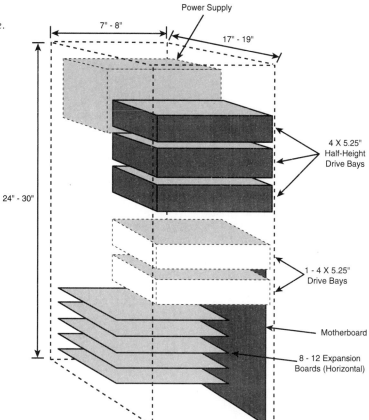

Power Supply

7" - 8"

17" - 19"

24" - 30"

4 X 5.25" Half-Height Drive Bays

1 - 4 X 5.25" Drive Bays

Motherboard

8 - 12 Expansion Boards (Horizontal)

As the display monitor sizes have increased, it is difficult to maintain a proper viewing position when it is placed on top of a PC AT six-inch high desktop unit. One solution to this problem was the development of the slim line or pizza box design as illustrated in Figure 2.7. IBM and several other companies produced this style package with from two to four horizontal expansion bus slots. In general, this style of package has fallen out of favor. It is more expensive to manufacture due to the riser card required to create the horizontal expansion bus orientation. Further, the horizontal adapter board orientation was very difficult to cool, creating reliability problems. Finally, this packaging style did not easily support the new VESA local bus or the PCI bus standards where the extra connector and extra physical distance created by the riser card could lower bus performance and reliability and limited the number of slots capable of being supported to two or three.

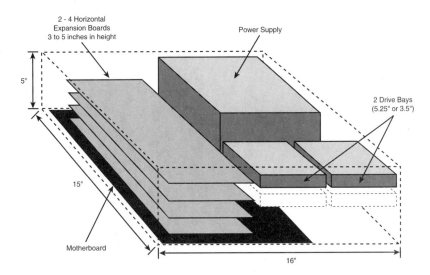

**Figure 2.7.**
*PC slim line or pizza box packaging style.*

An alternative to the slim line design that uses little desktop space and permits the monitor to be set on the desk is the mini-tower design illustrated in Figure 2.8. This design is very popular, easier to manufacture, and supports PCI and VESA local bus slots. This design is simply a PC AT desktop system turned on its side; thus many components are shared between a desktop and mini-tower design. This packaging style can sit on the desktop beside the display monitor or on the floor.

There are a number of packages supporting mobile PC systems. These range from the large, barely transportable systems to the very small palmtop devices. The basic concept of a mobile systems design is to integrate all the PC systems functions into a single mobile device. Naturally, some compromises have to be made to achieve the size and weight desired. Displays are usually smaller flat panel devices, expansion slots are limited, and keyboard size and layout are reduced in most mobile designs. In the smallest designs, floppy disk drives and hard disk drives are replaced with other more compact nonvolatile memory technologies. Figure 2.9 illustrates the major classifications of mobile systems. The larger transportable systems are still used in test and maintenance applications where portability is required along with space for some bus expansions slots.

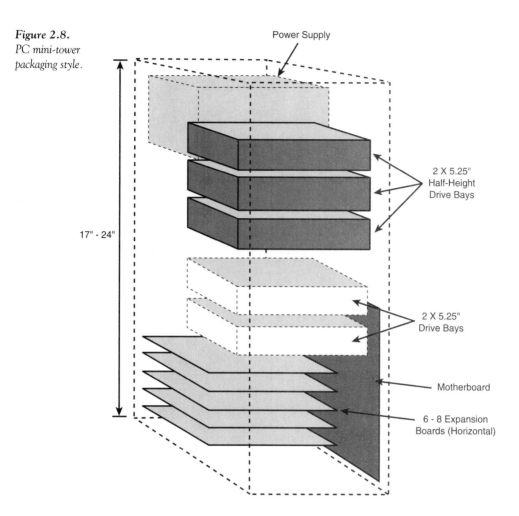

**Figure 2.8.**
*PC mini-tower packaging style.*

Power Supply

2 X 5.25"
Half-Height
Drive Bays

17" - 24"

2 X 5.25"
Drive Bays

Motherboard

6 - 8 Expansion
Boards (Horizontal)

Notebook designs have been partitioned into two basic categories: notebooks and sub-notebooks. The primary difference is the presence or absence of a floppy disk drive and the smaller screen size in the sub-notebooks. Sub-notebooks seem to be losing some of their popularity as notebooks become lighter, approaching the weight of a sub-notebook. Also contributing to their decline is the difficulty of typing on small keyboards and viewing Windows screens on the smaller screen sizes of the sub-notebooks.

Palmtop PC's were popular with the introduction of the HP LX95 device. But their popularity has declined as more and more applications move to Windows. It is not possible to support a Windows environment on the small screens and new DOS applications are simply not being developed. Further, custom PIM (Personal Information Managers) devices from Sharp and Casio perform the same function for less than half the cost of the PC-based palmtops. These devices now also support links to the desktop PC for PC-compatible data exchange, again further reducing the need for a DOS or Windows environment in the palmtop.

**Figure 2.9.**
*Mobile PC Packaging Styles.*

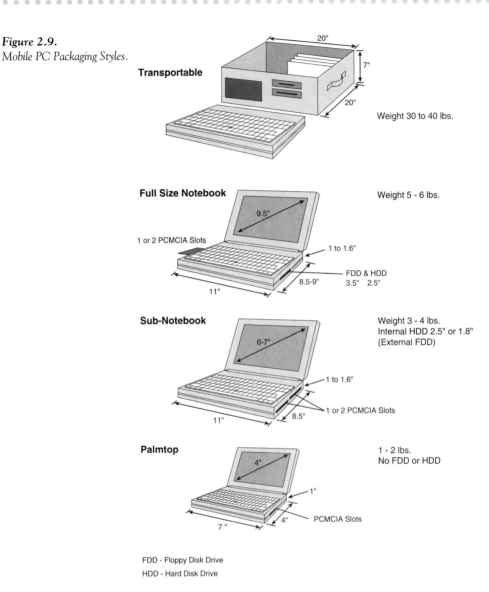

**Transportable**
20"
7"
20"
Weight 30 to 40 lbs.

**Full Size Notebook**
Weight 5 - 6 lbs.
9.5"
1 or 2 PCMCIA Slots
1 to 1.6"
FDD & HDD
3.5"   2.5"
8.5-9"
11"

**Sub-Notebook**
Weight 3 - 4 lbs.
Internal HDD 2.5" or 1.8"
(External FDD)
6-7"
1 to 1.6"
1 or 2 PCMCIA Slots
8.5"
11"

**Palmtop**
1 - 2 lbs.
No FDD or HDD
4"
1"
4"
PCMCIA Slots
7 "

FDD - Floppy Disk Drive
HDD - Hard Disk Drive

# Power Supply

The PC power supply converts the standard wall outlet 110 or 220 volt AC (Alternating Current) current to DC (Direct Current) voltages to run the electronics and peripheral devices in the PC's system unit. This power supply also can supply AC voltage to the systems display monitor through an AC convenience outlet on the power supply. The power supply also powers the PC's keyboard and mouse input devices through the interface ports and cables. The power supply converts the AC voltage to four DC voltages: +5 volts, +12 volts, –5 volts and –12 volts. Most of the power is supplied through the +5 volt and +12 volt outputs. The original PC was rated at 65 watts of power, the XT came with a power supply rated at 135 watts. The AT system had a 220-watt supply. Today most desktop units come with power supplies rated at between 150 and 220 watts. Tower designs are typically rated at 220 to 400 watts. If a large number of hard drives and adapter boards are to be installed in a tower system a minimum of 275 watts should be sufficient. In most desktop and mini-tower designs the system's cooling is provided by the power supply fan. This single fan is designed to cool both the power supply and the system unit electronics. In larger tower systems, separate independent cooling fans may be necessary. One fan cools the power supply and is often built into the power supply, and the second fan cools the motherboard and the adapter boards installed in the bus expansion slots. With the newer high-performance CPUs, often a fan is attached directly to the CPU.

In the United States, power supplies need to be approved by the UL (Underwriters Laboratory) and the FCC (Federal Communication Commission). The UL approval means that the power supply meets a set of minimum safety standards, whereas the FCC class B approval means the power supply does not create magnetic or electrical emissions that interfere with TV or radio reception. Actually the FCC approval also needs to be obtained on the entire system and its typical configurations. These approvals do not guarantee proper operation, quality level, or reliability!

# Floppy Disk Drives

All PCs, with the exception of some notebooks and palmtop devices, support one or more floppy disk drives. The name floppy is derived from the fact that the magnetic media is a soft, flexible mylar disk that rotates in the jacket of the disk. The floppy disk is called a data interchange or distribution media because it is removable after it is read or written. Data and programs can be moved from PC to PC by storing them on floppy disks. Also, most software is sold or distributed on floppy disks. Floppy disks can also be used to archive or back up system data on a hard drive. With larger hard drives and files, this can be very tedious. Early PCs used floppy disks that were 5.25 inches in diameter and stored from 160KB to 1.2MB of data. Later, a smaller 3.5-inch disk was introduced that stored up to 2.88MB of data (1.44MB is the more common standard). To maintain compatibility with older systems or interchange data with a PC owner with older 5.25-inch disks, most PCs are equipped with both a 5.25-inch and 3.5-inch floppy disk dives. New PC owners without the backward compatibility requirements should simply purchase 3.5-inch drives, since all software is now readily available on 3.5-inch disks. Most PCs support 5.25-inch drive bays that can be modified with a mounting kit to support 3.5-inch drives. Most PCs come with floppy disk drive adapters that support a minimum of two drives of any type. The floppy disk drive adapter and port are covered in more detail later in this chapter.

# Hard Disk Drives

For high-speed access and storage of both programs and data, the system's fixed disk drive is used. This is nonvolatile rotating magnetic media similar to the floppy disk drive. However, it is designed to be nonremovable and the media is not flexible, hence the name hard disk. Because the media is nonremovable and rigid, it is capable of storing much more data at significantly higher speeds than the floppy disk drives. Today's typical PC hard drive stores from 500MB to more than 5GB of data with access times below 10 milliseconds. Hard drives come in several package sizes with disk media or platter sizes from 8 inches to under 1.8 inches in diameter. Most PC hard drives are 3.5 inches in diameter, enabling them to fit in the same drive bays as 3.5-inch floppy disk drives. Hard drives attach to the PC system through an IDE (Intelligent Drive Electronics) or SCSI (Small Computer Systems Interface) adapter port. These two adapter ports are covered later in this chapter.

# CD-ROM Drives

CD-ROM drives are capable of storing over 600MB of data on a single 5-inch disk. This technology was derived from the same CD audio disks used in your audio CD player. However, instead of storing just digital audio data, it has been adapted to support any type of PC data or programs. CD-ROMs are great for distribution of large software packages and can contain all types of multimedia data. The CD-ROM technology is low cost and easy to produce, but it is a read-only media. You cannot save data or programs on a CD-ROM today. New technologies, however, are being developed that will soon permit the CD to also store data in real-time, similar to a floppy disk. CD-ROM drives can be installed in the same size drive bays as a 5.25-inch floppy disk drive. The CD-ROM drive interfaces to the PC through one of several port adapters. Often, a SCSI adapter comes with the CD-ROM drive, or it can use one that is often included on a sound board. However, many CD-ROM drives are now capable of being attached to the IDE adapter port, which also interfaces to the system's hard disk drive. The IDE Port adapter standard has recently been extended to support additional IDE ports with CD-ROM attachment capability. More information on the IDE and SCSI adapter ports is provided later in this chapter.

# The System Unit's Motherboard

The most defining element of a PC system and system unit is the motherboard. Motherboards have varied dramatically over time with new processors and expansion bus slot architectures. Before I discuss the motherboard's hardware features, a short review of the history of the PC architecture will be helpful. At this time several versions of the PC systems exist with different processor technologies and expansion slot bus architectures. Figure 2.10 illustrates the PC family tree from its origin—the original PC in 1981—to the present family of products.

**Figure 2.10.**
*The PC family tree.*

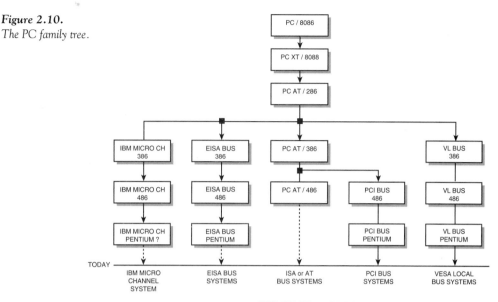

*NOTE: EISA, PCI, and VL BUS Systems also Support ISA Expansion Slots

---------- These Paths Phasing Out

Since the introduction of the original PC in September of 1981, thousands of models and versions have been designed and produced. Today there are literally hundreds of PCs offered with varying performance, features, and prices. Even if we were limited to the top name-brand manufacturers, it would be impossible to review and compare the models and versions offered. However, if one stands back and looks at the variety of PC architectures, it becomes apparent that there are two major defining factors that most will recognize:

1. The microprocessor type and speed: 386DX-25, 486DX2-66, Pentium 90, and so on

2. Bus Architecture: AT, ISA, EISA, IBM Micro Channel, VESA Local Bus, PCI

Each branch in Figure 2.10 represents a different design type or bus architecture and the paths along the branches represent the progression of processor types that have developed over time. At any point in time several processor types may be used in the marketplace with differing price and performance points.

# Motherboard Processors

Most would agree that the microprocessor type and speed are easy to understand. Faster is better, right? Surely it would seem that microprocessor performance can be measured and easily compared. Armed with a measure of relative performance, it would seem to be a simple task to select a system by comparing the microprocessors' performance at various price points. One would think that simply selecting the latest Intel microprocessor at the highest clock rate should give you the best performing system. Unfortunately, there are many complicating factors. First, there are now over 50 different processor types and speeds offered by both Intel and other suppliers producing "Intel-compatible" processors. Collecting and comparing "unconstrained" or raw microprocessor performance information can be a complex task in itself. It seems that suppliers tend not to measure their microprocessor's performance in the same ways. They don't want to make it too easy. For example, Intel only publishes performance numbers relative to other members of its family of processors. This is called the ICOMP Index. Since competitors don't know how to calculate the ICOMP index, they cannot easily compare their performances to Intel's. Secondly, many aspects of the system's design can dramatically affect the performance of the processor in a specific system design. For example, cache type and size, bus cycle efficiency of the "core chip set," performance of the system memory subsystem, and the basic "bus architecture" of the system can all affect system performance. A fast high-performance processor can be made to perform poorly in a bad or unbalanced system design. Third, the performance and capabilities of many other system components can dramatically affect the overall system performance in real applications. For example, a slow or older display adapter can have devastating performance impact on Window applications where display adapter performance is key. An older or slow hard disk subsystem can also dramatically affect real application performance, particularly in server applications and high disk I/O applications such as databases. For a much deeper understanding of the microprocessor options and their performance, see Chapter 3, "Brains: The Processors."

## What Is a Bus Architecture?

It's relatively easy for someone to comprehend how processor speeds and types affect a system design and performance. Also, the physical packaging styles discussed earlier are easy to comprehend. But when it comes to system expansion slot bus architectures, most have difficulty understanding what it is and why it's an important feature that deserves consideration. Exactly what is a bus architecture? Simply put, it is how the components of a PC system are connected together. It is how the microprocessor is attached to its memory—how the system's peripheral devices adapters such as hard disks, floppy disks, and keyboard are attached to the system. It is how expansion devices adapters such as display adapters, LAN adapters, sound cards, CD-ROM drives, and so on are attached to the system. It is sort of the "highway" that enables the microprocessor to talk to all the system elements. In the original PC and PC XT, the bus architecture was 8 bits wide and could transfer about one million bytes of information per second. Nowadays, to keep a Pentium class processor busy, the bus needs to be 64 bits wide and transfer data at speeds up to 500 million bytes per second. Obviously a Pentium processor running on the original PC bus architecture would be severely constrained. Over the years a number of competing bus architectures have been developed to cope with the increasing performance requirements of the PC. Picking a bus architecture is one of the most important decisions in selecting a PC. Figure 2.11 compares the data transfer rate of some of the existing bus architectures. Data transfer rate, of course, is not the only important feature of bus architecture. Compatibility with existing bus expansion adapter boards is also a very important issue. For example, the adapter you wish to purchase may only work in systems that support its expansion bus.

*Figure 2.11.*
PC system's bus
architectures and
data transfer rate
performance.

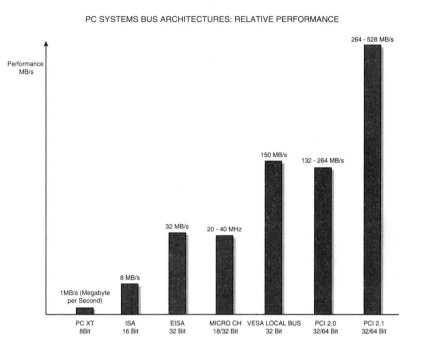

PC SYSTEMS BUS ARCHITECTURES: RELATIVE PERFORMANCE

# Why Is Bus Architecture Selection So Important?

First, you want a system design and bus architecture that enables the most performance possible for the system's microprocessor and its attached peripheral devices. Secondly, you want a bus architecture that is contemporary and will have ongoing support over the life of your machine. Many PCs that seem to be very attractively priced are older bus architectures that have no future or ongoing support and do not extract the maximum capability from the microprocessor. With the newer PCs offering processor upgrade capabilities, you will want to ensure that your system will be capable of fully utilizing the performance potential offered by CPU upgrading. Last, you will want a contemporary expansion bus architecture capable of handling the performance requirements of new multimedia applications. To support these new applications, you will need devices such as high-performance audio, video, hard disks, high-resolution and high-color depth displays adapters, full-motion video playback, CD-quality audio, video conferencing, Fast Ethernet (100 megabits) LANs, and ATM (Asynchronous Transfer Mode) LANs with 155 Megabits per second data rates. The new multimedia applications with new "rich data types" and an appetite for very high data rates place a heavy demand on the PC's bus architecture performance. Without recent innovations in the PC bus architecture, it would be impossible to enable these exciting new applications.

# The PC Family: A Historical Perspective

To better understand how the industry has arrived at its present state of supporting multiple processor types and speeds, multiple physical packaging styles, and multiple bus architectures, a short review of the PC family tree can be helpful. Figure 2.10 illustrates the evolution of the PC from the original PC to the present family of PC alternative bus architectures. Just as in nature, the evolution of the PC resulted in some dead ends. I will try to explain how and why each step was made and why some were more successful than others.

## The Original PC

The original PC project has it roots in a small laboratory in Atlanta, Georgia. This lab was part of the systems architecture group at the then IBM General Systems Division headquarters in Atlanta. This group supported the Rochester Minnesota Plant that developed and produced IBM's low-end systems products: the IBM S/3, System 34, System 38, and now the AS400. It also supported the IBM Boca Raton facility supporting the Series 1 mini-computer development. One of the tasks of the small lab was to investigate the competitiveness of outside technologies for building low-end IBM products. The lab focused on the emerging microprocessor technologies from Intel, Motorola, Zilog, and others.

In 1979 and 1980 the lab was successful in promoting the development of a number of new IBM products using microprocessor technology from outside IBM. Many believe that the IBM PC was the first product to use Intel Processors. The fact is that the IBM Displaywriter used the 8086, the IBM Datamaster system; IBM 5250 data entry terminals used the Intel 8085 8-bit microprocessor; the IBM 5100 portable system used the Intel 8080 microprocessor as a communications subsystem processor; and the IBM keyboards had adopted the 8048 8-bit single chip micro-controller as a keyboard controller. All of this happened before the PC development was even started! All of these systems products were a mix of IBM technology and closed designs and used IBM-developed software. These products used outside technologies but were still designed, built, and marketed under the IBM environment that was fixed and rigid, which resulted in long development cycles and expensive products. Since you probably never heard of these earlier systems that paved the way for the PC, you can guess how successful they were.

For a variety of reasons beyond the scope of this book, in the early summer of 1980 IBM began the PC project in Boca Raton. This project was not unique because of the use of outside technologies or Intel microprocessors, but it was a totally new development environment and approach that abandoned the existing IBM development methodology. The PC project benefited in many ways from these earlier efforts. Many of the original engineers were from the earlier IBM Datamaster project and therefore very familiar with the Intel Processor and peripheral chips. This time the development group did not have to use any IBM design methodology. Many features of the earlier Intel 8085 microprocessor-based Datamaster design were quickly adopted for use in the PC. The adapter card on motherboard packaging approach was taken from the Datamaster design. The PC's card size and right angle connector bracket mounting was adopted. Even the expansion bus connector and the bus signals were adapted. The 8085 microprocessors bus was very similar to the newer Intel 8088 microprocessors interface and only minor changes were made in the Datamaster's expansion bus architecture for use in the PC. It is a little-known fact that adapter boards designed for the PC would actually fit into and work in an older IBM Datamaster system! The adoption of the earlier Datamaster's key architectural and packaging features and its prior history of rigorous testing greatly enhanced the PC development schedule and its chances of success.

From this humble beginning the IBM PC became a floppy disk-based system with a maximum of 32KB of RAM on the motherboard. It supported one or two internal 160KB floppy dives with a connector supporting two external floppy drives. Five expansion slots were provided with three typically used in a system; one for a display adapter, one for the floppy disk drive adapter, and one for a parallel printer port adapter. This system used the Intel 8088 microprocessor running at a clock rate of 4.77 MHz. This weird speed was selected because the 8088 microprocessor's clock chip actually required a three-times clock input and the display adapter needed a frequency that was a multiple of the 3.56 MHz color burst frequency used in TVs. The nearest multiple of this frequency was four times or 14.318 MHz. When this frequency was divided by three for the processor, 4.77 MHz resulted. The system and expansion bus architecture was the extension of the processor's local bus with peripheral chips added to support DMA (Direct Memory Access), interrupts, and timer/counter functions. The bus architecture was straightforward and easy to understand and provided a very efficient, low-cost expansion bus capability. As a testimony to its longevity, expansion bus adapters designed for the original PC will still operate in state-of-the-art PC systems of today, even those with Pentium processors and PCI busses. The original PC chips used to create the PC bus architecture are still fully implemented in all contemporary PC designs. Figure 2.12 is a block diagram of the original PC and the closely related PC XT.

## The PC XT

The PC XT was introduced next by IBM and offered only moderate changes over the PC. The exact electronics were used on the motherboard; the processor remained the 4.77 MHz 8088 Intel microprocessor, and the support chip set from Intel was unchanged. The expansion bus slot architecture was exactly the same as that of the PC. The most important change was the addition of three extra expansion bus slots, which made a total of eight. The PC XT used the same mechanical package as the PC. The extra slots were accommodated by reducing the expansion bus slots spacing from 1 inch to .75 inch spacing. The floppy disk drive was also upgraded to a 360KB size, and the memory expansion capability on the motherboard was increased to 256KB. A hard disk adapter and drive option were also introduced. Also, to conserve expansion slots, a combination serial and parallel port adapter was made available. A typical system would use four of the eight expansion slots; display adapter, floppy disk adapter, hard drive adapter, and a combination serial and parallel port adapter. Memory expansion beyond the motherboard-supported 256KB required addition of a memory board in the expansion bus slots.

*Figure 2.12.*
*PC and PC XT*
*block diagram.*

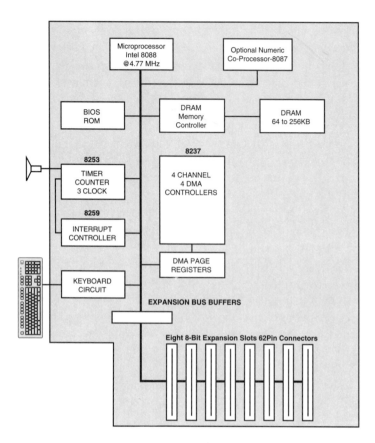

Typical System Used Four Expansion Slots
1) FDD Controller
2) HDD Controller
3) Display Adapter
4) Combination Serial & Printer Port

## The PC AT

In 1984, three years after the introduction of the PC, IBM announced the PC AT. The PC AT's major enhancement was the use of Intel's 286 16-bit microprocessor. This processor supported 16-bit bus transfers, 24-bit addressing (16MB as opposed to the 1MB available on the 8088), and memory management with protected-mode features. Protected mode feature allowed programs to be written such that one portion of a program could not destroy or effect another portion, a key feature required in multitasking operating systems such as UNIX. The 286 was introduced at a clock rate of 6 MHz and quickly upgraded to 8 MHz. The 286 AT offered a three to five times performance increase over the PC XT. The implementation still used the same Intel chips to support Direct Memory Access (DMA), interrupts, and timer/counter functions, but more chips were added to increase the number of interrupt levels and DMA channels. DMA is special circuitry used to transfer data at high speed between an adapter's I/O device and the PC's main memory. No new custom chip devices were used in the first PC AT. The physical package was significantly increased in size, with the system unit box size increasing by two inches in the horizontal dimension and one inch in height.

This change allowed support for the new larger PC AT form factor expansion cards. One of the most significant changes in the PC AT design was the enhancement of the 8-bit PC XT expansion bus with a scheme that increased the bus width to 16 bits and supported 24-bit addressing. This was done in a completely backward-compatible manner. This scheme allowed the existing PC and PC XT adapters to operate in the new bus expansion slots without hardware or software changes. This was accomplished by retaining the PC XT's 8-bit bus and 62-pin expansion slots, and supporting the enhanced features in an inline 36-pin slot. With this scheme, cards that supported or used only the PC XT bus features only attached to the 8-bit 62-pin slots and adapters that needed the 16-bit bus, and its added features were extended and attached to both slots. This evolutionary approach guaranteed the wide acceptance of the PC AT bus architecture. All PC designs still support the PC AT bus, enabling adapter boards designed in 1981 for the original PC to operate correctly in today's Pentium /PCI bus systems. Figure 2.13 illustrates the dimensions of the older PC XT adapter boards and the present-day PC AT adapter boards. Both board sizes work in all present-day PCs! Figure 2.14 illustrates the pin and signal definitions on both the PC XT and AT system's expansion bus slot connectors. Note that the upper 62-pin slot is the original PC XT 8-bit bus and the lower 36-pin slot is the 16-bit extension added by the PC AT.

**Figure 2.13.**
*PC XT and PC AT expansion bus adapter board sizes.*

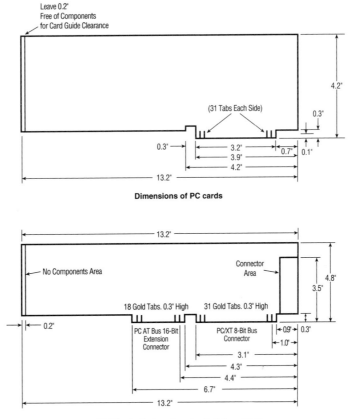

Dimensions of PC cards

PC AT adapter board mechanical dimensions

**Figure 2.14.**
*PC AT expansion bus slots signal/pin definitions.*

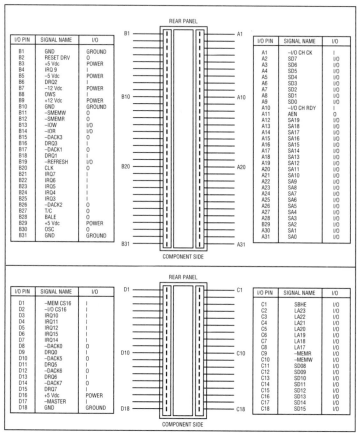

| I/O PIN | SIGNAL NAME | I/O |
|---|---|---|
| B1 | GND | GROUND |
| B2 | RESET DRV | O |
| B3 | +5 Vdc | POWER |
| B4 | IRQ 9 | I |
| B5 | –5 Vdc | POWER |
| B6 | DRQ2 | I |
| B7 | –12 Vdc | POWER |
| B8 | OWS | I |
| B9 | +12 Vdc | POWER |
| B10 | GND | GROUND |
| B11 | –SMEMW | O |
| B12 | –SMEMR | O |
| B13 | –IOW | I/O |
| B14 | –IOR | I/O |
| B15 | –DACK3 | O |
| B16 | DRQ3 | I |
| B17 | –DACK1 | O |
| B18 | DRQ1 | I |
| B19 | –REFRESH | I/O |
| B20 | CLK | O |
| B21 | IRQ7 | I |
| B22 | IRQ6 | I |
| B23 | IRQ5 | I |
| B24 | IRQ4 | I |
| B25 | IRQ3 | I |
| B26 | –DACK2 | O |
| B27 | T/C | O |
| B28 | BALE | O |
| B29 | +5 Vdc | POWER |
| B30 | OSC | O |
| B31 | GND | GROUND |

| I/O PIN | SIGNAL NAME | I/O |
|---|---|---|
| A1 | –I/O CH CK | I |
| A2 | SD7 | I/O |
| A3 | SD6 | I/O |
| A4 | SD5 | I/O |
| A5 | SD4 | I/O |
| A6 | SD3 | I/O |
| A7 | SD2 | I/O |
| A8 | SD1 | I/O |
| A9 | SD0 | I/O |
| A10 | –I/O CH RDY | I |
| A11 | AEN | O |
| A12 | SA19 | I/O |
| A13 | SA18 | I/O |
| A14 | SA17 | I/O |
| A15 | SA16 | I/O |
| A16 | SA15 | I/O |
| A17 | SA14 | I/O |
| A18 | SA13 | I/O |
| A19 | SA12 | I/O |
| A20 | SA11 | I/O |
| A21 | SA10 | I/O |
| A22 | SA9 | I/O |
| A23 | SA8 | I/O |
| A24 | SA7 | I/O |
| A25 | SA6 | I/O |
| A26 | SA5 | I/O |
| A27 | SA4 | I/O |
| A28 | SA3 | I/O |
| B29 | SA2 | I/O |
| A30 | SA1 | I/O |
| A31 | SA0 | I/O |

| I/O PIN | SIGNAL NAME | I/O |
|---|---|---|
| D1 | –MEM CS16 | I |
| D2 | –I/O CS16 | I |
| D3 | IRQ10 | I |
| D4 | IRQ11 | I |
| D5 | IRQ12 | I |
| D6 | IRQ15 | I |
| D7 | IRQ14 | I |
| D8 | –DACK0 | O |
| D9 | DRQ0 | I |
| D10 | –DACK5 | O |
| D11 | DRQ5 | I |
| D12 | –DACK6 | O |
| D13 | DRQ6 | I |
| D14 | –DACK7 | O |
| D15 | DRQ7 | I |
| D16 | +5 Vdc | POWER |
| D17 | –MASTER | I |
| D18 | GND | GROUND |

| I/O PIN | SIGNAL NAME | I/O |
|---|---|---|
| C1 | SBHE | I/O |
| C2 | LA23 | I/O |
| C3 | LA22 | I/O |
| C4 | LA21 | I/O |
| C5 | LA20 | I/O |
| C6 | LA19 | I/O |
| C7 | LA18 | I/O |
| C8 | LA17 | I/O |
| C9 | –MEMR | I/O |
| C10 | –MEMW | I/O |
| C11 | SD08 | I/O |
| C12 | SD09 | I/O |
| C13 | SD10 | I/O |
| C14 | SD11 | I/O |
| C15 | SD12 | I/O |
| C16 | SD13 | I/O |
| C17 | SD14 | I/O |
| C18 | SD15 | I/O |

PC AT 16-bit extension slot.

PC AT Expansion Bus slots signal/pin definitions

SD0-SD15 - System Data Bits 0 through 15
SA0-SA23 - System Address Bus bits 0 Through 24
IRQ2-IRQ15 - Interrupt Requests Levels 2 through 15
DRQ0-DRQ7 - Direct Memory Access Requests 0 thru 7
DACK0-DACK7 - Direct Memory Access Acknowledge 0 thru 7

Note:   The remaining signals provide Bus timing information, status and commands.  For a detatiled
description of these signals consult Interfacing to the PC (SAMS 1995) or the IBM Technical Reference Manuals.

The PC AT systems not only supported 16-bit bus transfers and 24-bit addressing, but also added three more DMA channels and seven more interrupt levels to the expansion bus. These additions used the same chips that were in the original PC. Most PC AT designs support eight slots with five or six of these slots supporting the extra inline connector for the full 16-bit bus support.

The original PC AT designs ran the expansion bus at the same clock rate as the microprocessor. (A 6 MHz 286 ran the bus at 6 MHz and an 8 MHz microprocessor ran the bus at 8 MHz.) As microprocessor speeds increased, early designs simply increased the expansion bus speeds. Many PC AT systems were built with expansion bus speeds of 10 and 12 MHz. Unfortunately, at these speeds some of the adapter boards did not work at all or became unreliable. Today most, if not all, PC AT busses run at 8 or 8.33

MHz. At this speed the vast majority of adapter boards work fine. To solve the growing disparity between processor speed and bus expansion speed, the clone manufactures began to develop chip sets that ran the PC AT bus asynchronously from the microprocessor's clock. This permitted the processor's clock speed to increase independently from the expansion bus speed. Today all designs use this asynchronous PC AT expansion bus approach. With the introduction of very high clock rate 286s and the 386 32-bit processors, the new chip sets partitioned the system designs such that memory was attached directly to the processor's local bus and was not constrained in bus width or speed by the PC AT expansion bus speed. Also, cache memory designs were attached at the local bus interface. This approach off-loaded memory accesses from the PC AT expansion bus, removing it as a bottleneck in system performance. The PC AT bus was relegated to supporting medium to low speed peripheral devices. By simply bypassing the PC AT expansion bus for memory accesses, the life of the PC AT expansion bus was greatly extended. Figure 2.15 is a block diagram of a contemporary PC AT or (ISA) expansion bus design that is still very popular in low-end systems.

*Figure 2.15.*
*Contemporary PC AT/ISA bus system block diagram.*

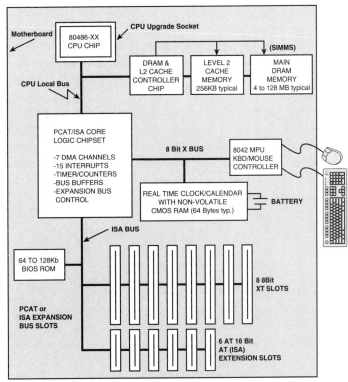

## ISA (Industry Standard Architecture) Bus

IBM never fully specified the PC AT bus with detailed timing and loading specifications. This made it difficult for an adapter designer to ensure his design would work in all PC or clone systems. To remedy this problem, Intel began to specify timing and loading information to force a de facto standard. Intel was able to gain the support for this standard from a number of clone manufacturers. The resulting specification was the AT bus with the clone maker consortiums best guess as to how IBM intended the bus to operate. This specification became known as the ISA bus (Industry Standard Architecture). At this point in time IBM was no longer in control of the PC architecture: it had taken on a life of its own. Many clone manufacturers were producing higher performance systems than IBM using highly integrated chip sets from numerous suppliers.

## EISA Bus Systems

Compaq became one of the leading clone manufacturers and began investigating extending the ISA architecture to support 32-bit busses and with much higher data transfer rates. A consortium of suppliers lead by Compaq and Intel began the development of the EISA standard (Extended Industry Standard Architecture). This standard had as a goal the development of a 32-bit bus with transfer rates up to 33 MB/second using a special burst mode DMA scheme. Considering the ISA standard was only 8 megabits/second, this was a significant improvement. The standard's goal was to also retain backward compatibility with the existing PC XT, PC AT busses and better specified the ISA bus functionally, electrically, and physically. This was accomplished by the clever design of a new slot connector that added new signals on a second tier of contacts below the existing ISA contacts. To support the existing ISA bus cycles and new faster and more complex EISA cycles, many new signals were added and the bus design complexity increased. EISA system chip sets were very expensive and systems designs were also very expensive. Very few mainstream applications saw any performance improvement in an EISA bus systems. As a result EISA systems never really caught on as a mainstream architecture. They were primarily used in high performance server applications where the benefits of the higher performance bus could be utilized. ISA bus systems had already solved most of the performance issues by allowing main memory to bypass the ISA bus and connect directly to the microprocessor's local bus. Figure 2.16 is a block diagram of a typical EISA bus system.

## IBM Micro Channel Architecture (MCA) Systems

Having lost control of the PC architecture and significant market share, in 1987 IBM made a bold move to recover its position. IBM introduced the PS/2 systems family of products. This family of products had many significant enhancements including a motherboard-integrated VGA display controller, motherboard-integrated floppy disk, serial and parallel ports, new keyboard and mouse ports, and a new high-performance hard disk adapter and interface. However, the most important new feature of the system was a completely new expansion bus architecture. Unlike the PC AT bus, this new bus was fully documented and specified by IBM with the obvious goal of creating a new PC standard. The new bus architecture added many innovations including well-supported bus mastering, the ability for an adapter to take over the bus from the microprocessor and transfer data to and from main memory independently. The level-sensitive interrupts feature was added, permitting MCA bus interrupt levels to be shared, unlike the ISA bus which allowed only one adapter to use an inter-rupt level at a time. Also added were features for adapter self-configuring support (early Plug and Play capability). Unfortunately, this bus had the same problems as the EISA bus. It was very expen-sive to build systems with MCA and the vast majority of applications saw no performance increase over an ISA bus system with main memory attached to the microprocessor's local bus. Further, the new smaller size expansion boards were difficult to manufacture at costs competitive with ISA boards. Figure 2.17 illustrates the dimensions of a typical MCA adapter board. Note its long thin outline, making it very difficult to compete with the much larger PC AT or ISA cards. MCA adapter boards also required multilayer printed circuit boards and custom chips to interface to the MCA bus. MCA also did not match the performance of the new EISA bus. In 1990 IBM introduced a number of MCA bus enhancements that were viewed as a ploy to "out spec" the more popular, EISA bus. However, when compared to EISA, MCA had one additional major disadvantage: it was not backward compatible with ISA or PC AT expansion slots and the vast market of ISA or PC AT adapters. MCA did not create a new standard to displace ISA or EISA, and IBM has let the micro channel architecture slowly fade from view while supporting ISA, VESA local bus, and PCI sys-tems. MCA did, however, introduce many new concepts that are now part of the PCI and VESA local bus implementations. Figure 2.18 illustrates the family of MCA busses and bus extensions defined by IBM. Figure 2.19 is a block diagram of a typical MCA bus architecture system design.

**Figure 2.16.**
*EISA Bus System*
*Block Diagram.*

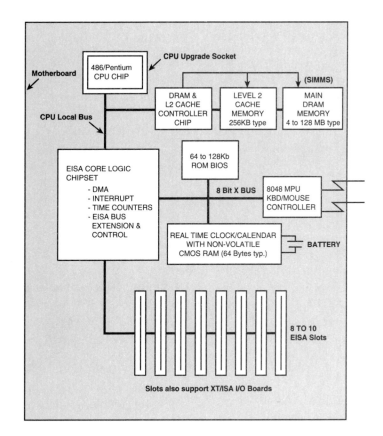

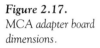

**Figure 2.17.**
MCA *adapter board*
*dimensions.*

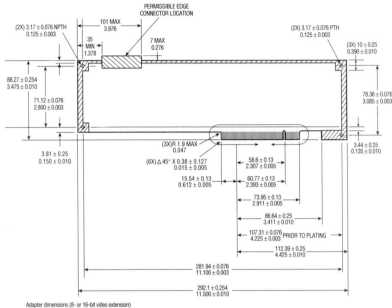

Adapter dimensions (8- or 16-bit video extension)

# VESA Local (VL) Bus Systems

With the introduction by Microsoft of its new display adapter bandwidth-hungry "Windows" Graphical User Interface (GUI), larger display monitors and screen resolutions—and applications using greater color depth—display adapter performance became the key bottleneck in PC system performance. VGA display adapters attached through the PC AT or ISA bus were reaching the limits of their performance. The primary bottleneck was the processor access to the display memory for Windows screen updates. The solution to the problem was obvious: move the display adapter and its memory to the local bus of the system—the same bus that the cache and memory subsystem was on. This scheme removed the 16-bit ISA bus bottleneck and dramatically improved Windows and thus system performance. Since the Video Electronics Standards Association (VESA) was trying to bring standards to PC monitors—screen sizes, refresh rates and timing standards, for example—they took on the task of standardizing the bus and connector for attaching devices to the processor local bus. To keep design complexity to a minimum and cost down, the VESA standard essentially selected the local bus of the Intel 486 microprocessor as the standard. Figure 2.20 is a table defining the 32-bit and 64-bit bus signals on the VL bus. The VL bus uses the same slot connectors as the IBM Micro Channel Architecture and the new Intel PCI bus standards. Depending on the loading on the local bus, up to three slots were typically available for local bus attachments. Loading refers to the electrical "load" added to the bus by the adapter; each device added to the bus loads the bus.

**Figure 2.18.**
*MCA bus definition and extensions.*

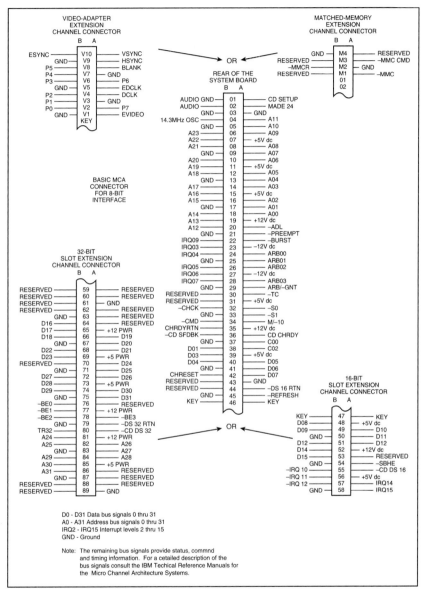

MCA bus definition and extensions.

**Figure 2.19.**
*IBM MCA(Micro Channel Architecture) system block diagram.*

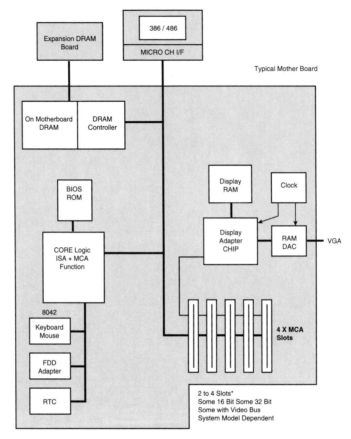

*One slot was typically used to support the Hard Disk adapter

For high-speed signals such as those on the VESA local bus, the load takes the form of added capacitance. The more devices attached, the higher the capacitance and the greater the bus loading. High capacitance values tend to slow the signals down and make the bus perform poorly. Table 2.1 defines the maximum bus clock speed and the number of slots permitted with various motherboard capacitance loads on the local bus. Table 2.2 defines the maximum theoretical data transfer rates for both 32- and 64-bit VL buses at various bus clock speeds. The VESA local bus slots are added as additional inline slots at the back of the existing ISA bus slots. This permits combining of local bus and ISA bus devices on the same physical card.

Figure 2.21 illustrates the combined ISA/VESA Local bus slot card dimensions. The VESA local bus was not intended to replace the ISA bus, but to augment its function in a system by providing a high-performance bus for high-speed peripherals. Today, the lowest cost high-performance systems are VESA local bus systems that support both VESA local bus and ISA slots. Although VESA local bus support 32-and 64-bit devices at speeds of up to 50 MHz, most systems are 32-bit 33 MHz designs. This is very competitive with the present implementation of standard PCI specification.

Devices other than the display adapter are often placed on the local bus, such as IDE (Intelligent Disk Electronics) hard disk adapters, SCSI adapters, and LAN adapters. The simplicity of VESA local bus design and its low-cost implementation made it a wide success for low-cost 486 class systems. Figure 2.22 is a block diagram of VESA local bus system.

Table 2.1. VL Bus Slots versus Bus Frequency and Loading.

| Max. VL Bus Freq. | Sys Board Capacitive Load | Max. Number of Slots |
|---|---|---|
| 40 MHz | up to 50 PF | 3 |
| 40 MHz | up to 75 PF | 2 |
| 50 MHz | up to 25 PF | 2 |
| 50 MHz | up to 50 PF | 1 |

PF is a measure of capacitance: 1 PF is one billionth of a Farad of capacitance.

Table 2.2. Maximum VL Bus Transfer Rates.

| VL bus freq. | Max. 32-bit bus bandwidth | Max. 64-bit bus bandwidth |
|---|---|---|
| 25 MHz | 80 MB/second | 133 MB/second |
| 33 MHz | 107 MB/second | 178 MB/second |
| 40 MHz | 128 MB/second | 213 MB/second |
| 50 MHz | 160 MB/second | 276 MB/second |

# PCI (Peripheral Component Interconnect) Bus Systems

In 1992 Intel began to develop a bus standard to connect peripheral components devices (chips) together. The original intent was to provide a standard to support high-speed chip interconnection on a motherboard. With each generation of new micro processors, Intel changed the processor's local bus architecture to gain more performance. This meant that with each generation of microprocessors, the peripheral chips interface also had to change. To solve this problem, Intel proposed the use of a new bus called the Peripheral Connection Interface (PCI). The PCI bus would attach to the microprocessor's local bus through a special local-bus-to-PCI bridge chip. Thus, each time the microprocessor and local bus were changed, only the bridge chip needed to be changed. All existing peripheral devices continued to work automatically with every new microprocessor Intel produced.

***Figure 2.20.***
*VL Bus slot pinout and signals.*

### VL-Bus Slot Pinout

Pinout shown is a top-view. The "A" side of the connector is the add-in board component side. The"B" side of the connector is the add-in board solder side. The 64 bit columns show the differences from the 32 bit signals during a 64 bit transfer.

DAT 00-DAT 63 - Data Bus bits 0 thru 63
ADR00-ADR31 - Address Bus bits 0 thru 31

Note: The remaining bus signals are used to indicate commands, status and timing information. For a detailed descrioption of the VL-Bus signals refer to the VESA Bus Standard.

| | B Side | | | A Side | |
| --- | --- | --- | --- | --- | --- |
| 64 bit | 32 bit | Pin # | 32 bit | 64 bit | |
| | DAT00 | 01 | DAT01 | | |
| | DAT02 | 02 | DAT03 | | |
| | DAT04 | 03 | GND | | |
| | DAT06 | 04 | DAT05 | | |
| | DAT08 | 05 | DAT07 | | |
| | GND | 06 | DAT09 | | |
| | DAT10 | 07 | DAT11 | | |
| | DAT12 | 08 | DAT13 | | |
| | VCC | 09 | DAT15 | | |
| | DAT14 | 10 | GND | | |
| | DAT16 | 11 | DAT17 | | |
| | DAT18 | 12 | VCC | | |
| | DAT20 | 13 | DAT19 | | |
| | GND | 14 | DAT21 | | |
| | DAT22 | 15 | DAT23 | | |
| | DAT24 | 16 | DAT25 | | |
| | DAT26 | 17 | GND | | |
| | DAT28 | 18 | DAT27 | | |
| | DAT30 | 19 | DAT29 | | |
| | VCC | 20 | DAT31 | | |
| DAT63 | ADR31 | 21 | ADR30 | DAT62 | |
| | GND | 22 | ADR28 | DAT60 | |
| DAT61 | ADR29 | 23 | ADR26 | DAT58 | |
| DAT59 | ADR27 | 24 | GND | | |
| DAT57 | ADR25 | 25 | ADR24 | DAT56 | |
| DAT55 | ADR23 | 26 | ADR22 | DAT54 | |
| DAT53 | ADR21 | 27 | VCC | | |
| DAT51 | ADR19 | 28 | ADR20 | DAT52 | |
| | GND | 29 | ADR18 | DAT50 | |
| DAT49 | ADR17 | 30 | ADR16 | DAT48 | |
| DAT47 | ADR15 | 31 | ADR14 | DAT46 | |
| | VCC | 32 | ADR12 | DAT44 | |
| DAT45 | ADR13 | 33 | ADR10 | DAT42 | |
| DAT43 | ADR11 | 34 | ADR08 | DAT40 | |
| DAT41 | ADR09 | 35 | GND | | |
| DAT39 | ADR07 | 36 | ADR06 | DAT38 | |
| DAT37 | ADR05 | 37 | ADR04 | DAT36 | |
| | GND | 38 | WBACK# | | |
| DAT35 | ADR03 | 39 | BEO# | BE4# | |
| DAT34 | ADR02 | 40 | VCC | | |
| LBS64# | NC | 41 | BE1# | BE5# | |
| | RESET# | 42 | BE2# | BE6# | |
| | D/C# | 43 | GND# | | |
| DAT33 | M/IO# | 44 | BE3# | BE7# | |
| DAT32 | W/R# | 45 | ADS# | | |
| | | KEY | | | |
| | | KEY | | | |
| | RDYRTN# | 48 | LRDY# | | |
| | GND | 49 | LDEV<X># | | |
| | IRQ9 | 50 | LREQ<X># | | |
| | BRDY# | 51 | GND | | |
| | BLAST# | 52 | LGNT<X># | | |
| | IDO | 53 | VCC | | |
| | IDI | 54 | ID2 | | |
| | GND | 55 | ID3 | | |
| | LCLK | 56 | ID4 | | |
| | VCC | 57 | NC | | |
| | LBS16# | 58 | LEADS# | | |

VL-Bus Slot Pinouts

**Figure 2.21.**
*VL bus/ISA adapter
board dimensions.*

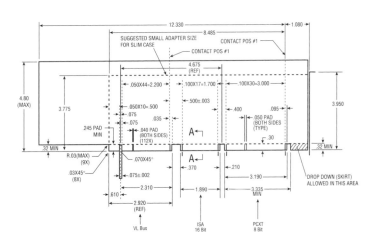

VL–Bus/ISA ADAPTOR CARD PHYSICAL LAYOUT

**Figure 2.22.**
*VESA local bus system
block diagram.*

**Typical VLB (VESA Local Bus System)**

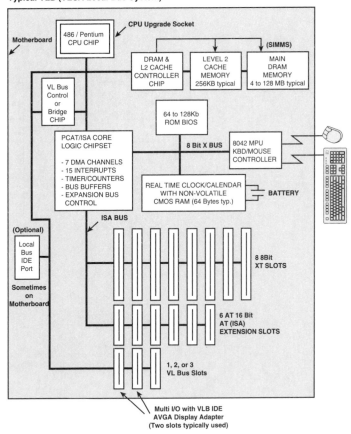

AVGA - Accelerated Video Graphics Array

This scheme essentially isolated microprocessor and local bus changes from affecting the larger family of peripheral chips. Unfortunately, the original PCI specification did not support expansion slots. With the introduction of higher speed 486 microprocessors and the Pentium chips, the industry became concerned over the life and viability of the VESA local bus, which was based on the 486 local bus. With urging from several industry sources, Intel upgraded the PCI specification so that it now supports expansion slot connectors. The PCI bus is extremely well-defined electrically and functionally, and is elegant in its simplicity. It is clear that it is becoming the dominant bus architecture. The PCI bus can be either 32 bits or 64 bits wide and runs at speeds from 25 MHz to 66 MHz, giving it a maximum throughput of 528 MB/second. This is more than 42 times faster than the ISA bus. Even with this overwhelming advantage, all PCI bus systems still support several ISA expansion slots, which enables the vast family of ISA bus adapters to still be used in PCI bus systems. This is accomplished using a special PCI-to-ISA bridge chip.

Figure 2.23 illustrates the PCI bus signals available on an expansion slot for both a 32-bit and 64-bit versions of the PCI bus. A minimum of 47 signals are required to implement a PCI bus slave device; two additional signals allow bus master support. A slave PCI device is one than cannot initiate a bus transfer; it can only respond to request for bus transfers. A master PCI device, on the other hand, can request control of the bus and initiate bus transfers. The PCI bus specification permits multiple bus master devices and defines an arbitration scheme to orderly service multiple simultaneous signals for the bus from bus masters.

**Figure 2.23.**
*PCI bus signals.*

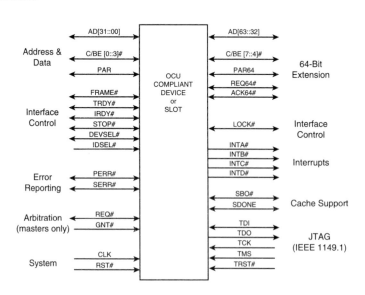

Note: For detailed information on the PCI Bus signals and bus operation refer to the PCI Bus specification. This specification is available from PCI Special Interest Group, M/S HF#-15A, 5200N.E. Elam Young Parkway, Hillsboro, Oregon 97124-6697

The PCI standard supports a total of 10 "loads" or devices on the bus, where a motherboard chip or device counts as one load and each expansion slot counts as two loads. If a typical system has a processor local bus to PCI bridge chip, an ISA bus bridge chip, a memory bus interface chip, and a PCI bus IDE controller chip, a total of 4 loads are used. This would leave 6 loads for expansion slots, or 3 expansion slots. One major difference between PCI and VESA local bus is the placement of the expansion slots. In the PCI implementations there are no inline ISA slots. It is not possible to design a single adapter with both ISA and PCI devices. However, one ISA slot is specified such that it is close to a PCI slot and can be shared. The cost of adapters that would use this approach is probably prohibitive. Figure 2.24 illustrates the PCI bus connector and its defined location on the motherboard relative to the ISA or PC AT bus slots.

**Figure 2.24.**
*PCI slot connector locations on ISA motherboards.*

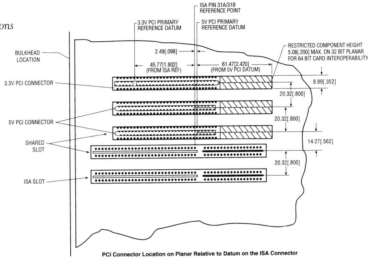

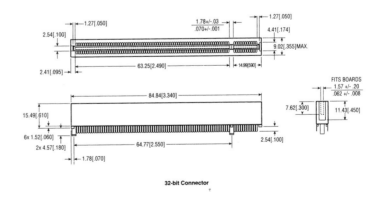

Figure 2.25 illustrates the PCI adapter board sizes proposed by the PCI standard. Note that short and long versions are defined where the long version is roughly the same size as a PC AT or ISA bus adapter board. The PCI expansion bus standard defines an IBM MCA-style expansion bus connector, the same connector as used on the VESA local bus standard. Actually, a family of connectors are defined supporting 5 volt adapters, 3.3 volt adapters and 32- or 64-bit versions of these. It's expected that most expansion bus adapters in the future will use 3.3 volt power sources instead of the

present 5 volt designs. Figure 2.26 illustrates how the PCI standard expects to migrate from the present 5 volt standard to a slot that supports both, and then to a future 3.3 volt only standard. Figure 2.27 is a block diagram of a typical PCI bus system design. Note that of this writing, all PCI bus systems are using 32-bit 5 volt slot designs that support 33 MHz clock speeds and a maximum burst mode transfer data rate of 132 MB/sec.

**Figure 2.25.**
*PCI bus adapter board size.*

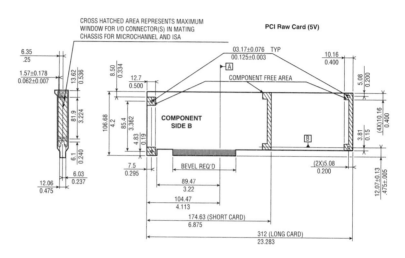

**Figure 2.26.**
*PCI adapter boards edge connectors for 5 and 3.3 volt designs.*

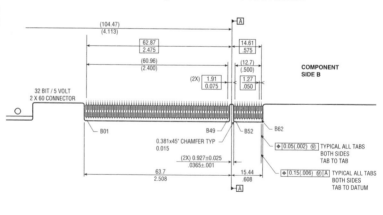

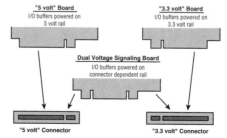

*Figure 2.27.*
*Typical PCI/ISA bus system block diagram.*

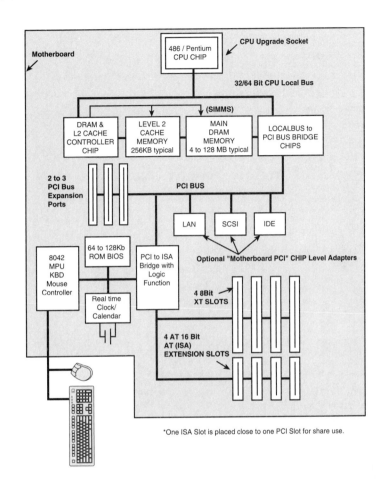

*One ISA Slot is placed close to one PCI Slot for share use.

## Multiprocessor Busses

The newer Pentium processors are all capable of supporting multiprocessor designs, with many motherboard designs able to accommodate two Pentium processors. The Microsoft NT operating system and IBM's SMP OS/2 system also supports multiprocessing if it detects this environment in the system. In high performance applications, such as file servers, multi-processor designs are very attractive and can offer performance that nearly scales with the number of processors added. Several new multiprocessor local bus architectures are competing for adoption as the de facto standard in the application segment. For most desktop applications, this is not likely to be an issue since the forthcoming Windows 95 operating system from Microsoft will not support multiprocessing.

However, high-performance servers using NT will be able to fully utilize new multiprocessor designs. Some of the busses contending for the multiprocessing standard are as follows:

- SIMPL bus from Corollary: 64 bit plus 8 ECC (Error Correction Code) bits at 50 MHz bus clock speed for a 290MB/second transfer data rate

- Intel's P6 local bus: 64 bits at a bus clock speed of 66 MHz for a 500 MB/second data transfer rate
- HydraXS bus from LSI logic: 64 bits at a bus clock speed of 50 MHz for a less than 500 MB/second data transfer rate
- Vbus from Vitesse: 64-bit bus at a bus clock speed of 66 MHz with a 500 MB/second data transfer rate

## Mixed Bus Architecture Systems

If you can't make up your mind on expansion bus architectures, it is possible, at a small cost premium, to purchase systems that support multiple busses. With the exception of the IBM MCA bus, all PCI and VESA Local bus systems support ISA slots. And of course EISA systems also support ISA slots as part of their basic design. To support all of the popular buses (except MCA), a single design with EISA slots, VESA local bus slots, and PCI slots is available. Standards for adding PCI and VESA Local Bus slots to MCA systems have been developed, but I don't know of any such systems in the market today. Figure 2.28 illustrates some of the popular mixed systems available.

## The PC Motherboard

The *motherboard* is the heart of the system. It is called a motherboard because all other features and peripherals must plug into it to operate. The following is a quick summary of the major elements on the motherboard. You can refer to the system block diagrams to see how these elements interact and are connected on the motherboard. The motherboard described is the more contemporary PCI/ISA design in Figure 2.27.

## The Microprocessor and Upgrade Socket

The most important item on the motherboard is the system microprocessor, sometimes called the CPU (Central Processing Unit) or just processor. In today's designs, that will mean an Intel 486 processor or an Intel Pentium processor, or compatible devices from a number of other suppliers. By the time this book is published, the dominant 486 processor will likely be the clock tripled Intel 486DX4 processor running at 100 MHz, or a similar device from one of Intel's competitors. On the high end, Pentium processors or their equivalent from non-Intel sources will be available in the 75 to 130 MHz performance range.

**Figure 2.28.**

*Combination expansion bus
architecture systems
available.*

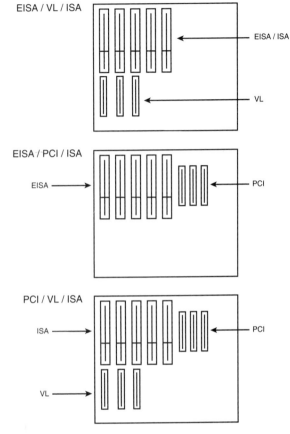

EISA / VL / ISA

EISA / ISA

VL

EISA / PCI / ISA

EISA

PCI

PCI / VL / ISA

ISA

PCI

VL

*Note: All present generation Systems (with the exception
of the IBM Micro Channel System) Support ISA Bus expansion slots!

*PCI/MCA & VL MCA systems have been defined by both the PCI
and VL standard, but are presently not produced!

ISA - Industry Standard Architecture
EISA - Extended Industry Standard Architecture
VL - VESA Local bus

PCI - Peripheral Component Interconnect
MCA - Micro Channel Architecture

Most systems designs today do not solder (electrically attach) the microprocessor permanently to
the motherboard. The processor is in a socket that permits the microprocessor's easy removal from
the motherboard. In fact, the socket is designed to support several microprocessor types and speeds.
This enables a system to be upgraded in the future with a more powerful processor by simply replacing the old processor with a better processor. This scheme was devised by Intel, and they call it the
"Power Up Socket or Overdrive Socket" For example, a system that was initially purchased with a
33 Megahertz 486SX processor could accept the following upgrades:

- A 486DX processor at 33 MHz (adds floating-point Coprocessor).

- A 486DX2 processor at 66 MHz (uses internal clock doubling).

- A 486DX4 Processor At 100 MHz (uses internal clock tripling).

- A Pentium Processor with a 486 bus interface.

- Further enhancement such as clock doubled and tripled Pentiums with 486 bus interfaces are also possible (Intel P54T or Pentium Overdrive).

Microprocessors are covered in much greater detail in the next chapter, as well as a further explanation of processor upgrade options.

## Cache Memory and DRAM Controller

The microprocessor obviously needs to attach to the system's main memory to access data and instructions. This memory is often called DRAM (Dynamic Random Access Memory), and is physically packaged on small circuit boards called SIMMs (Small Inline Memory Modules) The DRAM SIMMs are installed in SIMM sockets on the motherboard. Due primarily to historical reasons, the DRAM system memory cannot directly attach to the microprocessor's local bus. To meet the timing, interface, and "refresh" requirements of the DRAM, a DRAM controller device is needed to bridge between the local bus of the microprocessor and the DRAM devices. In modern designs with high-speed microprocessors, the main system memory (DRAM) cannot keep up with the performance requirements of the processor and becomes a performance bottleneck.

To overcome this limitation on performance, a second smaller memory, called *cache memory*, is placed between the microprocessor and the system memory. This smaller memory is much faster and can keep up with the processor's performance requirements. Typically built using SRAMs(Static RAMS), it stores small blocks of the system DRAM memory to create the illusion that all system memory is available at the high speed of the cache memory. Due to some characteristics of software execution, the cache memory can be very effective at making the system perform at cache memory speeds when most of the memory is much slower DRAM. The circuits that manage the filling of the cache memory from the slower DRAM memory is called a cache controller. The DRAM controller and cache controller functions are typically in a single chip on the motherboard. The high-speed cache memory is also on the motherboard and typically can be expanded in size by adding chips into empty sockets provided on the motherboard. Cache memory sizes range from 128 KB to 1MB—typical Pentium systems come with 256KB of high-speed cache memory. The DRAM or system memory size can vary from 4MB to 128MB and even larger with in some designs. A typical Pentium system is 16MB, although systems as small as 8MB can be built. For more detailed information on system memory and cache memory, see Chapter 15, "The Memory Workbench."

## Core Logic Chip Set

The core logic chip set is the glue that ties the system together. In ISA or VESA bus systems this included the basic Intel support chips that were originally designed into the PC and later expanded with the PC AT design. These core devices are known as the Intel 8237 DMA (Direct Memory Access) controllers, the Intel 8259A interrupt controller devices, and the Intel 8254 timer counter device. The Intel core devices are typically combined with ISA bus control and glue chips to create a single chip in most contemporary designs.

In newer PCI bus designs the "core logic" chip set includes the microprocessor local bus to PCI bridge chip, the system memory controller and cache controller chip, and the PCI to ISA bridge chip.

## PCI Bus Bridge Chip and PCI Expansion Bus

This chip converts the microprocessor's local bus to the PCI (Peripheral Component Interconnect) bus. This chip is different in each system design that uses a different microprocessor. For example, there is one design that converts a 486 local bus to PCI and a different design that converts a Pentium to a PCI bus.

## Keyboard/Mouse Controller and Ports

Each motherboard contains a keyboard and a mouse controller device and connector ports. Some older designs only support the keyboard port and assume the mouse is attached to one of the system's serial communications ports. The PC's keyboard is attached to the system unit's motherboard through a serial interface cable. The keyboard serial interface adapter and port sends and receives serial data in an isochronous transmission mode. This means that data is transmitted and received one bit at a time on the edges of a clock signal supplied by the keyboard adapter device, since the data and clock are synchronized transmission, timing is not critical and well adapted to a software implementation. For example, to send data, the adapter devices sets a bit value on a serial data line and then toggles a serial clock line on the interface. This process is repeated until a full block of data or a command is transmitted. Similarly, the keyboard responds by sending data to the motherboard adapter on each toggle of the serial clock line received from the motherboard adapter. As you may have surmised by now, the interface between the motherboard adapter and the keyboard is a two-wire interface supporting bidirectional data transmission over clock and data lines. The actual keyboard interface cable supports four lines, where the two additional lines carry 5 volts DC power and grounds, providing power to the keyboard. The keyboard cable is typically limited to 6 feet in length.

In pure PC AT designs, the keyboard attaches to a 5-pin DIN connector mounted on the back edge of the motherboard, which is accessible through a hole in the rear bulk head of the system unit's case. On systems that use the PS/2 style keyboard port, the connector is a mini-DIN type with 6 pins. The PS/2 style connector is often used on notebooks to save space. Often keyboards come with small adapters that allow them to connect to either style port.

The keyboard serial clock and data interface signals attach to an Intel 8042, or equivalent, micro controller chip on the motherboard. This chip in turn attaches to the system unit's microprocessor bus. Actually, the 8042 device connects to the sub-ISA bus used to communicate with other adapter devices on the bus. This sub-bus is often called the X bus and is only 8 bits in width. Figure 2.29

illustrates how the PC's keyboard attaches to the system unit and defines the signals on the two styles of port connectors. Note that in some designs, the micro-controller also supports a second auxiliary port typically used to attach a mouse pointing device. The 8042 controller sends and receives commands, status, and data to the system unit using the X bus and interrupt levels 1 for the keyboard and level 12 for the mouse, if the mouse function is supported. The 8042 micro controller chip is actually a small 8-bit microprocessor with 2KB of program ROM and 128 bytes of RAM. It is programmed to accept keyboard scan codes or mouse coordinates and report this information to the system unit's software.

**Figure 2.29.**
*PC keyboard/mouse adapter
and port block diagram.*

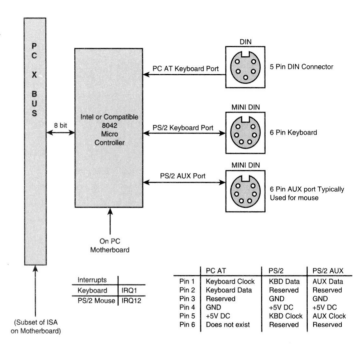

| | PC AT | PS/2 | PS/2 AUX |
|---|---|---|---|
| Pin 1 | Keyboard Clock | KBD Data | AUX Data |
| Pin 2 | Keyboard Data | Reserved | Reserved |
| Pin 3 | Reserved | GND | GND |
| Pin 4 | GND | +5V DC | +5V DC |
| Pin 5 | +5V DC | KBD Clock | AUX Clock |
| Pin 6 | Does not exist | Reserved | Reserved |

| Interrupts | |
|---|---|
| Keyboard | IRQ1 |
| PS/2 Mouse | IRQ12 |

At the keyboard end, a second micro-controller device installed in the keyboard attaches to the interface clock and data signals, and communicates with the 8042 device on the system board. The micro-controller device in the keyboard is typically an Intel or equivalent 8048 microprocessor. This microprocessor is programmed to periodically scan the keyboard keys and detect when a key is depressed or released. The 8048 device sends an 8-bit code for each key depression and also for each key being released. The 8048 can also detect when a key has been depressed for a long period of time and sends repeated scan codes performing a typematic function. The 8048 can also detect multiple simultaneous key depression and report all of them in order, which is called an N key rollover feature. The 8048 does not actually report keyboard character codes but special 8-bit scan codes that are then translated by the system unit's software to character codes.

# ROM BIOS

The ROM (Read-Only Memory) BIOS (Basic Input Output Service) device is a read-only memory device that contains software that is commonly used to talk to the system's hardware elements. In today's systems its primary purpose is to load the basic operating system software from the system's boot or start-up device and perform power on system tests. The operating system boot device is usually the system's hard disk or the LAN port. The read-only memory is from 64 to 128 kilobytes in size. Most of the time its contents are moved to faster DRAM memory for execution. Newer BIOS also incorporate features to support system configuration detection and resource allocation as defined by the new Plug and Play specification.

## Real-Time Clock and Calendar with Nonvolatile Memory

On every motherboard there is a chip called a real-time clock/calendar device. This device also contains a small amount of nonvolatile memory (normally 64 bytes). This device is always running, even when the system is powered off. Power is supplied by a small battery typically installed on the motherboard. The device supplies relatively accurate date and time information to the operating system software and stores basic system configuration information in the small nonvolatile memory. Loss of this information by disconnection of the battery or a low battery condition will likely temporarily cripple your system by destroying key configuration information.

# ISA to PCI Bridge Chip and ISA Slots

If the system is a PCI bus based design, it contains an ISA to PCI bridge chip. This chip performs the transformation of the PCI bus to the older ISA or PC AT bus. This chip contains all the original Intel core circuits including the 8237 DMA chips, the 8259 interrupt controller chips, and the 8254 timer counter chips. This chip creates the older PC AT or ISA bus, allowing backward compatibility with older expansion bus devices and adapters.

# Basic or Standard Adapter Boards

A typical non-IBM or Compaq system has two adapter boards installed in motherboard expansion slots. One board is a multi-I/O port board supporting several peripheral connection ports. This board is usually installed in a 16-bit ISA port slot. The second adapter board is usually a display adapter board supporting the VGA and SVGA standard with Windows graphic acceleration and installed in a PCI or VESA local bus slot. Some systems designs include one or both of these adapter boards functions on the motherboard, such as on some IBM and Compaq systems.

# Multi-I/O Port Adapter Board

This board supports a number of peripheral interfaces adapters and ports I describe in a moment. Figure 2.30 is a diagram of a typical multi-I/O port adapter board. Note that in some VESA local bus designs the board is extended to reach the inline VESA slot. This permits the board to attach the IDE (hard disk controller port) to the faster VESA local bus. This local bus connection can dramatically improve hard disk performance, particularly if the IDE port is the newer high-speed EIDE (Enhanced IDE) design. Typically, all the device adapters and ports on the multi-I/O port boards are integrated into a single chip called a *super I/O chip*. The following is a quick summary of the functions of each of the adapter functions port on the multi-I/O port adapter.

**Figure 2.30.**
*Typical PC multi-I/O adapter board.*

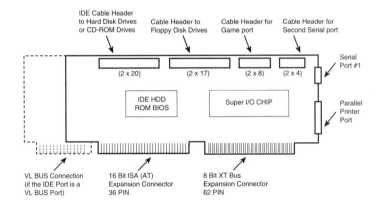

## Floppy Disk Drive Adapter and Port

This adapter function and port supports the attachment of (normally) two floppy disk drives. The drives can be either 3.5-inch or 5.25-inch devices or mixed. Most multi-I/O port boards also support the newer high-density 2.88MB 3.5-inch floppy dives. The original PC XT and AT designs actually supported up to 4 disk drives. In most modern PC designs, the floppy disk drive adapter functions are part of the super I/O chip on the multi-I/O port adapter board. The drives are attached through a 34-pin header organized as two rows of 17 pins each. The cable is then daisy chained from one drive to the other, as indicated in Figure 2.31. From the interface signal definition in Figure 2.31, four drive-select signals are provided. In early systems the leads of the cable were swapped to allow selection of a specific drive. Today, most floppy disk drives have jumper blocks that can be set to select the drive number. Most floppy disk drive adapters are capable of supporting drive data rates as high as 2 megabits/second and can also attach to backup tape drives.

**Figure 2.31.**
*Floppy disk drive adapter
and port block diagram.*

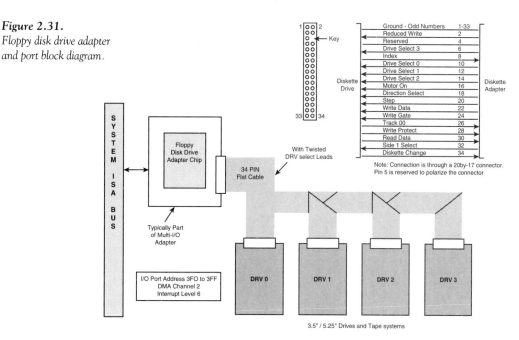

| | |
|---|---|
| Ground - Odd Numbers | 1-33 |
| Reduced Write | 2 |
| Reserved | 4 |
| Drive Select 3 | 6 |
| Index | 8 |
| Drive Select 0 | 10 |
| Drive Select 1 | 12 |
| Drive Select 2 | 14 |
| Motor On | 16 |
| Direction Select | 18 |
| Step | 20 |
| Write Data | 22 |
| Write Gate | 24 |
| Track 00 | 26 |
| Write Protect | 28 |
| Read Data | 30 |
| Side 1 Select | 32 |
| Diskette Change | 34 |

Note: Connection is through a 20by-17 connector.
Pin 5 is reserved to polarize the connector

Note: For more detailed information on the drive interface
signals refer to the IBM Technical Reference Manuals.

# The IDE Port

The IDE (Intelligent Drive Electronics), also known as the ATA (PC AT Attached) port, supports the attachment of two hard drives with a maximum capacity of 528MB each. When the PC AT was announced by IBM, the hard disk drive adapter was a separate adapter board installed in a PC AT or ISA bus expansion slot with a low level serial interface to the hard disk. Drive manufacturers saw an opportunity to move the adapter's functions to the drive and combine it with the drive-specific electronics. The new drive interface was actually a subset of the ISA bus signals used to communicate with the integrated hard drive adapter now on the drive. This scheme was transparent to the system software that saw the same hardware interface on the new IDE or ATA drives as was on the older nonintegrated separate adapter solution. Because the IDE interface was a subset of ISA bus signals, creating an IDE port was easy to do and was very inexpensive—normally involving less than $1.00 in parts! The very low cost of attaching IDE hard drives to the PC has accounted for their popularity versus the higher cost SCSI drives.

Most IDE interfaces and drives did not support DMA data transfers and all commands, status, and data are transferred using standard PC I/O port instructions. This data transfer mode is often called the PIO mode or Programmed I/O mode; in this mode the PC's software is involved in every data transfer operation. This would seem to be very slow and software-intensive, but the drives contained multiple sector buffers that could be read and written using the Intel X86 repeat I/O string instructions. The X86 processors have special instructions that can be repeated without being refetched each time they are used. When the repeat instruction is combined with an I/O port read or write instruction, high-speed data transfer is possible. Using this capability of the Intel processors actually resulted in a higher speed and lower bus utilization data transfer than achievable with DMA transfers. The IDE port also uses PC interrupt level 14 to notify the PC of incoming status or data from the hard drive. Figure 2.32 is a table defining the signals and connector pins used on the IDE port. Note that the data transfer interface is 16 bits wide and decodes two separate blocks of the PC I/O port address space. I/O port address space is a special block of 65,536 addresses that are used to talk to I/O adapters. They are similar to memory addresses except that the bits in each byte are typically tied to some hardware function in the adapter. The interface cable from the drives is attached to a 40-pin header organized as two rows of 20 pins, with pin 20 functioning as a key. Two drives are connected by a single cable connected in a daisy chain method, as depicted in Figure 2.33.

**Figure 2.32.**

*IDE port interface signals and connector pin locations.*

IDE Port Signals & Port Connector Pins

| Description | Source | Pin | Acronym |
|---|---|---|---|
| Reset | Host | 1 | RESET- |
|  | n/a | 2 | Ground |
| Data Bus bit 7 | Host/Device | 3 | DD7 |
| Data Bus bit 8 | Host/Device | 4 | DD8 |
| Data Bus bit 6 | Host/Device | 5 | DD6 |
| Data Bus bit 9 | Host/Device | 6 | DD9 |
| Data Bus bit 5 | Host/Device | 7 | DD5 |
| Data Bus bit 10 | Host/Device | 8 | DD10 |
| Data Bus bit 4 | Host/Device | 9 | DD4 |
| Data Bus bit 11 | Host/Device | 10 | DD11 |
| Data Bus bit 3 | Host/Device | 11 | DD3 |
| Data Bus bit 12 | Host/Device | 12 | DD12 |
| Data Bus bit 2 | Host/Device | 13 | DD2 |
| Data Bus bit 13 | Host/Device | 14 | DD13 |
| Data Bus bit 1 | Host/Device | 15 | DD1 |
| Data Bus bit 14 | Host/Device | 16 | DD14 |
| Data Bus bit 0 | Host/Device | 17 | DD0 |
| Data Bus bit 15 | Host/Device | 18 | DD15 |
| Ground | n/a | 19 | Ground |
| (keypin) | n/a | 20 | Reserved |
| DMA Request | Device | 21 | DMARQ |
| Ground | n/a | 22 | Ground |
| I/O Write | Host | 23 | DIOW- |
| Ground | n/a | 24 | Ground |
| I/O Read | Host | 25 | DIOR- |
| Ground | n/a | 26 | Ground |
| I/O Ready | Device | 27 | IORDY |
| Spindle Sync or Cable Select |  | 28 | SPSYNC:CSEL |
| DMA Acknowledge | Host | 29 | DMACK |
| Ground | n/a | 30 | Ground |
| Interrupt Request | Device | 31 | INTRQ |
| 16 Bit I/O | Device | 32 | IOCS16- |
| Device Address Bit 1 | Host | 33 | DA1 |
| PASSED DIAGNOSTICS |  | 34 | PDIAG- |
| Device Address Bit 0 | Host | 35 | DA0 |
| Device Address Bit 2 | Host | 36 | DA2 |
| Chip Select 0 | Host | 37 | CS0 |
| Chip Select 2 | Host | 38 | CS2 |
| Device Active or Slave (Device 1) Present |  | 39 | DASP |
| Ground | n/a | 40 | Ground |

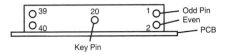

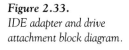

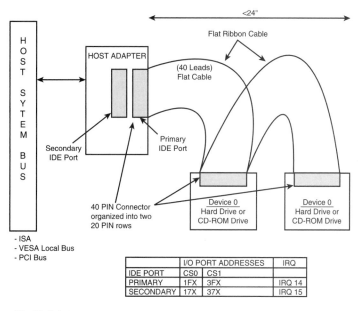

In notebook designs, the IDE port must attach to smaller hard disk drives, 2.5 or 1.8 inches in diameter, and require a smaller IDE connector. This connector also supports four additional drive-specific signals. These signals are used to supply power or provide power management functions in the notebook IDE drives. This 44-pin IDE connector is defined by the SFF (Small Form Factor) industry group.

## Enhanced IDE (EIDE) ATA-2

There have been several enhancements to this interface that allow for support of more than two drives and a significant increase in interface data transfer performance. The hard drive capacity limitation has been relieved and now supports up to 8GB on each drive. Also, it is now possible to attach CD-ROM drives to this port. These enhancements are part of an improved IDE specification called the EIDE (Enhanced IDE) or ATA-2 specification. In addition, a new standard called ATAPI (AT Attached Packet Interface) uses the IDE or ATA interface to support CD-ROM drives. The new ATA-2 or EIDE specification defines several improved data transfer modes and speeds. Besides the standard PIO (Programmed I/O) data transfer modes, a single-word and multiword DMA (Direct Memory Access) transfer are defined. The single word DMA transfer will transfer a single 16-bit word on each DMA request. The multiword transfer will continue to transfer 16-bit words as long as the DMA request signal is active and terminal count is not reached. Efforts are also now underway to define a PCI bus master transfer mode expected to support very high data rates (greater than 20 MB/second). As of this writing, this standard has not yet been solidified. Several PCI IDE adapters, however, are available that use the higher speed PIO modes now defined. Table 2.3 defines the newer IDE modes and their minimum IDE port bus cycle times.

Table 2.3. IDE Modes and Bus Cycle Times.

| Mode | Minimum bus cycle time in nanoseconds |
|------|---------------------------------------|
| PIO mode 0 | 600 ns |
| PIO mode 1 | 383 ns |
| PIO mode 2 | 240 ns |
| PIO mode 3 | 180 ns |
| PIO mode 4 | 120 ns |
| Single word DMA mode 0 | 960 ns |
| Single word DMA mode 0 | 960 ns |
| Single word DMA mode 1 | 480 ns |
| Single word DMA mode 2 | 240 ns |
| Multiword DMA mode 0 | 480 ns |
| Multiword DMA mode 1 | 150 ns |
| Multiword DMA mode 2 | 120 ns |

# Serial Ports

The multi-I/O port adapter typically contains two serial communications(COM) ports supporting standard start/stop asynchronous transmission protocols over RS-232-C electrical interface ports. Most new designs support data rates up to 115 kilobaud with deep FIFO, or both the transmit and receive register interfaces. Over the years the PC's serial communications ports have been implemented by a series of UART (Universal Asynchronous Receiver Transmitter) devices. The first device was the NS8250 used in the PC and PC XT. This device had several bugs and its speed was limited to 56 kilobits/second.(IBM specified its maximum speed at 9600 bits/second). In the PC AT design the device was upgraded to the NS16450 chip. This chip still ran at a maximum speed of 56 kilobits/second but fixed many of the bugs in the original NS8250 device. The latest PC designs use the NS16550 or equivalent devices. This device supports a 1X baud rate mode with a maximum data transfer rate of 115 kilobits/second. Note that this bit rate includes the start bit, stop bits, and parity bit if used, thus the actual data transfer rate of user data is somewhat less than the transmission bit rate. The NS16550 devices also provided 16-byte FIFO buffers on the transmit and receive data paths inside the chip. This feature limited the PC's need to service every data transaction, since multiple characters or bytes of data could be transmitted or received with only one PC interrupt per block. This dramatically increased the PC's ability to support the 115 kilobits/second transfer mode. Figure 2.34 is a block diagram of a stand-alone PC Serial communications port adapter board supporting two COM ports.

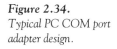

**Figure 2.34.**
*Typical PC COM port adapter design.*

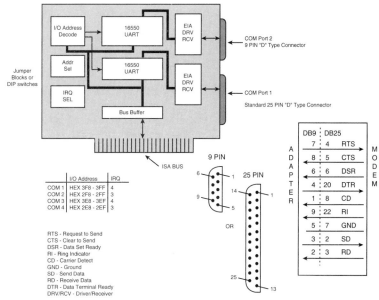

# Game Port

The PC's game controller adapter and port are typically integrated on either the multi-I/O adapter board or a sound board. It may also be offered as a stand-alone adapter board that plugs into one of the ISA 8-bit expansion slots. The game controllers connect to the PC adapter through a standard 15-pin D shell connector. (Note that this 15-pin connector is a different style and size than the "high density" 15-pin display adapter connector.) One or two game controllers can connect to this single port connector. When two game controllers are used, a special split cable is provided as depicted in Figure 2.35. The game controller port interface supports sensing of two joysticks or joypads, each with an X and Y position sensing capability. Also, a total of four switches or fire buttons can be sensed over the game port controller interface. The game controllers are expected to report X and Y positions as resistive values generated by X and Y potentiometers (POTs) built into the game controllers. The game controller port does not read the game controller POT's resistive values directly. The resistive values, however, can be calculated by measuring the time it takes to discharge the R/C (resistive/capacitive) time constant created by the POT's position and a fixed capacitance on the game adapter. The rate that a capacitor discharges an electrical charge is governed by the resistance of the discharge path. The game adapter's capacitor is first charged to +5 volts and then discharged through the resistive value of the current X or Y POT's position. By measuring the time it takes to discharge the capacitor, the POT's resistive value can be calculated. All four POT capacitors are discharged simultaneously by executing an I/O port write command to port address hex 201. The software can sense the discharge signal timing in a special read only I/O port register at I/O port address hex 201. The table in Figure 2.35 defines the bit positions to be read to measure discharge times and the read fire button switch states. By timing in software the discharge signal's length, the POT's present resistance value can be calculated using the following formula. This formula is relatively accurate for pot resistive values in the range of 0 to 100K ohms:

Discharge time = 24.2 + 0.011(Resistance)

Figure 2.35 illustrates how a game controller would attach to the game controller port. Note that on some sound boards that support a game port, pins 12 and 15 of the 15-pin connector are used to support a MIDI (Musical Instrument Digital Interface) serial port connection. The +5 volt and ground signals that were on these pins are obtained from other +5 volt and ground pins on the 15-pin connector.

***Figure 2.35.***
*PC game port and*
*controller connections.*

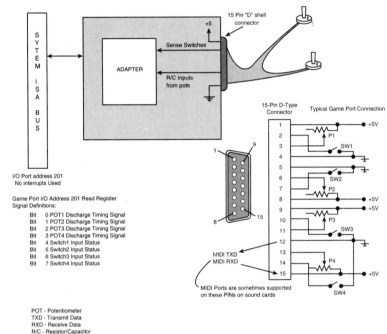

## Parallel Printer Port

Nearly every PC comes with a parallel printer port and adapter, which is often built into the multi-I/O adapter board. This port is called by various names including: Centronics printer port, parallel printer port, standard printer port (SPP), LPT (Line Printer) port, enhanced parallel port (EPP), extended capability port (ECP), and the IEEE 1284 port. The original PC designers selected an 8-bit output only port interface that was used on a family of printers designed by a company called Centronics, thus the name Centronics printer port. This port transferred 8-bit parallel data over a 17-wire interface using four output control signals and five status input signals. It was a simple, low-cost design that used software to control and transfer data from the system to the printer. The maximum transfer rate achievable over this original interface was about 150 KB/second. Later, IBM enhanced the interface by permitting 8-bit directional data transfer. This enhancement enabled attachment of all types of nonprinter devices such as scanners, LAN adapters, disk drives, and CD-ROM drives. This became known as the enhanced parallel port (EPP). Later HP and Microsoft defined further enhancement to the interface transfer protocol supporting command cycles, data cycles, and multiple logical device addressing. This became known as the extended capability port (ECP). Recently, the IEEE has further enhanced the parallel port interface standard under the IEEE 1284 committee. The EPP and ECP modes are also supported under the 1284 standard. This standard adds additional high-speed data transfer modes, better specifications for physical connections, and interface electrical specifications and protocols for mode negotiation. Figure 2.36 is a diagram of the PC's printer port and the interface connector and signal/pin definitions. Also, the tables in the diagram defines the I/O port addresses and the associated interrupt levels used by the printer port adapters.

**Figure 2.36.**
*PC parallel printer port.*

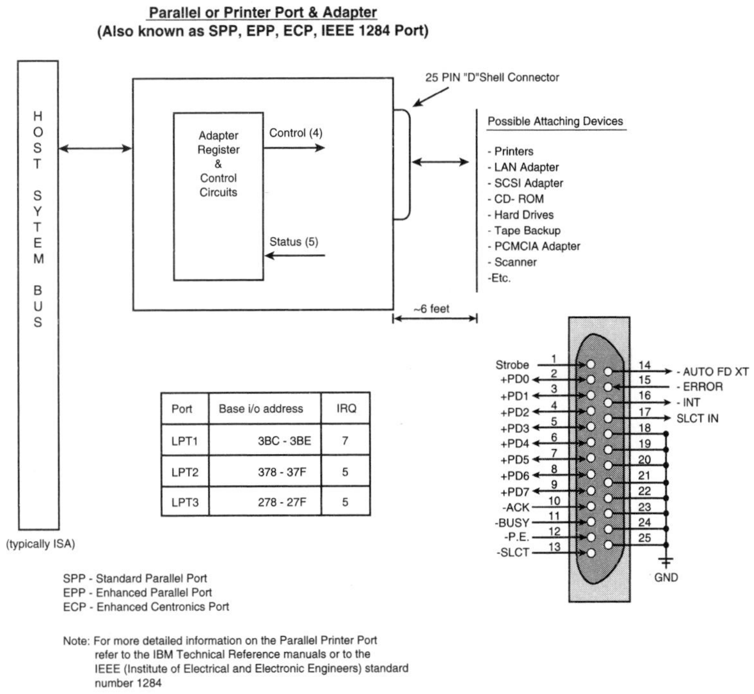

**Parallel or Printer Port & Adapter**
(Also known as SPP, EPP, ECP, IEEE 1284 Port)

| Port | Base i/o address | IRQ |
|------|-----------------|-----|
| LPT1 | 3BC - 3BE | 7 |
| LPT2 | 378 - 37F | 5 |
| LPT3 | 278 - 27F | 5 |

(typically ISA)

SPP - Standard Parallel Port
EPP - Enhanced Parallel Port
ECP - Enhanced Centronics Port

Note: For more detailed information on the Parallel Printer Port refer to the IBM Technical Reference manuals or to the IEEE (Institute of Electrical and Electronic Engineers) standard number 1284

# Display Adapter

The present PC display adapter is the result of a long progression of architectures starting with the original PC's CGA (Color Graphics Adapter) and MDA (Monochrome Display Adapter). What's interesting is that every present day PC display adapter supports all of the modes of the preceding display adapters, including the original CGA and MDA devices. Since most DOS-based software— and nearly all games on the PC—directly access the display adapter hardware, maintaining exact backward hardware compatibility has been a requirement of all display adapter designs. PC display adapters are usually separate adapter boards that plug into one of the PC bus expansion slots, but some systems integrate the display adapter function directly on the system's motherboard. Actually, the performance requirements of the PC's display adapter, driven by Windows GUI (Graphical Users Interface), has driven the PC's bus architecture innovations. Early display adapters were attached to the PC ISA or PC AT bus, but as the data rates increased with higher screen refresh rates, larger screens and more color per pixel, this bus became a significant performance bottleneck. Today's display adapters are designed to attach to either the VL bus or PCI bus.

Figure 2.37 is a basic block diagram of a PC display adapter. The major components are the AVGA (Accelerated Video Graphics Array) chip, display memory, RAMDAC, and a clock generator device. The graphic controller chip attaches directly to the PCI or VL bus and generates the CRT display horizontal and vertical sync signals, controls and provides software access to the local display memory where the screen image is stored, and supports local graphics manipulation functions such as line draws, area fills, image or data block moves, and color expansion. Normally when the system software wants to move a window on the screen, the display adapter is instructed to perform this function, and it occurs without the PC microprocessor's assistance. The RAMDAC (Random Access Memory and Digital to Analog Converter) takes the digital image data from the display memory and converts it to analog RGB signals (Red, Green, and Blue) that the CRT display monitor understands. The device also will convert 8-bit-color information to 24-bit color value using the RAM in the RAMDAC as a color palette. A clock generator device is used to convert a 14.318 megahertz frequency to the clocks required to control the display memory and output the pixels to the display. Some of the latest display adapter chips now incorporate the clock generator and RAMDAC in the AVGA device, making a true single chip display adapter solution. However, the highest performance systems still use independent clocks and RAMDACs.

The most important element of the display adapter is the display memory; its size, speed, and organization are major factors in defining the performance of a graphic display adapter. The size of the memory determines the screen resolutions possible. Depending on the number of colors per pixel, the memory size required to support a specific screen size can be calculated by multiplying the horizontal resolution by the vertical resolution in pixels and then multiplying this value by 1, 2, or 3, where 1 means one byte per pixel or 256-color, 2 means 16 bits per pixel or 65,536 colors per pixel, and 3 means 24 bits per pixel or 16.8 million colors per pixel. For example, on a 15-inch display monitor, it is possible to easily support an 800×600 pixel image. Thus, a 256-color screen requires 480,000 bytes or 480KB of memory, a 65,536-color screen will require 960KB or nearly 1MB of memory, and for a full 16.8 million full-color screen 1.44MB of display memory is required. If your display can support a screen size of 1280×1024 pixels, full color (16.8 million colors) requires 3,932,160 bytes of display memory, or nearly 4MB!

At high color depths and large screen resolutions, another problem begins to develop. The ability to move data in and out of the display memory—its bandwidth—can become a limiting factor. The memory bandwidth is measured in megabytes per second. Three devices contend for access to the display memory: display refresh, CPU, and the Graphics Accelerator engine or processor. First, the display itself must be refreshed or repainted quickly enough to eliminate display flicker. Most agree that the display must be refreshed at least 70 times per second to avoid annoying flicker. Multiplying the refresh rate times the screen horizontal resolution times its vertical resolution times the number of bytes (color depth) per pixel gives a rough measure of the refresh bandwidth requirement. For example, an 800×600 screen with 24 bits per pixel (true color), refreshed at a 76 Hz rate will require a display memory bandwidth of 109.44 MB/second, whereas a 1280×1024 screen at the same color depth and refresh rate will require roughly 393.216 MB/second bandwidth!

The latest 32-bit wide DRAM display memory technologies are capable of approximately 150 to 200 MB/second bandwidth. Unfortunately, the display controller and PC's microprocessor must also access the display memory to move windows and draw new windows fast enough to satisfy the user performance demands. A good rule of thumb is to reserve half of the display memory bandwidth for the display controller screen access updates. For the earlier example of the 800×600 16.8 million color screen at 76 hertz refresh rate, the 32-bit DRAM memory would be stretched to the limits of its performance. The large 1280×1024 full color screen cannot even be supported by the 32-bit DRAM solution! To meet the higher bandwidth requirements of large screens, most new display adapters support 64-bit wide DRAM designs with bandwidths of up to 300 to 400MB. Even with 64-bit wide DRAM designs, screen resolution of 1280×1024 at 16 and 24-bit colors per pixel at greater than 70 Hz are not feasible. For these performance levels, dual-ported memory designs are often used. The most commonly used dual-port memory is called VRAM (Video Random Access Memory). This memory has two access ports where data for refreshing the display is accessed on a port separated from the display update port. This effectively doubles the VRAM's bandwidth in display memory applications. State-of-the-art VRAM display adapters are capable of supporting memory bandwidth in excess of 800 MB/second. If your applications require high-resolution screens with high or full-color depth, the best performance is achieved using a display adapter designed with a dual-port memory scheme, such as VRAM.

The PC's display device connects to the display adapter through a high-density 15-pin D shell style connector. The pin and signal definitions for this connector are defined in Figure 2.37. In addition to this connector, most display adapters provide a special connector called a VFC (Video Feature Connector). This connector allows video images from other sources to be merged or mixed with the graphics images generated by the display adapter. This interface is often used to merge live TV images with computer generated images on the PC's display. Three versions of this connector are specified: the VFC, AVFC (Advance Video Feature Connector), and the VMC (VESA Media Channel. The primary differences between these interfaces is in the data rate and color depths of the merged video and where the data is actually merged. For more details on the PC's Display adapter, see Chapter 15.

# Optional Enhancement Adapters/Ports and Peripheral Devices

Following are brief descriptions of some of the more common enhancements added to PCs. Most of the devices described take an expansion bus slot and provide a new peripheral function or provide a new expansion port interface adapter capable of supporting attachment of new peripheral devices.

**Figure 2.37.**
*Block diagram of a
typical PC display
adapter.*

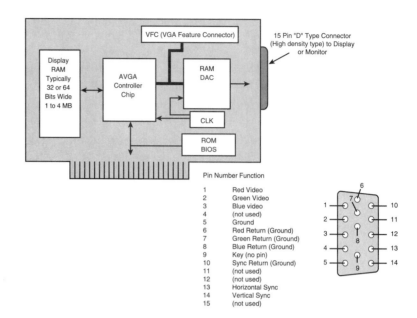

# SCSI Adapters

The SCSI (Small Computer System Interface), SCSI-2, and SCSI-3 specifications define a bus that
can connect one or more host computers (PCs) with a variety of peripheral devices. The SCSI specification first served the needs of the hard disk industry and was known as the SASI interface (Shuggart
Associates Systems Interface). The ANSI(American National Standards Institute) X.3T9.2 committee expanded the specification to define a generic parallel I/O bus. Table 2.4 summarizes the basic
characteristics of the SCSI bus.

Table 2.4. The SCSI Bus Characteristics.

| Interface type | Parallel I/O bus |
|---|---|
| Interface Protocol | Peer to Peer command blocks |
| Bus Configuration | 8-bit, 16-bit* or 32-bit* parallel |
| Connection Scheme | Daisy chain (terminator on last device) |
| Maximum total cable length | 6 meters(single ended drivers) |
|  | 20 meters (differential drivers) |
| Maximum number of devices | 8 OR 7 from a master port |
| Transfer modes and speeds |  |
| Asynchronous modes | 8 bits, 2 MB/second typical |
| Synchronous modes | 8 bits, 5 MB/second typical |
|  | 16 bits*, 10 MB/second typical |

| Interface type | Parallel I/O bus |
|---|---|
| Fast Synchronous modes* | 8 bits, 10 MB/second typical |
| | 16 bits, 20 MB/second typical |
| | 32 bits, 40 MB/second typical |

*Options in the SCSI-2 and SCSI-3 specifications

The SCSI specification defines a logical command set for each generic peripheral type as well as the physical and electrical characteristics of the bus. The specification requires that each device have local intelligence in the form of a controller. Any device can communicate directly with any other device over the SCSI bus. The specification defines bus phases that allow for bus arbitration and temporary disconnection and subsequent reconnection. Disconnection lets peripherals free the bus during long delays, such as disk seek operations. The SCSI specification defines multithreaded operations, in which more than one I/O operation can be active in the subsystem at a time. In fact, more than one I/O operation between the same two devices can be simultaneously active. SCSI devices can queue multiple commands in the local controller and execute them in the correct order. Therefore, a SCSI I/O subsystem can better handle the performance that a multiuser multitasking system application requires. The SCSI bus can also serve as a cost-effective single point connection to a variety of peripherals, such as both hard disk drives and CD-ROM drives and high-speed tape backup drives. Because SCSI is a host independent interface, it's also possible to easily move SCSI devices from, say, an Apple MAC system to a PC system.

## SCSI-2 and Wide Fast SCSI (SCSI-3)

The ANSI committee that developed the SCSI-2 specification went to a great deal of effort to ensure backward compatibility with the original SCSI specification. Thus a properly designed SCSI-2 adapter would work with virtually all older SCSI peripherals. The SCSI-2 specification defines the much heralded wide (16 and 32 bits) and fast synchronous data transfers as options, just as the original specification defined synchronous data transfers as options. In the SCSI-2 specification, the host and peripheral devices still perform all message, command, and status phases in the 8-bit asynchronous mode. The couple negotiate during the message phase to determine the fastest common method available to transfer data. Thus, all SCSI and SCSI-2 operate together in the baseline 8-bit asynchronous mode. Since SCSI-2 specifies the wide and fast modes as options, getting a SCSI-2 adapter or devices doesn't ensure the much higher data rates unless the features are specified. Wide Fast SCSI-2 (recently changed in name to SCSI-3) implementations often require balanced line drivers and receivers, doubling the number of signal lines in the cable. (These are the circuits that actually drive the cable between devices.) When two drivers and wires are used to drive a signal, the signal can be driven at a much higher speed, thus balanced or dual-line drivers are used in the fastest implementations of SCSI.

## SCSI versus IDE or ATA

In most PC applications where multitasking is not used, the new Enhanced IDE or ATA-2 interfaces cost less and provide similar performance to 16-bit fast SCSI-2 implementations. Now that
EIDE supports data rates to 16 MB/second, larger drives, multiple EIDE ports, and CD-ROM drives,
SCSI adapters and devices with their cost premium seem to be less attractive. However, in high-
performance networked file server applications, SCSI ports and hard disk drives are much preferred.

One additional concern with SCSI on the PC is that PC DOS does not support SCSI. Therefore, a
SCSI software device driver must be installed on the PC to support the SCSI port and devices. This
driver is typically provided by the SCSI adapter manufacturer. Figure 2.38 is a block diagram of a
typical SCSI port adapter on a PC system.

The SCSI standard is still evolving with the SCSI-3 proposed specification. This specification is
still not approved, but it intends to expand the scope of the standard to encompass a new high speed
serial version of SCSI, with higher speeds, lower connection costs, and new transmission mediums
such as fiber optic cables.

**Figure 2.38.**
*SCSI ports on PCs.*

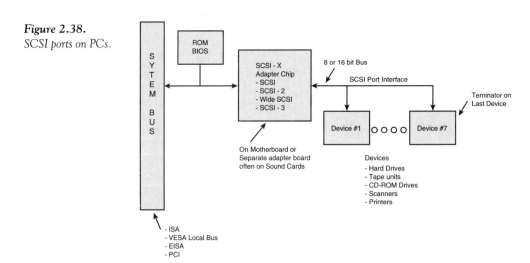

# PCMCIA Cards (PC Cards) and Slots

Several years ago, as notebook PCs became popular, it became obvious to many that expansion
devices, such as memory, fax and modems, LAN, and hard disk drives adapters needed to have a
standardized method of attachment to the notebooks. Each laptop or notebook manufacturer was
providing their own proprietary expansion ports; even simple upgrades such as memory expansion
were incompatible between manufacturers. Worse yet was the requirement to install expansion
upgrades by opening the system and fiddling with unfamiliar connectors and cables. To solve this
problem, the industry's efforts were initially focused on how to provide small but reliable form factor
memory expansion on devices such as notebooks without opening the notebook. Two organizations

began to develop similar standards for small form factor memory cards—JEIDA (Japan Electronic Industry Development Association) and in the United States, PCMCIA (Personal Computer Memory Card Association). In 1989, PCMCIA accepted the JEIDA-proposed 68-pin connector standard used today, and the two groups have since worked together to maintain a single uniform standard. The goal of the PCMCIA is to promote a single standard for small package form factor expansion cards, with a mechanical specification (size, socket, and connector), bus specification (signals, signal drive and loading, and timing), software driver, and Plug and Play specifications. The PCMCIA cards could be installed in a system by simply plugging them into externally accessible card slots.

Because of their very compact size (approximately the size of a credit card and about 1/5 of an inch thick), PCMCIA slots are most often found on mobile computer systems such as notebooks, personal digital assistants (PDAs), sub-notebooks, and palmtop systems. It is, however, possible to purchase an adapter that provides PCMCIA slots on a standard desktop computer. Desktop PCMCIA slots are often designed to fit into floppy drive mounting bays. These slots can be used as a method for exchanging data between a mobile system and a desktop system using a PCMCIA storage card.

The PCMCIA standard has gone through several revisions, the first version (1.0) only supported memory cards but defined the basic noncable-attached physical card size(Type I style/3.5 mm thick) and the initial bus specification supporting memory accesses. Version 2.0 of the specification adopted support for both memory and I/O port addressing, and expanded the mechanical specification to thicker cards (Type II/5 mm thick and Type III/10.5 mm thick), and cards supporting the attachment of external cables. The Version 2.0 standard also permitted programs to be executed directly from the PCMCIA card's memory(called execute in place mode). The PCMCIA standard has been plagued by software compatibility issues and much work has been put into carefully defining how software interacts with the PCMCIA slot and the installed adapters. Most of these problems have been resolved and operation on different platforms is generally satisfactory. Version 2.0 has several shortcomings that are being addressed by Version 3.0. The specification is now being updated to support 3.3 volt adapters, hot insertion and removal, power management, DMA and bus mastering, 32-bit operation, and functional compatibility with the PCI bus. The 32-bit version with PCI bus compatibility is often called the *CardBus Standard*.

Figure 2.39 defines the PCMCIA bus signals and the 68-pin connector used on the cards and slots. Note that the PCMCIA bus supports 26 bits of addressing or 64MB. Data can be transferred on either an 8- or 16-bit bus. Control signals on the bus support both memory and I/O ports with a single interrupt level input. The interface supports special voltages and control signals for real-time programming of nonvolatile Flash and EEPROM devices while they are plugged into a PCMCIA slot. Figure 2.40 illustrates how PCMCIA slots are created from ISA or PC AT bus signals. The most common device for performing this conversion is the Intel 82365SL controller chip, sometimes called a "host adapter" device. Several manufacturers produce clones of this chip—some with significant enhancements. Several manufacturers are now providing PCMCIA slots to PCI bus bridge chips, permitting the PCMCIA slots to access the higher performance PCI bus.

*Figure 2.39.*

*PCMCIA bus signals and connector definition.*

PCMCIA Bus Signals and Connector Definition

| Pin | Name | Description | Pin | Name | Description |
|-----|------|-------------|-----|------|-------------|
| 1 | GND | Ground | 35 | GND | Ground |
| 2 | D3 | Data Bit 3 | 36 | -CD1 | Card Detect 1 |
| 3 | D4 | Data Bit 4 | 37 | D11 | Data Bit 11 |
| 4 | D5 | Data Bit 5 | 38 | D12 | Data Bit 12 |
| 5 | D6 | Data Bit 6 | 39 | D13 | Data Bit 13 |
| 6 | D7 | Data Bit 7 | 40 | D14 | Data Bit 14 |
| 7 | -CE1 | Card Enable 1 | 41 | D15 | Data Bit 15 |
| 8 | A10 | Address Bit 10 | 42 | -CE2 | Card Enable 2 |
| 9 | -OE | Output Enable | 43 | RFSH | Refresh Input |
| 10 | A11 | Address Bit 11 | 44 | -IORD | I/O Read Strobe |
| 11 | A9 | Address Bit 9 | 45 | -IOWR | I/O Write Strobe |
| 12 | A8 | Address Bit 8 | 46 | A17 | Address Bit 17 |
| 13 | A13 | Address Bit 13 | 47 | A18 | Address Bit 18 |
| 14 | A14 | Address Bit 14 | 48 | A19 | Address Bit 19 |
| 15 | -WE/-PGM | Write Enable | 49 | A20 | Address Bit 20 |
| 16 | -IREQ | Interrupt Request | 50 | A21 | Address Bit 21 |
| 17 | VCC | Card Power | 51 | VCC | Card Power |
| 18 | VPP1 | Programming Supply Voltage 1 | 52 | VPP2 | Programming Supply Voltage 2 |
| 19 | A16 | Address Bit 16 | 53 | A22 | Address Bit 22 |
| 20 | A15 | Address Bit 15 | 54 | A23 | Address Bit 23 |
| 21 | A12 | Address Bit 12 | 55 | A24 | Address Bit 24 |
| 22 | A7 | Address Bit 7 | 56 | A25 | Address Bit 25 |
| 23 | A6 | Address Bit 6 | 57 | RFU | Reserved |
| 24 | A5 | Address Bit 5 | 58 | +RESET | Card Reset |
| 25 | A4 | Address Bit 4 | 59 | -WAIT | ExtendBus Cycle |
| 26 | A3 | Address Bit 3 | 60 | -INPACK | Input Port Acknowledge |
| 27 | A2 | Address Bit 2 | 61 | -REG | Register and I/O select enable |
| 28 | A1 | Address Bit 1 | 62 | -SPKR | Digital Audio Waveform |
| 29 | A0 | Address Bit 0 | 63 | -STSGNG | Card Status Changed |
| 30 | D0 | Data Bit 0 | 64 | D8 | Data Bit 8 |
| 31 | D1 | Data Bit 1 | 65 | D9 | Data Bit 9 |
| 32 | D2 | Data Bit 2 | 66 | D10 | Data Bit 10 |
| 33 | -IOIS16 | IO Port is 16 bits | 67 | -CD2 | Card Detect 2 |
| 34 | GND | Ground | 68 | GND | Ground |

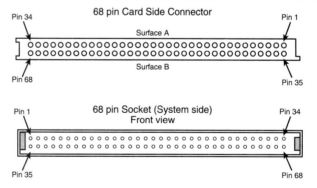

Note:    For more detailed information on the PCMCIA interface signals and their operation, refer to the PCMCIA standard.

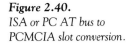

**Figure 2.40.**
*ISA or PC AT bus to PCMCIA slot conversion.*

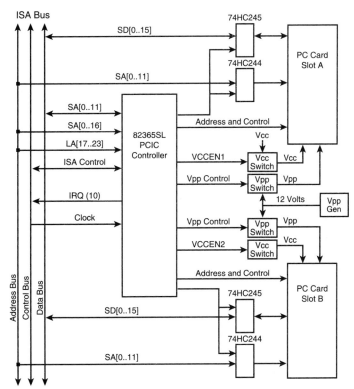

ISA or PC AT bus to PCMCIA slot conversion

Vcc - +5 Volts DC
Vpp - Typically +12 Volts used to program programmable memories
PCIC - Personal computer Interface Controller
SD0-SD15 - System Data Bus bits 0 to 15
SA0-SA15 - System Address Bus bits 0 to 15
LA16-LA23 - High order extended system address bits

Originally the PCMCIA specification defined only one card size that was 3.5 mm thick and provided no space for interface cables. This card was called a Type I style. When the need arose to attach cables to the card and support components inside the cards that were thicker than 3.5 mm, a Type II style was defined supporting 5 mm thick card bodies. The Type III style card was defined to enable packaging of very small removable hard drives. Also the specification was expanded to support longer or extended versions of the cards. Figure 2.41 illustrates the most popular card types now supported by the PCMCIA standard. When purchasing a system or notebook that supports PCMCIA slots, it is best to obtain a system that supports all three card types.

**Figure 2.41.**
*PCMCIA card types.*

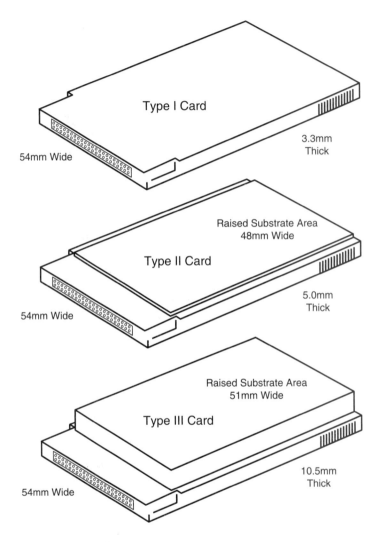

- Type I - 3.3mm thick
- Type II - 5mm thick
- Type III - 10.5mm thick
- TypeI Extended - 3.3mm thick, with 40mm extended length
- Type II Extended - 5mm thick, with 40mm extended length

Each PCMCIA card (sometimes now just called a *PC Card*) has an on-card data structure that can be read to reveal details about the card's function and capabilities. This complete structure definition is called the *Card Metaformat*. The Metaformat defines how the host is to read the Card Information Structures (CIS). The CIS is composed of a list of tuples (a group of related data structures). Each tuple has again a specific structure defining basic capabilities of the card and how it is to operate. On the PC side is a set of software called card and socket services that provide the interface between the PCMCIA socket hardware and card services that allocate and control the PCMCIA slots and services in the system. Many PCMCIA card tuples are now defined that support volatile and nonvolatile memory as memory or as simulated hard disk drives, actual hard disk drives as either IDE or SCSI devices, LAN adapters, communications adapters, modems and fax devices, CD-ROM drives, sound adapters, and wireless communications adapters.

In the past, purchasing a PC Card for use in a notebook that it was not packaged with or designed for was risky. Compatibility issues made it difficult to move PCMCIA cards from system to system. However, the latest systems and cards are now conforming to the latest standards, and interchange-ability has dramatically improved. Most of the compatibility issues arise from the loosely defined CIS structures, resulting in wide misinterpretation of the cards' identification and resources.

# MPEG Full-Motion Video Playback Adapter Boards

Using new video data compression technology, it's possible to decompress and playback full-motion video image from the system's hard drive or CD-ROM drive and display them in a window on the PC's display. The minimum standard for acceptable TV quality full-motion playback requires 320×200 pixel resolutions with 16-bit or higher color depths at minimum frame rates of 30 frames/second. This is nearly TV quality and, by using special zoom hardware in the latest display adapters, these images can be expanded to full-screen images on your PC display monitor. To achieve this resolu-tion and frame rate, special video decompression hardware is usually required. However, with new display adapters, technology with built-in full motion hardware-assist and a fast microprocessor, it will soon be possible to achieve this same level of full-motion video performance without any spe-cial hardware in the PC.

The compression technique that produces the best compression ratio and image quality is called the MPEG standards. *MPEG* stands for the Motion Picture Expert Group, a standards organization under the UTC (United Telecommunication Committee), which is part of the United Nations. This in-ternational standards organization has defined two basic full-motion video standards—MPEG 1 for VHS TV quality images, and MPEG 2 for broadcast quality and HDTV quality images. Most full-motion video playback boards available today use the MPEG 1 standard. An uncompressed full-motion video data stream has a data rate of approximately 27 MB/second. If the data was not compressed, it would take a huge amount of disk space to store even a few minutes of video. The MPEG 1 standard reduces the data rate to less than 1.5 megabits per second for a TV-quality frame rate and image. With this compression capability, it's possible to store 74 minutes of full-motion video and audio on a 600MB CD-ROM. The MPEG standard also defines audio compression and synchronization of the audio and video data streams, and playback boards usually contain an audio decompression chip and audio output ports. Full-motion video playback boards contain a special MPEG decompression chip that takes data from the systems hard disk or CD-ROM and either displays it on its own display adapter controller or attaches to the existing display adapter through the VFC (Video Feature Connector) or AVFC( Advanced VESA Feature Connector) ports on the display adapters. This permits the full-motion video images to be merged with computer generated graphics—for example, creating a full-motion video image in a window on the PC's screen. The full-motion video playback boards have low data rates and usually are installed in the PC ISA bus slots. For more information on full-motion video playback, see Chapter 25, "Multimedia."

# Sound Cards

Due to new multimedia applications and games on the PC, a popular expansion add-in board is the sound card. In general, most sound cards have additional features, such as game ports, CD-ROM ports, and MIDI ports. Figure 2.42 is a block diagram of a typical sound card. Most PC sound cards are "Sound Blaster-compatible or game-compatible," which means they have a certain level of audio function on the board and have maintained hardware compatibility with the Creative Lab's Sound Blaster products. At the heart of a Sound Blaster-compatible card is the audio processor or Sound Blaster controller, which accepts 8-bit commands that control the sound board. The Sound Blaster controller routes digital sound data in the system, decompresses compressed digital sound data for playback, and controls the sound mixer function. The Sound Blaster board can perform the following basic audio functions:

**Figure 2.42.**
*Typical PC sound adapter.*

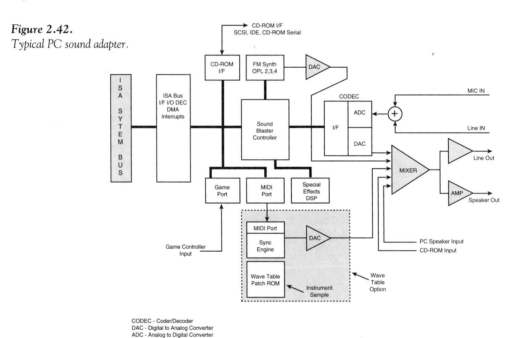

CODEC - Coder/Decoder
DAC - Digital to Analog Converter
ADC - Analog to Digital Converter

1. Record audio signals by converting them to digital data from either the "line in" port or from a microphone. In most systems the data can be recorded in stereo at sample rates as high as 44 KHz with a sample size of 16 bits each for each channel. This is equivalent to CD-quality audio sometimes called "Red Book" audio referring to the standards manual for CDs.

2. The sound card can also play back prerecorded digital data in either compressed or noncompressed formats, such as .WAV files. The playback audio can also be volume controlled and mixed with other audio sources attached to the mixer inputs. Playback of digital audio can also be supported at full CD-quality levels.

3. The sound card has a special audio signal generator that can be programmed to generate all types of audio tones and effects using FM (Frequency Modulation). The FM synthesis functions can be used to simulate musical tones and special effects for games. Its output can also be volume controlled and mixed with other mixer inputs. Music created using FM synthesis is not of very high quality and is typically limited to game applications.

4. For higher quality music reproduction, most sound cards have a wave table sound synthesizer, or at least an expansion header-supporting addition of a wave table synthesizer daughter board. The wave table header is a set of connectors on the audio board that allow the user to add a small board supporting wave table synthesis. A wave table synthesizer uses actual small prerecorded samples of musical instruments to reproduce music. Wave table synthesizers are typically controlled by commands from a MIDI port (Musical Instrument Digital Interface). The MIDI commands select instruments and describe how they are to be played. To ensure that all applications can expect to find a minimal level of wave table support, the General MIDI standard Patch Set supports a sample set for 24 instruments. The wave table synthesizer is capable of playing and mixing the output of 24 musical instruments to create a realistic orchestra effect. The musical effects created using a wave table synthesizer is vastly superior to that created by FM synthesis.

As indicated on the block diagram, most sound boards support attachment of peripheral devices such as the PC's game controllers, CD-ROM drives through secondary IDE ports or SCSI ports, and MIDI serial port interfaces supporting both MIDI in and MIDI out.

For much more information on sound cards, see Chapter 25.

# LANs and Network Adapters

The ability to connect a community of PCs and users together over a high speed connection medium has several advantages. First, they can communicate quickly and share data that is commonly owned and updated by the user group. For example, electronic mail (E-mail) can be sent between LAN-attached PCs, and common company or department databases can easily be accessed and updated by all LAN members. Secondly, they can share resources such as large arrays of hard disk storage, printers, modems, and fax machines. The ability to connect PCs together is accomplished through a special high-speed network called a local area network. They are called local area networks because they are typically within a building or campus of buildings. This is opposed to a wide area network such as the public-switched telephone system. Since local area networks are intended to share data and devices among a set of users, its speed is very important. If I want to access a data file on a server attached to the network, it would be ideal if the server's performance was equivalent to my local hard disks. For this reason, LANs are limited in distance and use very high speed transfer rates. Although anyone on a LAN can theoretically access any system and its resources on the LAN, most LANs are organized as servers and clients. A *server* is a LAN-attached device, usually a PC, that has a primary function on the LAN such as a *file server* that provides hard disk space, or a *print server* that provides access to a high performance laser printer, or a *communications* server that provides access to modems and fax machines. Most PCs attached to the LAN are client devices running local applications that access the LAN to make use of servers to share data with others or to share expensive hardware resources. The goal of any LAN is to make the user unaware of the LANs existence. For example, if a user obtains the same performance levels from a remote file server as he or she does from a local disk, the LAN is well designed and transparent to the user.

The most popular PC and workstation LANs are Ethernet and Token Ring LANs, with other LANs having a significantly smaller market share. Ethernet has the largest market share even though its data rate performance is less than Token Ring LANs. This is probably due to the cost of Token Ring adapters and the cost of wiring a Token Ring network. ISA bus Ethernet adapters are now available at costs approaching $50, and are capable of using low-cost, telephone-grade, twisted-pair wiring. Originally Ethernet was implemented as a single coax cable that looped through each LAN-attached device and supported a maximum data rate of 10 megabits/second. Ethernet used a half duplex transmission broadcast bus scheme where each device attempted to transmit anytime it needed to. If the commonly shared coax was busy serving another connection, a collision is detected and each transmitting PC would retry sending latter, hoping for a free time when no collisions would occur. Obviously, with a lot of PCs sending lots of data, many collisions would occur reducing the transmission capability of the network. This common bus approach not only reduces effective data transfer rates but makes problem determination very difficult—any PC on the LAN could potentially bring down the entire network. It's a little like having a string of Christmas tree lights. When one goes bad you have to check each one to find the bad bulb. To eliminate network-wide contention and limit problems caused by network faults, today's Ethernet systems are designed with devices called hubs. Hubs are used to divide the single common bus into short segments. This has the effect of isolating local data collisions to just that segment and permits the segment to more easily be wired in a nondaisy chained or loop bus topology. Further, network faults are easier to locate and isolate and don't bring down the entire network because the network is actually physically wired in a star topology. Figure 2.43 illustrates the difference between a conceptual network topology, or one without hubs and routers, and a physical topology using hubs and routers to create a star network.

The Token Ring LAN, as you may have guessed, attaches the network devices in a large ring topology with data time slots that are available for transmission of data from one device to another on the ring. A device that wants to transmit on the ring simply waits until a free token is detected and begins to transmit without worrying about data collisions. The Token ring architecture does not clutter the network with bad data frames that have been created by collisions. However, the ring topology is hard to wire and adapter costs are significantly higher than Ethernet adapters. Some of the wiring problems can be overcome using a similar hub architecture in token ring networks. Most Token Ring networks are limited in size and support data rates of up to 20 megabits/second, or twice the speed of Ethernet.

**Figure 2.43.**
*Network topology:*
*conceptual and physical.*

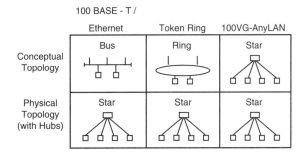

# Fast Ethernet and AnyLAN

With the demand for more network performance, faster Ethernet technologies are just now being deployed. Two competing standards—Fast Ethernet(100BASE-T) and 100VG-AnyLAN—are providing LAN speeds of up to 100 megabits/second over unshielded twisted-pair wiring (UTP). Several companies are now developing adapters that simultaneously support older 10 megabit Ethernet, Fast Ethernet and AnyLAN. Figure 2.44 compares the older Ethernet standard with the new Fast Ethernet (100BASE-T)standard and Fast Ethernet to AnyLAN. The primary benefits of Fast Ethernet is that it can be mixed with the older 10 megabit network and, by using the media independent interface, the same MAC (Media Access Controller) can be used with a variety of media types. Furthermore, Fast Ethernet is software compatible with existing Ethernet software and capable of full-duplex data transmission.

# LANs and Multimedia

Multimedia applications that use voice and full-motion video require a minimum sustained data rate to operate properly. For example, voice data must be contiguous to reproduce human speech and full-motion video must have smooth images without jerks and jumps distorting the picture. Unfortunately, existing LAN technologies cannot guarantee acceptable levels of continuous nonbursty data for these applications. For example, a 10 megabit/second Ethernet LAN connection may go several seconds without service if there are high levels of traffic on its segment. One solution to the problem is to provide each LAN user with a full 10 megabit/second point-to-point LAN connection. This is called a switched LAN service, and several LAN companies are now providing switched Ethernet LANs. With no other users or collisions on the LAN to your PC, sustained data rates capable of supporting voice and full-motion video multimedia data types are possible.

**Figure 2.44.**
*Comparison of Ethernet, Fast Ethernet and AnyLAN.*

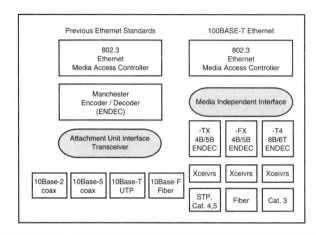

| 100BASE-T v.AnyLAN | | |
|---|---|---|
| | 100BASE-T | |
| MAC | CSMA/CD | Demand Priority |
| ENDEC | 4B/5B or 8B6T | 5B6B quartet signaling |
| Topology | Same as 10BASE-T | Hierarchical |
| Full Duplex Support | Yes | No |
| Data Rate | 100Mbps | 100Mbps |
| Cable Types | Cat. 3, 4, 5, STP, Fiber | Cat. 3, 4, 5 |

MAC - Media Access Controller
Cat. - Category
Mbps - Mega bits per second
UTP - Untwisted Pair
STP - Shielded Twisted Pair
CSMA/CD - Collision Sensing Multiple Access/Collision Detect
Xceivers - Transmitters and Receivers

Comparison of Ethernet, Fast Ethernet and Any LAN

# ATM (Asynchronous Transfer Mode): A Multimedia LAN Technology

First, some background. ATM is an international standard for cell-based transmission, multiplexing, and switching of high bandwidth/low delay digital data. Cell-based transmission used small blocks of data to eliminate long delays or network blockage caused by sending long data blocks. If the transmission is with small cells (blocks of data), it is easier to mix data from multiple sources on a single channel. New applications such as interactive video will require high bandwidth and very low delay through the networks. ATM has a very small cell size—53 bytes. This allows for low switching times, but also requires a nearly error-free transmission environment. With an error-free network as the goal, the network protocols (software) are significantly reduced. Most of the existing protocols are needed to do error checking and error correction, and to ensure that information packets arrive in the correct order. Standards activities on ATM started in the early 80's by the public-switched service providers (telephone companies).

Another important feature of ATM is the definition of an external user access interface. This means that private ATM devices, networks, and switches can attach to the public switch networks very easily. For example, a local ATM LAN could bridge to remote ATM LANs through the Public Switched Network (PSN). The ATM standard was originally defined for 155 megabits/second and 622 megabits/second service over fiber optic cable, but the ATM Forum—an industry group trying to apply ATM technology to LANs—has defined bit rates as low as 25 megabits/second on several copper wire media. Due to the high cost of ATM LAN adapters and the stiff competition from software compatible Fast Ethernet, wide use of ATM for LAN is likely to take place at a very slow rate. However, use of ATM to bridge remote LANs over wide area ATM networks is likely to be accepted quickly. ATM may also find wide application in LAN backbones connecting groups of high performance servers.

Figure 2.45 is a block diagram of a typical PC LAN adapter. LAN adapters for client PCs on the network are often simple low cost devices, whereas LAN adapters in PCs that provide server functions are designed differently. These adapters are designed with integrated intelligent subsystems, and often with powerful RISC processors that control and feed the LAN port.

**Figure 2.45.**
*Typical PC LAN adapter block diagram.*

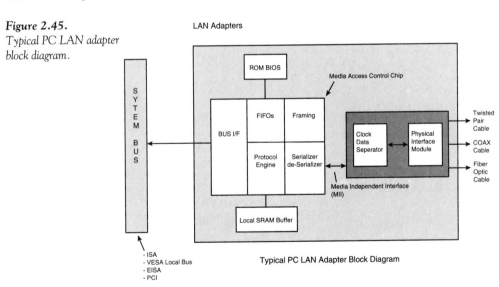

# Modems and the PC Connection

One of the most popular peripheral devices for the PC is the modem. The modem allows the PC to communicate with other computers over standard voice grade telephone lines. Most modern modems also support the transmission and reception of faxes. With the popularity of online services such as CompuServe, Prodigy, America Online, and the Internet, the modem is a required adapter in most home applications.

PCs can attach to modems in three primary ways:

1. As external standalone devices connected to the PC with a cable attached to one of the PC's serial communications ports

2. As an internal device that plugs into one of the PC's expansion bus slots (typically in an 8-bit ISA slot)

3. As a PCMCIA card that plugs into a PC's PCMCIA slot (usually on PC notebooks)

# The External Modem PC Connection

Figure 2.46 is a block diagram of an external fax/modem attached to one of the PC's serial communications ports. On the PC, the serial communications ports are often referred to as COM1, COM2, COM3, and COM4 devices. Most PCs today come with COM1 and COM2 ports either on the motherboard or on a Multi I/O adapter board installed in an ISA bus expansion slot. Sometimes one of the COM ports is used to attach a serial mouse to the system. On the PC, the COM ports are created using a chip called a UART (Universal Asynchronous Receiver Transmitter), which interfaces to the PC ISA bus and takes bytes of data and converts them to a serial bit stream. Each byte of data is framed in a start bit and followed by a parity check bit and 1, 1 1/2, or 2 stop bits. The UART also performs the deserialization process extracting data from the incoming framed serial stream. The UART generates a set of control signals and senses input signals from the modem—signals that are used to ensure that a connection with the external modem is in place. Both the serial send and receiver data streams and the modem control and status leads are then converted electrically to special voltage levels before being sent through a DB9 9-pin COM port connector at the rear of the PC. The standard that defines the signals, their function, electrical properties, and connector pin/signal assignments is called the EIA (Electronic Industries Association) RS-232-C specification. The PC uses a subset of the full specification on its serial ports.

# The PC Internal Modem Connection

External modems have several advantages. First, an external device can be used on any system that has a serial port is and not limited to just PCs. Secondly, external modems offer a small degree of additional protection if the phone line experiences a power surge such as a lightning strike. The modem may be destroyed, but the PC is still OK. One drawback of the external modem is that the PC's COM port may be implemented with one of the older style UARTs (NS8250 or NS16450 devices) and cannot support the higher data rates necessary to keep a high-speed modem with data compression busy. Most internal modes use the new NS16550 device that is capable of much higher data rates. Also, since the RS-232-C interface cable and its limitations are removed, the internal modems operate more reliably at high data rates.

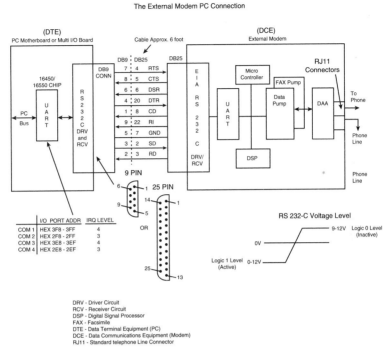

*Figure 2.46.*
*PC's connection to an*
*external modem.*

Figure 2.47 is a block diagram of a PC internal modem. Essentially, the RS-232-C interface is removed, and the UART in the modem replaces the PC COM port UART device. To the PC software, this internal UART looks identical to the PC serial COM Port. The result is that the PC software does not know if it is talking with an internal or external modem.

# PCMCIA Modems

The PCMCIA(Personal Computer Memory Card International Association), or credit card-sized modem, has become very popular in notebook designs. Its basic design is similar to that of the internal modem. PCMCIA modems are available as data/fax devices that support all the same standards and data rates as internal or external modems. The primary difference is their small size and ability to be easily plugged in and removed, which allows sharing of the slot with other devices. PCMCIA modems tend to be more expensive than either external or internal modems, primarily due to the higher cost associated with manufacturing small form factor devices.

Instead of interfacing directly to the PC ISA bus, these modems interface to the PCMCIA slot bus. This bus is a subset of the ISA bus optimized for the limited number of signal pins on the PCMCIA slot connector (68 Pins). Most PCMCIA modems are packaged in what is called a type 2 style card. This card is roughly 5 mm thick by 54 mm wide by 100 mm in length. The length is allowed to vary.

PCMCIA modems tend not to be software compatible with the PC's serial COM ports. For this reason a special device driver is often required to support PCMCIA modems.

**Figure 2.47.**
*Internal PC modem block diagram.*

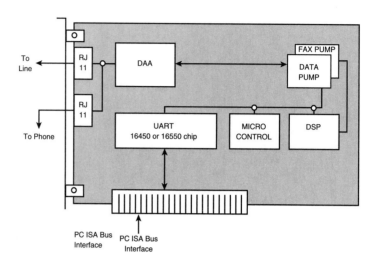

| | I/O Port ADDRS | IRQ Level |
|---|---|---|
| COM1 | HEX 3F8 - 3FF | 4 |
| COM2 | HEX 2F8 - 2FF | 3 |
| COM3 | HEX 3E8 - 3EF | 4 |
| COM4 | HEX 2E8 - 2EF | 3 |

DAA - Data Access Arrangement
RJ11 - Standard Telephone Line Connector

Figure 2.48 is a block diagram of a typical PCMCIA modem.

**Figure 2.48.**
*PCMCIA modem block diagram.*

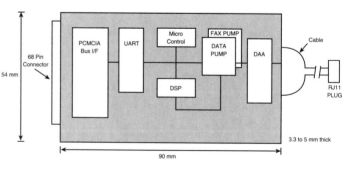

# 3

# Brains: The Processors

# PC Microprocessors

The PC's microprocessor is the key working component of the personal computer, and its selection can dictate the performance limits and cost of your system. If you want to understand the PC's capabilities and performance, you need to understand the microprocessor options available. Until recently, all microprocessors that ran PC software were derived from the early Intel 8086 or X86 architecture device. The X86 refers to the family of processors generated by Intel—and now others—since the introduction of the original 8086 device. Now even some of the RISC (Reduced Instruction Set Computer) processors can also execute PC software, either by emulating the Intel X86 microprocessors or, as proposed by several, incorporating compatible instruction execution units in the RISC devices. To further complicate the processor options, several manufacturers now sell Intel X86 clone processors. New Intel clone processors from AMD, Cyrix, and NexGen actually claim performance levels superior to the latest Intel microprocessors. At the present time, there are more than 50 Intel-compatible microprocessors used in PCs. Comparing and evaluating the costs, performances, and features of these processors is a complex task, but it's a necessary one if you want to get the best value and performance when selecting a PC.

One extraordinary feature of the Intel X86 processor family has been the manufacturer's devotion to maintaining 100 percent backward compatibility. Since the introduction of the 8086 in 1978, each new processor that has been introduced can still execute software written for all their predecessors. Even the latest Intel and clone Pentium-class microprocessors can execute software written for the original 14-year-old 8086 device. Intel's strategy of never rendering any PC software obsolete is a key marketing strength of the Intel X86 architecture. Today the Intel X86 architecture is being challenged by new RISC processors with superior performance claims. These new processors, however, cannot run the huge body of PC software the X86 processors can and thus will have a difficult time dethroning them. The newer Intel and clone X86 processors have also implemented many of the key features of the RISC processors, making the apparent performance gap significantly less. Today's new implementations of the older X86 architecture (such as Intel's Pentium, NexGen's 586, Cyrix's M1, and AMD's K5) are providing performance levels competitive with newer RISC processors. This melding of RISC and X86 features, combined with the X86 compatible PC software base, ensures a continuing presence for the X86 microprocessor architecture for the foreseeable future.

This chapter begins with a brief history of the PC's microprocessors and continues with a comparison of performance and key features of the latest microprocessors used in contemporary PC systems. Microprocessor upgrade paths are also covered. Finally, the chapter offers a glimpse of the future for microprocessors.

# The PC's X86 Processor Family

The original PC, announced by IBM in fall of 1981, used an Intel 8088 microprocessor running at 4.77 MHz. This was not the first or most powerful member of the Intel X86 processor family available at the time. In fact, it was not even IBM's first product to use the X86 processor. The IBM Displaywriter—a small stand-alone word processor designed in Austin, Texas—was introduced with the Intel 8086 running at 5 MHz. IBM's use of the X86 processor in a personal computer was not a first either. A small company called Seattle Computer Products had been marketing a S-100 system board with an 8086. This company's name may be familiar—they developed the first version of PC DOS that Microsoft purchased and converted to MS-DOS.

# Why the 8088?

The 16-bit 8086 processor was introduced in June of 1978, nearly three years before the introduction of the IBM PC. The IBM PC development group selected the less-powerful 8088 microprocessor in an attempt to keep the PC's costs down. The 8088 was similar to the 8086 in that it supported an internal 16-bit bus, but its external bus was only 8-bits wide. This made it easier to attach the standard 8-bit peripheral chips and enabled a smaller entry memory size in the PC design. This feature of the 8088 enabled the IBM PC to compete with popular, less costly 8-bit systems, yet have the performance advantage of a large address space and 16-bit internal processor. The 8088 selection also guaranteed a compatible performance migration path to the 8086 and the 286 processors.

The 8088's major distinguishing features over the existing family of 8-bit processors was its internal 16-bit data paths and one megabyte address space. The increase in address space was accomplished using a scheme called segmentation. Program instructions could not address any memory location in the 1-megabyte address space directly. A two-step process was used: First, a segment register was loaded that pointed to a 64KB block of data or instructions, which could be on any four-byte boundary in the one megabyte address space. Next, the normal X86 instructions could access any data or instructions in the 64KB block. To access data outside the 64KB block, the segment registers needed to be reloaded with new pointers. Four 16-bit segment registers were provided: one each of instruction accesses, data accesses, stack accesses, and a special extra segment register. Programmers hated this scheme because it meant that the programmer had to be constantly aware of the segment registers' values and to adjust them when spanning a segment boundary. It was not until the introduction of the 80386 processor that new addressing modes permitted full linear addressing in the X86 architecture. Figure 3.1 is a block diagram of the 8088 microprocessor. It's interesting to compare this block diagram to the latest Intel Pentium processor block diagram presented later in this chapter. The 8088 was implemented with 29,000 transistors and was packaged in a 40-pin package. The latest Pentium processors are implemented with 3.1 million transistors and require a 296-pin package.

The basic programming model of the 8086 is still intact in the latest Pentium devices. Basically, all the application level resources such as registers, data types, and addressing modes have simply been extensions to the original 8086 set of resources, primarily to support larger data types and addresses. Figure 3.2 illustrates how the physical memory addresses are generated using the X86 architecture segmentation registers. Figure 3.3 defines the 8088's register set available to the programmer through the processor's instruction set. One of the major criticisms of the X86 architecture is its limited number of registers and the fact that some registers must be used for specific functions. One of the strengths of the X86 architecture was its complex addressing modes; later, as more highly pipelined execution units were developed, these same addressing modes came to limit the system's performance.

*Figure 3.1.*
*Block diagram of the PC's*
*8088 microprocessor.*

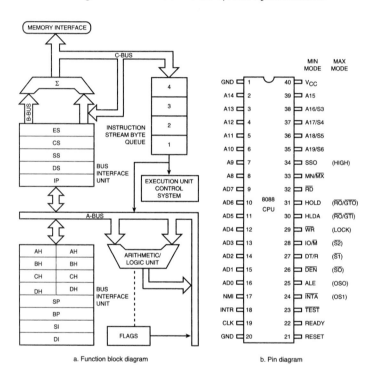

a. Function block diagram          b. Pin diagram

**Figure 3.2.**
*Segment register address generation on the 8088.*

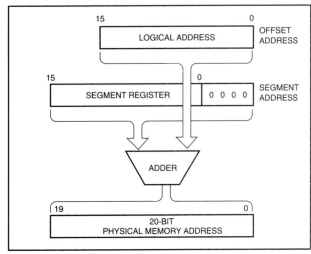

**8088 memory address generation.** *(Courtesy Intel Corporation)*

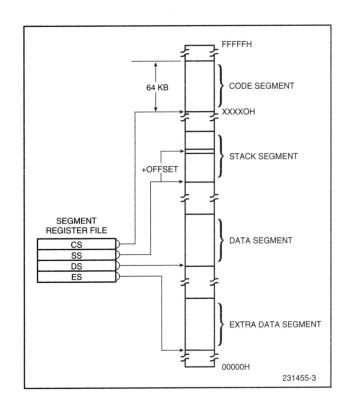

**Figure 3.3.**
*The 8088's register set and addressing modes.*

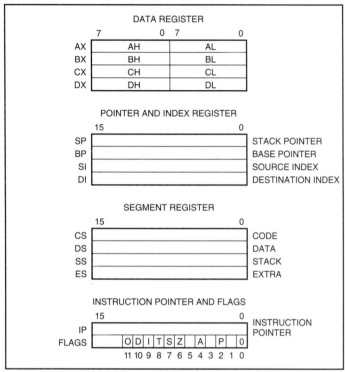

**The 8088 register set.** *(Courtesy Intel Corporation)*

*Effective Addressing Modes*

| Effective Address Modes | Registers Used |
| --- | --- |
| Displacement only | None |
| Base or Index only | BX, BP, SI, DI |
| Displacement + Base or Index | BX, BP, SI, DI |
| Base + Index | BP + DI, BX + SI + BP + SI, BX + DI |
| Displacement + Base + Index | BP + DI + DISP + BX + SI + DISP + BX + DI + DISP |

# Math Coprocessors

Early versions of the Intel X86 added floating-point and transcendental arithmetic (trigonometric and logarithmic functions) support through the use of a special math coprocessor chip. This special math coprocessor was given the designation X87 (8087). The original PC contained an open socket such that the math coprocessor chip could be added to the system. The math coprocessor extends the instruction set of the main microprocessor, and is physically attached directly to its local bus. The latest (Pentium or Pentium equivalent) versions of the X86 processors incorporate the X87 math coprocessor inside the microprocessor chip. Later in this chapter the math coprocessor family is covered in more detail.

# The X86 Processor Family Tree

As time went on and semiconductor technology advanced, Intel introduced newer and more powerful members of the X86 family. Most, but not all, of the Intel X86 processors were used in PC systems. Some family members were specifically designed for non-PC-embedded applications and others for use in notebook designs. Figure 3.4 illustrates the development of Intel X86 processors and math coprocessors to the present.

*Figure 3.4.*
*Intel X86 processor and*
*math coprocessor family.*

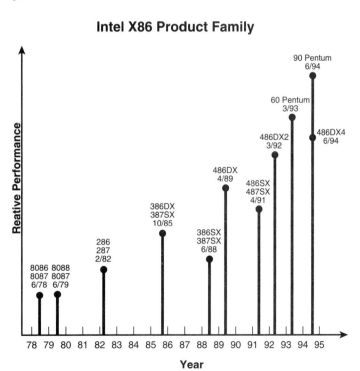

# The 80286 (286) Microprocessor

For the most part, major introductions of new PC capabilities is followed by the introduction of new and more powerful Intel processors. The PC AT (Advanced Technology) is such an example. Intel announced the 80286 processor in February of 1982, only 6 months after IBM announced the original PC with 8088! This new Intel processor had dramatic performance and function enhancements over the 8086. Figure 3.5 is a block diagram of the 286 microprocessor. This new processor used 134,000 transistors, and was packaged in a 68-pin package. The most important features were an increase in address space, which permitted memory sizes up to 16MB, and the processor's memory management features, which were expanded to support protected mode and virtual memory. Figure 3.6 illustrates how protected mode addresses were generated. The protected feature supported hardware task protection and allowed multitasking operating systems such as UNIX to operate on the processor. Without hardware task protection, one task could corrupt or interfere with another task and create a potentially unreliable system environment. Virtual memory enabled the software to operate as though there was up to one gigabyte address space available, even though a much smaller amount actually was. The processor could automatically detect that a memory reference was not in real memory, and go to the hard disk to load the required block of data or instructions into real memory. This could happen transparently to the application software. The processor was enhanced with a full 16-bit data bus that ran much faster than the 8086's bus (two clocks versus four clocks per memory access). Also, the speed at which many instructions were executed was improved by more efficient internal microcode. These features all combined to make an 8 MHz 80286 run 5 to 6 times faster than the older 8088. Figure 3.7 defines the 286's register set and the data types supported by the 286 and the companion 287 math coprocessor.

**Figure 3.5.**
*The 286 microprocessor block diagram.*

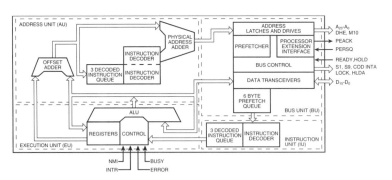

Even though the 80286 was introduced in 1982, IBM did not use it in a PC system until they introduced the PC AT in 1984. The PC AT was introduced with a clock speed of 6 MHz, which was quickly upgraded to 8 MHz. Over the life of the 80286, Intel and clone 286 chip makers gradually upgraded its speed to over 20 MHz. Even though the 286 had advanced features such as protected mode and virtual memory support, most PC software did not use these features, primarily to retain backward compatibility with the large installed base of older 8088 class systems.

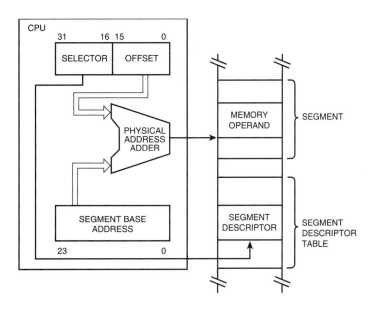

**Figure 3.6.**
*286 memory addressing
in protected mode.*

# The 80386 (386) Family

For nearly three and a half years after the introduction of the 286, there were no new major processor announcements from Intel—the 286 was king. Finally, in October of 1985, Intel introduced a new family of products called the 80386. Initially a single chip was introduced with a full 32-bit system bus, and later a special version of this chip—called a 386SX—was introduced that had a 16-bit bus. In these earlier processors, the SX designation referred to a 16-bit local bus interface and the DX indicated a full 32-bit local bus design. The 32-bit version was renamed the 386DX. The 386SX was very popular because it could be used in existing 286 designs with only minor changes. Also the 386SX worked well without an external cache memory. The very low system costs achieved with the 386SX—and aggressive processor pricing from clone chip supplier AMD—fueled the use of the PC in the consumer markets. For the first time, complete PC systems were available for much less than $1000. More importantly, for the first time PCs were differentiated by a family of X86 processors. Figure 3.8 is a block diagram of the 386DX processor. This processor was implemented with 275,000 transistors and housed in a 132-pin package.

## How Was the 386 Different?

The 386 family had a number of dramatic enhancements. The most important was the ability to process 32-bit information and access system memory on a 32-bit bus. Also, for the first time X86 processor's speeds were limited by system memory performance. To satisfy the processor's appetite for instructions and data, systems designers had to incorporate minicomputer and mainframe computer design techniques. This normally involved the use of bank interleaved memory designs (main memory was partitioned into multiple blocks that could be accessed simultaneously for increased speed), and inclusion of high-speed cache memories. Main memory subsystems were no longer attached to the PC AT's 16-bit bus but were attached directly to the processor's local bus.

**Figure 3.7.**
*The 286's register set and data types.*

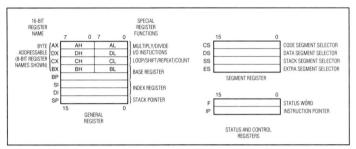

**The 286 register set.** *(Courtesy Intel Corporation)*

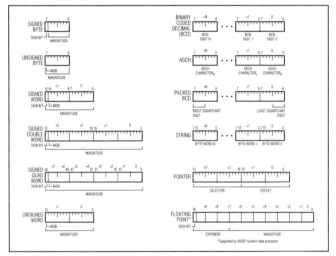

**286/287 datatypes** *(Courtesy Intel Corporation)*

**Figure 3.8.**
*The 386DX block diagram.*

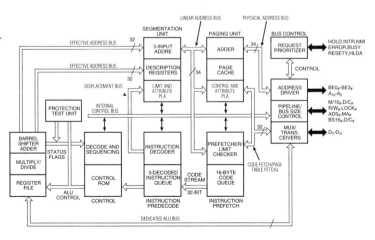

The 386 greatly expanded the X86's memory management modes to allow—for the first time—a full linear addressing mode(addressing without use of segment reqisters) and demand paging (the ability to automatically detect when a block of instructions or data is not in main memory and retrieve them from the hard disk drive as needed). Now the processor could directly address four gigabytes of information (two to the 32nd power). Virtual addressing was expanded to 64TB. Another important capability was virtual 8086 mode. (Figure 3.9 illustrates memory address generation on the 386 processor.) The 386 could be setup to simulate multiple 8086 real mode processors. This virtual machine mode allowed each user or task to operate as though it had an entire real mode 8086. As with the 286, many of the 386's advanced features were not used by PC software. With the announcement of Windows 95, it is only now that a 32-bit operating system and graphical user interface environment uses the full features of the 386 protected modes and offers true 32-bit support. The hardware was ready in 1985! It has taken nearly 10 years for the PC's software to evolve to take full advantage of the 386's capabilities. Figure 3.10 illustrates how the 386 extended the 286's register set to support 32-bit operations. Also, the data types supported were expanded on the 386 and 387 companion math coprocessor. Figure 3.11 illustrates the data types supported by the 386 and 387.

*Figure 3.9.*
*Memory addressing on the 386 processor.*

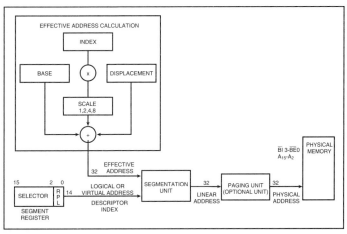

Memory address generation on the 386.
*(Courtesy Intel Corporation)*

**Effective Address Computation**

SEGMENT + BASE + (INDEX * SCALE) + DISPLACEMENT

$$\left\{\begin{matrix} CS \\ SS \\ DS \\ ES \\ FS \\ GS \end{matrix}\right\} + \left\{\begin{matrix} EAX \\ EXC \\ EDX \\ EBX \\ ESP \\ EBP \\ ESI \\ EDI \end{matrix}\right\} + \left\{\begin{matrix} EAX \\ EXC \\ EDX \\ EBX \\ EBP \\ ESI \\ EDI \end{matrix}\right\} + \left\{\begin{matrix} 1 \\ 2 \\ 4 \\ 8 \end{matrix}\right\} + \left\{\begin{matrix} \text{NO DISPLACEMENT} \\ \text{8-BIT DISPLACEMENT} \\ \text{32-BIT DISPLACEMENT} \end{matrix}\right\}$$

*Figure 3.10.*
*The 386's register set*
*extended to 32 bits.*

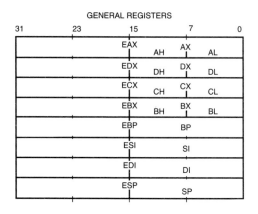

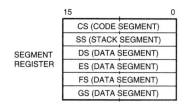

# 386 Fueled New PC Systems Designs

With the introduction of the 386 PC, systems designs changed dramatically. Memory subsystems were attached to the processor's local bus, and interleaved memory designs with high-speed cache memories became standard. The PC AT bus was relegated to a peripheral adapter board expansion bus, and the PC AT bus speed no longer tracked the processor's clock speed.

The initial 386 chips ran at 12.5 MHz but were quickly upgraded by Intel and clone suppliers to 16, 20, 25, 33, 40, and 50 MHz speeds. The most cost-effective and popular speeds were 25 and 33 MHz.

# The 386SL

Not only were speeds increased, but new versions of the processors were introduced. Intel introduced a product called the 386SL, which was a 386 processor specifically designed for the emerging notebook market. This processor incorporates some of the circuitry found in the notebook, added power management support, an 8-KB on-chip cache, a DRAM controller, and was capable of operating at 3.3 volts. This product had no second source and had significant competition from the standard 386SX from AMD that implemented power management as a standard feature and supported 3.3 volt operation. The 386SL had limited success, and was eventually withdrawn from the market by Intel.

**Figure 3.11.**
*386 and 387 data types supported.*

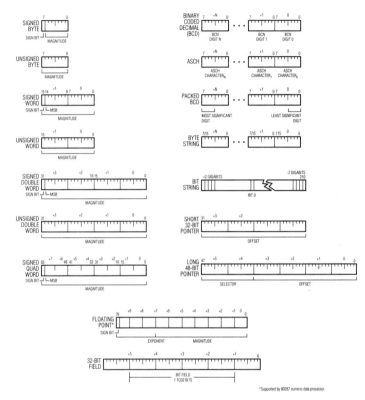

## The 387 Math Coprocessor

As with previous Intel processors, the 386 had a math coprocessor called the 387. More on math coprocessors later in this chapter.

# The 486 Processors

In April of 1989, Intel announced the 486 processor. This processor had very few new architectural features beyond the 386. In fact, the register set, addressing modes, memory management features, and data types were left pretty much unchanged from the 386. Its primary claim to fame was significant performance improvements coupled with integration of the math coprocessor and a small Level 1 cache on chip. Through the use of the latest silicon process technologies, it was now possible to build chips with over 1.2 million transistors! The original 486 used one micron (one millionth of an meter) design rules. This enabled the silicon chips to have transistors drawn with linear dimensions as small as one micron. Today's microprocessors are using 0.5 micron dimensions. It would seem that you would only get twice the number of transistors at .5 micron versus one micron. Since transistors are three-dimensional devices in the chip's silicon, however, changing a linear dimension can have dramatic effects. If transistor depth remained constant and the two-dimensional area sides are decreased from one micron to .5 microns, the transistor's area decreased from one square micron to .25 microns. Thus a change in a linear drawing dimension results in a much greater increase in transistor density—in this case a quadrupling. Thus, small changes in the silicon processing technology can have a dramatic effect on the number of transistors possible on a chip. Two secondary benefits result when smaller transistors can be created. First, the smaller transistors use less power and secondly, they can operate faster. The new 486 processors took full advantage of this progress. Figure 3.12 is a block diagram of the 486 processor.

*Figure 3.12.*
*The 486 processor*
*block diagram.*

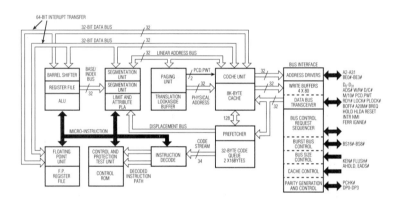

## Stealing from RISC Processors

The 486 was Intel's first processor to implement some of the same techniques that newer RISC architecture processors incorporated. To improve instruction execution speed, instructions were executed in a highly pipeline execution unit. On each tick of the processor's clock, a new instruction enters the pipeline. Although several clocks were required to actually execute the instructions, the results were that multiple instructions were being executed simultaneously, just slightly staggered in time. The effect was the capability to execute most instructions in what appeared to be one clock cycle, because a new instruction entered the pipeline every clock cycle.

## Internal or Level One 486 Cache

To feed this high-speed execution unit in the 486 processor, the 486 implemented an on-chip high-speed cache. The cache concept uses two important features of program execution. First, programs tend to use data and instructions that are close by. Secondly, programs tend to reuse the same blocks of code and data repeatedly—a program loop searching a block of data for a name and address field, for example. The cache concept takes advantage of these features by keeping small blocks of instructions and data that are to be used—or reused repeatedly—in a small high-speed memory. The cache is periodically filled from slower system memory. Cache schemes can be very effective. Typically, the data and instructions needed are in the cache over 95 percent of the time. The ratio of information being in the cache (called a cache hit) to not being in the cache (a cache miss) is called the cache hit ratio. This is a very important measurement of overall PC system performance. Cache technology and design is very complex and a complete technical treatment of the subject would take up the entire book. For the most part, larger caches are better and high cache hit ratios indicate superior performance. There are some key terms that you should have a familiarity with when it comes to cache designs and performance.

## Cache Basics

As mentioned earlier, the cache tries to keep instructions and data that are most often used and about to be used in its high-speed memory. When the processor requests an instruction or data, the cache assumes that there will be more references to the same data or data close by, and it begins to fill the cache with data from around the processor's reference. If the program is a short loop, the first time through the loop the cache may not be full and has to "warm up." If the program suddenly branches to a totally new area, the cache may have to be "flushed" and warm up (fill) from the new area. The rules for avoiding cache flushing and reducing warm ups are very complex. Ideally, the cache would like to keep track of all the areas of program references and keep small "sets" of data available in the cache. Unfortunately, a cache design of this type is prohibitively expensive and so compromises have to be made.

## Direct-Mapped Caches

The simplest type of cache is called a direct-mapped cache. This cache can keep only one "set" of data or data from frequently used areas of main memory. This cache is simple to design and is most effective when it is very large. It's well suited for older DOS programs on X86 processors, because these applications were written to avoid segment boundary crossings and tended to operate in 64KB regions.

## Set Associative Caches

The set associative cache design is much more sophisticated. It is capable of keeping sets of data from more than one frequently-used area of main memory. Two-way and four-way set associative designs are common, but some systems implement up to eight-way set associative designs. This means that eight sets of data are keep in the cache from the eight most frequently-used areas of memory. Set associative caches design can be very effective with small cache memory sizes. A small 16KB four-way set associative cache can often outperform a 64KB or 128KB direct-mapped cache. On most processors, the on-chip Level 1 caches are set associative designs.

## Write Back Versus Write Through

A cache design can also cache processor writes or simply write the data back to main memory immediately. Because only 25 percent of the systems cycles are typically write operations, simply avoiding the cache and passing all write cycles through to main memory is a reasonable option. If data is written back to the cache first, without updating main memory, the main memory will temporarily have bad or "dirty" memory. Caches that cache write data must detect accesses to memory locations that have not been updated, and hold off read accesses until the main memory is updated.

## Unified and Split Caches

Most cache designs use a single unified cache memory to hold both instructions and data. Spitting the cache into two caches creates a pseudo set associative environment—one set for instruction references and one for data references. Another advantage of split cache designs is the ability to simulate a Harvard architecture environment on a single address space machine. A Harvard architecture system has separate memory banks, one for instructions and one for data. Since instructions and data are in separate memories, they can be addressed simultaneously. The execution unit of the processor sees a separate memory space for instructions and data, which enables them to be fully overlapped or have two addresses active at once. Many of the latest systems designs are using split cache designs for the on-chip Level 1 cache.

## Cache Coherency and Bus Snooping

One of the difficulties of a cache design is that of ensuring the data in the cache corresponds with the data in main memory. Maintaining this correspondence is called *cache coherency*. This problem is particularly difficult if some other bus master or DMA channel can access main memory and change its contents without the cache's knowledge. Two techniques are used to solve this problem. The simplest approach is to declare some areas of memory as noncacheable and ensure that other bus masters only update in these areas. The second approach is to design the cache controller to watch or "snoop" the bus and detect alternate bus master access to data that is also in the cache. The cache controller can then invalidate the cache data and force it to be refilled with the latest data. This is only the beginning of cache coherency issues. Consider a multiprocessor environment and multi-level cache designs where the same data can exit in three different locations—Level 1 cache, Level 2 cache, and main memory—and is changeable by more than one processor!

# Level Two Caches

The 8KB four-way set associative internal cache in the 486 was a good match for system DRAM memory at processor clock speeds of 25 and 33 MHz. At higher clock speeds of 50, 66, 75, and 100 MHz, a second cache is often required. The small cache in the 486 is then called a Level 1 cache, and the external large cache is called a Level 2 cache. The Level 1 cache is filled from the Level 2 cache, which is filled from the system main memory DRAM. Level 2 caches are typically 256KB in size but can be larger or smaller. Increasing cache sizes have a diminishing return effect. A one-megabyte cache may have only a small percentage increase in performance over a 256KB cache. It may seem that simply adding a large Level 1 cache would be a better option than adding a Level 2 cache, but remember, often the Level 1 cache is built into the processor and cannot easily be expanded. Further, it is better to use a less expensive, slower Level 2 cache than more expensive, fast Level 1 cache memory.

# New Local Bus Architecture on the 486

The 486's local bus was changed significantly from the 386, which allowed for a significant increase in bus transfer rates. The 386 bus sent an address with each memory reference, whereas the 486 referenced data in up to 16-byte blocks. This scheme resulted in over a 50 percent increase in data transfer rate over the 386 at the same clock speed and bus width. Using the block transfer approach, only the initial or starting block address needed to be sent to the memory. This burst-mode block transfer scheme is ideally suited to cache memory systems like the 486, because cache memory fills were typically in small blocks of memory. The burst block transfer worked for both reads and writes, and took two clocks for the first 32-bit transfer and one clock for each additional 32-bit transfer. Up to a maximum of three additional 32-bit transfers were supported in this manner. Thus, with a 50 MHz system, a maximum block transfer was 32 bytes in five clock cycles, or 160MB per second. The original PC's 8088 had a maximum bus transfer rate of approximately one megabyte per second!

## Origin of VESA Local Bus

Many contemporary PC systems designs support high performance local bus slots where graphic display adapters and other high speed devices are often attached. The VESA (Video Electronics Standards Association) local bus standard essentially adopted the 486's local bus. The newer PCI (Peripheral Component Interconnect) bus standard also takes many of the features of the 486's local bus.

# Internal Clock Multiplying

Again, as semiconductor process technology advanced, chips became smaller and were able to run at much higher speeds. Unfortunately, the speeds of the external local busses were reaching their practical limits. The basic laws of physics dictated that bus speeds beyond 66 MHz were difficult to achieve using the present physical distances and bus driving and receiving technologies. Bus signals began to behave as waves versus logic voltage level signals. By incorporating very efficient on-chip Level 1 cache designs, it was possible to run the processor at much higher clock rates inside while keeping the external local bus at some lower speeds. This was accomplished by multiplying the external clock using a special phase lock loop circuit on the chip. A Phase Lock Loop (PLL) circuit can accept an input reference clock and multiply or divide the clock using a special analog circuit. For example, a 33 MHz 486 could clock double the external clock and run internally at 66 MHz.

Intel called their clock doubled 486 the 486DX2. With the on-chip first level cache and a good Level 2 cache, clock doubled processors run nearly 1.8 times the speed of the corresponding nonclock doubled processors. If clock doubling works, why not try clock tripling? The latest 486 processors are now capable of running internally at 100 MHz by using a clock tripling of the external 33 MHz bus clock. Intel calls their part the 486DX4 even though it is only clock tripled. The phase lock loop circuit can also generate clocks that are not integer multiples. For example, the 90 MHz Pentium uses a 60 MHz bus clock that is multiplied by 3/2 to achieve the internal 90 MHz operation. Well, if clock tripling works, why not clock quadrupling? This scheme approaches a point of diminishing return with the present internal cache technology and size. But as the internal level one cache size increases and becomes more efficient, higher clock rate multiples may become feasible.

## The 486SX and 487SX

The price difference between early 486 processors and high-clock rate clone 386 processors was so dramatic that Intel decided to offer a lower cost or entry version of the 486 family. This device became known as the 486SX. Its primary difference was the absence of the math coprocessor function. Even though the chip size and number of transistors were not greatly different, Intel offered the 486SX at between half to one third the price of a full 486DX. With the introduction of the 486SX, the full 486 was renamed the 486DX. In the 386 family SX meant a 16-bit bus chip; in the 486 family it meant the math coprocessor was missing. Makes about as much sense as calling the clock tripled 486 the 486DX4!

## Upgrade Sockets

With the proliferation of 486 processor types, clock doubled and tripled, DX and SX versions, Intel took what could have been a marketing nightmare and turned it into an advantage. They encouraged systems designers to place sockets on the processor motherboards such that a PC owner could upgrade his or her system by unplugging the older processor and replacing it with a full DX version or a clock doubled or tripled version. Some systems had two sockets and you did not even have to remove the old processor. To encourage this approach, Intel even gave away processor sockets to PC manufacturers. The message was your PC would never be obsolete! Intel even announced that a version of the new Pentium processor would be compatible with 486 processor pin outs, enabling 486 to Pentium upgrades. The clone processor manufacturers quickly jumped on the same bandwagon and proclaimed faster and better upgrade processors. Many even began to offer 486 class performance upgrades for the older 386 processors. Cyrix and IBM offer 486-like processors in 386 pin outs to upgrade older 386 systems. See the section on "Clone Processors" for more details on the 386 upgrades available.

Processor upgrades are very confusing to the average PC owner or user and have to be considered very carefully. First, upgrading a system involves opening the PC and handling electrical parts that many feel very uncomfortable with. Secondly, some systems do not have sufficient cooling to reliably support an upgrade processor. Third, the system's cache, chipset, and memory subsystems may not allow the upgrade processor to achieve its full potential performance increase. Fourth, often more than just the processor needs to be upgraded, such as the memory size, hard disk size, cache size, and display adapter type. Given the high cost of the upgrade processor, it may make more sense to simply upgrade the entire motherboard or even the entire system. Figure 3.13 illustrates some of the possible processor upgrade paths available to 486 class systems.

*Figure 3.13.*
*486 processor upgrades.*

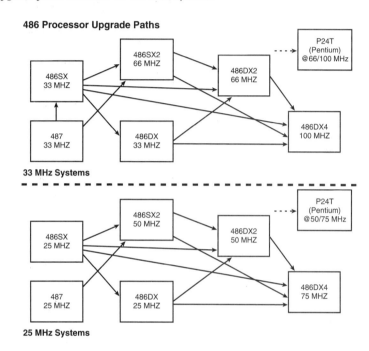

## The 486SL

Intel didn't learn its lessons from the 386SL, and introduced a 486SL processor targeted to notebook applications. It supported more advanced power management features and 3.3 volt operation, but as before, no second source existed. With the incorporation of 3.3 volt operation and advanced power management features in the standard 486 products, the 486SL never achieved the desired success. Intel also discontinued the 486SL.

## The 487SX

If one purchased a system with a 486SX and wanted to upgrade the system with a math coprocessor, Intel offered a 487SX device. If the 486SX was on a socket, as it was in early systems designs, it was possible to simply remove the SX part and replace it with a DX part containing an integrated math co-processor. However, to reduce systems cost, Intel offered the 486SX in a new package called a PQFP (Plastic Quad Flat Package). This lower cost device could not easily be placed in a socket, and was often soldered permanently to the motherboard. A second socket was placed on the motherboard for the 487SX upgrade. The 487SX upgrade was a special version of the 486DX device that simply disabled the 486SX and took control of the system.

## System Management Mode

The latest version of the 486 supports a new processor operating mode. With the introduction of the 386, three basic processor modes were supported: real address mode (old 8086 mode), protected mode (introduced in the 286), and virtual 8086 machine mode. The newest mode is called System Management Mode (SMM). This mode can be entered from any other mode by software or by detection of certain hardware conditions. This mode is totally hidden from the other modes and enables the processor to perform functions in software hidden from the applications software and even from the operating system software. This mode was originally developed to allow notebook power management functions transparent to the operating system and application software. This is still its primary function in most PCs, but other uses have emerged. A very useful capability enabled by the SMM feature is the virtualization of hardware that does not exist on the system. For example, the processor can be set up to enter the SMM state on detection of accesses to I/O port addresses, other system resources, or error conditions. An SMM software routine can emulate the existence of a specific sound board hardware on a different sound board hardware environment. This capability allows the system to deal with software that may be incompatible with the existing hardware support on the system. Figure 3.14 is a diagram of the possible modes and mode state transitions supported in the 486.

**Figure 3.14.**
*SMM modes and states transitions supported in the 486.*

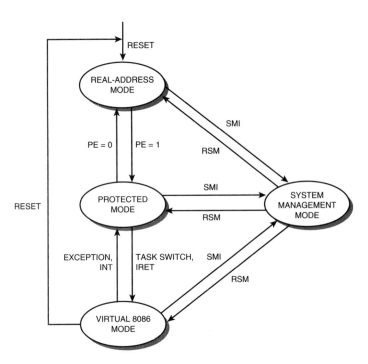

# Today's 486 Lineup

Figure 3.15 illustrates the present lineup of available 486 class processors from Intel and some of the 486 clone manufacturers. Note that AMD, IBM, and Cyrix also offer 486 class products. As of this writing, clone 486 processors are just emerging from Winbond, Texas Instruments, SGS Thomson, and UMC. In many instances, the early versions of these clone chips were actually 386 processors with internal caches of various sizes and types combined with clock doubling features. Because the 386 processors were nearly the same from an instruction set point of view, these hybrid designs often equaled or exceeded Intel 486 processors in performance at similar clock speeds. IBM has a license from Intel to produce X86 processors, and developed their own family of products primarily for internal use. Intel cleverly limited IBM's ability to sell just processors by requiring that they only be sold externally on boards. To overcome this limitation, IBM has licensed the Cyrix designs. The present IBM processor line is called the Blue Lightning series.

*Figure 3.15.*
*The 486 processor family.*

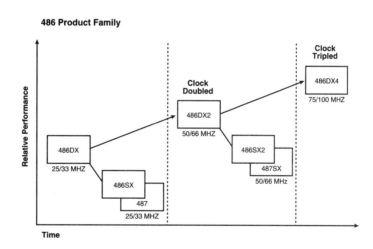

# The 486's Future

As of this writing (late fall of 1994), Intel claims that nearly 75 percent of their processor shipments are still 486 and below processors. They expect the crossover between 486 and Pentium shipments to occur by mid-1995. Intel's strategy has been to push the market to its latest technology when clone manufacturers begin to compete effectively with their existing designs. With this now happening in the 486 market, Intel will likely push the Pentium processor quickly into mid-range and low-end PC designs. Even their own 100 MHz 486DX4 product compares to the 60 MHz Pentium in basic performance. An indication of Intel's direction is the very aggressive pricing now being offered on the new 75 MHz Pentium just introduced. It seems to be clear that Intel will use this product to compete with the 486 clone market. From a performance point of view, the clock doubled and tripled 486s are adequate for most applications using Windows, however some of the emerging multimedia applications such as full motion video playback and capture, video conferencing, and 3-D graphics support will probably tax the limits of the 486 processors. It is likely that the 486 will continue to drop in price and find a large volume in the home/consumer markets. Who knows? Maybe the long awaited under $500 PC will use the 486. These 486 processors are also likely to find their way into new applications such as the emerging interactive TV top box markets.

# The Intel Pentium Processors

How do you make processor go even faster? Intel answered this question with the introduction of the Pentium processor in March of 1993. This new processor was implemented with over 3.1 million transistors. This was the first Intel X86 architecture processor to drop the X86 designation, although during its development it was referred to as the P5 or 586 device. Intel called it the P5, and the trade press called it the 586. To build a faster processor Intel used a three-pronged approach. First, Intel again took advantage of advancements in semiconductor technology to support more transistors on the chip and higher speed clocks internally. The Pentium processor was implemented with 3.1 million transistors or nearly three times that of the 486 processor. This dramatic increase in transistor count was used to significantly enhance the math coprocessor's performance, bring it up to workstation levels, and increase the internal cache size to 16KB. The original Pentium was offered at clock speeds of 60 and 66 MHz—compared to the 486's initial speeds of 20 and 25 MHz. Secondly, the Pentium increased the local bus width to 64 bits and upped its speed to 60 and 66 MHz. Third, the Pentium implements more RISC concepts in the processor execution unit. The Pentium was the first Intel X86 processor to implement a superscalar execution unit. This meant that the Pentium processor, under certain conditions, could execute two instructions in a single clock cycle. Figure 3.16 is a block diagram of the Pentium processor.

## Pentium's Superscalar Implementation

The key distinguishing features of the diagram are the two execution unit pipelines and the split cache design. There are numerous limitations on the instructions that can be executed in the V pipe and the U pipe. Therefore, two instructions are not always executed at once. Generally speaking, simple instructions can be executed in both pipelines, assuming both instructions don't share the same source or destination references. Instructions with prefixes and floating-point instructions are limited to execution on the U pipeline, as are instructions implementing shift functions (shifting a data field's bits to the right or left). Typically, more complex instructions are executed in the U pipeline, and simpler instructions are executed on the V pipeline. Due to these limitations, the superscalar effect is limited in the Pentium. The X86 instruction set is simply not well suited to superscalar environments because complex addressing modes and multiple memory reference in a single instruction are difficult to pipeline. The small number of X86 general-purpose registers makes it difficult to fill both pipelines without having instructions referencing the same registers. When one instruction has a dependence on the result of another in the other pipeline, their executions must be synchronized, which often stalls one of the pipelines. If the systems software is recompiled with a compiler that is aware of the superscalar environment, however, it can reorder instructions and limit its selections of instructions to the simpler types and realize a significant increase in performance, which is typically between 10 and 15 percent.

**Figure 3.16.**
*Pentium processor block diagram.*

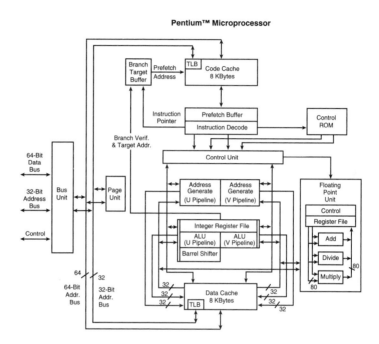

Although the Pentium has an external bus of 64 bits and two execution units, it's still considered a 32-bit processor. Note that each of the pipelines are 32 bits in width.

# Pentium's Dynamic Branch Prediction

The Pentium also implements dynamic branch prediction. Normally, instructions are prefetched (loaded from memory before needed) from the cache in linear manner and stored in the prefetch buffer awaiting execution in one of the superscalar pipelines. Branch instructions that are taken are very disruptive to the pipeline, for all the instructions following the branch in the pipeline must be flushed and the pipeline reloaded with the instructions at the branched to address. Most software has a branch instruction every six to ten instructions. Therefore, branches can be a severe problem for highly pipelined execution units. The Pentium addresses this problem by adding a *Branch Target Buffer*. This buffer remembers branch target addresses, and enables prefetching of the new instruction streams before a branch is taken. This technique reduces the effects of branches on the pipeline. In other words, both address paths of a branch are generated and available to the execution units.

## Pentium's Level 1 or Internal Cache

The internal or Level 1 cache size and design was also modified in the Pentium. A split cache was implemented with 8KB dedicated to instruction fetches and 8KB dedicated to data accesses. Both caches are two-way set associative designs. The two-cache approach allows the emulation of a Harvard architecture system where instruction space and data space are two separate memories. This scheme allows data and instruction accesses to be fully overlapped. Also note that the output of the eight kilobyte instruction cache feeds the prefetch stage over a full 256-bit wide bus!

## Pentium Architecture Enhancements

The Pentium processor also implemented a significant number of architectural extensions, including enhancements to the memory management unit, extension and enhancements to the SMM mode, new instructions (primarily to support new processor modes), new configuration registers, and new processor status bits. One significant enhancement was the addition of "hooks" to enable easier processor performance monitoring.

The Pentium's math coprocessor was totally redesigned from the older 486 implementation. It now supports a performance level of 3 to 10 times that of the 486. This new coprocessor implementation finally puts the X86 floating-point performance on a par with RISC workstation implementations. More on the math coprocessors later.

## Pentium's Local Bus

The Pentium's local bus was enhanced to a 66 MHz clock speed and bus width doubled to 64 bits. The Pentium's bus, like that of the 486, used a burst block transfer mode, and added the ability to support address pipelining, which allowed two outstanding bus transactions. This scheme nearly doubled the memory access time, which makes the Pentium work better on slower memory subsystems designs.

## Pentium System Integrity Features

The Pentium added a number of advanced system integrity features, including a built-in automatic self test. Parity is generated and checked on each byte of the external data bus transfers and generated on the address bus. Internally, parity checking is done on instruction and data caches. Also, parity is generated and checked on nearly all internal registers and internal ROM microcode. The Pentium also supports a system shutdown if internal errors are detected.

The Pentium also implements a function called *functional redundancy checking*. In this mode, a second Pentium can be added to the system to enhance the system's integrity. This second processor is called a *checker*, and runs in lock step with the main Pentium processor. The checker monitors all of the main processor outputs and compares them to the checker's values. If a mismatch occurs, the checker reports the error condition to the main processor.

## Latest Pentium Processors

The original Pentium processor was introduced at 60 and 66 MHz clock speeds, was a 5-volt device, and was implemented using .8 micron semiconductor technology. Recently, Intel introduced a newer Pentium processor called the P54C device. This device was implemented in .6 micron technology and supports clock speeds of 90 and 100 MHz. The device also runs on a 3.3 volt power source. Another key capability added to the P54C device was the inclusion of the on-chip APIC (Advance Programmable Interrupt Controller). This added support enabled glueless (no additional circuits required) dual processor systems designs. Many new motherboards are designed to support two Pentium processors.

Intel has also indicated that new higher clock rate Pentiums are due in 1995—120 and 150 MHz devices are expected soon. Intel has also demonstrated Pentium processors running at clock speeds of up to 180 MHz at technology conferences and trade shows.

Intel has also announced a Pentium processor called the P24T. This device is a special version of the Pentium processor that is pin-compatible with the 486 processor. The P24T Pentium is intended to be used for upgrading older 486 systems to Pentium class performance levels. The P24T will not achieve equivalent Pentium performance in a 486 socket since the bus width is only 32 bits and the Level 2 external cache may not be optimized for the Pentium's L1 cache operation. Table 3.1 is a summary of the Pentium processor family.

Table 3.1. Pentium Processors.

| Processor | Technology | Internal/External clock speeds | Voltage | Pins | Available |
|-----------|-----------|-------------------------------|---------|------|-----------|
| 60MHz | 0.8 micron | 60/60 MHz | 5 volts | 273 | 4Q93 |
| 66MHz | 0.8 micron | 66/66 MHz | 5 volts | 273 | 1Q94 |
| 75MHz | 0.6 micron | 75/50 MHz | 3.3 volts | 296 | 1Q95 |
| 90MHz | 0.6 micron | 90/60 MHz | 3.3 volts | 296 | 3Q94 |
| 100MHz | 0.6 micron | 100/66 MHz | 3.3 volts | 296 | 4Q94 |
| 120MHz | 0.6 micron | 120/60 MHz | 3.3 volts | 296 | 2Q95* |
| 132MHz | 0.6 micron | 132/66 MHz | 3.3 volts | 296 | 3Q95* |
| 150MHz | 0.4 micron | 150/60 MHz | 3.3 volts | 296 | 4Q95* |
| 200MHz (P6) | 0.4 micron | 200/66 MHz | 3.3 volts | 296 | 2Q96* |

* These are projected Pentium processors and have not been announced by Intel.

# A Closer Look at Clone Processors

For many years Intel was the only major supplier of X86 processors, with a few authorized and controlled alternate sources. Today a number of companies offer X86 compatible processors with no assistance from Intel. Often these processors fill niche product areas not well covered by Intel's products. Sometimes new and enhanced features are provided while others are more or less exact functional copies of the Intel devices.

## AMD's (Advance Micro Device) Processors

The primary early competitor to Intel for the X86 processor was AMD. AMD produced 286 processors under license from Intel, and later claimed this license also applied to 386 and 486 processors. So far they have had success in defending this position. AMD's strategy was to compete on improved specs and with slightly lower prices. In the 286, 386DX, and 386SX markets, they offered functionally and pin compatible devices at higher clock rates, with lower power dissipation and improved SMM functions. AMD has not had the same success in the 486 markets—its 486 devices were late to market and offered no real performance or functional advantage over Intel's devices. AMD's strategy with the 486 products was to compete on price and offer clock speed versions that Intel did not support. In anticipation of an adverse ruling concerning their license status, AMD has two 486 designs, one based on Intel technology and one based on their own "clean room" design. In an attempt to gain a leadership position in high end X86 processors, AMD has just announced a Pentium class product called K5. AMD claims that the K5 will outperform Intel's Pentium at similar clock speeds and will be available at higher clock speeds than Pentium. The K5 is not a clone of the Pentium, in that it does not use any Intel technology. AMD claims it performance advantage is due to a superior superscalar design. The K5's dual pipelines have less restrictions on simultaneous instruction execution, and the device not only supports branch prediction but also does speculative execution of the alternate path instructions in anticipation of taking the branch path. As of this writing there are not a lot of details about the K5, but it's clearly an attempt by AMD to take a leadership position in X86 processors instead of being an Intel follower. Figure 3.17 is a block diagram of the K5 device.

## Cyrix Processors

Cyrix has designed their own processors from the ground up with no technology from Intel. Intel still claims, however, that the Cyrix design violates Intel patents. Cyrix's solution to this legal problem was to build their devices at manufacturers that had Intel patent license agreements in place. This approach seems to have worked. As with AMD, Cyrix is also pursuing a path of new noninfringing designs. Cyrix's initial marketing strategy was not to produce exact clones of the Intel processors. Their initial products were actually hybrids of 386 and 486 processors. Their strategy was to fill the holes in the Intel price/performance/feature product line, provide lower-cost plastic packages, and aggressively pursue the processor upgrade market. All of their processors used a "486-like" processor with five-stage pipelines, which allow many instructions to be executed in single clock cycles. Also, by adding small one kilobyte instruction and data caches, they were able to keep costs low and equal or exceed Intel's performance levels. Recently, Cyrix has gone after exact Intel pin and functionally compatible devices, introducing 486SX, 486DX, and 486DX2 compatible devices. Cyrix is also designing a super-Pentium device called the M1 processor. Details are not available as of this writing, but Cyrix is targeting performances beyond those of Intel's Pentium by using approaches similar to AMD's K5. Figure 3.18 is a preliminary block diagram of the M1 processor, which indicates that it will be a two-issue superscalar design (it will execute two instructions at once) with a single unified cache. Table 3.2 is a summary of the present Cyrix processor offerings, excluding the M1. At present, clocks speeds of 20, 25, 33, 40, and 50 MHz are offered.

**Figure 3.17.**
*Block diagram of the AMD K5 processor.*

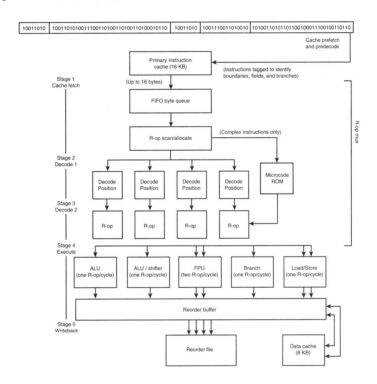

Table 3.2. Cyrix X86 Products.

| Processor | Processor class | Pinout | NPU | Cache | Clock-Doubled |
|---|---|---|---|---|---|
| Cx486SLC | 486 | i386SX | no NPU | 1KB I/D | no |
| 2Cx486DLC | 486 | i386DX | no NPU | 1KB I/D | no |
| Cx486SLC2 | 486 | i386SX | no NPU | 1KB I/D | yes |

*continues*

Table 3.2. continued

| Processor | Processor class | Pinout | NPU | Cache | Clock-Doubled |
|-----------|-----------------|--------|-----|-------|---------------|
| **Upgrade Processors** | | | | | |
| Cx486DRX2 | 486 | i386DX | no NPU | 1KB I/D | yes |
| Cx486SRx2 | 486 | i386SX | no NPU | 1KB I/D | yes |
| **Intel 486 pinout devices** | | | | | |
| Cx486s | 486 | i486SX | no NPU | 2KB cache | no |
| Cx486S2 | 486 | i486SX | no NPU | 2KB cache | yes |
| Cx486DX | 486 | i486DX | NPU | 8KB cache | no |
| Cx486DX2 | 486 | i486DX2 | NPU | 8KB cache | yes |
| M1 | Pentium class superscalar processor (not yet available) | | | | |

**Figure 3.18.**
*Cyrix's M1 processor block diagram.*

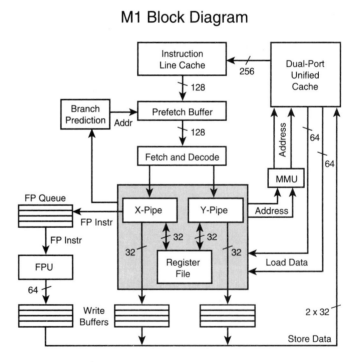

## M1 Block Diagram

Cyrix has also licensed its processor technology to IBM, SGS-Thomson, and Texas Instruments. The TI agreement, however, is now in dispute, and the intentions of IBM are unknown.

## Texas Instruments 486 Devices

Texas Instruments (TI) is an alternate source for the Cyrix 486SLC and DLC devices and has also developed its own versions with larger caches and PCI bus interfaces built in. At present, the TI versions are the TI486SXL and SXLC devices—both of which are also available in clocked doubled versions (SXL2 and SXLC2) and support an 8KB cache size. The SXL device is a 486 pinout device, and the SXLC is a i386SX pinout device. All devices have 3.3 volt versions available and operate at speeds up to 40 MHz. New devices are expected shortly from TI that offer more performance through larger caches and higher clock speeds.

## IBM X86 Processors

Agreements with Intel allow IBM access to 386 and 486 designs, but precludes IBM from selling the processor chips alone—they must be on boards or modules. IBM developed three basic products: the 386SLC, the 486SLC2, and the Blue Lighting. The 386SLC was a 486-like processor with an 8KB cache in an Intel 386SX pinout package, and operates at 20 and 25 MHz. The 486SLC2 was the same basic 486-like processor with a 16KB cache, clock doubling, and operated at speeds of up to 66 MHz internally. This device was also packaged in the Intel 386SX pinout. The IBM Blue Lighting was the same 486-like processor in the 486SL2, but was repackaged in the Intel 386DX pinout, and supports clock tripling for speeds up to 75 and 100 MHz.

Recently, IBM has indicated that it will no longer pursue X86 processor designs and will purchase devices from outside suppliers. However, they also recently obtained a license to the Cyrix technology. It's hard to predict what IBM will actually do with respect to X86 processors in the future. The IBM corporate push for the PowerPC, while still selling X86 products, gives them a split personality.

## NexGen

In 1993, NexGen sampled a chipset that they called a NX586, and which offered no significant advantage over the single-chip Intel Pentium. Since then, the NexGen chipset has been shrunk and is now a single chip device that is fabricated by IBM and uses a .5 micron technology. It seems to offer little by way of performance advantage and will probably compete on price alone. It has been criticized for not being Pentium pin-and-bus compatible, which makes it difficult to use with existing PCI core chipsets in systems designs.

# Math Coprocessor Basics

Until now, we've more or less ignored the math coprocessors in the X86 processor family. Now I would like to cover this subject in a little more detail. The math coprocessor function goes by several names—simply the coprocessor, the math coprocessor, the floating-point processor, and as Intel prefers, the NPX or Numerical Processor Extension. The main processor in the X86 family is an integer processor, which means it can only directly process numbers that are signed or unsigned fixed-point integers. To perform high-speed and highly accurate math functions, it is often necessary to represent the numbers in noninteger formats. Emulation of these other number systems can be accomplished in the systems software. However, these software routines are slow and can consume significant amounts of the main processor's power.

The designers of Intel X86 processors devised a method of attaching coprocessors to the main processor to perform functions that would accelerate math operations. The coprocessor interface is very general and could support all types of specialized function coprocessors, but the interface is primarily used to add the X87 Numeric Processor Extensions coprocessor. The X87 Math coprocessors are capable of performing numeric operations from 20 to 100 times faster than equivalent software routines using integer arithmetic. This blinding numeric performance is not required for many applications, such as word processors or data base transactions. However, math-intensive applications such as complex spreadsheets, engineering and scientific applications, and many new multimedia applications benefit greatly from accelerated math capabilities. Applications such as Computer Aided Design (CAD) and 2-D and 3-D graphics require a math coprocessor to be effective on the X86 architecture. Up until the introduction of the 486DX processors, the math coprocessor was a separate chip that needed to be installed in the PC in an empty socket. Ordinarily, PC's came without the coprocessor installed. Now 486DX and Pentium processors have the math coprocessor integrated on the same chip with the integer processor. Table 3.3 lists the X86 integer processor and its companion X87 math coprocessor along with the IEEE floating-point standard supported.

Table 3.3. Math Coprocessors.

| X86 Integer Processor | X87 Math Coprocessor | IEEE Standard Supported |
|---|---|---|
| 8088 | 8087 | Proposed IEEE 754 |
| 8086 | 8087 | Proposed IEEE 754 |
| 286 | 287 | Proposed IEEE 754 |
| 386SX | 387SX | Final IEEE 754 |
| 386DX | 387DX | Final IEEE 754 |
| 486SX | 487SX | IEEE 753 & 854 |
| 486DX | Built into 486DX | IEEE 754 & 854 |
| Pentium | Built into Pentium | IEEE 754 & 854 |

As with the main integer X86 processor, several other manufacturers now produce compatible math coprocessors. The trend is clearly to have the math coprocessor integrated on-chip with the main integer processor. In the past—even with the X87 coprocessors installed—the floating-point math performance on the Intel-based computers was not comparable to that on RISC-based workstations.

Intel finally addressed this problem with the Pentium math coprocessor by totally redesigning this function. On the Pentium, the floating-point performance is 5 to 10 times that of the 486 coprocessor and finally is competitive with floating-point performance found on RISC workstations.

## Numeric Data Types Supported In the Math Coprocessor

Not only can the math coprocessor handle floating-point numbers, it is also capable of handling integers and packed decimal (two decimal digits per 8-bit byte) numeric data representations. Figure 3.19 lists the numeric data types, significant digits, and ranges supported in the latest Intel math coprocessors.

**Figure 3.19.**

*Math coprocessor data types.*

**Numeric Data Types**

| Data Type | Bits | Significant Digits (Decimal) | Approximate Normalized Range (Decimal) |
|-----------|------|------------------------------|----------------------------------------|
| Word integer | 16 | 4 | $-32{,}768 \leq X \leq +32{,}768$ |
| Short integer | 32 | 9 | $-2 \times 10^9 \leq X \leq +2 \times 10^9$ |
| Long integer | 64 | 18 | $-9 \times 10^{18} \leq X \leq +9 \times 10^{18}$ |
| Packed decimal | 80 | 18 | $-99...99 \leq X \leq +99...99$ (18 digits) |
| Single real | 32 | 7 | $1.18 \times 10^{-38} < |X| < 3.40 \times 10^{38}$ |
| Double real | 64 | 15-16 | $2.23 \times 10^{-308} < |X| < 1.79 \times 10^{308}$ |
| Extended real* | 80 | 19 | $3.37 \times 10^{-4932} < |X| < 1.18 \times 10^{4932}$ |

*Equivalent to *double extended* format of IEEE Std 854.

Figure 3.20 lists the main math coprocessor instructions and the arithmetic and transcendental functions, and embedded constants supported. Note that the math coprocessor contains a number of embedded constants that are often used in advanced math functions.

**Figure 3.20.**

*Math coprocessor numeric instructions.*

**Principle Numeric Instructions**

| Class | Instruction Types |
|-------|-------------------|
| Data Transfer | Load (all data types), Store (all data types), Exchange |
| Arithmetic | Add, Subtract, Multiplt, Divide, Subtract Reversed, Divide Reversed, Square Root, Scale, Extract, Remainder, Integer Part, Change Sign, Absolute Value |
| Comparison | Compare, Examine, Test |
| Transcendental | Tangent, Arctangent, Sine, Cosine, Sine and Cosine, $2^X-1$, $Y \cdot Log_2(X)$, $Y \cdot Log_2(X+1)$ |
| Constants | 0, 1, $\pi$, $Log_{10}2$, $Log_e2$, $Log_210$, $Log_2e$, |
| Processor Control | Load Control Word, Store Control Word, Store Status Word, Load Environment, Store Environment, Save, Restore, Clear Exceptions, Initialize |

Even though the math coprocessor can accept and output numeric data in several formats, it converts all data into a standardized 80-bit internal representation before performing the math operations. This internal data representation is called *temporary real.* To the programmer, the math coprocessor appears as a set of additional register types, data types, and instructions. Basically, there are eight 80-bit real-mode data registers that act like a data stack or can be accessed independently. The coprocessor instructions allow manipulations and operations among these eight data registers, embedded constants, and transcendental functions. Figure 3.21 is a diagram that illustrates the floating-point data registers in the coprocessor.

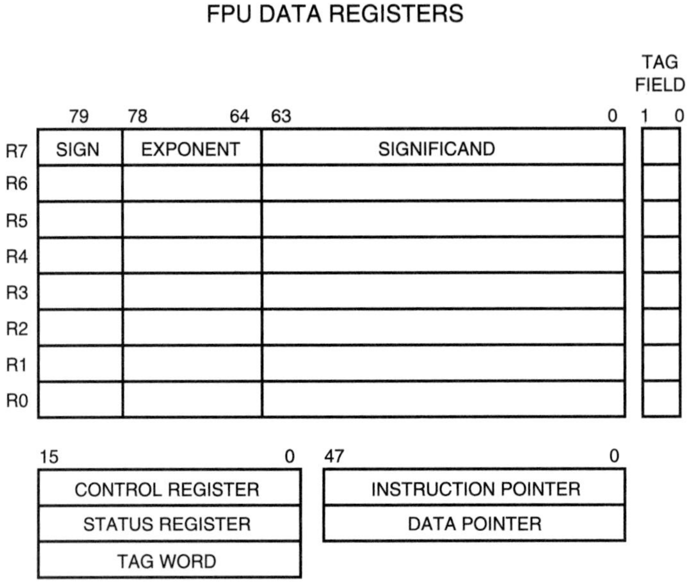

*Figure 3.21.*
*Math coprocessor floating-point unit register set.*

FPU DATA REGISTERS

To activate the math coprocessor, the main or integer processor sends a special escape code to the coprocessor. The two processors then work in concert to send instructions and data to the coprocessor. Once this is completed, the coprocessor proceeds to executes the desired functions while the main processor continues, typically setting up the next coprocessor session. This separate simultaneous operation is somewhat blurred in the Pentium where the two execution pipelines are also used for part of the floating-point operations. It's possible to write programs that automatically take advantage of the math coprocessor if it's present and default to software emulation routines when it's not present. Intel and others offers a suite of math coprocessor emulation software to support X86 platforms without coprocessors installed.

# DSPs (Digital Signal Processors)

The term coprocessor, taken in broader terms, could encompass many functions in the PC. A typical PC system has several coprocessors that perform specialized functions. For example, the keyboard/mouse controller is an independent coprocessor that handles the detailed chores associated with scanning the keyboard and tracking the mouse's position. Other coprocessors may be embedded in your graphic display controller, SCSI port controllers, and LAN adapters. Coprocessors may be loosely coupled to the main processor through a block of shared memory or through I/O registers. Others may be more tightly coupled and act as system bus masters.

One of the more important types of coprocessor now finding its way into PC designs is the DSP or Digital Signal Processor. These processors are specifically designed to handle real-world analog signals that have been converted to digital representations. They have very high performance instruction sets specifically designed to handle analog signal processing. Some of the applications that DSP can support are as follows:

- Sound and music synthesis
- Modem functions
- Audio and video compression and decompression
- Speech synthesis
- Speech recognition
- 2-D and 3-D graphics acceleration
- Video image processing

Spectron recently announced a new interface for downloadable DSP coprocessors in the PC. This interface—called the RMI (Resource Manager Interface)—allows a coprocessor DSP to be downloaded from the main processor with several applications, which in theory, could run simultaneously on the DSP coprocessor subsystem. At this time, several companies are providing PC add-in DSP coprocessor boards to support these multimedia applications. These boards are now very expensive, but the market strategy is to use one DSP to replace several stand-alone functions in the PC.

# Native Signal Processing

With the computing power available on the Pentium class processors and Intel's desire to create a demand for this level of performance, it is only natural that Pentiums try to take on some of signal processing functions now done by DSPs. Intel is now promoting the concept of Native Signal Processing or NSP. Intel's message is that with the power of a Pentium, many of the DSP's signal processing functions can be done directly on the Pentium. The Pentium has two limitations in signal processing: first, it does not have the specialized instructions of the DSP, and second, it doesn't support the real-time performance available on stand-alone DSPs. By most estimates, a fully dedicated Pentium is capable of approximately 6 to 10 DSP MIPs (Millions of Instructions Per second). Most dedicated DSPs offer performance in the range of 20 to 40 MIPs. Many of the newer RISC processors have gone one step further, and actually added new DSP-like instructions to their instruction set. It is very likely that Intel will take this same approach in future processors. Right now, the question of a separate DSP coprocessor in your future is still open. But it seems that the introduction of higher speed main processors with DSP enhancements has made stand-alone DSP coprocessors questionable as PC components.

# Summary of X86 Processors

I've pretty much covered the present state of the PC's X86 processors. By the time this is published there will undoubtedly be numerous additions to the family of products from each of the reviewed suppliers, as well as products for new suppliers. Semiconductor process technology will soon be able to support processor designs with 10 to 20 million transistors, which will enable new levels of functionality and performance and further complicate the X86 processor options.

# RISC Processors

I've mentioned the RISC (Reduced Instruction Set Computer) processor several times and alluded to the fact that they have many advanced features over the older CISC (Complex Instruction Set Computer) processors, such as the Intel X86. Now I would like to cover this subject in a little more detail and explain the differences between RISC and CISC and how it impacts the PC. Use of RISC technology in PCs is not a question of *if* but of *when* and *how much*. We now see RISC techniques being adopted by both the 486 and Pentium processors in an attempt to compete with a family of powerful RISC processors challenging Intel's dominance in the PC markets. The question is can will X86 architecture evolve to RISC, and will this happen before a specific RISC processor architecture gains dominance over the X86.

# RISC Basics

So what are the differences between a RISC and CISC processor? To answer this question we need to go back into history. It has been long recognized that it was possible to sacrifice memory efficiency in the encoding of an instruction set to gain performance. Simple fixed-length instructions with large register space were easier to implement and executed much faster. This technique was used in the early 50s and 60s to implement the IBM 360 mainframe architecture instruction set. The IBM 360's instruction set was a classic CISC design, but the microcode engine that actually executed the instruction set was a simple RISC processor. (Microcode is the term often used to describe the low-level software that is used to direct the execution of a processor's instruction set.) At the time, these RISC processor were called horizontal microcode controllers. The benefits of RISC design were not unknown, but the high cost of memory favored the much more storage efficient CISC designs. Given the very high cost of system memory, making a single instruction do more seemed to be the right way to go. So RISC concepts are not new, they were just waiting for the cost of technology to help justify the RISC approach to system design.

RISC got a significant boost as the result of software work being done at IBM. As a result of IBM's work on compiler technology, it was discovered that most of the complex instructions in the CISC designs were rarely used. The compiler is a software tool that takes instructions written in high-level languages and converts them to basic machine language instructions for execution on the computer.

By inspecting the compiler's generated machine language output, you can tell that often as little of 10 percent of the CISC machine language instruction set accounted for over 90 percent of the total code generated by the compiler. To some the conclusion was obvious: build better compilers. This proved much more difficult than first anticipated. To others, the better approach was to build simpler computers that better matched the capabilities of compilers. IBM and several universities began to do research into the development of simple computer designs that had very few instructions, large register arrays, simple load-and-store access to main memory, and with most instructions executed in one clock cycle. As expected, this resulted in very small processor designs with superior performance. Unfortunately, they also used 20 to 50 percent more memory and required expensive cache memories to keep the RISC processor busy. In other words, you could get superior performance from RISC, but you had to pay a premium for it in the form of high-cost memory subsystems—something the designers of horizontal microcode controllers had discovered more than 20 years earlier.

For a time, the higher cost of RISC designs precluded their wide acceptance in low-cost consumer and commercial applications. However, they were extensively used in high-performance workstations for scientific and engineering applications where performance at the cost premium could be justified. As the RISC processors evolved, their true advantage began to emerge. It wasn't the smaller instruction set that proved to be their advantage but the simplicity of their instructions. In fact, most modern RISC processors have just as many or more instructions than CISC designs. The fact that RISC instructions have simple addressing modes, reference main memory only once, and can be executed in a single clock cycle, meant that it was easy to pipeline the execution of RISC instructions. Further, since instructions were simple and often unrelated, it was possible to design superscalar execution units, or execute multiple instructions simultaneously. The true advantage of RISC finally prevailed, but it was in the simplicity of the basic instructions and not in a smaller instructions set! With highly pipelined and superscalar execution units, the high-level language compilers became much more important. RISC machine instructions were selected based upon keeping the pipeline full and allowing multiple pipelines to operate simultaneously. As IBM had first surmised, RISC hardware and software compilers must go hand-in-hand to achieve the best performance from RISC systems. As the cost of main memory came down and new applications fueled the demand for performance, RISC processors began to compete with CISC very effectively.

# RISC or CISC—Which Is Superior?

A question often asked is: *Why not combine the best of CISC and RISC?* In many instances, this has happened. CISC machines are now more highly pipelined and have superscalar units, and RISC designs now implement some of the CISC instructions to reduce storage requirements. In the final analysis, RISC designs are superior. No new CISC architectures have been introduced in the last 10 years! At similar internal clock speeds, RISC processors consistently outperform CISC processors. Since RISC processors don't require lots of silicon, it's easier to add superscalar execution units, more powerful floating-point units, and larger on-chip caches. Or more simply put, RISC designs take up less space and allow more functions on a chip than CISC designs.

# So Why Are We Still Using CISC Processors?

Even with all of RISC's advantages, the performance differences are not overwhelming. By adopting RISC implementation techniques and using the massive transistor densities now available with modern semiconductor technology, CISC processors such as the Intel X86 can come close to matching RISC performance. However, the major point favoring continued use of X86 CISC processors is that of software compatibility. A massive base of software now runs on the X86 processors. Even the new Windows 95 operating system and graphical user interface from Microsoft will only run on X86 processors! If one were to buy a new RISC-based PC, the full set of PC industry software would not be available to run on the machine. Most PC software is designed for and compiled to run exclusively on the X86 PC platforms. Three basic problems exist in trying to run PC software on RISC PCs:

1. PC software expects to see the Microsoft operating system environment and services on the PC.

2. The applications have been compiled to operate only on X86 instruction set processors.

3. Many older DOS applications and games expect to see the exact PC hardware environment and often directly access the PC's hardware resources.

The first problem was somewhat solved by Microsoft when they ported their NT operating system to the MIPs and Alpha RISC processors. Unfortunately, NT has not caught on as a mainstream operating system, and is primarily used on servers. To date, Microsoft has declined to port its new Windows 95 operating system to anything but X86 PC platforms. Overcoming the lack of Microsoft OS support on RISC processors is a major hurdle facing RISC PCs.

If, for the moment, you assume that a compatible OS exists on the RISC PC, the next problem is to get your application recompiled to operate on the RISC processor's instruction set. Many applications are now available in multiple versions where they have been compiled to target-specific RISC processor and either run under NT or some version of UNIX available on the RISC platform. Unfortunately, the number of applications available is still relatively small and there is great reluctance from developers to support two or more versions of the same applications. First, the market is still too small to justify the development and, secondly, keeping the version levels of the software in step is very difficult. The classic chicken-and-egg problem exists: no RISC PCs because of the lack of software, and no software due to the lack of RISC PCs.

For problems one and two above, the solution is technically straightforward: recompile and install the correct OS port. However, for item three, their is no simple universal technical solution. Applications written specifically for the PC hardware environment will not work on new RISC processors. Each application will require a rewrite to eliminate hardware dependencies. For older software, this is often simply not justifiable, given the low installed base of RISC processor platforms.

# PC Software On RISC Processors

For years a classic approach to migrating older software to new machines was to emulate the older machine's architecture and instruction set in software on the new machine. Typically, an emulation package is first installed on the new machine, and then binary software—just as it was to be run on the older machine—is loaded on the new machine. Even the older operating system environment can be loaded and emulated. This scheme is very effective in migrating software written for one target hardware and software environment to a new environment. It can be thought of as using the RISC processor to decode and execute the older machine's instructions. Unfortunately, this is just what happens—each of the older machines instructions take several RISC instruction's to execute. Even though the RISC processor is very powerful, the emulation scheme results in the older software running much slower than on the native hardware. Emulating X86 applications written for a Pentium on a more powerful RISC processor typically results in the applications running much slower than on the Pentium. This is not much of an incentive to buy a RISC processor to run PC applications.

New techniques in emulation have dramatically narrowed the gap in performance. Using a technique called binary recompilation, significant performance gains are possible in emulated software. The emulation software does not try to emulate each instruction, but looks at a block of instructions and tries to implement exactly the same function using the equivalent RISC instructions. Also, when a loop is discovered, it's only emulated once and then stored in a special cache so that the next time through the loop it does not have to be re-emulated. Using these techniques enables emulated software to achieve nearly 50 percent of the performance available on the native RISC processor. This performance increase does have a memory usage penalty. For example, on the PowerPC RISC processors, to emulate the Windows and PC X86 environment, an extra 4MB of memory is required. At this time, even the most powerful RISC processor using binary recompilation techniques cannot match the performance of a 486 executing its native code. It is rumored that IBM is taking the emulation scheme one step further on its new PowerPC 615 RISC processor chip. Special hardware is being added to accelerate the emulation of X86 instructions. Of course, the ultimate environment is to support both a RISC and CISC processor in the same chip. Many expect this to be the way of the future—a single chip supporting both an X86 processor and a RISC processor. Perhaps this is what is behind the recent joint development work between Intel and Hewlett Packard (HP)?

# Popular RISC Processors

There is now no shortage of powerful RISC processors in the industry. The most popular architectures are as follows:

1. SPARC—used in Sun workstations
2. PA-RISC—used in HP workstations

3. MIPs—used in Silicon Graphics workstations

4. PowerPC—used in new Apple and IBM PCs

5. Alpha—used in Digital Equipment's (DEC) new workstations

With the exception of the DEC Alpha processor, all the preceding RISC processors are manufactured by multiple sources. As a result, fairly large families of processor performance and cost ranges are available. RISC processors designed for embedded applications cost as little as $12 to $50. The highest performance versions designed for workstations can range from $200 to well over $1000 each. Competition is fierce in RISC processors, and new versions are constantly being introduced. As of this writing, the Microsoft NT operating system is available on both the MIPs and DEC Alpha processors, with plans announced for implementation on most of the others.

All of these architectures are evolving in the same direction:

- Full 64-bit implementations
- Highly pipelined execution units
- New instructions to support multimedia and DSP applications
- Very high internal clock rates, 200MHz and beyond
- Superscalar implementations, typically 4- or 6-issue implementations (can simultaneously start 4 to 6 instructions)
- Extremely powerful floating point units
- Large on chip caches, 16 to 64KB

The following is a brief summary of the key features of these RISC processors and block diagrams of their present high end implementations.

# SPARC RISC Processors

SPARC is one of the older RISC architectures, but has been continuously updated. Texas Instruments has been a major supplier of chips as part of a joint development with SUN. The latest product is called the UltraSparc, which implements the SPARC V9 specification. The new device is a full 64-bit design with a four-issue superscalar implementation. It is implemented in a 0.5 micron semiconductor process, which allows it to operate at over 200 MHz. A key new feature of the architecture is the addition of new instructions to accelerate graphics and video processing; up to eight pixels can be processed in a single instruction or clock cycle. This device is scheduled to ship in early 1995. Performance values as high as 250 SPECint92 are expected.(See the later section on processor performance for an explanation of the SPECint92 benchmark.) Figure 3.22 is a block diagram of the new UltraSPARC RISC processor.

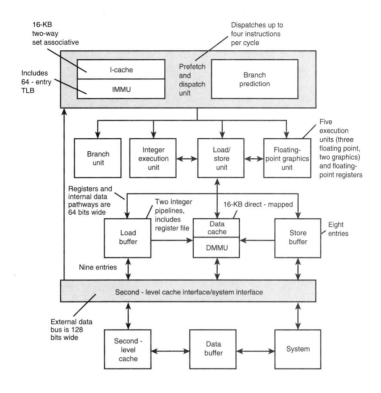

**Figure 3.22.**
*UltraSPARC RISC processor block diagram.*

# Hewlett Packard's PA-RISC (Precision Architecture)

Hewlett Packard has not as of yet officially announced support for Microsoft's NT, but it is a PA-RISC licensee. Samsung has indicated that it will port NT to its upcoming PA-RISC chip. The PA-RISC architecture is a new modern implementation specifically targeted to high performance workstations. The floating-point performance on the PA-RISC is excellent, outperforming most competitors. The PA-RISC architecture has recently added new instructions to support accelerated video and graphics functions similar to those of the new UltraSPARC. The PA-RISC design uses a very small on-chip cache and expects to be mated to very large Level 2 caches. HP's 7100LC device is now used in their low cost workstations and offers performance comparable to Pentium processors. At this time, HP seems to be concentrating its efforts on high-end workstations and taking a wait-and-see attitude to the PC RISC market. Figure 3.23 is a block diagram of the HP 7100LC dual execution unit.

**Figure 3.23.**
*HP 7100LC RISC processor*
*dual execution unit block*
*diagram.*

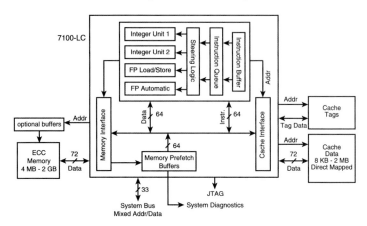

7100LC System Block Diagram

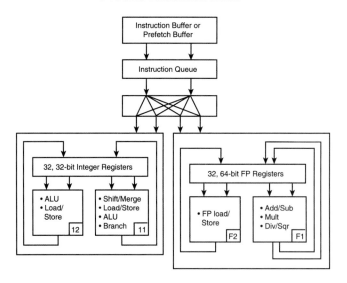

7100LC Execution Units

# MIPS RISC Architecture Processors

The latest product of MIPS Technology and Silicon Graphics is their MIPS T5 processor (recently renamed the R10000). The T5 is a totally new 64-bit superscalar design that is backward-compatible with the older Rxxx series chips that is expected to operate at internal clock speeds of over 200 MHz. It is a five-issue superscalar design with 64 internal registers and a 32KB on-chip Level 1 cache with a 3.3 volt design using .35 micron semiconductor technology process. It is expected to achieve 250 SPECint92 and 350 SPECfp92 performance levels, (see the section in this chapter on performance for an explanation of SPECint92 and SPECfp92 benchmarks), making it one of the highest performing devices on the market. Shipments of the T5 or R10000 are expected in early 1995. Figure 3.24 is a block diagram of the MIPS T5 RISC processor.

**Figure 3.24.**
*MIPS' T5(R10000) RISC processor block diagram.*

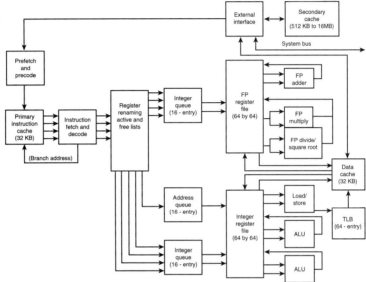

# PowerPC RISC Processors

From a marketing point of view, the PowerPC has a lot of clout. Backed by the powerful IBM, Apple, and Motorola combination, it is aggressively being pushed as the major competitor to the Intel X86 architecture processors. The PowerPC has the potential to be the only platform that can support Apple, PC, and UNIX software. With IBM's OS/2 and AIX UNIX ported and Apple's System 7 and new System 8 operating systems, more and more software will become available on the PowerPC platforms. Motorola has also promised a port of Microsoft's NT. By using state-of-the-art Binary Recompilation techniques and/or the new 615 PowerPC chip with built-in X86 accelerated emulation, PowerPC will be able to run most of the industry's operating systems and software on a single platform. Recently, IBM and Apple have defined a common hardware platform specification intended to enable cross operating system and application support on all PowerPC products developed by either party or its licensees.

The PowerPC is an older RISC architecture that has evolved from the IBM RS6000 Power workstation products. It's not as clean and elegant as new architectures, but it's more than adequate. It is a full 64-bit design with a family of products:

- PowerPC 601, First PowerPC chip (Pentium Performance levels)
- PowerPC 604, Latest Desktop PowerPC chip, Pentium Plus performance

- PowerPC 603, special version for portable products
- PowerPC 615, Special version with X86 accelerated emulation
- PowerPC 620, highest performance version for workstations/servers

PowerPC chips tend to be smaller chips and thus are much more cost-effective than some of the other RISC chips. They use superscalar techniques combined with very efficient large on-chip cache designs to achieve their performance levels at modest internal clock speeds. The highest performance device, the PowerPC 620, is planned to operate at 133 MHz with a 128-bit data bus. The present PowerPC 601, 603, and 604 operate at speeds up to 100 MHz. The PowerPC 620 has a superscalar implementation capable of issuing six instructions simultaneously. It also contains two massive 32KB caches, one for instructions and one for data. This split cache design allows emulation of an internal Harvard architecture. The PowerPC 620 chip is implemented with over seven million transistors, whereas the Intel Pentium has 3.1 million transistors. At the rated clock speed of 133 MHz, the PowerPC 620 is expected to achieve performance levels of 225 SPECint92 and 300 SPECfp92. Figure 3.25 is a block diagram of the PowerPC 620 chip.

**Figure 3.25.**
*PowerPC 630 RISC Processor Block Diagram.*

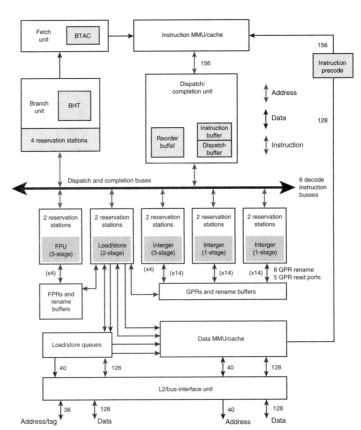

# Digital Equipment Corporation (DEC) Alpha Processors

The DEC Alpha RISC chip family has the distinction of operating at the highest clock rates of all the available chips. Devices are now available at speeds of up to 275 MHz and over 300 MHz devices are promised. The architecture is a modern 64-bit RISC design, and of all the presently shipping RISC devices, it has the highest performance levels. As mentioned earlier, Alpha's high clock rate accounts for most of it performance edge. The present design is just a two-issue superscalar implementation. A natural future extension is a four- or six-issue superscalar design. The following is a brief list of the Alpha RISC processor family members.

- 21064—First Alpha device, 200 MHz, 8KB on-chip cache
- 21064A—Highest performance device 275 MHz, 16KB on-chip cache
- 21066—Low cost Alpha, on-chip PCI bus, DRAM interface
- 21068—Embedded controller version of Alpha

Figure 3.26 is a basic block diagram of the DEC Alpha 21064A architecture.

*Figure 3.26.*
*DEC Alpha 21064A RISC*
*processor block diagram.*

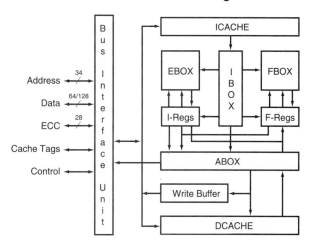

## 21064A Block Diagram

- cache size 16K each
- 1.68 million transistors
- clock rate 275MHz
- Die size 164 mm² in 0.6-micron, 4-layer-metal CMOS

# How To Compare Processor Performance

With over 50 different X86 processors on the market and now a similar number of RISC processors, and many capable of running PC software, how does one compare their capabilities? In the past, external clock speeds were a relatively accurate performance indicator and a 32-bit data bus was better than a 16-bit bus device. Now with internal clock multipliers, superscalar designs, and on-chip caches, these simple rules for judging performance don't apply. Simple measurement such as how many instructions are executed per second (MIPs, Millions of Instructions Per second) can be misleading when comparing RISC and CISC processors. Clearly, a more sophisticated approach is needed. The most accepted approach is to "benchmark" the processor's performance by running a set of well-defined tasks. Using this approach, a well-defined set of tests are run on the processor and the time it takes to execute the tasks are measured. Normally a set of common tasks are selected and both the individual and total times are used to create a relative performance level measurement number.

Benchmark tests can be run at three different levels:

1. On the target processor assuming an unconstrained system design. This level assumes that no other aspect of the system's design is constraining the processor's performance. For example, the attached memory subsystem is not causing the processor to slow down. Microprocessor chip designers like to use this type of processor benchmarking.

2. In a real system design. In real system designs the processor will likely be constrained from reaching its ultimate performance. For example, cache sizes and speeds are realistic and DRAM memory performance is not infinite. Often the same benchmarks on different systems with the same processor at the same speeds will yield dramatically different results.

3. In a real application environment. The ultimate test of any microprocessor and system is in a real application. In this case special benchmarks must be designed to measure the application. Often the application's performance is dictated more by the performance of other subsystems capabilities than by the processor. For example, the memory subsystem, disk subsystem, and display adapter subsystem performances can outweigh the effects of processor performance. Even software such as device drivers, operating systems, and BIOS implementation can dramatically affect a system's performance.

In other words, microprocessor designers like processor benchmarks, systems designers like system benchmarks, and users like real applications benchmarks. Processor benchmarks can also be used on systems, and are a good indication of the raw processing power of the system. System level benchmarks typically use processor benchmarks plus additional benchmarks to test the performance of other components of the system. And, of course, application benchmarks are designed to test the system's capabilities when running real applications, often a series of different types of applications. In general, processor benchmarks are a good indication of performance potential of a system, while system and application benchmarks are a further test of the total system's capabilities. The best approach is to first compare processor benchmarks to select a processor type, and then compare the same processor benchmarks on similarly configured systems, and finally compare application benchmark results on similarly configured systems.

# Where to Get System Level and Application Level Benchmark Results

It would be impossible to provide an accurate and up-to-date list of all of the PC systems and their benchmark results here. Further, the results would likely be out-of-date by the time this is published. Your best approach it to consult the many excellent PC magazines that publish extensive reviews of contemporary PC systems. These reviews often publish extensive benchmark test results. Unfortunately, each publication uses its own set of benchmarks. Therefore, it's difficult to compare systems from different magazine reviews. However, most publications offer the benchmark test software to their readers for a small fee. You can conduct your own benchmark tests if you can get access to the target systems. A popular set of PC Windows application benchmarks has been jointly developed by Microsoft and Ziff Davis Publishing (*PC Magazine*) called Winstone95.

# SPECint92 and SPECfp92 Benchmarks

Given the large numbers of benchmarks and the lack of portability between processors and operating systems and their complexity, many simply revert to the unconstrained processor benchmarks as an indicator of performance. The most widely accepted industry processor performance measurement benchmarks are the SPECint92 and SPECfp92. These well-defined tests can be run on all processors and give a very good indication of both integer performance (SPECint92) and floating-point performance (SPECfp92). (The 92 refers to the date of the last revision of the benchmark tests.) Most PC applications are primarily integer based and the results of the SPECint92 benchmark are typically more important. But if the application is an engineering or scientific application, the floating-point benchmark will also be important. The following table, Table 3.4, is a summary of SPECint92 and SPECfp92 results for popular X86 and RISC processors. Remember that these same processors in real system designs may yield lower results than indicated below, depending on the actual system design.

Table 3.4. SPECint92 and SPECfp92 Results for X86 and RISC Processors.

| Processor | Clock Speed | SPECint92 | SPECfp92 |
|---|---|---|---|
| 386SX | 25 MHz | 3.8 | - |
| 386DX | 33 MHz | 8.4 | - |
| 486SX | 33 MHz | 18.6 | - |
| 486DX | 33 MHz | 18.6 | - |
| 486DX | 50 MHz | 27.9 | - |

*continues*

Table 3.4. continued

| Processor | Clock Speed | SPECint92 | SPECfp92 |
|-----------|-------------|-----------|----------|
| 486DX2 | 66 MHz | 32.4 | - |
| Pentium | 66 MHz | 67 | 62 |
| Pentium | 90 MHz | 91 | 84 |
| Pentium | 120 MHz | 122 | 113 |
| Pentium | 150 MHz | 150 | 141 |
| PowerPC 601 | 80 MHz | 85 | 105 |
| PowerPC 603 | 80 MHz | 75 | 85 |
| PowerPC 620 | 133 MHz | 225 | 300 |
| HP 7100LC | 80 MHz | 84 | 130 |
| HP 7150 | 125 MHz | 135 | 200 |
| SuperSPACE+ | 60 MHz | 77 | 98 |
| UltraSPARC | 200 MHz | 250? | 350? |
| MIPS R4400 | 150 MHz | 96 | 105 |
| MIPS R10000 | 200 MHz | 250 | 350 |
| Alpha 21066 | 166 MHz | 70 | 105 |
| Alpha 21064A | 275 MHz | 170 | 290 |

**Note:** Many of the processors shown in Table 3.4 are not available and the values are projected based on extrapolation of clock speeds and simulations of the chips in development. Actual performance values will probably have minor variations from the above projected results.

## Intel ICOMP Ratings

Recently, Intel has been rating its processors using a value they call an ICOMP index number. Because ICOMP numbers are only available for Intel processors, you cannot use them to compare RISC processors or X86 processor from other manufacturers. The following chart in Figure 3.27 illustrates the ICOMP values published by Intel for their processors.

*Figure 3.27.*
ICOMP *ratings for*
Intel *processors.*

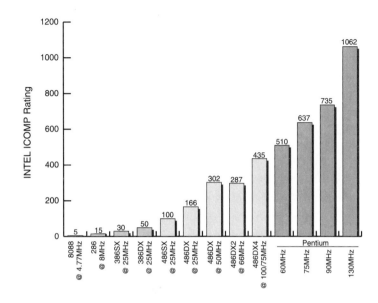

# Multiprocessor Systems

For years, mainframes and minicomputers have offered multiprocessor systems as a way to enhance overall system performance. Typically, adding multiple processors does not result in a linear increase in performance. For example, in a two-processor system, a 1.3 to 1.8 increase is about the expected range in performance gain. Of course, the processors need to be designed for multiprocessor environments or extra circuitry needs to be added to the systems. Also the operating system needs to understand and manage multiprocessor environments. However, the best performance is gained when the application is also designed for multiprocessor environments.

Multiprocessor techniques are now being applied to PCs and workstations. For example, the new Pentium P54C processor from Intel has been designed for multiprocessor support. Further, Microsoft's NT operating system can also support multiprocessor environments.

# Future Processors

On the X86 front, significant performance increases can be expected by simply taking advantage of further advances in semiconductor technology. The existing Pentium design will likely be extended through simple increases in cache size, cache efficiency, and increased clock speeds. Speeds of 120, 130, 150, and 180 MHz are expected. The new P6 processor from Intel rumored to be available by second quarter of 1995 is expected to double Pentium performance by increasing the superscalar design to support four instruction issue capability along with a more efficient pipeline with less simultaneous issue restrictions. The P6 is expected to have over 6 million transistors and be competitive with the latest RISC processors, offering 300 SPECint92 performance levels. Of course, RISC processors will not be standing still and will benefit similarly from semiconductor advances.

# Beyond RISC and CISC: VLIW

Microprocessor designers are now taking a new look at another old design technique that semiconductor technology makes practical. It has long been observed that most software programs execute blocks of instructions between branch instructions. These blocks are typically very small, ranging from 6 to 10 instructions in length. The VLIW (Very Long Instruction Word) processor design techniques take advantage of this characteristic of software. The basic idea is to pack several simple nonrelated instructions into a single super instruction word and deliver it to the VLIW processor where it could be divide up among a set of parallel execution units for simultaneous execution. The key to making this scheme work is not so much in the hardware as it is in the software compiler that creates the instruction block. The compilers would have to become much smarter by looking at more of the application at a time and determining how it could arrange the instructions and tasks such that the long word contained no sub instruction dependencies. This problem is similar to the present-day compiler's task of ordering the instructions such that the pipelines don't stall, but on a much larger scale. It is rumored that the joint development work being done by Intel and HP is targeting a new processor using VLIW techniques.

# New Memory Architectures

With the enormous processing power available in new processors, they are beginning to be constrained by the performance of their attached memory subsystems. The present memory technology and design approaches simply cannot feed the processors fast enough to keep them busy. Also, the cost of multilevel cache designs is keeping the cost of PCs high and limiting their access to the enormous consumer market. While processor performance has increased by a factor of 100 over the last 10 years, memory performance has increased only by a factor of three to four. The industry is now developing new memory designs that will support processors of the future in a more cost effective manner. Present DRAM memories can operate at speeds of up to 50 MHz and, with a few tricks, can achieve speeds near 100 MHz. One of the new more promising alternate memory design approaches is able to achieve speeds of 500 MHz. This new approach is called the RAMbus memory. You are likely to see several new memory technologies emerge over the next few years to better support the growing appetite of high-performance PC processors.

# 4

# Microprocessor Traffic Control

So far, I've talked about the history of the processors and coprocessors you can find installed in PCs. I've talked about performance, operating speed, and voltage requirements. I've shown you how the processors use the main and local buses to talk to the rest of the world and transfer information.

In this chapter, I delve a little deeper into how the processor itself functions and where it stores data. I'll also show you some simple program code to demonstrate a few key features. Don't let that idea put you off, though. There's information here that will help you make decisions and understand marketing mumbo-jumbo in the future. On the other hand, while this is not an engineer's discussion, it may go beyond what you want if you are a savvy user but couldn't care less about deep internal operations. If that's you, skip ahead to Chapter 5, "Disks: The Basic Story."

You'll remember (hey, you're still here!) from our discussion in Chapter 3, "Brains: The Processors," that today's processors are based on the old 8086. You'll also probably remember that the 8086 is quite similar to the 8088. Both work with 16 bits at a time and follow the same instructions. The major difference is that the 8086 sends and receives 16 bits of data at a time, while the 8088 sends and receives only 8 bits at a time. The X86 architecture is the foundation of the original PC, although IBM's original PC used the 8088 processor specifically. More importantly, it is also the foundation of DOS.

When you're exploring the Intel family of processors, it's very useful to get a firm grasp of how the X86 works. So first, we'll look at the inner workings of the Intel family of processors, based on the 8086. Then I'll explain how the newer processors have improved things. In fact, for the purposes of this book, most of what you learn about the 8086 processor applies to the entire processor family. Regardless of how fancy the Intel family of processors becomes, the first key to understanding your PC is understanding the 8086 at a relatively low level.

If you want a little more background on how the processor does what it does, stick with me for the next few pages.

# What the Processor Can Do

The best place to start to understand what a processor does is with its fundamental instruction set. (Again, for this technical level of discussion, I concentrate on the 8086. This keeps things relatively simple and, as I mentioned, if you understand the basics of this chip, understanding the Pentium isn't a giant step, believe me.)

Anything you ask the computer to do is a complex task from the computer's viewpoint. (Remember the maze in the introduction?) The computer must perform a series of steps built out of its own instruction set. These basic instructions are called machine language, or assembly language. (When it's in the form that programmers write, it's called assembly language; when it's in the form that the computer works with, it's called machine language.) These simple tasks are the only things the computer can really directly do; everything else from emulating an answering machine to automatically translating your typing into a foreign language as you telecommunicate is built upon combinations of these very basic abilities. One of the best ways to grasp the power of a computer is to see what its basic machine language instructions can do and how quickly they can do it.

## Processor Speed

Now that desktop PCs have reached and even overpowered the abilities of traditional mainframe computers, it's not uncommon to see a PC's abilities measured in the same terms that were formerly used for those mainframe systems. The term MIPS (pronounced with a short *i* sound) stands for Millions of Instructions Per Second and is a measurement of how many instructions—the basic instructions that we're talking about in this section— the processor can perform in a single second. While the original Intel chips delivered little more than one-third of one MIPS, current Pentium processors are pushing past 150 MIPS.

Another common method of measuring processor speed is MHz, short for MegaHertz. This is a measurement of the processor's clock speed, and I explain more about it later in this chapter.

If you tried to look at a computer's basic instructions in depth, you'd get bogged down in lots of tedious details, the details with which assembly language programmers have to work. That isn't my purpose here; instead, I help you explore what a computer's skills are. I start with simple arithmetic because arithmetic forms the basis for a great deal of what the computer does.

A PC processor can perform the four basic operations of arithmetic: addition, subtraction, multiplication, and division. Addition and subtraction are the simplest and by far the most common operations. Because the 8086 and 8088 are 16-bit processors, you know that they can do their adding and subtracting on 16-bit numbers, but they also can perform arithmetic on individual 8-bit bytes. You might wonder why computers need to do both 8- and 16-bit operations. If 16-bit operations are inherently more powerful, why bother with 8-bit numbers?

There are at least three good reasons for using 8- instead of 16-bit arithmetic. First, if you are working with numbers that can be accommodated in an 8-bit byte, why use twice as much memory as is really needed? When working with lots and lots of numbers that could be stored in 8-bit bytes, the added efficiency of using only single bytes can be very worthwhile. The second reason for using 8-bit arithmetic appears when you want to work on individual bytes.

Here's an example. Sometimes (more often than you might think) you need to convert alphabetic character data to all uppercase. If you look at the numeric equivalents of letters, you find that the lowercase letters fall 32 places above the corresponding uppercase letters in the ASCII coding scheme. (For more information on the PC character set, see Chapter 12.) A program can convert a lowercase letter into uppercase simply by subtracting 32 from the byte that holds the lowercase letter, and that's done with an 8-bit subtraction command. You can demonstrate this by trying this simple command in QBasic:

```
PRINT "a", ASC("a"), ASC("a") - 32, CHR$( ASC("a") - 32 )
```

Finally, the third good reason for using 8- in addition to 16-bit arithmetic is that 8-bit arithmetic easily can be used as the building blocks of more powerful operations. For example, suppose you want to add and subtract numbers that are larger than 16 bits can handle. You may need to work with numbers that are as large as 24 bits, or 3 bytes. You can see how the computer can do this by looking at how you add numbers together. For example, when adding 123 and 456, you do it digit by digit, starting on the right side. You add 3 and 6, getting 9, and then move left to the next place. If any pair of digits gives you a sum over 10, you carry 1 to the next place. Computers can do the same thing using 8-bit arithmetic. With 8-bit addition and subtraction operations, processors can work byte by byte with numbers of any size. Carries from one byte position to the next are handled by a special feature called a carry flag. (For more on flags, see "The PC's Flags" section later in this chapter.)

> **Technical Note:** With the widespread use of 24-bit color graphics, 8-bit arithmetic has gained another reason for existing. It is an important part of performing speedy color-component operations at 24-bit and higher color depths.

Note that 8- and 16-bit numbers can be treated as signed or unsigned. The signed formats enable the computer to use negative numbers, and the unsigned formats enable the computer to use larger numbers. Processors have variations on the basic addition and subtraction operations that enable programs to choose between 8- and 16-bit size, signed or unsigned values, and using or ignoring carries from previous operations. All of these operations concern the computer's basic binary (base 2) number system. There also are some auxiliary instructions that make it practical for the computer to work with decimal (base 10) numbers.

While processors handle just about every possible variation on addition and subtraction, they take a slightly less complicated approach to multiplication and division. Computers can multiply 8- or 16-bit (byte or word) numbers and treat them as signed or unsigned. For division, computers always divide a 32-bit (or double-word) dividend by an 8- or 16-bit divisor, signed or unsigned.

That's the basic arithmetic that the 8086 processor can do. If you need anything richer, such as larger numbers or floating-point format, the arithmetic usually is handled by a math coprocessor or by special-purpose subroutines (small programs) that can build a larger operation from simple arithmetic building blocks. Interestingly, the 8086 was the first processor family to partition the processing unit to support high-performance number crunching. The companion 8087 coprocessor for this family handled these duties when required.

The 486 family and the 386, 386SX, and 386SL can be programmed to work directly with 32-bits, which enables you to use larger numbers (although most DOS programs do not do so). Remember that the 486 was the first X86 family processor with a built-in math coprocessor. PCs based on a 486 always have a coprocessor available and never have to resort to the special-purpose arithmetic subroutines mentioned above.

# Snooping at Code

If you want to learn more about the power and features of the PC's instruction set, there are several ways you can do so without taking on the often difficult and tedious task of learning assembly language. This requires some cleverness on your part in deciphering some of the cryptic codes used in assembly language, but the effort can be rewarding in the satisfaction of knowing some of the most intimate details of how the PC works.

The trick is to get your hands on some assembly language programs that you can read and inspect to see just how things are done directly with the PC's instruction set. The best of all is to see some assembly language programming complete with the programmer's comments, which explain a great deal of what is going on.

One source is the *IBM Technical Reference Manual* for a pre-PS/2 computer. These manuals contain fully annotated listings for the ROM-BIOS programs that are built into all PCs. Unfortunately, with the introduction of the PS/2s, IBM stopped publishing the BIOS listings. (Figure 4.1 shows a page from one of these manuals.)

If you can't get your hands on an *IBM Technical Reference Manual*, you can try decoding (unassembling) some code (from unintelligible machine language into the slightly more readable assembly language) using an unassembler. One crude but usable unassembler is available as a part of DOS. It's included in the DEBUG program.

You can use DEBUG to unassemble any programs to which you have access, including the PC's built-in ROM programs. You can find an example of how to do this later in this chapter in the "Looking at an Interrupt Handler" section. However, it is important to remember that computer programs are proprietary. You can look, but don't even consider using the routine you find in your own programs. In some cases, it is technically a violation of your software license to even look at the code with a disassembler.

Although arithmetic forms a large part of the important core of the computer's operations, the computer's processors can do more than arithmetic. If all computers could do was arithmetic (and other straightforward manipulation of data, such as just moving it around), they would be nothing more than glorified adding machines. What makes computers much more powerful than simple calculators is a variety of instructions known as computer logic.

*Figure 4.1.*
*ROM-BIOS code from the*
*IBM PC AT Technical*
*Reference Manual.*

```
                        TITLE TEST1 11/28/83 ROM POST

;                                                                          :
;  BIOS I/O INTERFACE                                                      :
;                                                                          :
;       THESES INTERFACE LISTINGS, PROVIDE ACCESS TO BIOS ROUTINES         :
;       THESE BIOS ROUTINES ARE MEANT TO BE ACCESSED THROUGH               :
;       SOFTWARE INTERRUPTS ONLY.  ANY ADDRESSES PRESENT IN                :
;       THE LISTINGS ARE INCLUDED ONLY FOR COMPLETENESS,                   :
;       NOT FOR REFERENCE.  APPLICATIONS WHICH REFERENCE                   :
;       ABSOLUTE ADDRESSES WITHIN THE CODE SEGMENT                         :
;       VIOLATE THE STRUCTURE AND DESIGN OF BIOS.                          :
;                                                                          :
    PAGE
;--------------------------------------------------------------------------
;  MODULES REQUIRED
;       DATA.SRC        -->   DATA AREA
;       TEST1.SRC       -->   TEST.01 THRU TEST.16
;       TEST2.SRC       -->   TEST.17 THRU TEST.22
;       TEST3.SRC       -->   PROCEDURES
;                             ROS_CHECKSUM
;                             BLINK_INT
;                             ROM_CHECK
;                             XPC_BYTE
;                             PRT_HEX
;                             PROT_PRT_HEX
;                             PROC_SHUTDOWN
;       TEST4.SRC       -->   E_MSG
;                             P_MSG
;                             BEEP
;                             ERR_BEEP
;                             KBD_RESET
;                             D11 DUMMY INT HANDLER
;                             INT13 - X287 HANDLER
;                             PRT_SEG
;                             DDS
;                             HARDWARE INT 9 HANDLER (TYPE 71)
;       TEST5.SRC       -->   EXCEPTION INTERRUPTS
;       TEST6.SRC       -->   STGTST_CNT
;                             ROM_ERR
;                             XMIT_8042
;                             BOOT_STRAP
;       TEST7.SRC       -->   PROTECTED MODE TEST
;       SYSINIT1.SRC    -->   BUILD PROTECTED MODE DESCRIPTORS
;       GDT_BLD.SRC
;       SIDT_BLD.SRC
;       DSKETTE.SRC     -->   DISKETTE BIOS
;       DISK.SRC        -->   HARD FILE BIOS
;       KYBD.SRC        -->   KEYBOARD BIOS
;       PRT.SRC         -->   PRINTER BIOS
;       RS232.SRC       -->   RS232 BIOS
;       VIDEO1.SRC      -->   VIDEO BIOS
;       BIOS.SRC        -->   MEM_SIZE
;                             EQUIP_DET
;                             NMI
;                             SET_TOD
;       BIOS1.SRC       -->   DUMMY_CASSETTE (INT 15)
;                             DEVICE OPEN
;                             DEVICE CLOSE
;                             PROGRAM TERMINATION
;                             EVENT WAIT
;                             JOYSTICK SUPPORT
;                             SYSTEM REQUEST KEY
;                             WAIT
;                             MOVE BLOCK
;                             EXTENDED MEMORY SIZE DETERMINE
;                             PROCESSOR TO VIRTUAL MODE
;       BIOS2.SRC       -->   TIME OF DAY
;                             TIMER1 INT
;                             PRINT_SCREEN
;       ORGS.SRC        -->   PC COMPATABILITY AND TABLES
;                             POST ERROR MESSAGES
;--------------------------------------------------------------------------
      C  INCLUDE POSTEQU.SRC
      C  ;--------------------------------------------------------------------
      C  ;                    EQUATES                                  :
      C  ;--------------------------------------------------------------------
      C
 = 0000  C  TEST          EQU   0            ; CONDITIONAL ASM (TEST2.SRC)
 = 0000  C  KY_LOCK       EQU   0            ; CONDITIONAL ASM (TEST2.SRC)
 = 0000  C  KEY_NUMS      EQU   0            ; CONDITIONAL ASM (KYBD.SRC)
      C  ;--------------------------------------------------------------------
 = 00F0  C  X287          EQU   0F0H         ; MATH PROCESSOR
      C  ;--------------------------------------------------------------------
 = 0020  C  LOOP_POST     EQU   020H         ; MFG LOOP POST JUMPER
      C  ;--------------------------------------------------------------------
 = 0010  C  REFRESH_BIT   EQU   010H         ; REFRESH TEST BIT
      C  ;--------------------------------------------------------------------
 = 0000  C  POST_SS       EQU   0H           ; POST STACK SEGMENT
 = 8000  C  POST_SP       EQU   8000H        ; POST STACK POINTER
 = FFFF  C  TEMP_STACK_LO EQU   0FFFFH
 = 0000  C  TEMP_STACK_HI EQU   0            ; SET PROTECTED MODE TEMP_SS
      C                                      ; 0:FFFFH
      C  ;--------------------------------------------------------------------
 = 0060  C  PORT_A        EQU   60H          ; 8042 KEYBOARD SCAN/DIAG OUTPUTS
 = 0061  C  PORT_B        EQU   61H          ; 8042 READ WRITE REGISTER
 = 00C0  C  PARITY_ERR    EQU   0C0H         ; RAM/IO CHANNEL PARITY ERROR
 = 00F3  C  RAM_PAR_ON    EQU   11110011B    ; AND THIS VALUE
 = 000C  C  RAM_PAR_OFF   EQU   00001100B    ; OR THIS VALUE
 = 0040  C  IO_CHK        EQU   01000000B    ; IO CHECK?
 = 0080  C  PRTY_CHK      EQU   10000000B    ; PARITY CHECK?
      C
 = 0064  C  STATUS_PORT   EQU   64H          ;8042 STATUS PORT
 = 0001  C  OUT_BUF_FULL  EQU   01H          ; 0 = +OUTPUT BUFFER FULL
 = 0002  C  INPT_BUF_FULL EQU   02H          ; 1 = +INPUT BUFFER FULL
 = 0004  C  SYS_FLAG      EQU   04H          ; 2 = +SYSTEM FLAG -POR/-SELF TEST
 = 0008  C  CMD_DATA      EQU   08H          ; 3 = -COMMAND/+DATA
 = 0010  C  KYBD_INH      EQU   10H          ; 4 = +KEYBOARD INHIBITED
 = 0020  C  TRANS_TMOUT   EQU   20H          ; 5 = +TRANSMIT TIMEOUT
 = 0040  C  RCV_TROUT     EQU   40H          ; 6 = +RECEIVE TIME OUT
 = 0080  C  PARITY_EVEN   EQU   80H          ; 7 = +PARITY IS EVEN
 = 00FE  C  SHUT_CMD      EQU   0FEH         ; CAUSE A SHUTDOWN COMMAND
 = 00AB  C  INTR_FACE_CK  EQU   0ABH         ; CHECK 8042 INTERFACE CMD
 = 00ED  C  KYBD_CLK_DATA EQU   0EDH         ; GET KYBD CLOCK AND DATA CMD
 = 0001  C  KYBD_CLK      EQU   001H         ; KEYBOARD CLOCK BIT 0
      C  ;--------------MANUFACTURING PORT--------------
 = 0080  C  MFG_PORT      EQU   80H          ; MANUFACTURING CHECKPOINT PORT
      C  ;--------------MANUFACTURING BIT DEFINITION FOR MFG_ERR_FLAG+1--------
 = 0001  C  MEM_FAIL      EQU   00000001B    ; STORAGE TEST FAILED (ERROR 20X)
 = 0002  C  PRO_FAIL      EQU   00000010B    ; VIRTUAL MODE TEST FAILED (ERROR 104)
 = 0004  C  LMCS_FAIL     EQU   00000100B    ; LOW MEG CHIP SELECT FAILED (ERROR 109)
 = 0008  C  KYCLK_FAIL    EQU   00001000B    ; KEYBOARD CLOCK TEST FAILED (ERROR 304)
 = 0010  C  KY_SYS_FAIL   EQU   00010000B    ; KEYBOARD OR SYSTEM FAILED (ERROR 303)
 = 0020  C  KYBD_FAIL     EQU   00100000B    ; KEYBOARD FAILED (ERROR 301)
 = 0040  C  DSK_FAIL      EQU   01000000B    ; DISKETTE TEST FAILED (ERROR 601)
```

The computer's logic operations enable it to adjust what's being done to the situation at hand. There are three main kinds of logic operations that computers have in their repertoire: tests, conditional branches, and repeats. As an example, let the computer play the role of a parking lot attendant.

If a parking lot charges, say, $3 an hour with a $15 maximum, the parking lot attendant has to cal-culate your hourly charge and then check to see if it's over the maximum. The attendant multiplies $3 times the number of hours you were parked and then compares the amount with $15. In com-puter logic, that comparison is the test, and the result of the test is noted in some special-purpose flags, like the carry flag already mentioned. Generally, the test is some form of arithmetic (such as comparing two numbers, which is the equivalent of subtracting one from the other to see if one is bigger or if they are equal). The flags that are used have an arithmetic meaning. The zero flag means the result of an arithmetic operation was zero or that a comparison of two numbers found them equal. Similarly, the sign flag means the result was negative. These flags, which are the result of any gen-eral arithmetic operation or any test comparison operation, set the stage for the second part of com-puter logic—conditional branches.

Conditional branches enable the computer to adjust its operation to the situation. A branch is a change in the sequence of steps the computer is carrying out. A conditional branch skips from one set of commands to another based on a condition, such as how the flags are set. The parking lot attendant computer, after comparing your total hourly parking charge with the $15 maximum, would charge you only $15 if the total hourly charge were higher.

Conditional branches are used in computer programs in two quite different ways. The instruction, the conditional branch, can be the same, but the use to which it's put is quite different. One use, which you already have seen, simply is to select between two courses of action, such as charging the hourly rate or the maximum limit. The other way to use a conditional branch instruction is to use control looping, repeating a series of instructions. The parking lot attendant computer, for example, repeatedly performs the operation of parking a car as long as there are parking spaces available and customers waiting to leave their cars. The parking attendant loops through, or repeats, the process of parking a car, as long as the test and conditional branch instructions show that there are cars to park and places in which to put them.

A regular conditional branch instruction can be used for either purpose—selecting between two courses or controlling a loop—in a computer program. But, because loops are so important to com-puter work, there are also special-purpose instructions that are customized for the needs of looping. These are the repeat instructions. Some of them are designed to repeat a series of instructions, and some repeat a single instruction—a tightly coupled operation that can be executed with amazing speed and efficiency.

What you've seen so far of the instructions that the computer's processors can perform is really just a sampling of their full repertoire of commands. However, it is a summary of the most important things that the computer can do and should give you some feeling for the basic building blocks out of which programs are constructed.

Whether you are looking at a fast or a slow PC, you should be aware that the processor executes instructions with blinding speed—hundreds of thousands or millions of instructions every second. And, as you may expect, newer processors are continually faster than their predecessors. Indeed, Intel Pentium processors are even capable of executing two or more instructions at a time, under certain circumstances. As you would expect, this can dramatically increase your system's performance speed. For more details on the Pentium class of processors, see Chapter 2.

And, one reason performance at the instruction level is so important to consider is the fact that even the simplest thing you ask a computer to do involves hundreds and thousands of individual, detailed instructions. Moreover, most of the programming done with a processor is conducted at a relatively high level. If you issue a JUMP instruction through an assembler, for example, there is a lot of complicated underlying code required to carry out that seemingly low-level instruction.

# Tools at Hand—Memory, Ports, Registers, and Stacks

So far, I've talked about the kinds of operations processors can perform by themselves and with the help of coprocessors. Now, it's time to take a look at the tools that the processor has at its disposal to help it carry out these instructions. In this section, I explain how the processor uses memory, ports, registers, and stacks.

The computer's processor has only three ways of talking to the world of circuitry outside of itself. One of the three is the special communication that it has with the 87 coprocessors through the ES-CAPE command. The other two are much more ordinary and play a key role in the core of the computer's operation. These are the computer's memory and the use of ports.

Remember that memory acts as the computer's desktop, playing field, and workplace. The memory is the place where the processor finds its program instructions and data. Both data and instructions are stored in memory, and the processor picks them up from there. The memory is internal to the computer, and its essential function is to provide a work space for the processor. I take a closer look at memory in Chapter 15.

If memory is essential for the processor's internal use, there has to be a way for the processor's memory to communicate with the world outside. This is what ports are for. A port is something like a telephone line. Any part of the computer's circuitry with which the processor needs to talk is given a port number, and the processor uses that number like a telephone number to call up the particular circuit or part. For example, one port number is used to talk to the keyboard, and another is used for the programmable timer. Controlling the disk drives and transferring data back and forth also is done through ports. The display screen, too, is controlled by using ports. However, the data that appears on the display screen is handled through memory rather than ports, as you see in Chapter 11, "On-Screen Video."

Note that I'm using the word "port" here in a slightly different way than I did in Chapter 2 when I discussed the parts of the computer. In Chapter 2, I used the word to refer to a connection where the cable from a peripheral plugs into the system unit. The two meanings are related, however. A port is an interface through which data passes—either to and from the processor (as in this section) or to and from the system unit (as in Chapter 2).

The 8086 processor has 65,536 port "telephone numbers" available to it. Not all of them are connected. The designers of any microcomputer decide which port numbers to use for various purposes, and the circuit elements of the computer are wired to respond to those port numbers. The computer's bus (covered in Chapter 2) is something like a telephone party line, which is used in common by every part of the computer that is assigned a port number. When the processor needs to talk to one circuit part or another, it signals the port number on the bus, and the appropriate part responds.

**Technical Note:** Ports can be either 8, 16, or 32 bits in width. In a circumstance such as the 8086, with 65,536 ports available, each port is 8 bits wide.

The processor has a number of special assembly language commands that are used to communicate with ports. The OUT command sends one byte or one word (or one double word, OUT DX,AL OUT DX,AX OUT DX,EAX) of data to a port number; the OUTS and REP OUTS commands send multiple bytes or words of data (so does OUT; OUTS and REP OUTS send a string to a port). Similarly, the IN, INS, and REP INS commands request data from a port number. (Note: The 8086 and 8088 processors support only the simpler OUT and IN commands.)

You usually have no way to experiment with assembly language instructions, such as IN and OUT commands, unless you work directly with assembly language. But, in the case of these two instructions, QBasic provides two commands, called INP and OUT, that do exactly what the assembly language instructions do. You can use them to experiment with the computer's ports, although it's very tricky to do. To give you a quick example, here is a short program that turns the PC's sound on and off simply by using the ports:

```
SOUND 500, 1
X = (INP(97) MOD 4) * 4
PRINT "Press any key to stop this infernal noise!"
DO
OUT 97, X + 3 ' turn sound on
FOR I = 1 TO 250: NEXT I  ' kill time
OUT 97, X ' turn sound off
FOR I = 1 TO 250: NEXT I  ' kill time
LOOP WHILE INKEY$ = ""
```

To get some firsthand experience in toying with the PC's ports, give this program a try.

Unless you're doing some very special and unusual kinds of programming, you never have any reason to do anything directly with ports. Ports are almost exclusively reserved for use by the BIOS or other device driver code. The purpose of this discussion is so that you understand that ports are the mechanism the processor uses to talk with other parts of the computer's circuitry.

Next, I discuss registers and stacks, the tools available to the computer's processor to carry out its work. As you read, remember that I am describing the architecture of the 8086 and 8088—the architecture that is used in real mode by the 286, 386, 486, and Pentium series processors and in virtual 8086 mode by the 386, 486, and Pentium series processors, respectively. This architecture describes how PCs work most of the time when you are using DOS. I also try to differentiate these early processors from the 386 and later CPUs. Later in the chapter, I discuss a few of the special features that these processors offer in protected mode.

A register is basically a small special-purpose kind of memory that the processor has available for some particular uses. There are several groups of registers in each processor. One group of registers is designed for programmer control. The number of this type of register ranges from 14 in the pre-386 units to 16 in the later processors. In addition, there are many more registers that really aren't designed for programmer control, but that the CPU uses during some of its operations.

Registers are similar to main memory in one way. They are a set of places where data can be stored while the processor is working on it. However, the computer's main memory is large and is located outside the processor. It can be used for just about anything and is referred to through memory addresses; the registers are different in each of these respects. Figure 4.2 shows the registers used by early PC processors.

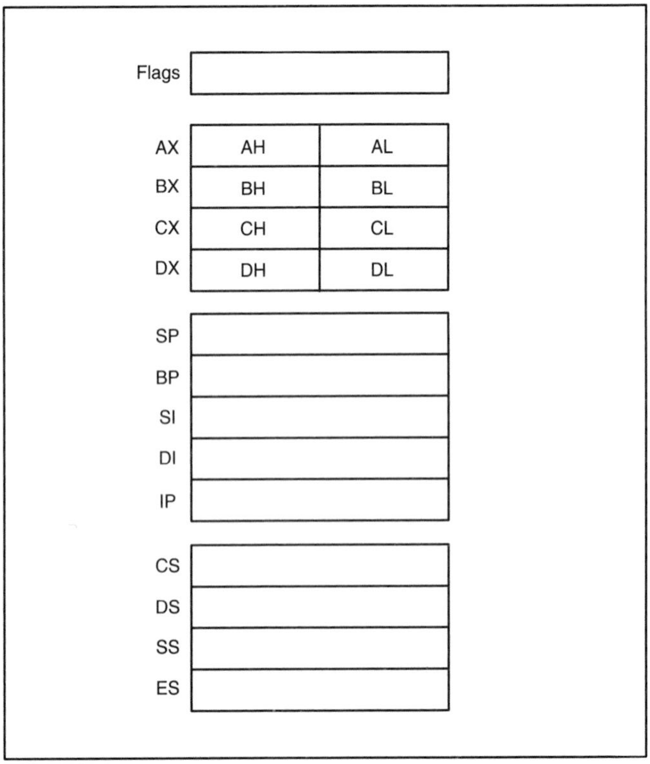

**Figure 4.2.**
*Registers used by the 8088, 8086, 188, 186, and 286 processors.*

The registers are 14 16-bit places where numbers can be stored. Each is an integral, internal part of the processor. Later processors, from the 386 through the Pentium, have a couple more registers, some of which are designed to hold 32 instead of 16 bits of information. Figure 4.3 shows the 16 Pentium processor programmer-oriented registers.

**Figure 4.3.**
*The Pentium register set.*
*(Drawing courtesy of Intel.)*

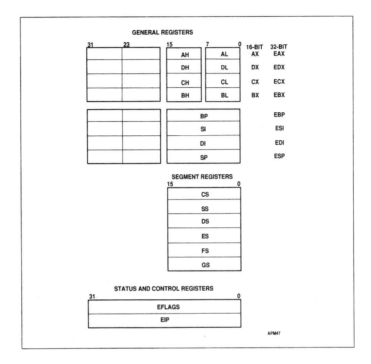

In effect, each register is a small scratch pad that the processor uses for calculations and record keeping. Some registers are dedicated to one special use, while others have a broad, general use. I take a quick look at each of them. Their actual use, however, really matters only to assembly language programmers.

The first group of registers is the general-purpose registers, which truly are used as scratch pads for calculations. There are eight of them (in the pre-386 processors), and they are known as AX, BX, CX, DX, SP, BP, SI, and DI. The 386 and later processors also have eight general-purpose registers. All of these general-purpose registers are 32-bit registers and are called EAX, EBX, ECX, EDX, ESI, EDI, EBP, and ESP.

Programmers can use each general-purpose register as a temporary storage area and scratch pad for calculations. Each register is either 16 or 32 bits in size, depending on the processor. If you want to work with just half of any register, you easily can do so because they are divided into high- and low-order halves (8-bit slices), called AH and AL, BH and BL, and so on. These same subsets are available in all processors. Plus, 386 and later processors can access 8 or 16-bit subsets of the 32-bit registers not available on earlier processors. A great deal of the work that goes on inside computers takes place in these general-purpose registers.

**Technical Note:** One of the major advantages of RISC processors over CISC processors is that RISC processors typically have a larger number of registers, and these registers are not generally restricted in the ways they can be used.

The forthcoming successor to the Intel Pentium processor, known now as the "Inte P.," is an interesting hybrid. While it is still a CISC processor, it has a large number of registers. Additionally, the P6 contains what is being called "Register Renaming," a scheme under which one register can be, essentially, shared. Here's how it works. The P6 actually contains a much larger number of registers than is directly available to programs. If program A requires the use of a specific register, it is allowed that access. Now, if program B requires the use of the same register (while A is already using it), the P6 will automatically, and transparently, redefine one of its "hidden" registers as a second copy of the conflicted register, and the processor will keep track of which program gets the data in which of the two registers, the original one and the renamed one. There is no very good analogy for this process, but it's a little like saying the P6 can walk and chew gum at the same time. Prior to the P6, most register conflicts would generate a disaster.

The next group of four registers (six on 386 and later processors, including the Pentium) is used to assist the processor in finding its way through the computer's memory. These are called the segment registers. Each one is used to help gain access to a section, or segment, of memory. Earlier processors access memory in 64KB blocks, but later CPUs use segments of varying length. A segment can be as little as 1 byte or as much as 4 gigabytes.

The code segment, or CS, register indicates where in memory a program is located. The data segment, or DS, register locates data that a program is using; the extra segment, or ES, register supplements the data segment. The stack segment, or SS, register locates the computer's stack, which I discuss shortly. There are two more registers on 386 and later processors. These are the FS and GS registers, two more segment designations for memory. These segment registers store information about memory locations, giving programmers the flexibility to choose from several possible memory organizations. You get a clearer idea how registers are used in Chapter 15, when I take a closer look at memory.

While the segment registers are used to gain general access to large chunks of memory, the last group of registers is used in conjunction with a segment register to help find specific bytes in memory. There are five of these registers, each used for a particular purpose. The instruction pointer, IP, register retains the processor's place in the program being executed. The stack pointer, SP, and base pointer, BP, registers are used to help keep track of work in progress that is stored on the stack (a holding area that records information about what the computer currently is doing). The source index, SI, and destination index, DI, registers are used to help programs move large amounts of data from one place to another.

Finally, there is the flag register, which is used to hold the condition flags that I talked about earlier. The various flags tell the programs the state of the computer: the results of arithmetic operations, whether interruptions are allowed, and similar status conditions.

# The PC's Flags

The PC's processor is controlled largely through a series of 1-bit flags, each of which signals or sets a particular state in the computer. The flags operate independently of each other, but they are, for convenience, gathered together in the flag register, or EFLAGS register in later chips. Individual flags can be tested and set with special-purpose instructions, and the entire group of flags can be read or set with a pair of instructions.

There are nine standard flags in all in the 8086. The EFLAGS register in later chips is a 32-bit location that stores 13–17 flags, depending on the processor. The Pentium supports 17 flags, for example, and the 386SX has 13 flag positions within the EFLAGS register. Six flags are used to indicate the results of arithmetic and similar operations: the zero flag, ZF, indicates a zero result (or equal comparison); the sign flag, SF, indicates a negative result; the carry flag, CF, indicates a carry to the next position; the auxiliary carry flag, AF, indicates a carry from the first four bits; the overflow flag, OF, indicates a too-large result; and the parity flag, PF, indicates the odd or even parity of the result.

The next three flags are used for control purposes. The direction flag, DF, controls whether repeated operations (such as a byte-by-byte data move) go right to left or left to right. The interrupt flag, IF, controls whether interrupts are enabled or temporarily suspended. The trap flag, TF, causes the computer to generate a special "trap" interrupt after executing a single instruction. This makes it possible to step through a program, tracing the results of each individual instruction.

To these nine flags, the 286 processor adds two more special flags. One, called NT, is used for nested tasks, and the other, a 2-bit flag called IOPL, controls the I/O privilege level. The 386SX and 386 add two more flags: RF, resume flag, is used for debugging, and VM, virtual mode, switches the processor into virtual 86 mode. The 486 adds one flag: AC, alignment check, which is used to indicate whether or not references to memory locations are aligned properly with certain boundaries. Finally, the Pentium, with 17 flags in all, has three additional flags: the virtual interrupt flag (VIF), the virtual interrupt pending flag (VIP), and the ID flag (ID).

The VIF flag replaces a required flag in multitasking environments that programmers previously had to emulate in software for 386 and 486 environments. Programs written for the 8086 sometimes set and clear the IF flag to control interrupts. In a multitasking environment, this can be a problem. Now, instead of having to maintain a virtual interrupt in software, the Pentium processor handles it. The virtual interrupt pending flag also helps in this process. Finally, the ID bit in the EFLAG register is used to help programs determine with which processor class a given application is running. Programs designed for earlier CPU environments traditionally determined the CPU class by setting a bit pattern within the flag register. Obviously, because early processors had only a 16-bit register for flags, if bits beyond that could be set, the processor must be in the 386-and-above class. In addition, by testing for the capability to change the AC flag—unique to the 486 until the arrival of the Pentium—a programmer could determine when a 486 was present. Now, if a program can change the AC flag and set the ID bit, the processor must be a Pentium because the ID flag doesn't exist on 486 CPUs.

You can see and tinker with the flags, and all the other registers, by using the R command of DOS's DEBUG program. For example, if you activate DEBUG and then press R and Enter, DEBUG displays the current register contents and the settings of all the flags. The register dump of a 66MHz 486DX machine is listed below:

```
-r
AX=0000  BX=0000  CX=0000  DX=0000  SP=FFEE  BP=0000  SI=0000  DI=0000
DS=258D  ES=258D  SS=258D  CS=258D  IP=0100  NV UP EI PL NZ NA PO NC
258D:0100 8AFF         MOV    BH,BH
```

There is one remaining tool at the command of the processor that enables it to perform the complicated juggling act needed for the computer to do all the things that users want. As the computer is working, it gets buried in an increasingly complicated stack of work and needs a way to keep track of where it is and what it's doing. To switch from one part of its work to another, the computer also needs a way to put work on hold without losing sight of it. Thus, the stack serves as a computerized holding area that records all the current information about what the computer is doing. When the computer passes into a subroutine, or temporarily interrupts one task to look after another, the stack is used to take note of where the computer was and what it was doing so that it can return to its interrupted subroutine or task without difficulty. As the computer switches to something new, information about the new operation is placed on top of the stack, indicating what is current. When the computer finishes the new work, information for that task is removed from the stack, and the prior work becomes the current and top item on the stack. In that way, the computer returns to its prior operation.

**Technical Note:** As it so happens, it's generally the contents of the processor's registers that is saved to the stack during a task switch or the servicing of an interrupt. This is because the processor registers serve as the primary indication of a processor's state during one or the other task. By restoring the registers, the processor's state is restored, as though no interruption had ever taken place.

Now you have seen what processors can do—the general power and features of their instruction sets—and some of the tools they have to help them do it—the memory, stacks, and so on. However, I barely have mentioned interrupts, a driving force in the process. That's what I look at next.

# Interrupts: The Driving Force

One of the key things that makes a computer different from any other kind of man-made machine is that computers have the capability to respond to the unpredictable variety of work that comes to them. The key to this capability is a feature known as interrupts. The interrupt feature enables the computer to suspend whatever it is doing and switch to something else in response to an interruption, such as the press of a key on the keyboard.

Interrupts solve what otherwise would be a very difficult problem in getting the computer to work effectively. On the one hand, you want the computer to be busy doing whatever work you've given it; on the other hand, you want it to respond instantly to any request for its attention, such as pressing keys on the keyboard. If the computer could only slog along doing just what it's been told to do in advance, it couldn't respond promptly to keystrokes unless it were constantly checking the keyboard for activity. Interrupts, however, make it possible for the processor to respond to keystrokes—or anything else that needs attention—even though it's busy working on something else. And, the interrupt processes enable this type of immediate response without having to waste CPU time and program code checking all of the possible side tasks that might need doing at any given time.

The computer's processor has the built-in capability to be interrupted combined with a convenient way of putting the work that's been interrupted on hold while the interrupt is being processed. The processor's stack (described above) is used for this. When an interruption occurs, a record of what the processor was doing at the time is stored on the stack; thus, when the interruption has been handled, work can resume exactly where it left off. This is one of several uses to which the stack is put and is a very key one. Without the stack as a place to put work on hold, the interrupts wouldn't work.

Every part of the computer that might need to request the processor's attention is given its own special interrupt number. The keyboard has its own interrupt, so that every time you press a key on the keyboard (or, interestingly enough, release a key you've pressed), the processor finds out about it. The PC's internal clock also has its own interrupt to enable the computer's timekeeping program to know each time the clock has ticked—which is about 18 times each second. (That sounds like a lot of interruptions, and I'd be inclined to think that being interrupted 18 times a second would be a bother. However, the processor can perform many thousands of instructions between each clock tick, so the clock interrupts don't take up much of the processor's time.) The computer's disk drives and printers have dedicated interrupt numbers, too. The disks use theirs to signal that they have finished work that the program asked to be done; the printers use theirs to signal when they are out of paper.

Interestingly, interrupts were not part of the original concept of a computer. In fact, computers had been used for decades before the interrupt feature came into widespread use. Today it's hard to imagine a computer doing much of anything useful without the interrupts that enable it to respond to demands for its attention.

Although interrupts are used to make the processor respond to outside events, such as the printer running out of paper, that isn't the only thing that they are used for. The concept of an interrupt has turned out to be so useful that it has been adapted to serve a variety of purposes within the computer. There are essentially three kinds of interrupts used in PC computers. The first is the kind I already have discussed—an interrupt that comes from another part of the computer's circuitry reporting something that needs attention. This is called a hardware interrupt. The other two kinds of interrupts relate to software.

Sometimes, while the computer is running a program, something goes wrong with either the program or the program's data. It's as if you were reading along on this sentence and then suddenly found yourself reading rbnss zmc jduhm zmc gzqkdx—some gibberish that didn't make any sense. Although it's not supposed to, that also can happen to the computer. The processor might run into some instructions that don't make any sense or some data that drives it wild, such as trying to divide a number by zero. When this happens, the processor generates an exception interrupt.

The last category of interrupt, unlike the others, doesn't occur unexpectedly. The whole idea of interrupts is so powerful that they have been put to use as a way of enabling programs to signal that they want some service to be performed by another part of the computer's programs. This type is called a software interrupt. I've mentioned before that PCs come equipped with built-in service programs called the ROM-BIOS. The computer's application programs need a way to request the services that the BIOS provides, and software interrupts are the way they do it. Software interrupts function in exactly the same way as the other kinds of interrupts. The only thing that's different about them is what causes the interrupt. In this case, instead of happening unexpectedly, software interrupts are generated intentionally by a program. There is a special assembly language instruction, called INT, that is used by a program to request an interrupt.

# Interrupts and the Interrupt Handler

There is a wider variety of types and uses for interrupts than you may imagine. In the text above, I outlined three broad categories of interrupts: hardware, exception, and software. But, there is another way of looking at interrupts that is closer to the way they are used in the PC family. You can break the basic interrupts into six different kinds.

First, there are the Intel hardware interrupts, which are the interrupts that are designed into the processor by its designer, Intel. These include the divide-by-zero interrupt mentioned before and others. These interrupts are universal to any computer using an Intel 86 processor regardless of how unlike the PC family the computer might be.

Next are the IBM-defined PC hardware interrupts. These are interrupts that report hardware events—printer out of paper or disk action completed, for example—to the processor. The PC hardware interrupts are universal to the PC family.

Then there are the PC software interrupts. These also are defined by IBM and universal to the whole PC family. They are used to activate parts of the PC's built-in ROM-BIOS software—to display a message on the computer's screen, for example.

Then there are DOS software interrupts. Unlike the previous three types, these interrupts aren't built into the computer; they are added on by software—in this case by DOS. Because you normally use the same operating system all the time, these interrupts are, in reality, there all the time, even though they aren't fundamental to the computer's operation. These interrupts are defined and handled by routines internal to DOS (or any other operating system you may be using).

Next are the application software interrupts, which are established temporarily by the program you are running (including BASIC, which uses quite a few of its own special interrupts). These interrupts are defined and handled by the specific application programs.

The sixth category, the table interrupts, is an odd one because it doesn't truly involve interrupts at all. As you see in Chapter 17, "BIOS: Digging In," part of the interrupt mechanism involves a vector table that holds the memory addresses of the interrupt handlers. This table is a convenient place to store some important addresses that actually have nothing to do with interrupts. For each of these, there's a corresponding interrupt number—one that can never be used because there's no interrupt-handling routine for it. All this table does is store the addresses where interrupt routines are stored. You can learn from this table where interrupt-handling routines are located.

Just how does an interrupt work? Each distinct interrupt is identified by an interrupt number. For example, one interrupt number is used for the disk drives (all *drives attached to the same disk controller* share the same interrupt). The clock, the keyboard, and the printer all have their own interrupt numbers. For the BIOS services, interrupts are grouped by category; for example, there are more than a dozen different BIOS services for different operations on the display screen, but they all share one interrupt number.

For each interrupt number there is a special program, called an interrupt handler, that performs whatever work the interrupt requires. A special table, kept at the very beginning of the computer's memory, records the location of each interrupt handler. When an interrupt occurs, the interrupt number is used to look up the proper interrupt-handling program. Before the interrupt handler begins work, however, the processor's interrupt-processing mechanism saves a record (on the stack) of the work that was in progress. After that is done, control of the processor switches over to the interrupt-handling routine.

### How Are Interrupt Numbers Generated?

Interrupt numbers are generated in one of two ways. In the case of a hardware interrupt, a dedicated chip on your motherboard—the hardware interrupt controller—must be factory-programmed to send the correct interrupt number when it receives specific input for an

IRQ that is dedicated, for example, to the internal hard disk. Some of the interrupts, such as those for the COM ports, are readdressable on some motherboards.

A software interrupt occurs as the result of a program executing an Assembly Language command called an INT instruction (for INTerrupt). In this case, the program itself must specify a specific IRQ number when the INT command is given to the processor.

The interrupt handler begins its operation temporarily protected from further interrupts, in case it has to perform critical or delicate operations that must not be disrupted. Usually, this involves changing the segment registers that control memory access and saving on the stack any further status information that's needed. After that is done, the interrupt handler safely can reactivate further interrupts of other types and do whatever work the interrupt calls for. When the work is done, the interrupt-handling routine restores the status of the machine to what it was before the interrupt occurred. Finally, the computer carries on with the work it was doing.

# Looking at an Interrupt Handler

To give you an idea of what some of the program code in an interrupt handler looks like, I show you how to view some. The fragment I show you is unassembled from the ROM-BIOS of an AT computer. The particular code shown is taken from the beginning of the routine that handles requests for video (display screen) services.

Begin by activating the DEBUG program, as follows:

```
DEBUG
```

Tell DEBUG to unassemble some program code, which translates the computer's machine language into the slightly more readable assembly language format. I happen to know where to find the routine I want to show you, so I tell DEBUG to unassemble it at its hex address:

```
U F000:3605
```

In response, DEBUG gives an unassembled listing that looks like this:

```
F000:3605 FB        STI
F000:3606 FC        CLD
F000:3607 06        PUSH   ES
F000:3608 1E        PUSH   DS
F000:3609 52        PUSH   DX
F000:360A 51        PUSH   CX
F000:360B 53        PUSH   BX
F000:360C 56        PUSH   SI
F000:360D 57        PUSH   DI
F000:360E 55        PUSH   BP
F000:360F 50        PUSH   AX
F000:3610 8AC4      MOV    AL,AH
```

```
F000:3612 32E4      XOR    AH,AH
F000:3614 D1E0      SHL    AX,1
F000:3616 8BF0      MOV    SI,AX
F000:3618 3D2800    CMP    AX,0028
```

The very first column (F000:3605, etc.) is a set of reference addresses that you can ignore. The next column of information (FB, FC, 06, and so on) is the actual machine language code, in hex. After all, this is what you're interested in—the assembly language equivalent of the program code you've unassembled.

The listing begins with the instruction STI, which reactivates interrupts. When an interrupt occurs, further interrupts are suspended in case the handler needs to do anything critical. In this case, there's nothing important to do, so the handling of other interrupts is turned on first.

The next instruction, CLD, sets the direction flag to its normal, forward state. This ensures that any data movement the program performs goes forward, not backward. This isn't a particularly important operation, but it's interesting to see that the programmer took the time to make sure the direction flag was set forward before anything else was done.

After that is something much more interesting: a series of nine PUSH instructions. The PUSH instruction saves data on the computer's stack. You see that each of these nine PUSH instructions names a register (ES, DS, and so on) that is being saved. These register values are being saved on the stack, so that this interrupt handler can be sure they are safeguarded. When the interrupt handler is done, it restores these values from the stack to the registers, so that regardless of how the registers have been used in the interim, they are returned to their former state.

After the register-saving PUSH operations, you find three data-manipulating instructions (XOR, SHL, and MOV) that grab a number and prepare it for comparison. Although it's not easy to tell just by looking at these instructions, what is going on here is fairly simple. This interrupt handler can provide a variety of display screen services, each of which is identified by a request code number. Before proceeding, the program gets its hands on that code number and puts it into the form in which this program wants it.

Having done that, the interrupt handler needs to make sure that the service code requested is a proper one, and that's what the last instruction does. Using the CMP (Compare) instruction, the computer compares the number with the value 28, which is the highest number corresponding to a proper service request. After that, the program branches on the basis of that test, either performing the service requested or rejecting the invalid service number.

This isn't an in-depth look at assembly language code, but it should give you a sampling of what assembly language looks like and how to go about decoding it. You can use the techniques shown here to inspect other parts of your computer's ROM-BIOS or other programs. When you do, remember that the ROM-BIOS varies from one model PC to another. The example shown here was from an old PC AT model. Unless you have the same computer, you will not find the same instructions at the same addresses.

Interrupt handlers, for the most part, appear in the computer's built-in ROM-BIOS programs or as a part of the operating system. However, they aren't restricted to just those systems programs. Applications programs—word processors, spreadsheets, and the like—also can have their own interrupt-handling routines. Any program can create an interrupt handler and use it either to replace a standard interrupt handler (so that its interrupts are handled in some special way) or to create a new kind of interrupt.

> **Technical Note:** Most TSRs that use pop-up hot keys work by inserting their own code in the way of the computer's keyboard interrupt handler. In this way, whenever a keyboard interrupt occurs (that is, whenever the user presses a key), the TSR gets first crack at analyzing the issued key codes to see if the programmed hot key has been issued. If the keystroke wasn't a hot key, the TSR's code itself sends the keystroke on. This type of code is called a "trap," inasmuch as it works by "trapping" keystrokes before the main system gets a crack at them.

In the beginning of this section, I described interrupts as the driving force of the PC. Modern computers, which are designed to use interrupts, are said to be interrupt-driven. That's because interrupts are the mechanisms that connect the computer to the world around it (including users). Interrupts drive the computer because, one way or another, most of the work that comes to the computer comes to it in the form of interrupts. More important, the internal organization of the computer is designed around interrupts—the forces that determine just where the processor turns its attention. Because the flow of interrupts directs the computer's attention where it's needed, it's quite accurate to think of interrupts as the driving force behind the whole machine.

Now that you've examined interrupts, you've seen all the basics that concern the PC's processor. You've covered the key things that are common to every member of the Intel 86 family. However, the more advanced processors—the 286, 386SX, 386SL, 386DX, 486SX, 486DX, and Pentium—add special features that are not part of the standard 8086/8088 architecture. These features, including virtual 86 mode and protected mode, are covered in Chapter 3.

# Keeping Up with the Clock

To run at a particular speed, a processor needs something that can provide an electrical pulse at regular intervals, like a metronome. Such a component is called a clock.

Before the 486, PC processors were designed to use a clock that ran at twice the processor speed. For example, a 25MHz 386 computer uses a clock that runs at 50MHz; it just internally divides the clock input by two. This is true for all the members of the Intel 86 family, from the 8086 to the 386. However, beginning with the 486, the newer CPUs use a clock with a matching speed. So, for example, a 50MHz 486 computer uses a 50MHz clock.

# Clock Multiplying: Technical Details and Real-Life Implications

Back in 1992, Intel introduced a new way for computer system manufacturers to provide faster machines to their customers, without requiring those manufacturers to totally redesign their system motherboards: clock-doubled processors. When you see a system that's referred to as being a 486DX2/66, the "DX2" lets you know that you're looking at a clock-doubled box. So, what does it mean, and what does it get you?

Clock doubling is a method through which the internal functioning of the processor—its performance of instructions from its basic instruction set—occurs twice as fast as the external functioning of the processor, such as its utilization of the bus, memory, disks, ports, and so on. This internal doubling is achieved by eliminating the "ignored" clock tick that I mentioned above, thereby allowing one instruction to occur on each single tick, theoretically, at least. Specifically, the bus interface unit (BIU) communicates with another part of the processor called a phase-locked loop (PLL). Data entering the processor passes through the PLL, which modifies the clock speed at which that data is moving. When data leaves the processor, the exact opposite happens, with the BIU and PLL reducing the clock speed of the data back down to the original rate. For example, then, our 486DX2/66 processor performs its internal functions at a full 66MHz, but accesses and communicates with all the other parts of the system at 33MHz.

**Technical Note:** You should be aware that the DX4 chips are not quadrupled, but are, instead, only tripled. The reasons for this relate to rather uninteresting issues of trademark law, actually, so I won't dwell on them here. However, you should be aware that a 100MHz DX4 processor is actually running an (approximately) 33MHz external bus, not a 25MHz external bus as you might suppose.

The performance gain you actually obtain depends on a number of factors relating to your system, and also to the kind of work you do on your computer. If you have accelerated video and very fast hard disks, your perceived system performance will shoot up because less time will be wasted, with the processor waiting for slow external devices. Further, with local bus systems (see Chapter 2), selected peripherals like video and disks are given more direct access to the processor and its resources. Additionally, just as the processor has to wait for external devices like disks, it also has to wait for external devices like main memory. On a clock-doubled system, main memory operates at the undoubled rate. The implication is that data which isn't already present in the processor's internal cache (see Chapter 3) must be brought in from main memory at the slower speed. Since the 486 family of processors comes with only 8K of memory in its internal cache, clock-doubled systems really benefit from large external cache memory. This memory is connected directly to the processor—thus obviating the need to access the bus, which controls main memory at the undoubled speed—and further benefits from a specialized addressing system that allows the processor to use fewer clock cycles to access the cache's contents than would be necessary to access main memory.

**Technical Note:** Many designs for cache memory have been optimized such that the cache functions as an independent system from the processor, with its own clock speed. The cache clock may or may not have any relationship to the processor's clock, depending on the specific design.

In terms of the tasks you do, as you'd expect, calculation-intensive programs will generally obtain significant benefit from clock doubling, as these calculations are internal processes. The kinds of software that will give you the largest return include everything from scientific design systems like CAD, to image-manipulation software, to 3-D video games. Anecdotally, you can expect that a DX2/50 will outrun a DX/33, but will not perform as quickly as a true DX50. Similarly, a DX2/66 functions at speeds comparable to a DX/50, on average. (Your mileage may vary.)

Additionally, Intel has developed a clock-*tripled* system, which it has given the somewhat misleading name of DX4. These systems are noticeably faster than DX2 processors. However, as of this writing, Intel itself has been aggressively lowering prices on Pentium machines, and has been actively discouraging users from purchasing DX4 systems, saying that the chips are in both low and limited supply. As I'm writing this, there are a few valid DX4 systems—notably a variety of high-end multimedia notebook computers, used for trade shows and corporate presentations. However, almost surely by the time you buy this book, Pentium notebook systems will be everywhere, and will be, by far, the economical choice, as I discuss in the next section, in closing.

# Processors: A Real-Life Summary

Economics works its magic on processors just as it does on every other aspect of computer hardware. The 386 has long supplanted the 286 as the absolute bottom-of-the-barrel, lowest-level processor you'd ever buy today, but the financial reality is that you can purchase a 486 for the same money— or even less—because of volume purchasing of 486-based systems. In fact, unless you're a "dealer discontinued" catalog shopper, you probably won't even be able to find a 386 system for sale, new, by the time you read this. And, as I was writing this chapter, one of the popular national computer magazines had a cover heralding the advent of Pentium multimedia systems for less than $1,500. Unless you have a price cutoff at $1,000—and, of course, you might—why would anyone today even consider a 486 machine?

It's a rhetorical question. You've already read my basic philosophy of hardware: Buy the best you can afford, and get the most you can get for your money. It sounds like common sense today, but there was a time not too long ago when the computing industry quibbled seriously over why a user would ever need anything more powerful than a 386. That'll barely run your kids' CD-ROM games today. And, further back in history, Bill Gates, of Microsoft, was quoted saying that no user would ever need more than 4MB of main memory. History has proved them all wrong, predictably.

Software developers, too, continue to push the limits of hardware, as they always have done. The brand-new 486 machine you purchased in mid-1994 with 8MB of RAM, 340MB hard disk, and a VESA Local Bus system is already antiquated. That isn't to say it's outlived its usefulness to you. But by the time this book reaches your hands, such systems will be blown off the retail shelves by 100MHz Pentium systems with PCI bus technologies, new hard disk standards (which I talk about in the next chapter), and continuously accelerated video, for the same sticker price. Moreover, new software will quickly grow to demand the performance capabilities of these new machines. The next version of Microsoft Windows—"Windows 95"—will demand at least 8MB of memory to run "efficiently." (Read, "to get baseline performance.") And that's just the operating system! That doesn't include running your word processor, or your spreadsheet, or Killer Ninja Quagmire.

**Technical Note:** On Pentium systems, the minimum requirements for Windows 95 may be a moot point. Since Pentium machines use a full 64-bit bus, 8MB of standard DRAM is the minimal configuration, regardless of what operating system you select.

So, I'll repeat: Buy the best you can afford. Buy the fastest processor you can get, and look for balanced systems in which a fast processor is coupled with fast memory, a fast bus, accelerated video, and a snappy hard disk. Unless you're buying a notebook system, there's little reason to look at 486 configurations today. Indeed, at the time of this writing, a major computer periodical has just run a cover feature opining that Pentium-based machines now match 486-based machines at price-point, and the 486 is truly antiquated. While it's not true that 486 systems are "antiquated," it is true that they probably aren't logical choices for anyone but the very lowest-dollar buyer. Even at that, you should understand that current pricing means that a very inexpensive 486 system is still probably not a good buy.

**Technical Note:** You will see advertisements for "upgradable" 486 systems that allow you to convert from VESA to PCI bus at a future date. Such a system may be a good purchase, but don't buy it with the idea of upgrading. Tests have indicated that the PCI bus works best with a Pentium processor and the VESA bus works best with a speedy 486. You might actually see a performance decrease if you convert your 486 VESA system to a 486 PCI system. If you know you want the PCI bus, look for a Pentium system.

# Some Things to Think About and Try

1. I've discussed how PC processors can do both 8- and 16-bit arithmetic. Is it really necessary to have both? What might be the benefits and costs of only having one or the other? What is the benefit of the 32-bit arithmetic that the newer processors offer?

2. You've seen, in the PC's arithmetic and in its logic looping instructions, some duplication—a variety of instructions that could be simplified into fewer instructions. What might be the advantages and disadvantages—for the computer's designers and programmers—of making a computer with lots of instructions that would provide many different ways of doing roughly the same thing or one with very few instructions that would provide just one way of doing things?

3. Few PCs have the X87 numeric coprocessor installed (many systems purchased in the mass market are of the SX variety), and few programs can take advantage of the X87. Why do you think that came about? What might have made the X87 more popular?

4. Using BASIC's INP and OUT commands, write a program to explore the PC's ports. Do you find anything interesting?

5. In the "Looking at an Interrupt Handler" section, I show you how to use the DEBUG U (Unassemble) command. Try using it on your PC at various memory locations to learn what's there. For the most part, each computer system is different, and what you find within memory depends on the type of peripherals you have installed, what programs you are running, and the type of ROM-BIOS you are using. Remember that the U instruction in DEBUG doesn't hurt anything, so feel free to try it.

**Warning:** Other DEBUG commands can cause you some real headaches with your system if you happen to write incorrect data to the interrupt table or the ports. If you stick with using the U command for your explorations, you'll have no worries.

# 5

# Disks: The Basic Story

This chapter is part one of a six-part exploration of your computer's disks. Only one other aspect of your computer—its display—is as richly varied and has as many fascinating aspects as the disks. Because so many options do exist, and because every piece of software that you use—from applications down to the documents you create with them—makes its home on disks, understanding disk storage will give you a tremendous amount of practical knowledge and will enable you to both make better use of what you have and make better purchase decisions in the future.

This first chapter of this series covers the basics so that you have a clear idea of exactly what a disk is. We'll get some of the jargon out of the way early. Because people use their disks under the supervision of DOS (Disk Operating System), Chapter 6 gives you a look at disks from the DOS perspective, and Chapter 7 gives you a more in-depth understanding of some of the more technical aspects of disks. Chapter 8 describes disk utilities. Finally, Chapters 9 and 10 describe removable and optical disks, respectively.

# Basic Disk Concepts

The disk storage that computers use is actually two things working together: a recording/reading technology and a quick-access design scheme.

For disks other than optical disks, the technology itself is magnetic recording. This is basically the same technology used in audiocassette and videocassette tapes. Magnetic recording works because iron and some other materials can be magnetized. You probably remember from science classes in high school that an ordinary iron bar becomes a magnetized iron bar if you expose it to a magnetic field. The magnetic field is, in a crude sense, "recorded" in the iron. All of our sophisticated magnetic recording is nothing more than a refinement of that simple science lesson.

Magnetic recording was first and most widely used to record sound, which is an analog form of information. Only later was magnetic recording adapted for the digital recording that computers require.

Digital magnetic recording is done on a surface of magnetically sensitive material, usually a form of iron oxide. Iron oxide is more commonly known as rust, and that's what gives magnetic media its characteristic color. The actual magnetic coating is quite thin; in fact, the thinner it is, the better it works. This coating is spread onto a supporting material. In the case of recording tape or floppy disks, this is usually flexible mylar plastic; a nickle/chrome plating on base metal is commonly used for modern hard disks.

Whether you're talking about hard disks, floppy disks, or digital tapes, the way the information is recorded on the magnetic surface is the same. The surface is treated as an array of dot positions, each of which is treated as a bit that can be set to the magnetic equivalent of 0 or 1. Because the location of these dot positions isn't precisely determined, the recording scheme involves some guidance markings that help the recorder find and match up with the recording positions. The need for these synchronizing marks is part of the reason that disks have to be formatted before you can use them.

Newer hard disks have additional servo tracks that are dedicated entirely to helping the drive mechanism make fine adjustments in alignment.

After you have physically stored data on a disk or tape, you need a way to access what you've stored. The second element that makes disk storage a reality is the quick-access design scheme of disks. A magnetic tape essentially is linear because information must be recorded and read on it from beginning to end. Even though it's not necessary to actually read every bit on a tape to access something stored near the end of the tape, it is necessary to fast-forward past all of that undesired data. This is incredibly time-consuming. A rotating disk, however, opens up entirely new possibilities.

Two things about a disk make it possible to get to any part of the surface quickly. The first is rotation. The disk spins around quickly, so any part of its circumference passes any given point without much delay. A floppy disk spins at 300 RPM, which means it takes, at most, 1/5 of a second for any given part to swing into place; hard disks commonly spin at about 5,400 RPM, or 1/90 of a second per rotation. Faster rotation speeds are coming on the market every day. As you would expect, faster rotation means lower access times.

The other thing that makes it possible to move around on the surface of a disk is the way the magnetic recording head moves. In a manner similar to that of the tone arm of a phonograph player (remember record-players?), it can essentially skip across the disk from outside to inside. It takes an average 1/6 of a second to move to any desired location on a floppy disk and 1/70 of a second on a hard disk, with faster-moving heads, predictably, premiering all the time. In addition to faster-moving heads, most new drives have multiple heads on each platter, further reducing potential access-times.

When you combine the two factors—moving the read/write head across the disk surface and rotating the disk into position under the head—you see that you can get to any part of the disk very quickly. That's why computer disks are called random-access storage; you can get to (access) any part of the recorded data directly without having to fast-forward through all the recorded information sequentially. Figure 5.1 illustrates this concept.

*Figure 5.1.*
*Direct disk access.*

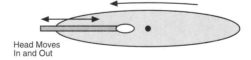

Head Moves
In and Out

A disk's surface is divided into tracks, which form concentric circles, starting at the outer edge of the disk. The number of tracks varies with the type of disk. Today's most common disk, the 3.5-inch, 1.44MB version, has 80 tracks. The low-capacity disks—the 3.5-inch, 720KB and 5.25-inch, 360KB versions—have 40 tracks. Hard disks typically have from 500 to more than 1,000 tracks. The tracks, however many there are, are identified by number, starting with track zero at the outer edge of the disk.

You might expect the tracks to spread across most of the recording surface, but they don't; they cover a surprisingly small area. For example, a 3.5-inch, 1.44MB disk records data at 135 tracks per inch. Because there are 80 tracks, this means that the space between the first and last track is only 80/135 or about 0.6 inches (1.5 cm). (In the technical literature, tracks per inch often is abbreviated TPI; if you run into that term, you now know what it is.)

Just as a disk surface is divided into tracks, the circumference of a track also is divided into sections called sectors. The type of the disk and its format determine how many sectors there are in a circular track. For example, a 3.5-inch, 1.44MB disk has 18 sectors per track. The newer 3.5 inch, 2.88MB disks have 36 sectors per track. Hard disks can have a variable number of sectors per track, with more sectors per track on the outer cylinders. The disk on which the files for this book are being stored has 63 sectors per track, and another disk on my PC has 56 sectors per track.

However many sectors exist, all sectors are a fixed size on any given disk. PCs can handle a variety of sector sizes from 128 to 1,024 bytes; however, 512-byte sectors are by far the most commonly encountered size. Figure 5.2 shows the relationship between tracks and sectors.

*Figure 5.2.*
*The tracks and*
*sectors of a disk.*

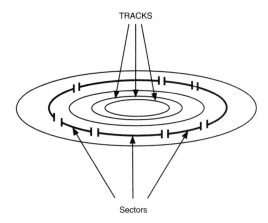

TRACKS

Sectors

All of the reading and writing of data that computers perform with disks is done in terms of complete sectors. As you'll see later, data can be any size and is made to fit snugly into the fixed storage size of sectors. However, the actual disk I/O (reading and writing of data) that the computer performs is done only in complete sectors.

The sectors in a track, like the tracks on the surface of a disk, are identified by numbers, starting with one rather than zero. (Sector number zero on each track is reserved for identification purposes, rather than for storing data.)

There is one final dimension to a disk that I haven't mentioned: the number of sides. While a floppy disk, like anything that's flat, has only two sides, hard disk drives often contain more than one disk platter, so they can have more than two sides. The sides of a disk, as you might expect, are identified by number; as with tracks, the sides are numbered starting with zero for the first side. You can see the arrangement of a two-platter drive in Figure 5.3.

**Figure 5.3.**
*The sides of a hard disk.*

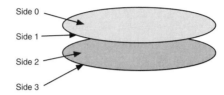

Sometimes it is convenient to refer to the set of all tracks, one on each side, that lie at the same distance from the center of the disk. This is called a cylinder. If a drive has two platters, such as the one illustrated in Figure 5.3, then each cylinder consists of four tracks.

Here's another example. Say that a hard disk has six sides, sides 0, 1, ..., through 5. Now consider the 26th track on each side—the 26th track on side 0, the 26th track on side 1, and so on. Collectively, these six tracks, the ones that line up at the same distance from the center of the disk, are referred to as the 26th cylinder. (You call it cylinder number 25 because tracks, like sides, are numbered starting from zero.)

On a hard disk, a cylinder includes one track on each of the recording surfaces. On a floppy disk, which has only two sides, a cylinder always consists of two tracks, one on each side.

When you combine all these dimensions, you arrive at the size, or storage capacity, of a disk.

Multiply the number of sides by the number of tracks per side by the number of sectors per track. This gives you the total number of sectors per disk. Multiply that by the number of bytes per sector—which is normally 512 bytes, or 0.5KB—to get the raw capacity of the disk. Naturally, some of that capacity is occupied with overhead of one kind or another, as you'll see in Chapter 6, "Disks: The DOS Perspective." Still, the number you calculate in this way is essentially the storage capacity of the disk; it should be the same as, or close to, the capacity that's reported by the DOS utility program SCANDISK (or CHKDSK before Version 6.2 of DOS).

If you are interested in learning more about your disks, you can use the System Information (SYSINFO) program that comes with the Norton Utilities. If you have an old version of the utilities (before Version 5.0) use the DI (Disk Information) program. These programs show you the four dimensions of your disk's storage together with some DOS-related information that you'll learn to decipher in Chapter 6.

One more basic disk concept remains to be covered: how disks are packaged and protected. However, because the method varies with different types of disks, I'm putting off exploring this concept until after I describe the main varieties of disks.

# Varieties of Disks

It may seem like there are more varieties of disks than can be used. It certainly isn't practical to undertake an exhaustive discussion of all the types of disks that exist, many of which are technically antiques. However, there's a lot of useful knowledge available to you if you examine the principal types and are aware of the existence of the more exotic varieties. That's what this section does. In this discussion, you need to keep clearly in mind that there are varying degrees of difference between the types; some differences are quite fundamental, and others, while important, are not major. Finally, some are purely minor variations. You'll see the distinctions as you go along.

Keep in mind that disk storage technology moves forward rapidly. Even as I'm writing this, both hardware and software solutions are being developed which will make all of this information antiquated very rapidly. Perhaps more than any other single part of the computer industry, the hard disk industry is extremely competitive. Manufacturers have the option of constantly pushing the envelope, or closing down shop. But, by understanding the fundamentals of disk storage, you'll be on solid ground when it comes time to evaluate those new technologies.

# 5.25-Inch Floppy

Although it's actually possible that you may personally have never seen one of these, the best place to begin exploring disks is where the PC family began: with the old, 5.25-inch floppy disk. Figure 5.4 shows a drawing of one.

**Figure 5.4.**
*A 5.25-inch floppy disk (top view).*

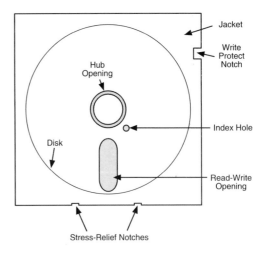

There are many variations on this disk, but let's look at the common characteristics first. The disk itself is made of soft flexible mylar plastic with a magnetically sensitive iron oxide coating. The coating is present on both sides, even for single-sided disks that are intended to be recorded on only one side. The second side of a single-sided disk may not have its second side finished, polished, and tested, but it still has the same coating. Whether it's safe to use the back side of a disk was once a heated argument, but as these disks are all but obsolete today, the question is really moot. (Incidentally, not many people know it, but the active side of a floppy disk is on the bottom, opposite the disk label, not on the top.)

These disks have two holes in them. One is the hub where the disk drive grabs it. This hub may have a reinforcing hub ring on it to help ensure that the disk is properly centered. The other hole, the index hole, is just outside the hub. It provides a reference point that defines the physical beginning of a track.

Surrounding and holding the circular disk is the disk jacket, which usually is black. On the inside surface of the jacket, almost completely out of sight, is a white felt liner. The liner is designed specially to help the disk spin smoothly around and to wipe it clean at the same time. A large oval slot provides the opening through which the disk drive's read/write head touches the disk. The two small cuts on either side of the read/write slot are called stress-relief notches; they help ensure that the jacket doesn't warp. Near the hub opening is an opening in the jacket for the index hole, which enables the disk drive to see the index hole in the disk. Finally, on one side, there is a write-protect notch. If this notch is covered, you cannot write to the disk.

If you find yourself using this type of disk, don't be surprised if you encounter some variations in the holes and notches. Some disks don't have a write-protect notch; this means that they cannot be written to. These disks, such as the disks that commercial software once came on, are used for the original copies of programs.

These days, 5.25-inch disks (which had a 1.2MB capacity in their most popular incarnation) are used primarily in older computers, although some people buy optional 5.25-inch disk drives for their new PCs to be able to read and write to the old disks.

# 3.5-Inch Floppy

The primary kind of floppy disk that you'll encounter is the 3.5-inch variety. A drawing of a 3.5-inch disk is shown in Figure 5.5.

**Figure 5.5.**
*A 3.5-inch disk*
*(bottom view).*

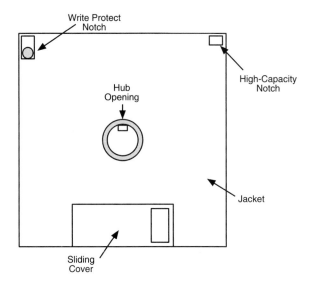

Write Protect
Notch

High-Capacity
Notch

Hub
Opening

Jacket

Sliding
Cover

The 3.5-inch disks are obviously smaller than 5.25-inch disks and are enclosed in a rigid protective case. Thanks to the smaller size and hard case, they are much easier and safer to post and to carry around (they fit nicely into a shirt pocket). Moreover, they hold more data than their older 5.25-inch cousins (1.44MB in their most common form, and 2.88MB in a rather unpopular format created by IBM.)

Inside, a 3.5-inch disk is the familiar soft flexible plastic, this time with a metal hub piece. Outside, the read/write opening is sealed by a spring-loaded sliding metal protector.

Write-protection is controlled by a sliding plastic tab. To write-protect a disk, simply slide the tab so that the little window is open. This works much better than the older 5.25-inch disks with the notches that had to be covered with sticky paper.

Almost all of today's computers use high-capacity, 3.5-inch disks that hold 1.44MB of data. As I mentioned, IBM created a newer format which holds 2.88MB, but there has been little industry acceptance of this format at the time of this writing. Older 3.5-inch drives commonly used only low-capacity, 720KB disks. The 1.44MB and 2.88MB drives are "backwardly compatible," and can read from and write to either 720KB or 1.44MB disks.

This variety of disk sizes once meant that software distributors felt obligated to cater to the lowest common denominator: the smaller disks. As the 1.44MB format has completely taken control of the market, distributors (except some game manufacturers) now commonly sell software on 1.44MB diskettes only. If you find yourself using a PC that only supports the lower-density format, you can either upgrade the floppy disk drive and controller card for about $150.00, or you can contact the software manufacturer for each product in question, and ask them to send you the software on low-density disks.

**Note:** My advice is to upgrade your hardware. There's nothing more frustrating than bringing home the latest hot software, only to discover you'll have to wait for weeks before you can use it because you have to ask the manufacturer to mail you low-density disks. Keep in mind also that those low-density disks hold less. While you may have to insert 10 high-density disks to install Microsoft Word, the same application requires 19 disk swaps on low-density disks. This is much more time-consuming for you, and you'll encounter the problem with each piece of software you install.

If you look at a high-capacity 1.44MB disk, you'll see a small hole in the corner opposite the write-protect switch. (See Figure 5.5.) This hole signifies that the disk is a high-density disk. In addition, most floppy manufacturers also print the letters HD somewhere on the disk case, either on the top beside the sliding metal cover or on the metal cover itself. The low-capacity, 720KB disks do not have either the extra hole or the printed HD letters.

# Hard Disks

Hard disks get their name from the fact that the magnetically coated disks themselves are rigid platters made of an aluminum alloy. Because of many factors, including the much faster speed of rotation and the higher recording density, hard disks need to be in an environment free from dust and other contamination. For this reason, hard disks are sealed inside the disk drive and commonly are not removable like other media. (There are significant exceptions to this, as you'll see, however.) Because hard disks are traditionally not removable, IBM actually used to refer to them as *fixed* disks.

There are many varieties of hard disks. They differ in speed, the number of platters and active recording sides, the number of cylinders, the number of sectors per track, and other characteristics. Generally, they are all lumped together in the collective category of hard disk.

While the smallest hard disks (now obsolete) held a meager 5MB, large new systems can theoretically hold over 8GB. A typical PC hard disk holds between 250 and 500MB. (Remember, though, that things change quickly. Don't be surprised if, by the time you read this, even these numbers are obsolete.)

Fortunately, all hard disks look pretty much the same from the user's viewpoint, and people rarely need to know what type of hard disk they have. (There was a time, however, when DOS could not recognize hard disks larger than 32MB. That restriction was removed with DOS Version 4.0. Before that, people with large hard disks had to use the DOS FDISK program to break them into partitions no larger than 32MB.)

# Disk Controller Types

Now that you know something about the physical design of hard and floppy disks, let's examine how information is moved in and out of the drive. I've already discussed computer ports as a way for the processor to share information with peripherals. This is how data gets from the hard or floppy disk surface into memory and back out again. I say into and out of memory because, ultimately, this is where the data has to be for the processor to interact with it and for your programs to use it.

Disk drives interface with the computer through controller ports or controller cards. These are plug-in hardware boards that use either the main computer bus or, more recently, the VESA VL or PCI local bus. In addition, a number of computer motherboards are designed with the floppy and hard disk interface built in. Almost uniformly now, except in the least-expensive models, when the disk interface is built into the motherboard, it uses a local bus technology—usually PCI—to communicate with the CPU and memory.

Beyond these general concepts, there are several popular disk controller standards, and any one of them may be in use on your computer. In general, as with much of the physical design of disk drives, you don't need to worry about interface standards when you're buying a PC system, because 95 percent of them come with the same type of interface. Your computer comes with the drive, the interface, and all the necessary cables preinstalled and preconfigured. You install whatever applications you want to use and go from there. However, when it comes time to add another disk drive or replace a defective drive, which type of interface you have becomes important. To this end, I describe each one of them briefly in the next section. There are four basic hard drive interfaces used by personal computers today. Some are more popular than others. These are the IDE, Enhanced IDE, and SCSI interface standards. Additionally, an entire new family of miniature hard disks exists that are all PCMCIA implementations. I talked a great deal about PCMCIA in Chapter 2, "Hardware: The Parts of the PC," and we look at PCMCIA disks again in Chapter 26, "Exploring and Tinkering."

## IDE

At the time of this writing, IDE (Integrated Drive Electronics) is still by far the most popular hard disk interface. IDE was developed primarily because in "the old days," there were too many incompatible ways to interface a drive to the computer, causing manufacturers, vendors, and users too much trouble and expense.

**Technical Note:** Bear in mind that the IDE port (or the E-IDE port or SCSI bus, for that matter) is a type of interface between the system and disks. Regardless of whether your system uses an ISA, PCI, or VL bus—and even if you are using a PCMCIA removable hard disk—the disk interface will still be IDE (or E-IDE or SCSI, of course).

Here's why I say trouble and expense. There are three parts of the drive-to-computer interface problem. The computer has to talk to the controller (and vice versa), the controller has to manipulate the data, and the controller has to talk to the disk drive (and vice versa). Until recently, the problem was approached from all perspectives, and it was up to interface designers and drive manufacturers to make it all work. Most of the intelligence for moving data back and forth from the computer to the disk drive was on the controller card in the computer.

That meant that to add a new hard disk or to replace an existing drive, you had to make sure your controller was completely compatible with the new hard drive. Moreover, this approach limited drive manufacturers in the number of improvements and innovations they could provide because of the inherent limitations in the interface. The IDE controllers changed much of this. With IDE, the controller on-board the disk drive took on a larger role in data transfer, so the actual interface between the drive and the computer could be comparatively simple.

As long as the drive you installed could interface properly with the electronics of the IDE interface in your computer, it didn't make much difference what went on inside the drive. Now the "standard" for drive interface is merely to maintain this IDE link between the IDE controller on your computer and the IDE interface inside the disk drive. This simplifies the electronics inside the computer and leaves drive manufacturers more flexibility in how they design the electronics for their drives.

IDE has its severe limitations, however. Multimedia applications quickly made it obvious that IDE's inherent 528MB limitation wouldn't be acceptable to users for very long. Think how quickly your hard disk will fill if DOS and Windows take almost 20MB, your word processor and spreadsheet each take another 10MB, and each game you load can easily take another 8MB! Combine all of that with the fact that an IDE controller only supports a total of two hard drives, and you have some serious expandability limitations. Adding insult to injury is the ever-present Apple Macintosh, which uses the SCSI interface standard. As we'll see below, SCSI drives have a capacity limitation of not 528MB, but approaching 8.4GB. Additionally, up to seven SCSI devices—which could be anything from hard disks to CD-ROMs to scanners, all using up only one slot in the computer—can be placed on a SCSI controller, and implementations exist for allowing multiple controllers on a Macintosh. IDE's two devices, which can only be hard drives, just can't compare.

# Enhanced IDE and Mode 3

In 1994, Western Digital and other major manufacturers of IDE hard drives introduced the *Enhanced IDE* interface standard and the Mode 3 data-transfer specification. By the time this book is in your hands, E-IDE hardware should be available everywhere. This new standard's primary purpose is to keep IDE hardware manufacturers in business in the wake of SCSI developments, which we'll talk about in the next section. The Enhanced standard wipes away the 528MB limit, replacing it with an 8GB limit that all but matches SCSI's potential. Additionally, E-IDE controllers will now support four devices, instead of only two. (This is still short, of course, of SCSI's seven-device potential.) And, while IDE itself could only control hard disks, the new Enhanced standard includes control for hard disks, CD-ROM drives, and tape-backup drives as well.

Data transfer rate, which has long been a battle that IDE always lost to SCSI, has also been improved under the Mode 3 specification. E-IDE Mode 3 drives should achieve sustained data transfer rates that are several times those of normal IDE drives, which all adhered to the Mode 2 data transfer specification. These Mode 3 transfer rates still don't even approach SCSI's fastest sustained rates, but at the time of this writing, a Mode 4 specification is in the works that should, at the very least, keep SCSI manufacturers on their toes.

> **Note:** Incidentally, be aware that simply buying an E-IDE-compatible drive will not give you the improved performance and capacity you might expect. You'll also need to have an E-IDE-compatible controller. While most new PCs will likely come with these enhanced controllers by the time you read this, older PCs will have to be upgraded, through a ROM BIOS upgrade to an on-motherboard controller, or through the installation of a new controller card into a PC expansion-bus slot (usually this would be a local-bus slot). Keep in mind, however, that if you install a new controller card, you'll have to disable any on-motherboard controller that exists, and you may not be able to successfully use four E-IDE products on your new E-IDE controller card if your PC's BIOS only supports two hard drives. (There may be device-drivers to get around that particular problem by the time you read this.)

# SCSI

The SCSI (Small Computer Systems Interface; pronounced "skuzzy," believe it or not) has been around a long time, and is widely available on the Macintosh and Sun platforms. Only recently, however, has it begun to rise quickly in popularity among PC users. SCSI, like other interface standards, was first used by a single drive manufacturer, Shugart Associates, and then became an industry standard as other vendors used it and refined it.

SCSI is an excellent choice for disk interfaces because it is more of a bus than just a simple interface. A SCSI port can daisy chain peripherals from a single interface card, supporting up to seven devices in addition to the interface board itself. This is important as the number of devices required in a PC continues to grow. Many users have more than one hard drive as well as a tape backup unit, an external or removable hard drive, a CD-ROM reader, scanner, and so on. If you must install a separate interface board for each device, you can run out of bus space quickly, especially in today's smaller desktop systems, and out of electronic room, experiencing conflicts with interrupts and other common bus signals.

SCSI can solve all of these problems. As I mentioned above, SCSI has also long had the 8.4GB capacity limit that IDE drives are only now beginning to approach, and that heavy-duty multimedia application development is already demanding. And, as with higher capacities, SCSI has always provided far faster data-transfer throughput than have IDE drives. While IDE drives commonly only deliver data transfer rates of 2MB/second, maximum, SCSI commonly delivers 5MB/second. Additionally, the Fast SCSI standard (SCSI-2) delivers up to 10MB/second, and the new SCSI-3 standard (which was formerly to be called "Fast and Wide" because it combined the SCSI-2 standard with a 32-bit data path, replacing the old 16-bit path) can reach transfer rates of up to 40MB/second. At its best, Enhanced IDE will likely top out at 16.6MB/second.

Additionally, SCSI devices are intelligent and are capable of communicating with each other without putting a load on your PC's main processor. Your processor has to take time out to participate in the progress of data-transfer between the passive IDE and E-IDE devices. However, SCSI devices take an active role in data-transfer, and can actually do all of their work internally to the SCSI bus, taking time from the main processor only to notify it when they are done. Therefore, SCSI may offer greater performance in circumstances when you are performing tasks that demand high performance of both your processor and hard disk simultaneously, such as in the rendering of a texture-mapped image from virtual memory, or in the compression/decompression of digital video.

While compatibility problems have plagued the SCSI world on the PC platform in the past—something that has never been a problem in the Macintosh SCSI world—that has recently changed with the SCSI-2 and SCSI-3 standards. SCSI is now *the* choice for disk storage on high-end, multimedia development and database systems. The primary element inhibiting the widespread adoption of SCSI drives today is economics. While a 1GB E-IDE drive can be had at membership shopping stores for as little as $400.00, the same capacity SCSI drive—because of the currently smaller market, and the cost of putting so much intelligent circuitry on each drive, rather than on the controller card—costs twice as much. Indeed, so much cheaper are IDE drives that even Apple Computer has started putting an IDE hard drive, instead of a SCSI drive, into their new low-end models of Macintosh.

# Some Things to Think About or Try

1.  The original PC used single-sided disks. The reasons had to do with availability and time constraints. At the time the PC was developed, single-sided disks were readily available and well tested. Double-sided disks were newer and more expensive. The PC design team had a limited amount of time, so it chose to go with a proven, economical technology. Eventually, it switched to double-sided disks. What were the advantages of the original choice? What were the disadvantages?

    Suppose that you were a software vendor at the time that IBM made the switch to double-sided disks. What type of disks would you have used to distribute your software? If you used double-sided, it would have been a problem for all of your customers who had single-sided drives. However, if you used single-sided disks, you would have had to use twice as many disks.

The same types of problems are with us today. Most DOS software vendors furnish both the old 5.25-inch disks and the new 3.5-inch disks. Moreover, distribution disks usually are the low-capacity versions.

Many disks are wasted in this way. Is there a solution to this problem? What would you do to avoid similar problems in the future? Do these issues arise with other PC components, such as displays, printers, modems, and so on? What advice would you give to someone on how to buy technology that will last as long as possible?

Thinking about these problems may help you understand a great deal about the realities that underlie personal computing.

2. An old IBM *Technical Reference Manual* states that a particular disk drive, which had 40 tracks, takes 5 milliseconds per track to move the read/write head. The manual says that the average move takes 81 milliseconds. Why is that and what does that tell you?

3. There are hard disks that have the same capacity but are shaped differently. For example, among the disk types that the PC AT can accommodate automatically, there is one with four sides and 614 cylinders and another with eight sides and 307 cylinders. The capacity of the two is identical. Is there any practical difference between them?

# 6

# Disks: The DOS Perspective

In this second chapter about disks, I take a look at computer disks from the DOS perspective; that is, how DOS (up through Version 6.x) lays them out and uses them. Disks by themselves are a kind of raw, unsurveyed land. It's only when an operating system, such as DOS, creates a map of how they are to be used that disks take on a useful form. Each operating system—the PC family has several, with more on the way—has its own plan for how the unbroken land of a disk should be turned into productive fields, if you will. Since at the time of this writing DOS is the only operating system that most PC users will encounter, DOS's way of organizing a disk is the only one I cover here.

**Note:** By the time you read this, Microsoft Windows 95 will likely be soon forthcoming. This new version of Windows, unlike all previous versions, will be a complete operating system unto itself, replacing DOS. Further, major differences in Windows 95 will mandate significant changes in the way that disks are formatted and organized, and the way data on them is referenced. If you are already using Windows 95, all of what follows will teach you the theory behind disk organization, but some or many of the technical details may have changed. Such is the nature of the high-technology beast, as we discussed in the Introduction.

First, I look at the basics of how DOS uses a disk, followed by the technical specifics that underlie a DOS disk. Then, I explore key elements of what DOS data files look like, so you have a better understanding of the working contents of your disks. In particular, I focus on the most common data format, ASCII text files.

This chapter gives you most of what you need to know about floppy and hard disks. What you don't find here, you will find in Chapter 7, "Disks: More Details."

# DOS Disk Overview

In Chapter 5, "Disks: The Basic Story," when you looked at the basics of the computer's disks, you saw how a disk is defined by three or four elements. These elements—track or cylinder, side, and sector within a track—locate the position of each sector on the disk. The size of each sector—expressed as the amount of data that can be stored inside a sector—is the fourth element. Multiplying the first three elements gives you the total number of sectors on a disk, the number of working pieces DOS has at its disposal when it uses the disk. Multiplying the number of sectors by the sector size gives you the data capacity of the disk, the number of bytes DOS has at its disposal in which to store data.

Sectors are the fundamental units of disk activity. All reading and writing on a disk is done with full sectors, not with any smaller amount. An important part of understanding how DOS looks at a disk is seeing how it handles sectors. A key part of this is that DOS "flattens" a disk, ignoring some of the elements that define it. Of course, DOS can't completely ignore these elements; to read and write disk sectors, DOS has to work with sectors in terms of their location and identity. That, however, is just to accommodate the physical nature of the disk. For its own purposes, DOS thinks of a disk as a linear object.

This means that DOS treats the sectors of a disk as a sequential list of sectors, from the first sector on a disk to the last. The diagram in Figure 6.1 shows how this is done. For its own purposes, DOS numbers the sectors sequentially, from 0 (for the first sector on the first side of a disk) to 1 (for the second sector on the first side) and so on to the last sector in the sequence (which is the last sector of the last side). Everything that DOS does in working with and planning the use of disk sectors is done in terms of these sequential sector numbers. Only at the last moment, when information actually is read or written on the disk, does DOS translate between its internal notation (the sequential numbers) and the disk's own three-element notation.

*Figure 6.1.*
*A three-element disk*
*meets a linear DOS.*

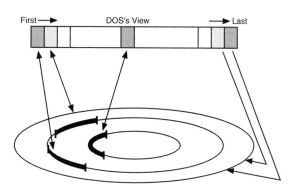

This linear approach greatly simplifies DOS's job of organizing a disk. However, it does have a price. One part of the price is that DOS can't take advantage of the fact that it takes quite a bit longer to move from one sector to another when they are located on different cylinders than it does to move between sectors in the same cylinder. Basically, DOS doesn't know which sectors are on the same cylinder because it ignores the cylinders. There used to be another price, too. At one time, the traditional way that DOS handled disks set a limit on the size of disk you could use. This particular limitation was removed with DOS 4.0.

### Old Limitations—32MB

At one time, the linear, sequential approach that DOS uses to organize disks led to a limitation that wasn't expected to be a problem when DOS was young. The size of a disk DOS could use was limited to 32MB.

This limitation came about as the natural result of two simple things. First, the standard size of a disk sector for DOS is 512 bytes. Second, DOS numbers all the sectors sequentially.

At the time, DOS stored these numbers in the PC's most natural format: 16-bit positive integers. However, there are only 65,536 different 16-bit positive integers. (Remember $2^{16}$ = 65,536). This meant that DOS could work with, at most, 65,536 sectors. And, because each sector is 512 bytes long, this set a limit of 32MB ($65,536 \times 512 = 33,554,432$) as the largest disk DOS could handle.

In the early days of DOS and the PC family, few people imagined that anyone would want a disk that big on a computer so small. But the history of computing has proven that however much you have, it's not enough for long. The solution to the 32MB limit, which came with DOS 4.0, was to change the DOS file system so that it could use more bits to store sector numbers.

DOS takes a similar approach when it comes to storing data on the disk. As I've mentioned, all reading and writing of data on a disk is done in complete sectors. But, when you work with data—or when programs, acting on your behalf, work with data—it may be any amount of data. You as the user can work byte by individual byte or you can work with huge amounts at a time. This points to one of the main jobs that DOS performs in managing disks: DOS acts as a translator between the way the disk works with data (one 512-byte sector at a time) and the way you want to work with it (any of a hundred ways).

DOS's disk-management routines handle the conversion between the amounts of data you want and the amounts of data the disk stores. In effect, DOS does it by running a warehouse and shipping operation. It packages and unpackages data, so that the data is bundled in appropriately sized quantities. DOS can save any amount of data you want and writes that data to the disk in 512-byte sectors. This also works in reverse. DOS reads information stored in appropriately sized sectors and makes it available for you to use as you need it. You can see how this works in Figure 6.2.

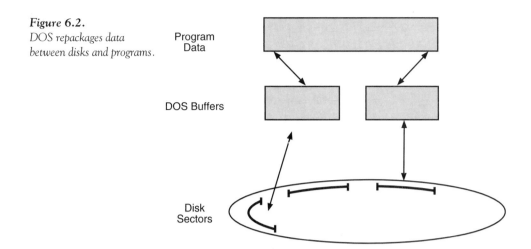

**Figure 6.2.**
*DOS repackages data between disks and programs.*

Program Data

DOS Buffers

Disk Sectors

# Physical and Logical Formatting

The formatting of a disk requires two steps: physical and logical formatting. You'll want to be aware of the distinction.

Physical formatting—sometimes called low-level formatting—involves the creation of physical sectors on a disk. The sectors are created, complete with their address markings (used like name tags to identify them after the formatting is done) and with the data portion of the sector (the part you and your programs know about) established and filled in with some dummy data. Until recently, new floppy disks normally came without physical formatting, but economies of scale have now reduced the price of pre-formatted floppy disks such that the latter are everywhere. A new hard disk is almost always physically formatted when you buy it.

**Note:** The decreasing price of SCSI hard disks has made them increasingly popular on the PC platform. But be careful. If you purchase a SCSI hard disk that was pre-formatted for use with the Apple Macintosh, you will have to redo the formatting to set up the disk for use with your PC. Three major hard disk manufacturers have told me that they won't honor their own warranties if you reformat a Mac hard disk for PC use, or vice-versa. You may find a disk for the other platform on a sale, but check with the manufacturer about their cross-platform policy before you jump at that great deal, or you may be sorry later. If you ever have a problem with the disk, you'll very likely spend a lot more by losing your five-year warranty than you originally saved by buying the discounted drive.

Logical formatting is essentially the conversion of a disk to the standards of the operating system. When a disk is formatted for DOS, the DOS-style structure of the disk is created. The logical formatting is the road map that DOS, or any other operating system, uses to navigate through and make sense out of a disk.

In terms of physical and logical formatting, the FORMAT command of DOS acts differently on floppy disks than it does on hard disks, which is why it is important to understand the distinction between logical and physical formatting. The FORMAT command always does the logical formatting because it is essential to DOS's use of a disk. What differs between floppy disks and hard disks is whether or not DOS is free to perform the physical formatting.

The FORMAT command performs the physical as well as the logical formatting for a floppy disk—unless the floppy disk is already formatted—because a floppy disk "belongs" to the operating system that formats it. A hard disk, on the other hand, may be partitioned into sections that can belong to different operating systems. (This is explained in more detail in Chapter 7.) On a hard disk, the FORMAT command does not dare perform the physical formatting, even within a partition that DOS "owns," because doing physical formatting on even part of the disk may interfere with the rest of the disk.

**Technical Note:** There are ways to force DOS to physically format a floppy disk, even if the disk has already been physically formatted. By using the /U switch (for "Unconditional"), you tell DOS to do a low-level format on the floppy, regardless of what's on the disk. This technique is useful if you want to quickly make certain that the average person can't retrieve the data that used to be on the floppy disk, even if they use an "unformat" utility program. (Disk wipers, like Norton Wipe Disk, give you many more wiping options, much greater confidence that your old data has been eradicated, and may be required for such purposes if you work for a large company or the government).

You will also cause DOS to physically reformat a floppy disk if you use the /F switch to change the size of a floppy disk; for example, to reformat a 1.44MB diskette as a 720KB diskette, for use in an older floppy drive. (DOS will warn you that a size-change format cannot be unformatted.) I do not personally recommend using the latter technique; your data is too valuable to risk, so run out and buy a box of the right-sized floppy disks, if you can. You'll find a good deal more information about DOS's FORMAT command, and its various options, in my *DOS Guide*, which is also in Sams' Premier Series.

DOS doesn't include a program to physically format a hard disk, and no newer hard disk should ever require low-level formatting. In fact, certain types of hard disks and hard disk controllers won't even allow you to perform a low-level format yourself. If you think—or know—that you have a drive that needs to be physically formatted, call the manufacturer for technical support before proceeding.

Depending on what software you use to perform a new low-level format, you may be at risk of using drive areas the manufacturer had identified as being error-prone during the initial low-level format. Additionally, even among drives that are of the same "type," hardware differences between manufacturers may uncover incompatibilities when you attempt to redo a physical format.

Incidentally, Symantec's Norton Utilities package includes a program called Calibrate that performs a special type of low-level format, called a "nondestructive physical format." Over many years, the sector markings on your hard disk may slowly fade. When they've faded, your data may still be on the disk, but will likely be unreachable. Calibrate scans for such "faded" markings and rewrites them fresh, without ever endangering your data, hence the name "nondestructive." Indeed, your data may be *more* safe once *this* type of low-level reformatting is complete.

The DOS FORMAT program uses a special BIOS command (see Chapter 18, "The Role of DOS") to format a disk track by track. The mechanism of physical formatting requires that the formatting for all the sectors in each track be laid down in one coordinated operation. When FORMAT formats a floppy disk, it sets the sector data to a default value—hex F6—in each byte. Because the FORMAT command overwrites each byte of the disk, all old data on the disk is completely obliterated. Without a utility program or the latest version of DOS, formatting a disk eliminates any hope of recovering any data on the disk after it has been reformatted. However, FORMAT does not overwrite the old data on a hard disk, so it is possible to recover data from a reformatted hard disk.

Special features of DOS 6 and later make formatted data recovery a lot more reliable and a lot easier. Unless you tell DOS otherwise, an image of the original data is saved on disk before it is formatted, enabling you to recover as much information as is not physically overwritten between the time you format the disk and the time you try to unformat it. Of course, if you choose to do the unconditional format I mentioned above, no "unformat" information is saved.

If you don't have DOS later than Version 6.0, but you do have the Norton Utilities, you can use the Safe Format program to format disks in such a way that the data is not erased. This process is faster, and it protects you from accidentally erasing the wrong data. If a disk is safe-formatted, you can unformat it as long as you have not already used the space for new data.

# The Structure of a DOS Disk

To organize disks, DOS divides them into two parts: a small system area that DOS uses to keep track of key information about the disk and the data area, the bulk of the disk, where data is stored. The system area uses only a small portion of a disk—two percent for a floppy disk and a tenth of a percent, or less, for a hard disk.

The system area that DOS uses is divided into three parts: the boot record, the FAT, and the root directory. Figure 6.3 shows these disk components.

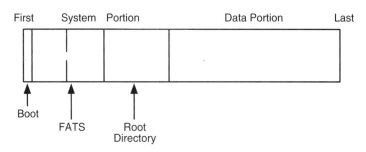

**Figure 6.3.**
*The parts of a DOS disk.*

# The Boot Record

The boot record is the very first part of a DOS disk. It holds a very short program—one that's only a few hundred bytes long—that performs the job of beginning the loading of DOS into the computer's memory. The start-up procedure is called "booting," based on the old expression "pulling oneself up by the bootstraps." Metaphorically speaking, that's exactly what your computer does. In this phase, DOS actually loads itself; it loads the programs that are necessary for it to carry on its work. The job of the boot record program is to start DOS from a disk by reading the first part of the DOS program from the disk into memory. Interestingly enough, the boot record itself is on every disk, even those not formatted as system disks. If you ever try to boot a disk that isn't a system disk, the boot record program will alert you to the fact by producing an error and asking you to insert a system disk to continue booting.

Incidentally, some very interesting information is recorded on some disks' boot records. I look into that as well as some of the more technical information in Chapter 7.

The next part of the system portion of a disk is called the file allocation table, or FAT. DOS needs a way to keep track of what you store in the data portion of a disk, so that it knows what's already being used and what's available for new data. The FAT records the status of each part of the disk. To manage the data space on a disk, DOS divides it up into logical units called clusters. When a file is being recorded on the data portion of a disk, disk space is assigned to the file in these clusters. The size of a cluster varies from one disk format to another, but it can be as small as an individual sector or much bigger. Table 6.1 lists the cluster sizes that DOS uses for floppy disks. (Remember, 0.5KB, 512 bytes, is the size of one sector.)

Table 6.1. Cluster Sizes for Floppy Disks.

| Diskette Type | Cluster Size |
| --- | --- |
| 3.5-inch 2.88MB | 1.0KB = 1,024 bytes |
| 3.5-inch 1.44MB | 0.5KB = 512 bytes |
| 3.5-inch 720KB | 1.0KB = 1,024 bytes |

| Diskette Type | Cluster Size |
|---|---|
| 5.25-inch 1.2MB | 0.5KB = 512 bytes |
| 5.25-inch 360KB | 1.0KB = 1,024 bytes |

FAT entries are 12 or 16 bits long, depending on the size of the disk. With a longer FAT entry, DOS can keep track of more clusters and therefore supports a larger disk. For floppy disks, DOS uses a 12-bit FAT entry. For hard disks, DOS uses a 12-bit entry if the disk is smaller than 17MB and a 16-bit entry if the disk is larger than 17MB.

In addition, the cluster size varies, depending on the total size of the hard disk and the way the disk is designed. Cluster size will normally be between 512 bytes and 8K bytes. Whatever the cluster size, DOS carves up the data portion of the disk into these relatively small clusters and then uses them as the unit of space that it allocates to the disk files.

## A Personal Example Using Norton System Information

Let's look at one of my disks just to get a "real" example of what we've talked about so far. As you can see in Figure 6.4, my drive D: is a 516MB disk. In this case, each cluster contains 16 sectors, and each sector is the usual 512 bytes, for a total of 8,192 bytes (8K, exactly) per cluster. There are 64,411 clusters on this disk, which makes for 1,030,576 sectors total, as you can also see. Because this is a relatively large disk, the 16-bit type of FAT is in use. You will also see that this disk has the normal set of *two* FATs: one for regular use, and a backup FAT, as a safety precaution.

If you have the Norton Utilities, you can see a similar screen for your own disks by running the System Information program and selecting Disk Characteristics from the Disks menu.

**Figure 6.4.**
*Characteristics of my Drive D, from Norton SysInfo.*

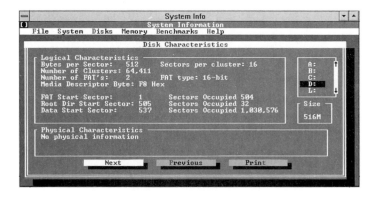

The allocation of disk space to files is managed by the FAT, which simply is a table of numbers with a place in the table for each cluster on the disk. The number that's recorded in each cluster's FAT entry indicates whether the cluster is in use by a file or available for new data. A zero in the cluster's FAT entry means the cluster is free. Any other number indicates it's in use. Because a data file may be larger than the size of a cluster, the numbers in the FAT are used to link clusters that contain one file's data.

The FAT gives DOS a place to keep track of the allocation of the disk's data space. This isolates the space and record-keeping function, which helps protect it from possible damage. If you think about it, you can see why the FAT is the most critical part of a disk, the part that most needs to be protected. As I mention in the preceeding sidebar, the FAT is so critical that DOS records two separate copies on each disk. Only the first copy is normally used; the second copy is there to help make it possible to perform emergency repairs on damaged disks.

# The Root Directory

The last part of the disk's system area is the root directory. This is the file directory that every disk has; it's the basic, built-in directory for the disk. Disks also can have subdirectories added to them. However, subdirectories are an optional part of a disk that you create as necessary. The root directory is not optional.

A directory, of course, records the files that are stored on the disk. For each file, there is a directory entry that records the file's eight-character filename, the three-character extension to the filename, the size of the file, and a date and time stamp that records when the file was last changed. All those parts of a file's directory entry are familiar because they're shown in the DIR listing. Two other pieces of information about a file are recorded in its directory entry. One is called the starting cluster number, which indicates which cluster in the disk's data space holds the first portion of the file. The other is called the file attribute, which is used to record a number of things about the file. For example, subdirectories have a particular directory attribute marking; DOS's system files have a special pair of attributes called system and hidden. There are also two attributes that serve users more directly. The read-only attribute protects files from being changed or deleted, and the archive attribute is used to help keep track of which files on a disk have been backed-up, or are in need of it.

The root directory of each disk, like the other items in the system portion of a disk, is a fixed size for each disk format. This size determines how many entries there are for files in the root directory. Each directory entry occupies 32 bytes, so 16 of them fit into a single sector. A 3.5-inch, 1.44MB disk has 14 sectors set aside for the root directory, so it has room for 224 (16×14) files in the directory. A 2.88MB disk has 15 sectors for the root directory, making room for up to 240 entries (16×15). Hard disks typically have something like 32 sectors, making room for 512 (16×32) directory entries in the root directory.

I mentioned before that the FAT is used to chain together a record of where a file's data is stored. Here is how it works. Each file's directory entry includes a field that gives the number of the cluster in which the first part of the file's data is stored. The FAT table has a number entry for each cluster. If you look up the FAT entry for the first cluster in a file, it contains the number of the next cluster used by the file, and the FAT entry for that cluster points to the next one. This way, the FAT entries are chained together to provide DOS with a way of keeping the contents of a file together. When the end of the file is reached, the FAT entry for the last cluster holds a special code number that marks the end of the file. Such a chain is called a linked list. You can see a typical file's space allocation in Figure 6.5.

**Figure 6.5.**
*A file's space allocation in the FAT.*

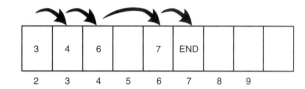

That finishes this survey of the system portion of a disk. What remains is the majority of the disk, the data portion. But you already know the basics about this part of a disk.

# The Data Portion

The data portion is used to record the data contents of your disk files. The data space, just like the system space, is divided into units called clusters. (Clusters are made up of one or more sectors. Clusters on a disk are all the same size, but their size varies between disk formats and types.) Each file's data is recorded on one or more clusters, and the record of which clusters, and in which order, is kept in the disk's FAT. It's worth noting that a file's data can be scattered all over a disk in disjointed clusters. DOS generally tries to keep a file's data together in contiguous sequential clusters. However, after many disk reads and writes, files can end up being stored on different parts of the disk.

When too many files get scattered in bits and pieces all over the disk, the disk is said to be fragmented. When a disk is badly fragmented, it slows things down because DOS must constantly move the read/write head from place to place. If you have DOS 6 or later, you have a program called DEFRAG that is an integral disk defragmentation utility. You may also own the Norton Utilities, which comes with the SpeedDisk defragment utility. SpeedDisk has an advantage over the free DEFRAG in that it can defragment your hard disk in the background, while you're running under Windows 3.1 or later. This allows you to get on with other work while the utility is doing its job. Contrastingly, DEFRAG can't be used while Windows is running, and you lose the use of your computer while it does its job, which can take anywhere from 30 seconds to 60 minutes, depending on the degree of file fragmentation and the size of your disk.

Whichever one you have, vow that you will use it relatively frequently. This keeps your drive running at optimum performance.

I've mentioned subdirectories, and at this point I should explain that each subdirectory acts like a mixture of a data file and the disk's root directory. As far as the way a subdirectory is recorded on the disk, it's no different than any other disk file. The subdirectory is stored in the disk's data space, and a record of where the subdirectory is located is kept in the FAT, exactly like any other file. However, when it comes to using its contents, a subdirectory acts like the disk's root directory. It holds a record of files and other subdirectories that are stored within it, and DOS works with subdirectories just as it works with the main, root directory. There are two major differences between subdirectories and root directories. One is that there is only one root directory on each disk, but there can be numerous subdirectories. The other is that each root directory has a fixed size and capacity, while subdirectories, like files, can grow to any size that the disk can accommodate. So, while you can only have a fixed number of entries in your root directory itself, the number of entries you can have in a subdirectory is limited only by the size of the largest file your disk can maintain. My basic recommendation is that you keep only your CONFIG.SYS and AUTOEXEC.BAT files in the root directory, and place all of your other files in a well thought-out subdirectory structure.

What you've seen so far gives you all the fundamental information you need to understand the basics of the structure of DOS disks. There is more to know about them, of course; there are plenty of fascinating technical details left to explore. (For more on file management, take a look at my book, *Peter Norton's Guide to DOS 6.22, Premier Edition*, from Sams Publishing.)

# Learning About File Formats

Each file stored on your disk potentially has its own unique data format, the structure of the data that's recorded in the file. The physical recording of data on the disk still must adhere to the format DOS and the drive's controller use, but the logical format of data varies with the application and the file type. It may seem that there is little I can say in general about the format of disk files, and in many ways that is true. However, there are a few important observations that I can make about files to help you understand what's going on inside your disks.

First, note that the three-character extension of a filename is intended to be used as an indication of the format and use of a file. Some filename extensions are standard and must be used to correctly identify the file type; most, however, don't have a strict use, just a conventional one.

The strictly enforced extensions primarily have to do with programs. DOS requires that all programs be recorded in one of two special program formats and that they be identified by the standard extension names of COM and EXE. Batch command files must use the BAT extension.

Most other filename extensions are optional, but application programs usually are designed to work more easily with files that have standard extensions. For example, the BASIC interpreter expects BASIC program files to have the BAS extension and C expects source files to have a C extension. Similarly, programs such as spreadsheets and word processors have their own conventional extensions. For example, Microsoft Word files typically have the DOC extension, and Lotus 1-2-3 files have extensions like WK1. You may be able to use names that don't adhere to a particular program's extension convention, but working with files from within an application usually is easier if you use the filename convention the program expects.

The contents of data files can be very interesting, but you have to make a special effort to look inside your files by using snooping tools like DEBUG or the Norton Utilities, both described in Chapter 26, "Exploring and Tinkering." Often it's hard to decode or otherwise make much sense of what you see inside a data file. However, by looking, you sometimes can find some very interesting things.

There is one very good reason for taking a look at and learning about the data formats created by the programs you use: you may need to do repair work on your disks, such as unerasing deleted files or other such file-recovery operations. If you learn what your data looks like in advance, you have a better chance of finding and recovering it in an emergency.

As a general rule, the data files created by programs have an internal structure that seems completely jumbled to the human eye. Certain parts—including such character text data as the names and addresses in a mailing list database—are easy to recognize. However, the parts of the data that hold numbers and formatting information usually are recorded in a form that is cryptic and can be deciphered only by the programs that work with the data.

One special kind of file, though, has a pattern to it that you should be able to recognize fairly well. These are data files made up of what are called fixed-length records: a repeated pattern in which content of the data varies, but each element has the same length. This is the kind of data that BASIC uses for its random-access files. Because the data records in this kind of file are all the same length, BASIC can calculate its way to the location of any randomly specified record number without having to search through the file from the beginning. Whenever you look at a data file that is built from fixed-sized elements, you may be able to recognize the pattern and decode some of the file's data.

By exploring and digging through some file data, you can learn a great deal about how computers and programs work with disk data.

# ASCII Text Files

The ASCII text file format is one file format that every PC user will encounter. ASCII text files, which also are called ASCII files, or text files for short, are the closest thing the PC family has—at least at the time of this writing—to a universal format for data files. While most programs have their own special way of recording data, the ASCII text file is a common format that can be used by almost any program and, in fact, is used by many of them. Even certain programs that display pictures on your monitor can obtain the data that makes up each picture from long strings of numbers, stored in an ASCII text file.

> **Note:** You very likely already know that ASCII stands for the American Standard Code for Information Interchange. It was originally a set of 96 upper-case and lower-case letters and numbers, plus 32 nonprinting *control* characters. The ASCII code is a simple replacement code that your computer uses to store text data. For example, every capital letter "A" is stored as the number 65, every capital letter "B" as the number 66, and so on.

ASCII text files were designed to hold ordinary text data, like the words you are reading. These files are used by many simple text editing programs, such as the DOS EDIT program, and some word processing programs also work directly with ASCII text files. However, most programs, including word processors, spreadsheet programs, and many others, use the ASCII text file format as an alternative to their own native data formats. These programs are prepared to work with ASCII text files simply because the ASCII text file format is something of a last-resort way of transferring data from one program to another. Often, however, rather than a last resort, it's the only way to get data from here to there. ASCII text file data *is* rather naked. It isn't clothed in the rich formatting that most programs use for their data, but when you need to pass data from one place to another, it's often the only reasonable way to get it done. It's the least common denominator.

When I say that most programs have their own special data formats, I am referring to applications programs such as databases and spreadsheets. There are many programs that expect to work only with ASCII text files. Programming language compilers and assemblers generally expect to read program source code from plain ASCII text files. Among programs that are, one way or another, writing tools, there is an informal division between the simple ones that use ASCII text files, such as many text editing programs, and the complex ones that use their own custom data formats, such as most word processing programs. Finally, batch command files, which enable DOS to carry out a series of commands with one instruction to the computer, are all actually ASCII text files.

The data in a text file is composed of two character types: ordinary ASCII text characters and the ASCII control characters. The regular text characters are the principal data in an ASCII text file, while the control characters format the text, for example, marking line and paragraph divisions.

There is no strict definition of the way programs and computers are supposed to use ASCII text files. Instead, all programs that work with ASCII text files use the most basic elements of this file format, but some programs go further and use the less common formatting control characters as well. I start by describing the most common elements.

A pair of ASCII control characters is used to mark the end of each line of text in the file. The characters Carriage Return and Line Feed—known in ASCII terminology as CR and LF—are character codes 13 and 10, or hex 0D and 0A. These two, taken as a pair, are the standard way to mark the end of a line of text.

One ASCII control character is used to mark the end of a text file. It's the Control-Z character—code 26 or hex 1A. In most tables of ASCII control characters, this code is called SUB, but because it usually indicates the end of a file, it also is called EOF. Normally, ASCII text files have an EOF character at the end of the text data.

The Horizontal Tab (HT) character is used as a substitute for repeated spaces. Its character code is 9. Tabs appear in many ASCII files, even though there is no universal agreement about just where the tab stops are. Most programs (but, unfortunately, far from all) handle tabs on the assumption that there is a tab stop every eight positions (at the 9th column, 17th column, and so on).

The Form Feed character is used to mark the end of one page and the beginning of the next. Its character code is 12, hex 0C, and the ASCII name is FF. This control character also is called Page Eject.

An ASCII text file can contain any control characters (these are summarized in Table 14.1), but the most common ones are the five I just described. And, in many cases, even the last two—Horizontal Tab and Form Feed—are avoided to keep the coding as simple as possible.

There are several commonly used ways to indicate the division of text data into paragraphs. The most common form marks the end of each line of text with a Carriage Return/Line Feed pair. This is the form in which compilers expect to find their program source code. When this form is used to mark words, sentences, and paragraphs, it's common to indicate the end of a paragraph with a blank line; that is, two pairs of Carriage Return/Line Feeds in a row. Sometimes, though, you see ASCII text files in which each paragraph is treated as a single, very long line with a Carriage Return/Line Feed pair at the end of the paragraph, but nowhere inside the paragraph. Some word processing programs create ASCII text files like this.

Because there are different ways of laying out an ASCII text file, there often are conflicts between the way one program expects to find a text file and the way another program expects to find it. Different programs often are at odds with one another when you try to use ASCII text files as a way of transferring data between them. For example, if you try to use ASCII text files to pass something you've written from one word processing program to another, you may find that what one program considers lines in a paragraph the other program considers separate paragraphs. This sort of nonsense can be very annoying. Nevertheless, ASCII text files are the closest thing PCs have to a universal language, and that's why you may find yourself working with ASCII text files more often than you expect, particularly if you are active on any online services or BBS's. (As an aside, you should know that most word processors and communications software support the saving and opening of files in a variety of ASCII and ANSI text formats, so if your program doesn't perform the proper translation automatically when you open the file, check your manual to see how to force the program to import the file with a specific type of filter.)

People usually think of ASCII text files as containing either words, like the sentences and paragraphs you are reading here, or program source code, like the programming examples you have seen throughout this book. However, any form of data can be translated into ASCII text format. Thus, you may find some text files that consist only of numbers written in ASCII characters. Some programs use ASCII text files to exchange data that isn't made up of words. For example, the Data Interchange File, or DIF, standard uses ASCII text files to transfer data among spreadsheets and other programs that know how to interpret DIF data. DIF files are simply ASCII text files that describe, among other things, the contents of a spreadsheet.

To get a more concrete idea of what an ASCII text file looks like, here's an example. Suppose you have a text file with these two lines in it:

```
Columbus sailed the ocean blue
In fourteen hundred and ninety two.
```

To see what that looks like inside an ASCII text file, I write it out in a way that represents the text file data. Note the control characters <CR>, <LF>, and <EOF>.

```
Columbus sailed the ocean blue<CR><LF>
In fourteen hundred and ninety two.<CR><LF><EOF>
```

The more advanced the tinkering you do with your computer, the more likely it is that you will find yourself working with or looking at ASCII text files. When you do, you should know about one anomaly you may run into. It has to do with the way ASCII text files are ended and the size of the file.

I mentioned earlier that the Control-Z (EOF) character, code 26, normally is used to mark the end of a text file's data. There are several variations on how that is done. The cleanest and strictest form has the EOF character stored right after the last line of text, as I show it in the preceding example.

The length of the file, as recorded in the file's disk directory, includes the EOF character in the size of the file. Sometimes, however, a file appears to be bigger, judging from the size recorded in the disk directory. This is because some programs work with text files, not byte by byte, but in chunks of, say, 128 bytes at a time. When this kind of program creates a text file, the Control-Z (or EOF) character shows up where the true end of the file is, but the file's disk directory entry shows a length that's been rounded up to the next highest multiple of 128. In such cases, the real length of the file is slightly smaller than you would expect based on the size in the directory.

There is another way that an ASCII text file may appear odd. It may be recorded without a Control-Z character. In that case, the file size recorded in the directory indicates the true size of the file, and there's no end-of-file marker on the theory that none is needed because the size tells you where the end is. Any time you take a close look at an ASCII text file or any time you write a program to read one, you should be prepared for variations like this in the way the end of the file is indicated.

# Some Things to Think About or Try

1. If you have the Norton Utilities, use the System Information program to explore the dimensions of your disk, as I suggested in the sidebar earlier in this chapter. (If you have an older version of the utilities, before Version 5.0, use the Disk Info program.) If you don't have the Norton Utilities, you can use CHKDSK from DOS to see a limited subset of information about your disks. This DOS utility shows you the original size of your disk, how much of it is in use, what kinds of files are stored there, and more.

2. Think about why the FAT is the most critical part of a disk. What makes it more important than the directory portion? There is a DOS file recovery utility called RECOVER that can recreate a disk directory if the directory is damaged but the FAT is not. How do you think this is possible? Could there be a similar program to recreate a damaged FAT if the directory were intact?

> **Warning:** Incidentally, if you're using Version 6.0 or later of DOS, you don't have access to the RECOVER command. If you're using a version of DOS before 6.0, *don't* try the RECOVER command, or you will likely discover why Microsoft removed it from DOS. Simply put, the RECOVER command used to search through the FAT, finding all of the files on your entire disk—whether in subdirectories or no—and rewrote *all* of your files into the root directory. (At least, it tried to do this, until the root directory ran out of space for entries.) Adding insult to injury, RECOVER renames each and every file—after moving it—to a sequentially numbered list, in the format of FILE0001.REC. I am almost never one to discourage exploration, but the RECOVER command is one place where I can confidently say, "Don't!" Even though there are utilities now to help you recover from RECOVER, you will, at the very least, experience tremendous stress and inconvenience from the exercise, and you may risk every piece of data on your disk.

3. If you have a version of BASIC that is earlier than QBasic (QBasic only saves its files in ASCII format), try this exercise to see how BASIC can record its program files in two forms—BASIC's own coded format and the ASCII text file format—enter a short BASIC program (just a line or two of any BASIC program, such as the maze program from the Introduction of this book) and then save it to disk in both formats, using these commands:

```
SAVE "BASFORM"
SAVE "TEXTFORM",A
```

Examine the two files. Compare their sizes using the DIR command. See how their contents differ by using the TYPE command to print them on your computer's display screen. If you know how to snoop in files using DEBUG or NU, inspect the contents of the two files.

4.  If you don't have a pre-QBasic version of BASIC, try using your Word Processor to save a few lines of text in both the word processor's native format and in ASCII text. You'll find a "save as text" option in the "Save File" dialog box of most Windows-based Word Processors. Using the same technique that I suggested above—DOS's TYPE command or DEBUG or the Norton Utilities—examine the file contents to see the differences. Their number may surprise you. Also, look at the directory listing to see variances in file size.

# 7

# Disks: More Details

This is the last leg of our journey through basic disk storage technology. The next three chapters provide information on disk utilities and special disk types: removable and optical drives. In this chapter, I move into some of the more technical details of how computers use disks, covering hard disks and the way computers work with them. Then I look at how DOS works with disks, expanding on the material in Chapter 6, "Disks: The DOS Perspective."

This chapter contains technical information, and readers who want to focus on understanding the PC can pass over the more technical parts. However, there is one part that I don't want you to miss: the discussion of hard disks and hard disk partitions. If you want to understand the most important practical things about the PC family, you do need to know about hard disks.

# Hard Disk Features and Partitions

Hard disks present some special challenges to the designers of computers. The most obvious thing is that a hard disk has a much greater storage capacity than a floppy disk. In nearly everything in life, there comes a point when a quantitative difference becomes a qualitative difference—when more isn't just more, it's also different. That's the case with hard disks. Their storage capacity is so much greater than the floppy disk's that they must be treated differently. Greater capacity and faster speed are part of what is special about a hard disk. Oddly enough, however, those two items do not constitute the most critical difference. What is most different about a hard disk is that it is not removable.

Or, I should say, it *generally* is not removable. For years hard disks have been called "fixed" disks because you couldn't access them from outside the computer or take them from machine to machine. However, this is no longer the case.

Now there are drive manufacturers, such as SyQuest, that make hard disk drives with removable platters. In nearly all other respects, these drives are like the nonremovable drives I've talked about already and describe further in this chapter. The difference is that the rigid platter (and sometimes the read/write heads as well) can be removed from the drive mechanism.

Also, many manufacturers offer very small, removable PCMCIA drives in which the entire drive mechanism is removed from a carrier so it can be put away for safe storage, carried to another computer to share data, or swapped for another disk with different information. As you might imagine, these removable drives are extremely popular with notebook computer users because they enable you to remove a drive from the laptop or notebook machine, insert it into your desktop computer, and transfer files easily. (You do need a PCMCIA socket in your desktop machine, but these are already common.) They also are ideal solutions for situations in which two or more people use the same computer, especially if business associates share a notebook computer. Removable hard drives enable each user to have a drive for personal programs or data.

In this chapter, I'm going to use the term "hard disk" because that's what nearly everyone calls them. IBM tended to call them "fixed disks" until very recently. The fact that a hard disk is fixed presents a special problem. You're stuck with the disk that came with the computer; you can't easily switch it for another one in a different format or set it up to accommodate another operating system. While most people work exclusively within the framework that DOS creates, DOS isn't the only operating system around; other systems include OS/2, UNIX, and the forthcoming Microsoft Windows 95, commonly referred to by its development name, "Chicago."

With floppy disks, the fact that they are owned by an operating system such as DOS—owned in the sense that they have a format and logical structure that applies only to the system (DOS) with which they work—should not be a problem, just as there is no fundamental problem with a game program using its own peculiar disk format (which many used to do for copy-protection). Although odd floppy disk formats can be a nuisance, they do not present a fundamental problem because computers themselves aren't committed in any sense to always using the same format; you can switch disks any time you want.

With a hard disk, the situation is completely different. If your hard disk is "owned" by one operating system, you can't easily or quickly use it with another operating system. Because almost everything you do with your PC is based on DOS—at least, as of the time of this writing—you may be tempted to ask, "So what?" The world of computing is always changing, however, and it's quite likely that the operating system you use today will be different from the one you'll use in a year, or even a few months. The Windows 95 operating system, for example, will use a completely new disk structure. And even today, some PC users find good reasons to use systems other than, or in addition to, DOS. How do users accommodate different operating systems with incompatible ways of structuring disks on one hard disk?

The answer is partitioning, or dividing a hard disk into areas that can be owned by different operating systems. Within the confines of each partition, the disk can be formatted and logically structured to meet the needs of the operating system that owns the partition. Together, all the partitions on a disk can occupy the entire disk or leave parts of it open.

This arrangement allows for a great deal of flexibility but relies on some across-the-board standards that every program using the disk must follow. There must be a master format within which all of the operating systems on the disk must operate. Part of this common ground is the physical formatting of the disk, which sets, among other things, the sector size that applies to every partition on the disk. (This points up the distinction between physical and logical formatting, which I talk about in Chapter 6.) However, a common sector size isn't all there is to the common ground and rules of coexistence that apply to a partitioned hard disk. There also must be a standard way of marking off the boundaries of a disk partition, and each operating system using a partitioned disk must agree to stay within its own bounds and not encroach on another partition's territory.

Here is how it's done. The very first sector of a hard disk is set aside for a special master record, which contains a partition table describing the layout of the disk. This table shows the dimensions of the disk, the number of partitions, and the size and location of each partition. A disk doesn't have to be divided into more than one partition; in fact, most PCs have only one partition, a DOS partition, which occupies the entire disk. Figure 7.1 illustrates a partitioned hard disk.

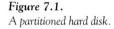

*Figure 7.1.*
*A partitioned hard disk.*

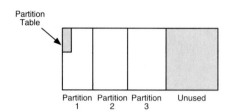

Most PC owners can safely ignore the extra complexity and possibilities that disk partitioning encompasses. Instead, most simply create a single DOS partition that fills the entire hard disk. This, in fact, is the most sensible thing to do. Until you need another partition—which may never happen—there is no reason to set aside hard disk space.

To deal with partitions on hard disks, DOS has a program called FDISK, which can display and change partition data. FDISK can list up to four partitions. Each partition in the list has a starting and ending location and size in disk cylinders. A typical listing of partition data is shown below:

```
Display Partition Information
Current fixed disk drive: 1
Partition  Status   Type    Volume Label    Mbytes    System Usage
C: 1         A    PRI DOS   STVBEAR           505      FAT16   100%
Total disk space is 505 Mbytes (1 Mbyte = 1048576)
Press ESC to continue
```

The FDISK program enables you to manipulate the disk partitions while working with DOS. If you're working with another operating system, it should have an equivalent program. FDISK enables you to create or delete a DOS-owned partition. Beginning with Version 5.0, DOS can now delete non-DOS partitions; earlier versions of DOS could not do so. While this restriction of early DOS versions may seem like a good safety feature, it has disadvantages. If you ended up with an unwanted partition from another system, you couldn't delete it from DOS, so you could be stuck with a bum partition. (This has happened to acquaintances of mine.) If you're using a version of DOS prior to 5.0, my suggestion  would be to update your DOS to the latest version, and then delete the non-DOS partition with the built-in ability of the newer DOS.

Suppose you've devoted your entire hard disk to DOS and now want to surrender some of the space to make room for another partition. Can you simply give up the space? Unfortunately, because of the way DOS structures its partitions, you cannot simply shrink a partition to make room for another. If you need to resize a DOS partition, you must back up the contents of the partition, delete the partition (with FDISK), create a new partition, format it (with FORMAT), and reload the data from your back-up tape or disks. That can be a laborious process. But, as I said, unless you know that you will need another partition, you're better off letting DOS use the entire hard disk and facing the chore of repartitioning if the need ever arises.

Also, the majority of computer systems are delivered to you today with the hard disk already partitioned and DOS and application software preinstalled.

In the FDISK listing above, notice that the sole partition is marked with status A. That means the partition is the active partition. On any partitioned disk, only one partition at a time can be active. This has to do with the start-up, or booting, process. Remember that every ordinary disk has a boot program on its first sector, which begins the process of starting up the operating system. The same thing applies to a partitioned hard disk, but there is an extra step involved. The first sector of a partitioned hard disk contains a master boot program along with the table that describes the partitions. This master boot program looks at the partition table to see which partition is active. Then it fires up the boot program that starts that partition. Each partition has its own boot program (just as each floppy disk has a boot record), which is tailored to the needs of the particular operating system that owns that partition. The master boot record does the job of finding the right partition boot record and getting it going.

You can see that partitions are a special key to making the large storage space of hard disks work with extra flexibility not available with floppy disks. With this large capacity and extra flexibility, though, comes an additional degree of complexity. And, if you want to take full advantage your hard disk, you must master this complexity.

Next, I look at the structure DOS places on disks and see some of the fascinating technical details of how DOS manages disks.

# Detailed Disk Structure

To help you better understand what's going on with disks, this section gives you a closer look at the way DOS structures a disk. The insight you gain here will help you appreciate and use your disk when everything is going right, and may help you work your way out of trouble if something goes wrong.

As I describe in Chapter 6, DOS divides each disk into two parts: the system part, used for DOS's record keeping, and the data part, where files are stored. The system portion has three parts: the boot record, the FAT (file allocation table), and the root directory. In the next sections, I give you a closer look at what's stored in each one.

# The Boot Record

The boot record is always the very first data on the disk. It's used to hold a short program that begins the process of starting DOS. The boot record is present on every disk, even those from which you can't boot. (You can't boot from them because they don't contain a copy of the DOS system files that are necessary for booting, in addition to the boot record).

The boot program is small enough to fit easily into a single disk sector, so it doesn't require more than one sector. However, DOS allows for the possibility that the boot area may have to be larger in the future.

There are more interesting things in the boot record of a disk than you may imagine. You can use the DOS DEBUG program to inspect the contents of a boot record. It only takes the two simple DEBUG commands listed below. The first reads the boot record from the hard disk C into memory; the second displays the boot record's data in hex and ASCII.

```
L 0 2 0 1
D 0 L 200
```

The following information shows what a DOS Version 6.2 boot record looks like. (Yes, it still says MS-DOS 5.0, because that's the basic structure on which DOS 6 was built.)

```
00000000: EB 3C 90 4D 53 44 4F 53 - 35 2E 30 00 02 10 01 00   .<.MSDOS5.0.....
00000010: 02 00 02 00 00 F8 CB 00 - 38 00 0F 00 38 00 00 00   ........8...8...
00000020: A8 A9 0C 00 80 00 29 CA - 1C 48 24 4E 4F 20 4E 41   ......)..H$NO NA
00000030: 4D 45 20 20 20 20 46 41 - 54 31 36 20 20 20 FA 33   ME    FAT16   .3
00000040: C0 8E D0 BC 00 7C 16 07 - BB 78 00 36 C5 37 1E 56   .....|...x.6.7.V
00000050: 16 53 BF 3E 7C B9 0B 00 - FC F3 A4 06 1F C6 45 FE   .S.>|........E.
00000060: 0F 8B 0E 18 7C 88 4D F9 - 89 47 02 C7 07 3E 7C FB   ....|..M..G..>|.
00000070: CD 13 72 79 33 C0 39 06 - 13 7C 74 08 8B 0E 13 7C   ..ry3.9..|t....|
00000080: 89 0E 20 7C A0 10 7C F7 - 26 16 7C 03 06 1C 7C 13   .. |..|.&.|...|.
00000090: 16 1E 7C 03 06 0E 7C 83 - D2 00 A3 50 7C 89 16 52   ..|...|....P|..R
000000A0: 7C A3 49 7C 89 16 4B 7C - B8 20 00 F7 26 11 7C 8B   |.I|..K|. ..&.|.
000000B0: 1E 0B 7C 03 C3 48 F7 F3 - 01 06 49 7C 83 16 4B 7C   ..|..H....I|..K|
000000C0: 00 BB 00 05 8B 16 52 7C - A1 50 7C E8 92 00 72 1D   ......R|.P|...r.
000000D0: B0 01 E8 AC 00 72 16 8B - FB B9 0B 00 BE E6 7D F3   .....r.......}.
000000E0: A6 75 0A 8D 7F 20 B9 0B - 00 F3 A6 74 18 BE 9E 7D   .u... .....t...}
000000F0: E8 5F 00 33 C0 CD 16 5E - 1F 8F 04 8F 44 02 CD 19   ._.3...^...D...
00000100: 58 58 58 EB E8 8B 47 1A - 48 48 8A 1E 0D 7C 32 FF   XXX...G.HH...|2.
00000110: F7 E3 03 06 49 7C 13 16 - 4B 7C BB 00 07 B9 03 00   ....I|..K|......
00000120: 50 52 51 E8 3A 00 72 D8 - B0 01 E8 54 00 59 5A 58   PRQ.:.r....T.YZX
00000130: 72 BB 05 01 00 83 D2 00 - 03 1E 0B 7C E2 E2 8A 2E   r..........|....
00000140: 15 7C 8A 16 24 7C 8B 1E - 49 7C A1 4B 7C EA 00 00   .|..$|..I|.K|....
00000150: 70 00 AC 0A C0 74 29 B4 - 0E BB 07 00 CD 10 EB F2   p....t).........
00000160: 3B 16 18 7C 73 19 F7 36 - 18 7C FE C2 88 16 4F 7C   ;..|s..6.|....O|
00000170: 33 D2 F7 36 1A 7C 88 16 - 25 7C A3 4D 7C F8 C3 F9   3..6.|..%|.M|...
00000180: C3 B4 02 8B 16 4D 7C B1 - 06 D2 E6 0A 36 4F 7C 8B   .....M|.....6O|.
00000190: CA 86 E9 8A 16 24 7C 8A - 36 25 7C CD 13 C3 0D 0A   .....$|.6%|.....
000001A0: 4E 6F 6E 2D 53 79 73 74 - 65 6D 20 64 69 73 6B 20   Non-System disk
000001B0: 6F 72 20 64 69 73 6B 20 - 65 72 72 6F 72 0D 0A 52   or disk error..R
000001C0: 65 70 6C 61 63 65 20 61 - 6E 64 20 70 72 65 73 73   eplace and press
000001D0: 20 61 6E 79 20 6B 65 79 - 20 77 68 65 6E 20 72 65    any key when re
000001E0: 61 64 79 0D 0A 00 49 4F - 20 20 20 20 20 20 53 59   ady...IO      SY
000001F0: 53 4D 53 44 4F 53 20 20 - 20 53 59 53 00 00 55 AA   SMSDOS   SYS..U.
```

There are several obvious things that looking at this boot record tells you. The error messages and the names of the two DOS system files (IO.SYS and MSDOS.SYS) give you an idea of some of the things that can go wrong during the boot process and also indirectly tell you that the boot program checks for these two names in the disk directory to see that it is a system disk. The DOS version marker at the beginning of the record is just the first element in a table that describes the characteristics of the disk to DOS. The table includes key information, such as the number of bytes per sector, sectors per track, and so on (the physical dimensions of the disk) as well as the size of the FAT and directory (the logical dimensions of the DOS structure on the disk). This table and an identifying signature at the end of the record (hex 55 AA) are included on all disks except those formatted for versions of DOS earlier than 2.0.

DOS must identify all the characteristics of each disk with which it works. In the earliest DOS versions, when there were only a few disk formats, knowledge of those characteristics was built into DOS, and all DOS needed from a disk was a single-byte ID code (which was stored in the FAT) to know everything it needed to about a disk. Now that approach isn't really flexible enough, so DOS learns what it needs to know about a disk from the information table in the boot record.

If you want to decode the boot program to study it, you can use DEBUG's U (Unassemble) command. To see all of it, you have to unassemble it in pieces and look to the addresses used in any jump commands to see where other parts of the program code begin. For the boot record shown above, the following two commands get you started:

```
U 0 L 2
U 3E
```

# The File Allocation Table (FAT)

Immediately following the boot record on each disk is the FAT, which controls the use of file space on the disk. As discussed in Chapter 6, the data portion of a disk is divided into clusters of segments, and the clusters are the units of space that are allocated to files. Each cluster is identified by a sequential number, beginning with 2 for the first cluster on a disk (clusters 0 and 1 are reserved for DOS). Regardless of the cluster size (which can be as little as 1 sector for a low-capacity disk to as much as 64 sectors for a 2GB hard disk), each cluster has an entry in the FAT that records its status.

Because what's stored in each cluster's FAT entry is the ID number of another cluster, the total number of clusters identifies how large a FAT entry needs to be. Originally, the FAT entries were stored as 12-bit numbers, which could accommodate numbers as large as 4KB and set a limit of about 4,000 on the possible number of clusters. However, today's hard disks may have many thousands of clusters, depending on how they are designed. This requires a larger 16-bit FAT design. The way the FAT is used is the same for both sizes.

If a FAT entry is 0, that indicates that the corresponding cluster is not in use and is free for allocation to any file that needs it; 1 is reserved for a technical reason. For clusters that hold data, the FAT entry contains either the ID number of the next cluster or a special number that marks the end of a file's space allocation chain. The clusters in which a file is stored are chained together by the numeric links stored in the FAT. The file's directory entry indicates the first cluster number, and each cluster points to the next cluster or indicates the end of the chain. (The end marker is hex FFF for a 12-bit FAT and FFFF for a 16-bit FAT.) This enables DOS to trace the location of a file's data from front to back. Portions of a disk that are defective and shouldn't be used—bad track areas—are identified by a FAT entry of FF7 for a 12-bit FAT or FFF7 for a 16-bit FAT. Other special FAT codes, FF0 through FFF (12-bit FAT) and FFF0 through FFFF (16-bit FAT), are reserved for needs that may arise in the future. (Except, of course, FF7 and FFF7 which already are in use.)

Note that the special FAT codes are kept to the 16 highest values (for either FAT format). This is so that there are as many usable cluster numbers as possible—up to 4,078 for 12-bit FATs and 65,518 for 16-bit FATs.

Although both 12- and 16-bit FATs are used in the same way, each is recorded in its own way to take account of the difference in the size of the entry. There's nothing special about how a 16-bit FAT is stored; 16-bit numbers are part of the PC's natural scheme, so the numbers in a 16-bit FAT simply are stored as a list of 2-byte words. For 12-bit FATs, things were more complicated. The PC's processors don't have any natural and convenient way to record numbers that are 1.5 bytes long. To deal with this problem, the FAT entries were paired, so that two FAT entries took up 3 bytes. The method of coding two 12-bit numbers in 3 bytes was set up to be as convenient as possible to handle with assembly language instructions, but it's rather difficult to understand if you look at the hex coding for this kind of FAT.

Each FAT begins with the entry for cluster 0, even though the first actual cluster is number 2. The first two FAT entries are dummies and are used to provide a place to store an ID byte that helps DOS identify the disk format. The very first byte of the FAT contains this code. For example, the hex code F8 identifies a hard disk.

To help safeguard the FAT, DOS records more than one copy. The two copies are stored one right after the other. From time to time, DOS checks one FAT against the other, making sure that they are identical. If they are not, DOS knows an error has occurred.

# The Root Directory

The final element of the system portion of each disk is the root directory, which is stored immediately following the FATs. The directory works as a simple table of 32-byte entries that describe the files (and other directory entries such as a volume label) on the disk.

The directory entries record, as noted in Chapter 6, the 8-byte filename, the 3-byte filename extension, the size of the file, the date and time stamp, the starting cluster number of the file, and the file attribute codes. There are also unused bytes in each directory entry that can be used for future needs. There are many interesting things to discover in these directory entries. For example, there are two special codes in the filename field that are used in the first byte of the filename. If this byte is 0, it indicates that the directory entry (and any following entries in this directory) has never been used; this gives DOS a way of knowing when it has seen all the active entries in a directory without having to search to the end.

Another code, hex E5, is used to mark entries that have been erased. That's why, when you work with erased files (using my UnErase program or a similar utility), you don't see the first character of the erased file's name. When a file is erased, the first character of the filename is overwritten with this hex E5 erasure code. Incidentally, when a file is erased (or a subdirectory removed), nothing else in the directory entry is changed; all the information is retained. The only thing that happens when a file is erased is that the filename is marked as erased, and the file's space allocation in the FAT is released.

There's one more special and interesting thing to know about the filename and extension fields. For files and subdirectories, these two are treated as separate fields. But, when a directory entry is used as a disk's volume label, the two together are treated as a single 11-character field. When a disk's volume label is displayed (as it is by the DIR, CHKDSK, and VOL commands), the label isn't punctuated with a period the way filenames are.

The size of each file is stored in the file's directory entry as a 4-byte integer, which accommodates file sizes much larger than any disk you could use. This guarantees that files won't be limited by the size that can be recorded in the file directory. Incidentally, the file size is recorded only for true files. Other types of directory entries have their file size entered as zero. That makes sense for the directory entry, which serves as a volume label, but is a little surprising for subdirectories. Even though subdirectories are stored in the data portion of a disk the same way files are and even though a subdirectory has a size, it's not recorded in the subdirectory's directory entry.

The date and time stamp in each directory entry is formatted in a way that can record any date from January 1, 1980 to the end of 2099; the time stamp records times to an accuracy of two seconds, although DOS only displays the time to the minute. The date and the time are recorded separately in two adjacent 16-bit words, and each is coded according to its own formula. However, the way they are stored enables the two to be treated as a single 4-byte field that can be compared in a single assembly language instruction to learn if one stamp is earlier or later than another. The date is coded by the following formula:

```
date = day + 32 × month + 512 × (year  1980)
```

The time is coded by this formula:

```
time = seconds/2 + 32 × minutes + 1,024 × hours
```

The final item of interest in a directory entry is the file attribute byte. This byte is treated as a collection of eight flags, each controlled by a single bit. Six of the eight are currently in use, while the other two are available for future use. Two of the six attribute bits are special and are used by themselves without any other bits set. One marks a disk's volume label directory entry; the other marks a subdirectory entry, so DOS knows to treat it as a subdirectory and not as a file. The other four attributes are used to mark files and can be set in any combination. One marks a file as read-only, not to be modified or erased; another marks a file as having been changed. This is used by back-up software to indicate which files need to be backed up.

The final two attributes, called hidden and system, are used to make a file invisible to most DOS commands. There is essentially no difference between hidden and system status. The two DOS system files that are on every bootable system disk are both marked as hidden and system. As an interesting oddity, hidden and system files are invisible to the DOS commands DIR, COPY, and DEL, but are seen by the TYPE command; you can verify that by entering the following command on a system disk:

```
TYPE MSDOS.SYS
```

However, beginning with DOS 5.0, you can use DIR with the /A (Attribute) option to display hidden and system files. Hidden files also are seen by the CHKDSK command when you use the /V option, which tells CHKDSK to display the name of every file along with the directory in which it resides.

Like the other elements of the system portion of a disk, the root directory has a fixed size for each disk, so DOS knows exactly where to find the beginning of the directory and the beginning of the data area that follows it. This means that the root directory can hold only so many entries, which is a rigid limit. Subdirectories, on the other hand, don't have that problem. While subdirectories work in essentially the same way that the root directory does, they are stored in the data portion of the disk just as though they were ordinary files and can grow to any size that the disk can accommodate. Using subdirectories, which were introduced with DOS Version 2.0, avoids any arbitrary limit on the number of files a disk can hold.

As I mentioned, each particular disk format uses a fixed size for each element of the system area. The boot record is always 1 sector. The size of the FAT (file allocation table) varies. For example, on a 3.5-inch, 1.44MB disk, each of the two FATs occupies 9 sectors; on a large hard disk, each FAT can use up to 256 sectors. The size of the root directory also varies.

If you have the Norton Utilities, you can use the System Information (SYSINFO) program to check out the size of each part of the disk. An example of this information (from the NU program) for a standard 1.44MB disk is listed below:

```
[]                         NU 8.0 System Information
    File  System  Disks  Memory  Benchmarks  Help

                          Disk Characteristics

  _
  _ + Logical Characteristics ------------------------------+  +--------+ _
  _ _ Bytes per Sector:   512      Sectors per cluster: 1    _ _  A:     _ _
  _ _ Number of Clusters: 2,847                              _ _  B:     _ _
  _ _ Number of FAT's:    2       FAT type: 12-bit           _ _  C:     _ _
  _ _ Media Descriptor Byte: F0 Hex                          _ _  D:     _ _
  _ _                                                        _ _         _ _
  _ _ FAT Start Sector:      1     Sectors Occupied 18       _  +--------+ _
  _ _ Root Dir Start Sector: 19    Sectors Occupied 14       _  + Size -+ _
  _ _ Data Start Sector:     33    Sectors Occupied 2,847    _ _        _ _
  _ _                                                        _ _ 1.44M  _ _
  _ +--------------------------------------------------------+  +------+ _
  _ + Physical Characteristics ------------------------------------------+ _
```

```
_ _  Sides: 2      Tracks: 80     Sectors per Track: 18              _  _
_ _  Drive Number: 0  Hex                                            _  _
_ _  Model: Unknown                                                  _  _
_ +--------------------------------------------------------------+   _
_                 Next      _   Previous   _    Print         _      _
_              _____    _____     _____            _
+----------------------------------------------------------------+
```

# Data Storage Area

The final and largest part of each disk is the data space. As you can imagine, there aren't quite as many fascinating details to discover about this part compared with the system part of the disk. You know your file data can have any length, but the file data always is stored in complete 512-byte disk sectors, and the sectors are allocated to files in complete clusters. Because of this, there usually is some unused space in the last sector of a data file and there may even be completely unused sectors at the end of the last cluster.

When DOS writes data to a disk, it doesn't clean up any data that may have been previously recorded. Thus, slack space in the new data file can contain pieces of whatever was stored earlier in a sector or cluster. If you inspect the slack area at the end of a file, you can find odds and ends of previous files stored there.

# Some Things to Think About or Try

1. Can you explain why the size of a DOS partition on a hard disk can't be changed without reformatting it? Is it possible to write a conversion program that can resize a partition? Describe the steps that would be involved.

2. Using the techniques described, inspect a boot record from one of your disks, and compare it with the one shown. Then, using the U (Unassemble) command of DEBUG, get an assembly language listing of the boot program and discover how it works.

3. For every disk format that your computer handles—high-capacity, low-capacity, etc.— format a disk with the DOS system files and then inspect the disk to see what the differences are in the boot record and other elements.

4. If you have the Norton Utilities, use the Disk Editor program to inspect the slack area at the end of your disk files. Select a file, display it, and then press the End key to jump to the end of the file. What do you see? What do your findings imply to you about the security of data you have deleted from a disk, even if you think you have over-written the erased data?

# 8

# Disk Utilities

I wouldn't have spent so much time describing disk drives and how they work if I didn't believe you have a lot to gain by knowing about this topic. After all, you can spend a lot of time, energy, and money understanding how the processor works, learning about how the computer uses memory, and procuring the best and fastest machine available, but if you can't store information safely, use it when you need it, and recover data if something goes wrong, then everything else is a waste.

In this chapter, I tell you about some important software utilities and procedures you can use to keep your hard disk in good shape and to get the most out of it.

This isn't a sales guide because there simply are too many software programs out there for me to know about them all; there isn't even room in this book to tell you about all the ones I do know. What you will find here, however, will make you aware of some of the software available to help you manage your disks, give you a basic understanding of how they work, and let you know some of the pros and cons of using them. That way, you'll be ready to head off on your own for some investigation and research, if necessary.

The three main areas I discuss in this chapter are disk compression utilities, disk optimizers, and disk troubleshooting utilities. I already have mentioned my Norton Utilities package several times, and I recommend it to you again here. It is a comprehensive collection of disk inspection and error recovery that most users find indispensable. Obviously, there are other software utilities that you also may need. I talk about them in this chapter—by type, not by name—so you at least know what to look for.

# Disk Compression

If you have ever purchased a new, larger disk drive in the hopes of finding enough storage for all those programs and data files you needed a place to put, only to run out of room on the new drive, then you are a candidate for disk compression or disk doubler software.

Many companies offer these utilities, not the least of which is Microsoft with its DOS 6.22. I'll tell you briefly how Microsoft goes about achieving disk compression in a moment. First, I explain about the two sides of disk compression: the good and bad, the Dr. Jekyll and Mr. Hyde.

As I mentioned, disk compression software can help you solve the never-ending problem of running out of room on your hard drive. You can't just keep adding more space forever, of course, but with a good disk compressor, you can generally double your amount of available space without buying another hard drive.

The technology of disk doubling is quite complex. A detailed explanation is well beyond the scope of this book. However, in general, here's how it works.

Nearly every file you store on disk—data and programs alike—contains a lot of redundant information. Data files, particularly, may be full of blank spaces or information that is repeated over and over. You can see this concept by looking at a color computer screen. What is the background color?

A dark blue, perhaps? Suppose that you were going to store the screen you're looking at as a data file, recording every piece of information faithfully to disk.

Can you see that the number of instructions for dark blue background dots is quite large, one for every location on the screen? If you have a 1,024×768 display, and every position is filled with a blue dot, that's a lot of dots. In fact, it's 786,432 dots! Blue, blue, blue, blue, and so on, and so on.

Now, suppose that you were to use a data compression utility to store the same information. The utility software looks at the data and notices that there are many blue dots. Sensibly, the software says, "Why not just store the idea of a blue dot once, and then store some information about how many more blue dots are needed?" In fact, that's what compression utilities do with the data they compress, whether the data is display information or text. Any time a file contains repetitive, re-dundant information, the software stores the repeated data once and notes how many times the information should be repeated.

To install such a utility, you need enough space on your hard drive for "scratch pad" work so that the software can inspect existing data, have room to work on it, and have room to move informa-tion around as it works with your drive. As you can imagine, if you have a couple of hundred mega-bytes of data already on a hard drive, it can take some time for the compression utility to scan all this data, decide how to compress it, and store it away on the disk in a new format. How much time isn't too relevant, however, because you can't use your machine for anything else while it is doing this. This particular task is the sort of thing that you set in motion and go to lunch or home for the evening. You'll find your disk storage nearly doubled in size when you return.

I've used several of these utilities at one time or another. It truly is amazing to run a piece of software and then discover when you issue the DIR or SCANDISK (or CHKDSK) command that you have about twice the free space you had before running the software. That's the good news.

In addition to the fact that you effectively can double your disk space, there is another good side. Because the data is compressed into half the normal space—yet the rotational speed of your disk drive hasn't changed—you can read and write data noticeably faster with most compression soft-ware than you can without it. The improvement isn't twice as fast because there is some overhead in compressing and decompressing the information on the fly as you use it. A RAM-resident driver, however, usually can perform these conversion functions much faster than your drive can read or write uncompressed data. Thus, the overall result is an improvement in read/write speed with data compression software.

The bad news is that after the information on your disk is compressed in this way, neither DOS nor any other application that uses DOS or reads and writes directly to the drive can make heads nor tails out of it. So, after compressing a disk in this way, you always must run a device driver (as I mentioned in the previous paragraph) when you boot your system. This memory-resident software grabs any software calls to the disk drive, interprets the request to read or write information, and puts its own "spin" on the request.

If DOS or another program asks for something from the compressed disk, the utility finds it on the disk and then decompresses it before passing it to the requesting program. If a program writes something to the disk, the driver grabs the write request and scans the data to remove as much redundant information as it can before storing the information to disk. In this way, anything you write to the disk, from word processor and spreadsheet data files to new programs you install, first goes through the compression routine so that you can continue to store about twice as much information as you could without a compression utility.

The reason this is bad news is that, because this utility must always run for you to access compressed data, it takes up memory, either conventional or high memory. It also is bad news that you have to preread and prewrite data in this way. And, depending on how sophisticated the program you're using is, it may put an additional burden on you as you maintain your disk drive. Certain types of compression utilities don't allow you to use some of the tried-and-true utility software you have become accustomed to. You may have to use utilities (provided by the compression software company) especially designed to work with compressed data.

Is there anything else wrong with data compression? That depends on several factors, including which compression utility you are using, what other software you are using, what hardware you have, what operating environment you are using, and so on.

At the theory level, there should be no problem with data compression. The software takes out unnecessary information before the data is stored to disk, carefully remembering how it did so, and then reverses the process when you want to read the compressed data. That's the ideal situation.

The real world of computers is different from the ideal, as you probably already know. Why? People and machines do things the software designer didn't expect, unforeseen events occur, and errors occur. This was demonstrated graphically when Microsoft released DOS 6.0 with an integral disk compression utility.

In theory, bundling compression software with DOS made a lot of sense. Properly done, this approach could remove the objections and potential traps of on-the-fly data compression because the compression utility would be tightly coupled with the operating system. Unfortunately for Microsoft, this wasn't the case with the initial release of DoubleSpace, their DOS compression utility. Many people who upgraded from previous versions of DOS to DOS 6 and used DoubleSpace experienced problems ranging from software incompatibility to lost data.

It is unfortunate, but this early experience probably gave data compression in general a bad name, and it took a little while for the reputation of compression software to recover from that. Today, however, most people do compress the data on their hard disks, and the new DriveSpace program (which replaced DoubleSpace, and which is a part of DOS 6.22 and later versions) has been carefully rewritten. While DriveSpace does still eat up a chunk of available memory (39K in my case), the problems of the first version of DoubleSpace are a thing of the past. (It should be noted that DoubleSpace had new technology added to it—DoubleGuard—in DOS 6.2, so the DoubleSpace program, running under DOS 6.2 and later, is safe to use. DriveSpace simply offers some additional functionality.) I have, as I said, used a couple of these compression utilities on perhaps five or eight machines and, aside from an occasional inconvenience (which I describe in more detail in a moment), I never had any problems with the software.

> **Technical Note:** You should know that if you put files that are already compressed, as is the case with many graphics formats, onto a compressed disk, the disk compression software will try to double-compress the data. Ironically, this attempt to compress what is already compressed can actually increase the amount of disk space required by the file. If you have a lot of graphic files or similarly precompressed files (like .ZIP files), you may want to keep them on an uncompressed drive to minimize this problem.

# Disk Optimizers

A disk optimizer is one class of disk utility that you should definitely have. This is a relatively broad type of software that can include a variety of features and functions. In general, disk optimizers are designed to handle some or all (and perhaps more) of the following functions:

- Defragmenting your disk
- Physically rearranging the files on your disk
- Locating and marking bad storage locations
- Determining and setting the optimum disk interleave factor
- Providing disk read/write cache

I discuss each of these features in the following sections.

# Defragmenting Your Disks

Disk fragmentation occurs after DOS has written different versions of your files several times. When you first create a file, all the information in it is stored end to end in contiguous disk locations. Using letters to symbolize files, this looks something like:

AAAAAAAAAABBBBBBBBBB

If you create another file, either as data for an application or by installing a new program, this file starts right after the previous file on the disk and stores all its information contiguously as well (the "B's" in the example, above). If you go back to the first file—let's say it's a word processor document—and add several pages to it, when you store it, the entire file no longer fits in one place because you have stored another file behind it. In this case, DOS leaves the old piece of the file where it was and stores the rest of the file in the next available open space, which is at the end of the second file you saved. Using letters again, this looks something like:

AAAAAAAAAABBBBBBBBBBBAAA

If you add some data to file B and save it back to disk, the two files are stored like this:

AAAAAAAAAABBBBBBBBBBBAAABBB

This is what happens, not with two files, but with hundreds on your disks. As you can see, over time your disk will look more like a pot of spaghetti someone dropped on the floor than an orderly arrangement of data files. Because you can't see the data on the disk, you don't personally care about the appearance, but it is a problem for DOS, nevertheless. Each time DOS loads one of these fragmented files, it has to move the drive's read head several times, perhaps jumping to wildly separated locations on the disk. This means that data retrieval can become extremely slow.

That's why you need to run a defragmenter utility on a regular basis. These programs scan the directory and FAT entries to determine which files are fragmented and then rewrite the files in new locations keeping them together. You should notice a definite improvement in disk performance when you clean up a heavily fragmented disk.

**Technical Note:** If you have an older hard disk with an interleave factor of anything other than one, the defragmenting utility will organize your files so that the data are located in sequentially-*accessed* sectors, which may not be physically sequential sectors. For example, on a drive with an interleave of 3, "defragmented" files will actually be placed on disk with each file's data located in every third physical sector. (For more on disk interleave, read on.)

Another benefit to using most of the defragmenter utilities is that, while they are scanning the disk and moving all this information around, they scan the disk surface looking for locations where data cannot be stored reliably. When a bad spot (usually called a bad "block") is found, the utility marks the spot in the FAT as questionable so that no new information will be written there.

# Physically Rearrange the Files on Your Disk

Individual file fragmenting is only one way your disk gets slowed down. Another way is when you load more than one file at a time and these files are widely separated on the disk. This separation happens naturally as you create and delete files or run defragmenter utilities. It is better to have related files physically stored together on the disk.

Sometimes you also may want the files to be stored on the disk in the order that they appear in the directory. This can be a convenience and also can be the way the computer uses the files, depending on your applications.

For whatever reason, you can store files in a sorted order or an order you specify with a utility designed to physically move files. Sometimes this is done as part of the defragmenting process, and sometimes it is done with a separate utility. Either way, it can take a long time if you have a large disk and haven't sorted files in this way in a long time. If you run the routine once a week or twice a month, however, it won't take too long, and you may notice benefits in improved computer performance.

## Locate and Mark Bad Storage Locations

I mentioned this service in the discussion of defragmenting utilities. Some defragmenters test the surface of the disk before writing any new data to it, even if something else is already stored there. Whether your defragmenter does or not, you should run a separate utility like SCANDISK, which is part of DOS 6.0 and later, to do a surface scan and test each storage location. You need to do this because if you write information to a portion of the disk that is not stable, you could lose that data. True, DOS handles this chore when you format the disk, but format markings fade over time, just like any other magnetic recording, and you may have several "faded" spots on your disk where data should not be placed, for fear of never seeing it again.

**Technical Note:** Prior to DOS 6.0, the CHKDSK utility was provided to serve the repair functions now performed by SCANDISK. SCANDISK is much more sophisticated in terms of its repair capabilities, and if you're used to using CHKDSK, you should really move up to SCANDISK. CHKDSK is still one of your best DOS tools, however, for obtaining information about your disks (SCANDISK does not provide this informative function.)

## Determine and Set the Optimum Disk Interleave Factor

If your hard disk was properly installed and configured in the first place, then you'll never need to reset the interleave factor. Similarly, if you have a hard disk that was manufactured after January 1994, you probably don't even need to think about your interleave factor, unless that disk is being installed into a very old machine, like a 286 or 386. This is because January 1994 is roughly the time at which computer processors were universally able to read and write data to hard disks at the speed required for an interleave factor of one. Previously, slower processors required that sectors be skipped — achieved with an interleave factor greater than one—so that the processor had time to "catch up" with the hard disk. If your disk drive is older than that date, or if you've upgraded your processor, there's a chance that you could speed up the operation of your hard disk considerably by correcting an interleave problem.

Disk interleave or "the interleave factor" is expressed as a ratio. It represents how many sectors your disk controller skips between each write operation. Information always is written to disk in multiples of whole sectors. This is because only so much memory is onboard the controller and inside your disk drive and because only so much data can be ready to write at any given time. Thus, the controller and disk work together to bundle up the information to be written to disk in a single operation. The bundle is sent to the disk read/write heads and recorded to disk.

Next, the electronics in the controller and disk have to fetch another cluster of information, send it down the wires to the read/write heads, and record it to disk. The hard disk platter, however, is spinning at least 3,600 RPM. Unless the electronic process is pretty quick, as it is with the combination of a newer computer and drive, a lot of blank disk has moved under the disk head before any data is ready to be recorded. The way around this problem is to specify how many sectors need to be skipped between writes to give the controller time to find the next block of data, format it, and get it to the drive's heads.

If the controller is fast (as most of them are today), then no sectors are skipped, and the disk interleave is 1:1. A 1:1 disk interleave means data can be written and read at disk speed without waiting for the controller to catch up. If one sector has to be skipped after each write, the interleave factor is 1:2 because every second sector is written. For a really slow controller, the interleave may be as much as 1:9.

Again, if the drive were configured properly in the first place, you shouldn't have to adjust the interleave, but it doesn't hurt to check—although checking can be one of those lengthy processes to start at night and let run until morning. A utility program that can check the interleave and adjust it if it isn't correct can improve disk performance. If you think you want to investigate your interleave factor, you can use the CALIBRATE program that is part of my Norton Utilities.

# Provide Disk Read/Write Cache

Even with the disk properly defragmented and the interleave properly set, the electronics inside your computer—the RAM, processor, and even disk controller card—are much faster than the physical drive. You simply can't read from and write to the disk as fast as the memory and the processor would like. Yet, if you could speed up read/write speed, the processor would be free quicker to go on about other duties.

That's where read/write cache comes in. A cache program does a couple of things to help speed up data transfer. First, a segment of memory, either part of system RAM or dedicated memory on the controller, is set aside to store temporarily the data going to and from the disk. With cache memory established, when you write data to the disk it goes first to the cache memory. This is all electronic, and no mechanical mechanisms are involved that slow down the process. Then, when the processor has time between other tasks, it can write the data to the physical disk.

The opposite happens during a read operation. Information coming off the disk is read first into temporary RAM, the read cache. In fact, more data than the calling program asked for is read into memory. Now, when a program asks for information, the cache memory is searched first. If the required information is there, it is sent along without the need to go to the physical disk. And, depending on the sophistication of the caching program, this routine may be able to teach itself about the applications running at any given time, predicting with increasing accuracy what the next requested information will be. That means that, as the predictions get more and more accurate, the program has to read from the physical disk drive fewer and fewer times.

If you have Windows 3.1 or later, you have a cache routine. In fact, you already may be using it. The SMARTDRV utility usually is installed automatically when you install Windows. Likewise, if you have DOS 5.0 or later, you have SMARTDRV, which you can elect to install, depending on your needs.

In general, disk-caching programs are a good thing, and I recommend that you use one. You should, however, be aware of several things. If you are using any type of high-density removable media, such as a SyQuest cartridge, make sure that your caching program can tell whether the disk has been swapped out. If your cache program doesn't recognize when you swap disks and then dumps the RAM buffer from the previous disk to a new disk, you will lose data.

Also, be aware of how your caching program handles file writes. If the writes are delayed (which they are in many cache programs to improve overall system performance), then you can't turn your computer off the moment you get a software indication that the write operation is complete. If you're working in DOS, for example, and save a file and exit the program, you might think it is safe to turn off the computer as soon as you see the DOS prompt. However, the cache buffer may still be full of the last data written, data that may not have gone to the disk. In this situation, you need to be aware of how long it takes to flush the write buffer and get in the habit of watching the disk drive light to make sure it has finished writing before turning your machine off or rebooting. Many hard drives also have their own buffer-memory which may be used for caching data. If power is lost before that buffer is written to disk, that data is similarly gone. Unfortunately, there is no prevention for this other than vigilance on your part and a backup power supply to protect against brown- or black-outs.

**Technical Note:** In the latest versions of SMARTDRV, Microsoft has greatly eliminated the danger of losing data in an unflushed cache by setting write-caching to "off" as the default. This means that all data is written directly to disk, and only reads are actually cached. However, in many circumstances, you may want to set SMARTDRV's caching to "on." If you do, the same concerns of data loss will apply to you as they did to everyone under older versions of SMARTDRV.

# Troubleshooting and Repair Tools

Troubleshooting and repair software is like fire insurance. It is the most useless thing in the world—that is, until you need it. Then there is no substitute for having the software you need. Obviously, you can't wait until you need it to buy it, either. You can't buy fire insurance after the fire starts, you can't buy health insurance after you get sick, and you can't wait to buy troubleshooting software until after you have an emergency.

The following sections highlight the features you can expect to find with this type of utility. (If you would like to have a more detailed understanding of these utilities than you find here, take a look at another of my books, *Peter Norton's Complete Guide to DOS 6.22*, from Sams. You'll find extensive technical and practical information about all of these tools there.)

# Unerase and Unformat Routines

These are some of the most useful utilities you'll ever own because they can frequently get your data back for you when you think it's been destroyed forever, either by being deleted or even because you've reformatted your hard disk.

Most undelete or unerase utilities work based on the fact that, when you normally "delete" something from your hard disk, your file isn't actually erased. Instead, changes are made in the disk's directory and FAT to indicate that the space occupied by the "deleted" file is now available to use. (Technically, only the first entry for the file is changed in the FAT...the chain of successive sectors used by the file remains intact.) Eventually, this space will be overwritten with new files. However, this overwriting doesn't usually happen immediately, and until it does, the "erased" files can usually be ressurrected.

Programs such as UNDELETE (which comes with DOS) and UNERASE (which is part of my Norton Utilities) can usually provide multiple levels of security against accidental erasures. At the simplest level, technically speaking, and the highest level in terms of security, the utility will install a memory resident program that creates a hidden subdirectory on your disk. When you "delete" files, they aren't deleted, but are simply moved to the hidden directory. If you decide you need one of those deleted files back, the utility simply displays a list of everything that has been moved to the invisible directory, you select your file, and back it comes. The downside of this technique, of course, is that you don't gain any free space on your disk when you delete files, since they're not actually deleted at all. You can specify the maximum amount of space for the hidden directory to use (up to 7 percent of your hard disk size with Microsoft's UNDELETE, for example). When that space is full, the oldest files in the directory will actually be erased to make room for new entries. If you install and uninstall a lot of software—for example, if you're trying out a lot of products like I do—this technique isn't particularly useful, because you'll quickly fill up the hidden directory with the thousands of uninstalled files that you generate. You cannot specify that certain types of files (like your word processor documents, for example) remain in the hidden directory longer than, say, Alien Zonko Blasters. When the directory is full, the oldest files get the axe. (Until that push-off happens, however, this level of protection is 100 percent sure, unless something goes wrong with your disk itself.)

Another level of security that utility software can provide causes the utility to maintain a list of all files that have been deleted, and their locations on disk. Once such a list exists, it's simple for the utility to keep track of which of the deleted files are still intact on your disk (that is, which ones haven't been overwritten yet) and if you need to "unerase" something, the utility will provide you with a list from which to choose. Such lists almost always include an assessment of how likely you are to find your deleted file in one piece, once the unerase process is complete. This protection level also involves a memory-resident program, but doesn't keep disk space "busy," like the first method I mentioned. Since files are actually deleted when you use this level of protection; it's not nearly as safe as the method I mentioned above.

A final level of protection isn't really any "protection" at all, in the strict sense of the word. At this level, the utility program doesn't do anything while you are normally using your computer. If you determine that a file has been accidentally erased, you can then run the utility that will search the entire disk's directory for deleted files. The actual unerasing process is no less reliable with this method than with the former method, but since the search process is not infallible, this method may be the least reliable, in practice.

Both the Norton Utilities and MS-DOS's UNDELETE provide all three levels of protection. For PowerUsers, the Norton Utilities also provides you with significant additional functionality through a "Manual Unerase" tool, which allows you to scan through your entire hard disk and manually re-assemble data files which are otherwise unrecoverable.

# Finding Lost or Misnamed Files

Both the Norton Commander and the Norton Utilities provide excellent tools that enable you to locate files you may have misplaced, or whose names you have forgotten. With either utility, you can search for files containing certain data that you define, whether you know any portion of the file's name or not. You can also search your disks for files which have names that match a certain criteria you select. For example, I could easily quickly search through all of my hard disks to find any file that contains the name "Scott," and I could similarly look for any file that has a name starting with the letter "S," or that is an ".EXE" file, and so on.

Additionally, the FINDFILE program in the Norton Utilities enables you to search for files created before or after certain dates you select, files of a certain size, files with certain file attributes set (such as "HIDDEN" or "ARCHIVE"), and even files on a network drive that are owned by an individual whom you select.

MS-DOS itself does not include any advanced file-search function of this sort, nor does it enable you to search for filenames you have forgotten, unless you know some of the file's content. DOS does enable you to search for data files that contain a text-string that you specify.

# Memory Testing and Reporting

Several utilities exist that provide a variety of information about your computer's use of its memory. The simplest of these is the MEM program, which is part of DOS. MEM can either provide you with a quick rundown of how much of each type of memory (conventional, high, and so on) is in use or is free, or, by using MEM with the /C switch, you can obtain a complete list of memory-resident programs that are loaded, and find out how much of each conventional and high memory each program is using.

The MSD (Microsoft Diagnostics) program that comes with Microsoft DOS and Microsoft Windows can give you a great deal more technical information about memory usage, as well as semigraphical representations of that usage. Whether you'll find those last to be useful or not is something you'll have to decide for yourself. MSD was actually designed to aid Microsoft's technical support staff in sorting through problems you may be having with your system. It was not designed specifically to give you personal insight into the depths of your machine.

In contrast, the SYSINFO program that is part of the Norton Utilities can provide you with significantly more information than MEM or MSD, and—in my opinion, of course—it gives you much more intelligible explanations of how your memory is used than those you'll find in MSD.

# Backup

Everybody needs to back up data, although too few of us actually do it. If your hard disk crashes or if files are deleted when your granddaughter runs amok at the computer, a frequent backup will guarantee that you'll get your data back, safe and sound, and usually with much less hassle than other methods afford you.

However, data backup is a subject that could easily fill several chapters. In fact, it does exactly that in my *Peter Norton's DOS 6.22 Guide*, published by Sams. If you want a technically detailed understanding of the methods and available techniques of backup programs, that's the best place to look. For the time being, let me say that backup software—though some of the most important software you'll ever own—is traditionally some of the most unfriendly software you'll ever buy. This is changing a lot, and Norton Backup, for example, is strides beyond everything the market has previously seen. However, you should take the time to explore different backup programs before you select one. When you do buy, make sure that the program you want to use supports the backup media you also want to use. Some programs only support backing up to diskettes (MSBACKUP which comes with DOS and is actually a scaled-down version of Norton Backup, is one of these), while others only support certain types of tape, like QIC-80, but not SCSI DAT tapes.

My personal recommendation: don't buy any backup product that doesn't support DAT. You'll almost surely have a DAT drive at some point if you have a lot of data to backup. It's extremely cost-effective per megabyte, and is one of the most reliable methods of backup available.

# Virus Protection and Other Security Features

Like backup software, virus protection deserves a long discussion of its own. At this juncture, let me simply make you aware that software exists that can significantly diminish your chance of ever experiencing a viral infection of your computer. MSAV, or Microsoft Anti-Virus, comes with DOS 6.22, and Norton Anti-Virus is available as a stand-alone product. Both will install memory-resident programs that will watch out for and alert you to events in your system (such as protected files being modified) that look like a viral infection. Similarly, both will scan all of the files that are currently on your hard disk to verify that none of them currently contain any viruses that may just be waiting for the right moment to erase your hard disk forever.

Unlike MSAV, however, Norton Anti-Virus is a fully upgradable solution that can be modified simply to provide you with ongoing protection against new viruses as they are discovered. Viruses are really nothing more than bits of program code, and NAV has been designed to let you make it aware of new "signatures" or telltale code fragments that signify the presence of new infectious agents. These new agents can enter your system from a friend's floppy disk, or from a file you've downloaded from a BBS or an online service, or they can be placed on your computer intentionally by someone with malicious intent. Whatever the method of infection, the upgradability of NAV enables you to combat new viruses as they become known.

**Note:** It's very true, incidentally, that all reputable online services like America Online and Compuserve, and most BBSs, scan software for viruses before making available for downloading. However, a second check never hurts, especially as new virus signatures are becoming known every day... viruses that the online service's software might not have known how to check for. Additionally, it's unlikely that you'll obtain all of your new software from this kind of source, and even your best friend could have a virus hiding on his system. Indeed, the father of a friend of mine bought six new PCs from a reputable dealer, only to discover that the infamous Michelangelo virus was on every single one of these new machines! Clearly, something at the dealer had been infected and this infection was being spread to each new machine they sold. You really can't be too careful with your data.

With either of these programs, or with any other anti-virus program, if a virus is found or suspected, the utility will identify the offending file and recommend that you delete it and restore it from a backup. With viral infections, it is frequently not possible to extract the virus code from, say, the code of an infected word processor program. For that reason, backup is a vital part of your complete anti-virus process.

# System Speed Testing with SYSINFO

The SYSINFO program from Norton Utilities provides a large set of benchmark tests with which to compare the speed of various parts of your system with industry-standard hardware.

Additionally, SYSINFO (and MSD, also) can display and print information about the assignment of your system's interrupts, ports, types and sizes of disks installed, and additional information that can be crucial in helping you install new hardware or diagnose system problems.

With this discussion of common types of disk utilities, our coverage of your PC's basic disks is complete. The next two chapters explain two kinds of storage that were "less" basic until very recently: removable disk storage and optical storage.

# 9 Removable Storage

When hard disks first became popular, they did so for some very good reasons. One of the main reasons was the density of storage they offered. The only way, however, these drives could provide highly reliable, dense storage was to fix the read/write mechanism inside the drive and not enable the recording media to be removed from the drive.

It was this removing the media (usually along with the heads and other parts of the mechanical mechanism) that caused unreliable operation in previous removable rigid drives. When the fixed drive came along, users felt a new surge of confidence in the storage medium, so the limitation of not being able to remove the platters didn't seem particularly severe.

As drive technology advanced and users became accustomed to large amounts of storage, the desire to move back toward some form of removable medium was natural. After all, if 40MB of fixed storage was good, how much better it would be to have 40MB over and over again in the form of a removable disk?

To make a long story short, that's what happened over a period of years. Yes, there were times when the media weren't particularly reliable, but  today, several technologies exist for providing high-density, removable, and reliable storage. I discuss these technologies briefly in this chapter.

# Removable Disk Types

There have been a number of successful and not-so-successful removable disk designs over the years. For the most part, the PC world has settled on several drive types:

- Hard drives with removable rigid platters
- Floppy cartridge drives on which the read/write medium is soft instead of hard
- A variety of removable hard drives on which the entire drive mechanism, including read/ write heads, drive motors, and electronics slip in and out of a plug-in slot

Several designs exist in each of these broad categories, and a number of companies are competing for the top slot in each category. There are, however, some high-profile players already on the field.

# Hard Disks

Well over a decade ago, removable hard platter disks were the computing industry's standard. These were huge, 14-inch or larger cases with four or more platters inside a (sometimes) clear cylinder with a large twist-off lid that looked more like a giant Tupperware container than a computer component. These drives held between five and twenty megabytes (MB) of data. These were the disks of the day on minicomputers in the 1970s, but they were notoriously temperamental and prone to crashes. Nobody liked them, but they were the only way to achieve enough storage for office-based minicomputers that were doing such work as payroll, accounting, inventory, and billing. A different disk or set of disks was used for each task.

When hard disks came out for PCs, they were a sufficient revolution over the floppy disk that people naturally ignored the fact that they were not removable. As data storage needs increased—and, particularly, as the range of applications for which PCs were used increased—various companies started working on removable hard disk media. There were and are several brand names of drives with removable hard disk cartridges; however, they all are made by one or two major companies. Easily the most common end-user label is SyQuest. Originally available in 44MB capacities, SyQuest became the industry standard for moving data between applications like graphic design and service bureaus where such images are printed on high-quality printers. As industry demands for portable storage have grown, SyQuest cartridges have similarly increased in capacity, first to 88MB, then to 105 and, as of this writing, 270MB. The reliability of this technology —which is truly the same technology as is found in a nonremovable hard disk—has been refined and proven, particularly over the last five years when its popularity and capacity have both soared. In the early days of large removable drives, there were many stories of crashed drives and lost data. Today, even the worst drives have a mean time between failure (MTBF) of at least 30,000 hours, and some units report an MTBF of 150,000 hours or more. That's a rating of 3.5 years on the low end to 17 years on the high end. In fact, some manufacturers offer a 5-year warranty on the media itself, a long time in computer terms. This assumes normal usage. If you're looking for long-term archival storage, and assuming that you store the drives properly, the data should be quite safe indeed.

# "Soft" Disks

Several versions of the removable soft platter drive exist, but the most visible in the industry is the Bernoulli cartridge system from Iomega. This system uses cartridges with a floppy-type recording medium. Normally, you couldn't record multiple megabytes of data on a 3.5-inch floppy medium. Because of the way the cartridge is designed, however, the floppy becomes very rigid as it spins, enabling dense recording. These drives can hold up to 150MB on each cartridge. (See the discussion of Bernoulli technology later in this chapter.)

Floptical drives that use magnetic media and an optical-assisted positioning mechanism also are being offered. Although floptical drives haven't caught on like Bernoulli, they also are a viable technology. These drives can't hold as much data in a given floppy, and the hardware costs a little more than Bernoulli. I talk more about optical storage in the next chapter.

# PCMCIA Disks Revisited

Removable hard drives are probably the newest of the technologies and will likely be the one destined to see the broadest service. Removable hard drives are appearing in many laptop and notebook devices. These drives are extremely small and light, don't make much noise, have low power requirements, and can be pulled out of one machine and put into another.

Removable hard drives fit into at least two categories: those that slide into a proprietary disk cage or slot and those that use one of the newer PCMCIA external expansion slots. (For more information on PCMCIA, see the discussion in Chapter 2, "Hardware: The Parts of the PC.") PCMCIA has easily eclipsed proprietary implementations in terms of popularity and cost-efficiency.

If you are using a drive with a proprietary hardware interface, you have to buy all your drives from the same manufacturer. And, if you want to install a removable disk slot in your desktop machine to match your laptop, you have to purchase the same kind of cage or slot from the same company that made the one in your mobile computer. As you would expect in a market economy, such a lack of choices doesn't exactly help drive prices down.

If you're using PCMCIA disks, on the other hand, the theory is that one drive should be able to slide into any compatible slot. As this new technology was getting under way, there were some problems with compatibility, and a few drives simply wouldn't work properly outside their manufacturer's environment. This little unpleasantness was just early growing pains and is a thing of the past. Now, so long as you are attempting to put the drive into a properly configured slot—there are PCMCIA drives that fit into Type II, Type III, and Toshiba's extended Type IV slots—they will work with any computer system.

## PCMCIA Types

As conceivable applications for the tiny PCMCIA form-factor have evolved, so has the standard itself. Originally, only Type I cards existed. These are the smallest of the PCMCIA devices, not any bigger than three credit-cards stacked on top of each other. Because of their size, Type I cards are useful primarily for nonvolatile flash RAM. Type II cards, which are about twice as thick as Type I cards, are large enough to contain surface-mounted circuitry for applications as diverse as modems, pagers, network connections like ethernet, sound cards, and SCSI adapters. As the size of hard disks shrunk dramatically over the last few years, PCMCIA Type III cards have come into existence. These are approximately twice as thick as a Type II card, and have, to date, been used almost exclusively to contains hard disks with capacities up to 1GB. Type IV cards exist, and are even larger than Type III cards, but they are a technology that is proprietary to Toshiba, and are used exclusively, to date, for removable hard disks.

The PCMCIA adapter socket is a rather unique implementation. Only the very smallest of notebook computers actually comes equipped with a Type I socket. Instead, Type I and Type II cards both fit properly in a Type II socket. The Type II socket is spring-loaded and compresses slightly within the space of its frame to hold a Type I card snugly. When a Type II card is inserted, the same spring-loaded glides expand to accommodate the larger card. The Type III card is designed to fit in a set of two Type II sockets, and this is a very common PCMCIA configuration for all but the smallest of notebook computers. Type IV cards fit only inside a proprietary Type IV socket.

As an aside, I should mention that PCMCIA devices are now being commonly referred to as "PC-CARD" devices. "PCMCIA" was apparently too cumbersome to pronounce. If you see references to PC-CARD II, or PC-CARD III, youll know that this simply refers to PCMCIA devices of Type II and Type III, respectively.

Whatever the standard or size of your removable disk, the concept behind the technology is the same. A very small drive—frequently not much bigger than a credit card—slips into a hole in the case of your computer where it meets with a set of pins at the other end. Like plugging in an expansion card, you simply slide the drive into the case until it seats firmly, making power and data connections automatically. From that point, the disk operates as if it were a regular, hard-wired drive. The drive contains hardware that actually tells your computer about the capacity of the drive and other technical details, and so PCMCIA disks are actually self-configuring.

Removing the drive simply is the reverse. When you're ready to take the disk to another machine to exchange data, you simply pop the cover on the access door to the drive, pull a handle or press a lever that releases the drive, and pull it out of the slot. In most systems, PCMCIA drives are designed so that you don't even need to power-down your computer before inserting or removing these drives, although you obviously want to make sure the drive isn't in use at the time.

The first time you see one of these drives, you may think someone is playing a joke. PCMCIA drives are a lot tinier than most people expect. These very small drives can hold several hundred megabytes of information, yet several of them can fit easily in the palm of your hand. Additionally, many PCMCIA drives come preloaded with compression software, effectively increasing their storage capacity by as much as a factor of two.

These tiny wonders are moving out of the mobile-only environment and showing up on desktop machines. Why not? They offer capacity similar to larger, hard-wired units, are smaller and lighter, require less power, and pop in and out as needed for information interchange or security purposes. The only downsize, at present, to the use of PCMCIA drives in desktop units is that, since this particular implementation is a new one, the desktop PCMCIA drive base units (which may be internal or external boxes) are relatively expensive. As more and more users own both a portable and desktop system and demand the ability to move data painlessly between these systems, desktop PCMCIA implementations should become as inexpensive as tape backup devices.

# Removable Storage: Real-Life Implications

The advantages to removable storage are probably obvious to you. The most obvious advantage is the capability to use one piece of hardware for multiple blocks of storage. In the case of cartridge systems like SyQuest-compatible drives, you pay once for the drive electronics, read/write heads, motors, and so on, and then can build the system to an unlimited amount of storage simply by adding new cartridges or disks. With PCMCIA systems, you are buying all of the drive hardware with each disk that you buy, but market demand and miniaturization have made these very economically sound purchases.

Security is another obvious advantage. If you record sensitive data on a removable disk, you can take it out of the machine and lock it up in a secure place. Then, the chances of someone making off with your information are very slim, indeed. In fact, this is a popular application in military and industrial research circles. The Bernoulli and SyQuest drives are particularly popular because of the high-density storage they offer compared with the cost of the storage media.

You can use removable media to exchange data or whole software systems among different machines. I like to use some type of removable device to store installed software applications that I don't use very often, but which I need to be able to access. I can install the software, create any data files I need, and then put the disk away on a shelf until I need that particular package again. That way, I don't take up conventional hard disk space for an application that I rarely use, yet I have it when I need it.

Removable hard disks can be useful for backup as well. If you have very large systems, you can compress the data or use backup utilities and still place the information on a removable disk to cut down the number of disks required as compared with backing up to floppies. With smaller systems, you can treat backup as I just described for infrequently used applications. Simply dedicate an entire disk—80, 150, or even 270MB—to a single application and copy the whole thing and its data files to the removable media. Now you have a backup that is more than a backup, it is also a working system. In the event that you need the backup, you don't have to copy it over to your regular hard disk because it is usable directly from the backup medium.

There are a few disadvantages to using removable media, but only a few. Still, you should be aware of them so that you aren't surprised as you try to use the technology.

For one thing, with today's technology the basic removable drive—the base unit—costs more than a comparable fixed disk. That's because the removable part of the design adds complications and hardware to the basic disk. As you add more storage to the basic disk mechanism, however, the price falls fairly quickly. A basic SyQuest 270MB cartridge may cost only $70 through discount channels, for example. That's fairly cheap storage.

With most removable cartridge systems (not systems on which the entire drive is removable), you must run driver software so that DOS recognizes the drive. This requires another level of concern during system configuration and use, and these drivers use some of your available RAM.

Moreover, not all disk-caching software recognizes when a removable hard drive cartridge has been taken out of the drive. If you cache a removable drive with software that doesn't know when you've swapped disks, you could lose a whole platter's worth of data by swapping disks before the cache software has flushed the RAM buffer. The answer to this problem is to make sure that your caching software can recognize disk swaps or simply to turn off caching for that drive.

Depending on how you look at it, the required interface for removable drives may be a problem. By far the majority of removable storage units I know about on desktop machines use some variant of the SCSI interface standard. If you already have a SCSI interface installed, then this is not a disadvantage. If, on the other hand, you have to purchase a separate SCSI interface to use the removable drive, that raises the cost, requires another slot in your machine, and gives you one more device— the SCSI interface card—to install and configure.

In general, however, SCSI is an excellent technology and is becoming more and more popular in PCs as more drives use it. Scanners, for example, almost always use SCSI interfaces, and with the rise in popularity of removable drives requiring SCSI, you will see this high-speed interface showing up on more PCs in the future.

# Removable Disk Technology

Removable technology matches the drive types I discussed earlier in this chapter: removable hard platters, removable soft platters, and removable drives. As I already mentioned briefly, there are also optical technologies, which I talk about in the next chapter. For now, I look a little more closely at each of the conventional removable technologies.

# Removable Hard Platters

At first look, a removable hard platter probably seems like the most reasonable solution to the removable media problem. After all, it was the first technology used by minicomputers, is well understood, and is accepted by the user community. In fact, it does work well and is a reasonable solution for many users.

Although they are marketed under different labels, today the majority of removable hard platter devices are manufactured by either SyQuest or Ricoh. For a long time, the standby standard for removable hard drives was the Sequester/Ricoh 44MB cartridge, which was about the size of a 5.25-inch floppy disk, except that it was 0.5 inches thick. Today, that same SyQuest drive may store six times as much data and many capacities fit in a 3.5-inch form factor.

Whether the drive is sealed or uses removable media, a hard disk is composed of certain basic components:

- Rigid disks with magnetic media for data storage
- Read/write heads, usually one per surface
- Head movement mechanics
- Electronic interface between the heads and the computer interface
- A computer interface/controller
- One or more cables between the drive and computer

With current removable cartridge technology, the design is limited to only a single platter. With fixed devices—and with PCMCIA drives—there may be two, four, or more platters; the more platters or disks, the more information a given drive can store.

The SyQuest design places very lightweight read/write heads above and below the spinning medium, floating on a cushion of air. Current drives can store up to 270MB, but the newer drives also are designed to read older 44MB and 88MB cartridges.

Some users I've talked to about this technology have expressed concern over the integrity of data stored on a removable cartridge. However, from what I can determine, these drives are very reliable. It is true that some of the very early cartridge units had some reliability problems, but that was years ago.

Today's devices use essentially the same technology as conventional hard disks. The biggest weakness, I believe, is the potential for damaging the plastic case that encloses each cartridge. If the case is damaged, the platter might not rotate properly. The media, however, is no more susceptible to damage than a floppy disk and, because it is enclosed in stronger plastic, maybe even less so.

Even early SyQuest cartridges were certified for a 36-inch drop onto a hard surface. According to the company, the case shouldn't break and there should be no internal damage in a drop from this height. Although the cartridge actually may withstand much more abuse, the company doesn't guarantee it beyond that. This is, however, a pretty liberal rating. If you keep the cartridges in their soft plastic storage boxes when they aren't in use, then dropping them, shipping them, and any other normal wear and tear should be no problem.

One of the technical factors that makes these drives reliable is that the majority of the drive mechanism stays with the drive. Earlier designs removed the read/write heads and the positioning mechanics with the platters. Thus, when one of these cartridges was dropped, there was much greater potential for damage caused by misalignment.

# Removable Soft Platters

High-density floppy cartridges use either a magneto-optical technology or a Bernoulli technology. I talk about optical drives in the next chapter.

The Bernoulli principle was first defined in the mid-1700s by Swiss mathematician Daniel Bernoulli, a specialist in hydrodynamic principles, calculus, and probability. The basic Bernoulli principle states that the higher the speed of a flowing fluid or gas, the lower the pressure. Conversely, as speed decreases, pressure increases.

This principle explains the lift of an airplane wing, among other things. An airplane flies because the wing is shaped to force air to travel faster across the top of the surface than it does underneath. This pressure differential exerts an upward force.

The Bernoulli cartridge from Iomega Corporation, shown in Figure 9.1, functions in this way. The Iomega box basically uses floppy disks that can store large amounts of information because they become semirigid in operation.

When the floppy disk spins rapidly inside a properly designed enclosure, the medium "flies," forming a reliable surface for high-density storage. In the Iomega design, the Bernoulli effect is caused by a rigid plate on top of the flexible medium. Air flowing between the plate and the medium causes the floppy disk to rise toward the plate. A read/write head protrudes through the plate, causing an even stronger and local Bernoulli effect, pulling the medium at the point very close to the head.

The disk is stabilized in 10 millionths of an inch of the head, which is even closer than standard hard disk tolerances. The read/write head does not actually touch the storage medium.

One of the advantages of this design is that the read/write head is on top of the medium. When the disk spins down, the floppy medium falls away from the head. There is no need for a special landing zone on the disk, nor is there a chance of a head crash in the event of mechanical or power failure.

Current Bernoulli boxes store from 35 to 150MB on each cartridge; 3.5- and 5.25-inch cartridges are available. One advantage to the Bernoulli design is the ruggedness of the cartridge. Because the storage medium is soft when at rest, the cartridge can withstand a lot of abuse without compromising data integrity.

## Removable Drives

There's not much to be said for removable drives except that they have gotten smaller and smaller over the past few years. Inside, these drives are much like any conventional hard disk. The newest designs have some advantages over older drives manufactured just two or three years ago. They contain extremely lightweight components, such as read/write heads, making them quick and reliable. In addition, many of them use the new 3.3-volt power supplies that are becoming common in mobile and "green" computers. Together, these features mean that they run quietly, use a relatively small amount of energy, and are extremely tolerant of shock and other abuse, making them reliable. And, prices are less than you may think for this technology.

# Some Things to Think About or Try

1. Removable technology of one kind or another can be a good primary or secondary storage choice for most users. One application is when your present storage needs are modest, 100MB or so, but you know that through data acquisition over the next months or years, you will need 1GB or more of storage.

   Suppose that this is your situation. How many removable cartridges that store 88MB would be required? What if you are using 270MB cartridges? You might need to know what the relative costs are of purchasing 1GB drive or of spreading the costs over several months by purchasing cartridges or removable drives. Many users compare prices by computing cost per megabyte. If the basic drive mechanism costs $525 and each 270MB cartridge is $64, what is the total per-megabyte cost of a 1GB drive? How does this compare with a 1GB hard drive that costs $700?

2. Consider your computing situation. How could removable technology fit into what you are doing? Would it save time or change the way you handle any of your computing chores? What about cost? Could changing at least some of your storage to removable media reduce costs in any area?

   If you use both a desktop and a notebook system and are used to copying data between them via floppies or a cable, compare that experience with the idea of using removable PCMCIA hard disks in both of your systems.

3.  Think about the technologies I've described in this chapter. What are the relative benefits
    of each one? Can you think of one technological advantage to Bernoulli technology?
    Under what sorts of circumstances would you choose a removable drive over a removable
    cartridge system?

# 10

# Optical Storage

I've spent the last few chapters talking about the technology of magnetic storage. This is because magnetic disks form the foundation of computer storage today. Magnetic disks were the storage of the past, are the storage of the present, and will be the storage of the foreseeable future.

Another technology, optical-based storage, has steadily gained ground. Optical storage brings data integrity and promises data density that is unheard of in the world of magnetic storage.

Today there are really two optical-based technologies in the PC world, each with different characteristics and some different applications: CD-ROM and magneto-optical (MO) technologies. Until recently, CD-ROM was a read-only technology; today, special drives enable you to write data once and then read it many times. MO technology is true read-many and write-many technology. Neither of these has yet threatened to take over from conventional magnetic storage for mainstream and day-to-day use, but each has a strong place beside or inside your PC for some applications.

In this chapter, I describe the general optical technology and then talk a little about each of the major optical-based types of storage you're likely to find on a PC.

# An Optical Technology Overview

The operation of all optical storage devices depends on laser technology. A laser is a highly focused, highly controlled beam of light, either visible or, more commonly in storage devices, infrared. Depending on the type of technology involved, this laser beam can be used to record data on special optical media, to enable traditional magnetic recording on special magneto-optical material, or to read prerecorded data.

This laser technology is similar to that used in the popular audio CDs. In fact, many computer optical disks can be used to "play" computer data or music depending on the software you use with them.

When information is recorded on optical media, a laser beam burns out any location that stores a logical one and leaves blank any location that stores a logical zero. This laser is controlled by electronics that translate the computer data into the appropriate burn and no burn instructions and that tell the laser mechanism where to place the data on the disk. Until recently, such laser activity was reserved for the software company or data provider that generates the master disk. I talk about recordable CD-ROMs later. Generally, however, when you use a CD-ROM in your computer, the laser device inside your drive produces only enough light to read the holes burned in the disk or to precisely position a read/write head for conventional magnetic recording (in the case of magneto-optical drives).

In most cases, the result is a rigid platter similar to an audio CD that contains 600MB or more of read-only data. You can place this disk into an optical reader that uses a laser beam to scan the disk, pick up the pitted locations, and translate that information into usable computer data.

# Optical Storage Advantages

The most obvious advantages to optical technology are storage density and data integrity. The latter feature is particularly important when recordable CD-ROM drives are used for data backup or archiving.

Just how reliable is optical technology? Consider your audio CD player. Sure, you should be careful when handling the disks, but even if you aren't, the sounds play back reliably, and except when scratches or other physical changes occur, you'd never know how dirty the disks were or how often they were handled.

When optical technology was relatively new, officials at Digital Equipment Corporation wanted to demonstrate just how reliable these devices were for its minicomputer customers. Computer industry writers were assembled at one of Digital's Boston-area facilities for sweet rolls, coffee, and a slide show on optical technology. After everyone had eaten what they wanted from the tray of sticky doughnuts and rolls, Digital personnel dumped the remaining food off the tray, which turned out to be an optical platter. The "tray" was washed, wiped clean, and then placed into an optical reader, where it performed flawlessly.

You still should store and handle your disks carefully, but optical media are extremely durable and reliable under normal use. Because the surface of the disk (sealed in its plastic coating) is never touched by anything but light, and because the medium itself is virtually unaffected by moisture or temperature conditions, information written to an optical disk should last a very long time.

One reason optical technology is so reliable is that the read head is several millimeters away from the disk surface. Magnetic read/write heads, on the other hand, ride about 2,000 times closer to the disk surface than the heads in a CD-ROM reader. That means even a microscopic flaw in the disk surface, including particles of dust or smoke, can cause a head crash and loss of data in traditional drives.

**Technical Note:** CD-ROMs are also as reliable as they are because a large amount of the disk's storage space is dedicated to error detection and correction. Because of these checksum values that are stored on the disk, even a large amount of data that is misread can be corrected automatically.

However, even if the read head were to somehow contact the optical disk surface—and this is virtually impossible—the chance of losing data this way is negligible. This is because the surface of the platters is physically strong, for one thing, and also because the electronics that read the data are smart enough to fill in the blanks where there is a minimal amount of data loss.

In addition, the actual data on a CD-ROM platter is isolated from the outside world by a strong protective layer of plastic. When the laser shines on the disk to pick up data, it isn't reading the very top surface of the disk where small scratches and dirt reside. It looks through such data detractors in much the same way as you can take a picture through a chain-link fence and not see any of the fence if the lens is focused on a distant object.

Optical technology offers some advantages from the data distributor side as well. A master laser platter is made with an electronically controlled laser that physically burns or pits the surface of the disk as data is written. After this master disk is produced, however, distribution disks that contain graphics, maps, reference text, or computer software can be "pressed" in much the same way as old-fashioned phonograph records.

You already see a good deal of software distributed on CD-ROM. This makes for relatively inexpensive software distribution and is also changing the way people look at software. In fact, several major software companies are passing on the lowered cost of producing CD-ROMs to their customers. Recent versions of Borland and Corel applications have cost up to $150 less on CD-ROM than they cost for the same application on traditional floppy disks.

# Optical Disadvantages

Although the disadvantages to optical storage are minimal, there are a few considerations of which you should be aware. One disadvantage is cost. You can purchase a good quality, dependable audio CD player for under $75. However, by the time you make the design more rugged, build it to exacting tolerances, add computer interface electronics and cables, and send it through the distribution chain, you pay $250—500 for a computer CD-ROM drive. If you specify faster performance or add any other extras, the price can climb to $800 and beyond.

With today's technology, you also have to be aware of access and transfer speed. Although a SCSI II interface is capable of more than 10MB/second data transfer, writable optical drives typically max out at 300KB/second. In addition, except for magneto-optical technology, optical products offer extremely slow data access time when compared with most hard disks.

A typical internal hard drive can find the data your application asks for in 10 milliseconds, for example; a CD-ROM drive takes up to 300 milliseconds (that's nearly a third of a second!) for the same task. Newer drives offer faster access times, but, if you need high-speed, online storage, a high-capacity hard disk is a better choice than a CD-ROM.

# CD-ROM: Technical Details and Real-Life Implications

CD-ROM technology is the most common optical technology in use with PCs. Particularly for software distribution and for multimedia applications, such as graphics, photographs, sound, and motion video, there simply is no substitute for this method of distributing information and for using it on your PC.

A CD-ROM disk is a rigid plastic platter 1.2 millimeters thick and 120 millimeters (4.7 inches) across with a center spindle hole that is 15 millimeters in diameter. Data is written to the disk by burning pits in the recording surface with a carefully focused laser. Each pit is 0.12 micrometers deep and about 0.6 micrometers in diameter. CD-ROM tracks are 1.6 micrometers apart for a track density of 16,000 tracks/inch (tpi). Compare this with the floppy disk track density of 96 tpi or a typical hard disk with a track density of only a few hundred tpi. CD-ROM data begins at the inside of the disc—the shortest tracks—and is written toward the outside. Figure 10.1 shows a typical CD-ROM.

**Figure 10.1.**
*A typical CD-ROM.*

Original data is enhanced with error correction information before it is written to the optical platter. Coupled with intelligent electronics in the ROM reader, this error correction code can help rebuild correct data even if the disk surface is damaged.

Data is written one sector at a time. Each sector consists of 2,048 bytes of data surrounded by error correction information: 16 bytes in front of each sector and another 288 bytes of error code. In addition, many systems write this entire sector again using a Reed-Solomon (cyclic redundancy check, or CRC) scheme. CRC breaks the encoded block of data into 24 bytes of information and adds another 8 bytes of error correction data before writing it to disk.

With all this error correction and the inherent physical reliability of the CD-ROM design, CD-ROM data is extremely reliable. For example, the mastering process is considered accurate to one bit in each quadrillion bits (1015 bits). That's actual wrong data read and detected. At the same time, because of error correction code, the electronics in your CD-ROM reader might fail to find a wrong bit once in two quadrillion discs—that's discs, not bits. Pretty good, huh?

Okay, so now it is time to consider purchasing a CD-ROM reader for your system. You could opt for the lowest cost unit you find. This unit will read data in standard PC formats, but you may find it is too slow for anything but text searches or software distribution.

As you look for a CD-ROM drive, keep the following specifications in mind. Believe me, it is worth spending the extra money to get a drive that meets at least these specifications:

- Average access time: 250 milliseconds or better.
- Data transfer rate: 300KB/second or better. (These are generally referred to as double-speed drives, because the mechanisms can transfer data twice as fast as was possible with the first-generation of CD-ROM drive.)
- Audio: direct audio out.

Specifications are getting better across the board. Today there are triple- and quadruple-speed CD-ROM drives that have average access times three or four times faster than first-generation drives, but these are the newest systems and you can expect to pay a little extra for them. In the long run, of course, you'll be glad you spent the money. Even with today's standard double-speed drive, if you try playing a cutting-edge interactive game with one of these drives or using it for any but the most basic multimedia application, you'll soon pull out your hair if you're at all like me.

Start looking around now for a CD-ROM drive. If you don't think you need one now, you probably will before long if you keep using computers. And, given their popularity, you will very likely find that any new computer system you may buy will come with a CD-ROM drive preinstalled.

# Magneto-Optical Drives: Technical Details and Real-Life Implications

MO drives use magnetic media to store information under laser control. MO drives use 5.25- or 3.5-inch cartridges filled with magnetic read/write media. The magnetic disk surfaces in an MO cartridge are slightly different from conventional magnetic material. MO offers more permanent data storage than conventional hard disks and floppies.

MO disks use the polarity changes that occur in magnetic material when it is heated. As the laser beam heats the magnetic material on the disk, it becomes very easy to change the polarity of the material. After the material cools, the polarity becomes fixed in the new orientation. Depending on which direction the magnetic material is polarized, it is interpreted as either a logical one or a logical zero.

Data is written in blocks of 512 bytes. The problem is that, to change a portion of this information, the disk must change all of it because there is no way to know which bits are ones and which are zeros. Thus, the entire block is initialized during the first pass, and the new data is written when the proper disk sector rotates around under the read/write heads the second time. Therefore, it takes twice as long to write MO data as to read it.

Until recently, MO drives were pretty much reserved for minicomputers. MO drives simply were too expensive for most PC users. Prices still are high—from $1,000 to $3,000 depending on interface, speed, and capacity. But, if you need high-capacity, removable, secure data storage, MO drives can be a good choice.

An MO drive uses a removable cartridge that is written on one side at a time. The most common format is 5.25-inch platters that can store about 300MB of data on each side. To access information on the other side of the disk, you have to remove the cartridge, flip it over, and put it back in the drive. As technology evolved, it has become more feasible, technically and economically, to read and write from both sides of the platter at the same time as is done with conventional hard disks, but most of these systems still require that the disk be flipped by the user.

Large data capacity and the removable platter design are two very strong MO advantages. In addition, manufacturers are promising a data shelf life of 10 to 15 years, which is another advantage for research and other archive data.

The primary disadvantages to MO technology today are cost and compatibility. The price of the drive mechanism is far higher than most PC installations can justify, and the $200 or so for a 5.25-inch replacement cartridge is a relatively large chunk of change to lay out at one time, even if it does store 600MB of information.

The newer 3.5-inch MO packages are cheaper, typically $800—1,200, but also store less information. The 3.5-inch platter generally holds only 128MB. When compared with competing technology, such as the Bernoulli 150MB removable cartridge system, the cost is high. The Bernoulli system costs under $700 and stores only a little less data.

The standards issue also is a problem. You can't take an MO cartridge written on a Ricoh drive, for example, and play it back on a Sony drive. The formats are different enough to prevent even this level of compatibility. And, MO drives may be slower in access and data transfer than standard drives. This may not be an issue for archival and backup applications, but if you want to use the MO technology for primary online storage, you have to pay a slight speed penalty.

# Recordable CD-ROM: Technical Details and Real-Life Implications

Recordable CD-ROM technology is used mainly to archive and back up large systems rather than to distribute information in the way traditional CD-ROM is used. Recordable CD-ROM works just the way the name implies. A laser source is used to burn information into the platter, like with a ROM computer chip or CD-ROM data. After the data is written in this way, you can't change it. You can read it as often as necessary and can rewrite the information to another portion of the disk, but you can't modify data that already has been written. Recordable CD-ROM drives use 5.25-inch platters. As with traditional CD-ROMs, the capacity of these discs is about 600MB. And, also as with traditional CD-ROMs, the discs usually are written only on one side. (Actually, this isn't quite true. When traditional CD-ROMs are made professionally, the same data is pressed onto both sides of each disc. However, because each disc has a label silkscreened onto one side, only one side is ever used by your CD-ROM drive.)

An important consideration when using recordable CD-ROM drives is the type of metaphor they use. Earlier recordable CD-ROM products, which evolved from the now-antiquated WORM, or write-once/read-many drives, were designed to emulate tape drives, which meant the read/write process was different than it was for a hard disk. Data was harder to access and slower to retrieve. These drives originally required that all data they were to place on a single disk be made available—say, from a hard disk source—at one time, and only one time. In other words, if you wanted to store a bunch of pictures on a recordable CD-ROM, you had to have all of the pictures available and online at one time because you couldn't write some pictures to the CD today, and more pictures tomorrow, and so on. All of this was the result of the way the CD-ROM's directory, the catalog of everything that's stored on the CD, was handled by these early drives.

Today, you really only want a recordable CD-ROM that emulates a standard hard drive. You can write some data to a CD today, and more tomorrow. This works best when keeping archived data available online or nearly online as in the case of a platter that has to be turned over or manipulated by a jukebox mechanism. When disk emulation is used, the standard DOS commands for manipulating data on a hard disk can be used, and the drive becomes more or less transparent to the end user.

The main advantages of recordable CD-ROM technology are its data reliability and the fact that after data is written, it can't be erased. This technology is very useful for data archiving or storing large volumes of data that don't change very much. This might include historical stock data, scientific test results, long-term accounting, patient or customer records, engineering or architectural data, design drawings, and the like. Best estimates predict that recordable CD-ROM data is good on the shelf for at least 10 years.

As with other optical technologies, cost may be the primary deterrent to placing recordable CD-ROM technologies in most PCs. Also, the fact that information can be written only once raises the cost of media for holding data over time.

One of the strengths of recordable CDs—large data capacity—is also a disadvantage. After you have filled a few platters with data, how do you know where to find the information you need? This problem is somewhat alleviated by jukebox technology, but most serious recordable CD users also use a software utility to track information by platter name or number and even location. When you first start using such a technology, the amount of storage seems unlimited. As time goes on, however, and many disks fill up, careful management of stored information is an important part of its use.

# Looking Around the Corner: Super-Dense Optical Storage

In March of 1994, Philips Consumer Electronics and Sony Electronics previewed a forthcoming CD-ROM standard for several industry journals. This new standard, which is yet to be named or licensed, will reportedly bring four times the data density to CD-ROMs. Technically, this means a storage capacity of around 2.4GB; in practice, it means that—allegedly—140 minutes of NTSC-quality video and sound will fit on a single CD-ROM. These high-density disks will require a completely new type of CD-ROM reader drive and are at least two years away at the time of this writing. Similar technologies with similar increases in capabilities will surely come to market before a leader emerges.

Other developments, like work on three-dimensional holographic memory, have been building on what is already a decade of research. Lambertus Hesselink, a research professor at Stanford University, announced in August, 1994, what may prove to be a long-awaited breakthrough in holographic technology. Previously, holographic memory remained elusive because the act of reading holographic memory gradually erased it. Hesselink's technique, using two lasers, seems to solve this tremendous problem. If his work proves to be the enabling key technology, then holographic memory—capable of storing 120 *billion* bytes of data in one cubic centimeter—may be a part of your desktop computer system in the first decade of the next century.

## How Holographic Memory May Work

Holographic memory is still in the pre-prototype stage, but there are some solid ideas about how it may be made to work in the future. The idea is that, while current technology only allows us to read/write from one layer of data on a CD-ROM—similar to a single platter in a hard disk—holographic memory will allow us to put together data in multiple layers that will be randomly accessible. A look a Figure 10.2 may help you grasp the idea. Imagine that you have a way of storing one bit of data—a single zero or a one—in one grain of sugar. If you place ten rows and ten columns of sugar grains down on your breakfast table, then you've got storage space for 100 bits, or $10^2$ sugar grains. That's a little bit like today's optical technology: data fits into spaces in a two-dimensional plane (the single layer of pitted metal sealed inside a CD-ROM), and you can randomly access any one of those spaces by (remember, this is just an analogy) specifying the X and Y coordinate of the sugar grain on your table.

Now, instead of a single layer of sugar grains, think of a sugar cube. For the sake of argument, let's say that sugar cubes are 10 grains across in each direction, and ten grains high. That gives us 1000 storage spaces ($10^3$) in a sugar cube.

Here's where your imagination has to do a little work. We said you can access the data in a grain of sugar by specifying that grain's X and Y location. If you could somehow specify X, Y, and Z locations (as the figure shows, the Z coordinate indicates the "layer" of sugar grains in the cube), you could store data in every grain in a solid three-dimensional sugar cube, and still be able to access any single piece of data randomly.

Holographic memory works a bit like that. Rather than having one layer of nontransparent material, like today's CD-ROM or like a single platter with a single read/write head in a hard disk, tomorrow's holographic storage will have multiple layers of transparent or semi-transparent material. You'll be able to store data in all layers of this material, and your new laser drive will be able to focus the beam in such a way as to select which layer (the Z coordinate)—in addition to which X and Y coordinates—the data is read from.

Whether this technology ultimately comes to market in a science fiction-like transparent cube, or whether we first see it in a form that resembles several CD-ROMs all glued together, who can say? But if you consider the "glued-together CD-ROMs" concept, you can see that in a case no larger than today's 120MB SyQuest cartridges, we  might be able to store 6GB of data—and probably more.

**Figure 10.2.**
*An analogy for
holographic memory.*

"Grain of Sugar"
Can hold a single bit
of data

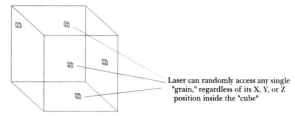

Laser can randomly access any single
"grain," regardless of its X, Y, or Z
position inside the "cube"

"Cube of Sugar", made up of "Grains"
Capable of holding hundreds of
millions of bits of data

# 11

# On-Screen Video

PC users generally agree that their most important interface with the PC is the video display. Applications direct the user and report results through the PC's display system screens. In the past, the PC's display system produced boring character-only screens in monochrome. Today's PCs and applications depend on the power of the display subsystem to produce color text and 2-D and 3-D graphics output with response times well under a second. Operating systems such as DOS were built around character-based text output. Now, graphical user interface operating systems such as Windows 95 depend on the PC's display subsystem to support all types of new multimedia applications. The capabilities and performance of the PC's display and display adapter are now nearly as important as the speed and performance of the PC's processor!

The PC's display subsystem can make or break a PC's perceived performance. For example, a high-performance Pentium-based PC with a poor display subsystem will likely be severely limited in reaching its full performance potential in many newer multimedia applications. Similarly, a slower 486 class system's performance can be significantly enhanced by a powerful display subsystem. As more and more applications mix live or full-motion video with high-performance 2-D and 3-D graphics, and the user demands realistic color images on high-resolution screens and large displays, the PC's display subsystem becomes the key enabling factor.

In this chapter I examine the components of the PC's display subsystem and identify the key characteristics that are important to users. Most of the information applies to both the standard CRT (Cathode Ray Tube) display monitors used on most nonportable PCs and the LCD (Liquid Crystal Displays) used on most portable PCs. Several other technologies are available, such as gas plasma and elector luminous displays, but these are not very common and have very small markets.

# Basics

As discussed briefly in Chapter 3, "Brains: The Processors," the major elements of the PC display subsystem are the display adapter, the display device (CRT or LCD), and the display subsystem software. All three are critical to the display subsystem's capabilities and performance. Before I get into specifics about those elements, however, this section covers some basic concepts about how the PC's display subsystem works.

When the PC's application software or operating system wants to communicate with the user through the PC's screen, it first builds a message in a virtual screen in the PC's memory. The message to be displayed is next passed from the application to the operating system as a block of memory. The operating system then formats the message and transfers it to the display adapter's memory as a pattern of pixels (picture elements) that represent the image or text message. The display adapter hardware then reads the formatted message out of its display memory and paints it on the PC's display adapter device so the user can read the application's message (image) and respond appropriately via the keyboard or mouse. Figure 11.1 illustrates this process flow, identifying the key components in the message path. Note that the figure also indicates several alternate paths commonly used by older DOS applications and games that bypass the operating system and directly communicate with the

PC's display subsystem hardware. These paths have required that the BIOS and hardware be exactly compatible with the IBM PC's earlier implementations or they will not work. This is why PC display adapters have tended to maintain a strict backward compatibility with the hardware environment over time. Typically, software that worked on the original PC will continue to work on the latest PC display subsystem hardware!

**Figure 11.1**
*Displayed message data flow.*

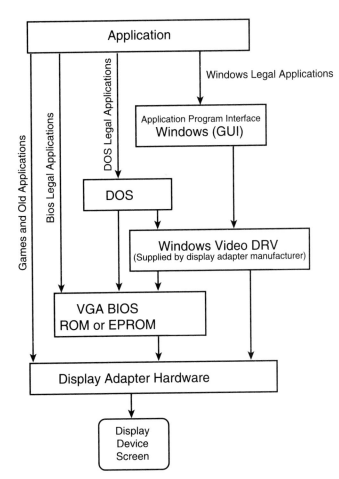

On the PC's display device, be it a CRT or LCD, images are created by forming a pattern of dots of varying colors and intensities. If the dots are small enough and enough colors are available, the image formed looks natural. If you look very closely at a screen's images, you can detect the individual dots used to form the images, either text or pictures.

# Pixels and Dot Pitch

The dots used to form the image on the screen are referred to as pixels, shorthand for picture elements. The minimum displayable pixel size on a display is determined by the dot pitch of the display device. Note that dot size is not measured, but the pitch is specified. Most display devices measure the dot pitch in millimeters. Typically, PC display devices support dot pitches from .39 to .22 millimeters or .0155 inches to .00873 inches. Smaller dot pitches are possible, but display devices supporting these pitches are very expensive. In a CRT display device, the smallest possible pixel is actually a dot trio—a red, green and blue phosphor dot set. An electron beam is used to strike the phosphor, causing it to emit light. Depending on which phosphor dots are struck and with what intensity, the dot trio emits a range of colors created by the mixing of the primary colors red, green, and blue. Even though the smallest possible pixel in a system is governed by the dot pitch, many times the pixel is made of several dot trios, so a pixel does not necessarily mean a single dot trio. A pixel is the smallest display picture element generated by the display adapter. The next technical note explains more about dots and dot pitch.

**Technical Note:** The dot pitch specification of a CRT display can be a little confusing because of the complexity of the definition and differing display technologies. The dot pitch is actually the shortest distance between two dots of the same color. Since the dots are trios and are packed together, the closest dots of the same color are typically measured on a diagonal proportional to the aspect ratio of the screen. This is true if the CRT uses circular dots. The Trinitron CRTs, however, actually use a set of strips rather than dots. The dot pitch is still measured the same way (distance for same color strips), but the result is different due to the different geometry of the phospors. A strip of slot mask display actually has less resolution at the same dot pitch as a circular dot design. For example, a 0.25 mm dot pitch slot or strip Trinitron display is roughly equivalent to a 0.28 conventional CRT. Figure 11.2 is a rough estimation of the horizontal and vertical resolutions achievable on different size displays with different dot pitches. In general, after calculating the theoretical resolutions based on dot pitch and aspect ratios, a fudge fact is added to reflect the quality of the displays and the analog nature of the system. In other words, Figure 11.2's values can vary and the dot pitch specification is only a guide line. The best way to judge a display is to actually observe the output at the resolutions and refresh rates you desire.

# Resolution of the Display Device

If we know the dot pitch and the size of the display, we can calculate the maximum resolution in pixels that can be displayed. CRT display devices are measured like TVs, by measuring the screen diagonally. Most PC screens are not square, and the ratio of the vertical dimension divided by the horizontal dimension is referred to as the aspect ratio. Typical aspect ratios are .75 for computer monitors and .8 for TV screens. Figure 11.2 is a table of typical PC CRT sizes and dot pitches available, with theoretical maximum pixel resolutions calculated. The table includes the most common screen pixel resolutions supported by the dot pitch and screen sizes. Note that in some instances the typical resolutions are higher than the calculated values. This is because most CRT displays display screen sizes larger than those calculated due to the analog nature of the phosphor dot trio and the geometry of their packing on the face of the screen. The larger the screen size and the smaller the dot pitch, the more expensive the display device. Today, most PCs are sold with 15-inch displays with .28 mm dot pitches that can comfortably display a 1024×768 pixel resolution image. To give you a feel of what this means, a typical TV screen has a dot pitch of .65 mm and displays an image of 352×480 pixels. A broadcast studio-quality TV image is 704×480 pixels. The original PC's monochrome display adapter displayed an image of 720×350 pixels. To produce an 80-column text screen with characters 8 pixels wide, a minimum of 640 horizontal pixels is required. The minimum screen resolution supported by Windows is 640×480 pixels. Thus, the ability to display a specific resolution image on a specific size display monitor is dependent first on its dot pitch and secondly, on the viewers' ability to read a screen. For example, a small dot pitch display that is also small in physical size may be able to display the image correctly, but the viewer many not be able to easily read the screen.

*Figure 11.2.*
*Pixel resolutions versus dot pitch and display size.*

| | | Pixel Resolutions vs. Screen Size and Dot Pitch | | | | | | |
|---|---|---|---|---|---|---|---|---|
| Screen | Aspect | | | Dot Pitch (in Millimeters) | | | | |
| sizes | Ratio = | 0.75 | 0.39 | 0.31 | 0.28 | 0.26 | 0.24 | 0.22 |
| Diag. Inches | 12 | | | | | | | |
| Horz. Inches | 9.60 | typ. horiz. pixels | 620 | 780 | 864 | 930 | 1008 | 1100 |
| Vert. Inches | 7.20 | typ. vert. pixels | 465 | 585 | 648 | 698 | 756 | 825 |
| | | typ. res. supported | 640x480 | 800x600 | 800x600 | 800x600 | 1024x768 | 1024x768 |
| Diag. Inches | 14 | | | | | | | |
| Horz. Inches | 11.20 | typ. horiz. pixels | 724 | 910 | 1008 | 1086 | 1176 | 1283 |
| Vert. Inches | 8.40 | typ. vert. pixels | 543 | 683 | 756 | 814 | 882 | 962 |
| | | typ. res. supported | 800x600 | 800x600 | 1024x768 | 1024x768 | 1024x768 | 1280x1024 |
| Diag. Inches | 15 | | | | | | | |
| Horz. Inches | 12.00 | typ. horiz. pixels | 775 | 975 | 1080 | 1163 | 1260 | 1375 |
| Vert. Inches | 9.00 | typ. vert. pixels | 582 | 732 | 810 | 872 | 945 | 1031 |
| | | typ. res. supported | 800x600 | 1024x768 | 1024x768 | 1024x768 | 1280x1024 | 1280x1024 |
| Diag. Inches | 17 | | | | | | | |
| Horz. Inches | 13.60 | typ. horiz. pixels | 879 | 1106 | 1224 | 1318 | 1428 | 1558 |
| Vert. Inches | 10.20 | typ. vert. pixels | 659 | 829 | 918 | 989 | 1071 | 1168 |
| | | typ. res. supported | 800x600 | 1024x768 | 1024x768 | 1280x1024 | 1280x1024 | 1600x1200 |
| Diag. Inches | 19 | | | | | | | |
| Horz. Inches | 15.20 | typ. horiz. pixels | 982 | 1236 | 1368 | 1473 | 1596 | 1741 |
| Vert. Inches | 11.40 | typ. vert. pixels | 737 | 927 | 1026 | 1105 | 1197 | 1306 |
| | | typ. res. supported | 1024x768 | 1280x1024 | 1280x1024 | 1280x1024 | 1600x1200 | 1920x1440 |
| Diag. Inches | 21 | | | | | | | |
| Horz. Inches | 16.80 | typ. horiz. pixels | 1086 | 1366 | 1512 | 1628 | 1764 | 1924 |
| Vert. Inches | 12.60 | typ. vert. pixels | 814 | 1024 | 1134 | 1221 | 1323 | 1443 |
| | | typ. res. supported | 1024x768 | 1280x1024 | 1600x1200 | 1600x1200 | 1920x1440 | 1920x1440 |

note: most CRT displays will display higher resolution images than calculated with dot pitch and screen size, due to the analog nature of the phosphor dot trio and the geometry of their packing.

# Color Depth

The number of colors that can be displayed is primarily a function of the display adapter. A color CRT display monitor can display a continuously variable color image with more than 16 million colors possible. However, the display adapter typically limits the number of colors displayable to a smaller number. Depending on the amount of display memory dedicated to each pixel, different color depths (numbers of colors displayable per pixel) are possible. For example, if one byte of memory is used to represent a pixel's color, 256 colors are possible for each pixel. If 16 bits or 2 bytes are used for each pixel up to 65, then 768 colors are possible. If 3 bytes or 24 bits are used, each pixel can have 16.8 million colors. In PC terminology, 8-bit mode is called 8-bit *pseudo color*, 16-bit mode is called *high color*, and 24-bit mode is called *true color*. Figure 11.3 illustrates how data in PC display adapter memory represents pixel colors. The data is converted to three analog signals, which are sent to the CRT to drive the electron beams, which strike and excite the phosphor trios to emit the desired colors. The device that converts the digital data to analog RGB (Red, Green, Blue) signals that drive the electron guns is called a DAC (Digital to Analog Converter), and it resides on the display adapter. Most display adapters use 8-bit DACs capable of producing 256 different component color intensity levels. (Some older PC adapters used DACs that were only 6 bits.) Thus, with three 8-bit DACs, a 24-bit color value is required; 24 bits can produce 16.8 million combinations or colors.

**Figure 11.3.**

*Pixel color representations in display adapter memory.*

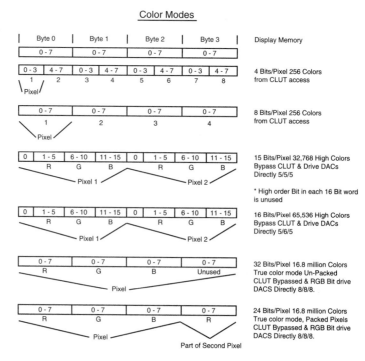

Many applications don't require that many colors and use a simpler, single 8-bit color value supporting 256 colors. But which 256 colors out of the 16.8 million available are to be used, and how is this 8-bit value converted to a 24-bit value to drive the DAC? The conversion from 8-bit value to a 24-bit value is accomplished through a color palette device built into the display adapter. The conversion from 8-bit pseudo color to 24-bit color is accomplished using a simple color look-up table (CLUT) memory scheme. A 256 word×24-bit memory is used. In each 24-bit word of the memory is stored the 24-bit true color RGB value that is to be displayed. This memory can thus store 256 possible 24-bit color values. The 8-bit color value is applied as an address to this memory and the data out at this address is sent to the DAC. (Some older PC adapters use an 18-bit wide memory and thus only support 262,144 colors.) This scheme will convert any 8-bit value to any of 256 24-bit values stored in the CLUT memory. Thus, the application can choose to display any 256 colors from a palette of 16.8 million. By simply changing the 24-bit word value in the CLUT memory, a new color can be defined for the 256-bit code that corresponds to this address. Figure 11.4 illustrates how the 8-bit pseudo memory mode and CLUT works.

**Figure 11.4.**
*Color palettes operation.*

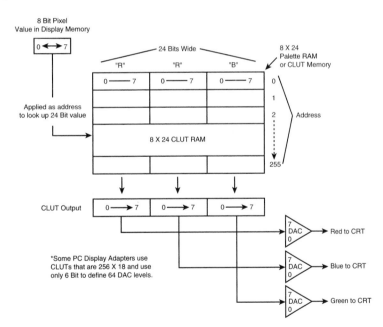

# Memory Size versus Color Depth and Screen Resolutions

You may have realized by now that the amount of memory needed to hold and display an image is dependent on the color depth and the screen size in pixel resolutions. The memory that the image is stored in is typically part of the display adapter subsystem and is not counted as program or data memory directly attached to the processor. It is very important to note that the display adapter memory can be accessed directly by the processor; this is how the images are initially moved to the display adapter subsystem memory for display. As was discussed earlier, each pixel requires a different amount of memory depending on the number of colors supported. I indicated that pixel color depths of 8 bits, 16 bits, and 24 bits are the most commonly used color depths, but other color depths are also possible and supported in older display adapters. Table 11.1 summarizes the most commonly used memory representations of pixel color depth in the display memory.

Table 11.1. Pixel Color Representations in Display Memory.

| Bits/pixel | Mode name | Palette colors | Max. pixel colors |
|---|---|---|---|
| 4 bits/pixel | 4-bit pseudo-color | 262,144 | 16 |
| 4 bits/pixel | 4-bit pseudo-color | 16,777,216 | 16 |
| 8 bits/pixel | 8-bit pseudo-color | 262,144 | 256 |
| 8 bits/pixel | 8-bit pseudo-color | 16,777,216 | 256 |
| 15 bits/pixel | 15-bit high color | palette bypassed | 32,768 |
| 16 bits/pixel | 16-bit high color | palette bypassed | 65,536 |
| 24 bits/pixel | 24-bit true color | palette bypassed | 16,777,216 |

In the 15, 16, and 24 bits per pixel modes, the palette memory or CLUT is bypassed and the memory bits directly drive the DAC inputs. Thus, in a 15-bit high color mode, 5 bits each are used to directly drive the DAC. If the display adapter's DAC is a 6- or 8-bit DAC, the 5 bits drive the high order DAC inputs. In 15-bit high color mode, the high order 16th bit is unused and is wasted memory in most cases. Later you will see how this bit can be used to assist in supporting live video overlays. In a 16-bit high color mode, typically 6 bits are used to drive the green DAC and 5 bits each for the red and blue DACs. In 24-bit true color mode, the 8 bits each drive the DACs.

# Packet Pixel Mode

In many display adapter designs, 24-bit true color mode actually uses 32 bits per pixel where the high order byte of the 32-bit word is not used. This scheme simplifies the display adapter design but wastes a significant amount of memory. Newer display adapter designs use a *packed pixel* mode in which each 32-bit word contains 1⅓ pixels of data. Not only does the packed-pixel mode save memory, it also reduces the bandwidth needed to display the image. One of the most important measures of a display system is its speed in moving or updating images; wasting time moving an extra unused byte of data has a significant impact on performance.

Today, most PC display adapters come equipped with display memory in 1, 2, or 4MB sizes. Due to the way memory chips are designed, other sizes are not practical. Since memory costs are the primary cost of a display adapter, the ability to display the largest possible images in these memory increments is important. Packed pixel mode enables the use of the least amount of memory for a 24-bit true color image.

Figure 11.5 shows the memory size requirements for different screen resolutions and color depth modes.

From the chart, it can be seen that high color depth large screen resolutions can require a lot of memory. Note how the packed pixel modes allow for larger true color screens in smaller memory increments. Also, remember that display adapter memory only comes in 1, 2, or 4MB increments, and if the image size and color depth require a small amount over the memory you have available, you will need the next full memory increment to display the image!

*Figure 11.5.*
*Memory size for screen resolutions and color depth modes.*

| Memory requirements in bytes for color modes and screen resolutions | | | | | | |
|---|---|---|---|---|---|---|
| | | | **Screen Pixel resolutions** | | | |
| color modes | 640x480 | 800x600 | 1024x768 | 1280x1024 | 1600x1200 | 1920x1440 |
| 4 bit 16 color | 153,600 | 240,000 | 393,216 | 655,360 | 960,000 | 1,382,400 |
| 8 bit 256 color | 307,200 | 480,000 | 786,432 | 1,310,720 | 1,920,000 | 2,764,800 |
| 15/16 bit true color | 614,400 | 960,000 | 1,572,864 | 2,621,440 | 3,840,000 | 5,529,600 |
| 24 bit non packed | 1,228,800 | 1,920,000 | 3,145,728 | 5,242,880 | 7,680,000 | 11,059,200 |
| 24 bit packed pixel | 921,600 | 1,440,000 | 2,359,296 | 3,932,160 | 5,760,000 | 8,294,400 |

# Raster and Scan Rates

Now that you understand how image pixels are represented in display memory, it's time to see how they end up on the screen. As mentioned earlier, the image to be displayed is stored as a virtual screen in the display adapter's memory. The display controller chip generates a raster, which moves the electron beams across the screen from left to right and then down the screen from top to bottom. When the beam reaches the end of a horizontal line, it is turned off and moved to the left edge of the screen one line down and begins to scan the next line. A scan created using this technique, horizontal lines left to right and vertical lines top to bottom, is called a *raster scan*. At each pixel position of this raster scan, data is fetched from the virtual screen in the display adapter's memory and applied to the DAC inputs to control the intensity of the red, green, and blue electron beams. Once the entire screen is painted by the raster scan, the entire process is repeated. The speed at which frames (individual screens) are painted is a very important characteristic of a display subsystem. The screen repaint rate is often called the refresh rate, vertical scan rate, or frame rate, all generally meaning the same thing. Figure 11.6 illustrates how the display adapter's memory is organized to create a screen using the raster scan approach.

As the beams pass over the phosphor dot trios, they are appropriately excited and emit the desired color light. After the beam passes, the light intensity begins to decay. The rate of decay is called the phosphor's *persistence*. *High persistence* means that it takes a long time for the light intensity to decay and *low persistence* means its light intensity decays quickly. If the phosphor decays too slowly, moving images on the screen may appear to smear as they are moving. But the screen refresh rate (frame rate or vertical scan rate) can be slow with high-persistence phosphor. If the phosphor is fast to decay, the screen refresh rate must be high. The problem with high refresh rates is that they place high performance requirements on the display adapter and its memory. Early PC display adapters refreshed the screens at 50 and 60 Hz rates or 50 and 60 times per second. Even with high-persistence phosphors that smear the images, most users were able to detect annoying screen flicker. Today's PC display subsystems tend to use relatively fast (low persistence) phosphors with screen refresh rates above 70 Hz. Screen flicker is most detectable at the edges of one's field of vision; therefore, as PC screens get larger, flicker is easier to detect. Some studies indicate that on large screens, refresh rates as high as 80 to 100 Hz are required to eliminate flicker. Since each individual's sight is different, what may be acceptable frame rates for one person may be totally unacceptable for another. For 15-and 17-inch diagonal screens, refresh rates of 75 Hz seem acceptable to most.

**Figure 11.6.**
*Display adapter memory organization for an APA (All Points Addressable) raster scan display.*

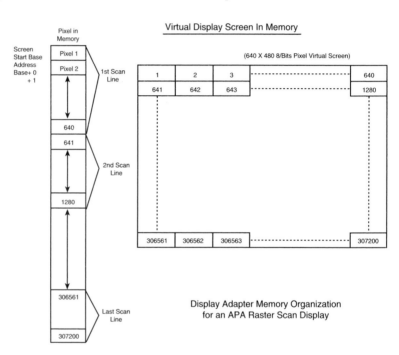

# Interlacing

One way to reduce the performance demands of high refresh rate screens is to interlace the raster. In this mode, two frame times are required to paint the entire screen. Odd lines are painted, and then even lines are painted. This results in halving the data rate from the display memory. This is exactly the way your TV works. The idea is that your eye will not detect the flicker if every other line is scanned at a high rate. This works just fine for TV images; because they are moving images, it is very difficult to detect flicker. But on mainly still images on computer screens, interlaced images often result in annoying flicker. Many of the later IBM display adapters used interlaced images for large screens. This is perhaps one of the reasons these display adapters did not become a popular standard. The low scan rate and interlaced operations also make TVs a very poor choice for computer displays. In general, avoid displays and display adapters that require interlaced operations.

# Text Characters On-Screen

So far I have primarily discussed formation and display of images on the PC's screen. One particularly important type of image is text characters, such as the characters on this page. The early PC display adapters contained special hardware that scanned text characters out of a character generator ROM. The pixel patterns that made up screen characters were stored in the ROM, where each bit represents a pixel. Earlier in this chapter, I explain how individual pixels are stored as color codes in a virtual screen raster in the PC's display adapter memory. Each pixel of the image is addressable by the processor and can be modified or moved by the processor to change the image or create a new image. Such a display system is called an All Points Addressable display system (APA). Today's PC display adapters are APA devices. Early display adapters for the PC used character generator schemes for displaying text characters. Instead of storing the exact bitmap that represented the character's pixel pattern in display memory, the data in memory was used as a character code pointer. The character code values was applied to the address inputs of the character generator ROM, which locates a block of ROM data that contained the bitmap pattern that represented the character to be displayed. Figure 11.7 illustrates how the bitmap pattern for a character was stored in the character generator ROM.

*Figure 11.7.*
*Character generator ROM bitmap pattern for the text character A.*

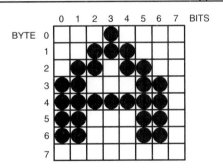

Character generator-based display adapter designs are very inflexible, since you can only display the limited number of text characters in the ROM. It is not easy to support, simultaneously, different style and size character patterns or fonts. Supporting features such as proportionally spaced characters, bold characters, italicized characters, or mixed size and font styles are very difficult to achieve using a character generator-based display adapter. Today's PC display adapters still support the older character generator modes, primarily to maintain compatibility with DOS-based text software. One change, however, has been made. Instead of storing the character's bitmap patterns in a ROM, they are stored in the display adapter's RAM, typically in an off-screen undisplayed area. This at least permits easily changing the character font style and size.

# APA Character Generation

Due to the limitations discussed earlier, graphical user interfaces such as Microsoft Windows do not use ROM character generator modes. Instead, all text characters are generated in APA mode, either by the processor directly accessing the display memory or by the display controller chip, acting on behalf of the processor, accessing the display memory. Bitmaps of the text characters are typically stored in off-screen display memory and fetched as needed by the processor or controller. In newer display adapters, this monochrome bitmapped image of the character is sent to a color expansion feature in the display adapter. The image is not actually expanded, but the color is "expanded" or added. Here a specified background color and text pixel image color is added and the full color text character expanded into the display adapter's displayable region by the display adapter's hardware. Color expansion hardware assist is a very important feature in modern PC display adapters and is the key to accelerating display performance in Windows' APA display mode.

By now you are probably wondering where the character bitmap patterns come from. They can be generated in two ways. The simplest method is to simply store the bitmapped text character patterns as a bit per pixel in memory. This is called a bitmapped font. Bitmapped fonts take up a lot of memory but are fast to access and require no processing to use. You can imagine how quickly memory requirements can grow using bitmapped fonts, as each font style and size must be stored. The biggest problem is with large size fonts. Since a memory bit is required for each pixel, as the font size increases, much more memory is required to store the font. Storing bitmapped fonts on a hard disk seems reasonable, but having to store several font styles and sizes in system or display adapter memory can become unreasonable.

# Size-Independent or Scalable Outline Fonts

A solution to the bitmapped font memory size is to store the fonts for a particular style in a size-independent form and let the processor expand the font to the desired size as it is needed. The scheme most popular today is to store the fonts as scalable outline fonts. This scheme stores a set of mathematical expressions and coefficients that represent a series of lines and curves that, when attached end to end, form the outline of the character. The PC's processor then can expand or shrink the character as needed and generates the desired size bitmapped font from the outline font information. The software that converts the outline representation to a bitmapped pattern is called an outline font engine. A particular font style—for example, Helvetica—is typically stored as four different outline files: standard, bold, italicized, super-, and subscript modes. The Windows TrueType fonts are an example of an outline font. Figure 11.8 illustrates how text characters are generated in a typical PC display adapter environment.

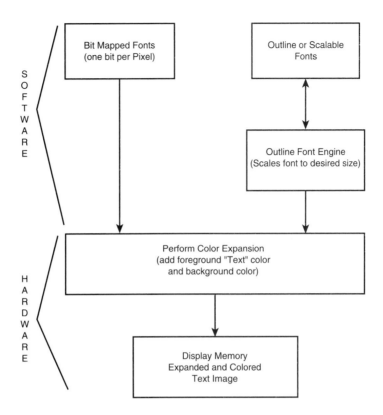

**Figure 11.8.**
*PC text character generation.*

# The Display Adapter Components

Now that you have some basic idea about how the PC's display adapter works and how graphic images and text characters are represented in the PC's virtual display adapter memory, it's time to explore the basic components of the display adapter hardware. Most modern PC display adapters are made of three major components: a controller chip, display adapter memory, and a ROM BIOS chip. It turns out that in some of the higher performance display adapters, some of the features in the controller chip are separated into individual parts. This is particularly common in dual-ported memory systems designs such as VRAM design, which are discussed later.

# Older Standards

Since the introduction of the PC in 1981, several families of display adapters have been developed for the PC. I will not dwell on the history of the PC's display adapters, but a quick summary will serve to familiarize you with some of the terminology. Figure 11.9 summarizes the evolution of the PC's display adapter technology. The original PC was announced with two display adapter options, the Monochrome Display Adapter (MDA) and the Color Graphics Display Adapter (CGA). The monochrome display adapter also included a printer port and displayed a raster of 720×350 pixels in character generator mode only, supporting an 80 column by 25 line text display using a 9×14 pixel box for each text character. No APA graphics were supported. The CGA supported both APA and character generator modes with up to 16 colors in a 160×200 APA raster, 4 colors from a 16-color palette in a 320×200 raster and 2 colors from a 16-color palette in a APA 640×200. In character generator mode, 320×200 raster supported 40 characters×25 lines and the 640×200 raster supported 80 characters×25 lines. All character modes used a character generator with an 8×8 pixel bit map. The MDA used a 50 Hz noninterlaced frame rate and the CGA used a 60 Hz noninterlaced scan rate but could be programmed to use interlace mode. The CGA was a TV scan rate compatible device.

**Figure 11.9.**
*PC display adapters family history.*

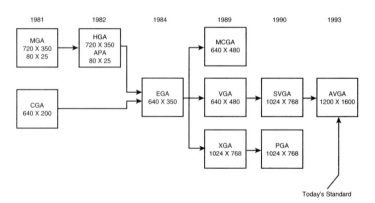

The next innovation in display adapters did not come from IBM, but from a small company called Hercules Graphics. They modified the MDA such that it could support an APA mode with a raster size of 720×348 monochrome pixels. This device also supported the standard MDA character generator mode.

Both the MDA and CGA had digital pixel interfaces to the monitors; this meant that the DAC function was in the monitor.

With the introduction of the PC AT, IBM announced a new Enhanced Graphics Adapter (EGA). This device continued to support the older modes of the CGA and EGA but supported higher scan rates and refresh rates with 64 colors at screen sizes of up to 640×350. This device also had a digital pixel interface to the monitor.

Next IBM introduced the VGA (Video Graphics Array) adapter. This device continued to support the backward compatibility modes of the MDA, CGA, and EGA devices while supporting APA graphic rasters of 640×400 and 640×480 at 31 KHz scan rates and 60 Hz refresh rates with up to 256 colors per pixel from a palette of 262,144 colors. The VGA adapter also supported an RGB analog interface to the monitor and incorporated the VGA Feature Connector interface. This interface now allowed graphics and video from other devices and adapters to be merged with the PC graphics. The VGA was a major enhancement to PC graphics and several third party chip developers began to design and build chips to support and extend the IBM VGA standard.

Meanwhile, IBM developed three other graphics adapters: the MCGA (Monochrome Color Graphics Array), the XGA (Extended Graphics Array), and PGA (Professional Graphics Array) devices. These devices had little success in the industry and IBM was the only major supplier. Most clone PC manufacturers selected the lower cost, better-defined VGA standard. The XGA and PGA adapters were not well accepted due to IBM's reluctance to publish a full register-level specification. Also, the designs used expensive VRAM display memory and only supported interlaced modes at the higher scan rates and resolutions.

# VESA SVGA Standard

With the industry's reluctance to accept the XGA and PGA IBM display adapter standards, many display adapter chip manufacturers began to extend the more popular VGA standard. The first extension was to support an 800×600 16-color mode at a slow 56 Hz noninterlaced frame rate. As technology permitted high speeds in the VGA controllers and display memory, there was a proliferation of noncompatible modes in the industry. At this time the VESA (Video Electronics Standards Association) standards group documented a set of VGA extensions, (actually a set of Video BIOS calls) to support a family of display modes. This set of standards became known as the Super VGA modes. Display modes of up to 1280×1024 pixel rasters with 24-bits per pixel and refresh rates of up to 75 Hz were defined. Nearly all of today's display adapters support the Super-VGA modes. Display adapters supporting this capability are now called SVGA (Super-VGA) devices. When the operating system wants to select a display mode, it sends a mode code to the display adapter BIOS, which then sets up the display adapter to support the mode. Early VGA adapters used a 7-bit code in the mode field. The VESA standard expanded this mode field to 15 bits and assigned 15-bit mode numbers to each of the new super-VGA modes. Figure 11.10 defines the present SVGA modes. (The numbers in parentheses in Figure 11.10—for example 5:5:5—refer to the numbers of bits used to represent each of the primary colors R:B:G.) It should be noted that the VESA standards committee will probably have expanded the modes by the time this is published! To obtain information on the VESA standards, you may contact the standards group at the following address:

Video Electronics Standards Association
2150 North First Street, Suite 440
San Jose, CA 95131-2029

**Figure 11.10.**
*VESA Super-VGA modes.*

GRAPHICS

| 15-bit mode number | 7-bit mode number | Resolution | Colors |
|---|---|---|---|
| 100h | - | 640x400 | 256 |
| 101h | - | 640x480 | 256 |
| 102h | 6Ah | 800x600 | 16 |
| 103h | - | 800x600 | 256 |
| 104h | - | 1024x768 | 16 |
| 105h | - | 1024x768 | 256 |
| 106h | - | 1280x1024 | 16 |
| 107h | - | 1080x1024 | 256 |
| 10Dh | - | 320x200 | 32K (1:5:5:5:) |
| 10Eh | - | 320x200 | 64K (5:6:5) |
| 10Fh | - | 320x200 | 16.8M (8:8:8) |
| 110h | - | 640x480 | 32K (1:5:5:5:) |
| 111h | - | 640x480 | 64K (5:6:5) |
| 112h | - | 640x480 | 16.8M (8:8:8) |
| 113h | - | 800x600 | 32K (1:5:5:5:) |
| 114h | - | 800x600 | 64K (5:6:5) |
| 115h | - | 800x600 | 16.8M (8:8:8) |
| 116h | - | 1024x768 | 32K (1:5:5:5:) |
| 117h | - | 1024x768 | 64K (5:6:5) |
| 118h | - | 1024x768 | 16.8M (8:8:8) |
| 119h | - | 1280x1024 | 32K (1:5:5:5:) |
| 11Ah | - | 1280x1024 | 64K (5:6:5) |
| 11Bh | - | 1280x1024 | 16.8M (8:8:8) |

TEXT

| 15-bit mode number | 7-bit mode number | Columns | Rows |
|---|---|---|---|
| 108h | - | 80 | 60 |
| 109h | - | 132 | 25 |
| 10Ah | - | 132 | 43 |
| 10Bh | - | 132 | 50 |
| 10Ch | - | 132 | 60 |

# Today's Standard: AVGA

As applications began to use the new high-resolution and increased color depth modes, the on-screen performance of the Windows GUI in APA mode began to suffer. The VGA controller chip manufacturers responded by adding Windows acceleration hardware to the SVGA chips. Display adapters that now support Windows acceleration in hardware are generally known as AVG (Accelerated VGA) devices. Since Windows has a very well-defined software interface for applications, the AVGA acceleration hardware need not be compatible between devices and can be isolated from the user and Windows by providing a Windows driver. The Windows driver interfaces to the Windows API (Application Program Interface) and converts Windows graphic commands to the unique hardware of the Windows accelerator hardware in the AVGA chip. This means that each AVGA chip or adapter supplier must also provide a unique Windows driver to support its specific accelerator hardware functions. The AVGA chip Windows drivers software can have a dramatic effect on the system's display performance. Display adapter manufacturers often offer driver upgrades that can significantly improve the performance of existing older display adapters. A cheap way to improve a systems graphics performance is often to simply get the latest Windows driver software for your display adapter.

## AVGA Chip

Most of today's PCs are equipped with an AVGA display adapter function. Sometimes it is installed in an expansion slot, either VL-Bus or PCI bus slot, or it is integrated on the system's motherboard and attaches to one of these busses. A few AVGA adapter boards are still sold with PC AT or ISA bus interfaces, primarily to enable performance upgrades on older PC systems. Figure 11.11 is a block diagram of a AVGA adapter function. Low- to medium-performance designs use a single-chip AVGA device combined with display adapter memory and a ROM or EPROM BIOS.

**Figure 11.11.**
*Block diagram of an AVGA*
*display subsystem.*

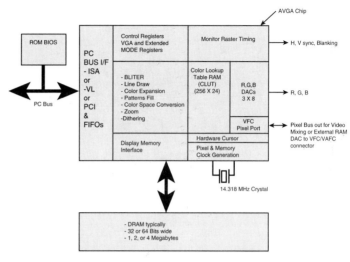

VFC - VGA Feature Connector
VAFC - VESA Advanced Feature Connector

Most of the basic controller functions are in the AVGA chip. This includes the clock generation for the memory, AVGA controller and pixel dot clock, the CLUT, the DAC, the VGA and SVGA controller, the AVGA accelerator, and the bus interface.

# Bus Interface

Figure 11.11 illustrates that a major portion of the AVGA chip is used to create a bus interface to one of the popular PC busses. Since many graphics operations entail copying of memory images or blocks of data from system memory to the display adapter's on-screen memory, the speed of the interface is critical. Also in many designs that have minimal hardware supporting Windows acceleration, this task falls back to the PC's processor; thus, the performance of the bus interface can become a serious bottleneck.

As PC designers learned that moving the system's main memory to the processor's local bus gains significant performance, it was only natural to also move the display adapter and its memory to the processor's local bus. This was the primary force behind the development of the VESA local bus (VL Bus) specification. Today's AVGA chips are designed to attach to either the 32-bit VL bus or the newer 32-bit PCI bus. Both bus interfaces allow for very high performance data paths to and from the display adapter's memory. Typical data rates in excess of 100 MB/second are possible using the VL or PCI bus interfaces. This compares to a maximum data transfer rate of 8MB/second on the older PC AT or ISA bus.

Two important performance features should be supported on the AVGA bus interface. First, burst mode data transfers should be supported. A burst mode data transfer transfers a block of data at one time by only specifying the start address and length. If burst transfer mode is not supported, the effective data transfer rate is nearly cut in half! Secondly, the bus interface should support zero wait state operation during burst mode transfers. This is particularly important on display memory read accesses. On the write accesses to display memory, an 8- to 16-word (32 bits/per word) FIFO memory should be used to ensure efficient data writes or screen updates. AVGA display chips that have these features will achieve the best bus interface performance.

## GUI Acceleration

The graphics engine is the heart of the AVGA chip and can be thought of as a local processor for performing graphic image creation and manipulation independent from the PC's processor, yet under its control. Some of the functions typically provided in the graphics engine are Bit and Block Transfers (Bliter functions), line draw, area fills, and color expansion.

**Technical Note:** The Bliter function is used to create and move rectangular blocks of data (pixels); for example, a window on the screen. Bliter performance is key to Windows performance and the hardware is often designed to specifically perform the Windows API functions in the display adapter hardware. A key consideration in evaluating a display adapter is the Bliter speed. It is also very important that the hardware operates efficiently on all pixel data types and color depths. Many early display adapter designs only support hardware Bliter functions on 256-color or 8-bit pixels and were very slow in 16- or 24-bit pixel color depth modes. Most new AVGA chips also support hardware line draw. This hardware can draw a vector, in all color modes, between two arbitrary points on the screen. Color expansion, as described earlier, is the ability to take a monochrome bit map and place the image on the screen in any position using a preselected image color and background color. It is important that the color expansion hardware feature also works in all color depth modes. Another graphics engine feature often provided is the area or polygon fill feature. This feature will fill an arbitrary polygon with a prespecified color or pattern.

## Display Memory

The major display subsystem feature that dictates screen performance of an AVGA display subsystem is the display memory size, type, and performance. You have seen how the screen raster size in pixel and color depth dictate the memory's size. (See Figure 11.5.) The display memory is mapped into the system's memory address space in a 128 or 64KB block in the A and/or B segments in the lower 1MB spaces of the system's memory. Since many screen sizes and color depth modes do not fit fully in this region, the AVGA controller maps small blocks at a time into this region where the PC's processor can access the APA pixel images. Some of the newer AVGA controllers can map or move the entire display memory into the PC's protected mode address space above the 1MB boundary. When moved to this address region, the full display memory is available without paging. This type of linear memory address remapping can significantly improve the display system's performance, since paging is eliminated.

The display memory's performance is measured by how many bytes of data can be accessed per second. The maximum access rate is called the memory's bandwidth and is usually measured in millions of bytes per second (megabytes/sec). Several functions of the display adapter subsystem contend for and use the display memory bandwidth. The largest user of the display memory's bandwidth is the screen refresh. As the raster scans the virtual screen in display memory, pixel data is read out and applied to the CLUT or directly to the DACs. It is fairly easy to calculate how much bandwidth (megabytes/sec) is required to simply refresh the screen. A rough value can be calculated by simply multiplying the screen raster horizontal size by the vertical size in pixels time the number of bytes per pixel times the screen refresh rates. For example an 800×600 pixel raster size with 256 color (one byte per pixel) running at a screen refresh rate of 60 Hz is: 800×600×1×60 = 28.8MB/second. Unfortunately, other display adapter functions also need bandwidth to access the screen to change it or update it. For example, the system's CPU may want to move a window or image from system memory to the display memory, or the AVGA BLITER will want to create a new window, move a window, or perform a color expansion creating a new set of text characters. The amount of bandwidth needed to perform these functions, by either the CPU or AVGA graphics engine, is dependent, again, on screen size and color depth. A good rule of thumb is to reserve 25 to 50 percent of the display memory bandwidth for nonscreen refresh functions such as processor access and graphic engine functions. Figure 11.12 shows display memory bandwidth requirements based on screen pixel raster size, color depth, and screen refresh rates. Remember, this table only accounts for the bandwidth needed to refresh the screen; roughly an additional 25 to 50 percent bandwidth is required to change or update the screen!

The organization of the display memory is very important to its bandwidth capabilities. For example, a memory that is 64-bits wide has twice the bandwidth of a 32-bit wide memory. It is also possible to use a technique called bank interleaving to achieve nearly 64-bit wide bus performance from a 32-bit memory system. This scheme allows two or more banks of 32-bit memory to be simultaneously accessed and the data from multiple banks multiplexed into the controller or DACs quickly. Thus a 2-bank interleaved 32-bit wide memory design is nearly as fast as a full 64-bit wide memory. Also, some memories are dual-ported, allowing simultaneous access on both memory ports. Usually one port is dedicated to the display refresh function and the other to the CPU or graphic engine access. Dual-port memory designs are more expensive but support much higher performance systems.

Figure 11.13 shows block diagrams of single-port and dual-port memory display adapter designs. Single-port memory systems use a single data port to both refresh the screen and provide CPU and controller accesses. Standard DRAM memory devices are used for most display memory, the same memory devices that are used for main system memory. Two recent enhancements in the DRAM memory technology have significantly increased its performance in display memory applications. One is called an EDO (Extended Data Out) DRAM, which does not disable the data bus out signals between access cycles thus allowing the memory to run at a higher speed. The other emerging DRAM technology is called synchronous DRAM or SDRAM. This technology allows data to be accessed synchronously at very high speeds with an external clock; that is, a pixel clock. Another single-port memory technology that is likely to be applied to display memory applications in the future is RAMbus. This technology permits data rates as high as 500MB/second on narrow 8-bit memory ports. Data is accessed in 256-byte blocks at a time, which works well for display refresh and not so well for CPU and controller updates. For single-port memory designs, standard DRAMs or EDO DRAMS are most commonly used in display adapters and a 64-bit wide memory system can achieve bandwidths as high as 400MB/second.

*Figure 11.12.*
*Screen refresh bandwidth requirements.*

| Screen refresh rate bandwidths in Megabytes/second | | | | 60 Hertz | 70 Hertz | 75 Hertz | 80 Hertz |
|---|---|---|---|---|---|---|---|
| screen size | color depths | | | refresh rate | refresh rate | refresh rate | refresh rate |
| 640x480 | 8 bit pseudo color | | | 18.432 | 21.504 | 23.040 | 24.576 |
| | 15/16 bit high color | | | 36.864 | 43.008 | 46.080 | 49.152 |
| | 24 bit packed Pixel true color | | | 55.2296 | 64.512 | 69.120 | 73.728 |
| | 24 bit unpacked true color | | | 73.728 | 86.016 | 92.160 | 98.304 |
| 800x600 | 8 bit pseudo color | | | 28.800 | 33.600 | 36.000 | 38.400 |
| | 15/16 bit high color | | | 57.600 | 67.200 | 72.000 | 76.800 |
| | 24 bit packed Pixel true color | | | 86.400 | 100.800 | 108.000 | 115.200 |
| | 24 bit unpacked true color | | | 115.200 | 134.400 | 144.000 | 153.600 |
| 1024x768 | 8 bit pseudo color | | | 47.186 | 55.050 | 58.982 | 62.915 |
| | 15/16 bit high color | | | 94.372 | 110.100 | 117.965 | 125.829 |
| | 24 bit packed Pixel true color | | | 141.558 | 165.151 | 176.947 | 188.744 |
| | 24 bit unpacked true color | | | 188.744 | 220.201 | 235.930 | 251.658 |
| 1280x1024 | 8 bit pseudo color | | | 78.643 | 91.750 | 98.304 | 104.858 |
| | 15/16 bit high color | | | 157.286 | 183.501 | 196.608 | 209.715 |
| | 24 bit packed Pixel true color | | | 235.930 | 275.251 | 294.912 | 314.573 |
| | 24 bit unpacked true color | | | 314.573 | 367.002 | 393.216 | 419.430 |
| 1600x1200 | 8 bit pseudo color | | | 115.200 | 134.400 | 144.000 | 153.600 |
| | 15/16 bit high color | | | 230.400 | 268.800 | 288.000 | 307.200 |
| | 24 bit packed Pixel true color | | | 345.600 | 403.200 | 432.000 | 460.800 |
| | 24 bit unpacked true color | | | 460.800 | 537.600 | 576.000 | 614.400 |
| 1920x1440 | 8 bit pseudo color | | | 165.888 | 193.536 | 207.360 | 221.184 |
| | 15/16 bit high color | | | 331.776 | 387.072 | 414.720 | 442.368 |
| | 24 bit packed Pixel true color | | | 497.664 | 580.608 | 622.080 | 663.552 |
| | 24 bit unpacked true color | | | 663.552 | 774.144 | 829.440 | 884.736 |

*Figure 11.13.*
*Single- and dual-port*
*memory display adapter*
*designs.*

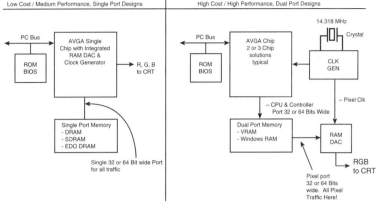

SDRAM - Synchronous Dynamic Random Access Memory
EDO - Extended Data Out
AVGA - Accelerated Video Graphics Array

# Dual-Port Memory Systems

For the higher performance and more expensive dual-port memory designs, VRAM is most commonly used. VRAM (Video RAM) is a special DRAM that has two data ports. One port is just like the single port on a standard DRAM and is used by the CPU or Controller to update or manipulate the image's pixel data. The second port is a serial access port that is typically used to access display data to refresh the screen image. VRAM designs totally separate the display refresh bandwidth requirement from the bandwidth needed by the CPU and Controller for screen updates. VRAM memories are typically 1.5 to twice as expensive as DRAM systems, so they are only used in the highest performance designs. Recently, several companies are providing a new dual-port memory called Windows RAM. This memory is a cost-reduced version of VRAM, yet provides most other dual-port memory performance benefits. Windows RAM achieves its lower cost by removing some of the seldom-used features of VRAM. Figure 11.13 shows block diagrams of both single-port memory designs and dual-port memory designs. Note that the dual-port solutions always require an external RAMDAC because the serial data output port does not return to the AVGA controller.

If we know the width of the display memory and the technology type and speed, it is possible to easily calculate the maximum total bandwidth that it can support. Figure 11.14 defines the typical maximum total bandwidth from common single-port memories for a range of memory device speeds and bus widths. DRAMs are very slow on initial random accesses but are very fast when contiguous memory locations are accessed. Contiguous access can use a special mode called page mode accesses that runs at what is called a CAS (Column Address Strobe) speed. The tables assume that 80 percent of the DRAM's accesses are the faster page mode CAS accesses.

For the dual-port memory, data can be accessed simultaneously on both the standard port and the serial port, nearly doubling the bandwidth available. Figure 11.15 estimates the bandwidth available on both ports for typical VRAM configurations and speeds.

*Figure 11.14.*
*DRAM or single-port*
*memory bandwidths.*

| BANDWIDTH AVAILABLE FROM DRAM MEMORY SUBSYSTEMS TYPES | | |
|---|---|---|
| (ALL VALUES IN MEGABYTES/SECOND | | |
| **32 BIT DRAM** | PAGE MODE CYCLES ONLY | DERATE BY X.8 FOR PAGE ACCESS FAULTS |
| 70NS (40NS CAS) | 100.00 | 80.00 |
| 60NS (35NS CAS) | 114.29 | 91.43 |
| 45NS (30NS CAS) | 133.33 | 106.67 |
| 15NS EDO BURST MODE CYCLE | 266.67 | 213.33 |
| | | |
| **64 BIT DRAM/32 BIT INTERLEAVED** | | |
| 70NS (40NS CAS) | 200.00 | 160.00 |
| 60NS (35NS CAS) | 228.57 | 182.86 |
| 45NS (30NS CAS) | 266.67 | 213.33 |
| 15NS EDO BURST MODE CYCLE | 533.33 | 426.67 |
| | | |
| **128 BIT DRAM/64 BIT INTERLEAVED** | | |
| 70NS (40NS CAS) | 400.00 | 320.00 |
| 60NS (35NS CAS) | 457.14 | 365.71 |
| 45NS (30NS CAS) | 533.33 | 426.67 |
| 15NS EDO BURST MODE CYCLE | 1066.67 | 853.33 |

CAS - Column Addressable Strobe (a key timing parameter in DRAM access times)
EDO - Extended Data Out (a new special mode for DRAM increasing their performance by nearly a factor of 1.5x)

*Figure 11.15.*
*VRAM or dual-port*
*memory bandwidths.*

| BANDWIDTH AVAILABLE FROM VRAM MEMORIES (ALL VALUES IN MEGABYTES/SEC) | | |
|---|---|---|
| **4 Mb TI VRAM** | DATA PORT(X.8) | VIDEO PORT |
| **32 BIT VRAM** | | |
| 70NS WITH: | | |
| 40NS CAS / 22NS SERIAL CYCLE | 80 | 181.82 |
| | | |
| 60NS WITH: | | |
| 35NS CAS / 18NS SERIAL CYCLE | 91.43 | 222.22 |
| **64 BIT OR 32 BIT INTERLEAVED VRAM** | | |
| 70NS WITH: | | |
| 40NS CAS / 22NS SERIAL CYCLE | 160 | 363.64 |
| | | |
| 60NS WITH: | | |
| 35NS CAS / 18NS SERIAL CYCLE | 182.86 | 444.44 |
| **128 BIT OR 64 BIT INTERLEAVED VRAM** | | |
| 70NS WITH: | | |
| 40NS CAS / 22NS SERIAL CYCLE | 320 | 727.27 |
| | | |
| 60NS WITH: | | |
| 35NS CAS / 18NS SERIAL CYCLE | 365.71 | 888.89 |

CAS - Column Address Strobe (a key timing parameter in determining memory performance)
VRAM - Video Random Access Memory (a special dual port memory designed for use in video display adapters)

If one compares the screen refresh bandwidth requirements in Figure 11.12 for different screen pixel resolutions, color depths, and screen refresh rates with the bandwidth available from dual-port and single-port memory systems, it is possible to determine which display memory subsystem is best for a specific screen size, color depth, and refresh rate. If one assumes that some portion of the display memory's bandwidth must be reserved for CPU or controller updates (25 to 50 percent), it is possible to determine what a specific memory speed, type, and width can support in terms of screen pixel size, color depths, and refresh rates. Figure 11.16 summarizes of the screens that can be supported by typical types and speeds of display memory. Note that it is possible to display large screens in some modes, but you would not have acceptable screen update speeds.

**Figure 11.16.**
*screen size and color depth versus display memory types and speeds.*

| 32 BIT 70ns DRAM @ 75 HZ | | | | | |
|---|---|---|---|---|---|
| | 8 BIT | 16 BIT | 24 BIT | 32 BIT | |
| 640 X 480 | Y | Y | Y | N | |
| 800 X 600 | Y | Y | N | N | |
| 1024 X 768 | Y | N | N | N | |
| 1280 X1024 | Y | N | N | N | |
| 1600 X 1200 | N | N | N | N | |

| 64 BIT 70ns DRAM @ 75 HZ | | | | | |
|---|---|---|---|---|---|
| | 8 BIT | 16 BIT | 24 BIT | 32 BIT | |
| 640 X 480 | Y | Y | Y | Y | |
| 800 X 600 | Y | Y | Y | Y | |
| 1024 X 768 | Y | Y | N | N | |
| 1280 X1024 | Y | N | N | N | |
| 1600 X 1200 | Y | N | N | N | |

| 64 BIT 70ns/50MHZ VRAM @ 75 HZ | | | | | |
|---|---|---|---|---|---|
| | 8 BIT | 16 BIT | 24 BIT | 32 BIT | |
| 640 X 480 | Y | Y | Y | Y | |
| 800 X 600 | Y | Y | Y | Y | |
| 1024 X 768 | Y | Y | Y | Y | |
| 1280 X1024 | Y | Y | Y | Y | |
| 1600 X 1200 | Y | Y | N | N | |

| | (CANNOT BE SUPPORTED) |
|---|---|

* SOME DRAM RATES CAN BE REFRESHED BUT
THERE IS TOO LITTLE BANDWIDTH LEFT FOR
BLITER ACCESS TO SUSTAIN REASONABLE
PERFORMANCE, SO "N" IS SELECTED IN THESE
CLOSE CASES

* 24 BIT MODES ASSUME PACKED PIXEL 24 BIT COLOR
IF THE CONTROLLER DOES NOT SUPPORT PACKED
PIXEL MODE FOR 24 BIT COLOR USE THE 32 BIT
NUMBERS AND RESTRICTIONS

* PACKED PIXEL MODE ALSO SAVES MEMORY & ALLOWS
24 BIT COLOR IN 1280 X 1024 MODE WITH 4MB OF RAM

# ROM BIOS

Each display adapter subsystem comes with a ROM BIOS. This Read Only Memory (ROM) contains a minimal amount of software to support setting up the AVGA controller to support a desired screen environment. Also, the BIOS software interfaces the AVGA's hardware to a standard set of DOS functions. BIOS software is primarily used in DOS applications and mostly bypassed in Windows environments. To improve system performance, often the contents of the BIOS is moved from the ROM to system DRAM, where it can be accessed much faster. This is called BIOS shadowing and is a standard feature in nearly all systems.

# DAC Speed

In most low-cost and medium-speed display adapter designs, the DAC function is built into the AVGA chip. For higher performance designs and VRAM or dual-ported memory designs, the DAC and CLUT RAM (RAMDAC) function is a separate chip. The speed of the DAC is very important and can limit the screen resolution and refresh rates of the total system. Note that the DAC speed is independent of the color depth because it accepts all color modes either directly from the display memory or from the CLUT RAM. Table 11.2 indicates the DAC speeds necessary to support popular screen resolutions at a 75 Hz screen refresh rate.

Table 11.2. DAC Speeds vs. Screen Sizes at 75 Hz Refresh Rates.

| Screen size | DAC Speed at 75 Hz Refresh Rate |
| --- | --- |
| 640×480 | 31.5 MHz |
| 800×600 | 49.5 MHz |
| 1024×768 | 78.75 MHz |
| 1280×1024 | 135 MHz |
| 1600×1200 | ~170 MHz |
| 1920×1440 | ~200 MHz |

# Gamma Correction

Sometimes it is very important that the display's colors reflect exactly the colors the user expects to see and use. Unfortunately, some displays do not exhibit an exact true color over the full range of the 16.8 million colors. The 256 color steps available through each the DACs may be not be uniform, or equal, steps. To correct this type of problem and get more of a true color representation from the display, some display adapters support gamma or color correction. This correction is accomplished by using the R, G, and B digital colors that would normally drive the DAC as addresses to a color component look-up table. The value in the correction memory is used to replace the component color value and is sent to the DAC. This is very similar to the color palette scheme used to change an 8-bit color to a 24-bit color, except it is performed on each RGB color component. In some designs the CLUT RAM is also used to perform color correction. By preloading the correction look-up table memory, it is possible to change any color component value to a new value, thus correcting color problems within the display system.

# The Display Device

Of course the display adapter is only part of the display subsystem. The display device, usually some type of CRT, is required to actually view the generated images. The CRT device is attached to the display adapter though a standard 15-pin high-density D shell connector. Figure 11.17 defines the connector's pins and signals on the interface.

**Figure 11.17.**
*Display adapter pin and connector interface to the CRT display.*

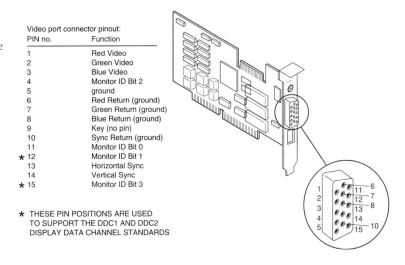

Video port connector pinout:

| PIN no. | Function |
| --- | --- |
| 1 | Red Video |
| 2 | Green Video |
| 3 | Blue Video |
| 4 | Monitor ID Bit 2 |
| 5 | ground |
| 6 | Red Return (ground) |
| 7 | Green Return (ground) |
| 8 | Blue Return (ground) |
| 9 | Key (no pin) |
| 10 | Sync Return (ground) |
| 11 | Monitor ID Bit 0 |
| ★ 12 | Monitor ID Bit 1 |
| 13 | Horizontal Sync |
| 14 | Vertical Sync |
| ★ 15 | Monitor ID Bit 3 |

★ THESE PIN POSITIONS ARE USED
TO SUPPORT THE DDC1 AND DDC2
DISPLAY DATA CHANNEL STANDARDS

Sync - Synchronization timing signals

Most CRT display monitors today are of the multisync design. This means that it will automatically adjust and display images independently of the applied horizontal and vertical synch frequencies within a band of scan rates. Most low-cost to medium-cost multisync CRT display monitors work in the horizontal frequency range of 31.5 to over 100 KHz and the vertical frequency range of 50 to 80 Hz. From a raster timing standpoint, three monitor specifications are important:

1. Maximum pixel clock rate supported. For VESA super VGA screens up to 1280×1024, a minimum clock rate of 135 MHz is required.

2. Maximum horizontal scan rate. For VESA super VGA screens up to 1280×1024 at 75 Hz refresh rates, a minimum horizontal scan rate of 80 KHz is required.

3. Maximum vertical scan or refresh rate. At the desired horizontal scan rate a minimum of 75 Hz is generally recommended.

Of course a major specification is the dot pitch of the CRT. This was discussed earlier in the chapter and Figure 11.2 defines the dot pitch requirements of various size CRT screens versus the pixel rasters size.

One of the more important features of a CRT display are the controllers available to adjust the screen. The following is list of the basic controls needed:

- Color adjustment, sometimes called intensity or brightness adjustment
- Contrast adjustment
- Horizontal raster position control
- Vertical raster position control
- Size controls, controlling both horizontal and vertical sizes

Of course the best way to judge a display's quality is to observe images at the screen resolutions, color depths, and refresh rates you intend to use on your PC. One thing to check is the quality of the screen images under bright lighting conditions. Reflections on the screen can be very annoying under adverse lighting conditions. Some CRT surfaces are treated with an anti-reflective coating to reduce reflective glare. Also, the linearity of the image should be checked. This can be accomplished by filling the screen with an *H* character and observing how well the horizontal and vertical lines line up. Another simple test is to open a full-screen window with a bright border color and check to see if the edges are straight. If they are curved, the display is exhibiting a pin cushion effect. Often the pin cushion effect is dependent on the display's brightness and contrast control setting, so adjust these controls full scale while observing the edges of the full-screen window. Often a display is very sensitive to noise generated by the computer that exists on the analog R, G, and B signals. Two forms of noise are common, low frequency and high frequency. An easy way to check for video signal noise is to create a light-colored screen that uses all of the R, G, and B signals at low intensity levels. Low frequency noise will manifest itself as a darker or lighter horizontal band that rolls slowly in the vertical direction. High frequency noise will be exhibited as Moiré patterns (semi-circle) of lighter or dark patterns on the screen. These patterns do not move but will come and go depending on the color on the screen. Most displays will exhibit some Moiré patterns and total elimination of this effect is difficult. Darker colors tend not to exhibit this effect.

# Low Radiation Displays

Another feature that's gaining popularity is Low Radiation CRT Displays. There is significant controversy over the issue of the effects on the human body of radiation from electric and magnetic fields created by the CRT display. Several European countries have imposed strict standards for emission from CRT displays. These are part of the ISO9000 Standards; not all monitors meet all of the specs of the ISO9000. Most low radiation monitors state that they are MPRII-Compliant, which deals with the radiation aspect of the specs. In response to concerns by PC users, many CRT display manufacturers are now offering low radiation CRT displays. Low radiation displays, which typically encapsulate the CRT in a metal shield inside the covers to reduce the electric and magnetic field emission, are available for a small price premium.

# (DPMS)
# Display Power Management Signaling

With the concern for energy conservation, the Display Power Management Signaling (DPMS) feature is gaining in popularity and is often specified by government agencies. The display adapter controller and BIOS software can signal the attached CRT display adapter to enter several levels of power down states. Figure 11.18 defines the DPMS states and how they are signaled across the interface using the RGB analog signals and the sync signals on the display connector interface. The defined power down level states are varying levels of image recovery speed, depending on the amount of power saved. The amount of power saved and the level of recovery time between states is not defined in detail by the standard; thus, different implementations of the standard are prevalent.

*Figure 11.18.*
*DPMS states and*
*signaling.*

Display Power Management Summary

| State | Signals | | | DPMS Compliance Requirement | Power Savings | Recovery Time |
|-------|---------|---------|-------|---------|---------|---------|
| | Horizontal | Vertical | Video | | | |
| On | Pulses | Pulses | Active | Mandatory | None | Not Applicable |
| Stand-by | No Pulses | Pulses | Blanked | Optional | Minimal | Short |
| Suspend | Pulses | No Pulses | Blanked | Mandatory | Substantial | Longer |
| Off | No Pulses | No Pulses | Blanked | Mandatory | Maximum | System Dependent |

# (DDC)
# Display Data Channel

Another feature that is being added to CRT display devices is the Display Data Channel (DDC). This feature enables the CRT display to inform the display adapter subsystem in the PC about the capabilities of the attached display device. This enables the display adapter's BIOS to select operational characteristics, such as scan rates, that are compatible with the attached monitor. The early VGA connector contained four signals that could be encoded with a monitor-type ID value. The DDC standard expanded the functions of this interface to allow the display to send detailed information serially over this interface to the display controller. Two basic levels of the DDC standard exist. Level 1 or DDC1 supports a continuous data stream from the display to the display adapter;

the display controller or adapter cannot send any information or requests to the display. Level 2 or DDC2 permits bidirectional communications between the display adapter controller and the display. The serial interface used to perform the communications is on pins 12 and 15 of the display adapter 15-pin connector. The DDC2 interface is also called the ACCESS.Bus standard. This is a standard based on the old Phillips I 2 C serial bus and is capable of supporting attachment of other devices such as keyboards and scanners. The DCC2 Standard is also part of the Plug and Play standards being developed by Intel and Microsoft to simplify device attachment and expansion on the PC.

# TVs on PCs

As emphasized earlier, TVs make poor display devices for PCs because of the large dot pitch and slow screen refresh rates. However, there are some instances when it is desirable to attach a PC to a TV. Consider the PC presentation applications, where the presentation is to be displayed to a large audience. This application is perfect for a large-screen TV or projection TV application. If a presentation is prepared on the PC such that it considers the limitation of the TV, some impressive results can be achieved. So how do you attach a PC's display adapter output to a TV? Most modern TVs have an RCA jack for composite video input. The PC has a 15-pin direct RGB drive connector. Also, the raster scan rates of the PC are not compatible with the TV's standard raster scan rates. Two solutions are possible to overcome these differences. The first solution is to reprogram the AVGA controller chip to approximate the TV's scan rates and then convert the direct drive signal to TV composite signals through a device called a Composite Encoder. This scheme is rarely used because the composite encoder needs to be built into the display adapter and adds cost to the design. An alternate solution is to purchase a VGA to TV scan converter box. This device simply attaches to the display adapter connector, captures the PC's display image in a special frame buffer memory, scans the same image out at the TV scan rates, and feeds the image into a composite signal encoder such that it can be displayed on any TV with a composite video input. Numerous manufacturers now provide PC to TV scan converter boxes at minimal cost.

# Video in the PC

Many new multimedia applications want to mix or display TV video on the PC's screen. This could be live video from a camera or prerecorded video from a laser disk, CD-ROM, or VCR. Another rapidly expanding application is live video conferencing on the PC. In all cases, it is necessary to display a TV moving image on the PC's high resolution display. If the video image comes from a TV camera, broadcast source, VCR, or laser disc, it is not compressed, and is normally a composite video or S-Video analog signal. If the video is stored on a CD-ROM or hard disk, it has already been converted to a digital representation and is probably compressed to save storage space.

In any case, the first step in moving either a live video or pre-recorded video signal to a PC display is to convert the analog video signal to digital information. This step is accomplished by a device known as a composite video digital decoder, which samples the incoming analog video signal and converts it to a digital representation. For U.S. TV standards, the sampled digital data output rate is typically 27MB/second. At this data rate, even a few seconds of video will quickly fill a typical PC's hard disk. Most sampled digital data needs to be compressed to a manageable size and data rate to be useful in PC multimedia applications. Unfortunately, the sampled digital data is not in a familiar digital R, G, and B component notation that the AVGA display adapter can recognize. The video industry uses a different digital representation that permits what is called *subcolor sampling*. This means the color (Chroma) portion of the signal is sampled at a slower rate than the brightness (Luminance) portion. The video signal is thus converted from the analog domain to a special "YUV" digital representation. The letters YU and V are not abbreviations, but commonly used letters used to define the Y (Luminance or lightness component of a color) and the UV or color difference component (color content).

To get the image on the PC's screen, the YUV digital data must be converted to the more familiar RGB digital representation that is understood by the PC's display adapter. This conversion is called color space conversion. Once the analog signal is decoded and color space conversion is completed, it can then be put into the PC's display adapter memory for display. The quality level of the digital image is dependent on the sampling rate and is typically specified by a series of three numbers, such as 4:4:4, 4:2:2, or 4:1:1. These three numbers refer to the sample rates of the Y:U:V color components. The value 4, for example, means roughly 4 times the base color burst frequency of 3.5 MHz or 13.5 MHz sample rate. The U and V components in the YUV system contain the color information; therefore, the 4:2:2 mode indicates that the color portion of the signals is sampled at one-half the rate of the Luminous portion. When the color portion is sampled at a lower rate than the Luminous component it is called subcolor sampling. To get acceptable conversion of a composite TV signal to a digital signal, a minimum of 4:2:2 sampling is usually required. If 8-bit samples are used, the Luminous (Y) component requires a 13.5MB/second data rate and the two Chroma components (U and V) require a 6.75MB/second data rate each for a total of 27 MB/second. Sampling of the color portion of the signal at a lower rate works well because the human eye does not detect color changes well in moving screen images.

# Merging Video and PC Graphics

Once a video signal is converted to the digital domain, it must next be merged with the PC's graphic image screen for display on the PC's CRT display. This hardware merging of the PC's graphics and the video images can occur in three different ways: DAC attached method, analog method, and the shared frame buffer method. Figure 11.19 depicts the three hardware schemes and how software only merging at the application level is supported. The simplest is to simply not convert the video image to digital data and mix the signals in the analog domain. This requires careful synchronization of the two analog signals and does not permit the PC to manipulate the video image to scale it or clip it into an arbitrary window size on the PC's CRT display screen. The second method is to merge the video data at the input to the RAMDAC in the digital domain. It turns out that the VGA display adapter design defined a port just for this purpose. The interface and connector for supporting video overlays onto PC screens is called the VFC or VGA Feature Connector. The VFC interface does have some limitations; for example, the interface is only 8 bits wide and only supports a 256-color mode. The VFC interface has a maximum bandwidth capability of approximately 40MB/second. Even though this is higher than the 27MB/second needed to support live video, when the video image is placed on the PC's higher refresh rate screen, it must merge at the PC refresh rates, which can be significantly higher than 40MB/second. To overcome these performance problems, the VESA standards have defined a new VESA Advanced Feature Connector interface (VAFC). This interfaces supports true color pixels (16.8 million colors) with data rates as high as 150MB/second over a 16- or 32-bit interface. Many of the newer display adapters support the newer VAFC interface and connector. If live video is to be added later on a PC display subsystem, it would be wise to purchase a display adapter with the newer VAFC interface and connector capability. Since the digital video and PC graphics are merged at the DAC input, the VFC or VAFC interface is also sometimes called a *DAC attached* video merging scheme. It is also possible for the PC application software to mix digital video and graphics before they are sent to the PC's screen. This scheme is called application level mixing and requires a very fast CPU and display adapter but no special hardware

**Figure 11.19.**
*Mixing of video and PC graphics options.*

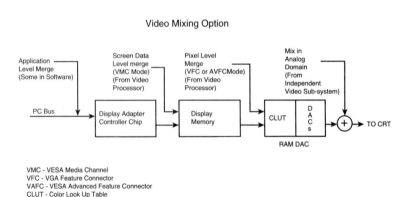

VMC - VESA Media Channel
VFC - VGA Feature Connector
VAFC - VESA Advanced Feature Connector
CLUT - Color Look Up Table

The analog mixing and DAC attached or VFC/VAFC can be very expensive since a full independent video input subsystem is needed. The most expensive piece is the frame buffer memory (also called the scan convert memory), which holds the digitized image before it is scanned out to the DAC's pixel input port. As the display adapter's display memory performance has improved with faster and wider memories, it is possible to place the video image directly in the PC display memory, eliminating the need for a separate video frame buffer memory. This scheme not only costs less, it also allows the PC and AVGA controller chip access to the video image for capture and manipulation purposes. This method of merging video and PC graphics is called the Shared Frame Buffer

(SFB) approach. Several AVGA chip manufacturers now support the SFB architecture for merging Video and PC graphics into a single unified display memory. Unfortunately, most use a proprietary interface. The VESA organization has attempted to standardize a high speed bus or channel called the VESA Media Channel (VMC), which would be used to move noncompressed video at their native data rates and color space representation between components of a graphics and video sub-system. At this time the specification calls for a full 32-bit bus running at a maximum of 33 MHz for a maximum data rate of 132MB/second. The VMC is ideally suited to support the transfer of digital video to a SFB memory. At this time, the VMC has little success in attracting a following. The Intel PCI bus has the same performance and is likely to be used as a video systems pixel bus in future designs. Figure 11.20 illustrates the SFB and DAC attached approaches to supporting video in a window on the PC's display. The SFB approach normally assumes that the AVGA chip has video processing capabilities built in.

**Figure 11.20.**
*Video in a window,
shared frame buffer
and DAC attached
schemes.*

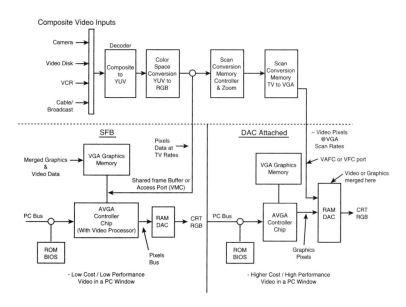

# Video Processing

As mentioned earlier, most TV video is generated or encoded to produce a TV resolution screen in the YUV format. To display the TV digital image on the PC's CRT at the full screen size, the digital TV image must first be color-space converted from the YUV format to the PC's RGB format and then expanded to the desired size on the PC's screen or window on the PC's screen. Zooming an image up or down in size and converting it from YUV to RGB representation cannot easily be done in PC software at full-screen sizes and high-frame rates. These functions are normally accomplished by a special piece of hardware called a video processor. The video processor may also perform image clipping, special effects such as fades and transitions, and Chroma keying. Chroma keying uses a specified color code (RGB) value to tell the video processor to overlay the video image at this pixel location. Sometimes the extra unused high-order bit in the 16-bit 5,5,5 high-color mode is used to indicate an overlay condition at the pixel location.

To scale or zoom an image, video pixels either need to be thrown away, duplicated, or created. The simplest way to scale an image is to either throw away pixels when scaling an image down in size or to duplicate pixels when scaling an image up in size. This scheme does not provide smooth scaling and creates large blocks of pixels with the same colors that are easy to detect and detract from the image's scaled up quality. Another, more preferred, method is to create new pixels by interpolation. This scheme creates a much smoother image when scaling up or down. Some video processors only interpolate in the horizontal direction and use pixel duplication or removal in the vertical direction. A good video processor will do both horizontal and vertical pixel interpolation. Recently, several AVGA controller manufacturers have been able to add the video processor's function inside the AVGA chip. This makes the video processor's features available both for live motion video in a window on the PC and to support the playback of compressed video stored on a CD-ROM or hard disk. Figure 11.21 illustrates a typical video processor hardware feature. The video processor hardware can be a separate board attached to the PC's display adapter via the VFC, AVFC, or VMC ports on the display adapter or, as with many new AVGA chips, it can be designed into the basic AVGA chip.

*Figure 11.21.*
*Video processor*
*block diagram.*

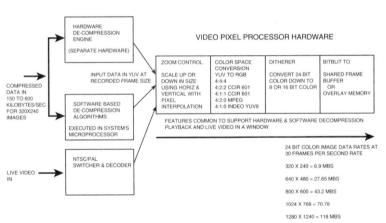

# Full-Motion Video Playback

Playback of compressed full-motion video on a PC can originate from a hardware decompression engine from companies such as C-Cube, SGS Thomson, Motorola, Winbond, TI, Zoran, or from a software decompression package (Cinepak, Indeo, Xing MPEG-1, CompCore MPEG-1, Captain Crunch, and so forth). However, displaying the decompressed images on the PC's AVGA system is still very compute-intensive and restricts the frame rates, image sizes, and color depth to unacceptable levels. Most video processors assume that actual decompression is done in software and the video processors assist in the display of the decompressed images. The video processors accept decompressed TV image in YUV format (from software or hardware decompression engine or from a live video source) and scales the image to the desired window size, clips the image if necessary, color space coverts the image to RGB, dithers the image for low color environments, and then transmits it to either the shared frame buffer or the overlay memory/direct DAC-attached subsystem. Until very recently, the functions of the video processor were not easily accessible in the Microsoft Windows environment. Windows required all display accesses to go through the Windows API (Application Program Interface) and did not permit use of or access to the advanced features of the video processor.

Microsoft has recently announced support for the DCI (Display Control Interface) specification. This new Windows standard allows Windows applications access to the features of the video processor and direct frame buffer access. This change alone accelerated playback of compressed data by over 50 percent, encourages the use of video processors, and makes software decompression much more viable. It has been estimated that almost 50 percent of the PC's CPU time during software decompression of an MPEG-1 data stream is spent in color space conversion and updating the screen window. Thus, a video processor that performed these functions in hardware could have a dramatic effect on playback performance. Scaling of the image up or down in size, as mentioned before, is also very compute-intensive and can be off-loaded to a video processor. See Chapter 25, "Multimedia," for more information on video compression/decompression and video playback acceleration of AVI (Audio Video Interleaved) files. Obviously, selecting a PC display adapter with built-in video processing would be wise if you wish to support multimedia applications requiring playback of video files or support for video in a window on the PC.

# 3-D Graphics

Realistic 3-D images on a low cost PC have great appeal in a number of applications areas. The market and applications for 3-D graphics can be segmented into two areas with vastly different technical requirements. The most familiar area is the traditional application of 3-D rendering in workstation applications. In this area, resolution, image quality, accuracy, and rendering speed are key. Today, this market is dominated by very high performance RISC workstations, often with specialized 3-D rendering hardware. It is not at all uncommon for a 3-D workstation to cost $20,000 to $70,000 and the rendering software packages to cost an additional $20,000. With Pentium and Power PC-based systems, the natural path is to move these applications to these lower-cost PC platforms. This is a well-understood market, since it is moving existing applications to a lower-cost platform and has a set of well-established application interfaces standards. In this area, Open GL from Silicon Graphics is the accepted industry standard API for most 3-D software. Thus hardware that accelerates the Open GL application interface will have immediate access to a large set of existing 3-D applications. The initial industry thrust will probably be to support low-cost 3-D rendering for existing workstation applications.

The second and more exciting area for 3-D is in games and multimedia applications, such as education and virtual reality. Here the need is for real-time 3-D rendering at 30 frames/second where game and user interactively allow lighting and viewing positions to change with game action and events. Sega, Nintendo, 3DO, and Sony all are developing game consoles with real-time 3-D rendering in hardware. The natural path is to enable this same capability on the PC. As with decompression of full-motion video, the developers are hesitant to support and require specific hardware for 3-D. With the compute power of high clock rate 486s and Pentium processors, game developers have opted for software-only 3-D rendering. To support the portability of games, several 3-D rendering libraries and application interfaces have developed. These include the following:

- Criterion (Render Ware)
- Argonaut (BRender)
- Reality Lab (Render Morphics)
- Intel (3DR)

Most games today are written for the DOS environment on the PC. This is again due to the overhead of the Windows graphics interface. In an effort to promote the use of Windows in game applications, Microsoft now provides a new game interface called WinG. WinG is not a 3-D rendering package, but it enables 3-D hardware and software access to the display memory without the overhead of the Windows API.

Since speed is the most important feature of real-time 3-D games, many tricks and short cuts are taken to create the 3-D images. Image quality, resolution, and accuracy are sacrificed for speed and color depth. Many functions that would normally be done in floating point are done with fixed point arithmetic. Further, many special effects such as warping, transparency, clouds, fog, star bursts, and flares are done at the scan line level versus the 3-D transformation level. For game applications, traditional 3-D rendering engines are too costly in memory and complexity or too inflexible. Hardware-specific acceleration of game 3-D graphics in a generalized manner is difficult to implement. Each API has unique features and the flexibility to change the underlying software implementation, as each new release further complicates hardware acceleration.

The 3-D rendering process is broken into two steps: the geometry transformation process (floating point-intensive) and the scan line rendering process (CPU cycle-intensive). Due to the high performance floating-point capabilities of the Pentium and Power PC chips, most new chips are now concentrating on the scan line rendering acceleration function. However, existing designs are still targeting the high-end applications with complex polygon vertices list-driven engines. These engines take a list of polygon coordinates that define the image (just the vertices of the polygon) and render them in the 2-dimensional mode for display on the PC's flat screen. The 3-D Lab's "Glint" chip and the Austec/Cirrus DG6472 devices fall into this range. Both devices will render 200 to 300KB 50-pixel triangles per second on a Pentium system. This is acceptable for games but probably not competitive with workstations. Unfortunately, these devices fall into no man's land: too slow to compete with workstations and too costly for games and multimedia applications.

### Hardware for Transforming and Rendering 3-D Images

3-D images are represented by a data structure that defines the vertices of a mesh of connected polygons in a 3-Dimensional space. As a viewer walks around in this space and lighting sources are moved, the objects or image must change as it is projected for a specific view on the display's flat, two-dimensional screen. A you can imagine, the transformation of a 3-D image for a specific viewing position and lighting situation to the flat screen set of polygons is very compute-intensive. Such transformations entail many floating-point operations. A 3-D Geometry Transformation Engine is a special set of hardware that can perform may simultaneous floating point operations. For most 3-D game applications, the transformations are done using the processor's floating-point processor or the arithmetic is done in fixed point. Once the transformation process is completed, the 2-D polygons are sent to the scan line rendering engine for shading and display.

This hardware is used to perform the pixel-level operations associated with building and displaying a 3-D image. Once a 3-D image is created with a mesh of polygons (typically triangles), it has to be transformed to a 2-D representation on the flat surface of the display, and then the polygons need to be shaded (colored). This is a very software-intensive operation and can be done much more efficiently in hardware. Some of the latest AVGA chips are now supporting 3-D scan line rendering as extensions to the hardware graphics engine.

Cost-effective real-time 3-D hardware acceleration of the PC is the area that new AVGA controller chip manufacturers are likely to pursue next. This capability would add greatly to the multimedia and entertainment capability of the PC.

# Measuring PC Graphics Performance

One sure way to determine the performance level of a PC's graphics subsystem is to run special benchmark software designed to exercise and measure the graphics performance of the system. Several benchmarks are available and their results are often published in PC magazines reviewing PC graphics adapters. One of the most popular PC graphics benchmark programs is published by Ziff-Davis Benchmark Operations and is part of a total PC systems benchmark package called Winbench 95, which measures system performance in a Windows environment. In the Winbench set of tests are a series of WinMark benchmark tests that measure the performance of both the graphics and the disk subsystem. A special set of tests for graphics is called the Graphics WinMark tests. These tests report both a combined graphic performance in millions of pixels per second and individual test results for specific graphics functions.

When comparing benchmark results between systems, it is imperative that the systems be configured similarly, if not identically. For example, comparing a 486 system to a Pentium system may not provide a fair comparison of their graphics subsystems. Also, only compare benchmark results between graphics systems that are running the same screen resolutions, color depths, and screen refresh rates. Do not try to compare results from different revision levels of the benchmark test software. To obtain the best results, make sure that your display adapter under test is using the latest Windows drivers available from the manufacturer. The Winbench Benchmark software is available from:

> Ziff-Davis Benchmark Operation
> One Copley Parkway, Suite 510
> Morrisville, North Carolina 27560

# Summary

As you can see, PC graphics and video adapter subsystems are fairly complex. The best advice I can offer is this: Don't scrimp on the graphics capabilities of your system. With the performance requirements of Windows and multimedia applications rapidly expanding and with the manufacture of larger displays with higher color depths and large resolution screens, investing in a high-performance graphics subsystem is money well spent. Remember, a high-performance Pentium PC can be crippled by a poor display subsystem, and an older, slower system can be revived by a good display adapter subsystem.

# 12

# The PC
# Character
# Set

Up to this point, I've mentioned the PC's character set several times, but I haven't taken the time to really describe what it is and how it works—and why you should care. That's because I think that the character set is an interesting enough subject that it merits its own chapter to give you a closer look. First, I give you an overview of the whole character set, then I show you how the PC's characters relate to a widespread standard known as ASCII, and I dig into and analyze the full set of special PC characters. Finally, I give you a look at the implication of the computing community going international.

# An Overview

Characters in the PC, as in most modern computers, occupy an 8-bit byte, so that there can be as many as $2^8$, or 256, distinct characters. These characters are shown in Figure 12.1.

*Figure 12.1.*
*The full PC character set.*

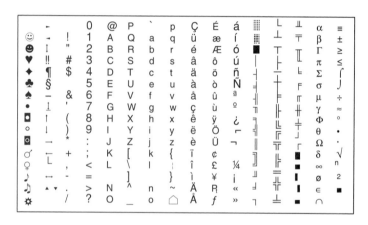

There are two easy ways for you to display all the characters on the screen of your computer. One is to use the program called ALL-CHAR. (You can find it in Appendix B, "QBasic Program Listings.") This program was used to create Figure 12.1. The other way is to use a utility program that offers a quick and handy display of the PC's full character set. Some such programs even pop up on top of other applications when you need them. When you use ALL-CHAR or a utility program, you see the PC character set in exactly the way your computer's screen shows them, which can vary somewhat depending on the type of display you have. (For more information on video displays, see Chapter 11, "On-Screen Video.") Figure 12.1 shows the characters in more or less their ideal form and gives you a quick and accurate way of seeing just what each character is like.

To give you a handy reference, Figure 12.2 shows each character's appearance together with the numeric character codes in decimal and hex. For each character, the decimal and hex code have the same numerical value but different representations. I refer to this figure frequently throughout this chapter. If you want to see the information from this figure on your computer screen, you can use either the REF-CHAR program listed in Appendix B or a utility program.

**Figure 12.2.**
*The PC character set with decimal and hex codes.*

| char | dec | hex | char | dec | hex | char | dec | hex | char | dec | hex | char | dec | hex | char | dec | hex | char | dec | hex | char | dec | hex |
|---|---|---|---|---|---|---|---|---|---|---|---|---|---|---|---|---|---|---|---|---|---|---|---|
|  | 0 | 0 |  | 32 | 20 | @ | 64 | 40 |  | 96 | 60 | Ç | 128 | 80 | á | 160 | A0 | └ | 192 | C0 | α | 224 | E0 |
| ☺ | 1 | 1 | ! | 33 | 21 | A | 65 | 41 | a | 97 | 61 | ü | 129 | 81 | í | 161 | A1 | ┴ | 193 | C1 | β | 225 | E1 |
| ☻ | 2 | 2 | " | 34 | 22 | B | 66 | 42 | b | 98 | 62 | é | 130 | 82 | ó | 162 | A2 | ┬ | 194 | C2 | Γ | 226 | E2 |
| ♥ | 3 | 3 | # | 35 | 23 | C | 67 | 43 | c | 99 | 63 | â | 131 | 83 | ú | 163 | A3 | ├ | 195 | C3 | π | 227 | E3 |
| ♦ | 4 | 4 | $ | 36 | 24 | D | 68 | 44 | d | 100 | 64 | ä | 132 | 84 | ñ | 164 | A4 | ─ | 196 | C4 | Σ | 228 | E4 |
| ♣ | 5 | 5 | % | 37 | 25 | E | 69 | 45 | e | 101 | 65 | à | 133 | 85 | Ñ | 165 | A5 | ┼ | 197 | C5 | σ | 229 | E5 |
| ♠ | 6 | 6 | & | 38 | 26 | F | 70 | 46 | f | 102 | 66 | å | 134 | 86 | ª | 166 | A6 | ╞ | 198 | C6 | µ | 230 | E6 |
| • | 7 | 7 | ' | 39 | 27 | G | 71 | 47 | g | 103 | 67 | ç | 135 | 87 | º | 167 | A7 | ╟ | 199 | C7 | γ | 231 | E7 |
| ◘ | 8 | 8 | ( | 40 | 28 | H | 72 | 48 | h | 104 | 68 | ê | 136 | 88 | ¿ | 168 | A8 | ╚ | 200 | C8 | Φ | 232 | E8 |
| ○ | 9 | 9 | ) | 41 | 29 | I | 73 | 49 | i | 105 | 69 | ë | 137 | 89 | ⌐ | 169 | A9 | ╔ | 201 | C9 | θ | 233 | E9 |
| ◙ | 10 | A | * | 42 | 2A | J | 74 | 4A | j | 106 | 6A | è | 138 | 8A | ¬ | 170 | AA | ╩ | 202 | CA | Ω | 234 | EA |
| ♂ | 11 | B | + | 43 | 2B | K | 75 | 4B | k | 107 | 6B | ï | 139 | 8B | ½ | 171 | AB | ╦ | 203 | CB | δ | 235 | EB |
| ♀ | 12 | C | , | 44 | 2C | L | 76 | 4C | l | 108 | 6C | î | 140 | 8C | ¼ | 172 | AC | ╠ | 204 | CC | ∞ | 236 | EC |
| ♪ | 13 | D | - | 45 | 2D | M | 77 | 4D | m | 109 | 6D | ì | 141 | 8D | ¡ | 173 | AD | ═ | 205 | CD | Ø | 237 | ED |
| ♫ | 14 | E | . | 46 | 2E | N | 78 | 4E | n | 110 | 6E | Ä | 142 | 8E | « | 174 | AE | ╬ | 206 | CE | ∈ | 238 | EE |
| ☼ | 15 | F | / | 47 | 2F | O | 79 | 4F | o | 111 | 6F | Å | 143 | 8F | » | 175 | AF | ╧ | 207 | CF | ∩ | 239 | EF |
| ► | 16 | 10 | 0 | 48 | 30 | P | 80 | 50 | p | 112 | 70 | É | 144 | 90 | ░ | 176 | B0 | ╨ | 208 | D0 | ≡ | 240 | F0 |
| ◄ | 17 | 11 | 1 | 49 | 31 | Q | 81 | 51 | q | 113 | 71 | æ | 145 | 91 | ▒ | 177 | B1 | ╤ | 209 | D1 | ± | 241 | F1 |
| ↕ | 18 | 12 | 2 | 50 | 32 | R | 82 | 52 | r | 114 | 72 | Æ | 146 | 92 | ▓ | 178 | B2 | ╥ | 210 | D2 | ≥ | 242 | F2 |
| ‼ | 19 | 13 | 3 | 51 | 33 | S | 83 | 53 | s | 115 | 73 | ô | 147 | 93 | │ | 179 | B3 | ╙ | 211 | D3 | ≤ | 243 | F3 |
| ¶ | 20 | 14 | 4 | 52 | 34 | T | 84 | 54 | t | 116 | 74 | ö | 148 | 94 | ┤ | 180 | B4 | ╘ | 212 | D4 | ⌠ | 244 | F4 |
| § | 21 | 15 | 5 | 53 | 35 | U | 85 | 55 | u | 117 | 75 | ò | 149 | 95 | ╡ | 181 | B5 | ╒ | 213 | D5 | ⌡ | 245 | F5 |
| ▬ | 22 | 16 | 6 | 54 | 36 | V | 86 | 56 | v | 118 | 76 | û | 150 | 96 | ╢ | 182 | B6 | ╓ | 214 | D6 | ÷ | 246 | F6 |
| ↨ | 23 | 17 | 7 | 55 | 37 | W | 87 | 57 | w | 119 | 77 | ù | 151 | 97 | ╖ | 183 | B7 | ╫ | 215 | D7 | ≈ | 247 | F7 |
| ↑ | 24 | 18 | 8 | 56 | 38 | X | 88 | 58 | x | 120 | 78 | ÿ | 152 | 98 | ╕ | 184 | B8 | ╪ | 216 | D8 | ° | 248 | F8 |
| ↓ | 25 | 19 | 9 | 57 | 39 | Y | 89 | 59 | y | 121 | 79 | Ö | 153 | 99 | ╣ | 185 | B9 | ┘ | 217 | D9 | • | 249 | F9 |
| → | 26 | 1A | : | 58 | 3A | Z | 90 | 5A | z | 122 | 7A | Ü | 154 | 9A | ║ | 186 | BA | ┌ | 218 | DA | · | 250 | FA |
| ← | 27 | 1B | ; | 59 | 3B | [ | 91 | 5B | { | 123 | 7B | ¢ | 155 | 9B | ╗ | 187 | BB | █ | 219 | DB | √ | 251 | FB |
| ∟ | 28 | 1C | < | 60 | 3C | \ | 92 | 5C | \| | 124 | 7C | £ | 156 | 9C | ╝ | 188 | BC | ▄ | 220 | DC | ⁿ | 252 | FC |
| ↔ | 29 | 1D | = | 61 | 3D | ] | 93 | 5D | } | 125 | 7D | ¥ | 157 | 9D | ╜ | 189 | BD | ▌ | 221 | DD | ² | 253 | FD |
| ▲ | 30 | 1E | > | 62 | 3E | ^ | 94 | 5E | ~ | 126 | 7E | ₧ | 158 | 9E | ╛ | 190 | BE | ▐ | 222 | DE | ■ | 254 | FE |
| ▼ | 31 | 1F | ? | 63 | 3F | _ | 95 | 5F | ⌂ | 127 | 7F | ƒ | 159 | 9F | ┐ | 191 | BF | ▀ | 223 | DF |  | 255 | FF |

The characters in the PC character set are designed to do many things, and some of them take on different functions, depending upon how they are used.

If you look at Figure 12.1, you see that it begins with two columns of very curious characters (the first 32 characters, with decimal codes 0 through 31) followed by six columns of the characters with which you are most familiar: the digits 0 through 9, the letters of the alphabet in upper- and lowercase, and a lot of punctuation characters. These eight columns are the first half of the PC's character set. They are called the ASCII (American Standard Code for Information Interchange) char-acters because they follow a widespread standard used in most computers.

ASCII proper consists of only 128 characters—the characters with decimal codes 0 through 127. The PC character set has twice as many entries, including the codes 128 through 255. These higher codes, which make up the other half of the PC character set, usually are called the extended ASCII characters. Strictly speaking, only the first half, the codes 0 through 127, are ASCII characters, but you often find people using ASCII to refer to any character or the coding scheme that defines how characters are represented in patterns of bits. There's no harm in that, but you ought to be aware that, depending on how it's used, ASCII can have a precise technical meaning or a broader meaning.

The ASCII half of our character set has an official meaning and definition that ranges far beyond our PC family. ASCII is a universal code used by many computers and other electronic devices. The extended ASCII characters, however, are another story. There is no universal convention for which symbols codes 128 through 255 should represent; however, the characters shown in Figures 12.1 and 12.2 were especially designed for the PC. Because of the importance and popularity of the PC, these particular extended ASCII characters have been used not only by the entire PC family but also by many computers that are only distant relatives of the PC.

This particular group of characters has become a *de facto* standard, usually referred to as the IBM character set. However, you may find that some non-IBM printers do not support the second half of the character set. In fact, printers, word processors, spreadsheets, and other applications can decide what characters to support and what characters to display or print when certain codes are entered. In today's computer world, you can use many more than 256 characters simply by using a software or firmware font that supports other characters. However, for the purposes of this book, I describe the basic—and mostly standard—PC character set. (Incidentally, issues like whether your printer hardware supports the entire character set aren't really issues these days; Windows and TrueType fonts mean that on all but the most antiquated printers, you can print all of the printable characters out of the 256 characters that make up any font, whether those characters are letters, line-drawing characters, or detailed drawings that make up a symbol font.)

It's time to dig into the details of the PC character set. I do that in three parts—two covering the ASCII characters (first the ordinary ASCII characters and then some special control characters) and one discussing the extended ASCII characters and some other unique characteristics of the PC character set.

# The ASCII Characters: Alphanumerics

The ASCII character set, character codes 0 through 127, breaks into two different parts that can be seen in Figures 12.1 and 12.2. The first part, which I discuss separately, is the first 32 characters, codes 0 through 31. These are called the ASCII control characters and are quite different from what they appear to be in Figures 12.1 and 12.2. I'll come back to them after I talk about the more conventional characters, codes 32 through 127.

If you look at the characters represented by codes 32 through 127, you see that these characters are the ones usually thought of as characters—the letters of the alphabet, digits, and punctuation.

Although these characters look ordinary, there actually are quite a few subtle details of which you should be aware.

It is obvious that there are separate characters for upper- and lowercase—that A isn't the same as a—but there is something else here you shouldn't miss. Whenever you're using any program that arranges data in alphabetical order or searches for data, this matters, unless the program takes special pains to treat upper- and lowercase characters the same way (some programs do, some don't, and some enable you to choose). A search for the letter a may not find the letter A, and unless you specify otherwise, in alphabetical order, lowercase a (decimal ASCII code 97) comes after capital Z (decimal ASCII code 90). You also should note that numbers come before uppercase letters.

The next characters you need to consider are the punctuation and other special symbols. One thing to note is that they are scattered all around the digits and letters—before, after, and in between. This means that the punctuation characters as a group don't sort into any one place relative to the alphabet and digits. For example, the commercial "at" sign (@) is decimal ASCII code 64, just before capital A, while left bracket ([) is decimal ASCII code 91, after capital Z. Falling before the numbers is forward slash (/), the plus sign (+), the dollar sign ($), and some other symbols. And, way down in the list numerically speaking are the braces ({ and }), vertical bar ( | ), tilde (~), and more. As you work with these characters—particularly if you need to sort or display them—keep Figures 12.1 and 12.2 handy.

The blank space character has a decimal character code of 32—the lowest of all the punctuation characters, so it appears at the beginning of any alphabetic sort. (In the character charts in Figures 12.1 and 12.2, you see three different characters that appear to be a blank space. See the "Spaces and Nulls" section for more about that.) Note that besides parentheses, there are two other pairs of characters that can be used to enclose things—the brackets, [], and the braces, {}. People also use the less-than and greater-than characters, < >, as a way of enclosing things, like <this>. It's good to know about all four of these embracing pairs because they all come in handy.

Consider quotation marks. In the type used in a book, you see left and right quote marks, but ordinary typewriters don't have them; neither does our PC character set. The PC character set has only one double-quote mark ("), decimal ASCII code 34; and one single-quote mark, or apostrophe ('), decimal ASCII code 39. Using the PC character set, the same double-quote mark is used to both open and close a quotation. There is also a curious character known as a reverse quote (`)—the one just before the lowercase a with a decimal character code of 96. This character should not be paired with the ordinary single-quote character. The reverse quote is used in combination with letters of the alphabet to form non-English characters. Other characters used this way include the circumflex (^), code 94; the tilde (~), code 126; the single-quote ('), code 39; and the comma (,), code 44. This idea of combining characters works only when you can overstrike one character on top of another, which you can do on a computer printer or a typewriter but (usually) not on a computer display screen. To make them easier to use, these non-English alphabetic characters have been incorporated into the extended ASCII characters. I talk more about them in a few pages.

**Technical Note:** When you attempt to use the overstrike characters, you should keep two things in mind. First, you won't see anything on your computer screen when you type the first half of the overstrike series. A character is displayed only when you press the second keystroke component, and the two key codes are interpreted together as one extended ASCII symbol. Additionally, overstrike only works for letters that actually take the overstrike-symbol (known as a *diacritic* in phonetics) you're typing. So, for example, you cannot have a tilde (~) over letters such as *e*, *i*, or *w*, none of which take a tilde in any of the Western languages. You'll notice that this restriction is new to you if you have previously worked with diacritics on the Apple Macintosh. It treats overstrikes very differently than do PC-compatibles, and the Macintosh can combine any letter with any diacritic, even if the combination is meaningless.

There are other characters that call for a brief mention. In addition to the regular slash character (/), code 47, there is a backslash (\), code 92. As far as I know, use of the reverse slash is limited to computing. For example, in the BASIC programming language it indicates whole-number division, while a regular slash indicates regular division, including fractional results. When working with DOS, the backslash indicates directory paths. Also take care not to confuse the hyphen character (-), code 45, with the underscore character (_), code 95. Finally, the circumflex (^), code 94, is sometimes used to indicate special control characters (or a number raised to a power in some text programs) rather than standing as an independent character. This can cause confusion, so when you see a circumflex, check carefully to see whether you are dealing with the circumflex character or a reference to a control character.

# More About ASCII: Spaces and Nulls

In Figures 12.1 and 12.2, you see three characters that appear to be blank spaces. Only one of them actually is the proper blank character: the one with character code 32. The characters with codes 0 and 255 are called nulls, or null characters. They aren't supposed to be treated as true characters, but as inactive nothings. For example, if you send code 32 (the true space character) to a printer, it leaves a space and moves on to the next location. However, if you send one of the null characters, nothing happens. The printer ignores the character; it doesn't move to the next location or leave a blank space.

In the proper ASCII character set, there are two nulls: codes 0 (NUL) and 127 (DEL). In the PC character set, code 127 is a real, visible character with an appearance something like a little house. To substitute for the ASCII null code 127, the PC character set treats code 255 as a null.

> **Technical Note:** Recall that the proper ASCII character set is composed of only seven bits, containing values from 0 to 127, inclusive. In the proper ASCII set, the last character in the set—127—is a null. However, the PC-compatible's extended ASCII set is an 8-bit set, consisting of values from 0 to 255. In order to expand the character set, the graphics symbols (like the small house that code 127 produces) were added to the proper ASCII set. However, to retain backwards-compatibility with documents created under the traditional 7-bit scheme, the PC was designed to automatically map character 127 to the last of the extended characters: 255, where the extended ASCII null is found.

Null characters don't have any everyday use. They are used primarily in communications to mark time; transmitting nulls is a way of keeping a line active while no real data is sent.

# ASCII in Charge: Control Characters

The first 32 of the ASCII characters, codes 0 through 31, have a very special use that has nothing to do with their appearance. For the moment, I ignore their appearances because this section looks at these characters from an entirely different perspective.

When a computer talks to a printer, it must tell the printer what to print and how to print it. It must indicate, for example, where the ends of the lines are and when to skip to the top of a new page. When you're printing directly from DOS and some DOS applications (as opposed to most Windows applications), the ordinary ASCII characters are the what-to-print part of the ASCII character set. The how-to-print part is the subject of this section.

The first 32 codes in the ASCII character set are reserved for passing special information to a printer, to another computer through a telephone line, and so forth. These codes aren't used to pass information or data, but to provide action commands, formatting signals, and communication control codes. I cover the main items here to give you a broad perspective on these characters and their uses.

First, you should know that these 32 codes have special names when they are used as ASCII control characters rather than the picture characters shown in Figures 12.1 and 12.2. Table 12.1 provides a summary of these codes and their names.

Table 12.1. ASCII Control Characters.

| Decimal Code | Hex Code | Control Key | Name | Description |
|---|---|---|---|---|
| 0 | 00 | ^@ | NUL | Null Character |
| 1 | 01 | ^A | SOH | Start of Header |

*continues*

Table 12.1. continued

| Decimal Code | Hex Code | Control Key | Name | Description |
| --- | --- | --- | --- | --- |
| 2 | 02 | ^B | STX | Start of Text |
| 3 | 03 | ^C | ETX | End of Text |
| 4 | 04 | ^D | EOT | End of Transmission |
| 5 | 05 | ^E | ENQ | Inquire |
| 6 | 06 | ^F | ACK | Acknowledge |
| 7 | 07 | ^G | BEL | Bell |
| 8 | 08 | ^H | BS | Backspace |
| 9 | 09 | ^I | HT | Horizontal Tab |
| 10 | 0A | ^J | LF | Line Feed |
| 11 | 0B | ^K | VT | Vertical Tab |
| 12 | 0C | ^L | FF | Form Feed |
| 13 | 0D | ^M | CR | Carriage Return |
| 14 | 0E | ^N | SO | Shift Out |
| 15 | 0F | ^O | SI | Shift In |
| 16 | 10 | ^P | DEL | Delete |
| 17 | 11 | ^Q | DC1 | Device Control 1 |
| 18 | 12 | ^R | DC2 | Device Control 2 |
| 19 | 13 | ^S | DC3 | Device Control 3 |
| 20 | 14 | ^T | DC4 | Device Control 4 |
| 21 | 15 | ^U | NAK | Negative Acknowledge |
| 22 | 16 | ^V | SYN | Synchronize |
| 23 | 17 | ^W | ETB | End of Text Block |
| 24 | 18 | ^X | CAN | Cancel |
| 25 | 19 | ^Y | EM | End of Medium |
| 26 | 1A | ^Z | SUB | Substitute |
| 27 | 1B | ^] | ESC | Escape |
| 28 | 1C | ^/ | FS | File Separator |
| 29 | 1D | ^: | GS | Group Separator |
| 30 | 1E | ^^ | RS | Record Separator |
| 31 | 1F | ^@ | US | Unit Separator |

Before I look at these control characters in greater detail, I should mention a few things about Table 12.1. The first two columns of the table are, of course, the numeric character codes in decimal and in hex. The third column shows the key combinations that evoke the characters. Each of these characters can be keyed in directly from your keyboard by holding down the Control key and the Shift key and pressing the indicated character—A (for code 1), B (for code 2), and so on.

**Note:** The conventional way of indicating these Control-Shift codes is to place a circumflex (^) before the name of the key to be pressed, as shown in the third column of the table. When you see ^A, it doesn't mean the circumflex character (^) followed by the character A. It means Control-A, which is invoked by holding down the Control key and the Shift key and pressing the a key. This combination is sometimes shown as Ctrl-A.

This "circumflex notation" is used quite often. You may run across ^Z or ^C—Control-Z or Control-C—both of which have special meaning for the PC, as you'll see shortly.

In the fourth column of Table 12.1 is a two- or three-letter code, which is a standard abbreviation for the full descriptive name of the control code character. You sometimes find these short codes used in writing about computers and communications. And, in the last column, is a descriptive name for each of the 32 special codes.

Some of the ASCII control characters are interesting and useful; others have rather obscure and technical uses. Instead of discussing them from first to last, I cover them in order of their importance.

First, I talk about the ones that are on your keyboard.

# Keyboard-Available Control Characters

As I mentioned, any of these characters can be entered easily from the keyboard, but the most important keyboard control codes also have regular keys assigned to them. There are four of these: Backspace (BS, code 8), Tab (HT, 9), Enter or Carriage Return (CR, 13), and Escape (ESC, 27). The Delete key on your keyboard is not, however, equivalent to the ASCII Delete (DEL, 16) code.

Notice the relationship between the control codes and the other characters on your keyboard. When you hold down the Control-Shift keys and press a character, the keyboard routine subtracts 64 from the value of the letter. (Applications can make use of Shift-Ctrl-character, but in DOS if you press Ctrl-character, the uppercase character is assumed by the keyboard conversion routine.)

To discover what keys to press to duplicate some of the control codes, simply add 64 to the value of the control code. To enter a Backspace (BS, 8) from the keyboard, for example, you either can press the Backspace key or hold Control and press H. The BS code is ASCII 8. If you add 64 to that, you get 72, the ASCII code for the letter *H*. The Line Feed code is Ctrl-J. LF is ASCII code 10. When you add 64 to that, you get 74, the code for the letter *J*.

One group of these control codes is used to indicate the basic formatting of written material. They function as both logical formatting codes, which help programs make sense out of data, and as printer control codes, which tell printers what to do. The most common ones include some I already have discussed, such as Backspace (BS), Tab (HT or Ctrl-I), and Carriage Return (CR). Others are Line Feed (LF, code 10, or Ctrl-J), which is used in conjunction with Carriage Return; Form Feed (FF, code 12, or Ctrl-L), which skips to a new page; and Vertical Tab (VT, code 11, or Ctrl-K).

Several other characters are of general interest and use. The Bell character (BEL, 7) sounds a warning bell or beep. If you send this character to a printer or console, you get an audible signal. Want to "ring the bell" on a remote system with which you are communicating via modem? Hold down the Control key and tap the letter G. (The BEL code is ASCII 7. When you add 64 to that, you get 71, the ASCII code for the letter G.)

The Control-C character (ETX, 3) is also known as the Break character. Pressing Ctrl-C usually has the same effect as pressing the Ctrl-Break combination. The Control-S (DC3, 19) and Control-Q (DC1, 17) characters sometimes can be used as Pause and Restart commands, particularly when you're working with a communications service such as CompuServe or MCI Mail. The Control-S Pause command is not, however, the same as the Pause key on your computer. (For more information, see Chapter 15, "The Memory Workbench.") (If your computer has an old-style keyboard, the Pause key is the Ctrl-Num Lock, and Break is Ctrl-Scroll Lock.) The Pause key actually stops your computer, while the Control-S Pause command pauses only the program with which you're working.

DOS follows the Ctrl-S and Ctrl-Q convention. If you type DIR at the DOS prompt, you can use Ctrl-S to stop the scrolling of a long directory listing and you can use Ctrl-Q to start continue the listing. In some early versions of DOS, however, the Ctrl-Q combination can cause the display to lock instead of releasing. If you have this problem, just repeat Ctrl-S to start the display again instead of using Ctrl-Q. (And while you're at it, consider upgrading to a newer, more reliable, version of DOS!)

Another useful control code character is the Ctrl-Z key combination (SUB, 26). This code is used to mark the end of text files stored on a disk. I discuss this code and the Carriage Return and Line Feed codes in Chapter 6, "Disks: The DOS Perspective."

Those are the ASCII control characters that are of the widest interest. I finish this section with an overview of some of the more technically oriented control characters. You can skip over the following paragraphs if you're not interested.

The rest of the ASCII control characters are used for a variety of purposes that assist in communications, data formatting, and the control of printers and other devices. I don't cover this topic exhaustively, but I do give you an idea of what these characters do.

Codes 1 through 4 (SOH, STX, ETX, and EOT) are used in communications transmissions to indicate the boundaries of header (descriptive) information, text data, and the entire transmission. Those codes are oriented particularly toward text data. Other codes, such as 28 through 31 (FS, GS, RS, and US), are used as punctuation marks in other forms of data and to mark the boundaries of files—

groups, records, and units—that take on different meanings depending upon the type of data being transmitted.

Other codes are used for the control of communications. For example, Acknowledge (ACK, 6) and Negative Acknowledge (NAK, 21) are used to indicate if data is passing successfully. ENQ, SYN, ETB, CAN, and other codes also are used in the control of communications (which is much too complex and specialized a subject to get into here).

A number of the ASCII control codes are used to control printers and other devices. Although the exact control codes vary widely from printer to printer, some of the more commonly used codes are worth mentioning. The Shift Out (SO, 14) and Shift In (SI, 15) codes commonly are used to instruct a printer to print wide or compressed characters. The four Device Control codes (DCI-4 are codes 17–20) also are used by many printers for such commands as turning off wide printing.

However, because most printers have more formatting and control commands than there are ASCII control characters available, it is normal for the Escape character (ESC, 27, or Ctrl-[) to be used as a catch-all command prefix. When a printer receives an Escape character, it knows that a special command follows. Instead of printing the next few characters, the printer interprets them as a command—a command to set the location of the tab stops or turn on underscoring, for example. If you want to know more about printer control codes, see the reference manual that comes with the printer you are interested in.

# Extended ASCII: The Graphics and Line-Draw Characters

It's time to look at the special characters that make up the extended ASCII characters, codes 128 through 255, and the PC-specific character pictures, codes 0 through 31. I discuss these characters in groups, pausing to make comments and point out interesting features.

Before proceeding, I need to discuss again a major source of confusion. There are two completely different ways of viewing the first 32 characters, codes 0 through 31. I discussed one way—interpreting them as ASCII control characters—earlier in this chapter. When these characters are interpreted as ASCII control characters, there is no displayed image associated with them. They serve as hidden codes to control communications or a printer, so there is nothing to see. In this section, I examine the other interpretation of these character codes—as characters that have an image or symbol associated with them, as shown in Figures 12.1 and 12.2.

What determines whether the same character code is interpreted as an ASCII control command or as a visible character? Basically, it all depends on how the code is used. In most circumstances, these codes are treated as ASCII control characters. But, if you manage by one means or another to get them to appear on our PC's display screen, then they take on their other interpretation, which is as part of the PC's special character set. It is up to the application you are running to make this interpretation.

If you look at the pictures of the first 32 characters in Figures 12.1 and 12.2, you see that they form a fascinating hodgepodge of graphic characters that can be used for a variety of purposes, none of them really essential. Because the use of these character codes is relatively restricted (they usually are interpreted as control characters), IBM decided to put the most important special characters into the extended ASCII area and use this section for some of the more amusing and dispensable characters.

Nevertheless, you can find some useful characters, including the card group (codes 3 through 6), the paragraph and section marks (codes 20 and 21), the arrow group (codes 16 through 31), and the "have a nice day" group (codes 1 and 2). There are real uses for these characters, but they frequently are used in entertainment contexts.

Moving on to the extended ASCII characters, codes 128 through 255, you find more special characters. They are organized into three main groups—the foreign characters, the drawing characters, and the scientific characters.

The foreign characters use codes 128 through 175 and include essentially everything that is needed to accommodate all of the major European languages other than English. (ASCII is oriented toward the needs of the English language.)

There are three main subparts to the foreign character group. One part, codes 128 through 154 and 160 through 167, provides the special alphabetic characters (with diacritical marks) used in various European languages. I mentioned earlier that the regular ASCII character set contains most (but not all) of the diacritical marks needed for European languages. They only can be used, as on a printer, when you can overstrike them onto letters of the alphabet, something you can't do on the PC's display screen. These special alphabetic characters solve that problem in an attractive way. The necessary diacritical marks are part of the defined extended character.

The second part of the European set provides currency symbols: the cent sign (code 155), the pound sign (156), the Japanese yen (157), the Spanish peseta (158), and the franc (159). The dollar sign (36) is part of the regular ASCII set.

The third part of the European set provides some special punctuation, including the Spanish inverted question mark and exclamation point (codes 168 and 173) and the French-style quotation marks (codes 174 and 175). These French quotes are worth noting because they can be used for many graphic purposes as well as their intended use.

Buried among the European characters are four symbols that have general use—the one-half and one-quarter symbols (codes 171 and 172) and two angle marks (169 and 170). Look them up in case you might have a use for them.

The next major section of the extended ASCII character set includes the drawing or graphics characters. These characters enable programs to produce drawings using only the PC's character set. There are three subgroups of drawing characters.

The most interesting and most widely used set of drawing characters are the box-drawing characters. These characters enable you to draw precise rectangular outlines (boxes) on the computer's
display screen. These box-drawing characters are sophisticated enough to draw vertical and horizontal dividing lines within an outline and to draw with either single or double lines. There are four
sets of characters for box drawing—a set for double lines, another for single lines, and two mixed
sets for double-horizontal, single-vertical lines, and vice versa. Figure 12.3 illustrates all four sets
and shows the character codes used to call them. If you want to see the boxes in action on the screen,
the program called BOXES, listed in Appendix B, reproduces Figure 12.3.

**Figure 12.3.**
*The box-drawing characters.*

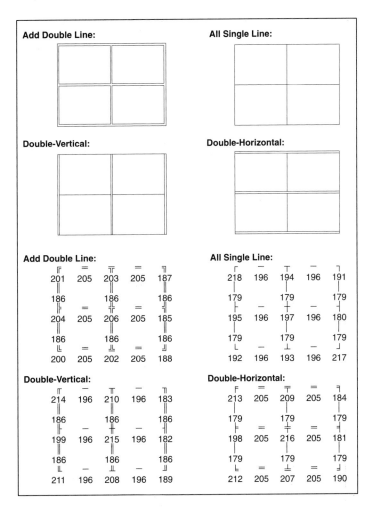

Because they look so good on the computer's display screen, practically every important DOS program for the PC makes heavy use of these box-drawing characters. (Bear in mind that they are frequently now redefined for more customized use by each such program. The redefinitions disappear

when a specific program quits.) I've taken the trouble to produce Figure 12.3 and the program that draws it to make it easy for you to look up the codes for these box-drawing characters and use them in your work.

The next group of drawing characters is used to provide shaded areas. Code 176 provides the lightest fill, approximately one-quarter dense; code 177 is one-half dense; code 178 is three-quarters dense; and code 219 is completely solid. Together with the blank character, they provide a range of four or five shades of gray that can be used either to fill an area on the screen or to produce bar charts of distinctly different appearance.

The final group of drawing characters consists of codes 220 through 223. Each of them is half of the all-solid character (219) that was just mentioned. One is the top half, another the bottom, another the right, and another the left. They can be used to draw solid, filled-in shapes that are twice as fine-grained as could be drawn with the all-solid character alone. For example, they can be used to make more detailed bar graphs.

Many amazing drawings can be produced on the screen of the PC using just the PC's standard characters, including all the drawing characters mentioned here along with some of the regular characters. With some imagination you can do wonders this way.

The final part of the PC's extended ASCII special character set consists of the scientific character group, codes 224 through 254. These include the Greek letters commonly used in math and science, the infinity symbol (code 236), various special mathematical symbols, including two (244 and 245) that, when stacked together, form a large integral sign. There are even square and square-root symbols (253 and 251). While these symbols don't cover everything that might be needed for mathematics, science, and engineering, they do take care of some of the most common requirements.

# Some Character Development: The Internationalized Character Sets

As personal computing grew in popularity worldwide, the PC's support for almost exclusively Western languages became a real liability. In order to handle the symbol sets of other cultures' languages, some of which contain up to 10,000 symbols, work had to begin to expand the PC beyond the 256 characters allowed by ASCII.

Originally, this problem led to a number of custom solutions, most of which were somewhat Rube Goldbergian, and all of which were created on-the-fly as they were needed to perform specialized tasks. You will recall, for example, that ASCII has the 256 characters it has simply because the PC's standard 8-bit byte is capable of handling 256 unique values. The earliest implemented solution to ASCII's limitations, then, was to use more than one byte to store each character.

# The Motherboard

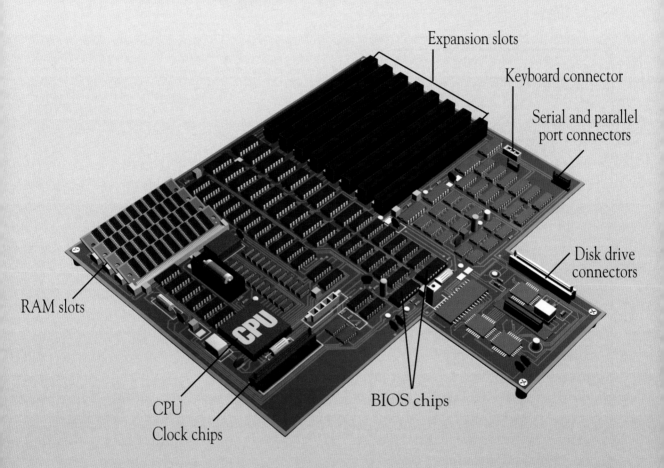

Expansion slots

Keyboard connector

Serial and parallel port connectors

Disk drive connectors

BIOS chips

RAM slots

CPU

Clock chips

CPU

The most defining element—the very heart—of a PC system and system unit is the motherboard. It is called a motherboard because in order for other peripherals to operate, they must be plugged into it. Motherboards have varied dramatically over time with new processors and expansion bus slot architectures. Here you see a typical motherboard, including the microprocessor—the key working component of the personal computer. For an integral description of each of these components, see Chapter 2, "Hardware: The Parts of the PC."

# Looking Inside a PC

The major components of a PC system are a set of input/output (I/O) devices and the main system unit. The main system unit is the heart of any PC system and contains the microprocessor (CPU), high-speed memory (RAM), low-speed memory devices (ROM), input and output adapters, expansion slots, and ports that permit the system to attach to other system components. The most common input/output devices are the keyboard, mouse, display monitor, and printer, all of which attach to the main system unit. There also are other components that form part of the packaging and support for these basics, such as the power supply and cooling system (fan). See Chapter 2, "Hardware: The Parts of the PC," for a detailed description.

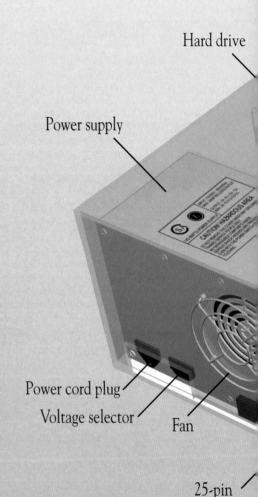

Hard drive

Power supply

Power cord plug

Voltage selector

Fan

25-pin serial port

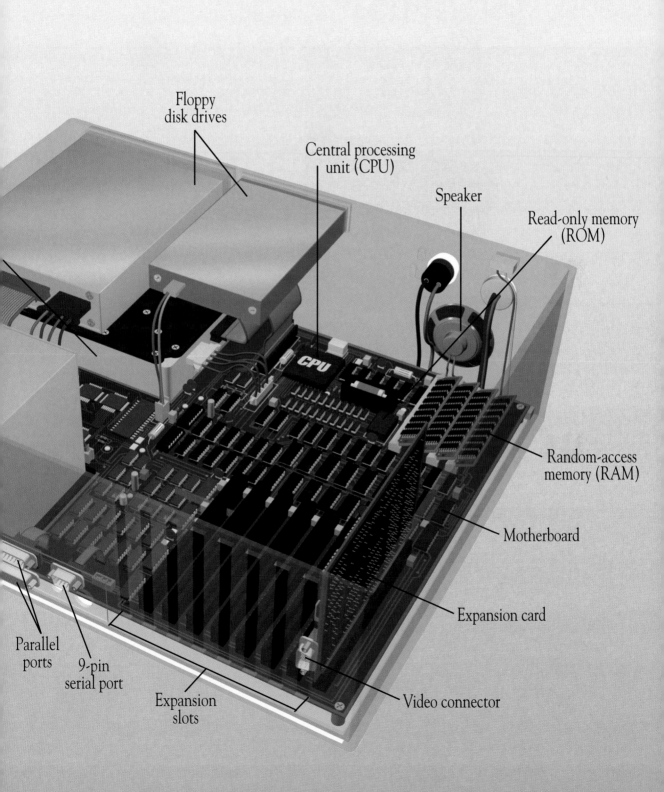

Floppy disk drives

Central processing unit (CPU)

Speaker

Read-only memory (ROM)

CPU

Random-access memory (RAM)

Motherboard

Expansion card

Parallel ports

9-pin serial port

Expansion slots

Video connector

# The System Bus

A bus architecture is how the components of a PC system are connected together. It is how the microprocessor is attached to its memory; how adapters are attached for peripheral devices such as hard disks, floppy disks, and the keyboard; and how the display, the LAN, sound cards, CD-ROM drives, and so on are attached to the system. It is the "highway" that allows the microprocessor to talk to all the system elements.

In the original PC and PC XT, the bus architecture was 8 bits wide and could transfer approximately 1 million bytes of information per second. Today, in order to keep a Pentium class processor busy, the bus needs to be 64 bits wide and transfer data at speeds up to 500 million bytes per second. Over the years several competing bus architectures have been developed to cope with the increasing performance requirements of the PC. Picking a bus architecture is one of the most important issues in selecting a PC. For information, see Chapter 2, "Hardware: The Parts of the PC."

# RAM and ROM

RAM chip ————

ROM chip

The microprocessor needs to attach to the system's main memory in order to access data and instructions. This memory is often called dynamic random-access memory (DRAM), and it is physically packaged on small circuit boards called small inline memory modules (SIMMs). The DRAM SIMMs are installed in SIMM sockets on the mother board. In modern designs with high-speed microprocessors, the main system memory (DRAM) cannot keep up with the performance requirements of the processor and becomes a performance bottle neck. To overcome this limitation, a second, smaller but faster memory is placed between the microprocessor and the system memory. This memory is called a *cache memory*. It stores small blocks of the system DRAM memory, creating the illusion that all system memory is available at the high speed of the cache memory.

The ROM-BIOS (Read-Only Memory Basic Input/Output System) is a set of programs built into the computer that provide the most basic, low-level, and intimate control and supervision operations for the computer. The task of the BIOS is to take care of the immediate needs of the hardware and to isolate all other programs from the details of how the hardware works. In modern systems, the primary purpose of the ROM-BIOS is to load the basic operating system software from the system's boot or start-up device and perform system tests when you turn on the power. Chapters 16 and 17 discuss ROM in detail.

# Parallel Ports and Serial Ports

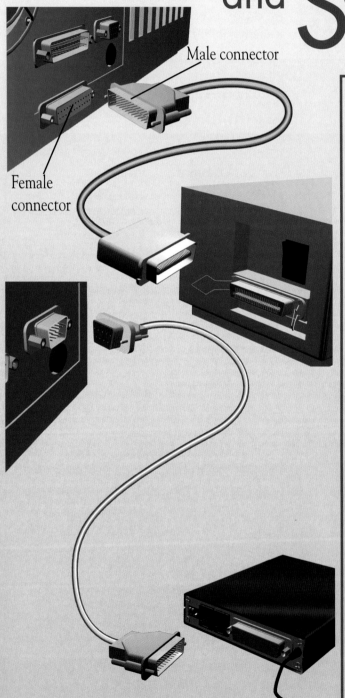

Male connector

Female connector

The *parallel port* is the most common printer connection. It is so called because data moves from the computer to the printer along parallel wires—all 8 data bits travel together. The 8 data lines carry the 8 bits of a byte of information. This transfer of information is accomplished digitally, with a high voltage on a line meaning a set bit, and a low voltage or no voltage meaning a clear bit.

As the name implies, the *serial port* differs from the parallel port in that each data bit, as well as control information, is sent along the wire in a serial stream—one bit at a time sent one behind the other. This movement slows data transfer to some extent, but it enables you to communicate over long distances.

For the exact definition of the different signals carried by each operative pin of the parallel and the serial port, see Chapter 21, "Printers and Communications."

# Portable Storage Media

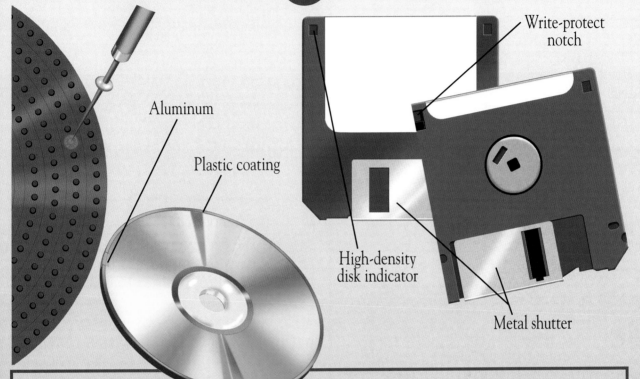

Aluminum

Plastic coating

Write-protect notch

High-density disk indicator

Metal shutter

Floppy disks—generally 3.5-inches wide—continue to be the most popular portable storage device. These disks are called *random-access storage* because you can get to (access) any part of the recorded data directly without having to fast-forward sequentially through all the recorded information. For more information on how the surface is divided in tracks and clusters with an addressing scheme (and partitions) see Chapters 5, 6, and 7.

CD-ROM technology is the most common optical technology in use with PCs. This media is used particularly for software distribution and multimedia applications such as graphics, photographs, sound, and motion video.

*Magneto-optical* (MO) drives use 5.25- or 3.5-inch cartridges filled with magnetic read/write media to store information under laser control. By using the polarity changes that occur in magnetic material when it is heated, MO offers more permanent data storage than conventional hard disks and floppies. Data is written in blocks of 512 bytes. To change a portion of this information, the disk must change all of it because there is no way to know which bits are 1s and which are 0s. Therefore, it takes twice as long to write MO data as to read it. Optical-based technology is discussed in Chapter 10.

# Adapter Cards

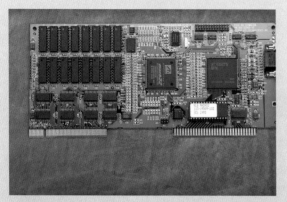

A local bus card.

An 8-bit adapter card.

A 16-bit adapter card.

The original IBM PC provided 5 expansion slots (8 in the PC XT), 3 of which were typically used in a system, 1 each for the display, floppy disk drive, and parallel printer port adapters. The bus architecture was straightforward, easy to understand and provided a very efficient and low-cost expansion capability. Bus adapters designed for the original PC will still operate in state-of-the-art PC systems, even those with Pentium processors and PCI busses. The original chips used to create the PC bus architecture are still fully implemented in all contemporary PC designs.

The PC AT design enhanced the 8-bit PC (XT) expansion bus with a scheme that increased the bus width to 16 bits and supported 24 bit addressing. Complete backward compatibility was maintained by retaining the PC XT's 8-bit bus and 62-pin expansion slots and supporting the enhanced features in an inline 36-pin slot. With this scheme, cards that supported or used only the PC XT bus features attached to the 8-bit 62-pin slots alone, whereas adapters that needed the 16-bit bus and its added features were extended and attached to both slots. This evolutionary approach guaranteed the wide acceptance of the PC AT bus architecture. All PC designs still support the PC AT bus, thus enabling adapter boards designed in 1981 to operate correctly in today's Pentium /PCI bus systems.

For the specifications of the different expansion bus architectures and their systematic comparison, see Chapter 2, "Hardware: The Parts of the PC."

As you can probably imagine, this led to problems. The first of these is the fact that there never used to be a standard regulating exactly how many additional bytes would be used to store each character. In some UNIX systems, up to three bytes are used. In versions of Microsoft Windows that are sold to Far East markets, a combination of one- and two-byte systems are used, right within Windows! (Incidentally, these far- and mid-Eastern languages will also be supported by Windows 95). From the user's point of view, this generally means text files that are from two- to four-times larger than their ASCII "equivalent" files. Storage space, always at a premium, is the first thing to go. You might also expect that double-byte character set (DBCS) files take a lot longer to transmit over a modem. You'd be right. A byte is a byte, and two-for-one isn't a sale in this case.

From a programmer's point of view, this combination of byte-group lengths can make coding much more difficult. Text-related code in applications must be written to handle the fact that in any given document, one-, two-, and three-byte characters may all be present. Further, since different systems— and different releases of any given system—may use different numbers of bytes to store symbols, it's nigh impossible to write simple code that can be moved directly from one platform to another without modification. For example, a word processor that's written to work with single-byte characters will show you little but garbage if you feed a double-byte file into it. Similarly, things users take for granted, like where the vertical-bar insertion point appears in a word processor, all have to be custom-programmed to work with DBCS files. If they're not, the text insertion point may appear in the middle of DBCS letters, rather than at their left, where it belongs.

Many of the problems that have plagued the PC throughout its history have been the result of having no standards. To move towards solving the PC's evolving DBCS problems, a group of companies and entities got together to come up with a new standard. This standard, known as Unicode, was originally developed at Xerox PARC, from which it was borrowed by Apple Computer. In 1991, Unicode became the baby of the Unicode Consortium, a nonprofit group consisting of such giants as Microsoft, Apple, IBM, HP, Novell, and Symantec. Together they created Unicode 1.1, an international standard which, in 1993, was merged with the ISO's ISE10646 (until then, a competing international standard).

The new Unicode standard attempts to solve the variety of user and programmer problems I've already mentioned by establishing a standard 16-bit scheme for character encoding. Each character, whether representing a letter in English or an ideograph in Chinese, uses 2 bytes. Period. Programmers don't need to fuss over coding for seven hundred different implementations, and users don't have to worry about moving documents between language-based platforms: a Unicode document will open in China just as nicely as it will in Sweden, or in the United States, so long as it's opened on a Unicode system.

As of this writing, there is only one such system: Microsoft Windows NT. However, others are on their way. Microsoft's forthcoming Windows release, Windows 95, does not yet support Unicode. However, it is a widely held industry opinion that Windows 95 will be quickly eliminated by Microsoft, with Windows NT and its forthcoming successor, code-named Cairo, the surviving entity. When that happens, Unicode will be ubiquitous.

# What Are the Implications?

Well, for one, you should get used to the idea of larger files. Unicode, however, isn't entirely responsible for that. In a November 1994 article in *Microsoft Systems Journal*, Microsoft acknowledges that plain text files under Unicode can, indeed, be twice as large as their ASCII equivalents. However, they point out, very few programs, including word processors, save files as plain text any more. Microsoft Word 6.0, for example, saves files in a rich binary format. The point of knowing that is that you've probably already noticed that the short word processor document which used to be a 700-byte letter is now a 12KB letter. File sizes have already exploded, and Unicode will *not* cause those already-exploded binary files to increase by an additional 100% as you might otherwise expect. Microsoft additionally observes in *MSJ* that users like you and me are incorporating sounds and pictures and other multimedia elements into our files, and so our files are getting bigger anyway. While this is true, it doesn't alter the fact that, according to Microsoft, "...English plain text data... would double in size."

Microsoft claims, however, that proper use of compression can guarantee that a Unicode file generated by your word processor won't be larger than an ASCII file of the same content. Of course, Microsoft is putting the onus of providing that wonderful degree of compression on the developers of individual applications. (You can be sure that Microsoft applications will include that compression and that fact will be a marketing point in favor of Microsoft.)

Another potential cost to users is that, according to *MSJ*, Microsoft is doing the same thing in relation to the transfer of files from a new Unicode system to an older, non-Unicode system. The responsibility of understanding Unicode lies with the otherwise non-Unicode platform, not with Unicode itself or the new Unicode systems. (In other words, *MSJ* says that a Unicode system may not provide "save as non-Unicode" capability; the non-Unicode system that wants to access a Unicode file will have to provide "read from Unicode and translate" capabilities, instead.)

On the one hand, this might slow down the adoption of Unicode, as people desiring backwards compatibility hold on for dear life. On the other hand, if individual developers don't do a good job of providing backwards translation, users will be inclined to upgrade to Unicode simply to *stay* compatible with new systems as they are sold.

On the other hand, Microsoft says that Unicode-compliant systems will run faster than today's DBCS systems. A standard process for text-handling will allow for the streamlining of code. Shorter code runs faster, you might say. Will you and I notice the difference? That's hard to say, since a lot of Microsoft's claims are based on the assumption of ever-larger hard disks and ever-faster processors running applications. But in general, yes, the international computer user should notice a speed increase after she adopts a Unicode platform.

Overall, will you and I notice the difference between ASCII and Unicode in our day-to-day computing? Not if you're not an international user. While the coming of Unicode today may be, as

Microsoft says, "comparable in magnitude to the introduction of ASCII 30 years ago," it seems unlikely that the average user will even need to be aware of its existence, until she picks up the ninth or so edition of this book. Unicode *will* provide a more universal degree of information compatibility, but whether that compatibility will take us to a new paradigm of computing (as happened with the enablement provided by ASCII) remains to be seen.

# Some Things To Think About or Try

1. Experiment to find out how your computer's screen and printer respond to the 32 ASCII control characters. Write a program in BASIC, for example, to send these characters one by one to the screen and printer. (Hint: If you precede and follow each control character with a printable letter, such as an X, you can get a clearer idea of what the response is to each control character.)

2. Do your computer's printer and display screen respond differently to the same control characters? Try to explain why.

3. Look at the ALL-CHAR and REF-CHAR programs in Appendix B that generate Figures 12.1 and 12.2 on your computer's screen. Find how they write the characters onto the screen. Why don't they use the ordinary PRINT command?

4. If a program sorts data treating upper- and lowercase letters alike (which is often what you want), it either treats both as uppercase or both as lowercase. Does it matter which way? What effect does that have on punctuation?

5. The design of the PC's drawing characters was limited by the number of character codes available. Suppose there had been another 50 or more codes available. What sort of additional drawing capabilities might have been added? Try to produce your own extensions to the PC's set of drawing characters.

6. Using the PC character set's line-drawing characters under Microsoft Windows is a good example of using the wrong tool for the job. Think about why this is true today.

7. Using the Windows File Manager or the Norton Commander, take a look at the lengths of text and word-processor files on your computer today. Assuming that your data was not compressed any more than it is today, what percentage of your files do you think would be significantly larger under Unicode, rather than ASCII?

8. If you are a programmer, you may already know that ANSI C and Microsoft Visual C++ do not support DBCS (including Unicode) files as source text. Since this is true, consider the implications—if any—to the size of your final executable files after a widespread adoption of Unicode.

# 13 Keyboarding

Now that you've looked at the PC family's display screens and character set, it's appropriate that the next topic be the keyboard—the other half of your primary interface with the computer. While the keyboard may seem simple compared to the display screen, the PC's keyboard contains complexities that make it much more interesting to explore than you might think. You see why in this chapter. You also see how some programs work with the keyboard in some very unusual ways.

# Basic Keyboard Operation

To understand what's going on with the computer keyboard, you need to understand two key things, no pun intended. First, there is more to keyboard operations than you might think; and second, keyboard information undergoes several transformations before it emerges as what you expect to see when you press a key. To make sense out of this, I explain why the keyboard works so indirectly before I show you how it works.

You might logically expect the keyboard to work in a relatively crude way: press the A key, and the keyboard says to the computer, "A." It doesn't work that way for a simple reason: If the keyboard is assigned the task of making the A key mean the letter A, then the keyboard is in the business of giving meaning to what you do when you pound away on the keyboard. There are two things wrong with that. One is that it's not the business of computer hardware to assign meaning to what you're doing. Hardware is supposed to be like a blank slate. Software, on the other hand, is supposed to bring the hardware to life, giving it activity and meaning. So, the first thing that is wrong with the keyboard deciding that the A key means the letter A is that the hardware is intruding on a job that belongs to software.

The other thing that's wrong—and the reason why the first thing that's wrong *is* wrong—is the inflexibility of that scenario. You may think that it is stupid for the A key to mean anything else, but as much as possible, a computer should be flexible and adaptable, and if the hardware doesn't impose any meaning on keystrokes, so much the better.

In fact, under certain circumstances it may be convenient to change completely the way the keyboard works. The keyboard layout commonly used is called the QWERTY design, named after the letters at the top-left of the keyboard's main section. Another layout, the Dvorak (named after a person, not a letter arrangement), was designed to be easier to use and, allegedly, to ease repetitive-task injuries. Because PCs have a flexible software-based keyboard system, you can change the position of the keys by telling the computer which key represents which letter and have a Dvorak keyboard for no additional cost.

# The Scan Code: How Your Keyboard Works

Those are the ideas behind what may seem like a curious relationship between the keyboard and the computer (and the built-in ROM-BIOS programs). Here is what actually happens when you press a key on your computer's keyboard: The keyboard recognizes that you've pressed one of the keys and makes a note of it. (The keys are assigned an identifying number, called a scan code, and that scan code is what the keyboard notes.)

After the keyboard notes that you've pressed a key, it tells the computer that something has happened. It doesn't even say what; it just says that something has happened on the keyboard. That's done in the form of a hardware interrupt. The keyboard circuitry sends your computer's microprocessor an interrupt using the interrupt number assigned to the keyboard, interrupt 9.

**Technical Note:** Actually, the keyboard interrupt comes in on IRQ level 1 in the hardware. This is converted to interrupt 9 in the interrupt table.

Interrupts (you can refer back to Chapter 4, "Microprocessor Traffic Control," for more information) cause the microprocessor to put aside what it is doing and jump to an interrupt-handling program. In this case, the interrupt handler is an integral part of the ROM-BIOS software.

At that point, the keyboard interrupt handler swings into action and finds out what took place on the keyboard. It does that by sending a command to the keyboard to ask what happened. The keyboard responds by telling the ROM BIOS which key was pressed. These commands and responses are sent via ports (also discussed in Chapter 4). The ROM BIOS issues its command by sending a command code out to a port address to which the keyboard responds. The keyboard replies by sending the scan code of the key to the port address that the ROM BIOS reads. In a moment, you see what the ROM BIOS does with that information, but first you need to know what takes place in the keyboard itself.

The keyboard, of course, must keep track of which key was pressed and wait until the ROM BIOS asks for it. (It isn't a long wait—usually less than 1/10,000 of a second; still, for computer hardware, that's a wait.) To do this, the keyboard has a small memory, called the keyboard buffer, which is large enough to record a number of separate key actions—commonly 16—in case the microprocessor does not respond to the keyboard interrupts before more keys are pressed. Although it's rare for the microprocessor not to respond immediately, the keyboard design makes allowances for that possibility. After the keyboard reports the details of a key action to the microprocessor, that action is flushed from the keyboard's memory, making room for new scan codes.

There are two more things you need to know about the keyboard, the first of which is critical, to your computer at least. The keyboard doesn't just note when you press a key; it also notes when you release a key. Each separate key action is recorded by the keyboard, turned into an interrupt, and fed to the ROM BIOS on command. To distinguish between the press and release of a key, there are separate scan codes for each action.

That means that the ROM BIOS is interrupted twice as often as you may have guessed. It also means that the ROM BIOS knows whether a key is being held down or has been released, enabling it to know, for example, if you're typing in capital letters by holding the Shift key down, and when you are issuing special keystrokes, like the Ctrl-Alt-Del combination.

The other thing you need to know about the keyboard is that the keyboard hardware governs the repeat-key action. The keyboard hardware keeps track of how long each key is held down and, if a key is held down for more than a certain period of time (about half a second), the keyboard hardware generates repeat-key scan codes at a regular interval. These repeat-key signals appear to the ROM BIOS just like regular keystroke signals. If it needs to, however, the ROM BIOS can distinguish keys held down by the absence of key release scan codes.

IBM calls this repeat-key action the Typematic feature. If you want, you can change the initial delay and the repeat rate by using the DOS MODE command like this:

```
MODE CON RATE=r DELAY=d
```

For this command, $r$ is a number between 1 (slow) and 32 (fast), and $d$ is a number between 1 (short delay) and 4 (longer delay). Note that this command is not available with versions of DOS prior to 4.0. Keep in mind also that the changes you make with the MODE command will revert to your ROM BIOS's defaults when you reboot. You can put the MODE command in your AUTOEXEC.BAT file, so that it will be issued at each boot. Most of today's computer systems allow you to directly edit the ROM-BIOS settings, and to change the default there. You should refer to your hardware manual or your computer manufacturer's technical support department for instructions.

What I've described so far is exactly how the standard PC family keyboards work. The oldest members of the PC family, however, used different keyboards. The older keyboards work in more or less the same way but have different layouts. I'll talk about that in the "Keyboard Differences" section, later in this chapter.

# How the Scan Code Works

When the ROM-BIOS's keyboard interrupt handler springs into action, it receives one of the scan codes from the keyboard and must interpret that code. The ROM BIOS quickly goes through several stages of analysis to discover how it should interpret the key action and what it should do about it. First, it tests to see if the key action applies to one of the shift-type keys—the left and right Shift,

Alt, and Ctrl keys. If so, the ROM BIOS makes a note of the shift state because this affects the interpretation of any action that follows. Next, the ROM BIOS tests to see if the key action is one of the toggle keys—the CapsLock, NumLock, ScrollLock, and Ins keys. The toggle keys, like the shift keys, affect the meaning of other keys, but the action is different. The shift keys apply only when they are held down, and the toggle keys apply depending upon whether they are toggled on or off.

For both the shift and toggle keys, the ROM BIOS must keep track of the current state of these keys. This record is kept in two bytes of low memory. Each of the bits in these two bytes separately records one part of the keyboard status, recording if one of the keys is pressed or whether one of the toggle states is on or off. You can inspect and play with these keyboard status bits using the KEYBITS program listed in Appendix B, "QBasic Program Listings." KEYBITS demonstrates how the keyboard status is recorded and shows you some surprising things about the information that the ROM BIOS tracks. You see, for example, that the ROM BIOS keeps separate track of the left and right Shift keys and whether the toggle keys are pressed. Experimenting with KEYBITS tells you a lot about how the ROM BIOS works together with the keyboard. Using the KEYBITS program, you can find out the status of the various bits, as shown in Figure 13.1.

**Figure 13.1.**
*Keyboard status bits of an IBM system.*

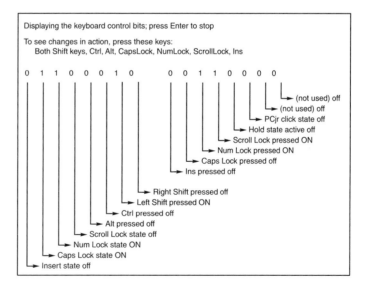

There is another memory location that is used only with newer keyboards. This location stores the bits that tell whether or not the right Alt or Ctrl key has been pressed. These keys do not appear on the old-style keyboards. Because the KEYBITS sample program was designed to work on all keyboards, it does not test these bits. You may want to extend the program to do so.

After the ROM BIOS has taken care of the shift and toggle keys, it needs to check for special keys and key combinations, such as Ctrl-Alt-Del, which reboots the computer, and the Pause key. I discuss these special keys and key combinations in the following section.

# Advanced Keyboard Functions

It's natural to think that keyboard information flows in only one direction. After all, you press the keys, and the data ends up in the computer. Actually, the keyboard system is a complex mechanism. Because keyboard information is passed back and forth to the main processor, the keyboard requires its own controller, just like any other I/O device.

In most systems today, the keyboard controller also offers several variations of password security, all of them dependent on the keyboard. First, you can set a power-on password. This means that, when you turn on the computer, it doesn't start until you type in the correct password.

Second, you may be able to set a keyboard password. This enables you to lock the keyboard without turning off the computer. When the keyboard is locked, it does not respond until you type in the correct keyboard password. This is useful if you have to leave your desk for a short time and want to ensure that no one can play around with your PC while you are gone. Of course, all popular screen-saver software offers this same type and degree of protection. And speaking of degrees, don't be fooled: All that's necessary to get past a locked keyboard is to hit the reset key on the system unit. The system will reboot, and the keyboard protection won't be active. If you lock your keyboard (or use a screen saver that provides password protection) with unsaved data, you may also lose all of that data if someone resets your machine to get past the password protection.

Finally, on some systems, you can set a network server password. This is important when a PC is acting as a file server for a local area network. In such a case, the PC provides data to the network and must be left on, unattended, all the time. In this situation, you don't want people to be able to enter commands at the keyboard. You can set the PC so that the keyboard is locked but so that other computers on the network can access the hard disk. To unlock the keyboard, you type in the network server password.

On IBM PS/2s, and some other systems, the keyboard controller can control a pointing device as well as the keyboard. Usually, this is a mouse, although it can be a touchpad, trackball, or special keyboard. To provide this support, the keyboard controller maintains a special serial interface for the pointing device.

Bear in mind that the password and mouse controller keyboard features I've just described are available on IBM PS/2s, but they may or may not be available on non-IBM brand computers. Indeed, other vendors offer other keyboard features that may or may not be available on the PS/2s. Gateway 2000, for example, supplies a keyboard with its machines that can be easily programmed for special key functions, including keyboard-level macros.

You can see the keyboard has a great deal more functionality than most people think. To help you understand this, Table 13.1 summarizes the keyboard-type services that the BIOS provides for programs with the help of the keyboard controller.

Table 13.1. BIOS Keyboard Services.

| Service | Description |
|---------|-------------|
| Keyboard ID | Find out the keyboard ID number. (Different keyboard types have different ID numbers.) |
| Scan codes | Find out if any scan codes are available from the keyboard buffer or if it is empty. |
| | Read scan codes from the keyboard buffer. |
| | Write scan codes to the keyboard buffer, just as if those keys had been pressed by the user. (This is useful if a program wants to simulate the pressing of keys on your behalf.) |
| Status keys | Find out the current status of the Insert, CapsLock, NumLock, and ScrollLock keys. |
| | Find out if one of the Shift, Alt, Ctrl, or SysReq keys is being pressed. |
| | Reinitialize the keyboard and turn off NumLock, CapsLock, and ScrollLock. |
| | Set NumLock, CapsLock, and ScrollLock off or on. |
| Typematic support | Set the Typematic (repeat-key) delay and rate. |
| | Find out whether or not the keyboard supports changeable Typematic features (the older keyboards do not). |
| Security | Enable or disable the keyboard's capability to pass data to the system. |
| | Turn the keyboard password security system off or on. |
| | Set a specific keyboard password. |
| | Set which scan codes should be ignored when a password is being typed in. (For example, it shouldn't matter if you press a Shift key while you are typing a password.) |
| | Lock the keyboard until the correct password is typed in. |
| | Unlock the keyboard after the correct password has been typed in. |

# Ctrl-Alt-Del, Pause, PrintScreen, and More

The keyboard ROM-BIOS routines do more than supervise the raw keyboard input and translate it into meaningful characters. They also oversee some built-in features of the PC family.

The three best-known features that the keyboard routines invoke are the system reboot (the Ctrl-Alt-Del key combination that you're likely very familiar with), print screen (Shift-PrintScreen), and system pause (Pause). (On the oldest keyboards, print screen was invoked by pressing Left Shift-Asterisk, and the system pause was invoked by pressing Ctrl-NumLock.)

Both reboot and print screen are services that always are available to any program that wants to invoke them. Print screen, for example, is invoked by issuing an interrupt 5. In the case of these two services, the keyboard routines simply provide the user with a way of getting at a service that normally only is available to a program.

> **Note:** When you're running under Microsoft Windows, Windows traps the PrintScreen keystroke, and—rather than printing the current screen to the printer—places a copy of the current screen onto the clipboard, including text, graphics, and whatever else is visible. You can then use the Paste command in a graphics editing program and save the screen shot to a file for future use and editing. Additionally, if you're working in a MS-DOS prompt (also called a DOS box) from inside Windows, pressing the PrintScreen key by itself will copy all of the text on the DOS screen to the Windows clipboard, so you can paste that text into a Windows text file for later use. In a DOS box, the Shift-PrintScreen key combination still sends text directly to the default printer.

Pause, however, is a special feature peculiar to the keyboard ROM BIOS. When the keyboard routines recognize this key combination, the ROM BIOS makes a note of it and goes into a never-ending, do-nothing loop, effectively suspending the operation of any program running. When this pause state is in effect, the machine is not locked up, and it continues to respond to any hardware interrupts that occur, such as disk and timer interrupts. However, when those interruptions are completed, control passes back to the keyboard routine, which refuses to return control to the program that has been suspended. Only when you press one of the PC's regular keys does the ROM BIOS reset its pause bit and return the microprocessor to active duty. If you run the KEYBITS program, you can see the pause bit that the ROM BIOS uses to keep track of this state. However, KEYBITS can't show the pause bit set because, when this bit is set, no program, including KEYBITS, can run.

Finally, if a key action passes through all that special handling, it means that the key is an ordinary one and can be assigned a meaning—that is, if the action is the key being pressed and not released. Releasing a key ordinarily means nothing unless the key is one of the special shift or toggle keys. When you press an ordinary key, the ROM BIOS recognizes it and produces a keyboard character in the ordinary sense, such as the A key. To give an ordinary key meaning, though, the ROM BIOS must translate the key into its character code. This is the point at which the A key becomes the letter A. In this translation process, the shift states are taken into account to distinguish letter *a* from A and so forth.

When a keystroke is translated, it can have one of two sets of meanings. The first is one of the ordinary ASCII characters, such as A or Control-A (ASCII code 1). The second is for the PC's special keys, such as the function keys. These keys, which include the function keys, the cursor keys, and the Home key, have special codes that distinguish them from the ordinary ASCII character keys.

# The Alt-Numeric Keypad Trick

There is one more special trick that the keyboard ROM-BIOS routines perform that many PC users don't know about. I call it the Alt-numeric keypad trick.

Most of what you want to type is right there on the keyboard in plain sight—the letters of the alphabet and so forth. And, much of the more exotic stuff can be keyed in by combining the Ctrl key with the alphabetic keys; for example, Ctrl-Z produces the ASCII code 26, which is used as an end-of-file marker for text files. But, you can't key in every item in the PC's character set that way. For example, if you wanted to key in the box-drawing characters that you saw in Chapter 12, "The PC Character Set," you could not do that.

To make it possible for you to key in virtually anything, the ROM BIOS provides a special way to enter any of the characters with ASCII codes 1 through 255. Oddly, though, you can't key in ASCII code 0 in any way.

To key in the ASCII codes 1 through 255, hold down the Alt key and then key in the ASCII code number. You enter the code in decimal and must use the numeric keys on the right side of the keyboard, not the number keys on the top row. When you key in a character this way, the ROM BIOS makes a note of it and calculates the code number you keyed in. When you release the Alt key, it generates an ASCII character just as if you had pressed a single key that represented that ASCII character.

Try it yourself, using the ASCII code for capital A, which is 65. Hold down the Alt key, press and release 6 and then 5 on the keypad, and then release the Alt key. The letter A should appear on your screen, just as if you had typed in a capital A.

This special scheme works under most, but not all, circumstances. QBasic (and many applications programs such as graphics-oriented word processors or drawing programs that take over control of the keyboard) changes the keyboard operation, so it doesn't work. However, under most circumstances, you have access to this special ROM-BIOS facility.

To accommodate both the plain ASCII codes and the PC's special codes, the ROM BIOS records each key character as a pair of bytes. If the character at hand is an ASCII character, the first of the two bytes is nonzero and holds the ASCII character. (In this case, the second character can be ignored. It generally holds the scan code of the key that was pressed.) The special PC characters are identified by a zero in the first byte. When the first byte is zero, the second byte contains the code identifying which of the special key characters is present.

QBasic gives you access to these two-byte keyboard codes with the INKEY$ function. With it, you can inspect the keyboard codes. The little program below shows you how. Just run this in QBasic and start pressing keys. The Enter key stops the program.

```
DO
K$ = INKEY$
```

```
L = LEN(K$)
IF L = 1 THEN
PRINT "ASCII character   "; ASC(LEFT$(K$, 1))
ELSEIF L = 2 THEN
PRINT "Special key code "; ASC(RIGHT$(K$, 1))
END IF

LOOP WHILE K$ <> CHR$(13)
```

After a real keystroke has been recognized and translated into its two-byte meaning, it's stored in the ROM BIOS's keyboard buffer. This is the second time that the keyboard information is stored in a buffer—once in the keyboard's internal memory and then in the ROM BIOS's storage area. The ROM BIOS has a buffer large enough to store 32 characters. If it overflows, the ROM BIOS issues the complaining beep on the speaker to which experienced PC users are accustomed and then throws away the latest key data.

After key actions have been received and translated into meaningful characters by the ROM BIOS, they are available for programs to use. Programs can either take them directly from the ROM BIOS, using the ROM-BIOS keyboard services, or get them from DOS, using the DOS keyboard services, which indirectly takes them from the ROM BIOS. Either way, programs end up using the keyboard characters that have been constructed by the ROM BIOS from key actions.

That, anyway, is the way things work when things proceed in a straightforward way. However, the whole elaborate scheme for processing keystrokes that I've described so far is intended to enable programs to sidestep the normal keyboard operation and start pulling rabbits out of hats. Next you see how some of that is done.

> **Note:** You may already know that if you're running Microsoft Windows, there is now an easier way to access those special characters. The CHARMAP.EXE program in your \WINDOWS subdirectory will display a graphical representation of all characters in any font that's installed on your system. You can easily copy individual or multiple special characters to the clipboard from CHARMAP.EXE, and then into your own data files. Certain applications, like Microsoft Word 6.0 for Windows, also allow you access to these special symbols without jumping out of the application.

# Keyboard Remapping

Under Microsoft Windows *all* keyboards are remappable, as we'll see in a moment. Additionally, many manufacturers' keyboards can be remapped at the firmware (firmware is, essentially, the software in the hardware) level. For example, the Gateway 2000 AnyKey keyboard has a REMAP key right on the keyboard. To remap a key from one value to another, you simply press REMAP, then the key you want to remap, and finally the new key you want the first key to remap as.

So, if you happen to have grown up with typewriters (remember typewriters?!) and are used to using the lowercase letter l instead of the number 1, it might be easier for you to remap the key while you're entering numeric data into a spreadsheet. You would simply press REMAP, then l, then 1. Ta-Da! Whenever you press a lowercase l now, you'll actually get a "1". To reverse the process, press REMAP, then strike the lowercase l key twice. This little trick works by causing the first key—the letter l in this case—to produce the scan code of a different key, such as the number one.

Probably much more useful is Microsoft Windows' software keyboard mapping. Through the "International" Control Panel, you can immediately remap all of the keys on your keyboard at once. In this Control Panel, you'll see a drop-down box labeled "Keyboard Layout." Drop down the list and— if you're in the United States of America—you'll likely see that you are using the "US" layout. Also immediately available to you are a Dvorak layout for U.S. users, many non-English keyboards, and a special variation of the U.S. keyboard that enables you to enter special international characters like ü, ñ, and ç.

# Keyboard Differences

There are three principal keyboard designs used with PS/2 computers. The most common is the standard keyboard shown in Figure 13.2. IBM calls this the enhanced keyboard. This name was given when the keyboard was first introduced (with the last model of the PC AT computer). The name refers to the new features this keyboard offered compared with the oldest PC keyboards.

**Figure 13.2.**
*The enhanced keyboard.*
*(Photo courtesy of IBM.)*

The original keyboard that came with the PC and PC XT and a second version that came with the first PC AT preceded the enhanced keyboard. Although most PCs sold these days use the enhanced keyboard, you may run into an older machine with one of the PC or PC AT keyboards. For this reason, I have made sure that the sample keyboard programs in this chapter and in Appendix B work with all the variations.

The Gateway 2000 AnyKey-101 Keyboard, shown in Figure 13.3, combines the left-hand function keys of the regular keyboard with the extra keys and the topmounted function keys of the enhanced keyboard, creating a *really* enhanced keyboard.

**Figure 13.3.**
*The Gateway 2000 AnyKey-101 Keyboard. (Photo courtesy of Gateway 2000.)*

And, of course, there are many non-IBM vendors that supply keyboards of their own design. Some of these, like Gateway 2000's AnyKey-101 keyboard, include programmable features. Other keyboards are hybrids of the old style and the enhanced keyboard. They may, for example, have a set of function keys along the top of the keyboard plus a set of function keys at the left of the keyboard. Other designs may include additional keypads or cursor movement keys and some vendors frequently duplicate some frequently used keys such as the asterisk (*) or backslash ( \ ). Individual placement of keys varies from keyboard to keyboard and from brand to brand.

In addition to the enhanced keyboard and its variations, there are also space-saving varieties that are popular with smaller desktop units because of their smaller footprint.

# Some Keyboard Tricks to Try

The PC's design enables programs to work with the keyboard in many, many ways. Even when a program isn't doing anything exotic, it has a choice between two ways of obtaining its keyboard data: either obtaining it directly from the ROM-BIOS or getting it through the DOS services. However, those certainly aren't the only ways a program can come by keyboard information.

I can't give you an exhaustive rundown of keyboard tricks for many reasons. One is that ingenious programmers are inventing new keyboard tricks all the time. The biggest reason is that the tricks are far too technical. They are advanced programmer's tricks that have nothing to do with the goal of this book, which is to help you understand the PC family. However, more and more, users find themselves using programs that are based on keyboard tricks, and it's very worthwhile to know the basics of how they work.

There are a number of unusual ways in which a program can respond. One of them is indirectly demonstrated in the KEYBITS program. Any program can monitor the keyboard status bytes and act accordingly. Here's an example:

```
DEF SEG = 0
PRINT "Please press both shift keys at once!"
WHILE PEEK(&H417) MOD 4 <> 3: WEND
PRINT "Thank you!"
```

This code enables a program to treat the shift-type keys in a special way. While ordinary programs have no good reason to do something like that, I'm not talking about ordinary treatment of the keyboard. Often the designers of game programs want to do something rather special, particularly with the shift keys. For example, a pinball program may want to use the right and left Shift, Alt, or Ctrl keys to control the right and left pinball flippers. To do that, the program must recognize when either of those keys is held down, which it can do simply by monitoring the keyboard status bits.

**Technical Note:** Many keyboards—particularly today's low-cost models—use the same scan code to detect, for example, the left or right Alt keys, and so software that requires you press one or the other to obtain different results will not function properly on these systems. Fortunately, it is primarily with games, not professional software, that such problems may be encountered. You don't need to worry about not being able to run your spreadsheet just because you couldn't resist that $5.95 keyboard sale.

One of the most interesting types of programs used on PCs is the memory-resident programs that sit, inactive, in the computer's memory until they are activated with a special key combination. I will show you some of the ways that this can be done.

You may remember from Chapter 3, "Brains: The Processors," that the PC has an internal clock that ticks many times a second. The clock tick is made audible, so to speak, by a special clock-tick interrupt, interrupt 8. Normally, the ROM BIOS receives that interrupt and uses it to update its time-of-day record. However, the ROM BIOS also makes the ticking of the clock available to programs by generating another interrupt, interrupt 28 (hex 1C), which does nothing unless a program has set up an interrupt vector to receive it. If a program has set up such a vector, it is activated as many times per second as there are clock ticks.

Consider how a memory-resident program might use this technique to spring into action. Say that the program is waiting for you to press a particular combination of keys. One way the program could do that simply is to use the timer interrupt to give it a frequent chance to check the keyboard status bits to see if you have both keys pressed (similar to the way the sample BASIC program above checks for Shift keys). If the bits are not set, the program simply returns control from the timer interrupt, and very little time has been wasted. However, if the bits are set, the program can keep running, performing its special magic.

In this example, the timer interrupt does not interfere in any way with the normal flow of keyboard data. Instead, it makes use of the timer interrupt and the keyboard system's willingness to enable a program to see the state of the Shift keys.

That, however, is far from the only way a program can make special use of the keyboard. For even more exotic operations, a program can interpose itself in the middle of the keyboard data flow so that it can monitor, and possibly modify, the information.

If a program wants to take control of the keyboard or at least know exactly what's going on in the keyboard, it can interpose itself in the path of the keyboard hardware interrupt simply by placing an interrupt vector pointing to the program in place of the standard vector that directs keyboard interrupts to the ROM BIOS. Then, when the keyboard causes a hardware interrupt, the new program, instead of the ROM BIOS, sees the interrupt.

There are two main things that such a program might do. One simply is to take full control of the keyboard data so that the ROM BIOS never sees it. This can be done by a program that wants to take ruthless and total control. Most programs that intervene in the keyboard data process, though, aren't interested in stopping the flow of information from the keyboard to the ROM BIOS; they merely want to monitor it and, when appropriate, modify it. This sort of program inspects the keyboard data as it goes by, but generally permits the normal flow of information. That's how most keyboard-enhancing programs work. They step in to monitor and modify the keyboard data. To do that, they may have to replace the ROM BIOS processing programs with their own program steps, but they don't stop the processing of the keyboard data in the way in which the ROM BIOS normally does.

When you look at the wide selection of software available for the PC family, you find many programs that treat the keyboard in special ways, and if you look under their surfaces, you find different degrees of programming. What I've discussed concerning memory-resident programs represents the extreme case. There are, however, much less radical, but still special, ways to handle keyboard data.

Consider the example of Framework. Framework makes special use of the so-called gray plus and gray minus keys, the plus and minus keys that are on the far right side of the keyboard. In an ordinary program, there is no difference between these plus and minus keys and the plus and minus keys located in the top row of the keyboard. However, Framework (as well as WordPerfect for DOS and other programs) uses these gray keys to perform a special operation. Framework uses these keys to move up or down a logical level within its data scheme. To do that, however, Framework must be able to recognize the difference between the gray plus and the regular plus key. You might be tempted to think that Framework would have to tinker with the keyboard data, but it doesn't.

As you saw earlier, when the ROM BIOS presents keyboard data to a program, it presents it as a two-byte code in which the first byte indicates the ASCII code of the character data. Whether you press the gray plus key or the other plus key, this byte of information from the ROM BIOS is the same (ASCII code 43). However, the second byte that the ROM BIOS makes available to the program reports the scan code of the key that was pressed, so it is very easy for a program like Framework to tell the difference between the gray plus and the regular plus key. It also easily can tell when you generate the plus code by using the Alt-numeric scheme that I described earlier in this chapter.

Framework can respond to the special gray plus and minus keys simply by making full use of the standard information that's available, without having to perform any special magic or interfere with the operation of the ROM-BIOS or the flow of keyboard information.

That's an important thing to know because people often assume that it's necessary to use special and potentially disruptive tricks to accomplish special objectives in programs. This example illustrates that it is possible to accomplish what you need to accomplish without breaking out of the standard conventions that keep PCs working smoothly.

# Some Things to Think About or Try

1. For the toggle keys, like the CapsLock key, the ROM BIOS keeps track not only of the current toggle state but also of whether the key is pressed. Even though programs have no normal use for this information, there is a simple logical reason why the ROM BIOS records it. Can you discover why?

2. The scheme used to separate the PC's special character codes from the ASCII codes works quite well, but it has one technical flaw. Can you find it? How could you correct it?

3. There are some ways (though devious) in which a program can detect the keyboard pause state. Can you imagine how it might be done?

4. Earlier, I discussed the data areas that show which shift-type keys have been pressed. The KEYBITS program in Appendix B accesses the data area at locations 417 and 418 (hex). This program distinguishes between the left and right Shift keys but not between the left and right Alt and Ctrl keys.

   The BIOS keeps another data area at location 496 (hex) that shows whether or not the right Alt or Ctrl key has been pressed. If the right Alt key has been pressed, bit 3 is set on; if the right Ctrl key is pressed, bit 2 is set on. (The bits are numbered so that the rightmost bit is 0.)

   Modify the KEYBITS program so that it checks the data area at location 496 (hex) to distinguish between the two Alt and Ctrl keys.

# 14

# Data!

In this chapter, I introduce you to the basics of computer data and the main data formats that the PC uses. When you reach the end of this chapter, you should have a clear foundation for understanding what the PC really works with: data!

# Bits, Bytes, and Characters

The starting point of computer data, the smallest, most fundamental unit, is called a bit. The word *bit* is a contraction for binary digit. Everyone is familiar with the 10 decimal digits, 0 through 9, used to express the numbers with which we work. Binary digits, bits, are similar, but there are only two different values, 0 and 1.

The bits 0 and 1 may be said to represent off and on, false and true, and no and yes—whichever of those replacements you prefer. (Of course, even the values 0 and 1 are replacements we project onto the presence or absence of electrical voltage, but...you get the idea, I'm sure.) When voltage is present at a given location, that location is interpreted as holding the value 1; when no voltage (or a relatively lower voltage, sometimes) is present, that location is interpreted as holding the value 0. These 1s and 0s also have the obvious numerical meaning: the bit value 0 really does mean zero, and 1 does mean one. As I mention in Chapter 1, "Inside the PC," it is the concept of the bit that makes information-handling machines as we know them (computers) possible. Because it's practical to make electronic machines that work with on/off signals at great speed, it's possible to make machines that work with information that process data. It all depends, however, on the capability to match information that's meaningful with the model of information with which the computer can work. And that depends on the capability to construct real information out of the simple bits of 0 and 1.

Common sense and some heavy mathematical theory both indicate that a bit is the smallest possible chunk of meaningful, distinguishable information. Bits serve as building blocks that enable the construction of larger and still more meaningful amounts of information. By themselves, bits usually aren't of much interest or use, and only on occasion do I talk about individual bits in this book. It's when bits are strung together into larger patterns that something useful and interesting is made.

The most important and interesting collection of bits is the byte. A byte is eight bits taken together as a single unit. Bytes are important because they are the main practical unit of computer data. You undoubtedly know that the memory capacity of a computer and the storage capacity of a disk are measured in bytes. (Large numbers of bytes are measured in kilobytes, megabytes, gigabytes, and terabytes, all of which I discuss shortly.)

That's because the byte is really the main unit of data; a bit may be the smallest grain of sand of computer data, but the byte is the brick, the real building block of data. (OK, I promise, no more metaphors for a few paragraphs, at least.) Although computers can work with larger aggregates of bytes and get into the bits in a byte, they are designed to manipulate and work with bytes.

A byte contains eight bits, which means that there are eight individual 0 or 1 settings in each byte. Therefore, if eight bits each have two settings (0 and 1), then the number of possible distinct combinations of bit settings in a byte is $2^8$, which is 256. There are, then, 256 different values that a byte can have. The number 256 is important; you'll see it again and again. (Remember in Chapter 12, "The PC Character Set," that I say there are 256 basic elements in the PC character or symbol set. Now you can see the reason for this seemingly arbitrary number.)

Most of the time, you won't be interested in anything smaller than a byte. However, there are times when I need to refer to the individual bits in a byte—particularly when I get into some of the more technical matters. I give a brief introduction to this level of computer logic in the next section.

# The Bits in Bytes and Words

Before you can examine the bits in a byte, you need a way of referring to them. This is done by numbering them from the far right, or least significant, bit starting with the 0, as shown in Table 14.1. This method of specifying numbers is called binary. (Decimal and hexadecimal numbers have been discussed in previous chapters.) You probably already know that *bi-* means two, and there are only two values possible in this numbering system. The more familiar decimal system has 10 digits (0 through 9), and hexadecimal uses 16 numbers (0 through 9 and A through F).

Table 14.1. Binary Bit Pattern and Values.

| Bit Pattern | Bit Position | Numeric Value | Power of 2 |
|---|---|---|---|
| 00000001 | 0 | 1 | $2^0$ |
| 00000010 | 1 | 2 | $2^1$ |
| 00000100 | 2 | 4 | $2^2$ |
| 00001000 | 3 | 8 | $2^3$ |
| 00010000 | 4 | 16 | $2^4$ |
| 00100000 | 5 | 32 | $2^5$ |
| 01000000 | 6 | 64 | $2^6$ |
| 10000000 | 7 | 128 | $2^7$ |

It may seem odd to number the bits from the right and to start numbering them from 0, but there is a good reason for doing this. When interpreting the numeric value of a byte and the bits in it, the bit number is the power of 2 that corresponds to the numeric value of the bit. For example, bit 3 has a numeric value of 8, and $2^3$ is 8.

A similar scheme applies when you're looking at two bytes together. Instead of numbering the bits in the individual bytes separately, they are commonly numbered together: 0 through 15, 0 through 31, and so on.

A byte inside a computer is raw data that can be used for anything. Two of the most important things that you do with your computer is work with numbers and manipulate written text like the words you are reading here. Bytes are the building blocks of both numbers and text (character) data.

There is nothing fundamental about a byte, or any other collection of data, that makes it either numeric or text. Instead, it is simply a matter of what you want to do with your computer. If you're working with numbers, then the bytes in the computer are treated as numbers, and the bit patterns in the bytes are given a numerical interpretation. On the other hand, when you work with text information, the bytes are interpreted as characters that make up the written text information—although there is numeric information immediately beneath the character interpretation, as explained in Chapter 12, "The PC Character Set." Each byte represents one character of text.

Basically, as far as we're concerned as users, bytes work as either numbers or characters, depending on what program you are using. The same pattern of bits could be, for example, the letter A or the number 65, depending on what you are doing. The same bit pattern could represent 65 percent in a pie chart your spreadsheet has created. It's all numbers to the computer, but the interpretations are task-specific.

Most of the remainder of this chapter discusses how bytes can be used as numbers and characters and how several bytes taken together can be treated as more complicated numbers or strings of text characters.

By the way, when I refer to a computer as an 8-, 16-, or 32-bit computer, I am talking about the amount of data it can deal with in a single gulp. The PC family members are 16- or 32-bit computers, depending on which processor they use (more on that back in Chapter 3, "Brains: The Processors").

Before ending this introductory section, let's take a look at four more basic terms concerning computer data: the kilobyte (KB), the megabyte (MB), the gigabyte (GB), and the terabyte (TB).

It's always handy to be able to talk about things in round numbers, particularly when you're dealing with large quantities. Computers deal with large numbers of bytes, so people started expressing these values in round numbers, which are an approximation of the actual binary value. The most common of these terms is the kilobyte, which is $2^{10}$, or 1,024. The *kilo* in kilobyte comes from the metric term for thousand. In a computer context, however, kilobyte represents 1,024, not 1,000, bytes. When you hear people talking about 64KB, they mean 64 × 1,024, or 65,536 bytes.

Similarly, a megabyte is roughly one million bytes. To be exact, a megabyte represents $2^{20}$, or exactly 1,048,576, bytes. The sizes of computer hard drives often are expressed in megabytes. The last two terms have become important in recent years as disk sizes have grown. Gigabyte refers to $2^{30}$, or

1,073,741,824, bytes. Terabyte refers to $2^{40}$, or 1,099,511,627,776, bytes. These relationships are summarized in Table 14.2.

Table 14.2. Number Suffixes and Powers of Two.

| Term | Power of 2 | Approximate Value |
|------|-----------|-------------------|
| 1 kilobyte | $2^{10}$ | one thousand |
| 1 megabyte | $2^{20}$ | one million |
| 1 gigabyte | $2^{30}$ | one billion |
| 1 terabyte | $2^{40}$ | one trillion |

Now you're ready to move on to learn more about computer data. You can learn about the fearsome hexadecimal system and go on to explore numeric data in greater detail.

# Hexadecimal

If you really want to understand the inner workings of the PC or any other computer, you need a good working grasp of the computer-oriented number system known as the hexadecimal (or hex) system. Understanding hex certainly isn't necessary for you to be a very capable (or even an expert) user of the PC. However, if you want to comprehend the machine and use some of the more sophisticated tools for the PC, including the DEBUG program that is a part of DOS, you'll need to have a working knowledge of hex.

You already know that the smallest building blocks of computer data are bits that individually signify the values 0 and 1. If you write computer data in its binary, or bit, form, you get a rather long string of 0s and 1s. Just writing out a single byte in binary form is rather long: 01010101, for example. Because each byte, or character, contains 8 bits, it takes 88 bits to write out the pattern that represents the word hexadecimal (a typical floppy disk can store approximately 15 million bits). When you want to write out the exact data in a computer, you need a way to represent all the bits—one that isn't as long and tedious as binary. This is where hexadecimal comes in.

Hex, simply put, is a practical solution to a tedious problem. Hex is a shorthand for binary notation, in which one hexadecimal digit represents four binary digits (bits). If you look at bits individually, they have two values, 0 and 1. If you grouped them in pairs, there would be four possible combinations of bit values: 00, 01, 10, and 11. Taking that idea two steps further, if you organize four-bit groups, there are 16 possible patterns, starting with 0000 and ending with 1111. (The math of it is that the number of distinct combinations of the two-bit values taken four at a time is $2^4$, or 16.)

In the decimal numbering system, we use 10 symbols, 0 through 9, to represent 10 digit values. We can combine these decimal digits to make larger numbers, like 100. The same principle applies to binary notation; we can combine the two-bit symbols, 0 and 1, to make larger numbers. It works the same for hex, but instead of the two binary digits or the 10 decimal digits, hex uses 16 hexadecimal digits to represent 16 values. The 16 hex digits are 0 through 9 (which have the same numerical meaning as the decimal digits 0 through 9) plus six additional hex digits, which are written using the letters A, B, C, D, E, and F. These last six hex digits, A through F, represent the six values after the value nine: A is 10, B is 11, and so on, to F, which has a value of 15.

Each of the 16 hex digits represents a value between 0 and 15; it also represents a pattern of four bits. The hex digit A, for example, represents the bit pattern 1010, and F represents 1111. Table 14.3 shows a list of the 16 hex digits, their decimal equivalents, and their binary equivalents.

Table 14.3. The 16 Hex Digits.

| Hex Digit | Decimal Equivalent | Binary Equivalent |
| --- | --- | --- |
| 0 | 0 | 0000 |
| 1 | 1 | 0001 |
| 2 | 2 | 0010 |
| 3 | 3 | 0011 |
| 4 | 4 | 0100 |
| 5 | 5 | 0101 |
| 6 | 6 | 0110 |
| 7 | 7 | 0111 |
| 8 | 8 | 1000 |
| 9 | 9 | 1001 |
| A | 10 | 1010 |
| B | 11 | 1011 |
| C | 12 | 1100 |
| D | 13 | 1101 |
| E | 14 | 1110 |
| F | 15 | 1111 |

There are two ways to view these hex digits (and the four bits that each represents), and it's important to understand the distinction. It's a distinction that applies to all the computer data that you view. When you consider a hex digit—say, B—you might be interested in the numerical value that it represents (which is 11) or the pattern of bits that it represents (1011). Bear in mind that whether you're talking about hex, bits, or any other computer data, the same data takes on different meanings, depending on how you look at it. And, at the same time, regardless of how you (or an application program) interprets the data, it is stored in the computer only one way, as a pattern of 1s and 0s.

One question that might come to mind is, "Why hex?" It's easy to understand that bit notation is too long and clumsy and that something more compact is needed to express several bits at a time. But why hex? Why four bits at a time, when that leads to using the unfamiliar digits A through F? The answer is that hex is a reasonable compromise between what's closest to the machine and what's practical for people to work with. Because the most common unit of computer data is the byte, hex can conveniently represent all the bits in a byte with two hex digits, each one representing four of the byte's eight bits. Hex fits neatly into the fundamental scheme of computer data.

So far I've talked about individual hex digits, but you also need to be able to work with larger numbers, expressed in hex. Later in the book, I'll talk about the memory addresses used in the PC family that use four-digit (and larger) hex numbers. Therefore, you need to have a sense of the size of larger hex numbers and be able to do some arithmetic with them.

Hex arithmetic, of course, works just like decimal arithmetic, but the values of the numbers are different. The largest decimal number is 9, and the number after it, 10, is written using the individual digits 1 and 0. The same principle applies in hex (or any other number base). The largest hex digit is F (which has a value of 15); the number after it is written 10, which has a value of decimal 16; next comes the number 11 (which is 17 decimal); and so on.

Two hex digits are all you need to express all the possible bit combinations in a byte. You'll recall that with eight bits in a byte, there are $2^8$, or 256, bit patterns (00000000 through 11111111) to a byte. In hex, the binary 00000000 and 11111111 are hex 00 and FF. The first four bits are represented by the first hex digit, and the last four are represented by the second hex digit.

You can use Table 14.3 to translate between any pattern of bits and its hex equivalent. That's what you do when you're just looking at hex and bits as arbitrary data. When you want to interpret hex digits as a number (which you do from time to time in this book), you need to know how to convert between hex and decimal as well as how to do simple arithmetic in hex. (Well, to be honest, you don't really *have* to know how to do this as many calculator programs—including CALC.EXE, which comes with Microsoft Windows—support conversions, but you're reading this technical section for knowledge and greater understanding, so, here goes!)

First, let's see how to evaluate a hex number. It helps to pause and think of how you evaluate decimal numbers. Consider the number 123; it really means 3 + 20 + 100. Each position has a value that's 10 times higher than the place to the right. (As you would probably expect, the same basic rules for carrying numbers to the left in addition and so on apply to binary and hexidecimal math, just as they do to decimal math.) The same principle works in hex, but the multiplier is 16, not 10. So, if you interpret 123 as a hex number, it's $3 + 2 \times 16 + 1 \times 16^2$ (which is 256). Thus, 123 in hex is equivalent to 291 in decimal. Table 14.4 lists the decimal equivalents for the round hex numbers from 1 to F0000.

Table 14.4. Hex Value Table.

| Hex | Decimal | Hex | Decimal |
| --- | --- | --- | --- |
| 1 | 1 | 100 | 256 |
| 2 | 2 | 200 | 512 |
| 3 | 3 | 300 | 768 |
| 4 | 4 | 400 | 1024 |
| 5 | 5 | 500 | 1280 |
| 6 | 6 | 600 | 1536 |
| 7 | 7 | 700 | 1792 |
| 8 | 8 | 800 | 2048 |
| 9 | 9 | 900 | 2304 |
| A | 10 | A00 | 2560 |
| B | 11 | B00 | 2816 |
| C | 12 | C00 | 3072 |
| D | 13 | D00 | 3328 |
| E | 14 | E00 | 3584 |
| F | 15 | F00 | 3840 |
| 10 | 16 | 1000 | 4096 |
| 20 | 32 | 2000 | 8192 |
| 30 | 48 | 3000 | 12288 |
| 40 | 64 | 4000 | 16384 |
| 50 | 80 | 5000 | 20480 |
| 60 | 96 | 6000 | 24576 |
| 70 | 112 | 7000 | 28672 |
| 80 | 128 | 8000 | 32768 |
| 90 | 144 | 9000 | 36864 |
| A0 | 160 | A000 | 40960 |
| B0 | 176 | B000 | 45056 |
| C0 | 192 | C000 | 49152 |
| D0 | 208 | D000 | 53248 |
| E0 | 224 | E000 | 57344 |
| F0 | 240 | F000 | 61440 |

| Hex | Decimal | Hex | Decimal |
|-----|---------|-----|---------|
| 10000 | 65536 | 90000 | 589824 |
| 20000 | 131072 | A0000 | 655360 |
| 30000 | 196608 | B0000 | 720896 |
| 40000 | 262144 | C0000 | 786432 |
| 50000 | 327680 | D0000 | 851968 |
| 60000 | 393216 | E0000 | 917504 |
| 70000 | 458752 | F0000 | 983040 |
| 80000 | 524288 | | |

If you want to convert between decimal and hex manually, you can use Table 14.4 to look up the equivalents. To convert, for example, the hex number F3A into decimal, look up the value of hex A (it's decimal 10), hex 30 (48), and hex F00 (3,840). Adding them, you get 3,898 as the decimal equivalent of hex F3A.

To convert decimal into hex, you work the other way, subtracting as you go. For example, to convert the decimal number 1,000,000 to hex, you look up the largest entry in the hex table that's not over the decimal number. In this case, it's hex F0000 at the end of the table. Subtract its decimal value (983,040) from the starting number and continue the process until there's nothing left. Then the series of hex numbers you subtracted combine to make the hex equivalent of the decimal number. In this case it is hex F4240.

Fortunately, as I mentioned, there are tools readily available that do the work of hex-to-decimal conversion, so you don't have to resort to this manual process. In addition to the Windows Calculator, you can easily perform conversions in QBasic, which comes free with DOS:

```
INPUT "Enter a hex number", X$
PRINT "The decimal equivalent is " ; VAL("&H"+X$)
```

and

```
INPUT "Enter a decimal number ", X
PRINT "The hex equivalent is "; HEX$(X)
```

If you're forced to do hex arithmetic the hard way or just want to try your hand at it, type in the QBasic program HEXTABLE in Appendix B, "QBasic Program Listings." When you run this program, it generates a handy conversion table.

# Normal Numbers

Because numbers are so important to computers, you need to look at the kinds of numbers with which PCs can work. I start this section with the simple number formats that are part of the PC's basic repertoire of numbers, the numbers that the PC has a native capability to work with. In the next section, I look at some more exotic types of numbers that the PC can use when you stretch its skills.

You might be surprised to realize that the PC basically can work with only whole numbers (integers), and rather small numbers at that. The PC can work with only two varieties of numbers: one- and two-byte (one-word) integers.

Although today's PCs are 16-, 32-, or 64-bit machines, they operate in DOS in real mode (16-bit mode). That means the PC's built-in arithmetic skills can be applied only to single 8-bit bytes and 16-bit (two-byte) words. With the assistance of clever programs, the PC can work with larger numbers by combining two 16-bit words into a larger 32-bit number, for example. However, this can be done only with special software. When you're talking about the PC's natural skills, you're talking about only 8- and 16-bit arithmetic. (Under a 32-bit operating system, like the forthcoming Microsoft Windows 95, things are different and 32-bit math is possible).

Just how big can 8- and 16-bit numbers be? Not very big, really. As you already know from looking at 8-bit bytes, an 8-bit byte can have only 256 ($2^8$) distinct values. A 16-bit, 2-byte word can have $2^{16}$ (65,536) distinct values in all. That sets a rather tight limit on the range of numbers that you can work with using bytes and words. (If you want to explore 2-byte words or other longer integer formats, you need to know about back-words storage. See the "How Data Is Stored" section in Chapter 15, "The Memory Workbench.")

Each of these two sizes of integer can be interpreted in two ways, doubling the number of possible numeric formats. The two interpretations depend on whether you want to allow for negative numbers. If you don't have to work with negative numbers, the entire range of values of each of these two sizes of integers can be devoted to positive numbers. For a 1-byte integer, the range of numbers can run from 0 to 255, using all 256 bit patterns. For a 2-byte word, the range of positive integers is from 0 to 65,535.

On the other hand, if you need negative numbers as well, half of the range of values is devoted to negatives, and you can have numbers only half as large. In the case of bytes, the range of values is from −128 to +127; for words, the range is from −32,768 to +32,767. You don't get to choose the range, so you can't get a wider range of positive numbers by giving up some of the negative ones. (For more on negative numbers, see the following "Negative Numbers" section.) Notice that the range of negative numbers is one greater than the range of positives (there is a −128 but no +128). That's just an odd by-product of the way negative numbers are handled. Table 14.4 summarizes the range of numbers handled by the four integer formats.

Table 14.4. Range of Integer Formats.

| Integer | 1 Byte | 2 Bytes |
|---|---|---|
| Unsigned | 0 to 255 | 0 to 65,535 |
| Signed | –128 to +127 | –32,768 to +32,767 |

As mentioned before, the processor in your PC can do all of its standard arithmetic (add, subtract, multiply, and divide) on these four integer formats, but that is the extent of the basic calculating the PC processor can do.

> **Technical Note:** Your X86 processor can also perform what is known as BCD, or Binary Coded Decimal, number crunching. BCD is a specialized technique used for representing base 10 (decimal) numbers in sets of only four bits.

As you might imagine, few programs can get along with just those four simple integer formats. BASIC, for example, uses three kinds of numbers. Only one of them, called an integer in BASIC's terminology, is of these four formats; it's the signed two-byte word format. The other two, which BASIC calls single-precision and double-precision, have to be created by going beyond the PC's ordinary skills.

# Negative Numbers

Negative integers are represented inside the PC in a form known as two's-complement. It's a commonly used scheme in computers and is closely related to the borrow-and-carry tricks you were taught when you first learned to add and subtract. It's easiest to explain with an example done with decimal numbers that you make three digits long; that's analogous to the fixed length one- or two-byte binary numbers with which the PC calculates.

In the example three-digit decimal numbers, zero is written 000 and one as 001. If you subtract 001 from 001, you get 000. How can you subtract 001 again to get minus one? You can do it by borrowing from an imaginary one in the fourth place. Think of 000 (and all other positive numbers) as having a one in front that can be borrowed, like this:

```
(1)000 zero
 –001 subtract 1
 ─────
   999
```

Thus, –1 is represented as 999; –2 is 998, and so on.

The positive numbers start at 000, 001, 002, and go up to 499. The negatives are 999 (–1), 998 (–2), and so on, down to 500, which really means –500. The same trick works with the binary numbers inside your computer.

Notice that the value of a number can depend on whether you interpret it as signed or unsigned. As a signed number, 999 means –1; as an unsigned number it means 999.

# "Real" Hot Numbers

Most of your computing needs go beyond the simple integers that are native to the PC. Whether you're doing financial planning with a spreadsheet program, performing engineering calculations, or just balancing your checkbook, you need numbers more powerful than the integers discussed so far. Just dealing with money, the integers discussed so far couldn't handle anything more than $655.35 if you figure down to the penny. So you need some more numbers.

There are two ways that the PC can give you a wider range of numbers and two ways to calculate with those numbers. I look at the kinds of numbers first and then show you how those numbers can be calculated.

The first way to extend the range of numbers with which your PC can deal is simply to make longer integers. You already have seen one- and two-byte integers. You also can use integers of three, four, and more bytes. Anything is possible, but the most practical extra length of integer is four bytes, which gives you a range of numbers of about –2,000,000,000 to +2,000,000,000.

To handle fractional amounts and extremely long numbers, computers use a concept known as floating point. Floating point works like something you may have learned about in school called scientific or engineering notation. In this scheme, numbers are represented in two parts. One part represents the digits that make up the number; the other part indicates where the decimal point is located. Because the decimal point can be moved around freely, floating-point numbers can become very, very large (astronomical) or very, very small. Regardless of how large or small the number becomes, it remains accurate because the digits that determine accuracy, or precision, are independent of the numbers that specify where the decimal point is.

In the QBasic programming language, the style of numbers known as single- and double-precision are both floating-point formats. The difference between them is that the double-precision format allows you to store numbers with a higher level of accuracy.

**Note:** You're probably already familiar with this concept. If someone asks you the cost of an item and you know it costs $2.99, you'll likely tell them it costs three dollars. On the level at which the information is most commonly useful to shoppers, only the dollar amount is really significant. Less accuracy is acceptable (this is like single-precision accuracy). On the other hand, if your bank pays you 5.6485945921038529 percent interest on your deposits, it would certainly be unacceptable to you if they truncated this payment amount down to 5 percent. It works similarly for programmers. When they know the degree to which their program will require accuracy when it is performing calculations, they can set up their software to use single-precision values (which require less memory) or double-precision values (which use more memory, but guarantee that errors don't occur through rounding or truncation).

Other programming languages use floating point too. Spreadsheet programs also use floating point to represent their numbers because it gives them greater flexibility and greater precision in the calculations they perform.

The PC's number scheme can be extended in two ways: longer integers and floating point. As I mentioned, however, the PC's microprocessor has the natural ability to work with only the four simple integer formats covered earlier. How do you get any arithmetic done in these extended formats? The answer is through software and hardware.

Software is the most common solution. Every programming language, including QBasic—and nearly every calculating program, including spreadsheets—contains program routines that can perform calculations on floating-point numbers or long integer formats. These subroutines use the PC's basic arithmetic and logic skills as building blocks to perform the more complex calculations necessary to work with these other number formats. This goes on at a cost, however. Although the PC can perform its own integer calculations very quickly—typically, for a 486, in a less than a millionth of a second—a floating-point subroutine takes perhaps 100 times as long to do an equivalent calculation simply because the subroutine has to perform its work using 100 elementary steps.

For many purposes, the speed of these software-based calculations is fast enough, but not as fast as it could be. To get more speed, you must look to a hardware solution.

The processor inside the 486- and Pentium-based PC has a companion, the math coprocessor, designed for just one task: fast mathematical (floating-point) calculations. (On 386-based machines, these coprocessors were optional chips that plugged into a special socket on the motherboard. They were all members of the Intel X87 family of math coprocessors.) The 486 and Pentium processors come with a built-in coprocessor so they have no need for the X87 family. When a coprocessor is available (installed) and a program knows how to use it, the speed and accuracy of floating-point calculations can be improved enormously.

It's worth bearing in mind that many programs just don't do any floating-point calculations. Word processing programs, for example, have no need for floating-point numbers. These programs aren't slowed down by floating-point subroutines or sped up by the presence of an X87 coprocessor. (However, some of today's word processors include math or spreadsheet functions or links to external programs that handle numbers. In these cases a coprocessor could be helpful.) And, some programs that do perform floating-point calculations still don't take advantage of a coprocessor. Older versions of BASIC, for example, ignore any coprocessor that might be present, since coprocessors weren't around when those first versions of BASIC were written. Spreadsheet programs, on the other hand, use the coprocessor whenever it can help.

Unlike integer formats (discussed in this chapter) and unlike the PC character set (discussed in Chapter 12), there are no universal standards for the kinds of longer integers and floating-point numbers that can be used by a program. Next, let's look at some of the most common extended number formats.

Let's start with longer integers. Programs can work with any number of bytes to make a long integer, but one size is by far the most common: four-byte signed integers. These numbers can range from slightly over –2,000,000,000 to just over +2,000,000,000. Math coprocessors are designed to work with both four- and eight-byte integers, which get as large as nine billion billion. These coprocessors also can work with a special decimal integer format that holds 18 decimal digits, which is also in the billion billion range. This special decimal format is a unique example of a decimal orientation; everything else that your computer does is essentially binary rather than decimal.

The two most common sizes of floating-point numbers occupy four or eight bytes of storage, like QBasic's single- and double-precision formats. Four-byte, floating-point formats give the equivalent of about 6 decimal digits of accuracy, and eight-byte formats give about 16 digits of accuracy. The range (how large numbers can get) is in the neighborhood of $10^{38}$ power. Because there are several ways to code a floating-point number, there is some variety in the amount of precision and the range in size of floating-point numbers, so the figures I give are rough estimates. Coprocessors also can work with a slightly larger format that occupies ten bytes; it provides about 18 digits of accuracy.

The kinds of programs you use determines the kinds of numbers with which you can work. The discussion in this chapter applies to most programming languages, but specialty programs may have their own unique number formats. It's not uncommon, for example, for spreadsheet programs to use their own variations on the idea of floating-point numbers. This chapter should give you a clear idea of the kinds of "real" hot numbers that can be at your disposal when you work with your computer.

# Stringing You Along

Character or text data (letters of the alphabet and so forth) are very important in your use of the computer. In fact, computers are used more for working with text data than with numeric data, which is ironic because computers are, first and foremost, overpriced calculators. However, people have learned how to make these fancy calculators do a lot of useful work manipulating written text. For example, the words you are reading have been handled by a computer from the moment they were written. It's important to understand some of the fundamentals of how computers handle text data.

Text data is made up of individual characters, such as the letter A. Each letter is represented by a particular pattern of bits and occupies a byte of storage. A coding scheme is used to define the standard way of determining which pattern of bits represents which letter. (I go into great detail on this subject in Chapter 12).

Individual characters aren't terribly useful until you put them together to form words and sentences. Similarly, inside the computer, groups of character bytes are more significant than individual bytes. *String* is the term used to describe a group of characters handled as a single entity. A string is a group of consecutive bytes that is treated as a unit.

All computer programming languages and many of the most important kinds of software, such as spreadsheet programs, can work with strings of character data. Word processing programs are designed to work primarily with character strings.

Having emphasized the importance and utility of strings, there isn't a great deal more to say about them. There are, however, a few key things that you ought to know, particularly about how strings are stored and the limitations that are sometimes placed on what sort of string data you can use.

Inside the computer's memory and on the computer's disks, strings are stored just as common sense indicates: The character bytes are recorded one right after another. That's nothing special. What is special about strings is that something has to tie them together. Earlier in the chapter, you learned that every kind of numeric data has a specific format that rigidly defines the size of the number—how many bytes it occupies. Strings, however, are special because they don't have any fixed length. Some are long; some are short. Still, something has to define a string's length to tie together the characters that make it up.

This is not done in any universal way. Different programs and computer languages use their own methods and rules to define what a string is and what holds it together. Nevertheless, I can discuss some of the most common methods used to give you some insight into how programs work with strings and why the limitations on strings come about.

Programs define the length of a string in two main ways. One simply is to keep track of the length of the string as a number that is recorded separately from the string; usually, this length-of-string number is placed just before the beginning of the string. Here's an example:

4This2is1a6string2of5words

As you can see, each word in the example is a separate string, and the number of character bytes in each word is recorded just before it. This is a very common technique for dealing with strings and determining how long they are. If you think about it, you realize that this method places an inherent limit on the length of any individual string. The number that represents the length of the string is recorded in a numerical format like the ones I discussed. The maximum number that format allows sets a limit on the length of the string.

It's very common for the length of a string to be recorded as a single unsigned byte, which can't be larger than 255. Many programs limit the length of the strings they work with to 255. (Sometimes the limit is a few less than 255 because one or two bytes may be needed for overhead.) The older versions of BASIC that used to come with PCs worked this way, so strings in BASIC couldn't be over 255 characters; but compiled BASIC records its string lengths as two-byte words, so the string length for compiled BASIC can be over 32,000. Some word processing programs hold each line as a separate string and use a one-byte string length counter; these programs limit the length of a line to 255 characters.

There is another way to determine the size of a string that doesn't place any arbitrary limit on string length. With this technique, the length of the string isn't recorded; instead, the end of the string is marked with some sort of delimiter. Here's another example, using asterisks as delimiters:

```
This*is*a*string*of*words*
```

The   delimiter is used to mark the end of the string, but is not considered part of the string itself. There are two delimiters that are widely used. The first is a zero-byte, a byte with all the bits off. (A zero-byte isn't a bad choice of delimiter because it is not normally used as an ordinary text character.) The second commonly used delimiter is a byte with a numeric code of 13. Thirteen is the code for a Carriage Return character, which is normally used to mark the end of a line of text. Because it's common to treat each line of text as a separate string, it makes sense to use the same byte code to mean both end of line and end of string.

One obvious disadvantage to using a special end-of-string delimiter code is that the string can't include that code value in the string. This may not be a major problem in most circumstances, but it is a disadvantage and a limitation of which you should be aware.

Having looked at data and how it's organized and how the computer's interface gets it out of your head and into the computer, I next look at how the computer stores that data internally. Chapter 15 begins our exploration of the computer's memory.

# Some Things to Think About or Try

1. BASIC can easily convert numbers between hex and decimal as long as the numbers aren't any bigger than the equivalent of four hex digits. Try writing a program that converts larger numbers between hex and decimal.

2. Try your hand at some hex arithmetic. Add 1234 to ABCD. Subtract 1A2B from A1B2. Multiply 2A by 2 and by 3.

3. Can you figure out a way to test either the accuracy or range of numbers that a program can handle? Try writing a BASIC program that tests how large a number can become or how precisely a number is represented.

4. Analyze the problems inherent in the two ways of defining a string. Think of practical situations in which the limitations might matter. Can you think of a scheme that places no limit on the length or contents of a string? Are there any disadvantages to your scheme? Write a program in BASIC (or any other programmable software, such as a spreadsheet) that finds out how long a string can be by increasing a string character by character.

# 15 The Memory Workbench

Now it's time to get to know the computer's memory. In this chapter, I quickly look at what memory is and how data is stored in it. Then I look into the complex but fascinating details of how programs gain access to memory. You see how the PC's designers subdivided the memory into different uses and then take a look at two kinds of additions to the PC's memory. This may sound like a lot, but it's all intriguing.

You already know, from earlier parts of this book, most of the underlying ideas about the PC's memory, so I really don't need to introduce you to the fundamentals of computer memory. But, to help make sure that you're on the right track, I briefly pause to summarize the key things about computer memory. Then I dive into the really interesting details.

The computer's memory is a scratch pad where working information—which includes both program instructions and data—is kept while it is being worked on. For the most part, what's in the computer's memory is temporary working information (For the exception, see the discussion of read-only memory later in this chapter.)

Computer memory is organized into units of bytes, each made up of eight bits. (See Chapter 14, "Data!," for more details on how this works.) The same bit pattern can be seen as a number, a letter of the alphabet, or a particular machine language instruction, depending upon how you interpret it. The same memory bytes are used to record program instruction codes, numeric data, and alphabetic data.

While the computer's memory is divided into bytes, those bytes can be combined to create larger aggregates of information. One of the most important is the word, which is 2 bytes taken together to form a single 16-bit number. When 4 bytes are taken together to form a single 32-bit number, it's called a double-word. (Remember that the 386 through Pentium series can work with 32-bit quantities. When you interpret a series of bytes together as alphabetic text, it's called a character string. There are endless ways to combine bytes into meaningful data, but these are some of the most important.

To work with the computer's memory, each byte of the memory has an address; that is, a number that uniquely identifies it. The memory addresses are numbered, beginning with zero. The same numbers used as computer data also can be used to specify memory addresses, so the computer can use its capability to do arithmetic to find its way through its own memory. This integration of arithmetic, data, and memory addressing gives the computer astonishing power.

That's the essence of the computer's memory. Now, I take a closer look.

# How Data Is Stored

If you plan to explore the computer's memory, want to work with assembly language, or, like me, just want to know everything you can about your computer, you need to know about what's whimsically called back-words storage.

When you write down either numbers or names, you put what's called the most significant part first. That's the part that matters the most when you arrange names or numbers in order. In the number 1776, the 1 is the most significant, or high-order, part; in the name California, the C is the most significant letter.

In PCs, it doesn't go exactly that way. For character string data, which is the format used to store names like California, the most significant letter is stored first, in the leftmost byte (the byte with the lowest address), just as you write it. Numbers, however, are stored the other way. For numbers that take up more than one byte (such as a 16-bit number), the least significant byte is stored first. In effect, the number you know as 1776 is stored in the computer as 6771. (Please don't take that example too literally for reasons you'll see in a moment.)

This way of storing data, with the least significant byte first, is called the little endian data format. (If the processor stored data with the most significant byte first, it would be called the big endian data format.) However, the term that is used more often is *back-words*. This term indicates that a word (a 16-bit, two-byte integer) has its bytes stored backward from what you might expect. This doesn't apply just to two-byte words; it also applies to longer integer formats, such as 32-bit, 4-byte long integers. It also applies inside the complex bit coding used to represent floating-point numbers.

While PCs can work with any numeric format, the one that they use most is the 2-byte word format. That's because 16-bit words are used in every aspect of the PC's memory addressing (as you'll see in more detail below) and because 16-bit words are the largest numbers that the PC's instruction set handles when the processor is in real mode.

To explain the idea of back-words storage, I gave the example of the (decimal) number 1776 written back-words as 6771. But that doesn't exactly tell you what's going on. Back-words storage concerns binary integers stored byte-by-byte in reverse order. When you see binary integers written down, you see them in hex notation, which uses two hex digits for each byte. For example, when you write it front-words, the decimal number 1776 in hex is 06F0. To write the same hex number back-words, don't reverse the order of the individual hex digits, reverse the bytes (which are represented by pairs of digits). Hex 06F0 back-words is F006 with the two hex pairs (06 and F0) reversed.

Knowing about this back-words storage is more than a matter of simple intellectual curiosity. Any time you work with computer data represented in hexadecimal, you must know whether you're seeing numbers represented front-words (the way you write them) or back-words (the way they actually are stored). Generally speaking, whenever data is formatted for the user's consumption, it is in front-words order; whenever it's being shown as stored in the machine, it is in back-words order. You have to be careful not to get confused about which way you're seeing it.

Here's an example of how you may be shown a number in both forms. If you work with some assembly language, using either DEBUG or the assembler, and have an instruction to move the hex value 1234 into the AX register, you see something like the following:

```
B8 3412    MOV  AX,1234H
```

On the right side, you see the number in people-oriented, front-words form (1234); on the left side, you see the number as it actually is stored: back-words.

# Memory Segments: Technical Details and Real-Life Implications

There's a messy little problem inside the PC's processor, a problem that makes it complicated for programs to find their way around the computer's memory. The problem centers around 16-bit arithmetic.

Remember that when you use DOS, the processor is working in real mode. It is emulating an 8086, which means that it works best with 16-bit numbers, which can be no larger than 65,536. Because the computer uses numeric addresses to find its way through the memory, that suggests that the memory can't be larger than 64KB.

Experience has shown that 64KB is laughably too little memory for serious computer applications. PCs have come equipped with megabytes of memory for nearly ten years now. So how did the PC's designers reconcile the need for a larger memory with the use of 16-bit numbers to access it?

The solution that Intel designed into the 8086 processor family involves segmented addresses, and it's been a nightmare for PC users ever since it was created. You'll see why later.

Segmented addresses are built by combining two 16-bit words in a way that enables them to address 1,048,576 bytes (1MB) of memory. To see how it's done, you have to look at two things: the arithmetic involved in combining the two words of a segmented address and the way these segmented addresses are handled in the processor.

The arithmetic involves what is called shifted addition, which enables you to create a 20-bit binary number (which goes up to 1,048,578) from two 16-bit numbers. Suppose that you have two 16-bit words, which, in hexadecimal, have the values ABCD and 1234. Remember that each hex digit represents four bits, so four hex digits (ABCD or 1234) represent 16 bits all together. Take one of these two numbers, say ABCD, and put a 0 at the end: ABCD0. In effect, this shifts the number over one hex place (or four binary places); you can say that it has multiplied the value of the number by 16. The number is now five hex digits (or 20 bits) long, which brings it into the million range. Unfortunately, it can't serve as a complete 20-bit memory address because it has a 0 at the end; it can represent only addresses that end in 0, which only are every 16th byte.

To complete the segmented addressing scheme, take the other 16-bit number (1234) and add it to the shifted number, like this:

$$
\begin{array}{r}
\text{ABCD0} \\
+\ \ \text{1234} \\
\hline
\text{ACF04}
\end{array}
$$

When you combine these two 16-bit numbers, you end up with a 20-bit number that can take on any value from 0 to 1,048,577. That's the arithmetic scheme that underlies the PC's capability to work with 1MB of memory using 16-bit numbers.

The two parts of this addressing scheme are the segment and offset parts. In this example, ABCD is the segment value, and 1234 is the offset value. The segment part specifies a memory address that is a multiple of 16—an address that has a hex 0 in its last place. These memory addresses that are multiples of 16 are called paragraph boundaries, or segment paragraphs.

The offset part of a segmented address specifies an exact byte location following the segment paragraph location. Because the 16-bit offset word can range from 0 to 65,535, the offset part of the segmented address enables you to work with 64KB of memory, all based on the same segment address.

There is a standard way of writing these segmented addresses, which you encounter often when you're dealing with technical material about the PC. It's done like this: ABCD:1234. The segment part appears first, then a colon, and then the offset part. If you do anything with assembly language or use the DEBUG program, you see plenty of segmented addresses written this way. If you look at the DEBUG listing that appears later in this chapter, you see segmented addresses in the right column.

Usually, addresses inside the computer's memory are referred to in their segmented form. Occasionally, however, you need to see them in their final form, with the two parts of the segmented address combined. Whenever you need to do that, they are called absolute addresses, so as not to be confused with segmented addresses. In the example of combining ABCD and 1234, ACF04 is the resulting absolute address.

That's the arithmetic behind the segmented addressing scheme. Now, how does it work inside the computer? The segment part of segmented addresses is handled entirely by a set of four special segment registers, which I mentioned in Chapter 4, "Microprocessor Traffic Control." Each of the four is dedicated to locating the segment paragraph for a particular purpose. The code segment (CS) register indicates where the program code is. The data segment (DS) register locates the program's main data. The extra segment (ES) register supplements the data segment, so that data can be shifted between two widely separated parts of memory. And, the stack segment (SS) register provides a base address for the computer's stack.

(As I mentioned earlier, the 386 and 486 series processors have two extra segment registers, FS and GS. These generally are not used by DOS programs which, for the most part, follow the rules of the 8086 architecture.)

Most of the time these segment registers are left unchanged, and programs waltz around within the base set by the segment paragraph. Detailed addressing is done by working with the offset part of the address. While the segment part of an address can be used only when it's loaded into one of the four segment registers, there is much greater flexibility in how offsets can be used. A program can get its address offsets from a variety of registers, including the general-purpose registers AX, BX, and so forth, and the indexing registers SI and DI. Offsets also can be embedded in the program's machine language instructions or calculated by combining the contents of registers and the machine language instructions. There is a great deal of flexibility in the way offsets can be handled.

**Technical Note:** Let me give you an example of how these two methods of handling offsets might be implemented. If a programmer is creating a fixed, closed array containing, say, the days of the week, she knows that she only has seven offsets to work with, and she can, therefore, specify values directly in the code itself. If her program's week begins on Sundays, then an offset of three will always point to Tuesday; an offset of seven to Saturday, and so on. On the other hand, a serious database programmer is much more likely to be creating an open-ended array with who knows how many elements, arranged who knows how. It would be cumbersome at best—and probably, impossible—for him to permanently code offsets pointing to elements of that array. He doesn't know where elements will be until he's actually working with dynamic data. In that sort of instance, only a calculated offset makes any sense at all. Imagine if to begin designing a phone book program you had to first know the name of every person who would be entered in it! Trust me, you'd go back to your day job in a hurry!

The way that the PC's processor uses segmented addresses has many practical implications for the way programs work. For an important aside on that, see the "64KB Limits" section.

Fortunately, the tedious details of working with segmented addresses are kept out of the user's way as much as possible. For the most part, only if you're doing assembly language programming do you have to bother yourself with the tricky problems of segmented addressing. However, if you want to explore segmented addressing, BASIC gives you a way to do it. The DEF SEG statement in BASIC enables you to specify the segment part of a segmented address, and the number that's used with the PEEK and POKE statements provides an offset part that's combined with the DEF SEG's segment part. So, if you want to try your hand at tinkering with segmented addresses, you can do it with these features of BASIC. For some examples of how to use segmented address, see the program listings in Appendix B, "QBasic Program Listings," especially the ALL-CHAR program.

# 64KB Limits

Once in a while, you may encounter what are called 64KB limits. For example, when you use older dialects of BASIC, you're limited to a maximum of 64KB of combined program and data memory. Other programs mention that they can handle no more than 64KB of data at one time. Some programming languages can't build programs with more than 64KB of program code.

You know, of course, where the 64KB number comes from. It's the maximum amount of memory that can be addressed with one unchanging segment register value. Why are you restricted to one fixed segment pointer and why do you encounter such 64KB limitations in real mode? The answer lies in something called the memory model, which is based on the degree of sophistication that a program has in manipulating the segment registers.

As a program runs, it has to find its way to the various parts of the program and to its data. In simplified terms, each program uses the code segment (CS) register to locate parts of the program and the data segment (DS) register to locate the data. While the program is running, these registers can be independently treated as fixed or changeable. If either of them is fixed (that is, not being changed by the program), then that component (program code or data) can't be any larger than the 64KB that a single segment value can address. But, if either can be dynamically changed during the program's operation, there is no such limit to the size of that component. If both are fixed, you have the small memory model, which limits a program to 64KB of code and another 64KB of data. With both changeable, you have the large model, which is without the 64KB limits. There are two more models, which have one segment fixed and the other changeable.

Although the advantage—no 64KB limits—of changing the segment registers is obvious, the price isn't so obvious, but it's quite real. When a program manipulates the segment registers, it takes on both an extra workload, which slows down the operation, and an extra degree of memory management, which can complicate the program's logic. There is a clear trade-off to be made between speed, size, and simplicity on the one hand and power on the other.

As it turns out, the design of the processor's instruction set makes it relatively easy and efficient to change the CS register that controls the program code and relatively clumsy to control the data's DS register. Thus, you find a fair number of programs that are larger than 64KB but work with only 64KB of data at a time. Fortunately, both the art of programming the PC and the PC's programming languages are becoming increasingly sophisticated, so you run into the 64KB limit less and less frequently.

# Ringing in the New: Flat Memory Models and Windows 95

The information about segments and offsets that you've read in this chapter may not seem like it, but they are one of the biggest annoyances of the Intel hardware and DOS operating system in its history. And they're not only an annoyance to application programmers; they've done their share of driving users crazy, too. Before virtual memory in Version 3.1 brought Windows into the twentieth century, "out of memory" errors and system crashes because of memory problems were terribly common. Even today, if you are a power user, you've probably had to run the DOS program MEMMAKER to place boot-time device drivers into high memory so that you have enough conventional memory available to actually run DOS programs.

Windows 95 all but says "goodbye" to DOS, and it does say goodbye to this sort of memory annoyance. All of this segment, offset, conventional memory, expanded memory, extended memory, high memory, low memory nonsense will vanish through Windows 95's implementation of a "flat" memory model. In a phrase, under Windows 95, all memory is the same, and Windows itself—finally a full operating system under Windows 95, and not just an environment running on top of DOS—will take control over what loads where in memory and how memory is allocated and protected among applications and low-level devices. Memory will be used far more optimally than ever before and Windows 95 applications will be easier for programmers to design in some regards. Windows 95 is discussed in depth in Chapter 23, "Microsoft Windows: Role and Function." If you'd like more information about these memory issues right now, turn to that chapter and read the section entitled, "Understanding Windows Memory Models."

# The PC's Memory Organization

One of the most useful things you can learn about the inner workings of your PC is how the memory is organized and used. Knowing this helps you understand how the PC works, comprehend many of the practical limits on the kinds of work the PC can undertake, know how the display screens work, and learn the basis for the often-mentioned but little-understood 640KB memory limit. All of that, and more, should become clear when I take a look at the basic organization of the PC's memory space. As you read on, bear in mind that I am describing how things work in real mode or virtual 86 mode (which is what DOS uses).

You know, from seeing how the PC addresses memory through its segment registers, that there is a fundamental limit on the range of memory addresses with which the PC can work. This limit is roughly one million different addresses, each representing a byte of memory. That means that the PC has an address space of 1MB.

A computer's address space is its potential for using memory, which isn't the same thing as the memory that the computer actually has. However, the basic address space provides a framework for the organization of the computer's workings. When the designers of a computer figure out how it's going to be laid out, the scheme for the address space is a very important part of it. I explain how the PC's designers laid out the use of the PC's address space.

The easiest way to see it is to start by dividing the entire 1MB address space into 16 blocks of 64KB each. You can identify each of these blocks of memory by the high-order hex digit that all addresses in that block share. So, the first 64KB of memory is called the 0 block because all addresses in that block begin with 0 (for example, 0xxxx in five-digit absolute address notation and 0xxx:xxxx in segmented address notation). Likewise, the second block is the 1 block. Thus, the 1MB address space is made up of sixteen 64KB blocks, the 0 block through the F block. Table 15.1 summarizes how this memory generally is used. I give you more detail on that in the following sections.

Table 15.1. The IBM PC's Memory Blocks.

| Block | Address Space | Use |
|-------|---------------|-----|
| 0 | 1st 64KB | Ordinary user memory to 64KB |
| 1 | 2nd 64KB | Ordinary user memory to 128KB |
| 2 | 3rd 64KB | Ordinary user memory to 192KB |
| 3 | 4th 64KB | Ordinary user memory to 256KB |
| 4 | 5th 64KB | Ordinary user memory to 320KB |
| 5 | 6th 64KB | Ordinary user memory to 384KB |
| 6 | 7th 64KB | Ordinary user memory to 448KB |
| 7 | 8th 64KB | Ordinary user memory to 512KB |
| 8 | 9th 64KB | Ordinary user memory to 576KB |
| 9 | 10th 64KB | Ordinary user memory to 640KB |
| A | 11th 64KB | Video memory |
| B | 12th 64KB | Video memory |
| C | 13th 64KB | ROM extension area |
| D | 14th 64KB | ROM extension area |
| E | 15th 64KB | System ROM-BIOS |
| F | 16th 64KB | System ROM-BIOS and ROM-BASIC |

It's very important to note, when talking about these blocks, that there is no barrier of any kind between the blocks. Memory addresses and data flow in smooth succession through all of memory and across the artificial boundaries that separate these blocks. They are referred to as distinct blocks partly for convenience, but mostly because the overall scheme for the use of the PC's 1MB of memory is organized in terms of these blocks.

# Low Memory Fun

The very lowest part of the computer's memory is set aside for some important uses that are fundamental to the operation of the computer. There are three main divisions to this special use of low memory.

The first is the interrupt vector table, which defines where interrupt-handling routines are located. The first 1,024 bytes of memory are set aside for the interrupt vector table, with room for 256 interrupts—quite a few more than are routinely used. This occupies absolute memory addresses 0 to hex 400. (You learn more about this later in this chapter.)

The second area is used as a workplace for the ROM-BIOS routines. Because the ROM-BIOS supervises the fundamental operation of the computer and its parts, it needs some memory area for its own record keeping. This is the ROM-BIOS data area, one of the most fascinating parts of the computer's memory. Among the many things stored in the ROM-BIOS data area is a buffer that holds the keystrokes you type before your programs are ready to receive them, a note of how much memory the computer has, a record of the main equipment installed in the computer, and an indicator of the display screen mode.

An area of 256 bytes is set aside for the ROM-BIOS data area in absolute memory addresses hex 400 to 500. There are some amazing things in this area. If you want to learn more about them, take a look at my book, *The Peter Norton Programmer's Guide to the IBM PC*.

The third part of the special low memory area is the DOS and BASIC work area, which extends for 256 bytes from absolute address hex 500 to 600. This region was shared by both DOS and BASIC as a work area, similar to the ROM-BIOS work area that precedes it.

This low memory area is just loaded with goodies for the interested explorer. Anyone who wants to learn about the inner workings of the PC can get a graduate education in PC tinkering simply by digging deeply into this part of memory.

The key working area of memory is the part used for programs and their data. That's the area made up of the first 10 blocks, the 0 through 9 blocks. This area often is called the user memory area to distinguish it from the rest of the address space, which is, in one way or another, at the service of the computer system itself. When I talk about the amount of memory that PCs have, what I really am talking about is the amount of user memory installed in this area. In theory, user memory could be as little as 16KB or as much as 640KB with all 10 blocks of memory installed. Whatever amount of memory is installed forms one contiguous chunk from the 0 block to wherever the end of the memory is.

There are actually several different kinds of memory, and the kind installed here is regular read/write random-access memory (RAM). Two things characterize RAM memory. First, as read/write memory it can have the data in it inspected (read) and changed (written). Second, it is volatile, meaning that the data in it is preserved only as long as the computer is running.

This memory is dedicated to holding programs and data while the computer is working with them. The amount of RAM installed here in many ways determines the size and scope of the operations that the computer can undertake.

The basic design of DOS sets aside only 10 of the 16 blocks in the address space for this main working memory area. That's just over 60 percent of the total. That 640KB area seems much too small for today's problems, but at the time the PC was designed it seemed like a very generous amount. At that time, typical personal computers were limited to perhaps 64 or 128KB of total memory, and DOS's 640KB limit seemed enormous. (Underestimating the need for growth and expansion is a mistake that has occurred over and over again in the history of computing.)

It is possible to expand the 640KB user memory area slightly by encroaching on some of the system area that follows, but that isn't really wise because the memory blocks that come after the 640KB user area are reserved for some special uses that should not be sabotaged. However, there are new memory management routines — including those that have come with DOS since Version 5.0 — that do a pretty good job of using these memory areas safely. Third-party utilities also are available to make use of some of this memory between 640KB and 1MB. Note that few, if any, applications use this memory directly. They do so only through the manipulations of these DOS or third-party utilities. That's a safer and more predictable way to go.

Not every single bit of the user memory area is available for programs to use. The very first part of it, beginning at memory address 0, is set aside for some essential record keeping. You can find some deeper technical information about one part of it in the next section. But, except for that small (and interesting) part, this entire 640KB section of memory is set aside for use by programs. On the other hand, the rest of the memory blocks have some fascinating characteristics.

# The Interrupt Vector Table

When I introduce interrupts in Chapter 4, I explain that the interrupt mechanism causes the current program to be put on hold while an interrupt-handling program is activated. The processor needs a simple and straightforward way to find that interrupt-handling program, and that's accomplished using the interrupt vector table, a very simple table of the addresses of the stored interrupt-handling routines beginning with the vector (the pointer to the beginning of the routine) for interrupt number 0 at memory location 0. Each vector address is four bytes long; the vector for any interrupt number $x$ is found at memory location $x \times 4$.

The vectors are simply the complete memory address, in segmented form, of the routine to be activated when the interrupt occurs. A segmented address is made up of a pair of 2-byte words, so you can see why vectors are 4 bytes each.

You can inspect the interrupt vector table in your computer very easily by using DEBUG. Use the D (Display) command to show the beginning of memory like this:

```
D 0:0
```

DEBUG shows you the first 128 bytes, or 32 vectors. An example is shown below. When you try it on your computer, you probably will get different numbers. What you see depends on several factors, including the version of DOS you are using, the type of computer you have, and whether or not you have installed any memory-resident programs.

```
0000:0000   E8 4E 9A 01 00 00 00 00-C3 E2 00 F0 00 00 00 00
0000:0010   F0 01 70 00 54 FF 00 F0-05 18 00 F0 05 18 00 F0
0000:0020   2C 08 51 17 D0 0A 51 17-AD 08 54 08 E8 05 01 2F
0000:0030   FA 05 01 2F 05 18 00 F0-57 EF 00 F0 F0 01 70 00
0000:0040   90 13 C7 13 4D F8 00 F0-41 F8 00 F0 3E 0A 51 17
```

```
0000:0050   5C 00 B7 25 59 F8 00 F0-E2 0A 51 17 9C 00 B7 25
0000:0060   00 00 00 F6 8E 00 DE 09-6E FE 00 F0 F2 00 7B 09
0000:0070   27 08 51 17 A4 F0 00 F0-22 05 00 00 00 00 00 F0
```

The vectors are stored back-words, the offset followed by the segment. For example, the first four bytes that DEBUG shows above (E8 4E 9A 01) can be translated into the segmented address 019A:4EE8.

Generally, you find three kinds of addresses in the vector table. There may be ones that point to the ROM-BIOS, which you can identify by a hex F leading the segment number. There may be ones that point into main memory, as in the above example. These may be pointing to routines in DOS or in a memory-resident program or to DEBUG itself because DEBUG needs to have temporary control of the interrupt. Finally, the vectors may be all 0 because that interrupt number is not currently being handled.

If you want, you can chase down any of the interrupt-handling routines by first decoding its interrupt vectors as shown above and then feeding that segmented address to DEBUG's U (Unassemble) command to inspect the program code inside the interrupt handler.

Immediately following the user memory area is a 128KB area, consisting of the A and B blocks, which is set aside for use by the display screens. The data that appears on the screen of the computer has to be stored somewhere, and the best place to store it turns out to be in the computer's memory address space. That's a good idea because it enables programs to manipulate the display screen data quickly and easily. So, to make that possible, the 128KB area of the A and B blocks is set aside for the display screen's data. (I discuss in Chapters 11 through 14 how the display screens work and how they use this memory.)

In the original PC design, only part of the B block was used for the display screens; the A block was reserved but not used. This is why it has been possible for some PCs to have an additional 64KB of user memory installed. This has never been a wise thing to do, though, because it breaks important design conventions of the PC family. The first official use of the A block came with the appearance of the IBM Enhanced Graphics Adapter, which needed more working display memory than the previous display adapters.

The memory installed for use by the display screens operates just like the conventional RAM. Normally, it has one extra feature that helps speed the operation of the computer: it has two doorways, so that programs (using the processor) and the display screen can work with it simultaneously without interfering with each other. This is called dual-port memory. I show you an interesting example of how such interference can cause problems in the next section.

# Video Snow

The display circuitry and the processor usually can access the dual-port video memory at the same time without getting in each other's way. With the old Color Graphics Adapter (CGA), however, the display and the processor clashed under certain conditions. The result was video interference that showed up as snow.

To circumvent the problem, old software installation programs asked the user whether such snow was noticeable. If the user answered yes, the software took steps to avoid the interference.

There were two choices. The software could refrain from accessing the video memory directly and use the facilities of the BIOS. However, on older computers, this slowed down the program. Or the software could access the video memory directly but only during the intervals in which the electron beam that actually displays the dots was not in use. These times are called the horizontal and vertical retrace intervals. They occur when the beam is moving from the end of one row to the beginning of the next or from the bottom to the top of the screen.

After the display memory area come two blocks, C and D, which are set aside for some special uses. They are rather nebulously called the ROM extension area. There is no hard-and-fast assignment for this memory area. Instead, it is used for a variety of purposes that have arisen in the evolving history of the PC family. One use, which gives this section its name, is as a growth area for the very last section of memory, the ROM-BIOS which occupies the E and F blocks. When new equipment is added to the PC family and it requires built-in software support, the additional ROM-BIOS programs are added here. Another use for the ROM extension area, one which was not designed by IBM, is to support extended memory, which I discuss shortly.

The final part of the PC family's memory address space includes the E and F blocks, which are used to hold the computer's built-in ROM-BIOS programs. The memory used here is a special kind known as read-only memory (ROM). ROM is permanently recorded, so it can't be written to or changed, and isn't volatile, so turning off the computer does not disturb it. As you can see, ROM is very different from RAM, although their names are easy to confuse. I give you some additional information about ROM-BIOS in the next two chapters.

# Extended Memory

As discussed earlier, the amount of memory that the standard 8086/DOS architecture can use is 1MB. Out of this 1MB, only 640KB is available for programs and data. However, today's computers have multiple megabytes of memory. With DOS, any ordinary memory over 640KB is not directly accessible and is called extended memory.

OS/2 and other protected mode operating systems can take advantage of all this memory. And, special DOS control programs such as Microsoft Windows can as well. But what can you do with plain vanilla DOS to avoid wasting this extra memory?

The BIOS provides a service to transfer blocks of data in whatever size you need back and forth to extended memory. There are some special programs that take advantage of this feature to provide facilities that would normally not be available.

For example, DOS comes with a program named either VDISK.SYS or RAMDRIVE.SYS depending on your version of DOS that enables you to create a virtual disk. (A virtual disk is an area of memory that is used to emulate a real disk.) You activate VDISK.SYS by placing the appropriate command in the CONFIG.SYS file. If you want, you can instruct DOS to have VDISK.SYS create a virtual disk in extended memory. This saves as much as possible of the low-end 640KB for your programs and data.

When VDISK.SYS uses the BIOS transfer service to move data in and out of extended memory, it does so without having to change into protected mode or to manipulate the extended memory area directly.

If you carefully read the instructions in your DOS manual for setting up the CONFIG.SYS (configuration) file, you will see that there are a few more system programs that can use extended memory if you so desire. This is usually a good idea as the space below 640KB is precious.

# Virtual Memory

Remember that today's processors—the 286, 386, 486, and the Pentium—can use virtual memory in addition to real memory. Virtual memory is a service provided by a protected mode operating system (such as Windows, Windows 95, and OS/2) working in conjunction with the built-in features of the processor to use external storage (such as a disk) to simulate large amounts of real memory.

Back when the mainframe was king and all types of storage were expensive, it was said of virtual memory that "you pay for it, but you only think it's there."

Table 15.2 shows the maximum real and virtual memory with which various PC processors can work. Take a look at this table and then read on for an explanation of how virtual memory is implemented.

Table 15.2. Maximum Real and Virtual Memory Available to PC Processors.

| Maximum Processor | Real Memory | Virtual Memory |
|---|---|---|
| 8088 | 1MB | — |
| 8086 | 1MB | — |
| 286 | 16MB | 1GB |
| 386 | 4GB | 64TB |
| 386SX | 4GB | 64TB |
| 386SL | 4GB | 64TB |
| 486 | 4GB | 64TB |
| 486SX | 4GB | 64TB |
| Pentium | 4GB | 64TB |

To put this in perspective, Table 15.3 shows the same information expressed in bytes.

Table 15.3. Maximum Real and Virtual Memory Available to PC Processors (in Bytes).

| Maximum Processor | Real Memory | Virtual Memory |
|---|---|---|
| 8088 | 1,048,576 bytes | — |
| 8086 | 1,048,576 bytes | — |
| 286 | 16,777,216 bytes | 1,073,741,824 bytes |
| 386 | 4,294,967,296 bytes | 70,368,744,177,664 bytes |
| 386SX | 4,294,967,296 bytes | 70,368,744,177,664 bytes |
| 386SL | 4,294,967,296 bytes | 70,368,744,177,664 bytes |
| 486 | 4,294,967,296 bytes | 70,368,744,177,664 bytes |
| 486SX | 4,294,967,296 bytes | 70,368,744,177,664 bytes |
| Pentium | 4,294,967,296 bytes | 70,368,744,177,664 bytes |

Virtual memory is a sleight-of-hand operation that involves some carefully orchestrated cooperation among the processor, a virtual memory support program, and the disk drive.

When a program is being set up to run in the computer, the operating system creates a virtual memory space, which is a model of the amount of memory and the memory addresses the program has at its disposal. Then, a portion of the computer's real memory is given over to the sleight-of-hand operation that is the core of the virtual memory concept. Using a feature that's an integral part of the processor, the operating system's virtual memory support program tells the processor to make the real memory assigned to it appear to be at some other address. This other address is the virtual address that the program will use. A memory mapping feature in the processor makes the real memory appear to have a working memory address other than its true address.

So far what I've described is just a shuffling act, a trick that makes some real memory addresses appear to be, and work as, some other virtual addresses. The most important part of virtual memory comes in the next step, when a program tries to use more virtual memory than there is real memory.

A program starts out with some of its (large) virtual memory space mapped into a part of the computer's (smaller) real memory. (See Figure 15.1). As long as the program is working with only that part of its virtual memory, all goes well. The program actually is using different locations in memory than it thinks it is, but that doesn't matter. What happens when the program tries to use some of the large virtual memory that hasn't been assigned a part of the smaller real memory? When that occurs, the processor's mapping table discovers that the program is trying to use an address that doesn't currently exist; the processor generates what is called a page fault.

**Figure 15.1.**
*How virtual memory works.*

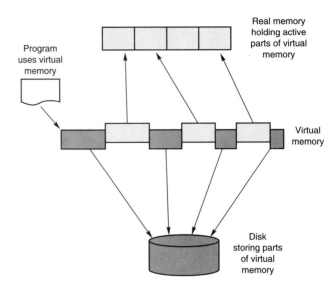

When there is a page fault, indicating that a program is trying to use a virtual address that isn't actively mapped into real memory, a special virtual memory support program swings into action. It temporarily places the program on hold while it deals with the crisis. The support program chooses some part of the virtual memory currently in real memory and saves its contents temporarily on the disk; that's called swapping out. That freed-up part of real memory is recycled to act as the needed part of virtual memory. When the swapped-out part of memory is needed again, it's copied back in from disk. As you can see, the disk is used as a warehouse for storing the parts of virtual memory that aren't in current use.

Depending on how things go, the virtual memory operation can run very smoothly or can involve so much swapping in and out of memory that a lot of time is wasted waiting for the swaps to take place. The latter is called thrashing; when a virtual memory system starts thrashing, very little work gets done. The practical operation of a virtual memory system can involve a very sensitive balancing act known as system tuning.

# Using More than 640KB of Memory

The future of the PC family's evolution belongs to the 486- and Pentium-based processors and to new operating systems, like OS/2, Microsoft Windows 95, Windows NT, and UNIX, that can take full advantage of the hardware. However, there are still millions of DOS-based machines that are dependent on the old 8086-based architecture.

As I explained earlier, the 8086/DOS architecture enables programs to directly access only 1MB worth of addresses. Moreover, the top 384KB of this area are reserved, leaving only 640KB of addresses that can be used by programs.

Remember that each byte of memory requires an address to be accessed by a program. Because DOS has only 640KB worth of nonreserved addresses, DOS programs can access only 640KB of general RAM.

When the PC was first developed, this was fine. Indeed, the very first PCs had only 64KB of RAM. Nowadays, however, 640KB is far from adequate. DOS has been straining at the seams, so to speak, for some time. Although today's computers have plenty of memory, DOS has no easy way to use it.

Through the years, solutions have been developed. However, these solutions aren't perfect, and not one of them is universally employed. The basic problem—that the memory addresses from 640 to 1,024KB have been reserved and that thousands of DOS applications are written to expect this—is a fundamental flaw within DOS. Even when you're running an environment like Microsoft Windows 3.*xx*, you can have problems because certain elements are still based on DOS, and certain types of drivers require specific memory locations. The only complete solution is to change to an operating system like OS/2 or Windows 95 that is designed to access large amounts of memory. Such programs don't "remember" the old requirements and can make more efficient use of available system resources.

# The Expanded Memory Specification (EMS)

Having said that, I take a look at some of the solutions that have been developed to help DOS solve this problem. I start with expanded memory, the first important solution.

You know that DOS can access any memory with addresses from 0 to 1,024KB. Expanded memory uses a 64KB block of addresses to access extra memory. Here is how it works. You buy a memory adapter board (or plug additional memory into the proper slot on the motherboard) that contains extra memory (RAM) chips. The board has a number of 64KB banks of chips. These banks are not assigned permanent addresses; instead, they are accessed one at a time using a 64KB page frame.

Here is an example. Your computer has an expanded memory board that has 16 banks of memory, each of which contains 64KB of RAM. When you install the board, you also install a program called an extended memory manager, or EMM. The EMM sets up a 64KB area of memory as a page frame.

Now, when your programs want to use expanded memory, they call on the EMM to fulfill the request. The EMM sends a signal to the memory board that turns on the appropriate bank. The EMM then helps your program access the bank via the 64KB page frame. The system that makes this all work is called the Expanded Memory Specification, or EMS. (Sometimes, this specification is known as LIM-EMS. LIM stands for the names of the three companies who developed the design—Lotus, Intel, and Microsoft.)

EMS usually uses a 64KB page frame that lies in the reserved area of DOS memory, which is somewhere between 640 and 1,024KB. Usually, this window is in the D or E block of memory and sometimes in the C block. (See Table 15.1.)

To enable your program to access the data in the page frame, the EMM divides the frame into four windows, each 16KB long. Any program that knows how to use EMS can call on the EMM to swap data in and out of a window. (See Figure 15.2.)

*Figure 15.2.*
*How expanded*
*memory works.*

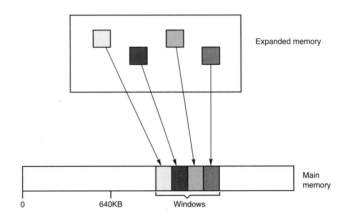

For EMS to work, however, several conditions must be met. First, you must have a special memory board, one that has the necessary hardware to perform bank switching. Second, the program you run must be written to take advantage of expanded memory. Finally, you must install an expanded memory manager to run the show.

The newest processors—the 386 and 486 families and the Pentium—have built-in facilities that can simulate bank switching. Thus, if you have a newer PC, you can use regular extended memory—plain vanilla extra memory—to simulate expanded memory. This means that you can use EMS-savvy programs without having an expanded memory board. All you need is a memory manager designed to take advantage of the enhanced capabilities of these processors. Beginning with DOS 4.0, such a program (EMM386.EXE) was included with the operating system. (Your DOS manual has the details.) Under Windows 95, none of these shenanigans will be necessary. (Take a look at Chapter 23 for more details on Memory under Windows 95.)

# The Extended Memory Specification (XMS)

The good thing about the EMS scheme is that it enables you to avoid DOS's 640KB memory limitation. There are two drawbacks, however. First, only programs that are written to use EMS can use expanded memory. The big memory hogs—the spreadsheets, databases, and so on—are, for the most part, written in this way. However, the vast majority of DOS programs do not support EMS, and no Microsoft Windows program can make use of expanded memory. In fact, if you are running Windows as your exclusive operating environment, you need not configure any memory as expanded. It is simply a waste of memory.

The second drawback is that, even if a program can use the extra memory, it cannot be accessed all at once. Although a program may think it is using a lot of memory, DOS only can access 64KB, that is, just the amount that fits into the page frame. And, within a program, data must be accessed via 16KB windows. Even with a fast computer, this can slow things down.

A newer solution enables DOS programs to access extended (extra) memory by using the Extended Memory Specification, or XMS. As with EMS, a program must be explicitly written to use XMS. However, after this is done, the memory can be accessed quickly; the program does not have to work via continued bank switching.

To use XMS, you need a 386-, 486-, or Pentium-based computer and an extended memory manager. (Such a program is included with DOS 5.0 and later as well as with Microsoft Windows.) As the use of extended memory becomes more and more common, you should find very few new programs that can't make use of it. In fact, as Microsoft Windows gains in popularity, the number of programs that require, or that even can use the older EMS standard, is waning.

The memory managers that come with DOS are called EMM386.EXE (expanded memory) and HIMEM.SYS (extended memory). In fact, some newer applications check your system configuration to make sure that one or both of these programs is installed properly. You can find more information on how these programs work with DOS and how you can use them to enhance your system in my DOS book, *Peter Norton's Complete Guide to DOS 6.22*, also published by Sams Publishing. And, of course, your DOS manual and DOS's online Help system (just type HELP at any command prompt) are good sources of information on these program utilities.

# An Exploration of Memory with the MEM Command

There's an easy way to get a great deal of direct insight into how your computer is using memory at any given moment: the MEM command, from DOS. If you've used the MEMMAKER program from DOS 6 or later, you've probably already used MEM, too. By using the different switches that are available to the command, you can get a fairly customized look at what memory's being used and what's free.

If you issue the MEM command with no switches

MEM

you'll get a quick but accurate overview of your system's memory status.

```
Memory Type      Total  =  Used   +  Free
---------------  ------    ------    ------
Conventional      640KB    123KB     517KB
Upper             139KB    139KB       0KB
Reserved          384KB    384KB       0KB
Extended (XMS)  15,221KB  14,197KB  1,024KB
---------------  -------   -------   -------
Total memory    16,384KB  14,843KB  1,541KB

Total under 1 MB  779KB    262KB     517KB


Largest executable program size      517KB (528,896 bytes)
Largest free upper memory block        0KB     (0 bytes)
MS-DOS is resident in the high memory area.
```

From this, you can see that I have a total of 16MB of memory in my computer, and that only roughly 1.5MB of that memory are currently free. You can also see that the largest DOS-based program I can run now is one that uses 517KB of my available 640KB of conventional memory, and that none of my upper memory area is free (DOS and several of my device-drivers are loaded there).

Adding the /CLASSIFY (or /c) switch to the MEM command breaks down your memory usage by program. It also shows you how much of each type of memory is being used by each program.

```
Modules using memory below 1MB:

Name        Total      =   Conventional  +  Upper Memory
--------  ----------       --------------    -------------
MSDOS     18,589  (18KB)   18,589  (18KB)         0   (0KB)
ASPI4DOS   5,472   (5KB)    5,472   (5KB)         0   (0KB)
HIMEM      1,168   (1KB)    1,168   (1KB)         0   (0KB)
EMM386     4,144   (4KB)    4,144   (4KB)         0   (0KB)
ASPICD    11,584  (11KB)   11,584  (11KB)         0   (0KB)
SJIIX      5,856   (6KB)    5,856   (6KB)         0   (0KB)
COMMAND    3,008   (3KB)    3,008   (3KB)         0   (0KB)
win386    48,608  (47KB)   13,744  (13KB)    34,864  (34KB)
MSCDEX    40,352  (39KB)   40,352  (39KB)         0   (0KB)
MOUSE     25,600  (25KB)      272   (0KB)    25,328  (25KB)
NC        13,456  (13KB)   13,456  (13KB)         0   (0KB)
COMMAND    3,216   (3KB)    3,216   (3KB)         0   (0KB)
WIN        2,096   (2KB)    2,096   (2KB)         0   (0KB)
COMMAND    3,248   (3KB)    3,248   (3KB)         0   (0KB)
SETVER       624   (1KB)        0   (0KB)       624   (1KB)
CSP        7,168   (7KB)        0   (0KB)     7,168   (7KB)
IFSHLP     3,904   (4KB)        0   (0KB)     3,904   (4KB)
DRVSPACE  39,936  (39KB)        0   (0KB)    39,936  (39KB)
SMARTDRV  30,368  (30KB)        0   (0KB)    30,368  (30KB)
Free     528,912 (517KB)  528,912 (517KB)         0   (0KB)

Memory Summary:

Type of Memory    Total   =    Used    +    Free
---------------  ----------    ----------    ---------
Conventional       655,360       126,448      528,912
Upper              142,192       142,192            0
Reserved           393,216       393,216            0
Extended (XMS)  15,586,448    14,537,872    1,048,576
---------------  ----------    ----------    ---------
```

```
Total memory       16,777,216   15,199,728   1,577,488

Total under 1 MB    797,552      268,640      528,912

Largest executable program size      528,896   (517KB)
Largest free upper memory block            0   (0KB)
MS-DOS is resident in the high memory area.
```

From this list, you can see all of my loaded device drivers and programs, including SMARTDRV, my scanner software, and Windows. Although DOS's MEMMAKER program will do the work for you under many circumstances, if you are having difficulty freeing up memory—or specific types of memory—a list like this can be invaluable in helping you see what's using what, and deciding where different software could be loaded to make a more efficient use of your resources.

The /DEBUG (or /d) switch breaks things down even further, showing the size and location in memory of each loaded element, type of each element, like "device driver," or "program," and so on. Here's an excerpt from a /DEBUG readout from my computer:

```
Conventional Memory Detail:

  Segment         Total        Name      Type
  ------          ----------   --------  --------
   00000        1,039  (1KB)             Interrupt Vector
   00040          271  (0KB)             ROM Communication Area
   00050          527  (1KB)             DOS Communication Area
   00070        2,752  (3KB)   IO        System Data
                               CON       System Device Driver
                               AUX       System Device Driver
                               PRN       System Device Driver
                               CLOCK$    System Device Driver
                               A: - D:   System Device Driver
                               COM1      System Device Driver
                               LPT1      System Device Driver
                               LPT2      System Device Driver
                               LPT3      System Device Driver
                               COM2      System Device Driver
                               COM3      System Device Driver
                               COM4      System Device Driver
   0011C        5,696  (6KB)   MSDOS     System Data
   00280       36,416 (36KB)   IO        System Data
   ...
   01A37          288  (0KB)   WIN       Environment
   01A49        1,808  (2KB)   WIN       Program
   01ABA          320  (0KB)   win386    Environment
   01ACE       13,088 (13KB)   win386    Program
   03498      439,920 (430KB)  MSDOS     — Free —

Upper Memory Detail:

  Segment Region     Total        Name       Type
  ------- ------    ----------   --------   --------
   0C801     2      39,920 (39KB) IO        System Data
                    39,888 (39KB)  DBLSYSH$ Installed Device=DRVSPACE
   0D1C0     2          48  (0KB) win386    Data
   0D1C3     2      30,368 (30KB) SMARTDRV  Program
```

```
0D92D       2     25,328   (25KB)   MOUSE      Data
0DF5C       2     31,296   (31KB)   win386     Data

XMS version  2.00; driver version  2.05
```

You'll notice that the DEBUG switch also tells you which version of extended memory manager you're using. Exciting, no?

If you should happen to want to find out what areas of memory a specific program or device driver is using, the /MODULE (or /m) switch is exactly what you need. By placing the name of the element you're interested in—say, the WIN386 program which, basically, *is* Windows—you can see exactly where in memory that module is located.

```
C:\WINDOWS>mem /module win386


WIN386 is using the following memory:

Segment   Region        Total        Type
-------   ------    --------------    --------
  00C25                  144   (0KB)  Data
  01608                  192   (0KB)  Data
  01ABA                  320   (0KB)  Environment
  01ACE               13,088  (13KB)  Program
  0B422       1        3,520   (3KB)  Data
  0D1C0       2           48   (0KB)  Data
  0DF5C       2       31,296  (31KB)  Data
                    --------------
Total Size:          48,608  (47KB)
```

Finally, the /FREE (or /f) switch will show you which blocks of memory remain free for use, and how large each of those blocks is.

```
Free Conventional Memory:

Segment         Total
-------    --------------
  01ECB            304   (0KB)
  01EDE         88,992  (87KB)
  03498        439,920 (430KB)

Total Free: 529,216  (517KB)

Free Upper Memory:

Region   Largest Free     Total Free      Total Size
------   --------------   --------------  --------------
   1        0   (0KB)        0   (0KB)    15,216   (15KB)
   2        0   (0KB)        0   (0KB)   126,976  (124KB)
```

One thing to keep in mind: many of MEM's readouts go on for screen after screen. It's a good idea to add the /PAGE (or /p) switch or the ¦MORE DOS pipe command to make your system pause after each full screen of data. You can get a lot of very useful information from the MEM command any time that you need it. It's been invaluable to me at times when I've been trying to cram one more device driver into place or make just enough room to run a particular piece of beta software.

A good deal more information about the MEM command is available in my book, *Peter Norton's Complete Guide DOS 6.22*, which is also published by Sams.

# Some Things to Think About or Try

1. Explain why the segmented addresses 1234:0005, 1230:0045, 1200:0345, and 1000:2345 all refer to the same memory location. Which of these refers to a different location than the other two: A321:789A, A657:453A, and A296:824A? Is there an ideal way to divide the two halves of a segmented address?

2. Using the DEBUG program's U (Unassemble) instruction, unassemble some of your computer's ROM-BIOS. For example, enter the following:

   ```
   U F000:A000 L 100
   ```

   Try to pick out examples of back-words storage.

3. How could you write a program in BASIC that finds out how much memory is installed in the computer by experimental means? Can this operation disrupt the computer? Write such a program and see what happens. (Incidentally, you can find a very fast version of such a test in the System Information program as a part of the Norton Utilities program set.)

4. What do you think are the advantages and limitations of expanded (bank-switched) memory? What does a program have to do to take advantage of it? What might the problems be for a program working with 16KB windows of data?

5. If you try using the MSG-HUNT program, which searches through the ROM-BIOS looking for messages, you may find that it gives some false alarms; for example, one "message" that it detects on my computer is "t'<.u"—nothing very fascinating or meaningful. That's because the program accepts as a possible message all characters from a blank space to a lowercase *z*. That enables you to capture punctuation inside of a message, but it also finds spurious messages, like the one above. What sort of test can you add to the program to filter out this nonsense? Try adding such a filter to MSG-HUNT (the listing for which is in Appendix B). Experiment with making your rules for an acceptable message tighter or looser and see what the result is.

6. Use the different switches available under the MEM command to find out what areas of memory are used in your system. Redirect the output to your printer using the command:

   MEM [switches go here] >LPT1:

   (assuming your printer is on the first LPT port) so that you can look at it at your leisure. One use of the MEM command can make you a real hero with your children: Many games require a specific minimum amount of free conventional memory, and won't run without it. You and the MEM command can be real heroes, believe it or not. Have fun!

# 16

# Built-In BIOS: The Basics

In this chapter, I begin to explore the software heart of the PC: its built-in ROM-BIOS. The task here is to understand the basic ideas behind the BIOS—the philosophy of how it is organized and what it tries to do. This lays the groundwork for Chapter 17, "BIOS: Digging In," where I explore the details of the services that the BIOS performs.

Before proceeding, to avoid confusion, note there are two things in the computer called BIOS. One is the ROM-BIOS, a built-in software feature; that's the topic for this chapter and the next. The other is the DOS-BIOS, the part of DOS that performs a similar service (but on a quite different level) for DOS.

# The Idea Behind BIOS

The ROM-BIOS has a clumsy name that only hints at what it's all about. ROM-BIOS is short for Read-Only Memory Basic Input/Output System. Ignore the name and concentrate on what it does. The ROM-BIOS is a set of programs built into the computer that provides the most basic, low-level, and intimate control and supervision operations for the computer.

Software works best when it's designed to operate in layers, with each layer performing some task and relieving the other layers' concern for the details of a task. Following this philosophy, the BIOS functions as the bottommost layer. It is the layer that underlies all other software and operations in the computer. The task of the BIOS is to take care of the immediate needs of the hardware and to isolate all other programs from the details of how the hardware works.

Fundamentally, the BIOS is an interface, a connector, and a translator between the computer hardware and the software programs that you run. Of course, properly speaking, the BIOS is simply a program like any other. However, if you want to understand the BIOS, you should think of it as if it weren't just software but a kind of hybrid—something halfway between hardware and software. Functionally, that's exactly what it is. (As a matter of fact, software that is permanently stored in hardware chips is called firmware to indicate this hybrid quality.)

# What's in the BIOS?

The ROM-BIOS contains a set of programs that provides essential support for the operation of your computer. There are three main parts to the ROM-BIOS programs. The first part is used only when the computer is first turned on; these are test and initialization programs that check to see that the computer is in good working order. Some of the delay between when you turn on the computer and when it starts working for you is caused by these test and initialization programs, which sometimes are called the power-on self-test (POST).

The second and most interesting part of the BIOS are its routines. These programs provide the detailed and intimate control of the various parts of the computer, particularly the I/O peripherals, such as the disk drives, which require careful supervision (including exhaustive checking for errors).

The BIOS, to help support the operation of the computer, provides a very long list of services that are available for use both by the operating system and by application programs. I have much to say about this part of the BIOS throughout the rest of the book.

The third part of the ROM-BIOS, which applies only to the older members of the PC family made by IBM, is the built-in ROM-BASIC. This was designed into the machine in the days when every user had to do a lot of programming to make the machine do much useful work. In fact, the earliest IBM machines didn't even have disk drives. They used cassette tape to load programs and store data. And, because there were no disk drives, there was no Disk Operating System (DOS). The machine started in BASIC, and this was the operating environment you used to interact with the machine, build programs, and load other applications. This BASIC was the core of the BASIC programming language, which is used either by itself or as part of the old dialect of BASIC (BASICA) that comes with IBM DOS. The new dialects of BASIC (like QBasic which comes with DOS 5.0 and later versions), does not depend on the ROM-BASIC, of course. And, the new IBM-brand PCs don't include BASIC as part of the ROM.

All of the BIOS programs are contained very compactly within the 128KB area of the E and F blocks of memory (E000 and F000 hex). (See Chapter 15, "The Memory Workbench," for more information on memory allocation and usage.) The amount of this block used varies from model to model. Generally speaking, the more complex computers need more software crammed into the BIOS. Thus, the E block is used for this purpose in newer computers. In older PCs, the ROM-BIOS is confined to the F block.

> **Technical Note:** Just for clarity, let me say that the ROM-BIOS I'm talking about here is the BIOS for your main system, which is stored in chips on your motherboard and may or may not be upgradable. Certain adapter boards, like VGA controllers and SCSI controllers, may contain their own ROM-BIOS to control their own functions. And, in some cases, such as select SCSI controllers, the ROM-BIOS on the adapter board may replace the functionality of the ROM-BIOS on your motherboard if you wish it to do so. This is generally an option that can be set through software during installation or through the setting of a switch on the card.

# What Does the ROM-BIOS Do?

What makes the ROM-BIOS so special? What does it do that makes it seem to be midway between hardware and software?

The answer lies in what the ROM-BIOS has to do and how it does it. The BIOS is designed to control the hardware directly and respond to any demands that the hardware makes. How it does this is largely through use of the ports that you learned about in Chapter 2, "Hardware: The Parts of the

PC." For the most part, all of the PC's components are controlled by commands or parameter settings sent through the ports, with each part of the circuitry having special port numbers to which it responds.

You already know that there are many important aspects of the hardware that don't work through ports, such as the memory addresses used to control what appears on the display screen. Most of the exceptions to the general rule that the hardware is controlled through the ports are exactly the parts of the computer that it's okay for programs to work with directly. These are the parts that the BIOS doesn't have to supervise.

I don't want you to get the impression that the BIOS concerns itself only with ports; it doesn't. Ports best symbolize what is special about the BIOS; it's the software that works most intimately with the computer's hardware and that takes care of hardware details (like ports) that other programs shouldn't have to touch.

# What's Special about the BIOS?

What's special about the ROM-BIOS is that it is written to work intimately with the computer's hardware. That means the ROM-BIOS incorporates lots of practical knowledge about how the hardware works. It isn't always obvious just what that knowledge is.

Up until the debut of the PS/2s, IBM published the listings of the programs that make up the ROM-BIOS. If you study these listings (which, of course, are unbelievably out-of-date), you easily can see what's so special about BIOS programming: it makes sure the right ports send the right commands to the PC's hardware components. What isn't anywhere near so obvious is that there is magic going on as well.

Not everything that it takes to make computer circuits work correctly is clear from their basic specifications. There are many subtleties as well, including things such as timing or just how errors actually occur.

For example, some circuits can accept a command at any time, but need a short amount of time to digest one command before they are ready to take another. In other cases, two separate steps may have to be performed with as little intervening time as possible. Hidden inside the BIOS are subtle factors like that. You might see a sequence of commands that appear straightforward and simple but that have a hidden element in them as well, such as carefully worked out timing factors.

This is a part of what makes BIOS programming so special and why many programmers think of BIOS programming as something of a magical art—an art that involves not just the logical steps from which all programs are built but also close cooperation between the programs and the computer hardware.

# How Does the BIOS Work?

Although the complete details of how the BIOS works are really of concern only to accomplished assembly language technicians, the basics of how the BIOS is organized and works will dramatically help you understand your machine. That's what I sketch out in this section.

To start with, the BIOS is roughly divided into three functional parts, as diagrammed in Figure 16.1.

**Figure 16.1.**
*The organization of the BIOS.*

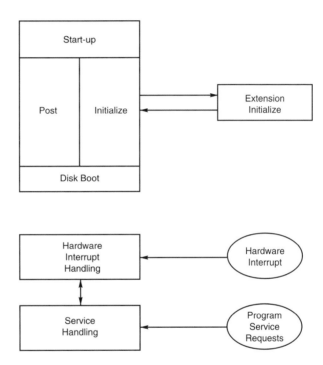

The first part of the BIOS contains the start-up routines, which get the computer going when you turn on the power. There are two main parts to the start-up routines. The first, as I mentioned a little earlier in this chapter, is the power-on self-test (or POST) routines, which test to see that the computer is in good working order. They check the memory for defects and perform other tests to see that the computer isn't malfunctioning. The second part of the start-up procedure is the initialization.

The initialization involves such things as creating the interrupt vectors, so that when interrupts occur the computer switches to the proper interrupt-handling routine. Initialization also involves setting up the computer's equipment. Many of the parts of the computer need to have registers set, parameters loaded, and other things done to get them ready to go.

The BIOS knows the full complement of standard equipment that a PC can have and performs whatever initialization each part needs. Included in this initialization are steps that tell the ROM-BIOS what equipment is present. Some of that is learned by checking switch settings inside the computer (in the case of the original PC) or by reading a permanent memory that records the equipment the computer has (in the case of the newer PCs). In some cases, the BIOS can find out if equipment is installed simply by electronically interrogating it and checking for a response. Whatever it takes, the BIOS checks for and initializes all the equipment that it knows how to handle.

Of course, you can add new equipment to your PC; people do it all the time. Some of this equipment is standard stuff, such as additional memory or extra serial and parallel output ports, but not all of it is. There is some optional equipment that isn't taken care of in the standard BIOS routines that need special BIOS support. To take care of that situation, the BIOS is prepared to search for additions to the BIOS.

# How Do You Add to the ROM-BIOS?

The BIOS in the PC is a fixed part of the computer's equipment, which leads to a fundamental problem: how do you add support for new options? The answer lies in an automatic feature, called BIOS extensions, that allows for additions to the BIOS.

The scheme is simple. Additions to the BIOS are marked so that the standard BIOS can recognize them and give them a chance to integrate themselves into the standard part.

Just as the main BIOS appears in memory at a specific location—the high, 128KB, E and F blocks of memory—additions have a standard memory area reserved for them as well—the C and D blocks.

Any new equipment requiring special BIOS support, such as an optical disk, places its read-only BIOS memory somewhere in that block and includes in it a special marking, hex 55 AA, in the first two bytes. The BIOS can't be located just anywhere. It has to be in a unique location that doesn't conflict with any other BIOS extensions and must begin on a 2KB memory boundary.

The standard (or you might say, master) BIOS, as part of its start-up routines, searches the BIOS extension area for the identifying 55 AA signature. When it finds one, it passes control over to the beginning of the BIOS extension, enabling the BIOS extension to do whatever it needs to do to initialize its equipment and integrate itself into the rest of the BIOS. For example, a BIOS extension for a new kind of display adapter might change the interrupt vector for video services to direct them to the BIOS extension rather than to the old BIOS video routines.

A BIOS extension performs whatever start-up and initialization work it has to do when the main BIOS passes control to it during the start-up procedure. When the BIOS extension is initialized, it passes control back to the main BIOS, and the computer proceeds in the usual way. Now, however, new equipment and new BIOS support for that equipment have been added.

All this is made possible by the mechanism that enables the main ROM-BIOS to search for and recognize BIOS extensions.

# ABIOS—The Advanced BIOS

So far, the BIOS and the memory usage I have discussed have been based on the 8086 architecture that is still used by DOS. With PCs that are based on the newer processors—the 286, 386, 486, and Pentium series—DOS runs in either real mode or virtual 86 mode. This means that, unless special control programs are used, DOS cannot take advantage of the protected mode features of these processors, such as large memory facilities, multitasking, and so on.

Other operating systems—in particular, OS/2 and Microsoft Windows—can take advantage of protected mode. However, such operating systems require a lot of system support that the regular BIOS does not provide. This support is provided by the Advanced BIOS, usually referred to as ABIOS.

If you want, you can write a short BASIC program that hunts through the ROM-BIOS looking for messages. In Appendix B, you find the listing for a short program, called MSGHUNT, that hunts through the whole F block looking for a string of five letters or punctuation characters in a row. When it finds them, it displays them and goes on hunting. If you want to learn more about what's inside your computer's ROM-BIOS, try MSGHUNT. After you have experimented with MSGHUNT, you might try to modify it to search another area of memory, such as the 0 or E block.

There's one final and quite interesting thing to know about the ROM-BIOS. In the original PC, IBM placed an identifying date at the end of the BIOS. I was among early users who found out where that date was located and talked about it in the original version of this book and in articles. I showed people how to find the date and display it with a simple BASIC program, like the following:

```
10 ' Display ROM-BIOS date
20 DEF SEG = &HFFFF
30 DATE.$ = "
40 FOR I = 5 TO 12
50 DATE.$ = DATE.$ + CHR$(PEEK(I))
60 NEXT
70 IF PEEK (7) <> ASC("/") THEN DATE$ = "missing"
80 PRINT "The ROM-BIOS date is ";DATE$
```

Here is the same program in QBasic:

```
 ' Display ROM-BIOS date
DEF SEG = &HFFFF
BiosDate$ = ""
FOR I = 5 TO 12
BiosDate$ = BiosDate$ + CHR$(PEEK(I))
NEXT I
IF PEEK(7) <> ASC("/") THEN BiosDate$ = "missing"
PRINT "The ROM-BIOS date is "; BiosDate$
```

After the days of the original PC, when other vendors started making PCs and writing BIOS code for them, an interesting thing happened. BIOS vendors, intent on duplicating the PC to the last detail, also included this date location. However, they weren't exactly sure how applications were using this date, so some companies were afraid to change the date. (One way the date was used was to tell an application whether the PC was capable of speed switching, which was implemented on late model PC ATs.) In Phoenix BIOS firmware, this date stayed the same for a long time. Then, sometime after 1990, the company decided it was probably okay to change the date for any major upgrades. Thus, you may find some later dates in your Phoenix BIOS if you poke around. And, Phoenix sold some BIOS packages to third-party companies who were licensed to take it and use it as they wanted. Some of these companies kept this original version of BIOS up-to-date with new processor and other computer technology, but they never did change the date inside the code.

Some computer vendors ignore this date when they install BIOS; others try to keep it current. One of my contacts at CompuAdd told me recently, for example, that they didn't use to change the date that the BIOS vendor used. However, so many customers complained about the date of their BIOS that they had to start maintaining that date. Even so, the date in your BIOS is probably not the precise date when the BIOS was updated.

Most manufacturers don't change this location with every minor change or version modification. They change it once a year or when there are major changes made to the BIOS. In short, don't be concerned if your BIOS date is relatively old. It really doesn't mean much.

That's why, even on newer machines, you may find very old dates when you run this program. The machine I used to write this book, for example, is a 486DX/2-66 with VESA local bus. It uses a Phoenix BIOS dated 1988. Obviously, if the BIOS were actually that old, the machine wouldn't run with all of its new equipment. It still can be fun to poke around in the BIOS and see what is there.

In addition to the date stamp, IBM has created a loosely defined model ID code, which can be used by programs that need to know when they are running on some of the more unusual models of the family. This simple BASIC program displays the ID byte:

```
10 ' Display machine id byte
20 DEF SEG = &HFFFF
30 ID = PEEK (14)
40 PRINT "The id byte is";ID;"hex ";HEX$(ID)
```

Here is the same program in QBasic:

```
 ' Display machine id byte
DEF SEG = &HFFFF
ID = PEEK(14)
PRINT "The id byte is"; ID; "hex "; HEX$(ID)
```

There are a number of codes that you may come across. They follow two separate patterns. At first, IBM decided to give each model of personal computer its own ID code. Later, they changed the scheme to focus on the architecture of the processor. For example, the PS/2 model 90, being a 486-based computer, has an ID code of F8. The PS/1, as an 8086-based computer, has an ID code of FA.

Non-IBM manufacturers have followed this code convention up to a point. To ensure PC compatibility, BIOS manufacturers (nearly all of them, I think) store FC in this location, indicating to any application that needs to know that the machine is PC AT compatible. Note that if the computer uses an ISA or EISA bus it is PC AT compatible, even if it uses a newer processor.

Because each model of computer has its own subtle but distinct characteristics, it can be beneficial for programs to make appropriate adjustments in the way they operate based on the machine ID. From this viewpoint, it's unfortunate that the most important of the non-IBM members of the family may not be easily identified by either a model ID byte or by the BIOS date. However, remember from the discussion in Chapter 3, "Brains: The Processors," that the newest processors include registers that, when properly accessed by applications, show what processor is being used.

# Upgradable BIOS

As strange as it may sound at first, the ROM-BIOS in most computers can now actually be changed. These upgradable BIOSs are stored on chips called EEPROMS, or Electronically Erasable Programmable Read-Only Memory, or in Flash RAM. Although the technology behind these chips is beyond the scope of this book, what you really need to know is that these chips remember the data that is stored in them—even when the power to your computer is turned off—until they receive instructions that erase their contents and replace those contents with a new BIOS.

For example, just before I went to work on the revision of this book, I paid a very small fee and received a floppy disk in the mail from my upgradable BIOS's manufacturer. By putting this diskette in my floppy drive and running an install program—which looked to me just like any other install program—I was able to erase my old BIOS and install a new one that enables me to use up to four EIDE hard drives of up to 8GB in capacity each! That's quite a change from only being able to use two IDE disks of up to 500MB each, just by running an update program.

On other hardware configurations, the "upgradability" of the BIOS may simply mean that the BIOS chip is in a special socket on the motherboard, from which it can be easily extracted and replaced with a completely new BIOS chip that already contains the new capabilities.

# BIOS and Booting

The very last part of the start-up routines in the BIOS is the boot routine, which tries to fire up DOS or any other operating system you may be using. The boot process involves the BIOS attempting to read a boot record from the beginning of a disk. The BIOS first tries drive A. If that doesn't succeed and the computer has a hard disk as drive C, it tries the hard disk. If neither disk can be read, the ROM-BIOS goes into its nondisk mode. Generally, this means that an error message of one kind or another is displayed, indicating that no valid boot device is available.

**Technical Note:** The setup program that enables you to set different defaults for your BIOS very likely enables you to specify, for example, that the floppy drives can be bypassed entirely during the boot process. However, keep in mind that if you make that change, and your hard drive crashes, you may experience significant inconvenience in getting your system up and running again. My personal suggestion: endure the five seconds it takes for your computer to poll the floppy disks each time you boot.

Normally, the BIOS can read a boot record from the disk and hands control of the computer to the short program on the boot record. As I explain in Chapters 6 and 7, the boot program begins the process of loading DOS (or another operating system) into the computer.

After the start-up routines are finished, the computer is ready to go. The other two parts of the ROM-BIOS play key roles in running the computer. These two parts are hardware interrupt handling and service handling routines. They function as two distinct but closely cooperating kinds of routines.

The service handling routines are there solely to perform work for programs (and for DOS) by carrying out whatever services the programs need. You see in more detail what these services are in Chapter 17, "BIOS: Digging In." They include such things as requests to clear the display screen, switch the screen from text mode to graphics mode, read information from the disk, or write information on the printer. For the most part, the BIOS services that the service-handling routines perform relate to hardware devices, such as the screen, keyboard, disks, printers, and so on. These are the basic input/output services that give the BIOS its name. However, there also are other services that the BIOS performs that aren't I/O related. For example, the BIOS keeps track of the time of day and reports the time to programs.

To carry out the service requests that programs make, the BIOS has to work directly with the computer's I/O devices. That's where the intimate and tricky part of the BIOS comes in, that is, using ports to issue commands and send and receive data to and from various devices. The key job of the ROM-BIOS here is to relieve the program of the tedious details involved in performing these tasks.

The program doesn't need to know which port is used to send data to the printer; it just asks the BIOS to send data to the printer, and the BIOS takes care of the details. That shields the program from the details of how the printer works, but even more important it shields the program from the very annoying and messy problems of error recovery. Surprisingly, the equipment that makes up a computer often is balky and can act up temporarily. Part of the job of the BIOS is to check for errors, retry operations to see if the problem is only temporary (as it often is), and only in the case of stubborn failure, report the problem to the program.

While some of the hardware parts of the computer require attention only when you want them to do something (that is, when a program is requesting a service from the BIOS), other parts call for attention completely separate from what the programs are doing. You already have seen a few examples of this: you know that, when you press a key on the keyboard, it generates a keyboard interrupt that demands attention from the BIOS.

Likewise, the PC's internal clock creates clock interrupts every time it ticks, about 18 times a second. There are other hardware interrupts as well; for example, the disks use an interrupt to signal when they need attention from the BIOS. To handle these needs of the hardware, there is the final part of the BIOS, the hardware interrupt-handling section.

The hardware interrupt-handling part takes care of the independent needs of the PC's hardware. It operates separately but in cooperation with the service-handling portion. In Chapter 15, where I discussed how the keyboard operates, you saw a good example of how that works. The keyboard-handling routines are divided into two separate but related parts that work together.

The hardware interrupt part of the keyboard handling responds to your actions on the keyboard, recording what you do and holding the resulting characters ready for use when your programs need them. The service-handling part of the keyboard routines accepts requests for keyboard data and passes on the keyboard characters that the interrupt handler has received. These two parts face in different directions—one to the hardware, and the other to the software—and service different demands. Together, they make the keyboard work for you and your programs.

That captures the essence of the BIOS and what it does for computers. With that groundwork in place, Chapter 17 shows what sort of services the BIOS can perform for programs.

# Some Things to Think About or Try

1. If you have the Norton Utilities, you can use the SI (System Information) program to search for the BIOS signature that identifies additions to the BIOS. Try using it on your computer and see what you find. You can get even more information about your BIOS if you use the MSD program that comes with Microsoft Windows. Run "MSD," and click on the "Computer" button. What do you recognize now, having read this chapter?

2. Think about how the interrupt-handling and service-handling parts of the keyboard ROM-BIOS routines work with each other. How do you think these two parts interact safely and successfully?

3. What do you think are the special needs and requirements to initialize an extension to the ROM-BIOS? How would an extension smoothly integrate itself into the rest of the BIOS without creating any disruption?

4. What sorts of changes to your computer system do you think would require not just device drivers, but actually updating your BIOS? Why?

5. Considering what you know about the new Plug and Play standard (see Chapter 2), will you likely be able to upgrade your current computer to be Plug and Play compatible simply by upgrading your BIOS? Why or why not?

# 17

# BIOS:
# Digging In

This chapter takes a more detailed look at what the PC family's built-in ROM-BIOS does for you and your programs, focusing on the standard services that the BIOS provides. This isn't, however, an exhaustive reference guide. Instead, it is a guided tour of the power that the BIOS puts at your command. The objective is to give you a feel for what the BIOS can do.

Before beginning the BIOS tour, though, you need to look at some of the principles and problems that underlie the services.

# Working Principles and Machine Problems

If you want to understand the workings of the ROM-BIOS and the list of the BIOS services and comments that follow in the next section, it helps to understand some of the principles that underlie the way the BIOS works and the way it's organized, as well as some of the design problems that are inherent in any software as sensitive as the PC family's ROM-BIOS.

The BIOS has to operate in a way that provides maximum flexibility, places the least caretaking load on the programs that use it, and works with the greatest possible safety (safety against disrupting the workings of the computer).

You already saw some of the ways the design of the BIOS works toward these ends when you learned about one of the BIOS's interrupt handlers in Chapter 4, "Microprocessor Traffic Control." One of the design considerations that the BIOS routines must meet is to suspend interrupts as seldom as possible. It's important not to shut down or even suspend interrupts because interrupts are the force that keeps the computer running. Recall from the discussion of the interrupt handler that interrupts are immediately activated. Sometimes this can't be done; sometimes it's necessary to perform a few critical steps free of the possibility of being interrupted, but the BIOS keeps those steps as short as possible.

Because the BIOS performs the bulk of its work with interrupts active, other interrupt-driven BIOS service calls can be invoked while the BIOS is carrying out an earlier service request. To avoid tripping over its own feet or confusing the work in-progress of one service call with that of another, the BIOS routines must be programmed following a special discipline called re-entrant coding. Re-entrant programs, such as the ROM-BIOS, are designed to keep the working data and status information that pertains to each service call separate from the others. This is done by keeping all data either in the stack or in registers that (by programming convention) are preserved on the stack if another interrupt occurs.

Although re-entrant coding is not difficult to do, it must be done carefully and places restrictions on the ways in which information can be passed between the BIOS and any program requesting BIOS services. Much of the design of the BIOS stems from the requirement that it be re-entrant.

As a separate but related issue, the BIOS services must be organized in a modular fashion. As you learn in the next section on the details of the basic BIOS services, these services are organized into groups. All the services for the display screen, for example, are grouped together under one interrupt number, and no other BIOS services use that interrupt.

This modular organization by group and interrupt has two obvious benefits. First, for the programs that use the BIOS services, the grouping makes it easier to deal with the complexities of the services. Second, if it becomes necessary to modify the operation of any particular kind of BIOS service—for example, modifying the video services to accommodate the special features of a new display adapter—it can be done in a relatively clean and uncomplicated way simply by replacing one interrupt handler.

There is one fundamental complexity and difficulty that has not been dealt with very well in the ROM-BIOS. There are two families of IBM PCs: the original ones and the PS/2s. Then, of course, there is the entire "other" family of desktop and deskside computers designed and manufactured by non-IBM companies. Each family has multiple members, and each member has its own version of the BIOS. Although much of the BIOS is the same for all PCs, different services are offered for different models.

This book covers BIOS only generally because not only do different manufacturers' products have different BIOS designs, but each motherboard in a product line has a different BIOS. The general operation and theory are the same, of course, but specifics, such as services offered, memory locations used, the size of program, and other details, are motherboard chip set dependent. By "chip set," I mean not only the CPU (processor) used, but the support set that handles memory I/O, manages the ports, and conducts other CPU interface duties. These chip sets are provided by several vendors; one of the most common is Opti. It is the technology of these chip sets (around which the rest of the motherboard is built) that determines the precise design and function of the BIOS on any given computer.

Fortunately, IBM's reference manual explains every BIOS feature (for IBM machines) thoroughly, showing exactly which services apply to which computers. In the old manuals, IBM used to print listings of the BIOS programs. Nowadays this information, which is copyrighted, is considered proprietary and is not published. The interfaces to the BIOS are well documented, however, and for those with a smattering of assembly language, easy to understand.

Other companies publish their own version of this manual to show programmers and system designers how to use the BIOS services available in a given BIOS design.

# BIOS Services: Technical Details and Real-Life Implications

The ROM-BIOS services are organized into groups, with each group having its own dedicated interrupt. Table 17.1 summarizes the groups as used by IBM computers. I cover them one by one, beginning with the richest, most complicated, and most interesting: the video services.

Notice that in Table 17.1 the BIOS services are identified by a hexadecimal number. This is the usual case. This table does not show every BIOS interrupt, just the ones that offer groups of services to programs. Unless it is specified otherwise, you can assume that an interrupt number is in hex. Likewise, all the services in a group are identified by their own hex number. Remember, too, that computer (and therefore BIOS) technology is changing rapidly. Although this table, and the information and tables that follow, generally are true, you may find individual differences in specific BIOS code used with specific computers. It isn't practical to try to give you a fully up-to-date list in this book because, even in a single vendor's line, things tend to change frequently.

Table 17.1. The ROM-BIOS Service Interrupts.

| Interrupt (Hex) | Service Group |
| --- | --- |
| 05 | Print screen |
| 10 | Video |
| 11 | Equipment determination |
| 12 | Memory determination |
| 13 | Floppy and hard disk |
| 14 | Asynchronous (serial) communication |
| 15 | System services (miscellany) |
| 16 | Keyboard |
| 17 | Printer (parallel ports) |
| 18 | ROM-BASIC (old) |
| 18 | Network interface card |
| 19 | Bootstrap loader |
| 1A | System timer, real-time clock |
| 4B | Advanced services (SCSI, DMA) |

# Video Services

There are 16 separate video screen services in the PC family's basic ROM-BIOS services. These 16 are the original complement used on the very first PC model, and they form a base for the video services of every member of the family. The services are numbered 00 through 0F. In addition to these basic services, there are nine other services used with the newer members of the PC family. The video services are summarized in Table 17.2.

Table 17.2. The Interrupt 10 Video Services.

| Video Service | Description |
|---|---|
| 00 | Set mode |
| 01 | Set cursor type |
| 02 | Set cursor position |
| 03 | Read cursor position |
| 04 | Read light pen position |
| 05 | Select active display page |
| 06 | Scroll active page up |
| 07 | Scroll active page down |
| 08 | Read attribute/character at cursor position |
| 09 | Write attribute/character at cursor position |
| 0A | Write character at cursor position |
| 0B | Set color palette |
| 0C | Read dot |
| 0D | Write dot |
| 0E | Write teletype to active page |
| 0F | Read current video state |
| 10 | Set palette registers |
| 11 | Character generator |
| 12 | Alternate select |
| 13 | Write string |
| 14 | Control character set for LCD display |

*continues*

Table 17.2. continued

| Video Service | Description |
|---|---|
| 15 | Return information about active display |
| 1A | Read/write display combination code |
| 1B | Return functionality/state information |
| 1C | Save/restore video state |

Bear in mind that all video services, the basic ones as well as the new ones, are accessed via interrupt 10 (hex). You may wonder how the BIOS knows which service you want. The answer is that an application prepares for interrupt 10 by loading the AH register with the code number of the service requested. Then the application invokes the interrupt. As soon as the interrupt handler takes over, it checks the contents of the AH register to see which service is requested.

Loading certain registers with specific values before invoking an interrupt is the standard way to pass information to the BIOS. Conversely, the BIOS passes information back to an application by loading data into registers before returning to the program. One of the main purposes of a BIOS technical reference manual is to describe what each interrupt and service expects in the way of register usage.

# The Twenty-Seven Services

The first service, number 00, is used to change the video mode. This service is used by the program to switch the display screen into whatever mode is needed. As you see later, there is a complementary service that tells the program what the current mode is.

Video service 01 controls the size and shape of the cursor. It sets the scan lines on which the cursor appears. This is the ROM-BIOS service that underlies the BASIC program statement LOCATE ,,,X,Y.

Video service 02 sets the cursor location on the screen, corresponding to the BASIC program statement LOCATE X,Y.

Video service 03 reports the shape of the cursor and where it is located. This service is the opposite of services 01 and 02 combined. It enables the program to record the current state of the cursor so that it can be restored after the program is done. You see an example of how useful that can be when I discuss the print screen interrupt.

Video service 04 is the sole service supporting the PC's little-used light pen feature. (Actually, support for pen computing is growing. Several manufacturers offer pen-based computers, but compared with regular PC products, pen computing is still a little-used technology.) When a program invokes this service, the BIOS reports whether the pen is triggered and where it is touching the screen. Interestingly, the service reports the pen position in two different ways: in terms of the grid of text character positions and in terms of the graphics pixel locations.

Video service 05 selects which display page is active (shown on the screen) for the video modes that have more than one display page in memory. (See Chapter 11, "On-Screen Video," for more information.)

Services 06 and 07 are a fascinating pair that perform window scrolling. These two services enable an application to define a rectangular window on the screen and scroll the data inside the window up from the bottom (service 06) or down from the top (service 07). When a window is scrolled, blank lines are inserted at the bottom or top, ready for the program to write new information into them. The purpose of these services is to enable the program to write information on just a part of the screen and leave the rest of the screen intact. This capability wasn't used very much in the early days of program development. Nearly all programs today, however, support some form of windowing interface; the capability to control (and scroll) multiple windows is an important feature.

The next three video services work with text characters on the screen. Video service 08 reads the current character (and its attribute) from the screen (or, rather, out of the screen memory). This service is clever enough, in graphics mode, to decode the pixel drawing of a character into the character code. Video service 09 is the obvious complement to service 08; it writes a character on the screen with the display attribute that you specify. Service 0A also writes a character, but it uses whatever display attribute is currently in place for that screen location.

The next three services provide operations for the graphics modes. Video service 0B sets the color palette, service 0C writes a single dot on the screen, and service 0D reads a dot from the screen.

Video service 0E is a handy variation on the character writing service, 08. This service writes a character to the screen and advances the cursor to the next position so that it's in place for the next character. (The other services require the program to move the cursor as a separate operation.) This is a convenient service that makes it easy for a program to use the display screen like a printer, printing out information with a minimum of fuss (and with flexibility). Therefore, this service is called write teletype.

The final basic video service, 0F, is the inverse of the first. It reports the current video state so that the program can adjust its operation to the video mode or record the current mode so that it can return to it after changing the mode. This service tells you what video mode is set but not what video standard is being used (XGA, VGA, and so on). To determine this type of information, you can use video service 1A.

In addition to the basic 16 services, there are nine newer services, too. For the most part, these nine services are used with only EGA and newer video standards (rather than with the older CGA and MDA standards).

Service 10 sets the registers in the hardware that control the colors displayed.

Service 11 is an interface to the character generator. You can change which character set is used for either text or graphics. You can specify one of the built-in character sets or even design your own. It sounds like fun to set up your own character set, but it requires a fair amount of work. You must first initialize a table of bit patterns to define each character.

The name of service 12, alternate select, comes from its original purpose, which is to specify an alternate way of handling the print screen function (more on this in the discussion of interrupt 05). With newer displays, alternate print handling is necessary to print screens that have more than 25 lines of text. The new functions added to this service are unrelated to printing; for the most part, they involve very technical display settings.

Video service 13 enables an application to write an entire string of characters to the display in one fell swoop. This is easier and faster than repeatedly calling on a video service, such as 09, 0A, or 0E, to display characters one at a time.

The next two services are used with the PC Convertible, which has a special liquid crystal display (LCD). Service 14 loads a particular character set, and service 15 returns information about the active display, which can be either the built-in LCD or a separate display. The PC Convertible is no longer a current model, but other machines do have LCD displays. Remember, as technology changes, BIOS designs change. This information should be considered to be general. The market is so broad today that an exhaustive list of all services, such as these BIOS calls, is all but impossible.

Services 16 and 19 are not used with PS/2s. These numbers may or may not be used with other vendors' hardware. Service 1A tells you what type of display standard is currently being used with what category of display (MDA with a monochrome display or VGA with a color display, for example). You also can find out whether there is an unknown display or even no display at all. By using this service, you can tailor a program to act appropriately with different types of systems.

Service 1B returns a table of detailed information about the current video mode and video hardware. This service provides a way for programs to determine the capabilities of the video system currently in use.

Finally, service 1C enables you to preserve the state of the video BIOS and hardware. You can change the current setup by changing video modes or reprogramming the color palette, for example, and later restore the setup to its previous condition.

These video reading and writing services constitute the officially approved way for programs to put information on the screen. Using these services has the advantage of ensuring that output heading for the screen is handled in a standard way and can be automatically adapted to new hardware. However, many programs avoid these services because the overhead involved is disappointingly high. Screen output can be performed much faster when programs do it themselves rather than using the ROM-BIOS services.

# The Print Screen Service

The next thing I look at is a special service, the print screen interrupt, which is different from all the others. The majority of the ROM-BIOS services work with specific peripheral devices, such as the display screen or keyboard. The remaining services are basically informational, handling the time of day or indicating the amount of memory installed in the computer. The print screen service, though, is a different animal.

The print screen service is designed to read from the screen the information displayed and route it to the printer. You can invoke this service directly by pressing the PrintScreen key on the keyboard. What makes this service particularly interesting is the fact that it is built from other ROM-BIOS services; it does nothing unique in itself. It just combines services to perform a new and useful service.

Print screen begins work by using video service 03 to determine the current cursor position and service 0F to check the dimensions of the screen. It saves the cursor position so that it can later restore the cursor to its original position. Then, print screen moves the cursor through every location on the screen from top to bottom. At each location, it uses video service 08 to read a character from the screen and a printer output service to copy the character to the printer. When this is done, print screen restores the cursor and returns control to the program that invoked it.

You may think of the print screen service as strictly an adjunct of the keyboard, something you get by pressing the PrintScreen key. Not so. Print screen is a standard ROM-BIOS service that can be invoked by any program just as any other service is invoked—by issuing an INT (interrupt instruction; for interrupt 05, in this case). The PrintScreen key works because the keyboard ROM-BIOS routines monitor keyboard activity to see whether you have pressed this key. Whenever you press the PrintScreen key, the keyboard ROM-BIOS uses interrupt 05 to request the print screen service. Any other program could do the same. This nifty service can be placed at the disposal of any program to be used in any way.

**Note:** The PrintScreen key (not the interrupt itself,  just the keyboard stoke), incidentally, is trapped by Windows and functions differently. Pressing PrintScreen under Windows places a snapshot of the current Windows screen onto the Windows clipboard. From there, you can paste it into any application that supports the pasting of graphic content.

# Disk Services

This section covers the other device services first and then the information services.

All the disk services are invoked with interrupt 13. You can divide these services into three groups: those that apply to both floppy and hard disks, those for hard disks only, and those for floppy disks only. The disk services are summarized in tables 17.3 and 17.4.

Table 17.3. The Interrupt 13 Hard Disk Services.

| HD Service (Hex) | Description |
| --- | --- |
| 00 | Reset disk system |
| 01 | Read status of last operation |
| 02 | Read sectors to memory |
| 03 | Write sectors from memory |
| 04 | Verify sectors |
| 05 | Format a cylinder/track |
| 06 | Format a cylinder and set bad sector flags |
| 07 | Format drive starting specified cylinder |
| 08 | Read drive parameters |
| 09 | Initialize drive pair characteristics |
| 0C | Seek |
| 0D | Alternate disk reset |
| 10 | Test drive ready |
| 11 | Recalibrate |
| 15 | Read disk type |
| 19 | Park heads |
| 1A | Format unit |

Table 17.4. The Interrupt 13 Floppy Disk Services.

| FD Service (Hex) | Description |
| --- | --- |
| 00 | Reset disk system |
| 01 | Read status of last operation |
| 02 | Read sectors to memory |
| 03 | Write sectors from memory |
| 04 | Verify sectors |
| 05 | Format a cylinder/track |
| 08 | Read drive parameters |
| 15 | Read disk type |
| 16 | Change line status |
| 17 | Set disk type for format |
| 18 | Set media type for format |

# Services Used with Floppy and Hard Disks

This discussion begins with the disk services used with both hard disks and floppy disks. These are services 00 through 05, 08, and 15.

The first, service 00, is used to reset the disk drive and its controller. This is an initialization and error recovery service that clears the decks for a fresh start in the next disk operation. Related to it is disk service 01, which reports the status of the disk drive so that error handling and controlling routines can find out what's what.

Disk service 02 is the first of the active disk services. It reads disk sectors into memory. The sectors don't have to be read individually; the service reads as many consecutive sectors as you want, as long as they are all on the same track. Disk service 03 works similarly, except that it writes sectors instead of reading them.

Disk service 04 verifies the data written on a disk, testing to ensure that it is properly recorded. This often-misunderstood service underlies the DOS option VERIFY ON that you see in the VERIFY command and the VERIFY feature of DOS's configuration file (CONFIG.SYS). It does not check the data stored on disk to see that it matches data in memory (data that you may have just read or written). Instead, the verify service simply checks to see whether the disk data is properly recorded, which means testing for parity errors and other recording defects. As a general rule, that helps ensure the data is correct, although it's no guarantee. If you have the wrong data properly recorded, the verify service reports that it's fine.

Disk service 05 is used to format a track of a disk. This is the physical formatting that underlies DOS's logical formatting of a disk. This formatting service is a fascinating business because it specifies, for each track, the number of sectors, how the sectors are identified, the order in which the sectors appear, and the size of each sector. Normally, all the sectors on a track are the same size (512 bytes) and are numbered sequentially beginning with 1. On floppy disks, sectors physically appear in numeric order. (They also may appear in sequential order on hard disks, but on slower hard disks, they don't.)

The next service, 08, provides information about the hardware characteristics of a particular disk. Finally, service 15 tells you what type of disk you have (hard disk or floppy).

This ends the discussion of the disk services that apply to both hard disks and floppy disks. Next, I discuss the nine services used with only hard disks.

# Services Used with Hard Disks

Services 06, 07, and 1A augment the formatting capabilities of service 05. Service 06 is a variation of 05 that can format a defective cylinder; service 07 formats an entire disk, starting with a specified cylinder; and service 1A formats an entire ESDI (Enhanced Small Device Interface) drive.

The next service, 09, is used to initialize a hard disk that is not recognized automatically by the BIOS.

Service 0C positions the disk's read/write head at a particular cylinder.

Three services help set up the hard disk. Service 0D resets the drive. It is similar to service 00, except that service 0D does not reset the floppy disk drive automatically. Service 10 tests to see whether a disk is ready, and service 17 recalibrates a disk.

## Services Used with Floppy Disks

The last set of disk services includes those that apply only to floppy disks. There are three such services: 16, 17, and 18.

With certain floppy disk drives, you can use service 16 to see whether the disk in the drive has been changed. This feature is called change line status. Actually, this service can tell an application only whether the disk drive door has been opened. If this is the case, you can have a program check an identifier, such as the volume serial number, to see whether the actual disk has been changed.

The last two services are used to prepare for formatting. Before you can use service 05 to format, you must use either service 17 or 18 to describe the disk. With service 17, you specify what type of disk; with service 18, you specify the number of sectors and tracks. This sort of knowledge is interesting, but generally you use features of DOS (such as FORMAT with its various switches) to handle this level of disk management for you. And, as DOS has gotten more sophisticated, it has become less necessary for users to know the specific BIOS locations and calls that make all this happen.

## Serial Port Services

The serial port (RS-232, communications line) services are invoked by interrupt 14. Sometimes these services are called asynchronous communications, reflecting the back and forth nature of the way in which data flow is controlled between serial devices and the computer. Table 17.5 summarizes the six serial port services.

Table 17.5. The Interrupt 14 Serial Port Services.

| Serial Service (Hex) | Description |
| --- | --- |
| 00 | Initialize a serial port |
| 01 | Write a character |
| 02 | Read a character |
| 03 | Write sectors from memory |
| 04 | Initialize a PS/2 serial port |
| 05 | Control modem control register |

Using the serial port is fairly simple. Everything is compared with the screen and the disk drives, and only six services are needed. Service 00 initializes the communications port, setting the basic parameters (discussed in Chapter 25, "Multimedia"), the baud rate, and so forth. Service 01 is used to write a byte to the port; service 02 reads a byte. Service 03, the last, is used to get a status report, which indicates things such as whether data is ready.

Services 04 and 05 are advanced services used with only PS/2s and newer AT-class machines that have improved serial ports. Service 04 is used instead of service 00 to initialize a port. Service 04 adds such features as support for communications rates above 9,600 BPS. Service 05 reads from and writes to a special modem control register.

# Other BIOS Services: Miscellaneous, Keyboard, and Printer

The next interrupt, 15, was at one time used only to control a cassette tape interface. However, IBM has expanded the interrupt to offer a grab bag of miscellaneous system services. Table 17.6 lists some of the more interesting services provided by this interrupt.

Table 17.6. The Interrupt 15 Miscellaneous Services.

| Service (Hex) | Description |
| --- | --- |
| 21 | Read the error log from the power on self-test |
| 80 | Open a device |
| 81 | Close a device |
| 82 | Terminate a program |
| 83 | Wait for an event to happen |
| 84 | Support a joystick |
| 85 | Test to see whether the SysReq key has been pressed |
| 86 | Wait for a particular length of time |
| 87–89 | Support extended memory and protected mode |
| 90 | Signal that a device is busy |
| C0 | Find out the system configuration parameters |
| C2 | Support a pointing device such as a mouse |

The keyboard services are activated with interrupt 16. Service 00 reads the next character from the keyboard input buffer. The characters are reported in their full two-byte form, as discussed in Chapter 15, "The Memory Workbench." When a character is read by service 00, it is removed from the keyboard input buffer. Not so with service 01; service 01 reports whether there is any keyboard input ready. If there is, this service also previews the character by reporting the character bytes in the same way that service 00 does, but the character remains in the keyboard buffer until it's officially read with service 00.

The final keyboard service, 02, reports the keyboard status bits, which indicate the state of the Shift keys and so forth. (This is discussed in Chapter 15, and you can see it in action in the KEYBITS program in Appendix B.) Although you know where to find that information in the low memory location where the BIOS stores it, this service is the official and approved way for programs to learn about keyboard status.

Services 00, 01, and 02 were designed for the old-style keyboard. Starting with the last version of the PC AT computer, IBM introduced what is now the standard 101/102-key keyboard. (American keyboards have 101 keys; some non-American keyboards have 102 keys.) All PS/2s use some version of this keyboard.

Because this keyboard has extra keys, it requires new services to replace 00, 01, and 02. These services are 10 (read), 11 (status), and 12 (shift status).

Service 03 controls the typematic rate; that is, how long you have to hold down a key to get it to repeat and how fast it repeats.

Service 04 was used with only the PCjr and PC Convertible. The keyboards on these computers did not make a clicking noise on their own, so a sound had to be generated via the speaker. This service was used to turn the clicking sound off and on. Table 17.7 summarizes the keyboard services.

Table 17.7. The Interrupt 16 Keyboard Services.

| Keyboard Service (Hex) | Description |
| --- | --- |
| 00 | Read (old keyboard) |
| 01 | Status (old keyboard) |
| 02 | Shift status (old keyboard) |
| 03 | Set typematic rate |
| 10 | Read (new keyboard) |
| 11 | Status (new keyboard) |
| 12 | Shift status (new keyboard) |

The next of the device support services are for the parallel printer port, using interrupt 17. There are three simple services: 00 sends a single byte to the printer, 01 initializes the printer, and 02 reports the printer status, such as whether the printer is out of paper.

The final interrupt that provides device services is a new one, 4B. This interrupt actually does two jobs. First, it provides services to control SCSI devices. SCSI is an interface that enables you to daisy-chain devices to use only a single port. IBM offers high-capacity SCSI hard disks on the high-end PS/2s.

The second set of services offered by interrupt 4B involves DMA, Direct Memory Access, which is the capability to transfer data between a device and memory without the constant control of the main processor. This part of interrupt 4B actually is supplied by the operating system, not by the BIOS.

That finishes off the ROM-BIOS services that are directly used to support the PC's I/O peripheral equipment. It's worth noting that there are two other I/O devices in the PC's standard repertoire, the speaker and joysticks, that have no support in the BIOS whatsoever.

# The Rest of the BIOS Interrupts

The remaining ROM-BIOS services are used to control information or to invoke major changes in the PC.

Interrupt 11 is used to get the PC's official (and now rather out-of-date) equipment list information. The equipment list was designed around the facilities of the original PC model and hasn't been expanded to include the new equipment that has been added to the family (mostly, I think, because it hasn't turned out to be necessary). The equipment list reports the number of floppy disk drives the machine has, but says nothing about hard disks or other disk types. It reports the number of parallel ports and serial ports. It also reports whether there is an internal modem installed, some rudimentary video information, whether a pointing device such as a mouse is installed, whether a math co-processor is installed, and whether a boot disk is present.

A companion service to the equipment list reports the amount of memory the computer has up to 640KB. Officially, it's requested with interrupt 12. The amount of memory is reported in kilobytes. (The amount of extended memory is reported by interrupt 15, service 88.)

The third and last of the pure information interrupts is 1A. This interrupt provides services that have to do with time. Some of the more interesting services are setting the time and date, using a timer, and using an alarm. The BIOS keeps a time-of-day clock in the form of a long, four-byte integer, with each count representing one clock tick.

The PC's hardware clock ticks by generating a clock interrupt 18.2 times a second, and the interrupt handler for the clock adds one to the clock count each time. The clock count is supposed to represent the number of ticks since last midnight. It shows the right time (that is, the right count) only if it has been properly set, for example, by the DOS TIME command or the battery-powered, real-time clock.

When you turn the computer on, the clock starts counting from zero, as if the time were midnight, until something sets the correct clock time/count. DOS converts the clock tick count into the time of day in hours, minutes, seconds, and hundredths of seconds by simple arithmetic. The BIOS routines that update the clock check for the count that represents 24 hours. At that point, the clock is reset to zero, and a midnight-has-passed signal is recorded. The next time DOS reads the clock count from the BIOS, DOS sees this midnight-has-passed signal and updates the record it keeps of the date.

Newer PCs have BIOS code to handle BIOS shadowing, as well. I've pointed out before that a computer's ROM operates much slower than RAM. Depending on the type of memory you are using, system RAM may be 70 percent or more faster than ROM in handling memory I/O. This is due not only to the speed of memory itself (ROM may operate at 200 nanoseconds, for example; RAM moves along at 70 nanoseconds), but also to the way ROM and RAM move data. ROM may be handling only 8 bits at a time; system RAM may handle 32 bits at a time.

The solution is to copy ROM-BIOS out of ROM and into system RAM as soon as the boot process is complete. Then, by disabling ROM, you can locate the RAM-based BIOS at the same memory address as the ROM-based BIOS. That's how "shadow" BIOS works. For each ROM address, there is an equivalent RAM address. So, even if you have shadow BIOS, it may be located at `F000` or `E000` just as it would be without shadow. It just runs a whole lot faster.

There are, finally, two more interesting BIOS service interrupts. They are used to pass control to either of two special routines built into the BIOS. One is the ROM-BASIC (on older machines; network interface on newer machines), and the other is the start-up routines. (By the way, keep in mind that only IBM's own older models of the PC family have the built-in BASIC; other family members, such as Compaq computers, do not.)

Many of today's computers use interrupt 18 (the old ROM-BASIC) for network interface card (NIC) control. One routine that is fairly common, for example, is for interrupt 18 to be called during start-up if both the floppy and the hard disk fail. That could mean that there are no local disk drives on the PC and that the DOS boot routine is handled by a ROM on board the NIC. You can boot a system over a network with the proper bootstrap ROM installed on the network interface card.

The normal way to activate the bootstrap program is by pressing Ctrl-Alt-Del. And, usually, you do not activate the ROM-BASIC at all. However, it's also possible for any program to activate either of these routines simply by invoking their interrupts. Unlike the ordinary service routines, which do something for the program and then return processing to the program that invoked them, these two routines are one-way streets. They take full charge of the machine and never return control to the program that invoked them.

If you do decide to play with these interrupts, remember two things. First, there is more to rebooting than invoking the bootstrap interrupt. You may hang up the machine so thoroughly that it must be turned off and on again. Second, if you do start up ROM-BASIC (something you can only do with an old PC anyway), there is no way to save any work that you do. ROM-BASIC was designed originally for a cassette device and cannot save files to disk. With those warnings in mind, the following is a simple way to test these interrupts by using DEBUG.

Start the DEBUG program. The DEBUG prompt is a hyphen ( - ). When you see the prompt, enter the Assemble command (A). This enables you to enter an assembly language command. Enter int 18 (for ROM-BASIC or to access your NIC) and int 19 (for bootstrap). Press Enter to end the assembly. Finally, enter the Go command (G) to execute the interrupt statement.

# The BIOS Future

Like  the rest of your PC, the BIOS isn't sitting still. It is changing as new technology evolves that requires some basic changes to this important, internal logic area of your machine.

Easily the most significant of these changes revolve around the implementation of the forthcoming Plug and Play interface standard, all of which you can read about in detail in Chapter 24, "Plug and Play." However, Plug and Play isn't the only new technology that has impacted the BIOS.

Energy Star, the federal government's conservation standard for computer energy use, is a BIOS-level implementation of features not unlike the power-management features of most notebook computers. When the system is left unused for periods of time (which are user-settable), system elements either turn off or slow themselves down to conserve energy. Processor speed, whether the hard disk is on or not, and how much power the monitor uses are among these elements. BIOS-level integration of these features ensures that power is conserved while user efficiency is not diminished. You wouldn't want to have to move your mouse every few minutes to keep your computer from shutting down during a long file download over your modem, would you? So, like some screen-saver programs, the Energy Star-compliant BIOS watches the ports to make certain that the desire to save energy doesn't abort the printing of your annual report or the sending of electronic photos to your kids' grandparents.

**Note:** Actual use of certain Energy Star features requires that you purchase particular types of compatible peripherals. Connecting a non-Energy Star monitor to your Energy Star system can actually permanently damage the monitor. If you're purchasing an Energy Star computer and you wish to be able to use the conservation features, make sure that the monitor you select is compliant.

The Enhanced IDE standard, which you read about back in Chapter 5, "Disks: The Basic Story," also has required changes to the PC's BIOS. Formerly only able to support a maximum of two IDE hard disks, drives of up to 540MB, and relatively slow data-transfer rates, BIOSs, with Enhanced IDE support, can now handle four drives of up to 9GB each, and data-transfer throughput that rivals

SCSI. Since your system hardware has to know how to efficiently address hard disks and how quickly it can write to them or read from them, BIOS changes have been necessary to bring these capabilities to our desktops.

For better (compatibility) or worse (antiquation), the PC's BIOS has changed little until recently. Now that the obvious importance and benefits of Plug and Play have broken that dam, the next ten years should be even more high-paced and amazing than the last.

# Some Things to Think About or Try

1. What would be the effect of combining all the ROM-BIOS services under one interrupt? Or giving each service its own separate interrupt?

2. Can you think of reasons why the bootstrap loader and the PC's built-in ROM-BASIC would be invoked by interrupts? Do you think it was to make them available for use by any program or just to make them easier to use by IBM's system programs?

3. At the end of the first section of this chapter, I mentioned that one of the reasons to study the BIOS services is to understand their level. Consider how the level of the services might be higher or lower. Take one example from the services and see how you could change its definition to be more primitive or more advanced. Analyze the video services and rank them in terms of relatively high or low levels.

# 18

# The Role of DOS

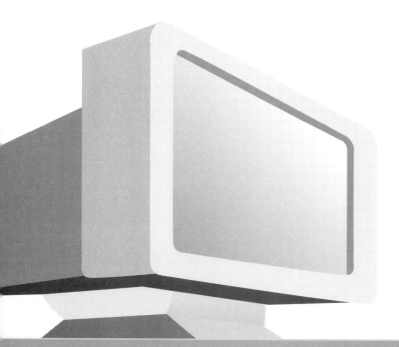

This chapter begins a three-chapter tour of DOS, the last major part of the PC epic. These chapters won't tell you all the details of every DOS command imaginable, so if you already know how to use DOS, don't worry that this is all repetition. It's not. The next two chapters investigate how DOS works for you directly and how it works for your programs, behind the scenes. However, before I get into that, I need to set the stage with some background information on DOS, and that's what this chapter is for. I start by looking at operating systems in general. Then I discuss the forces that shaped the character of DOS and the ideas that formed the basis for its design. Then you learn how DOS can be expanded in ways that are internal (such as device drivers) and ways that are external (such as visual shells).

# What Any DOS Is About

The DOS or Disk Operating System that you use on your PC is just one example of an entire class of computer programs that are known as supervisors, control programs, or operating systems. Operating systems, such as DOS, are probably the most complex computer programs that have ever been built. The task of an operating system basically is to supervise and direct the work, the operation, of the computer.

It's a tribute to the power and flexibility of computers that they are able not only to do computing work but to take on the complex job of looking after their own operation. And, it's a marvelous irony that the most sophisticated programs are created not to deal with the user's work, but to take care of the computer's own work. Computers are the most powerful tool man has ever created. They are so powerful, in fact, that users must have the intermediary of an operating system to make the tool manageable. Users give computers the task of supervising themselves so that they don't have to concern themselves with the extraordinary problems involved in making a computer work.

In Chapter 6, "Disks: The DOS Perspective," when you learned about interrupts, you saw just how demanding the task of supervising a computer can be. Every physical part of the computer's equipment requires some looking after, and some of those parts demand a lot. The PC's clock, for example, which is used to keep track of the time of day, demands attention with an interrupt 18.2 times each second. The keyboard, as you learned in Chapter 12, "The PC Character Set," demands attention every time a key is pressed or released. When you type the word *keyboard*, you cause the computer to be interrupted 16 separate times just to note the keystrokes, and an enormous, additional load of work is done after the keystrokes are recorded.

The task of orchestrating, coordinating, and supervising the breathtaking array of events that take place inside computers falls to the operating system. For PC users, this is DOS.

So what does the operating system do? Essentially, it manages devices, controls programs, and processes commands.

DOS's work in managing devices (printers, disks, screens, keyboards, and other peripherals) involves everything needed to keep the computer running properly. On the lowest level, that means issuing commands to the devices and looking after any errors they report. That's exactly the job that the PC's ROM-BIOS performs. In the broadest sense, any operating system that works on a PC includes the ROM-BIOS as one of its key components. On a much higher level, the operating system performs a major organizing role for the computer's devices. This is particularly evident with the disks. An important, even dominant, part of the operating system's responsibility is to work out the scheme for recording data on disks. This includes management of disk space, efficient storage of data, and quick, reliable retrieval.

The second broad job that DOS undertakes is the control of programs. That involves loading programs from disk, setting up the framework for a program's execution, and providing services for programs (more on this in Chapter 19, "DOS Serving Us"). Operating systems can also control things like what parts of memory and disk a given program has access to. While much of this control isn't available under MS-DOS as of this writing, it is available on the operating systems of many workstation and minicomputer systems, and developments in the near future will make this level of control similarly available on PCs.

The third major task that DOS performs is command processing, which is the direct interaction that DOS has with the user. Every time you type something at the DOS command prompt, you are working with the command processing aspect of DOS. In the case of DOS, your commands are essentially requests to execute programs, whether that program is a word processor, or just an internal program that shows you how much free memory you have. In some complex operating systems, commands can take on a wider scope, including things like directing the workings of the operating system itself. Whatever the scope of commands that an operating system provides, an important task for the operating system is to accept and carry out those commands.

That, in summary, is the heart of what any operating system does. Now, it's time to take a look at the history of DOS so that you can see some of the concepts that underlie the way DOS works.

# History and Concepts of DOS

The real history of DOS begins with the early planning for the IBM Personal Computer and the operating system used with the generation of personal computers that preceded the PC.

The PC was planned and designed at a time when most personal computers used an 8-bit microprocessor, and the dominant operating system for those machines was CP/M (Control Program/Microcomputer). Even though the PC was to be a much more powerful 16-bit computer, IBM wanted to build on the experience and popularity of CP/M machines. Although the PC was going to be quite different, and even though 8-bit CP/M programs couldn't be used directly on the PC, making the

PC's operating system similar to CP/M would make it easier to adapt programs (and users' experience and skills) to the new machine.

Apparently, IBM intended to have an updated, 16-bit version of CP/M, which became known as CP/M-86, as the PC's primary operating system, but that didn't work out. IBM ultimately decided to use an operating system sold by Microsoft, in Seattle, WA. That operating system was called DOS.

Today, after several years of developing and changing, there are two basic versions of DOS: Microsoft's, and everybody else's. Microsoft's DOS is called MS-DOS; another common version has been PC-DOS, from IBM. At one point there were as many as 26 different brands of DOS available. There are some differences—primarily minor ones—between all of the different brands of DOS, but all perform the same essential task. The industry leader today is clearly Microsoft's MS-DOS 6.22 (as of this writing), but, as with other areas of computing and technology, each company would like you to believe its way of doing things is the best. For the most part, really, you won't notice the differences between brands.

Although DOS was favored from the start, it was not the only operating system IBM introduced with the PC. Two other operating systems, each with its own base of supporters, were also introduced and given official IBM approval. These operating systems were CP/M-86 and the UCSD p-System, an operating system closely tuned to the needs of the Pascal programming language. In those days, however, nobody wanted to use more than one operating system because it was very inconvenient to switch from one to another and nearly impossible to share data or programs between them. For practical reasons, there could be only one winner in the battle for operating system supremacy, and that winner was DOS. (Modern operating systems, such as OS/2 and the UNIX-based PC systems—AIX, UNIX, and XENIX—can share files with DOS, making it feasible to use more than one operating system on a computer. With older operating systems, such sharing was just not possible.)

Although DOS was a competitor to CP/M for the PC, the design and operation of DOS were based on the facilities that CP/M provided. DOS, as it was initially introduced, had the flavor and style of CP/M for an important and deliberate reason. DOS developers wanted to make it as convenient as possible for computer users who were familiar with CP/M to learn to use DOS and to make it easy for existing 8-bit CP/M programs to be adapted for the PC.

The influence of CP/M appears in the very first thing you see when you use DOS: the command prompt. In addition, DOS shows the design influence of CP/M in many of the ways in which it works with you and your programs.

Although experienced eyes can see the similarities between DOS and CP/M, the most important ways that CP/M set the style for DOS aren't visible because they are ideas. Foremost among them was the scope and use that was intended for DOS from the beginning. DOS was built with the most primitive concepts of personal computing in mind. This included the assumption that only one person would be using the computer and that the one user would ask the computer to do only one thing at a time (not, for example, printing out one document while computing on something else, which would be performing two tasks at the same time). DOS was designed to be a single-user, single-tasking system. This was natural because its roots came from an operating system and a family of 8-bit machines that weren't suited to anything more ambitious.

The PC family, however, had more ambitious goals, and the limitations of the CP/M heritage would have severely restricted DOS's ability to grow with the PC. On the other hand, the UNIX operating system was widely admired for its broad features, and Microsoft had extensive experience with the UNIX style based on its work with XENIX, a variation of UNIX. So, when the time came to make a major revision of the features and internal structure of DOS, many of the concepts used in UNIX/XENIX were stirred into the DOS recipe. The result was DOS Version 2.0 and, eventually, all the subsequent versions.

The influence of UNIX is visible in the subdirectories that are available to you to help you organize and subdivide disks. It is even more apparent in the internal structure of DOS and the services that DOS provides for programs. Chapter 19 shows an important example of that when I discuss the two ways DOS provides for programs to work with files: an old CP/M method and a new UNIX-inspired method.

The DOS that you know and use today is a blend of the styles and design features of CP/M and UNIX. Although DOS contains many of the expansive and forward-looking features of UNIX, it still suffers from many of the limitations of CP/M. Because DOS originally gave every program total control over the computer and all its memory, it is difficult for more advanced versions of DOS to impose the limitations that are required to have two programs running at the same time. Like so many other things, DOS has been able to grow and develop far beyond what it was in its earliest days, yet it still feels the restrictive tug of its predecessor. Later in this chapter, and in Chapter 23 "Microsoft Windows: Role and Function," I discuss some of the techniques being used to transcend those limitations, which relate both to technical and usability issues. First, though, let's look at how DOS has evolved to become a flexible tool.

# Installable Drivers and Flexible Facilities

In its earliest form, DOS had a rigid structure that included totally predefined devices, disk formats, and other elements with which it could work. This was DOS Version 1, the release based solely on the model of CP/M. That version of DOS was unable to adjust itself to changing circumstances or to incorporate new devices, or new disk formats.

But, as the PC family grew, it became important to be able to adjust DOS to the special needs of each computer and computer user and to be able to make DOS accept and accommodate new peripheral devices, particularly the many kinds of disks that were being used with PCs. So, with DOS 2.0, which included many new UNIX concepts, DOS was made adaptable through a facility known as a configuration file.

The configuration file is the key to DOS's flexibility and adaptability. When DOS first begins operation, it looks on the start-up disk for a file with the name CONFIG.SYS. If it finds that file, DOS reads it and follows the commands that define how DOS is to be configured and adapted. Following is an example of a configuration file:

```
rem * ====================================
rem * CONFIG.SYS (October 11)
rem * -DOS version: 6.22
rem * ====================================
rem-Load memory management programs
device = c:\dos\himem.sys
device = c:\dos\emm386.exe NOEMS HIGHSCAN
dos = umb
dos = high

rem-Set options

break = on
buffers = 10,0
files = 60
lastdrive = f

rem-Install device drivers

device = c:\dos\smartdrv.sys 4716
devicehigh = c:\dos\ramdrive.sys 4096 /e
devicehigh  = c:\winapps\scanner\sjiix.sys


rem-Install memory resident programs

install = c:\dos\doskey.com

rem-Set up the command processor: 400 byte environment

shell = c:\dos\command.com /e:400 /p
```

DOS can be customized, modified, and configured in five important ways. As you can see, the CONFIG.SYS file is divided into five parts. If you want to learn more about CONFIG.SYS, you can look at my DOS book, *Peter Norton's DOS 6.22 Guide*, published by Sams Publishing.

The first part of the sample CONFIG.SYS file sets up the programs that manage extended and expanded memory. In this example, HIMEM.SYS is the extended memory manager, and EMM386.EXE is the expanded memory manager. These DOS commands control the loading of part of DOS into upper memory.

The next part tells DOS how to set up certain options and system values. The BUFFERS setting, for example, tells DOS how many disk buffers (temporary read/write areas) to use. Choosing the number of disk buffers involves a simple trade-off: the more buffers, the less often DOS has to wait for information to be read from the disk, but the less memory there is for programs to use.

The third part of the CONFIG.SYS file involves programs called device drivers that can be integrated into DOS. Naturally enough, DOS has built-in support for all the standard types of peripheral devices. However, you may want to add other components to DOS, and that's what the DEVICE and DEVICEHIGH commands enable you to do. DEVICEHIGH installs the driver in upper memory to leave more regular memory for programs.

The device drivers are written following a strict set of guidelines that enable them to work in close cooperation with DOS without disrupting any of DOS's other workings. The sample CONFIG.SYS file shows five examples of device drivers.

The first two device drivers, HIMEM.SYS and EMM386.EXE, are the memory managers already discussed. The next device drivers are SMARTDRV.SYS, which sets up a disk cache, and RAMDRIVE.SYS, which creates a virtual disk (a RAM disk). Finally, in the case of my computer, SJIIX.SYS is a device driver that supports my flatbed scanner.

The fourth section of the CONFIG.SYS file installs memory-resident programs. In this case, DOSKEY provides the ability to recall and edit previous DOS commands and to create macros (abbreviations for lists of commands).

The final configuration task uses the SHELL command to set up the command processor. In this case, you are using the default command processor, COMMAND.COM, that comes with DOS. It is also possible to specify an alternative program, such as the NDOS.COM command processor that comes with the Norton Utilities (Version 6.0 and later).

Whatever purpose installable device drivers and programs serve, they provide a way for you to modify, extend, and expand the capabilities of DOS within the basic design of the operating system. There are other ways to expand and change DOS, though, that don't work from within DOS. This is the subject of the next section.

# Shells: The Norton Commander and Microsoft Windows

Certain inherent characteristics of DOS define how DOS appears to you (the face it presents to the user) and what DOS is and isn't capable of doing. As you know from experience, DOS's user interface is based on a simple command prompt and commands that must be typed from the keyboard. You also know that DOS can run only one program at a time. DOS doesn't give you any way of having more than one thing going at a time (except for things such as the PRINT command, which can print while you run other programs). You also cannot suspend a program during operation (put it on hold) while you run another program and then return to the first program.

Just because DOS doesn't provide a way of doing these things, however, doesn't mean that they aren't desirable or can't be done. In fact, many of the most talented minds in the PC community have been working hard to provide you with programs that can add fancy facilities to DOS.

You can transform the operation of DOS by using any of a class of programs commonly called visual shells (although that name describes only part of what this class of program can do). Shells are programs that essentially wrap themselves around DOS and provide facilities that DOS does not have.

There are any number of things that such a program might undertake, but of the ones that have received the most attention from the PC community, two stand out. One is providing a more appealing and useful "face," that is, a nicer way to enter commands. The other is some kind of multitasking that enables you to use more than one program at a time. When a shell uses graphics, it often is called a graphical user interface, or GUI.

The best publicized program of this type is Microsoft Windows. I briefly discuss Windows to give you an idea of why this sort of program has been discussed and energetically worked on. This program stands as a representative of the broad class of shell programs that have appeared, and which you can expect to see more of. (For more information on Microsoft Windows, see Chapter 23.)

One of the reasons that there has been so much interest in the idea of shells is that DOS's command interface provides you with so little help in entering commands. To run a program with DOS, you must remember the name of the program and type it in along with any parameters that are needed. Until you figure out what command to enter, the computer sits dumbly, waiting, doing nothing.

Shell programs, like Microsoft Windows, on the other hand, show you a menu of all the commands that you might want to use. You simply can select a command and execute it without having to type the command name. Using a mouse or cursor keys, you can point to the command that you want performed and send it into action with a single click (or a press of the Enter key).

The command interface can be enriched even beyond that, from the verbal to the visual, by replacing the names of commands on the screen with drawings called icons, which represent the function that the command performs.

But, easier or more attractive command entry is not the main reason for the interest in visual shells. Equally important is the capability of some shells to work with more than one program at a time. This can be done in a variety of ways, each of which has its own unique technical challenges. Some shells actually have several programs in active operation at the same time, as Microsoft Windows does; others put programs on hold while other tasks are performed and then return to the suspended program without starting it from scratch. The DOSSHELL application, supplied as part of DOS Versions 5.0 through 6.0, is one of these. (The DOSSHELL is not available as part of DOS after Version 6.0, because Windows has all but taken control of the shell market. DOSSHELL is still available from Microsoft, however, as part of the MS-DOS Resource Kit, which can be mail ordered directly from Microsoft. These files can also be downloaded from most major online services and from Microsoft's own BBS.)

Shells are found in other PC operating systems besides DOS. OS/2, IBM's multitasking and multiuser operating system that competes directly with Microsoft Windows and Windows NT, uses an icon- and window-based GUI called the Presentation Manager. UNIX systems also have shells. One example is Motif which is based on the X-Window System developed at MIT.

Another approach to DOS shells is to forgo the icons and other pictures and to provide a simple, straightforward DOS interface. These types of shells (my Norton Commander and the integral DOSSHELL are examples) enable both experienced and novice users to navigate the world of DOS without having to deal directly with DOS commands or the DOS prompt. (DOSSHELL does work in "graphics" mode, but it still doesn't offer anything like the icon support of Windows.)

These simpler shells have two advantages over the more elaborate shells. First, they operate in text mode rather than graphics mode. Text mode requires less overhead and works with older text-based displays. Second, these shells work just as well on older PCs.

Each type of shell has its advantages. Microsoft Windows is actually a whole operating environment; the Norton Commander is a new face for DOS.

# Some Things to Think About or Try

1. Why is it that the PC's original processor, the 8088, can't safely run multiple programs at the same time? How can a program like Microsoft Windows try to overcome some of these problems? What advantages does Microsoft Windows have when it is running on a 386-, 486-, or Pentium-based PC?

2. If you were designing a shell for DOS, a new way of making it easier for the PC user to give commands, how would you design it? Work out the best approach that you can think of and consider what compromises you might have to make to balance different needs.

# 19

# DOS
# Serving Us

Chapter 18, "The Role of DOS," should have left you feeling that you now have a good understanding of why your PC needs DOS. In this chapter, we take a much closer look at exactly what DOS does for you, the user. Then, in Chapter 20, "DOS Serving Programs," you see what DOS does for software, providing universally available and standardized services that programs can use.

To understand what DOS does—and can do—for you, you need to look with me at the subject of DOS commands. Later in this chapter, I explain how batch processing enables you to chain series of DOS commands together to powerfully automate tasks.

# Command Processing

Of all the things that DOS does in supervising a computer, the one that you're most directly aware of is command processing: DOS's capability to accept and act on commands. The job of command processing falls to the one visible component of DOS's three key parts, the program known as COMMAND.COM.

COMMAND.COM issues the terse command prompt that you're used to seeing, which usually looks something like this:

```
C:\>
```

When you see the command prompt, it means that DOS (or more particularly, the COMMAND.COM command processor) is waiting for you to enter a command for it to carry out.

### The DOS Prompt Under Windows

If you've never seen the DOS command prompt, you probably work exclusively in Microsoft Windows—although, even in Windows, most users access the DOS prompt frequently. Windows, you'll recall, is an *environment* for users to work in, which floats, in a manner of speaking, on top of the actual operating system, DOS.

If you'd like to explore DOS and you've only worked in Microsoft Windows, you can access the prompt in two ways: a direct way, and an indirect way. The indirect way is one that you're probably familiar with, although you may have never recognized it as a DOS prompt. When you install new Windows applications, you generally select "Run" from the "File" menu. The dialog box that opens up has a text area where you are probably used to typing something like

```
A:\SETUP.EXE
```

You'll notice that there's a heading in that dialog box that says Command Line, and that's exactly what it is. "Command Line" is really just another name for "DOS Prompt," and you can type any valid DOS command—and running a program, like SETUP.EXE *is* technically a DOS command—from the Windows File | Run dialog box. Depending on which commands you issue, the behavior of Windows may be a bit bizarre—you might find your monitor flashing from the graphical Windows screen back to a DOS text screen, and then back into Windows. This is because Windows is designed to return you to the Windows interface whenever the program you're running from the Command Line finishes. If the "program" you choose to run happens to be a short DOS command, like CHKDSK, DOS will execute that command and display the results on a DOS text screen, and then Windows will bring you back to graphics. If you want to execute this type of DOS command from within Windows, first move to a MS-DOS Prompt by double-clicking that icon in your "Main" folder in Program Manager.

The direct way to access the DOS prompt from Windows is also the flexible way. From the File | Run dialog, you can only enter a single command. However, if you double-click on the MAIN panel in Program Manager, and then double-click on MS-DOS Prompt, that's exactly where you'll end up: at an honest-to-goodness, text, DOS prompt. From this type of prompt, you can issue as many commands as you like, run DOS programs, and so on. You'll still be running Windows, of course, and you'll get an error message if you try to start Windows or a Windows application from this kind of DOS prompt. You can temporarily switch between Windows and the DOS prompt by holding down the Alt key, and touching Tab, to cycle between DOS, Windows, and back. Further, if you'd like to be able to see the DOS prompt in a window in Windows—are you tongue-tied yet?—hold down the Alt key and press Enter. Ultimately, to leave the DOS prompt and return fully to Windows, just type EXIT and press Enter at the prompt.

By the way: you can't quit Windows with the File | Exit command while the DOS prompt is active. You'll need to return to the DOS prompt—press Alt-Tab—type EXIT and press ENTER at the prompt, and then select the File | Exit menu command again.

Just what is a command? It's really nothing more than a request to run a program. The command you issue—the first word you type on the command line—is simply the name of a program you're asking DOS to run. (Even if you're using a command like DIR to get a directory of files, that's still a very small internal program that DOS is running. More on internal and external commands in just a couple of paragraphs.) After the program name may come one or more command parameters or switches that control how the program operates. If, for example, you issue the following command, you're doing nothing but asking DOS to find a program named FORMAT and run it for you:

```
FORMAT A: /S /V
```

Everything in the command line after the word FORMAT (in this case, A: /S /V) is simply further instructions to the program, telling it what to do. You're giving parameters to the DOS command processor (actually the program, COMMAND.COM) and it passes them on to the program. To the DOS command processor they mean nothing, and it pays no attention to them.

The programs that the command processor can carry out for you fall into two main categories. It's important that you understand what they are and how they work because your effective use of the computer is based largely on how well these commands are put at your disposal. The two categories of commands are internal commands and external commands. External commands, in turn, can be thought of as belonging to one of three types: COM programs, EXE programs, and BAT (batch) commands. Let's start at the top with the differences between internal and external commands, and then we'll look at the three subclasses of external commands.

Most programs (that is, the commands that DOS can perform for you) are separate entities that are stored in files on disks. Not all of the commands that DOS can perform work that way, however; not all of them are kept in their own disk files. The COMMAND.COM command processor file contains some of the most important and frequently used command programs. This enables DOS to respond to these common commands very quickly, because it isn't necessary to fetch a program file from disk to carry out each command. These commands load when DOS boots and are resident in memory, ready to run at all times. External commands, on the other hand, stay on disk until you call for them by entering the name of the file on the DOS command line.

The list of internal commands varies from version to version of DOS. Table 19.1 shows DOS 6.x internal commands. Note that regular commands also can be used in batch files, but you normally can't use the commands specifically designed for batch programs at the DOS command prompt. In addition, some of the regular commands in Table 19.1—SET, PATH, DATE, TIME, LOADHIGH—most often are used in batch files. (Although you can use them at the command line, normally you use them as part of the booting process.) The commands listed in the CONFIG.SYS column are designed for system configuration and can be used only within the CONFIG.SYS file, with the exception of the ones marked with an asterisk, which also can be used at the DOS command prompt. (Note that I have included one external command in Table 19.1 just to make the list complete. COUNTRY is an external command that only can be used in the CONFIG.SYS configuration file.)

**Table 19.1. DOS 6.x Internal Commands.**

| Regular Commands | Batch Commands | CONFIG.SYS Commands |
|---|---|---|
| BREAK | CALL | BREAK* |
| CHCP | CHOICE | BUFFERS |
| CHDIR(CD) | ECHO | COUNTRY |
| CLS | FOR | DEVICE |
| COPY | GOTO | DEVICEHIGH |
| CTTY | IF | DOS |
| DATE | PAUSE | DRIVPARM |
| DEL(ERASE) | REM | FCBS |

| Regular Commands | Batch Commands | CONFIG.SYS Commands |
|---|---|---|
| DELTREE | SHIFT | FILES |
| DIR | | INCLUDE |
| EXIT | | INSTALL |
| LOADHIGH(LH) | | LASTDRIVE |
| MKDIR | | MENUCOLOR |
| PATH | | MENUDEFAULT |
| PROMPT | | MENUITEM |
| RENAME(REN) | | NUMLOCK |
| RMDIR(RD) | | REM* |
| SET | | SET* |
| TIME | | SHELL |
| TYPE | | STACKS |
| VER | | SUBMENU |
| VERIFY | | SWITCHES |
| VOL | | |

The command processor holds a table of these internal commands and the program code to carry them out. When you give DOS a command, COMMAND.COM first looks up the command name in its table to see whether you're asking for an internal command. If so, COMMAND.COM can carry out the command immediately. If not, COMMAND.COM must look on a disk for the file that holds the external command program.

The command processor identifies the files that hold external commands in two ways. First, the filename of the disk file is the name of the command; second, the extension to the filename identifies the file as one of the three types of external commands: a COM file, an EXE file, or a BAT batch command file.

**Note:** Because the filename of the program file defines the name of the command the program file will carry out, you have a great deal of freedom to change the names of your commands. You can do it simply by renaming the files (but keeping the extension the same) or by making a copy of the command file under another name so that the command is available under its original command name and under any other name you want to give it. I do this all the time and find it one of the handiest DOS tricks there is. I use it primarily to abbreviate the names of the commands I use most.

You can give your commands any name that's allowed under the DOS filename conventions, and you can give them alias names simply by duplicating the files under different names. For internal commands, you can use the new macro facility offered in the DOSKEY command (with DOS versions 5.0 and later). DOSKEY enables you to define any name as an abbreviation for a list of commands. So, for example, you could define the one-letter name T to stand for the TIME command as follows:

```
DOSKEY TIME = T
```

I use DOSKEY to add switches and optional features to DOS commands, too. For example, I like the DIR command always to sort the files by name order and pause when the screen is full. I do that with this DOSKEY command:

```
DOSKEY DIR=DIR $1 /on /p
```

The /on parameter tells the DIR command to order the file list by name, and the /p parameter tells DIR to pause when the screen is full. Note that I also add the variable $1 to enable me to specify file characteristics for any directory list. Without the $1 variable support, every DIR command would produce a full directory listing of the current directory only. By adding $1, I can issue commands, such as the following (which displays a list of all files with names beginning with PROG that have the TXT extension), and still get a sort by name and a pause when the screen is full:

```
DIR PROG*.TXT
```

Of the three kinds of external commands, two (COM and EXE files) are variations on the same principle. The BAT file is something entirely different. Both COM and EXE are proper program files that the command processor loads and executes for you.

From the point of view of the user who fires up programs through the command processor, the differences between COM and EXE program files have no practical importance, but it's interesting to know the difference. COM files have a simple, quick-loading format, and EXE files are more complex. A COM file is sometimes called an image file, which means that what's stored on disk is an exact image of the program as loaded and run in the computer's memory. A COM file needs no further processing or conversion by DOS to run; it's just copied into memory and away it goes.

You may think that all program files are like that, but many programs require a small amount of last-minute preparation before they can run. The crux of this load-time preparation is the one thing that can't be known in advance when a program is created, and that is the memory address to which the program will be copied. In general, the various parts of a program are closely linked. All sections of the executable code know where the other sections are (so that they can call each other), and the program code knows the memory locations of all the bits of data that come with the program. Although any program can know the relative location of its parts, no program can know in advance the absolute memory addresses of those parts. After all, where a program is loaded into memory depends on how much memory is being used by DOS and memory-resident programs, and that can change.

It is possible for a program to adapt itself automatically to wherever it happens to be placed in memory. That's exactly what COM-type programs do. Because they take advantage of segment registers and careful programming conventions, COM programs don't have to be adjusted depending on where they are located in memory. However, not all programs can work that way because the COM format is rather restrictive. Under normal circumstances, COM programs can't be any larger than 64KB, and that's not enough to accommodate more sophisticated programs. Thus, the EXE format exists to handle programs that can't be loaded as a pure memory image.

When DOS loads an EXE program into memory, it performs any last-minute processing needed to ready the program for execution. One main part of that preparation is to plug the memory address at which the program is loaded into all the parts of the program that need it. To do that, the EXE file format includes a table that shows which parts of the program need to be modified and how it should be done. Instructions that refer to particular addresses are modified to refer to the actual addresses into which the program loads. That's not the only special work that has to be done for EXE programs, though. Other things, such as setting up the program's working stack, also must be done. (COM programs take care of that for themselves.)

Also, COM programs and EXE programs are loaded differently, and there also are differences in the ways they are written. Slightly different programming conventions are used to accommodate the different ways they are loaded and run. Also, somewhat different steps are used by programmers to prepare these programs. (These steps are explained in Chapter 22, "How Programs Are Built.") All in all, though, this is just a technical matter that concerns program developers. From the point of view of the computer user, there is no difference between COM and EXE programs.

When DOS runs a program, either COM or EXE, the command interpreter finds the program on disk, loads it into memory (processing EXE as needed), and then turns control of the computer over to the program. When the program is finished, it passes control back to the heart of DOS, and DOS reactivates the COMMAND.COM command processor. Although the core parts of DOS are held permanently in low memory locations, most of the command interpreter is kept in high memory, the area that programs can use for their data. This is done to avoid permanently tying up much memory for the command interpreter. If a program needs to use the memory in which the command interpreter is located, it simply does so—without even being aware that it is overwriting the command interpreter. When a program finishes and hands control back to DOS, DOS checks to see whether the command interpreter has been disturbed. If it hasn't, DOS simply starts using it again; if it has, DOS loads a fresh copy from disk. That's why, with old PCs that did not have a hard disk, you sometimes had to have a copy of COMMAND.COM on your working disk even though COMMAND.COM was on the DOS system disk you used to start the computer.

That's the essence of the way DOS runs programs, DOS's own internal command programs, and the command programs (COM and EXE type) that are stored on disk. However, there is one more type of command that DOS can carry out for you: the batch file command.

# Whipping Up a Batch

Batch files represent a powerful expansion of DOS's capability to carry out commands for you. Properly speaking, however, batch files are not a fourth kind of program in the sense that DOS's internal commands and COM and EXE files are programs. Instead, batch command files are scripts of conventional program commands that DOS can carry out, by treating all the steps in the script as a single unit, when you enter a single command.

Batch files are identified by the BAT filename extension. Inside a batch file is simply data in the format of an ASCII text file. Each line of the text file is a command that the command interpreter will carry out.

The simplest kind of batch file is a series of conventional program commands that have been gathered into a batch file so that you can conveniently run them in sequence as a single unit. However, there is much more to batch file processing.

For one thing, parameters can be used with batch files just as they can with ordinary programs, and the command interpreter can take the parameters you give with the batch command and pass them on to the programs inside the batch file. And, even more sophisticated than that, there's a whole batch command language that enables the command interpreter to carry out logical steps to repeat the execution of programs or to skip steps depending on errors that occur, parameters you give, or whether the files you need actually exist.

**Note:** If you have the Norton Utilities, you can use the Batch Enhancer facility to supercharge your batch files. The Batch Enhancer offers an array of features to augment the standard DOS batch commands.

Although this isn't the place to go into the complexities of DOS's batch processing command language, it's worthwhile to note that it exists and that it's one of the most powerful tools you have to help you make effective use of DOS. Experienced users of DOS tend to do practically everything in DOS through the batch processing facility because it enables them to avoid the work of entering a series of commands repeatedly. To give you an idea of how much I use batch files, I just counted the number of batch files I've built for myself. They total an amazing 145! That might be a lot more than you need (I suspect it's more than I really need, too), but it gives you an idea of just how important batch files can be.

If you haven't already mastered the uses of the batch file, I highly recommend that you take the time to do so. Be aware, though, that there are advanced parts of the batch command language that can really be quite confusing when you first try to use them. I'd recommend that you try to learn about and take advantage of batch files in an incremental way, first using the simplest features and then, when you're comfortable with them, moving on to see whether you have any use for the more advanced ones. If you'd like some help, my book *Peter Norton's Complete Guide to DOS 6.22*, published by Sams Publishing, covers batch files in depth.

# Some Things to Think About or Try

1. Using any snooping tool available to you (such as DEBUG or DISKEDIT in the Norton Utilities), browse around inside your computer's COMMAND.COM and find the names of the internal commands. Do you find anything unusual? What else, besides the command names, does COMMAND.COM need to hold? (For information on how to use DEBUG or the Norton Utilities, see Chapter 23, "Microsoft Windows: Role and Function.")

2. How do you think a COM-type program can adjust itself to wherever DOS loads it into memory? What are some of the problems that might have to be solved, and how can a program overcome them?

3. If you're familiar with the ins and outs of DOS's batch command language, analyze it to see what you think are its strong and weak points. Particularly, look for the parts that are awkward to use. Think about inventing your own batch language. What features do you think would be the most useful or powerful?

# 20

# DOS
# Serving
# Programs

Now that you understand some of the basic ideas behind DOS and how DOS works for you, it's time to see how DOS works for programs. This chapter is a parallel to Chapter 17, "BIOS: Digging In," which covers the services that the ROM-BIOS provides for programs; this chapter does the same for DOS. The similarity is strong, of course, but there are two important differences. As you learned in Chapter 19, "DOS Serving Us," one difference is that DOS does much to serve the computer user directly, which the ROM-BIOS does not. The other difference is that the ROM-BIOS provides services for programs on a very low level, whereas many of the services that DOS provides for programs are complex and on quite a high level. That's one of the themes that will emerge as you tour the DOS services.

# DOS Services and Philosophy

The services that DOS provides for programs are subject to several conflicting tugs that have pulled them in multiple directions and which account for some of the contradictory nature that you'll see in them. Although the ROM-BIOS services that I mention in Chapter 17 were designed as a whole and created afresh in the best way their designers could manage, the DOS services have had the benefit neither of a single underlying purpose nor of being built in one integrated effort. Don't be too surprised if the phrase "hodge-podge" comes to mind.

Four main influences have shaped the DOS services into what they are today. Two of the four are other operating systems that served as the foundation of DOS.

The first influence, as you learned in Chapter 18, "The Role of DOS," was CP/M. Because CP/M was the dominant operating system for the eight-bit generation of computers that was the predecessor of the PC family and because there was so much CP/M-based software available, DOS was carefully designed to be enough like CP/M to make it relatively easy to adapt CP/M programs to the PC and DOS as well as to make it easier for experienced CP/M users to use DOS. The key to this was having DOS present to programs an appearance very much like that of CP/M. The appearance had to include identical or nearly identical operating system services and a similar philosophy in the design of the disk architecture so that CP/M programs would not have to be redesigned from scratch. Thus, DOS's first big influence was the desire to imitate CP/M.

The second major influence, which came later, was UNIX. Not long after the appearance of DOS and the PC, it became clear that the CP/M framework had too limited a horizon to accommodate the PC's future. The UNIX operating system, on the other hand, was highly regarded, and Microsoft (DOS's creator) had extensive experience developing its variation of UNIX, called XENIX. When it came time to revamp DOS into something more forward-looking, much of the style and many of the features of UNIX were stirred—you might prefer the word "dumped"—into DOS. This became DOS's second major design influence.

Two other factors have played a big part in the evolution of DOS. One was the desire to make and keep DOS as hardware-nonspecific as possible, that is, to have it be computer—and peripheral—

independent. Some of the working parts of DOS must be specifically adjusted to the hardware features of the machines on which it is working, but this is limited to a specific machine-dependent part, called the DOS-BIOS (and distinct from the machine's own ROM-BIOS). Outside of the DOS-BIOS, DOS basically is unaware of the characteristics of the computer with which it is working. This is beneficial because it makes DOS and, particularly, the programs that are designed to use DOS services, machine-independent. It also has some important drawbacks, however, because it tends to remove many of the most useful machine features from the realm of DOS services.

The most painful example is the use of the display screen. The services provided by DOS do not give programs a way to position information on the display screen. Software is faced with a choice of either using the screen in a crude Teletype-fashion (one character after another, and wrapping back to the left margin when each line on the screen is full of text) or giving up the machine independence that using only DOS services provides. For some time, that prevented users from having a wide range of powerful programs that automatically work on any computer that uses DOS. In any event, the reluctance to give DOS features like full-screen display output has been an important influence in DOS's evolution.

The final major influence that has shaped DOS has been the relatively *ad hoc* addition of features needed to support the new directions in which IBM and other manufacturers have taken the PC family. In general, features have been added to DOS on an as-needed basis, not designed in a unified way. Thus, the various parts have not fit together quite as smoothly as they might have otherwise. This approach has resulted in versions of DOS that, for example, had no memory management services. Designers then attempted to add memory management to what had been an unruly "please serve yourself" approach to the use of memory. The same has been true of the services necessary for shared resources and networking and for the multiprogramming and multitasking of programs.

When you stir together these four main influences, out comes the DOS that you know and use. Emerging from this DOS mishmash is the collection of services that DOS provides for programs.

# All the DOS Services

Now you're ready to work your way through the main list of services that DOS provides for programs. Read on if you want to get a good idea of what DOS can do for programs and, thus, for you. Some of them are remarkably interesting. I don't elaborate on each one individually because that would make this chapter impossibly long. Instead, I present an overview that hits the essence of the services DOS provides.

The DOS service routines are all invoked by a common interrupt instruction, interrupt 21 (hex), which is used as a master way of requesting the services. The specific services are requested by their service ID number through the simple process of loading the service number in one of the processor's registers, the same way they are used to request ROM-BIOS services in each service group (such as the video group).

The DOS services also are organized into groups of related services, but in a more informal way. I cover the services in terms of these groups, roughly in numeric order. One thing to bear in mind is that, unlike the relatively static list of ROM-BIOS services, the list of DOS services continues to grow, with new ones being added with each release of DOS. This is both good and bad. Although new features are constantly being added, this can create problems when program designers want to take advantage of the latest DOS features. Because many PCs continue to use older versions of DOS, programs that incorporate newer features can't run on machines that use earlier versions. In this discussion, I point out which services are included with particular versions of DOS.

> **Note:** Incidentally, if you want Peter's Principle of DOS Upgrading, it's basically this: upgrade. DOS has developed so significantly—even from Version 5.x to 6.x—that so long as you're not running very old hardware that won't support the new versions of DOS, there's really no reason to not upgrade. You'll get significant new capabilities for the relatively tiny investment of upgrading. Additionally, a lot of new DOS features alleviate the need to purchase certain types of third-party utilities, like disk compression, which is built-in under DOS 6.2x. (I say alleviate and not "eliminate," because most third-party utilities give you significant additional flexibility and power over the built-in DOS utilities.)

I begin with the most elementary group of DOS services, the ones designed for console I/O (interaction with the user). The input services read from the keyboard, and the output services display information on the screen in the simplest and crudest way, treating the screen like a printer and placing information on the screen without any sense of position. These services are a carryover from CP/M and are crude because they are intended to be completely machine-blind; that is, they are designed to work uniformly without any awareness of the features of a particular display screen. (This is why the screen output services cannot position information at particular locations on the screen.)

As part of the CP/M heritage, these services are a screwy conglomerate. There is, for example, a simple keyboard input service and a simple screen output service. In addition, there is another service that acts as input or output or combines both, depending on which way you use it. As I mentioned already, all these CP/M-style services were provided to make translating CP/M programs to DOS relatively easy. That was part of an effort to help the PC in its early days when there was a lot of CP/M software and very little DOS software. That thinking has long been obsolete, but these services remain.

Part of the same group of elementary DOS services are services that send output to the printer (the parallel port) and read and write data to the communications line (the serial port).

All the DOS services that fall into this group are matched by similar or, in some cases, even identical ROM-BIOS services. Why would DOS duplicate services that the BIOS provides? The answer lies in the theory that programs should turn to DOS for all their services so that they are not tied to the features of one machine. Using DOS services is, in principle, more adaptable and makes it possible for programs to run on dissimilar machines. DOS services also enable far more flexible handling of I/O, for example, by rerouting data. That's one of the functions the DOS MODE command provides: It enables you to direct printer output to the serial port. If a program used the ROM-BIOS printer services, that function would be impossible.

Unfortunately, that principle works well for only very simple input and output operations with the printer, serial port, keyboard, and the screen. Most programs have much more sophisticated needs, though, particularly for screen output. As I've said, DOS lets you down in that regard. Using the internal driver, ANSI.SYS, and some careful programming, however, you can position individual characters anywhere you want on the screen. This is another example of how DOS has expanded through add-on facilities that probably now should be part of DOS proper.

Although the first group of DOS services provides essentially nothing more than you already have available in the ROM-BIOS, the next group ventures into realms that naturally belong to DOS: high-level disk services, particularly file input and output.

This group of services also is related to old design features of CP/M and is based around an approach that has been made obsolete by new developments in DOS. These older file services are called, in DOS's terminology, the traditional file services, and they are based on the use of a file control block, or FCB. FCBs are used by programs to provide the names and identification of the files with which programs work. The FCB also holds status information while a file is in use. When programs use these traditional file services, DOS keeps records of what's what in the FCB, making these services vulnerable to tinkering by the programs you run. (Newer file services hold DOS's control information apart from the programs, ensuring safer and more reliable operation.)

These FCB-oriented traditional file services can do a variety of things. First, to track down files, a pair of services can locate files matching wild-card filenames that include the characters ? and *. Programs can use the wild cards either to find the first matching filename or to find the full list of files that match the specification.

Other traditional file services open a file (prepare for reading or writing data) and later close it. Then there are services that enable the computer to read or write a file sequentially from beginning to end or to read and write randomly, skipping to any position in the file.

The console services and the traditional file services make up the majority of the universal DOS services—the services that were available in the long-forgotten DOS 1.0. A handful of additional services exist in this universal group. These are services that read or set DOS's record of the date and time, end a program, turn disk verification on and off, and perform other technical services.

Because these universal services were available from the very beginning, they can be used with every version of DOS. The DOS services I discuss from this point on have been added in later releases of DOS, mostly beginning with the also-long-forgotten Version 2.0. Thus, programs that use these services must run on machines that use a version of DOS that supports these features.

The first of these services, which is now obviously an essential service, reports which version of DOS a program is running under. This service enables the program to find out whether the services it needs are there. If not, the program can adjust itself to what's available or at least exit gracefully, reporting that it needs a different version of DOS. Because this service was introduced in DOS 2.0, it would appear to have come too late. Fortunately, thanks to the way earlier versions of DOS work, if a program uses this service, these early DOS versions report themselves as version 0; that's not exactly correct, but at least it properly indicates a pre-2.0 version.

Beginning with DOS 5.0, an external utility, SETVER, enables you to fool an application expecting a certain version of DOS into thinking it is running with the correct version. An internal version table holds information about popular applications so that when one of these applications runs, DOS can scan the version table and tell the application what it wants to hear. If an application you want to run isn't already in the version table, you can add new programs to the list.

For file operations, DOS 2.0 and all later versions provide an alternative to the FCB-oriented traditional file services. These new file services work with a handle, which is simply a two-byte number that uniquely identifies each file in use by a program. When a program opens a file using these new file services, DOS gives the program a handle that identifies it for all subsequent file operations until it is closed. This use of handles enables DOS to keep all critical file-control information safely apart from the program, protecting it from damage or tinkering. These handle-oriented services provide all the facilities that the FCB-oriented traditional services provide, but they do it in a cleaner fashion. Programs are provided with several standard handles, one for writing ordinary information on the display screen, another for error messages (which appear on the screen even if the user tells DOS to reroute screen output), and so forth.

In addition, all versions of DOS from 2.0 on provide services that are closely related to the extra structure that has been added to DOS disks. These include services to create and remove directories, change the subdirectory, move a file's directory entry from one directory to another, and so forth.

There are also services that enable programs to work more intimately with the hardware, without having to break out of the DOS framework. Previously, programs could either look at devices, such as disks, in a dumb way through DOS or in a smart way on their own. These new device-control services bridge the gap. As an example, with these device services, a program can determine whether a particular disk drive is fixed (a hard disk or RAM disk) or removable (a floppy disk) and, for removable media, whether the drive can sense when you switched disks. (Most drives include a signal line that changes state when the drive door has been opened. This enables DOS or other applications to be aware that the same disk as before may not be in the drive.) All these services enable programs to use the computer in a more sophisticated way.

Additionally, there are memory services, which enable programs to work together with DOS in grabbing and releasing memory. Normally, each program that runs under DOS has the exclusive use of all of the computer's memory, but these memory services enable a broader sharing of memory.

Some of the services provided by DOS 2.0 and later versions enable a program to load and run subprograms and give them a degree of independence from the program that started them.

Many of the significant additions to DOS appeared with Version 2.0, but other features have been added in later versions. Version 3.0 added extended error codes, which enable a program to get a much more detailed explanation of what has gone wrong when an error is reported. The main additions that appeared in DOS 3.0 and 3.1 concerned the special problems of using networks. These new services provide the locking and unlocking of access to all or parts of a file, making it safe and practical for several computers to share access to the same file through a network without interfering with one another. Similar network-related services deal with the control and redirection of printer output.

DOS 3.2 added a new facility for the use of languages other than American English and support for IBM Token-Ring networks, 3.5-inch disk drives, and the PC Convertible. DOS 3.3—the "standard," for many years—enhanced the language support (with code pages) and added the capability to partition large hard disks (greater than 32MB) and to support up to four serial ports. DOS 4.0 added more language support, the capability to use large hard disks without making partitions, and a built-in extended memory facility.

DOS 5.0 added new services and features in several different areas. First, DOS's memory management capabilities were greatly enhanced, and new extended memory and expanded memory managers were added. In addition, DOS 5.0 could make use of unused memory addresses above 640KB to load device drivers, memory-resident programs, and even part of DOS itself. Programs can explicitly ask for and use this extra memory (called upper memory blocks).

Second, DOS 5.0 provided a way for programs to indicate that they are waiting for some event, such as for the user to press a key. This enabled multitasking systems, such as Windows, to take advantage of the waiting time.

Third, DOS 5.0 introduced built-in help. Programs can be designed to make use of this system so that the HELP command can provide help on any program, not just DOS commands.

Fourth, there are some programs that work with only specific versions of DOS. DOS Version 5.0 uses the SETVER utility I mentioned earlier to tell these programs that they are running under the version of DOS that they require.

Fifth, DOS 5.0 provided an easy way for programs to examine the volume identification information associated with a disk, such as the volume serial number. (This is a unique identifier assigned by DOS when the disk is formatted.) Checking this information enables a program to determine categorically which disks are present. Before a program updates a file on a floppy disk, for example, it can make sure that the disk has not been changed.

Finally, DOS 5.0 provided ways for programmers to ensure that their programs will work safely in multitasking (Windows) and task-switching (the DOS Shell) environments.

With the release of DOS 6.0, the PC operating system began moving toward providing the type of operating system services large machine users have had for years. It's not there by a long shot, but it's moving in the right direction.

The latest version of DOS—Version 6.22 as I'm writing this—for example, includes DRIVESPACE, a utility that compresses information as it is written to disk and decompresses it on the fly when it is loaded into memory. This feature essentially can double the amount of disk space available on each physical drive. A 100MB drive becomes a nearly 200MB drive. Just how much compression is possible depends on the type of data and programs you use, but a doubling of space is close to what most users get. There has been much written about problems with the first releases of this integrated utility, and the legal battles between Microsoft and Stac Electronics, Inc. which led to Microsoft rewriting the utility from its original implementation, DOUBLESPACE, to the DRIVESPACE with DOUBLEGUARD that we have today. With the possible exception of future legal squabbles, and a fall in the stock price of Stac, problems with DRIVESPACE are few today.

There are other new services in DOS 6.xx as well. The help facility has been much improved, making it an interactive, full-screen facility that you can read, search, and study, more like a Windows help system. And, memory management is the best yet provided with DOS. Using technology licensed from Helix software's Netroom memory manager, DOS can now automatically figure out the best use of your memory and install the proper program calls in your CONFIG.SYS file to make it happen. (All of this is achieved through a utility known as MEMMAKER.)

The backup and restore facilities have been greatly enhanced by using technology licensed from my Peter Norton Backup utilities. Additional utilities, including a CD-ROM support driver, facilities for building multiple configurations right into CONFIG.SYS, a CHOICE program to prompt a user for input from a batch file, a DEFRAG utility to eliminate disk fragmentation, and DELTREE, a command that enables you to delete an entire disk subdirectory and the directories it holds, have been added to DOS 6.

There also is INTERLNK, a utility that links two computers through serial or parallel ports so that they can share disks and printer ports. This isn't really networking, but it is a way to reduce the need for "sneakernet" (carrying floppy disks and walking down the hall) between two machines in the same office or workgroup. You also can use INTERLNK to transfer information quickly from your desktop computer to your laptop and back again.

The MSAV command scans the computer for viruses and removes them if you tell it to. A companion utility, VSAFE, installs itself as a RAM-resident scanner that continuously monitors for viruses.

In addition, some of these services are installed in a Microsoft Windows application window so that you can call them up easily from inside Windows.

There's another interesting addition to DOS 6.*xx*, the MSD utility that scans your computer's hardware and memory and reports on what it finds. This program was first included with very early versions of Windows 3.0 and was used primarily to report hardware configurations of beta sites to Microsoft. MSD is a useful utility when you are installing new software or hardware or when you simply want to know something about how your computer is configured.

As a preliminary move to support green PCs and the growing laptop generation, DOS version 6.*xx* includes a POWER utility that reduces power consumption when applications and the computer itself are idle. The POWER.EXE file is loaded as a device in the CONFIG.SYS file.

So far, I've discussed only the mainstream DOS services, but there are others that are quite interesting and useful. Probably the most fascinating of all are the terminate-and-stay-resident services that enable programs to embed themselves into the computer's memory and remain there while DOS continues to run other programs.

There are two stay-resident services that these types of programs use: an old one that's part of the universal DOS services and a more advanced one that's part of the services introduced with DOS 2.0. Both services enable programs to become resident in a part of the computer's memory that is not used by subsequent programs that DOS runs.

Related to the operation of these programs is a DOS service that helps a resident program tell whether it is safe to swing into operation. In Chapter 17, I discuss the fact that the ROM-BIOS programs must be re-entrant, so that they can be suspended or doubly active without difficulty. DOS, however, does not work in a completely re-entrant way, which means that, at certain times, if DOS is in the middle of one operation, it is unsafe for a program to request another DOS service. A special DOS service is used to report whether DOS is in that dangerous state. Some memory-resident programs use this interrupt to see whether DOS is in the middle of doing something before they pop up. If DOS is not to be bothered, the memory-resident program alerts you (by making a beep, for example).

Another interesting DOS service is the one used for country-dependent information, such as the currency symbol (dollar sign, pound sign, and so on) that should be used and the way numbers are punctuated (12,345.67, 12.345,67, and so on). DOS is designed to adjust to different national conventions and can report the country-specific information to your programs so that they can adjust. Not only can your programs learn the country information from DOS, they also can instruct DOS to change the country code with which it is working.

**Note:** Incidentally, the DOS country information exists independent of the Microsoft Windows International control panel I talk about in Chapter 13, "Keyboarding." You can easily have DOS configured for the fact that you live in the United States, and have Windows configured to assume—and operate on the assumption—that French is your primary language, for example.

There are more DOS services, but what you've seen should give you a sound feeling for the main range of DOS services as well as a peek at some of the curiosities. Two of the most common services that DOS provides are control over the parallel and serial ports, to which you connect printers, modems, and so on. We take a look at those technologies in the next chapter.

# 21

# Printers and Communications

So far, I've talked about the core hardware that makes up a PC and the software—DOS and Windows—that makes it run. In this chapter and later in Chapter 25, "Multimedia," I give you a quick look at some of the external components that help enhance and expand your computer. In fact, a printer and modem are such necessary parts of computer for most users that they almost could be considered inherently part of the computer. Indeed, many computer systems are sold with a modem preinstalled. I discuss printers first and then move on to communications.

# Printers: The Parallel Port

Beginning with the first PCs, computers have included a port through which you could attach a printer. The earliest computers I used had a current loop port to connect to a teletype machine. Then manufacturers began adding serial ports (see the next section), and today the parallel port is the most common printer connection.

> **Technical Note:** The original IBM PC could access printers that were originally designed for the IBM Datamaster system. They did this by using a "current loop" that was nearly identical to today's MIDI serial interface for electronic musical instruments. Data is sent across a two-wire loop as a changing current (as opposed to a changing voltage). Normally, both a transmit loop and a receive loop were required—a total of four wires—that could successfully transmit data over several hundred feet.

You sometimes hear the parallel printer port on a PC referred to as a Centronics port, after the company that popularized it. The technology of that port has changed very little over the years, except that the original interface used a 36-pin connector, and today's version generally uses a 25-pin D-shell connector (DB25). That reduces the real estate requirements for the connector and doesn't really compromise operation of the interface. About all that is dropped in the newer connector are a few ground leads. The original connector required multiple, redundant signal grounds. The new connectors simply use fewer of them.

This printer interface is called a parallel interface because data moves from the computer to the printer along parallel wires, that is, all eight data bits travel together. In a serial interface (see the next section), each data bit as well as control information is sent along the wire in a train-like fashion: one bit at a time sent one behind the other.

Figure 21.1 shows a drawing of a typical parallel port connector, and Table 21.1 shows the electrical connections for the computer side of the cable.

**Figure 21.1.**
A typical DB25 printer
cable connector. (Drawing
courtesy of Gateway 2000.)

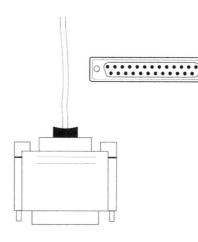

Table 21.1. Parallel Port Pinout Connections.

| Signal Name | Pin |
| --- | --- |
| -STROBE | 1 |
| Data 0 | 2 |
| Data 1 | 3 |
| Data 2 | 4 |
| Data 3 | 5 |
| Data 4 | 6 |
| Data 5 | 7 |
| Data 6 | 8 |
| Data 7 | 9 |
| -ACK (Acknowledge) | 10 |
| Busy | 11 |
| Paper Empty | 12 |
| +Select | 13 |
| -Auto FDXT | 14 |
| -Error | 15 |
| -Init | 16 |
| -Slctin | 17 |
| Ground | 18 |

*continues*

Table 21.1. continued.

| Signal Name | Pin |
|---|---|
| Ground | 19 |
| Ground | 20 |
| Ground | 21 |
| Ground | 22 |
| Ground | 23 |
| Ground | 24 |
| Ground | 25 |

You can see in Table 21.1 that there are a fair number of ground connections—eight to be exact. Why eight? These ground connections correspond to the eight data lines; there is one separate ground wire for each data line.

The -STROBE line on pin 1 is used to tell the printer when the current data stream is complete and that it is okay to print a character. Notice that the strobe line is identified by a negative sign in front of it. That means that the strobe pulse is a negative pulse. When the computer has finished sending a byte of data to be printed, the voltage on the strobe line is pulled low, an occurrence that the printer recognizes.

The eight data lines carry the eight bits of a byte of information. This is accomplished digitally, with a high voltage on a line meaning a set bit, and a low voltage or no voltage meaning a clear bit. As you may recall from Chapter 14, "Data!," information can be stored within a computer using binary digits of this nature.

The Acknowledge line, pin 10, is a signal from the printer back to the computer that says, in effect, "I am ready to receive more information." As long as this line is high, the computer doesn't send any new data. When the line goes low (notice the negative sign in front of it in the table), the computer knows the printer is ready for more information.

The Busy line signals the computer when the printer is busy. The computer waits until the printer buffer is emptied to send more information. Obviously, with parallel data lines the computer could outdistance the printer rather quickly if there weren't some way to tell the computer to wait before sending more information.

Like the Busy line, the Paper Out line tells the computer to stop sending information because the printer isn't ready to receive it. The printer could simply send a Busy signal, but then the computer has no way of knowing why the printer stopped. Some applications use the Paper Out line to report to the user that paper is needed.

The Select line shows that the printer is selected, meaning that the printer is online. (The front of your printer probably has an online switch and light.) When the printer is offline, it cannot receive characters from the computer.

The -AUTO FDXT (Auto Feed) line controls how the printer handles a new line. The printer either can advance the print head to the next line when a Carriage Return is received (the usual action) or can merely interpret the Carriage Return literally and move the print head back to the beginning of the line. When the computer holds this line low, the printer adds a Line Feed to the Carriage Return character. With -AUTO FDXT high, a Carriage Return means just that and nothing more.

The -ERROR (or Fault) line is a general-purpose line to signal any other printer errors. The computer may not be able to determine precisely what is wrong, but it knows that the printer probably is not out of paper and that some other unusual condition is preventing the printer from processing data.

The -INIT line is a way for the computer to control the printer. By signaling the printer on this line, the computer essentially resets the printer to its power on defaults. That prevents the printer configuration from the last program—a special graphics mode, for example—from being carried over to the next print job. With the -INIT line, an application can reset the printer to a known state before trying to send anything down the wire.

The -SLCTIN (Select Input) line is a way for the computer to control whether the printer is ready to accept data (online or offline). When this signal is low, the printer can accept data; when it goes high, the printer is offline and cannot accept data.

The good news about parallel connections is that with eight wires to carry data simultaneously, information can flow from the computer to the printer quickly compared with most serial connections. In fact, the parallel port is theoretically capable of sending around half a million characters per second down the line. A printer may be able to take this for a while, but eventually would fall behind, so the Busy line stops the computer while the printer catches up.

And, while you most often use your printer port to send information from the computer to the printer, you also can use it to accept data from an external device. (This wasn't true with early PCs, which had an output-only design on the parallel port.) There are software/hardware packages available today to do just that. By connecting two computers together through a null cable (one with the wires crossed so that the output wires of one machine are connected to the input wires of another) and installing some software, you can share data, transfer files, and the like.

You may wonder why, if the parallel port is so fast, parallel links aren't used for everything. One of the main reasons is the distance limitations of parallel lines. Because the data lines are parallel, there is more chance for interference—resulting in data errors—as the line length increases. Parallel communication is good for distances of 12 feet or less. For longer lines, use your serial port.

# Communication Lines: The Serial Port

The other standard communications port you can find on your PC is the serial port. In fact, today's PCs generally have at least two serial ports.

As the name implies, the serial port differs from the parallel port in that the data is sent down the line in a serial stream instead of in parallel. This slows down data transfer, to some extent, but enables you to communicate over long distances. Instead of the parallel port's maximum 1012-foot range, you can use a serial line for 50 or more feet and still get reliable communications. In fact, back in the days of minicomputers, I have run shielded serial cable through metal conduit inside walls and ceilings for 150 feet or more. That much distance isn't recommended, but with quality wire, conduit, and careful grounding, you can (sometimes) get away with it.

The RS-232 serial standard calls for 25 lines, but as a practical matter, you can get by with a lot less. Figure 21.2 shows the type of 9-pin D-shell connector commonly used for the COM 1 port on most PCs today. The COM 2 serial port uses the older DB25 connector. However, even the larger connector usually doesn't have all 25 pins connected to anything.

**Figure 21.2.**
*A typical 9-pin serial connector. (Drawing courtesy of Gateway 2000.)*

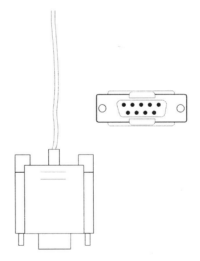

When you purchase a commercial serial cable, it rarely has all 25 lines connected. And, when you wire one yourself, you probably aren't going to string all 25 wires between connectors. In fact, the most common connections are those shown in Table 21.2.

Table 21.2. Common Serial Connections.

| Signal | Name | DB9 Pin | DB25 Pin |
|--------|------|---------|----------|
| DCD | Data Carrier Detect | 1 | 8 |
| RX | Receive Data | 2 | 3 |
| TX | Transmit Data | 3 | 2 |
| DTR | Data Terminal Ready | 4 | 20 |
| GND | Signal Ground | 5 | 7 |
| DSR | Data Set Ready | 6 | 6 |
| RTS | Request to Send | 7 | 4 |
| CTS | Clear to Send | 8 | 5 |
| RI | Ring Indicator | 9 | 22 |

The pin assignments shown in Table 21.2 are for the cable that attaches to your PC because PCs are considered DTE (Data Terminal Equipment) devices. Normally, when you purchase your own serial cable, the connections on the other end are the same. The wires connect straight through from DCD to DCD, for example, from RX to RX, from TX to TX, and so on. This can be done because normally two DTE devices don't connect to each other in the serial world.

When you plug a cable into a DTE device (your computer), the assumption is that you will plug the other end of the cable into a DCE (Data Communications Equipment) device, such as a modem. A DCE device has different serial pin assignments so that the TX line from a DTE device attaches automatically to the RX pin of a DCE device. Similarly, the TX line from the DCE unit hooks up to the RX pin of the DTE device.

Other lines require reverse connections as well. For example, the RTS line from one device must connect to the CTS line of another. That makes sense, when you think about it. The Request to Send line (RTS) is a query that must be answered by the Clear to Send (CTS). The DTR/DSR lines also must connect to each other, and the DCD line from one device usually connects to the DTR line of another.

Again, this kind of cross-connection takes place automatically when you are using one DTE and one DCE device. If you want to connect two DTR devices, as you would do if you wanted to hook up two computers via the serial line to exchange files, the cable itself must make the swap. Such a cable is called a null modem cable. You can see how this cable is wired by studying the drawing in Figure 21.3.

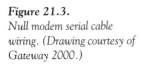

**Figure 21.3.**
*Null modem serial cable wiring. (Drawing courtesy of Gateway 2000.)*

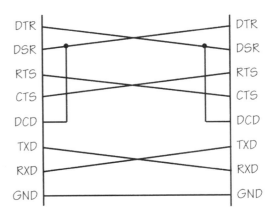

Depending on what you're using the serial line for, you might actually be able to get by with even fewer connections. In the minicomputer days when serial terminals were used extensively, I frequently ran serial lines with only three or four wires, the RX, TX, ground, and maybe one other line such as the DCD or DSR line.

Today, one of the main reasons for having a serial port in the first place is to connect your computer to a modem or other external device. And, because you don't always know what that device will be, it is best to have at least the lines shown in Table 21.2 connected. With that set of nine lines, you can support a modem, serial printer, plotter, and other common serial devices.

Now for a brief look at each of these serial signals so you can understand what each one does. This level of technical discussion also should help you understand the status lights on your modem and how to configure your communications software. I look at those topics in the next section.

The Data Carrier Detect (DCD) line (or simply Carrier Detect, CD) is used by modems to indicate they are talking to each other at some level. When your local modem links with the remote modem and gets a good carrier signal, the local modem places a positive signal on the DCD line. This tells your computer and its communications software that a modem-to-modem link has been established.

The Receive Data (RX) line is obvious. It is through this connection that your computer or the DCE device receives information transmitted to it from a remote device.

The Transmit Data (TX) is the channel over which your computer or the remote DCE unit transmits information. Notice that there are two data lines, one for send (transmit) and one for receive. That means that, with the proper software, two serial devices can send data at the same time.

The Data Terminal Ready (DTR) line carries a positive signal from the DTE device (normally, your computer) to the remote device to indicate that a DTE device is connected to the serial cable. The companion to this line is the Data Set Ready (DSR) line. For two devices to communicate, these two lines usually must be high, each telling the other it is there and ready for communications.

The Ground (GND) pin is a signal ground, or the other side of the transmit and receive signals. In most serial installations, this connection actually is not at ground potential. That is, it is not attached to the computer or DCE chassis.

The Data Set Ready (DSR) is the other half of the DTR/DSR pair I talked about earlier. DSR is a positive signal from a DCE unit that tells a DTR device it is online and ready to communicate.

The Request to Send (RTS) line also is part of a signal pair (the other half is the CTS line) that enables two connected units to tell each other when they are ready to receive data. The RTS line is controlled by the DTR device, while the CTS line is controlled by the DCE unit.

The Clear to Send (CTS) line is the other half of the RTS/CTS pair. Unless a positive signal is present on both the CTS and RTS lines, no data can flow across the serial connection in many communications links. There are exceptions, of course. The most common is the serial terminal attached to a remote computer. This link may or may not use the CTS/RTS lines. And, it is fairly common practice to hardwire these signals inside the local connector so that you don't have to run as many wires. So, for example, you can connect pins 4 and 7 as well as 8 and 6 inside the 9-pin connector that attaches to the PC. Then you only need to connect a lead from pin 3, Transmit Data, on the PC to pin 3, Receive Data, on the printer or other DB25-type device; connect a ground between pin 5 on the PC and pin 7 on the remote device; and connect a handshake wire from pin 6 on the PC to pin 19 on the printer or other device. Now you have a one-way PC-to-printer cable with only three wires.

The Ring Indicator (RI) is a way for the local modem to tell the computer to which it is attached that a call just came in. This enables the communications software to know that an impending modem connection is coming.

# Modems Reaching Out

As you know, the data in your computer is stored and manipulated as bits of digital information, 1's and 0's. However, telephone lines transmit analog data—information that varies continuously. To connect your PC to a remote system, you need to convert the PC's digital data to analog signals so it can be sent over the phone line. Similarly, at the other end, the signals must be converted back into computer data.

The process of converting digital computer-type data to an analog form is called modulation. Converting back again is called demodulation. Thus, the device that does the work is called a *modem*, a modulator-demodulator. The analog signal that carries the information is called a carrier.

The nice thing about using a modem is that once you have things set up properly, everything is done automatically. All you need to do is connect the modem to your PC and to the phone line and use the right software. In fact, as I mentioned at the beginning of this chapter, today most systems are sold with a modem preinstalled. Of course, external modems remain very popular, too. Most modems—internal or external—have their own small speaker so you can hear the modem work as it dials a number and connects to the remote computer. As your work with your modem, you pass through three distinct phases: power-up, in which the connection between computer and modem is established (this connection is usually initialized by your communications software), ready mode, during which time you can issue AT commands to make the modem dial the phone number you wish to connect with, and so on. (AT commands are discussed in the next section), and data mode, during which your modem is communicating with another modem and is actually sending and receiving data.

An external modem comes in its own case and will need its own source of electric power. Most external modems come with a separate transformer that plugs into a wall outlet. Some small modems can draw power from the serial cable or the phone line. Additionally, PCMCIA modems—used commonly now in notebook computers, and arriving on the desktop as prices drop—draw all of the power they need from their PCMCIA socket. (I introduce the idea of the PCMCIA bus in Chapter 2, "Hardware: The Parts of the PC.") PCMCIA modems are external devices, but they connect directly to the bus, just as if they were peripheral cards, like those you plug into your desktop computer.

An internal modem resides in your computer, of course, so you don't need to bother with a power cord or a serial cable. The modem draws its power directly from the computer and connects via the bus. All you will need to do is connect the modem to the phone line. The modem has a plug that you can access from the outside.

# Modem Commands—The AT Set

The basic set of modem commands was originally developed by the Hayes Microcomputer Products company and was released in 1981 with their first PC modem. Since then, this set of commands has become the accepted standard. In fact, modems that support this command set are commonly described as being "Hayes-compatible."

As you will see in a moment, all modem commands are prefixed by the letters *AT*, which stands for "attention." Thus, the commands have come to be known as the AT Command set. (When you say the name, it is customary to pronounce it as two separate letters: "ay-tee.")

Modems are actually small but sophisticated computers. They not only follow commands, but they store their own data in the form of different parameter settings that you can change. Most, but not all, modems have nonvolatile memory, which we talked about in Chapter 15, "The Memory Workbench." The AT commands enable you to set parameters the way you want or change them to default settings. At any time, you can save the current parameter settings to the nonvolatile memory. That way, every time you turn on the modem, it will be initialized the way you want.

As part of its data storage area, your modem has a number of registers. A register is a memory location that can hold a single number. The values in the registers control many aspects of the modem's performance. The AT commands allow you to specify the value of each register.

For example, register 0 controls whether or not the modem should answer the phone when it rings. If this register is set to zero, the modem will not answer the phone. If the register is set to a number greater than zero, the modem will answer the phone after that many rings.

Thus, if you want your modem to answer the phone after one ring, set register 0 to have the value one. As we will see in the next section, the command to do this is

```
AT S0=1
```

To have the modem answer after three rings, you would use

```
AT S0=3
```

To reset the modem so that it does not answer the phone at all, use

```
AT S0=0
```

When you tell your communications program to prepare for an incoming call (sometimes called "auto-answer"), it sets the value of register 0 to one. When you tell the program to stop waiting for a call, it sets the register back to zero.

The AT command set is certainly an important standard in that it enables all modems to be programmed similarly, but there are problems. First, as we will see later, there are low-speed and high-speed modems. Although the basic AT command set is adequate for low-speed modems, it does not provide all the commands needed for the more sophisticated modems. Unfortunately, each modem company has extended the AT command set in its own way and there is no standard—yet—for the highest-speed modems.

# Using Modem Commands

Most communications software will do everything necessary to program and set your modem. But there may be times when you want to enter your own commands. In this regard, your program will work in one of two ways.

All modern communications programs are menu-driven. Some start off with a main menu automatically. To type your own commands you need to pick a menu selection that connects you directly with the modem. Other programs work in the opposite way. When you start, you are already connected and everything you send goes right to the modem. To call up a menu you must press a special key combination.

The rules for entering standard modem commands are simple, but modem commands are like the DOS commands I talk about in Chapter 19, "DOS Serving Us": The more power you want to directly access, the more complicated it gets. For all commands, however, you type the two letters AT, followed by one or more commands, and then press Enter. The command line can be up to 80 characters long. Commands can be either upper- or lowercase, just as with DOS commands. If you want, you can use spaces to separate commands, but this is not required. Also as with DOS commands, nothing you type is processed until you press Enter.

All modem commands—after the "AT"—start with either a single letter or an ampersand (&) followed by a single letter.

Here are some sample modem command lines. Each line contains five commands, and all the lines are equivalent:

```
AT &F L2 M1 S0=0 S11=50
AT&FL2M1S0=0S11=50
at &f l2 m1 s0=0 s11=50
at&fl2m1s0=0s11=50
```

Although you can put as many commands as you want on a line (up to the 80 characters I mentioned), you can also use a separate line for each command. This can be handy when your commands are to be stored in a script to be executed automatically. Having each command on a separate line enables you to make changes easily and to test various configurations by including or excluding a particular command.

The following set of five command lines has the same effect as previous example:

```
AT &F
AT L2
AT M1
AT S0=0
AT S11=50
```

If you want to repeat the previous single command, simply enter

```
A/
```

This is the only command that is not preceded by AT.

# Modem Services

There are three types of AT commands. First, there are commands that tell the modem to do something. For example, the command:

```
AT A
```

tells the modem to answer the phone immediately. The command:

```
AT &F
```

tells the modem to reset all the parameters to the default (factory) settings.

The second type of command uses a number to set a particular parameter. This number follows the letter that identifies the command.

For example, the L command specifies the volume of the built-in speaker. (This is the speaker in the modem, not the PC's speaker.) To set the volume to low, medium, or high, you use the value 1, 2, or 3, respectively. The commands are:

```
AT L1
AT L2
AT L3
```

All commands that set parameters have defaults. These are the values that are built-in to the modem (and are reset by the &F command.) If you enter a parameter-setting command without specifying a value, the default will be used.

For example, the default value for the L command is 2, medium volume, for most modems. Thus, the following two commands are equivalent:

```
AT L2
AT L
```

The third type of command is used to set the value of one of the built-in registers. This command is S, followed by the number of the register, an equals sign (=), and the new value. For instance, to set register 11 to have the value 50, the command is

```
AT S11=50
```

Notice that there are no spaces before or after the equals sign. You can use spaces between commands, but not within a command.

If you want to examine the current value of a register, put a question mark after the register number. For example:

```
AT S11?
```

There are many services in the basic AT command set and, for the most part, they are rather technical. As a reference, I have included a technical section on the AT command set.

# Details of the AT Command Set

All modern PC modems support the AT Command set. However, there is no strict definition of all aspects of the commands. The Hayes company has its own version, but not all manufacturers follow it exactly. Similarly, there is no strict definition of what is meant by a Hayes-compatible modem.

Through the years, the AT Command set has been expanded to contain many different commands and to control many different registers. For reference, this section contains a list of the most basic commands, the ones that are more or less the same from modem to modem. However, the best reference is the documentation that comes with the specific modem that you are using.

As you will see, many of the AT commands set parameters or register values. Once you have configured a modem to your liking, there is a way to save all the settings for later recall. Unfortunately, there is no standard command to display all the current settings, although you can display register values, one at a time. Some, but not all, modem manufacturers have added a command to display the settings, but it has not been standardized.

## High-Speed Modem Commands: Some Problems

The basic AT command set does not provide all the functionality needed for sophisticated high-speed modems. For this reason, modem manufacturers have extended the command set. Unfortunately, there is no standard—each company has added new commands and registers in its own way.

As mentioned earlier, most communications programs are able to use any Hayes-compatible modem. However, the programs will not be able to use every type of high-speed modem efficiently; there are just too many nonstandard protocols and commands. Thus, you may have to program your modem yourself.

Usually this means entering a set of configuration commands, suitable for how you want to use the modem, and then saving the setup in the nonvolatile memory. Most high-speed modems enable you to save more than one configuration, called a profile. If you need to use your modem in two different ways, you can store two different profiles and recall each one as you need it. In addition, you may also have to customize your software to make sure that it sends the correct modem initialization commands at the start of each session.

Programming a high-speed modem can be difficult work and, for the most part, you will depend upon the documentation to tell you exactly what to do. Many times, you will find yourself entering commands from a list without really understanding what they do. For this reason, it is important that you choose a modem that comes with a clear, comprehensive manual.

Even more important, find out what kind of tech support comes for free with the modem. Most people with high-speed modems will, at some time, need tech support. It is not at all uncommon to have to spend some time on the phone with an expert. The nice thing is, of course, that once you get your modem programmed properly, you can save the configuration in a profile. However, be sure to keep a record of the exact commands that you used. Months later, you may need them again for some reason. If you haven't written them down, you may not remember them.

## The Fundamental AT Commands

Table 21.3 shows the most important of the basic AT commands that are common to all Hayes-compatible modems. Following the table is a brief discussion of each command. Most of these commands have default values, but you cannot count on their being the same in all modems.

Table 21.3. The Fundamental AT Commands.

| Command | Description |
|---------|-------------|
| A | Answer the phone immediately. |
| D | Dial a phone number, then wait for connection. |
| E | Set command echoing (0=off; 1=on). |
| H | Hang up (0); pick up phone line (1). |
| L | Set speaker volume (0,1=low; 2=medium; 3=high). |
| M | Speaker control: 0=off; 1=on while connecting; 2=always on; 3=on until a carrier is detected. |
| V | Set type of return codes (0=numeric; 1=verbose [words]) |
| Z | Reset parameters and register settings. |
| &C | Data Carrier Detect Control: 0=always on; 1=only when a carrier is detected. |
| &F | Reset parameters and settings to factory defaults. |
| &W | Write current parameter values and settings. |
| +++ | The break signal: change from data mode to command mode. |

A: This command tells the modem to answer the phone immediately. Example: You are using your communication program and someone dials your phone number to connect to your system so that you can exchange files. As soon as the phone rings you enter:

AT A

Your modem answers the phone and connects to the calling system. An alternative is to have your modem answer the phone automatically by setting the S0 register. (See the next section.)

D: Use this command to tell your modem to dial a phone number. The D command tells the modem to stop interpreting other commands, dial the number indicated, and wait for a connection. There are several modifiers that you can use after the D. First, you can specify either *T* or *P* to indicate tone or pulse dialing, respectively. Next, you can use the characters 0 through 9, *, and # to indicate the number to be dialed. Finally, you can use a comma (,) to specify a short pause. For example, to dial the number 987-6543, enter

AT DT9876543

To dial 9, followed by a pause, followed by the number 1-805-123-4567, enter

AT DT9,18051234567

If you need a longer pause, use more than one comma:

```
AT DT9,,,18051234567
```

Notice that there are no spaces within the command. However, most modems will ignore hyphens and parentheses; you can use these characters to make the number more readable:

```
AT DT1-(805)-123-4567
```

Once the D command is processed, the modem waits for a connection. If there is no connection within a specified time, the modem cancels the D command and returns to command mode. (If you want, you can change the time that the modem waits before canceling a call by modifying the value of register S7.)

Alternatively, you can deliberately abort a D command by typing any character before a connection is made. Here is an example: You have just entered a D command and you suddenly realize that you specified the wrong phone number. Press any key to abort.

E: As you type commands, it is convenient to see them displayed on the screen. The command:

```
AT E1
```

tells the modem to do just that. If, for some reason, you want to turn off command echoing, enter:

```
AT E0
```

Normally, you would not use E0, but your software might.

H: This command enables you to control the switch hook. This is analogous to hanging up the phone or taking the receiver off the hook. The H0 command hangs up the phone. The H1 command goes "off-hook". Just like a telephone, when you enter H1 and the modem goes off hook, you will hear a dial tone. This is not something you would normally do. However, you might use H1 to manually disconnect from a remote computer. As a convenience, the default is H0. Thus, you can hang up the phone by merely entering

```
AT H
```

L, M: The next two commands control your modem's built-in speaker. The M command controls whether the speaker will be on or off. M0 turns the speaker off. M1 turns the speaker on but only when the modem is dialing and connecting. Once the connection is established, the speaker goes off. This is the usual setting. M2 keeps the modem on at all times. If you want to hear what data communication sounds like, use M2. (You will probably get tired of it pretty soon and go back to M1.)

The L command sets the speaker volume (loudness). Both L0 and L1 set low volume; L2 sets medium volume; L3 sets high volume. Obviously, the actual loudness depends on your particular modem. Some modems have a volume control knob, just like a radio. Some of these modems do not implement the L command.

V: Whenever you enter a command, the modem sends back a result called a return code. If your modem is echoing (E1), the return code will be displayed on your screen. Normally, you would want the return code to be displayed as words. This is what the V1 (verbose) command does. The V0 command returns numeric codes. A program may set V0 so that it can test for a numeric return code after sending a command to the modem.

&W, Z, &F: These three commands enable you to save and restore a profile. Most modems have nonvolatile memory that retains its data when the power is turned off. At any time, you can use the &W command. This writes all the current parameter settings and register values—a profile—to the memory. The Z command recalls the profile.

The &F command restores the settings to the built-in factory defaults. &F is useful when you want to set everything back to a known value.

It is important to appreciate the difference between the &F and Z commands. &F restores the factory default settings. Z restores the profile that you have previously saved with an &W command.

Some modems do not have nonvolatile memory. For such modems there is, of course, no &W command. The Z command resets everything to reasonable values controlled by the modem's internal software. This may or may not be the same as &F.

&C: At certain times, the modem sends a signal to the computer to tell it that a carrier from the remote modem has been detected. This signal is called the DCD, or Data Carrier Detect Control. The &C command determines when this signal is to be sent. &C0 tells the modem to send the DCD signal continuously. &C1 tells the modem to track the actual state of the carrier. With &C1, the DCD signal is sent only when the carrier is actually detected.

+++ The Break Signal: There may be a time when you will want to deliberately change from data mode to command mode. For instance, say that you have logged out of a remote system but its modem did not disconnect you. You can't disconnect yourself by entering a command as your modem is still in data mode.

The solution is to type the break signal, three plus signs in a row (+++). The modem will change to command mode and you can enter an H command to hang up. The actual characters that you type, in this case plus signs, are called escape characters.

You might ask: What if, in the course of my work, the characters +++ happen to get sent over the modem? After all, this sequence might appear in a data stream. Will the modem stop what it is doing and go into command mode? The answer is maybe. (See the discussion on register S12 in the next section.) If this becomes a problem, you can change the escape character by modifying the value of register S2. (See the next section.)

## The Registers

Registers are built-in storage locations that hold numeric values. Each register is known by an identification number. Although some modems have many tens of registers, you can only count on the first thirteen (0 through 12) as being standard.

Most of the time you will not want to concern yourself with register settings. However, there are a few that are useful. Table 21.4 is a summary of the standard registers and what they contain. Following the table is a brief discussion of each register. Be aware that some of the defaults may vary from modem to modem.

The only registers that you are ever likely to change are S0, S7, and S11.

Table 21.4. Modem Registers.

| Register | Default | Description |
| --- | --- | --- |
| 0 | 0 | Answer on ring number |
| 1 | 0 | Count of incoming rings |
| 2 | 43 | The escape character |
| 3 | 13 | The carriage return character |
| 4 | 10 | The line feed character |
| 5 | 8 | The backspace character |
| 6 | 2 | Wait time before dialing |
| 7 | 30 | Wait time for carrier after dialing |
| 8 | 2 | Pause time for comma when dialing |
| 9 | 6 | Wait time to connect after carrier detect |
| 10 | 14 | Wait time to disconnect after carrier loss |
| 11 | 95 | Time delay between touch tones |
| 12 | 50 | Break signal guard time |

S0: Register 0 controls whether or not the modem answers the phone automatically. This facility is called auto-answer. With S0=0, auto-answer is disabled: the modem will not answer the phone unless you enter an A command.

To enable auto-answer, set S0 to a number greater than zero. The modem will answer the phone after that many rings. For example, the usual auto-answer command is S0=1, which tells the modem to answer after only a single ring.

S1: Register 1 is a read-only register that is used by communication programs. When the phone is ringing, S1 contains the number of rings that have been detected so far. At all other times, S1 is set to zero.

S2: Register 2 contains the ASCII code number (in decimal) of the escape character. This is the character that must be typed three times to tell the modem to switch from data mode to command mode. The default is character number 45, a plus sign. Normally, you would not change this setting.

S3, S4, S5: These registers let you change certain default characters that are used in command mode. The registers contain the ASCII code number (in decimal) of the carriage return character (S3), the line feed character (S4), and the backspace character (S5). The defaults are S3=13, S4=10, S5=8. Normally, you would not change any of these settings.

S6: Register 6 contains the length of time, in seconds, that the modem will wait after going off-hook before starting to dial. This delay is to give the telephone system time to detect the off-hook condition and apply a dial tone. The usual default is 2 seconds. Normally, you would not change this setting.

S7: Register 7 contains the length of time, in seconds, that the modem will wait for a valid carrier tone to be sent from a remote modem. If, after dialing a number, your modem is giving up before the remote system has time to answer, you may want to increase the value of S7. (You may also have to tell your communications program to allow more time before giving up.) The usual default is 30 seconds.

S8: Register 8 contains the length of time, in seconds, that the modem will pause each time it encounters a comma in the dialing sequence. The default is 2 seconds. Normally, you would not change this setting.

S9: Register 9 contains the length of time, in tenths of a second, that the modem will wait, after a carrier is detected, before connecting to the phone line. The default value is 6 (0.6 seconds). Normally, you would not change this setting.

S10: Register 10 contains the length of time, in tenths of a second, that the modem will wait, after a carrier is lost, before disconnecting the phone line. The default value is 14 (1.4 seconds). Normally, you would not change this setting.

S11: Register 11 contains the length of time, in milliseconds (thousands of a second), that the modem will pause between successive touch tones when dialing. The usual default is 95.

If you want to speed up your modem's dialing, set S11 to a smaller number. The usual minimum allowable value is 50. Try S11=50. If it works, the modem will dial very quickly. If it doesn't work, try a larger value.

S12: Register 12 contains a length of time, in 1/50 of a second (20 milliseconds), referred to as the escape sequence guard time.

As you recall, the break signal consists of three escape characters in a row. This signal causes the modem to switch from data mode to command mode. The default escape character is + (the plus sign). A problem can occur if the data stream happens to contain the character sequence +++.

To prevent unwanted break signals, the modem will not recognize a sequence of three escape characters unless they are preceded and followed by a time delay. This is the guard time. The default value is S12=50, which is 1 second.

That is, the characters +++ will not act as a break signal unless they are preceded and followed by a delay of 1 second. Normally, you would not change this setting.

# Communications Speed

Communications speed is measured in terms of how fast data is transmitted. As you would expect, the speed of a modem is usually expressed in bits per second, or BPS. As you also might expect, for a communications system to work, both modems must be transmitting and receiving at the same speed. Thus, there are standard speeds that modems use. They are 2400, 9600, 14400, and 28800 BPS. The latter two speeds are usually written as 14.4K and 28.8K BPS, respectively.

> **Note:** Incidentally, as I explain back in Chapter 15, when K is used to describe bytes of memory, it means 1024. However, when we use K for the speed of communications, we mean exactly 1000.

Two very slow speeds, 300 BPS and 1200 BPS, are obsolete and are rarely used anymore. The speeds you will generally see are from 2400 to 28.8K BPS, although even 2400 BPS will be largely antiquated by the time you read this.

If you want to approximate the speed of a modem in characters per second, divide the BPS value by 10. As you know, a character (1 byte) is stored using 8 bits. We can throw in the other 2 bits because there is some overhead.

For example, a 9600 BPS modem transmits about 960 characters per second. Bear in mind that this is only a rough estimate. The actual value can vary drastically depending on the software you are using, the quality of the phone connection, and whether data compression is being used.

> **Note:** Aside from "BPS," there is an older term, "baud," that describes the speed of a modem. With PCs, these two terms mean the same thing. That is, we can talk about a 9600 BPS or 9600 baud modem.

# Modem Hardware: Standards and Speeds

One of the key specifications of a modem is its maximum data transfer rate. The transfer rate is specified in what is called a baud rate. For modern modems, the baud rate is equivalent to a bit rate or the number of bits that can be transmitted per second. For the high-speed modems the baud or bit rate is specified in kilobits/second, where *kilo* means 1000s of bits. Thus a 14,400 bit/second modem is the same as a 14.4 kilobits/second modem. Since PCs use what is called asynchronous transmission protocols, each byte or 8 bits of information is packaged in a 10- to 12-bit data block for transmission. A good rule of thumb is to assume that the character or byte transfer rate is the baud or bit rate divided by 10. The data transfer rate can be significantly lower than this value if either a 12-bit data block is used (Parity is added and two stop bits are used), or the PC cannot feed data to the modem fast enough.

Disregarding the PC for the moment, the maximum speed of a modem is governed by several factors, including transmission quality of the voice grade circuit, noise levels on the circuit, the sophistication of the modulation/demodulation scheme, and its ability to deal with transmission quality and noise. Generally speaking, the fact that the phone line uses unshielded copper wire is not the factor limiting transmission speeds. Considering that digital data can easily be transmitted over voice-grade copper wiring at data rates of over 100 megabits/second in LAN environments and at speeds of over 1.544 megabits/second for distances of over several miles with the new ADSL (Asymmetric Digital Subscriber Loop) technology. Surprisingly, the bottleneck is in the digital portion of the modern telephone switching network. Modern telephone switching systems convert the analog voice signal to digital signals to enhance switching using digital computer technology. This process converts the audio signal to a 64 kilobit/second digital channel. This 64 kilobit/second channel uses 8 bit sampling at a rate of 8 KHz. For a frame of reference, modern audio CDs uses a sampling rate of 44 KHz with 16-bit samples. Passing complex modulated signals through this 64 kilobits/second system severely limits the maximum data rate achievable in a telephone switching network. To overcome this limitation, new all-digital services such as ISDN (Integrated Services Digital Networks) are being installed that support both digital voice and data on the same phone line. ISDN will be covered in more detail later.

# Modem Standards and Specifications

Typically, modems are referred to by their speed and the standards that they support—for example a V.32 (Standard) and 9600 baud rate (speed) modem. In this section I explain how the speed and standards define a modem. Before two modems can communicate over the voice network, they must use compatible modulation/demodulation schemes. For a number of years the old Bell Telephone company set the standards for modem compatibility in the United States. Unfortunately, they were not compatible with standards used in other countries. International data communications was difficult to impossible. The European countries set up a standards group called the CCITT (Comité Consultatif International Télégraphique et Téléphonique). This standards organization was eventually placed under the authority of the United Nations and renamed the International Telecommunications Union (ITU). Most modern modems support the older Bell standards and the newer CCITT and ITU standards. Along with these official standards, some industry *de facto* standards were developed. These *de facto* standards were usually the result of a specific modem manufacturer introducing a new modulation/demodulation scheme before international standards were complete in an attempt to gain a competitive advantage. One should be very careful when purchasing modems that implement nonstandard or *de facto* standard data rates and modulation schemes. First, these modems may not be able to communicate with other modems at the same data rates. Secondly, the *de facto* standards tend to become obsolete very quickly when official standards are available. For example, the 19,200 baud rate V.32terbo, and the 28,800 baud rate called V.fc (V.FAST) are not official standards and may not work with other modems supporting official standards.

Most modern modems will attempt to communicate at the highest data rate selected and supported, and will automatically fall back to older standards and slower data rates when line conditions or incompatible modulation/demodulation schemes are encountered.

# Modems That Support Both Data and Fax Transmission

With the ability to send and receive digital data, it was a simple step to the transmission of images. Images could easily be digitized and transmitted as digital data using any of the modulation/demodulation schemes. As with modulation/demodulation schemes, the two modems needed to use compatible image scanning methods, data formats, communications protocols and data compression/decompression schemes. A group of analog-based standards were developed supporting different image resolutions and data rates. Early analog standards, called Group 1 and Group 2, were slow and supported transmission speeds of approximately 3 minutes/page. In 1980 the CCITT adopted an all-digital standard that supported data rates up to 14,400 bits per second and resulted in full-page transmission rates of 20 seconds/page. The Group 3 standard did not set a specific speed for fax transmission but allowed a variety of speeds. On most fax/modem products, the fax transmission speed is higher than the data transmission speed. This is because the fax transmission is primary half duplex (one way at a time), allowing use of the full-line bandwidth for one-way transmission. Fax transmission speeds are defined by standards separate from data standards, even though a modem device can support both data and fax transmission and reception. The latest ITU V.34 standard for data rates up to 28,800 bits/second will also support fax rates at this same speed. Just like data modems, fax modems will fall back to facilitate communications with slower products supporting older standards.

Table 21.5 is a summary of the most common data modem standards. The table indicates the standard name or number and the maximum data rate supported by the standard.

Table 21.5. Data Modem Standards and Transfer Speeds.

| Modem Standard Designation | Speed | Duplex Mode |
|---|---|---|
| Bell 103 | 300 BPS | Full Duplex Transmission |
| Bell 212 | 1200 BPS | Full Duplex Transmission |
| CCITT V.21 | 300 BPS | Half Duplex Transmission |
| CCITT V.22 | 1200 BPS | Full Duplex Transmission |
| CCITT V.22bis | 2400 BPS | Full Duplex Transmission |

| Modem Standard Designation | Speed | Duplex Mode |
|---|---|---|
| CCITT V.32 | 9600 BPS | Full Duplex Transmission |
| CCITT V.32bis | 14400 BPS | Full Duplex Transmission |
| V.32terbo | 19200 BPS | Full Duplex Transmission |
| V.Fast (V.fc) | 28800 BPS | Full Duplex Transmission |
| CCITT(ITU) V.34 | 28800 BPS | Full Duplex Transmission |

Note: BPS stands for Bits Per Second

The V.32terbo and V.FAST (V.fc) modems standards are industry de facto standards and were produced by companies before the CCITT or the ITU-generated official worldwide standards for these data rates. These standards are not widely used and will likely be replaced by the official worldwide CCITT V.34 standard. In general, I would avoid modems that implement de facto industry standards.

Table 21.6 summarizes the fax standard designations and their associated data rates. A fax/data modem is designated by both a data standard and a fax standard. All of the fax standards are relative to the Fax Group 3 protocol standard. A Group 4 standard has been developed that supports significantly higher resolutions; however, it applies to and requires high-speed digital lines services such as ISDN or switched 56 services described later in this chapter.

Table 21.6. Group 3 Fax Standards and Data Rates.

| FAX Standard Designation | Speed | Duplex Mode |
|---|---|---|
| CCITT V.21 | 300 BPS | Half Duplex Transmission |
| CCITT V.27 | 2400 BPS | Half Duplex Transmission |
| CCITT V.27ter | 4800 BPS | Half Duplex Transmission |
| CCITT V.29 | 9600 BPS | Half Duplex Transmission |
| CCITT V.17 | V.29 Rates and 14400 BPS | Half Duplex Transmission |
| BPSCCITT X.XX (not fully defined) | 28800 BPS | Half Duplex Transmission |

# Making Sure the Data Gets Through Correctly

Like many things, modems and the public-switched telephone network are not perfect, so data transmission on modems is not error-free. Depending on the quality of the line and the associated noise levels, data can easily become garbled or even lost. Early modems provided no means to detect or correct corrupted or missing data. As a result, several error detection and correction protocols were developed and implemented in the PC's system software. These protocols were primarily devised to send and receive PC files containing binary information. They typically sent blocks of data with overhead added to detect missing or corrupted blocks. Error recovery normally entailed resending the entire block of data in error. Some of the more common system level file transfer protocols that implemented error detection and error correction features are Xmodem, Xmodem CRC, Xmodem-1K, Wxmodem, Ymodem, Ymodem-g, Zmodem, and Kermit. Most of these protocols use a software-generated checksum or Cyclic Redundancy Check (CRC) value that is transmitted with each data block. On reception of the data block, the check-sum or CRC is recalculated and compared with the value sent. If an error is detected, the entire block is re-sent. Some protocols also add a block count to ensure that blocks are not missing or received out of order. To perform a data transfer using these protocols, the two systems must be using the same protocol.

To modem manufacturers, a natural extension to the modem's capabilities was to include error detection and correction facilities. An early adopter of integrated error detection and correction was the modem manufacturer Microcom. Microcom devised a whole series of standards call MNP (Microcom Networking Protocols). MNP classes 1 through 4 are various protocols adding error detection and correction to modems. The error correction and detection protocols are speed-independent and can be used with all of the modem data rate standards. Some versions of the MNP protocol also provide a degree of data compression because of the error detection protocol used. To support a worldwide error detection and correction protocol, the CCITT developed a new standard called V.42. This is a state-of-the-art error detection and correction protocol that has gained wide acceptance and is implemented in most modern modems. Table 21.7 lists the MNP and CCITT error detection and correction protocols often supported in modern modems.

Table 21.7. Modem Error Detection and Correction Protocol Standards.

| Standard Designation | Description |
| --- | --- |
| MNP 1 | Microcom Network Protocol Level 1 |
| MNP 2 | Microcom Network Protocol Level 2 |
| MNP 3 | Microcom Network Protocol Level 3 |
| MNP 4 | Microcom Network Protocol Level 4 |
| V.42 | CCITT (ITU) Error Detection and Correction |

# Data Compression/Decompression Protocol Standards For Modems

Data transmission speed can be increased substantially if the information to be sent is first compressed. Many PC data types and files are easily compressed because of the repetitive nature of their contents. As with error detection and correction, data compression and decompression was performed in the PC using system software. Numerous protocols were developed. Some worked better on certain data types than others. Often, error detection and correction functions were combined with data compression/decompression. Again, it was natural to incorporate compression/decompression features directly in the modem. Microcom developed and promoted additional MNP standards for modem-based compression/decompression of digital data. Later the CCITT developed a worldwide data compression/decompression standard called V.42bis. The state-of-the-art compression/decompression standard can achieve a compression ratio of up to 4 to 1 on some data types. Effective data transmission rates of up to four times faster than the actual data rate of the modem can be achieved. For example, the new CCITT V.34 modem with a data transfer rate of 28.8 kilobits/second can achieve effective data rates of up to 115.2 kilobits/second.

With data compression, the modem output transfers data at a maximum rate of 28.8 kilobits/second; however, the input to the modem may see a data rate as high as four times this value (115.2 kilobits/second). This means that the PC software and hardware COM ports must deal with this much higher data rate! The PC's COM port or the COM port inside a modem board must be able to support this data rate, but many of the earlier PCs and modems use COM port serial chips that cannot. PCs with older chips like the NS8250 or the N16450 may not be able to keep up. Newer PCs use a serial COM port device called the NS16550 UART (Universal Asynchronous Receiver Transmitter) chip. This chip supports data rates up to 115.2 bit/second and has built-in FIFO memory. The FIFO (First In First Out) memory significantly reduces the software overhead when transmitting and receiving high-speed serial data on the PC's COM ports.

Table 21.8 summarizes the most popular modem data compression/decompression standards.

Table 21.8. Modem Data Compression/Decompression Standards.

| Standard Decryption | Max. Compression | Ratio |
| --- | --- | --- |
| MNP 3 * | Microcom Networking Protocol Level 3 | 1:1.16 |
| MNP 4 * | Microcom Networking Protocol Level 4 | 1:1.2 |
| MNP 5 | Microcom Networking Protocol Level 5 | 1:2 |

*continues*

Table 21.8. continued.

| Standard Decryption | Max. Compression | Ratio |
|---|---|---|
| MNP 7 | Microcom Networking Protocol Level 7 | 1:3 |
| V.42bis | CCITT (ITU) Compression Standard | 1:4 |

Note: MNP levels 3 and 4 were primarily error detection and correction protocols that also resulted in limited data compression/decompression features.

Microcom has also developed a number of additional standards that improve the connection efficiency and operation under adverse conditions. These standards are known as MNP Levels 6, 9, and 10.

# Synchronous and Asynchronous Transmission Modems

Most PC communications applications use asynchronous data mode in data communications applications. The PC's serial COM ports only support asynchronous data transfers. This is the data format that is sent between the PC's COM port and the modem, and the signal that the modem modulates for transmission on the telephone line. Each character or byte of data to be transmitted requires 2 to 4 additional framing bits. Thus to send 8 bits of data, 10 to 12 bits are transmitted. Asynchronous data transmission is not very efficient since up to 4 out of the 12 bits transmitted are overhead for each byte or 8 bits sent. Note that the asynchronous data contains no clocking information. Just data is sent. Each end of the communications link must mutually agree to the baud rate (1/bit cell time) before communication can occur. To extract the data from the asynchronous frame, a 16 to 32 times local clock is used to sample each data cell. The cell timing samples are started by the leading edge of the start bit. Any small error in sample timing or data cell times is accumulated over the frame, making asynchronous data difficult to properly recover at high speeds.

An alternative to asynchronous data transmission that provides better efficiency and higher speeds is synchronous data transmission. With this scheme, the modem generates a transmit and receive clock signal that is used to synchronously clock data bits in and out of the modem or Data Communications Equipment (DCE) and communications adapter in the PC Data Terminal Equipment (DTE). A single bit of data is transferred on each clock cycle. This scheme has higher efficiency since the start, stop framing bit and parity bit are removed. This scheme is also much more reliable at high data rates than asynchronous data transfer; no 16 or 32 times data rate sampling clocks are required for high-speed data recovery. Synchronous data transmission has been used by larger computer systems for years. The larger IBM systems used synchronous data transmission to connect remote terminals to mainframe computers and to interconnect mainframe computers. IBM's SNA network (Systems Network Architecture) is primarily a synchronous communications network.

Synchronous data transmission does have some problems that are unique to this mode of data transmission. First, if data is to be transmitted and received using a synchronous clock, there needs to be some way of sending the clock along with the data so that it can be used to recover the data at the other end of the connection. Sending the clock as an additional data stream would consume too much of the connection's bandwidth. This problem is overcome by using a clever scheme of encoding the serial data stream so that the clock can be recovered from the encoded data. A special electrical circuit called a Phase Lock Loop looks at the encoded data and regenerates the original synchronous clock at the receiving end. If the data stream contains long blocks of 0's or 1's data, the phase lock loop cannot extract the clock. The encoding scheme typically used to solve this problem used is called NRZ (Non-Return to Zero). This scheme sends data state changes for every consecutive 0 or 1 detected in the data stream.

A second problem occurs if a continuous stream of data bits is transmitted; it is difficult to determine the byte boundaries during data recovery, since no start or stop framing bits are transmitted. To overcome this difficulty, data is sent in special packets. The start of a packet is defined by a flag, a special field of encoded clock and data bits that violates the clock data encoding scheme. Once this start flag field is detected, it is followed by a header field. This contains information defining the packet data type, length, and destination addresses. This field is normally two to three bytes in length. Following the header field is a block of data, normally 256 bytes in length, but the length can vary. Following the data block is a special 2-byte field that contains a CRC (Cyclic Redundancy Check) value. This value is unique for each packet sent and is used to check that the packet was transmitted and received without error. At the end of the CRC field is a second flag field that indicates the end of the packet. Even with the flags, header, and CRC fields, the overhead associated with synchronous data transmission is very low compared to asynchronous overhead. In asynchronous mode, a byte of data required at least 10 bits of data to send; thus, transfers are at best only 80 percent efficient. In synchronous mode, a 256-byte packet requires only 6 or 7 bytes of overhead to frame the data packet, so it has an efficiency of nearly 95 percent. Also, this packet scheme makes it easy to detect errors and recover blocks of data by simply retransmitting the block. This data framing scheme is called a Data Link Layer protocol. Two very similar data link protocols dominate. One is used by IBM and is called SDLC (Synchronous Data Link Control). The CCITT is promoting an international standard called HDLC (High-level Data Link Control).

The standard PC COM ports do not support synchronous data transmission. If synchronous data transmission is required on the PC, a special synchronous data port adapter board must be installed. Synchronous data transmission is likely to become more important in the future. All of the new high-speed digital network services, such as ISDN (Integrated Services Digital Network), are synchronous networks. Even though these networks can still handle the PC's asynchronous data, significant performance and reliability gains are realized when synchronous data transmission modes are used. Also, multimedia applications with audio and video prefer synchronous data environments where clock synchronous data guarantees sustained data rates with low error rates and low delays.

Synchronous modems operate at the same data rates as asynchronous devices, and often at much higher data rates when on special conditioned lines (Higher Quality Lines). They also conform to the same electrical interface standards (RS-232-C, V.35, and RS-449, 485, 530) as asynchronous modes. Since higher data rates are more common, the higher speed RS-449, 485, 530, and V.35 interface standards are more common on synchronous modems. The primary differences on these interfaces is the addition of the transmit and receive clock signals, and the electrical interfaces are designed to handle higher-speed signals sent over greater distances.

Synchronous modes have one other anomaly that is the result of their historical use. Originally, synchronous modems were used on leased lines which were always active and did not require call setup. Therefore, to make a dialed connection on most synchronous modems, a special dialing port is provided. Often the dialing port is simply a standard asynchronous port which accepts D.C. Hayes AT commands for call setup and control. Sometimes a special parallel port is provided on synchronous modems to support call setup and control. This parallel port sends dialing information as 4-bit codes to the modem. This parallel port interface is specified by the Electronics Industry Association (EIA) standard RS-366.

# New Modems Can Do More Than Just Send and Receive Data and Faxes

Not only have the data rates improved with newer modulation schemes, but other advanced features have been added to modems. Some of the more interesting features include Caller ID, voice over data, and voice recording and response.

## Caller I.D. (Incoming Caller Identifications)

One of the new services now available in many areas allows identification of the calling parties number before the call is answered. This service is called Caller I.D. or ICLID (Incoming Call Line Identification). The service is available for a small fee in most areas. Some legal challenges concerning privacy issues have delayed this service's universal deployment. The calling party's phone number and date and time are sent as low-speed data between the first and second ring on an incoming call. Many modems can now read this data and make it available to the PC, assuming the application software supports this feature. The data can be used to selectively answer calls, look up data on a caller before the call is answered, and record incoming call data. In many areas the Caller I.D. service can only report incoming calls in the local area. Caller I.D. is also an extra charge feature, adding cost to your phone bill.

# Modems That Can Talk to You

Most modems are now implemented with DSPs (Digital Signal Processors), or small special-purpose microprocessors, and can also easily handle digitized voice. (See Chapters 2, 3, and 25 for more information on DSPs.) By providing a path through the modem to the PC's data bus, digitized voice can be recorded or played back through the modem, simulating answering machine functions or providing voice prompts to automated phone applications.

# Voice-Over Data Modems

With the newer modems, the high data rates permit the simultaneous transmission of digital data and voice. The voice is transmitted as digital data and is usually compressed to keep the data rate as low as possible. Both Intel and AT&T have proposed standards for simultaneous transmission of both data and digitized voice-over modems. This is a necessary feature to support effective shared applications and video conferencing, in which simultaneous voice and data over a single phone line is highly desirable.

# High-Speed Digital Services, An Alternative to Modems

Most of the public-switched network is already fully digital. Routing of voice signals in telephone office switches and between switches is nearly 100 percent digital. Each voice signal uses a 64-kilobit data channel in the digital network. These 64-kilobit channels can be combined to support very high-capacity trunks between switches. The telephone companies and long distance carriers have offered business customers access to their digital networks as switched 56 service (56KB/second digital links) and as T1 services (1.544 megabits/second), digital channels. These high-speed digital services are typically used to connect mainframes between remote sites, interconnect remote LANs at remote locations, and provide video conferencing services. These services are relatively expensive, often costing as much as hundreds to thousands of dollars per month, depending on the distance and actual bandwidth purchased. Access to the power of these digital public-switched networks is simply beyond the average residential customer's grasp, but it is close. The only portion of the phone system that is not already fully digital is the short distance between your phone and the closest substation, often less than a mile. Elimination of this "last mile" bottleneck would make available to the masses a high-speed all-digital network with worldwide connectivity, and with no modems! Upgrading this last mile would be very expensive, particularly if the actual copper wire needs to be replaced with coax cable or fiber optic links. In the early 1980s, an all new digital service was proposed that used the existing installed base of analog voice grade wiring. The service was called ISDN or Integrated Services Digital Network.

# ISDN Basic Rate Interface Service

ISDN is not a new network but an enhancement to the existing public-switched telephone network that extends the existing digital structure to the subscriber, much like switched 56 services, but at a much lower cost. ISDN is actually a set of digital service offerings. The lowest class of service was called Basic Rate Interface (BRI). This service was intended to provide all-digital service to existing residential and business analog subscribers. It would use the existing residential copper wiring and would support a total bandwidth of 144 kilobits/second. The 144 kilobits/second channel was divided into two 64KB/second Bearer ("B") channels that could carry either voice and/or data, and a 16 kilobit/second "D" channel used to setup and control and maintain the calls. The BRI service provided what was called 2B+D service, referencing the two 64 kilobit/second Bearer channels and the D signaling channel. When the D or signaling channel is not being used, it can also be used to transmit packet data through a packet switching service provided by the phone company. Since the D signaling channel is always active, it can also monitor incoming calls at the same time an existing call is active. This "out of data channel" signaling enables many of the advanced call features of ISDN, such as call forwarding, call transferring, call waiting, call conferencing, access to call detailed statistical information, calling party identification, and so forth.

ISDN is intended to be an evolutionary step, not a revolutionary technology. Although ISDN BRI services use the existing copper wiring, both the central office switch and the phone or CPE (Customer Premises Equipment) need to be replaced. The cost of this upgrade process has slowed the acceptance of ISDN as a widely available service. In anticipation of wider deployment of ISDN, most central office switches are now ISDN-capable. BRI ISDN services are now available in most major metropolitan areas as island services. This means ISDN was available only for local area calls. Long distance ISDN data call support is just now becoming available. ISDN BRI service costs vary by phone company and service area, but costs from 1.5 to 2 times the costs of a standard analog line (about $20 to $60 per month). Still, it's a real bargain compared to the cost of older switched 56 and T1 services.

ISDN services are delivered to you over the same two-wire copper lines that provide analog phone service. This two-wire ISDN BRI interface is called a "U" interface. Once at your location, a special device called a network terminator (NT1) converts the 2-wire interface to a 4-wire "S/T" interface. This 4-wire interface can support up to seven attached devices at a distance of up to 3000 ft. Since two B channels are provided, any two of the seven devices can have simultaneous 64 kilobits/second voice or data calls active. Figure 21.4 illustrates a typical ISDN connection.

**Figure 21.4.**
*ISDN network and connection topology.*

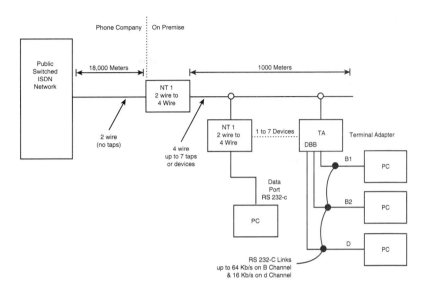

ISDN Network and Connection Topology

To use the ISDN BRI voice services, you need a new all-digital phone. These devices are still very expensive. If you don't need the advanced calling features of ISDN and plan to use only voice services, ISDN is hard to justify. ISDN will only make sense if you intend to use the digital data portion of the service. The device that converts the ISDN line to a digital data port is called a terminal adapter (TA). Some ISDN voice phones have built-in terminal adapters. It is a little like buying a phone and modem in a single package. A single terminal adapter can support two data ports, one for each B channel. It is like getting two modems in one package. The terminal adapter or phone/terminal adapter devices convert the 64 kilobit/second S/T interfaces to standard RS-232-C, V.35 or RS-449, 485, 530 modem interfaces. A PC's asynchronous COM ports can attach to the terminal adapter's ports just as though they were modems. The terminal adapters accept the PC's AT dialing commands and convert them to D or signaling channel commands, enabling existing modem software to operate without change in the all-digital network. The PC's asynchronous data is converted to synchronous data before it is sent on the 64 kilobit/second B channels.

The process of asynchronous to synchronous data conversion is called rate adaptation. Normally, a PC's 19,200 kilobit/second data rate is the maximum data rate that can be converted to the 64 kilobit/second channel. This poor asynchronous data to synchronous data conversion efficiency has also limited the acceptance of ISDN as competitive service over modems in PC applications. If the PC was using a synchronous communications port adapter, it would be able to take full advantage of the 64 kilobit/second bandwidth and the much greater efficiency and reliability of synchronous transfer modes. Unfortunately, most PC communications software is written for the PC asynchronous COM ports.

ssible to combine the two 64 kilobit/second B channels to create a 128 kilobit/second apacity on a single ISDN line. Unfortunately, the ISDN service cannot guarantee that the through the two B channels will be the same. Therefore, to use this capability the application ensure that data is synchronized so that it does not arrive out of order.

t as with modems, there are internal ISDN terminal adapters available for the PC. Several com-panies offer full ISDN terminal adapter voice and data functions on a PC adapter that connects directly to an ISDN line. Internal ISDN adapter boards are very competitive with standard high-speed modems, and, in theory, should cost even less than a modem.

At present the major problems with ISDN for PC applications are the high cost of terminal adapter equipment, low data rate for PC asynchronous software applications, and the limited deployment of ISDN capability. As new multimedia applications demand higher sustained data rates and greater reliability, ISDN offers a significant speed benefit.

# ISDN Primary Rate Service and Broadband Services

As mentioned earlier, ISDN is a family of services, and the BRI service is the lowest level of service. ISDN PRI(Primary Rate Interface) service offers access to two 64 kilobits/second channels on a single physical wire pair. Unfortunately, ISDN PRI service is much more expensive and not widely avail-able to nonbusiness customers. However, the high data rate available is capable of supporting live video transmissions using MPEG-1 compression and is more than five times the speed of the highest speed analog modes.

The highest performance service available in the ISDN service hierarchy is B ISDN or Broadband ISDN. B ISDN offers data rates from 155 megabits/second to 622 megabits/second. Of course these levels of service cannot easily be offered on the existing voice grade copper wire environment. This service must use coax or fiber optic transmission mediums and potentially could be used on the ex-isting cable TV systems. B ISDN uses the new ATM (Asynchronous Transfer Mode) protocols to transmit data. The ATM protocol breaks data into 53-byte packets and guarantees sustained data rates, with nearly error-free transmission and very low network delays. These feature are highly de-sirable in multimedia applications such as transmission of live video and audio data.

# Cable or Fiber Optics to the Home: The Super Highway Connection

With the desire to provide new interactive video services such as movies on demand, home shop-ping, games, and high performance online service, new high-performance residential digital services are needed. Both the cable TV industry and the telephone companies want to provide these new "Information Super Highway" services. The cable companies have the coax cable and fiber optic networks to the home, but have limited two traffic capability and switching capabilities. The phone companies have pervasive two connections and switching built into the basic network, but very low bandwidth capability. Many trials are now going on to help define the requirements and capabilities of high-speed digital networks to the home. Most services are planning coax cable or fiber optic links to the home with bandwidths of 3 to 6 megabits/second per subscriber. This data rate will be necessary to support reasonable full-motion compressed video. Obviously, once this capability exists in the home or office, PCs will be able to attach to these service ports and utilize the full bandwidth available on the network. There has been significant progress in transmitting high-speed data over existing copper wire voice grade lines in an attempt to provide reasonable video without coax or fiber optic links. Using a new technology called ADSL (Asymmetric Digital Subscriber Loop) is one way data rates of 1.5 to 6 megabits/second seem feasible over standard voice grade wiring. As with ISDN, the cost of deployment may slow its acceptance.

Some cable companies are now providing two way data and voice services over the existing cable networks through a device called a cable modem. These services are very limited and only support PC COM port data rates even though the networks are capable of much higher speeds.

# Satellite Communications: Direct PC

Since most multimedia applications are primarily receiving large data volumes versus sending large data volumes, most new high-speed digital networks are planning slower back channels. *Back channels* are communications from the PC back to the network or data provider. An interesting approach to providing high data rate multimedia service to PCs is now being planned by Hughes Network Systems using their Direct TV satellite technology, now called Direct PC. A PC would use a normal modem connection to request access to data such as images, software downloads, etc. The modem message would cause the requested data to be sent to a satellite via a master up link and then broadcast to the PC from the satellite.

As you can see, there are many new advancements in wide area data communications with all types of new services being planned with numerous experimental "trials" underway. These new high-speed services are needed to support the high performance needs of multimedia applications and expand the market for PC in the consumer markets. Exactly which technologies will succeed is still in question. High-speed analog modems are likely to remain the dominate wide area communications medium for the next few years with ISDN gaining popularity in major metropolitan areas. Then the battle will be between the phone companies with upgrade services and the cable companies with both entertainment and networking services. It will be very interesting to see how this all plays out in the future, but for sure, new high-speed multimedia wide area networks will emerge.

# ,s to Think About or Try

they were first developed, parallel connections were unidirectional, not bidirec-
.l as they are now. What sorts of capabilities were added to parallel devices because of
, evolution?

s a general rule, a parallel cable can move data faster than a serial cable. You'd expect
this, since a parallel cable can move an entire byte at a time. Why, then, did modems
evolve as serial devices? Moreover, why are common modems *still* serial devices, when
everyone is clammering for faster and faster communications?

3. Why do you suppose a parallel cable has so many wires dedicated to ground, while the
serial cable does not?

4. As a general rule of thumb, you should always set the Baud Rate or Communications Rate
setting of your terminal software to the fastest speed the software supports, regardless of
your modem's maximum external communications speed. Why does this practice make
good sense?

# 22

# How Programs Are Built

Among the most fascinating topics regarding the PC family is how programs are built. Whether you plan to create programs for the PC or just use PC programs and want to have the intellectual satisfaction of knowing what lies behind them, it's wonderful to understand the mechanics of creating a program. That's what I cover in this chapter.

I present a brief survey of how programs are constructed so that you get a feel for what's involved. For a deeper understanding of the steps involved in program building, you can turn to any number of specialty books on programming for the PC family.

# Programming Languages: An Overview

The reality of computers is that they carry out only the instructions they are given in machine language. However, most programmers don't write programs in machine language. They write programs in programming languages. Programming languages are the tools programmers use to create programs, just as English and other spoken languages are the tools writers use to create books.

If you want to understand programming languages, you need to know what they are like and how they are turned into machine language. In this section, I focus on the nature and characteristics of the programming languages. Later, I describe how the programming languages that humans use are translated into the machine language that the computer uses.

Perhaps the first thing you need to know about programming languages is the distinction between assembly language and all other programming languages, which are collectively called high-level languages.

Assembly language is essentially the same as the computer's own machine language, only it's expressed in a form that's easier for people to work with. The key thing about assembly language is that a programmer who writes in assembly language is writing out, one by one, the detailed instructions for the computer to follow when carrying out the program. You've had a few glimpses of assembly language before (for example, in the "Looking at an Interrupt Handler" section in Chapter 4, "Microprocessor Traffic Control").

The following listing is an assembly language subroutine that I use in my programs. It flushes the keyboard buffer. Flushing the keyboard buffer protects against a reply being typed in before the question is asked. If the buffer isn't properly flushed, the "y" key that you inadvertently struck while waiting for your computer to finish some job might be taken as a "yes" response to a potentially disastrous question like "OK to delete this file?" If you want to know what an assembly language subroutine looks like, complete with all its window dressing, you can learn a lot just by studying the following routine:

```
; FLUSHKEY - clears DOS keyboard input buffer
  DOS generic
```

```
            PGROUP  GROUP PROG
            PUBLIC  FLUSHKEY
PROG        SEGMENT BYTE PUBLIC 'PROG'
            ASSUME  CS:PROG
FLUSHKEY    PROC    NEAR
TEST:

            MOV     AH,11     ; check keyboard status
            INT     33        ; function call
            OR      AL,AL     ; if zero
            JZ      RETURN    ;   then done
            MOV     AH,7      ; read one byte
            INT     33        ; function call
            JMP     TEST
RETURN:

            RET
FLUSHKEY    ENDP
PROG        ENDS
            END
```

While machine language instructions appear in almost incomprehensible hexadecimal codes, assembly language codes are easily intelligible to experienced programmers. With just a little practice, you also can make sense of at least some of what's written in an assembly language program. For example, the first active instruction in the listing above is MOV AH,11, which tells the computer to move the number 11 into the register called AH. I don't claim that the meaning of MOV AH,11 should be obvious to anyone, but you can see how it shouldn't be too hard to get the hang of reading and even writing this kind of stuff.

To understand what assembly language programming is all about, you need to understand that there are essentially three parts to it. The first part is what people think of assembly language as being—individual machine language instructions written in a form that programmers can understand (like MOV AH,11). In this part of assembly language, each line of program code is translated directly into a single machine language instruction.

The second part of assembly language programming consists of commands that control what's going on, essentially setting the stage for the working part of the program. In this example, everything before MOV AH,11—for example, the line that reads ASSUME CS:PROG—is part of this stage-setting overhead. ASSUME CS:PROG indicates what's happening with the code segment (CS) register. (For information on registers, see Chapter 4.)

The third part of assembly language programming is a labor-saving device. Whenever a series of instructions is repeated, assembly language enables the programmer to abbreviate many instructions in a macro instruction, or macro for short. (Note that when I use "macro" here, I use it in a different sense than when I refer to spreadsheet macros or macros defined by DOS's DOSKEY command.)

This assembly language example doesn't include any macros, but it could. Notice that a pair of instructions (MOV AH,X and INT 33) appears twice with only a slight difference between them: the MOV has a different number in it. These instructions can be replaced with a single line of code, the macro, representing the pair of instructions. (The macro facility in assembly language can accommodate the difference between the two pairs of instructions by substituting a parameter that contains the appropriate number; macros can handle this trick and others that are much more elaborate.)

In a nutshell, these three elements—program instructions that are turned into machine language code, overhead commands, and macro abbreviations—are the heart of assembly language.

Writing a program in assembly language is an exceedingly long and tedious process. To give you an idea of just how many instructions are involved in a program (not just a brief subroutine, like the one listed above), a very early version of the main Norton Utilities program—a medium-sized program—contained about 20,000 machine language instructions. A large and complex program easily can consist of hundreds of thousands of separate machine language instructions. If such a program is written in assembly language, the programmer must write out all those separate commands, each of them intricate and each of them a potential bug. Think of it: if any of the words in this book are speled rwong, it doesn't necessarily destroy its usefulness, but any tiny mistake in a program can potentially render it useless. And, when a program written in assembly language has 500,000 or even 5,000 instructions (also called lines of code) in it, the possibilities for errors are enormous.

High-level languages—every computer language other than assembly language—are designed to eliminate the tedium and error-prone nature of assembly language by enabling the computer to do much of the work of generating the detailed machine language instructions. High-level languages rely on two ideas to make this possible. One is the idea of summarizing many machine language instructions into a single program command. This is the same idea as assembly language macros but applied in a broader way. The other idea is to remove from sight details that have to do with how the computer operates but that have nothing to do with the work you want to accomplish—for example, which registers are used for what.

If you ask a program to add three numbers, the program uses one of the computer's general-purpose registers, such as AX, BX, CX, or DX, but this information is not important to you. Assembly language programmers have to concern themselves with such details as which register to use for what (and using it consistently). High-level language programmers are spared that effort. High-level languages are characterized by the fact that they generate a lot of machine language code for each program command (a many-for-one saving of human effort that gives high-level languages their name) and by their avoidance of unnecessary detail (such as specifying which registers and memory addresses are used).

Assembly language and high-level languages have their benefits and drawbacks. I've focused on some of the drawbacks of assembly language—mainly that it requires more work to write because it requires more lines of program code and is more error-prone because it involves many details—but there are others. One important one is that assembly language requires more expertise to write than most high-level languages. However, it has important advantages as well. Assembly language programs are usually smaller and run faster because assembly language programmers use their skills to find efficient ways to perform each step. Also, using assembly language, programmers can tell the computer to do anything it's capable of doing, while high-level languages normally don't give people a way to use all the tricks the computer can do. Broadly speaking, you can say that high-level languages enable programmers to tap into 90 percent of the computer's skills, while assembly language enables them to use 100 percent, if they're clever enough.

So far, I've talked about high-level languages as a category, as if they were all alike. They do have a lot in common, particularly in contrast with assembly language, but there are many important differences among them. The next step is to look at the varieties of high-level languages, which can best be done by talking about the most important and widely used PC programming languages. There are literally hundreds of programming languages, and easily dozens that are used on the PC, but I only talk about an important few—BASIC, Pascal, and C—and use them to paint a representative picture of all high-level languages.

BASIC is the closest thing to a universal language for personal computers. Essentially, every DOS user has access to BASIC in one form or another. With IBM PC DOS before Version 5.0, the program is BASICA.COM. With MS-DOS, the program is GWBASIC.EXE.

The old forms of BASIC—BASICA and GWBASIC—have some major limitations. They run more slowly than other high-level languages and are severely limited in the size of programs and the amount of data they can handle. Also, from the point of view of professional craftsmanship, these forms of BASIC provide a clumsy set of tools. There are newer forms of BASIC that incorporate the features that programmers need to write well, but these features aren't available in the BASIC that comes free with DOS.

Fortunately, starting with Version 5.0, DOS includes QBasic, a new form of BASIC similar to Microsoft's QuickBASIC. QBasic comes with an online help system and an easy-to-use programming system. Its major limitation is that it cannot produce stand-alone executable programs. An optional compiler for QBasic programs is available for an additional price from Microsoft.

A relatively new version of BASIC that *can* indeed produce stand-alone applications is Microsoft Visual Basic. Visual Basic (notice that Microsoft has even changed the capital "BASIC" to a more friendly, "Basic") is so different, really, from any computer language that has come before it that it really requires some discussion at length to do it justice. You'll find exactly that kind of discussion in several of the good programming books on Visual Basic, including my own, *Peter Norton's Visual Basic 95 Programming*, from Sams Publishing. For now, however, you can get a quick inside look by reading the next section.

BASIC's strength is that it is easy to fiddle with and includes features that give users easy access to most of the PC family's special features, such as the capability to play music on the computer's speaker. (Most other high-level languages have only general features that can be used on any computer. To use the PC's unique characteristics, programmers using those languages have to use special methods, which usually means tapping into some assembly language. I discuss that later in this chapter.)

# Visual Basic

Microsoft's Visual Basic is a language like none we've ever seen before. Or, perhaps more accurately, it is a programming environment like none other. The underlying language itself is a new version of Microsoft BASIC, vastly improved-upon and expanded to provide a breathtaking range of new functionality. Have you ever wanted to program in Windows and produce programs that look as professional as anything that's actually for sale? Well, welcome to Visual Basic, where you can do exactly that.

Prior to the release of Visual Basic, programming in Windows was really nothing short of a nightmare. As you might expect, programmers who wanted to use windows, dialog boxes, and so on had to do a tremendous amount of work to bring these visual elements into existence. Of course, basic instructions to Windows like "draw a window of this size, here" were standardized. These standard instructions are called the Windows API calls, because when a programmer wanted to draw a window, for example, he "called" outside of his program to Windows to ask Windows to draw the window for him. On the one hand, this greatly eased the programmer's burden; imagine if each programmer had to come up with his own way of drawing a window on the screen! It also greatly helped users by creating a standardized interface, so that the menu bar would always appear at the top of the screen, the Minimize button would reliably work a certain way, and so on. On the other hand, it took hundreds of hours of study and practice for a programmer to master—indeed, to even understand—the best use of the many API calls available, and this relegated Windows programming to the professional and the very few serious hobbyists who were willing and able to dedicate themselves to that work.

Visual Basic has largely changed that. Using what was universally hailed as a revolutionary programming environment, Visual Basic allows programmers to graphically draw—using tools very much like those in drawing applications—graphical elements like windows; to graphically place elements like radio buttons, command buttons, menus, and so on; and to quickly link all of these elements together with very few lines of code. Visual Basic is able to provide this functionality through the use of a run-time interpreter (yes, as of this writing, Visual Basic is an interpreted, not a complied language) that translates the straightforward Visual Basic commands into an assembly-language version of the hellacious Windows API calls.

Visual Basic is such a step forward in functionality that even professional programmers use it—despite some industry disdain for the word "Basic"—to prototype sections of huge applications like Microsoft Word. This can dramatically decrease the prototyping cycle and allows programmers, graphic designers, and marketing people to try out a variety of possible interface techniques before dedicating tens of hours programming them in a more traditional language like C. That doesn't mean that Visual Basic itself isn't used to create final products. A built-in facility of Visual Basic can convert VB source files into executable EXE files that work just like anything you've ever purchased.

At the same time, as it now stands, Visual Basic remains an interpreted language, even after source files are converted to EXE files. The runtime interpreter library file, VBRUN300.dll (its current name, as of this writing), must be distributed with any VB program and has to be installed into the /WIN-DOWS/SYSTEM subdirectory of any computer on which a VB program is to be run. While the VB environment provides a setup program creator that vastly automates all of this, the fact that VB is interpreted means that it does execute slower than a comparable compiled language. For this reason, Visual Basic is unsuitable for many high-speed programming tasks, and professional programmers, to date, still rely on other languages—compiled or assembled languages—to produce most of their final products.

(Incidentally, if you're not familiar with the terms "compiled" and "interpreted" languages, stick with me. I'll talk about those concepts in depth under the upcoming "Translating Programs" heading.)

# Pascal and C

Two of the well-known languages ideally suited for professional programming are Pascal and C. Both have the features considered most useful in helping programmers create well-crafted programs that are reliable and easy to update. To see what each language is like, I've included two fragments of Pascal and C from my working programs. They give you a quick way to get a feel for what Pascal and C programs look like and how they are built. The following fragment is from a Pascal program:

```
{A Pascal Program to Count Words}
program count (output,input_file);
var
  input_file : text;
  i          : word;
  thousands  : word;
  units      : word;
  line       : lstring (255);
  alpha      : boolean;
  active     : boolean;
procedure report;
  var
    i, x : word;
  begin
    write (chr(13));
    if thousands = 0 then
      write (units:7)
    else
      begin
        write (thousands:3);
        write (',');
        x := units;
        for i := 1 to 3 do
          begin
            write (x div 100 : 1);
            x := (x mod 100) * 10;
          end;
      end;
  end;
procedure add_to_count;
  begin
    units := units + 1;
```

```
      if units >= 1000 then
        begin
          units := units - 1000;
          thousands := thousands + 1;
        end;
      if (units mod 100) = 0 then
        report;
    end;
begin
  thousands := 0;
  units     := 0;
  reset (input_file);
  while not eof (input_file) do
    begin
      active := false;
      readln (input_file,line);
      for i  := 1 to line.len do
        begin
          if active then
            begin
              if line 9i: = ' ' then
              active := false;
            end
          else
          if line 9i: in 9'a'..'z','A'..'Z': then
            begin
              active := true;
              add_to_count;
            end;
        end;
    end;
  report;
  write (' words.');
end.
```

This fragment is from a C program:

```
/* A 'C' Program to Draw a Double-Line Box Outline */
box ()
    {
      drow =  0; dcol = 1; vdup (205,78);
      drow = 24; dcol = 1; vdup (205,78);
for (drow = 1; drow < 24; drow++)
    {
      dcol =  0; vdup (186,1);
      dcol = 79; vdup (186,1);
    }
drow =  0; dcol = 0; vdup (201,1);
      dcol = 79; vdup (187,1);
drow = 24; dcol = 0; vdup (200,1);
      dcol = 79; vdup (188,1);
if (TEST)
    {
      if (swtchset ("X"))
        {
          int     i;
          unsigned x;
          char    s 940:;
          int     sl;
```

```
for (i = 1; i <24; i++)
  {
    sl =   0;
    decint (s,&sl,i,3);
    drow = i;
    dcol = 77;
    vstr   (s);
  }
drow = 24; dcol = 3;
x = spstart - splowest;
  decint0 (s,x);
  vstr   (" ");
  vstr   (s);
  vstr   (" stack used ");
dcol += 2;
  decint0 (s,poolleft);
  vstr   (" ");
  vstr   (s);
  vstr   (" pool left ");
dcol += 2;
  x = pool - poolsave;
  decint0 (s,x);
  vstr   (" ");
  vstr   (s);
  vstr   (" pool used ");
dcol += 2;
  x = poolends - poolend;
  decint0 (s,x);
  vstr   (" ");
  vstr   (s);
  vstr   (" heap used ");
  }
 }
}
```

Pascal and C have many similarities, including structural features that promote good programming practices. Both are very suitable for professional use in the building of large and demanding programs. Pascal finds its champions among those who have studied it in school (it is the language most favored for teaching computer science and, in fact, was originally created as a language for teaching rather than professional use) and those who have the inexpensive Turbo Pascal compiler. (Pascal will also be likely making a mainstream comeback because of the introduction of Delphi, a graphical programming environment, similar to Visual Basic, which is based on Object Pascal.) C has been favored by programmers who are looking for the utmost efficiency in a high-level language and who want their programs to be in tune with one of the directions in which personal computers are evolving. Later versions of the C language, including C++, for example, offer enhanced programmer tools, and expanded features.

I have used both Pascal and C in my own programming for the PC family. My Norton Utilities programs were first written in Pascal and later converted to C. I am fond of both languages. C is particularly good for writing programs that need to be tight and efficient and that work closely with the computer's BIOS and DOS. It's also worth noting that, for both the Pascal and C versions of my programs, I had to use assembly language subroutines to perform tasks that couldn't be done in the high-level languages. The assembly language subroutine shown in the beginning of this chapter is one of those. This illustrates an important point regarding the creation of professional-quality programs: often the best programming is done primarily in a high-level language (such as Pascal or C or even Visual Basic) with assembly language used as a simple and expedient way to go beyond the limits of the high-level language.

My experience points up some of the most important factors to be considered in the choice of a programming language. Usually a programming language is chosen on very pragmatic grounds: which languages the programmer already knows (or can easily learn) and how well suited the programming language is to the work that the program has to accomplish. Personal taste and convenience also play a major part in the selection of a programming language—and why shouldn't they?

So far, I have given you a short look at programming languages. What I look at next is how they are implemented—what turns them into usable machine language instructions that computers can carry out.

# Translating Programs

Before any program, regardless of what programming language it is written in, can come alive, it must be translated into the only thing a computer actually can execute: machine language instructions. There are three main ways for this translation to be done: interpreting, assembling, and compiling. Understanding each of these three ways of translating programs is important to your comprehension of what is going on in the computer as well as some of the important limitations of software and why some programs run fast and others quite slow.

Interpreting is a special kind of translation, in which the program essentially is translated into machine language on the fly, that is, as the program is being carried out. Interpreting on the computer is quite a bit like what's done at international conferences when the words of the person speaking are simultaneously translated into other languages.

The program to be interpreted (program P) is worked over by an interpreter program (interpreter I). When you use program P, the computer actually is running interpreter I, and interpreter I carries out the steps of program P. Interpreter I scans the text of program P and, step-by-step, performs the work of program P. In effect, interpreter I is translating program P word by word and step-by-step and carrying out (executing) the instructions on the fly.

Interpreting is inherently slow and inefficient, but flexible. It's slow because the translation is being done at the same time the work of the program is being carried out, so time is being taken up performing two tasks (translating the program and doing the program's work) instead of just one (carrying out the work). It's inefficient because the translation is done over and over again—not just each time the program is run but each time a step of the program is repeated. Because much of the power of programs comes from repeated steps (program looping, as it's called), plenty of instructions are repeatedly translated when a program is interpreted.

On the other hand, interpreting is flexible because an interpreted program can be adjusted, changed, or revised on the fly. Because the translation of an interpreted program is done continually, changes can be made on the spot and accommodated immediately.

I have plenty of experience with interpreted programs. The BASIC that comes with DOS and many programming applications, like spreadsheets and databases, is interpreted—as is the newer Microsoft Visual Basic.

There is an important technical issue concerning interpreted programs. When you run an interpreted program, such as any of the QBasic programs shown in Appendix B, "QBasic Program Listings," you think of that program as what's running in the computer. In a strict sense that's not true. From the computer's and the operating system's viewpoints, the program being executed is the interpreter, and what you think of as the program is just the data that the interpreter is working with. For a BASIC program, the actual program that's running is BASIC.COM, and the "program" is just data for the program. Of course, this is a very special kind of data—it's data that describes the steps that you want the computer to perform, which is exactly what a program is to users. Under most circumstances, this technical distinction is of no importance, but at times you may bump into some of its ramifications. For example, because the BASIC interpreter is designed to work with only a single 64KB data segment (recall the discussions of memory and data addressing in Chapter 15, "The Memory Workbench"), interpreted BASIC programs can't exceed a total of 64KB for both the "program" (which is technically data to the interpreter) and the program data.

With the newer QBasic, the same considerations hold, but the size limit for the program plus its data is extended to 160KB. The interpreter uses separate segments for each subprogram, the main data area, and certain types of arrays (lists of data elements). Thus, within the 160KB limit, each of these components can be up to 64KB long. Microsoft Visual Basic is more sophisticated still, providing the full 640K of conventional memory for a programmer's use.

Although BASIC, spreadsheet programs, and database programs often are interpreted, they don't have to be. While the normal form of these languages is interpreted, there are some compiled forms as well, and I come back to this later.

Interpreted programs, as I've said, are translated on the fly as the program is being run. The other two types of program translation—assembly and compiling—aren't done that way. Instead, they are translated in advance and permanently converted into the machine language. Assembly and compiling have more in common than they have differences, so I cover the similarities first.

Assembled and compiled programs are translated into machine language by the program developer before the program is used. For these programs, translation is part of the program development process. This means that the user of the program doesn't have to waste time translating the program and that translating software does not need to be available. Programs prepared in this way are complete in themselves. In contrast, interpreted programs only can be used if you have the interpreter as well. You only can run BASIC programs if you have the BASIC interpreter. (With the old versions of DOS, the interpreter is BASICA.COM [PC DOS] or GWBASIC.EXE [MS-DOS]. With DOS 5.0 and later, the interpreter is QBASIC.EXE.)

The people who design an assembler or compiler for any programming language must make many decisions about how the translator will work, including the exact details of what features the programming language will have. You may think of a programming language—say, Pascal—as being just one thing, but that's really not true. To anyone writing programs, a programming language like Pascal is the child of the marriage of two elements—the general form of the programming language (which defines the language's main form, its syntax, and principle features) and the specific implementation (which defines the specific features and the way they're used).

For these reasons, programmers don't really write programs in a general programming language. They write them using the characteristics of a specific implementation of a general programming language. Programs aren't written in Pascal or C; they are written in Turbo Pascal or Lightspeed C. Whether you are setting out to write your own programs or just want to understand how the choice of a programming language affects the programs you use, this is an important thing to know.

Most compilers and assemblers for the PC family follow a standard mode of operation that was created as part of the overall organization of DOS. In this standard operating mode, the translator converts a program from the language in which the programmer wrote it into the computer's machine language instructions. However, that doesn't mean the translated version is ready to use. Normally, it's not. Although a program has been converted into executable machine language instructions, the instructions aren't yet ready for action. (You see the reason for this and look at the additional steps that are needed to get programs ready in the next section.) Not all program language translators work that way, however. Some follow their own rules and have their own conventions for getting a program ready for work. The best-known examples of this are Borland's Turbo Pascal and Microsoft's QuickBASIC and Quick C. With these compilers, a program can be executed immediately after it's translated. The advantage of this is obvious, but there are real disadvantages as well. Translators like these go their own way and don't fit into the DOS world as comfortably as conventional ones do.

In the first section of this chapter, I note the distinction between low-level assembly language and the high-level languages (Pascal, C, BASIC, and so on). In assembly language, a programmer must write out the equivalent of every machine language instruction that the finished program will perform. In a high-level language, the programmer can write a program in terms of larger steps, steps that will be translated into many individual machine language instructions. In keeping with this distinction, the translators for assembly language are called assemblers, and the translators for high-level languages are called compilers. Depending on your focus, the distinction is either important or inconsequential. From one viewpoint, both are the same; they convert the programmer's high-level language program (the source code) into machine language instructions (the object code).

From another viewpoint, a compiler is given the very creative and demanding task of deciding what kind of machine language instructions will be used and making strategic decisions about how the computer's resources are to be used, for example, what the registers will be used for. On the other hand, an assembler performs a very mechanical and uncreative conversion of the programmer's instructions into the equivalent machine instructions. From this perspective, a compiler is a very complex beast, and there is enormous potential for differences in the quality of compilers (one compiler might generate very efficient code, while another could produce lousy code). These differences don't apply to assemblers.

When a programmer works with a compiler or an assembler, his or her source code is fed into the translator and checked for errors. If it's in workable shape, machine language object code is the result. You can identify any object code files that you might come across by their filename extension, OBJ. The object code is ultimately for use by the computer as a finished, executable program. For the programmer's use, the compiler or assembler displays error messages indicating flaws in the program (not logical flaws, or bugs, which are the responsibility of the programmer, but syntactic flaws, such as misspelled keywords and missing punctuation).

Because an assembly language programmer is working very closely with the computer's basic skills (its machine language instructions), an assembler gives the programmer lots of technical information about the results of the assembly. To give you an idea of what it looks like, here is the assembler listing for the assembly language program shown earlier:

```
                              ; FLUSHKEY - clears DOS keyboard input buffer
                              ; DOS generic
                              PGROUP   GROUP PROG
                              PUBLIC   FLUSHKEY
0000                PROG      SEGMENT BYTE PUBLIC 'PROG'
                              ASSUME   CS:PROG
0000                FLUSHKEY  PROC   NEAR
0000                TEST:
0000  B4 0B                   MOV     AH,11     ; check keyboard status
0002  CD 21                   INT     33        ; function call
0004  0A C0                   OR      AL,AL     ; if zero
0006  74 06                   JZ      RETURN    ;   then done
0008  B4 07                   MOV     AH,7      ; read one byte
000A  CD 21                   INT     33        ; function call
000C  EB F2                   JMP     TEST
000E                RETURN:
000E  C3                      RET
000F                FLUSHKEY  ENDP
000F                PROG      ENDS
                              END
```

One of the things an assembly listing shows is the exact machine language instructions in hexadecimal. Normally, a compiler does not give a programmer so much technical information; after all, one of the main purposes of using a high-level language is to avoid working with technical details. However, if a programmer wants to know more about the machine language code that a compiler is generating, most compilers can print out an assembly language equivalent of the object code that has been created. The object code listing enables an experienced programmer to evaluate the quality of the code the compiler generates and can be helpful in deciding which way of writing a program is most efficient.

Depending on how you look at the process of translating a program from source code to object code, you can think of compilers and assemblers as very different creatures or as minor variations on the same theme. Either way, compilers and assemblers are charged with the task of converting what programmers write into what computers can do. After that come the final steps of putting a program together into a working whole, and that's what I cover next.

# Putting Programs Together

One of the key elements in practical programming is the old principle of divide and conquer; any task becomes more manageable when it is broken down into smaller parts. Programming also works that way, so the process of program development has been set up in a way that makes it practical to break a program into functional, modular parts and then piece together the whole program from its parts. In this section, I cover the mechanisms that make it possible to put programs together from parts and how those mechanisms work.

Three things enable programmers to divide and conquer: subroutines, linking, and libraries. Subroutines, as you know, are relatively self-contained fragments of a program. In different languages they are known by different names. For example, in C they are called functions; in Pascal they are called procedures. They perform a particular part of the program's work, acting as a building block for the program. One of the key reasons for creating subroutines is to subdivide and therefore simplify the task of creating a program.

After a program is divided into logical parts, and those parts are made into subroutines, the next logical step is to remove the subroutines from the main program. After all, the point of subroutines is to reduce the logical clutter in a program by isolating work into discrete components. If you're going to sweep the subroutines off into a logical corner to tidy up the design and organization of the program, you may as well move them out of the way entirely. Programmers take the subroutines out of the program and treat them separately, including compiling or assembling them separately. This idea of separate compilation is a key adjunct to the idea of creating subroutines in the first place. Because the program is divided into logical modules, you may as well make them completely separate by putting the source code (what the programmer writes) into separate disk files for each module and compiling (or, in the case of assembly language, assembling) these files as separate items.

There are two main advantages to separating the subroutines from the main program. One is that it shortens and simplifies the source code of the main program. The other is that it makes the subroutines available for use by any program. If you had to keep your subroutines inside each program, then when you create a new program that could use some of the old subroutines, you'd have to copy the source code for the subroutines into the new program. By separating subroutines and compiling them separately, you keep them available for any program to use. You also save time and trouble by having to compile a subroutine only once.

The whole idea of separately compiled subroutines requires that you have a way of combining the different parts of a program into one piece. This is done in a process called linking and is performed by a program called LINK, which comes as a part of DOS. The process of linking is something like building models. In effect, a program that needs a subroutine named X has an empty slot marked X, and a separately compiled subroutine has the computer equivalent of a tab marked X. The job of the LINK program is to fit the two together.

Linking involves making all the connections between the pieces of a program to make them work as a whole. In the last section, I mentioned that compilers and assemblers generate their machine language instructions in a form called object code, which isn't completely ready to be run as a program. The reason for this is that object code is set up in the form that's needed for linking, with all the "tab" and "slot" markings. The job of LINK is to gather all the parts of object code, make the connections between them, and then output the results in a form that is ready to be run by the computer. Even when a program doesn't need any subroutine connections, standard DOS compilers and assemblers still translate their programs in the object code format.

You can see that creating a program involves two basic steps beyond writing the program in the first place: translating the program's source code into object code with a compiler or assembler and then converting the object code into a finished program with the linker.

It's worth pausing here to note that I'm talking about the standard DOS way of creating programs, which is used by most programming language versions. However, not every one follows the DOS standard. For example, the extremely popular Turbo Pascal and Quick C compilers go their own ways and avoid the use of object code and linking. Instead, this type of compiler creates executable programs, effectively combining compiling and linking into one step. This has the advantage of simplifying and speeding up the process of developing a program, but also eliminates much of the flexibility that comes with separate compilation and linking.

Another important example is the QBasic interpreter that comes with DOS (versions 5.0 and later). QBasic combines the speed of compiled programs with the flexibility of interpreting.

When you first load a program, QBasic immediately converts it into an intermediate, partially compiled, form. When you run the program, QBasic completes what is left of the compilation. Because a lot of the work has been done already, your program starts to execute almost immediately. When you make a change, QBasic reprocesses just the part of the program affected by the change—usually a single subroutine or less. All of this makes for an extremely fast program development environment.

However, QBasic has a significant limitation: It cannot create separate executable programs. You can run QBasic programs only within the QBasic environment.

Microsoft Visual Basic is something of a hybrid. While programs remain interpreted, the Visual Basic environment comes with a built-in facility for creating free-standing runtime programs. These must be distributed with the Visual Basic Runtime Library, however, through which VB program instructions are translated into executable commands as the program runs.

# Object Libraries

If you create lots and lots of subroutines, you will be faced with the problem of having lots and lots of object code files cluttering up your disks. There is nothing uncommon about a programmer developing dozens of subroutines, and for a large programming project or for a programming language that makes liberal use of built-in subroutines, the number easily can grow into the hundreds. For example, an early version of my Norton Utilities included approximately 175 subroutines and program modules, which is just too many to conveniently keep track of.

The solution to that practical problem is libraries of object modules. An object library is a file that can contain the object code for any number of program subroutines. After a subroutine is written, the programmer compiles (or assembles) the subroutine into object code and then uses a special DOS program called LIB, which takes the object code and stuffs it into a library with other subroutines. LIB makes it possible to gather the clutter of many subroutine object files into one tidy package— an object library file. You can identify any object libraries that you come across by their filename extension, LIB.

So far you've seen all the pieces of the programming puzzle. Now I put the pieces together so that you can see them in action. I run through a little example from my programming work to illustrate the main steps of the process.

I begin with the assembly language subroutine that you saw at the beginning of this chapter, FLUSHKEY. After FLUSHKEY has been written by the programmer (me), the programmer's source code is stored in a file named FLUSHKEY.ASM. Each programming language has its own standard filename extension for source code; for assembly language, it's ASM. To assemble FLUSHKEY, I use the assembler program named MASM (which is short for macro assembler) with a command like this:

```
MASM FLUSHKEY
```

This gives me an object file named FLUSHKEY.OBJ. Next, I can add FLUSHKEY to my object library, which I call OURLIB:

```
LIB OURLIB+FLUSHKEY
DEL FLUSHKEY.OBJ
```

Notice that the command line for LIB has a plus sign (+) in it. That's my way of telling LIB to add FLUSHKEY to the library. There are other operations that LIB can perform as well. You also see that, after adding FLUSHKEY to the library, I delete the object file because I no longer need it.

That takes care of subroutines. The next step is to compile and link a main program. For this example, I consider a program, called NU, written in the C programming language. The source code file for that program is called NU.C, and C is the standard filename extension for a C program. I have two choices for the C (I'm using Microsoft C) compiler. I can use one command to ask the compiler to call the linker automatically after compiling:

```
LINK C+NU,NU,,OURLIB
```

Or, I can use a separate command for each step:

```
CL -C NU.C
LINK NU.OBJ,,,OURLIB.LIB
```

To fully understand what's going on here, you have to know more about program building. However, even in this simple outline, you've seen the essence and all the key parts of how programs are built and put together.

In Chapter 26, I get into the business of snooping, tinkering, and exploring, and that includes snooping inside some of the programs that you use. It's another way of gaining insight into how programs are built. In the next chapter, I talk about one of the most important changes in the PC world ever, Microsoft Windows. Don't get me wrong. Windows certainly is not the best program around, but it solves many problems that have plagued PC users for years and is setting a new, widely accepted and much-needed set of standards. It probably is as important to you as DOS, so give the next chapter some time.

# Some Things To Think About or Try

1. In this chapter, I briefly mentioned the function of the LIB program. To manage a library well, LIB has to have a variety of skills. What are they? Work up a list of the separate functions that you think LIB needs to perform.

2. Batch command files are the key to combining program steps like the ones I've mentioned for building programs. Try your hand at writing a batch file to assemble a program and add it to an object library. Write another to compile and link a program. If you know how to use batch file logic, make your batch files adjust to any errors that occur.

3. As I explained earlier, the QBasic interpreter partially compiles your program before you start work. When you make changes, only small parts of your program have to be reprocessed. This makes for an especially fast and flexible working environment. Are there disadvantages to this system? Why do you think all language processors do not use these same techniques?

# 23

# Microsoft Windows: Role and Function

A cleaning product commercial of a few years ago coined a phrase that remains, in one form or another, part of our ongoing social chat: "I don't do windows." Some personal computer users still "don't do Windows"—although their numbers are quickly decreasing—because either the right applications aren't available or users perceive the environment as too restrictive or unfamiliar. Those who cut their computer teeth on DOS—or CP/M, UNIX, or other command-oriented operating systems— were slow to embrace Windows. I have to say that I still lean toward DOS as my favored operating environment, but I also use Windows—not necessarily because I want to, but because it doesn't make sense not to.

Since Microsoft Windows 3.0 hit the streets in the early summer of 1990, many software vendors have announced products to support this graphical user interface. The release of Windows Version 3.1, which includes many enhancements, has further fueled the growth of Windows-based applications. Windows for Workgroups and Windows NT added networking (and other refinements) to the Windows environment, further increasing its appeal to corporate America. (An interim release of Windows for Workgroups, Version 3.11, takes care of some reliability and speed problems found in previous versions.) Unfortunately, some people viewed Windows for Workgroups as too little because it doesn't provide a robust multitasking environment for some tasks, and Windows NT as too much because of its stringent hardware requirements. Enter Windows 95, Microsoft's latest entry in the Windows market. Now there are windowing environments for beginning, intermediate, and advanced users from the same source and with much the same interface.

Windows may be even more popular than users, buyers, and industry watchers predicted when Version 1.0 was first released. When Windows was first developed, it was competing with an entrenched GUI environment, the Macintosh, and the first few releases of Windows simply weren't as well done as the Apple Computer product. Besides, there weren't many applications that made use of the Windows interface. You could run programs in Windows, but there was little benefit.

Why has Windows become so popular? Windows-based programs simply are easier—*much* easier— to learn and use than conventional DOS applications. And, as most mainstream products—the ones most PC users already have and love—have joined the Windows ranks, the real power of computing is being made available to people who couldn't use it before. In fact, some Windows versions of products like WordPerfect are so popular that their vendors don't plan to release a new DOS version of the product, except to fix bugs.

I've saved the discussion of Windows until near the end of this book because this is primarily a book about PC hardware and how it works. I talked about DOS earlier because the operating system works so closely with the hardware as to be almost a part of it. But Microsoft Windows is also an important part of the changing PC world, and I feel any reader of this book needs to be comfortable with Windows as well as with DOS and the PC's hardware.

This chapter takes a detailed look at what Microsoft Windows does for you and your programs. It focuses on some of the standard services that the Windows can provide to an application. I also look at how Windows 3.1 and Windows for Workgroups 3.11 differ from Microsoft's newest release, Windows 95, forthcoming as I'm writing this. This isn't, however, an exhaustive reference guide.

Instead, it is a guided tour of the power that Windows in general, and Windows 95 in particular, puts at your command. The objective is to give you a feel for what Windows can do.

# What Is Windows?

Even if you have been using a PC with Microsoft Windows for a while, a clear definition of Microsoft Windows may elude you. Certainly, if your only experience with a PC is a DOS-level interface, understanding what the hullabaloo over Windows is all about can be difficult. Whether you already have installed Windows and are using it daily or are merely contemplating moving to the Windows environment, it is helpful to know a little bit more about this trend-setting software. This is particularly true as, after Windows 95 is released, new PC hardware will be sold almost exclusively with Windows 95 preinstalled, and with DOS all but absent. The decision to upgrade to Windows 95 will eventually be moot for non-UNIX PC users.

The earliest computer users were technical types who understood hardware and software design. They took to cryptic procedures and arcane commands easily. As computer power became available to a wider audience, however, users struggled with "computerese" and sought ways to ease access to applications. The Apple Macintosh (introduced in 1984) was the first business-oriented product to provide a natural, picture-oriented interface for the computer. The Macintosh operating system and other features were designed from the beginning with this graphical user interface (GUI) in mind.

A GUI is simply computer software, such as Microsoft Windows, that represents programs, procedures, and files as graphics symbols. Users interact with the computer by manipulating these symbols instead of typing discrete commands. Under DOS, the user has to remember where an application is stored and what its name is to start it. The reason that a GUI is so much easier to use is that the user doesn't have to remember anything except how to double-click to start an application. Windows provides a complete directory of all the applications the user can access; all the user need do is select one.

# Windows Evolution

Windows started out as little more than a task-switching environment. The initial 1985 release of Version 1.0 left a lot to be desired and its reception by the industry as a whole was, frankly, rather dismal.

The second version wasn't much better than the first. Version 2.0 of Windows—which appeared in 1987—didn't offer the GUI that people see today. In fact, it didn't even use the icons that most people associate with a GUI. This version of Windows provided a list of applications in text and not much more. In fact, it didn't offer much more than a menuing system. This was due in part to the memory restrictions and lack of horsepower provided by the 8086 processor. However, it still made DOS easier to use and enabled the user to start more than one task at a time (as long as the multiple tasks would fit in available memory). Windows 2.0 was a small but important step away from DOS. This version, like its predecessor, did poorly in the marketplace.

Microsoft introduced two other versions of Windows about this time; 80286 users could use all of their extended memory for applications by getting the Windows/286 version. Like its counterpart, this version offered task switching, not multitasking. The Windows/386 version—released in 1988—at least allowed the user to multitask applications. This wasn't the preemptive multitasking that provides a smooth transition from application to application that most people think about, but a cooperative multitasking that allowed one application to grab all the system resources if it wanted to. Think of cooperative multitasking as an honor system method of managing applications (and we all know how well the honor system works). Preemptive multitasking leaves Windows in charge, ensuring all the applications work together fairly. (See the "Cooperative Multitasking versus Preemptive Multitasking" section for a detailed discussion of this topic.) In other words, this version of Windows was a step in the right direction, but it was still a far cry from what Windows is today.

It was the 3.0 Version of Windows, which Microsoft introduced on May 22, 1990, that really got the ball rolling. This is the version that began to offer users a real reason for switching from DOS-based applications. Not only did Windows 3.0 offer enhanced memory support so that applications could do more, but it offered an attractive interface as well. (See Figure 23.1.) This is the first version that made extensive use of icons. It also offered the Program Manager interface that most people associate with Windows today. Most important of all, you could run more than one task simultaneously under Windows 3.0, a feat impossible with DOS alone. Of course, Microsoft had to make a few concessions to gain the support that Version 3.0 enjoyed. For example, Version 3.0 was the last version you could use on an 8088.

**Figure 23.1.**
*Windows versions 3.0 and above offer one of the things that users need to use a computer efficiently: a graphical user interface (GUI).*

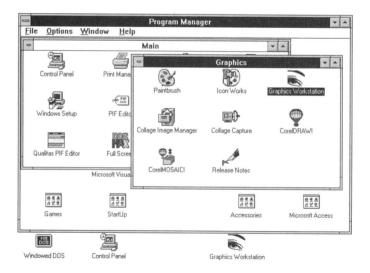

Even though the marketplace welcomed Windows 3.0 with open arms, users soon discovered problems. Most of the negative elements of Version 3.0 centered around the concessions Microsoft had to make for backward compatibility. For one thing, running Windows 3.0 in real mode meant that Microsoft could not make the system as reliable as they wanted it to be. (Remember our discussion of differences between real mode and protected mode in Chapter 3, "Brains: The Processors." In addition, you will want to read the section on Windows 95's and Windows NT's flat memory model in this chapter to get an idea of how this capability will affect you.) An operating system running in protected mode can intercept and deal with maverick applications that cause the system to crash. Using real mode drivers in some areas meant that Windows 3.0 safety net was pretty thin (or non-existent). One faulty application could cause a data-killing system crash. The biggest complaint that people had about this version, however, was its own inherent instability.

Another problem was the infamous UAE (Unrecoverable Application Error). Although Windows itself was responsible for some of these errors, they often had nothing to do with Windows itself but with the applications it ran. An application could try to grab a file handle to a nonexistent file—or some other system resource—and crash the system as a result.

Undaunted by these problems, Microsoft introduced yet another version of Windows. Version 3.1 offers even more to the user, but it's the hidden details that set this version apart from Version 3.0. The UAE disappeared in this version because Microsoft added methods for validating system requests. Every time an application wants to look at a disk file or perform some other task, Windows makes sure that task can succeed before it gives the go-ahead. This forced a lot of vendors to rewrite their software to actually look for potential problems before they requested a system service. Unfortunately, even with all these checks, some applications still violate system integrity. The result is a general protection fault (GPF). From a user point of view, the GPF doesn't look much different than the UAE did; both can cause the machine to freeze. However, Windows usually recovers better from a GPF. In addition, users see a lot fewer GPFs than they did UAEs. The GPF also shows that Windows at least recognized an error before the machine froze; the UAE always resulted from a failure to recognize a symptom. The difference means that Windows can now provide more information to a vendor in an effort to find and fix the source of a GPF. (This is why Windows 3.1 includes the Dr. Watson utility, which records the set of conditions that Windows detects right before a system failure.) Suffice it to say, Version 3.1 added a lot under the hood and forced developers to rethink their Windows programming strategy.

Microsoft also decided to provide a fully enhanced memory environment for Windows 3.1. For example, no longer does the user have to pay as much attention to the amount of actual system memory available for running applications. Windows 3.1 can use virtual memory, a method of using part of the hard drive to simulate RAM. (I discuss this in detail later). Microsoft uses part of this additional memory to provide enhanced driver support. A user can no longer run Windows on an 8088 by starting it in real mode because the 16-bit drivers need to run in protected mode. In addition, the extra memory allowed Microsoft to improve driver performance and the overall reliability of Windows. Needless to say, running everything in protected mode enables you to utilize all that memory sitting above the 1MB conventional memory boundary. Using protected mode also makes Windows 3.1 a little more stable than its predecessor. This version still has to call on DOS, however, to perform some tasks.

Now that Windows is entrenched in the corporate environment, certain failings have come to light. The biggest failing was the lack of good network support. I'm not talking about the big mainframe to PC connection here, but the small, intimate, Local Area Network (LAN) connections required for workgroup computing. These small groups of users don't have the monetary resources required to create a big network—what they really need something that allows them to share a few devices and some files. Windows for Workgroups solved this problem. A user can now create very inexpensive connections for a small group of people by installing a network card and some cable. This version also provides some simple network-related utilities like a meeting scheduler and an e-mail system. A peer-to-peer network that uses Windows for Workgroups may not provide the robust environment needed for enterprise computing, but it will work for a small company or other small organization.

This version of Windows also provides better reliability than its predecessor. For one thing, Microsoft provided many bug fixes to Windows-specific features. As a result of these bug fixes and the enhanced support provided by Windows for Workgroups, many pundits in the trade presses recommended that people switch to Windows for Workgroups even on stand-alone machines. Other than that, Windows for Workgroups provides essentially the same feature set as Windows 3.1.

Some people do use Windows for mission-critical applications. They want more reliability from Windows than either the 3.1 or Workgroups version can offer. For example, the reliability problems presented by the current Windows setup make it unfeasible to use as a database server. What if the server went down in the middle of a transaction? The results could be devastating, even in a workgroup setting. Windows NT solves this problem by getting rid of DOS altogether. It provides a totally new Windows environment that looks like the old one but runs completely in protected mode. Of course, Windows NT provides a lot of other features as well. For one thing, it isn't restricted to the Intel family of processors. The initial version of Windows NT came out with support for the Hewlett Packard Alpha processor as well.

Unfortunately, this new and improved version of Windows comes with a big price tag. Microsoft really designed NT as a server-based operating system. As a result, there is no way to run Windows NT with less that 8MB of RAM and a fast processor. Many users complain that the high hardware price tag just isn't worth the additional security that Windows NT provides. Enter Windows 95. This version of Windows doesn't rely on DOS for Windows application needs; all the Windows DLLs and supporting code run in protected mode. (Windows 95 does rely on DOS to run any DOS applications, to provide some low-level BIOS support on non-Plug and Play machines, and to support antiquated devices that use real mode drivers.) It also uses a subset of the Windows NT 32-bit programming interface and runs completely (except for real mode drivers) in protected mode. Not only does Windows 95 perform better, faster, and more reliably, but it sports a new interface as well. (See Figure 23.2.) Windows 95 represents a halfway point between Windows for Workgroups and Windows NT. It also represents the future of Windows. For example, Windows 95 is the first version of Windows to include Plug and Play as an integral part of the operating system.

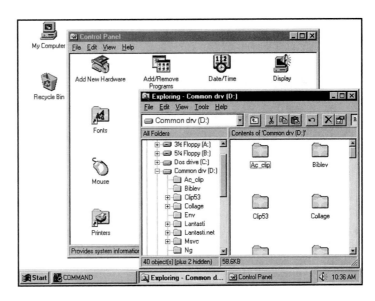

*Figure 23.2.*
*Windows 95 sports a new interface that should make life a lot easier for the novice user.*

# Why Windows Was More Successful Than OS/2 and GEM

Have you ever heard of the person who was at the right place at the right time? You could say the same thing about Windows. It was at the right place, at the right time, with the right features to make a difference. I hate to say it, but that's the big reason that OS/2 and GEM haven't succeeded like Windows has.

Technically speaking, OS/2 has a lot to offer and it had it to offer before Windows NT was even a glimmer in anyone's eye. The problem is that OS/2 came out at a time when users were unwilling to leave DOS for something completely different. The real need for a fully protected, secure environment just didn't exist. People wanted the familiarity of the DOS prompt.

Windows offered people the DOS prompt. It ran on top of DOS. Users could choose to start their machines and simply leave DOS running. They could also start Windows, run it for a while, then go back to their old familiar standby, DOS. Even though OS/2 came out with the protected features that people want today long before Windows NT was out, Windows was entrenched in corporate America first. Upgrading to Windows NT from Windows 3.1 is a lot easier than learning a new operating system.

If OS/2 was too early, then GEM was too late. By the time that GEM came on the scene, Windows was already deeply entrenched—too entrenched for a startup to divert anyone's attention. Even though GEM offers features that the average Windows user would like to have, it doesn't offer the level of application support that Windows users have come to expect. It's a matter of too little, too late.

# Windows Modes and Memory

Any discussion of Windows and its evolution has to include the modes of operation that Windows supports. Previous versions of Windows supported three modes: real, standard, and 386 enhanced. The real mode of operation went out with the 8088 and Windows 3.0. It's just too limited to perform any useful work, so I won't waste time talking about it here. Suffice it to say that real mode is limited to a mere 1MB of memory: hardly enough to load Windows, much less any applications. The following sections provide an overview of the other two modes of operation.

## Standard Mode

The only reason for the existence of standard mode is the 80286. This mode enables Windows to run on a chip that only provides access to 16MB of RAM as a maximum and doesn't provide all the features that the 80386 does. The important feature that the 80286 lacks is the ability to create virtual machines. Think of a virtual machine as a way of separating tasks so that they can't interfere with each other. Every application thinks that it is running on its own machine, but each virtual machine is really part of the "real" machine that you can see.

Standard mode has some important limitations. For one thing, you can't multitask under standard mode. Windows only task-switches in this mode. Essentially this means that you can open as many applications as memory will permit, but only the foreground task will actually do anything.

Another important limitation of standard mode is the lack of virtual memory support. Without this support, the user is limited to the physical memory provided by the machine. Since 80286 machines were never known for their surplus of memory, most users will run out of memory long before they run out of applications to run.

> **Note:** The only version of Windows that still supports standard mode is Windows 3.1. You access it using the /s switch at the command line. The new versions of Windows only support 386 enhanced mode.

## 386 Enhanced Mode

You have to have an 80386 or above processor to use 386 enhanced mode. This is the default mode that Windows 3.1 and above use to get the most out of your machine. It offers all the features that people normally associate with Windows now. Even though there might be someone out there trying to run Windows in standard mode, most of us switched to 80386 machines long ago. There are several important features that differentiate enhanced mode from standard mode:

- Multitasking—Using 386 enhanced mode enables Windows to perform more than one task simultaneously. There are various forms of multitasking; I cover them in the "Cooperative Multitasking versus Preemptive Multitasking" section of this chapter.

- Virtual Memory—Let's face it; have you ever used a machine that has enough memory? Most of us haven't. Applications always seem to require 1MB more RAM than you have installed. Virtual memory enables Windows to get past this problem so that you don't have to worry about whether your application will run.

- VxD Support—Virtual device drivers make Windows a lot safer environment to work in. (The actual acronym means Virtual Anything Drivers.) Not only are VxDs safer, but they're faster as well. Standard mode never supported the 32-bit enhanced disk services or any of the extended functionality that 386 enhanced mode can.

It's not too difficult to imagine why 386 Enhanced Mode is the way to go if you have an 80386 machine to run Windows on. In fact, I often wonder how people could expect to run Windows on an 80286 in the first place. (Frankly, as I said in a column I wrote for *PC Week* many years ago, I wonder why anyone ever *bought* an 80286, but that's another story entirely.) It's one of those hindsight is 20-20 situations, I guess.

# The Windows and DOS Partnership

As I said earlier, one of the reasons for Windows 3.0's success was that the user could upgrade DOS to use it. In other words, the user could make the transition slowly without having to give up a comfortable environment.

That relationship between DOS and Windows also causes some problems for the user. Consider the speed issue that many people bring up when you talk about using Windows. Since Windows rides on top of DOS, it must use some DOS services to access the hardware. The hard disk drive falls into this category. DOS provides all the file services that Windows 3.*xx* uses. In fact, this is about the only DOS service that Windows 3.1 does use.

What using DOS to provide file services means to the user is that the system has to slow down every time Windows wants to access the hard drive. To see what I mean, look at Figure 23.3. Every time that Windows wants to access the hard drive, it has to create a request in a format that DOS will understand, switch over to real mode so that it can access DOS, then wait for DOS to get the job done. Meanwhile, all those applications that are supposed to do something in the background get suspended. Remember, the Intel processor cannot multitask in real mode, it can only do that in protected mode. Once DOS finds the bit of information that Windows needs, Windows has to copy that information out of the conventional memory space into an area that it can reach in protected mode. It must then switch the processor from real mode back into protected mode.

**Figure 23.3.**
*Windows 3.1 needs to switch from protected mode to real mode to access the hard drive through DOS. Not only does this waste time, but it opens the door for a system crash if a rampant application decides to do something unexpected.*

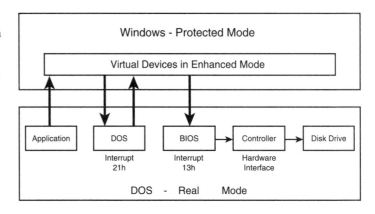

This is only where the problem starts, not where it ends. Every time Windows has to make the switch from protected mode to real mode, it becomes vulnerable to attack from a maverick application. When the processor is in real mode, the operating system can no longer track system activity. The processor won't alert the operating system when an application creates a memory fault. As a result, an application could crash the system before Windows 3.*xx* even knows what is going on.

## 32-bit Access Under Windows 3.1

Windows 3.1 provides a new feature called 32-bit access. This feature reduces the opportunity for system crashes and enhances overall system speed. However, before I talk about how 32-bit access affects your computing environment, you need to understand what it is.

If you tried to figure out what 32-bit access is by its name, you might suspect that it's some new technique for accessing the data on your drive 32 bits at a time. What 32-bit access actually provides is a little more complex.

Every time an application requests data from the hard drive, Windows intercepts the request to see if it can be fulfilled using data in protected memory. Usually this request asks to open a file or to read specific byte ranges of data. Once Windows determines that it can't fulfill the request, it switches to real mode and passes the request to the DOS interrupt 21h handler. This handler looks at the request and starts to take care of it by issuing interrupt 13h requests. You can look at interrupt 21h as the manager and interrupt 13h as the worker. Interrupt 21h gets the whole problem in one big chunk. It breaks the problem up into small pieces that interrupt 13h can handle. As a result, each interrupt 21h call can result in a lot of interrupt 13h calls.

Of course, since Windows is monitoring everything, the system just doesn't stay in real mode and take care of the entire disk request at one time. Windows intercepts each interrupt 13h call that the DOS interrupt 21h handler makes and sees if it can fulfill the request using data in protected memory. If not, Windows switches back to real mode and the BIOS handles the call. The BIOS performs the work required to fulfill the call and passes the information back to Windows, which passes it back to

DOS, which passes back to Windows, which finally passes it back to the application. This may seem like a lot of work just to read a few bytes of data from the disk, and it is.

Figure 23.4 shows the new 32-bit access method used by Windows 3.11. Notice that the BIOS is completely cut out of the picture. That's because FastDisk (a 32-bit protected mode driver) emulates the BIOS using protected mode code. This means that Windows not only eliminates two mode transitions for every interrupt 13h call, but that it can effectively multitask during more of the disk access cycle. We only lose the DOS processing time instead of both DOS and BIOS processing time. This improvement accounts for part of the noticeable speed-up in Windows 3.1. It also accounts for some of the improved stability that people experience.

*Figure 23.4.*
*Windows 3.11 provides a 32-bit access feature that reduces the opportunities for a system crash and enhances system throughput.*

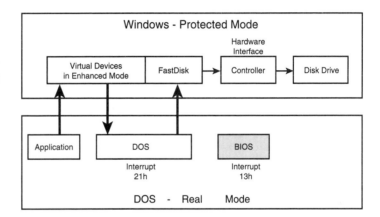

Windows 3.11 and Windows for Workgroups 3.11 add even more. In addition to 32-bit disk access, these versions add 32-bit file access. These versions of Windows use the DOS file access features to search for files and to perform other file-specific activities. (This differentiates a file access from a disk access, which deals with reading and writing sections of data.) This means even fewer transitions to DOS because the file system no longer keeps the BIOS in the picture. The result: an overall improvement in system speed and reliability.

## The Windows 95 Alternative to 32-bit Access

Windows 95 gets around the entire real mode access problem by incorporating all operating system functions into a 32-bit architecture. Microsoft has named this technique the VFAT interface. Its full name is the Protected Mode FAT File System. Figure 23.5 shows how this disk management system differs from the one used under Windows 3.x. Using protected mode drivers means there is less chance that a random application will cause a system failure because there is never a time where Windows 95 is unprotected. It always runs in protected mode. (The only exception to this rule is if you installed real mode drivers in CONFIG.SYS to support an antiquated device like a CD-ROM drive. Windows 95 does switch to Virtual 86 mode when accessing a device that uses a real mode driver.) Using protected mode means that the operating system constantly monitors every event taking place on the machine. It has the final say before a particular event takes place.

**Figure 23.5.**
*Windows 95 uses a totally different system than its predecessors to access this disk. This new system runs totally in protected memory, reducing the chance of system crashes due to disk-related problems to nearly zero and greatly enhancing disk access speed.*

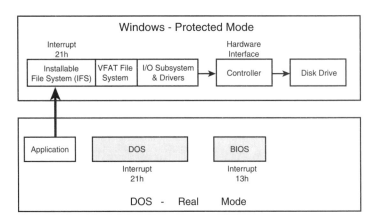

As Figure 23.5 shows, there are several discrete components in the Windows 95 file system. Actually, Microsoft refers to these components as layers. There are 32 possible layers in the Windows 95 file system, starting at the I/O subsystem. (The current configuration does not use all 32 layers.) Layer 0 is closest to the I/O subsystem, while layer 31 is closest to the hardware. Each layer provides hooks for third-party software used to support custom file systems and devices. For example, adding a network driver to the file system layer enables you to access drives on other machines. Unlike previous versions of Windows, a vendor can retrofit the Windows 95 file system to provide additional capabilities with relative ease. Each of these components performs a different task, as follows.

- Installable File System (IFS) Manager—This is the highest layer in the file system. The IFS is a VxD that provides the interface to applications. It doesn't matter whether the application uses the interrupt 21h interface or either the 16-or 32-bit Windows interface, this is the component that receives application requests. It is the responsibility of the IFS to transfer control to the appropriate file system driver (FSD). The VFAT FSD component appears in Figure 23.5, but Windows 95 also includes network and CD FSDs as well.

- File System Driver (FSD) Layer—The most common file system driver layer component is the VFAT FSD. This is the VxD that takes care of all local hard drive requests. It provides the long filename support and protected mode stability that makes Windows 95 better than its predecessors. Your machine may have several other FSDs, depending on the type of equipment you have installed. For example, Windows 95 installs a network file system handler if you install any form of a LAN. All of the FSDs talk with the IFS manager. They also send requests to the layers that directly communicate with the hardware.

- I/O Subsystem (IOS) Layer—This is the highest level of the block device layer. What do I mean by a block device? Any device that sends information in blocks (like a hard drive does) is called a block device. A hard drive usually uses some multiple of 512 bytes as its block size. Other devices may use a different block size. Network devices, tape drives, and CD-ROM drives all fall into the block device category. The IOS provides general device services to the FSDs. For example, it routes requests from the FSDs to various device-specific drivers. It also sends status information from the device-specific drivers to the FSDs.

- Volume Tracking Driver (VTD) Layer—Windows 95 may or may not install this driver. It handles any removable devices attached to your system. For example, if you have a floppy or CD-ROM drive, then Windows 95 will install this component. On the other hand, if you use a diskless workstation or rely on local and network hard drives alone, Windows 95 will not need to install this component. The VTD perform one and only one basic function. It monitors the status of all removable media drives and reports any change in media. This is the component that will complain if you remove a floppy prematurely (usually in the middle of a write).

- Type Specific Driver (TSD) Layer—Every type of device needs a driver that understands its peculiar needs. For example, the hard disk drive driver would not understand the needs of a floppy drive very well. This layer deals with logical device types, rather than specific devices. For example, one TSD handles all the hard drives on your system, while another TSD handles all the floppy drives. A third TSD would handle all network drives.

- Vendor Supplied Driver (VSD) Layer—This is where a vendor would install support for a proprietary bus CD-ROM or a removable media device like a floptical drive. Every specific device type needs a driver that can translate its requests for Windows. This is the layer that performs those services. The VSD knows things like the number of heads that a disk has or the amount of time it needs to wait for a floppy to get up to speed.

- Port Driver (PD) Layer—The PD performs the actual task of communicating with the device through an adapter. It is the last stage before a message leaves Windows and the first stage when a message arrives from the device. The PD is usually adapter-specific. For example, you would have one VSD for each hard drive and one PD for each hard drive adapter. If your system uses an IDE hard drive, then Windows would load the IDE PD to talk to the IDE adapter.

- SCSIzer—Don't let the strange-looking name for this layer fool you. It deals with SCSI command language. Think of the command language as the method the computer uses to tell a SCSI device to perform a task. It isn't the data that the SCSI device handles; rather it is the act that the SCSI device will perform. There is one SCSIzer for each SCSI device.

- SCSI Manager—Windows NT introduced something called the miniport driver. With Windows 95, you can use the Windows NT miniport binaries. However, before you can actually do this, Windows 95 has to translate its commands to a format that the miniport driver will understand. The SCSI Manager performs this service.

- Miniport Driver—This is a device driver that provides support for a specific SCSI device. No other device uses the miniport driver. The miniport driver works with the SCSI manager to perform the same task as a PD. Both Windows NT and Windows 95 use the same miniport drivers.

- Protected Mode Mapper—This layer performs a very special task. It enables you to use your DOS drivers under Windows 95. Without the support of this VxD, Windows 95 could not support legacy devices that lack Windows 95 specific drivers. Essentially the protected mode mapper disguises a real mode driver to look like a Windows 95 protected mode driver.

- Real Mode Driver—It is almost certain that some vendors will not supply drivers for every device that they ever made. In reality, there is no reason for them to do so. That old legacy device that still does the job for you is probably so far out of date that you are the only one still using it. Still, like a really comfortable pair of shoes, you hate to give that old device up. (I personally have a proprietary bus Hitachi CD-ROM hanging around; it still does the job, so I'm not going to give it up just yet). One of the goals of the Windows 95 development team was to allow you to keep that old legacy device hanging around until you are ready to give it up. Sure, it's going to cost some system speed to keep it, but that real mode driver will work just fine under Windows 95.

You can access the VFAT interface in a DOS application. Microsoft incorporated a new set of services into the interrupt 21h handler. Table 23.1 shows the various calls you can make to this new interface. Notice that the AL part of the service call corresponds to the current disk service call numbers. The contents of the other registers correspond to the old DOS register setups as well. If you know how to use the current set of interrupt 21h disk routines, then using the new ones means a simple change in the contents of the AX register (in most cases). Microsoft recommends that you use the Get Volume Information (71A0h) to detect if the current system supports long filenames. Set the carry flag before making the call. If the machine does not support long filenames, then the carry flag will be unchanged on return and DOS will clear the AL register. Never use the long filename calls on a system that does not support them. Remember that all of these service numbers go into the AX register and that the values are in hexadecimal.

Table 23.1. VFAT Interface Interrupt 21h Functions.

| AX Code | Function Name |
| --- | --- |
| 7139h | Create Directory |
| 713Ah | Remove Directory |
| 713Bh | Set Current Directory |
| 7141h | Delete File |
| 7143h | Get/Set File Attributes |
| 7147h | Get Current Directory |
| 714Eh | Find First File |
| 714Fh | Find Next File |
| 7156h | Move or Rename File |
| 716Ch | Extended Open/Create File |

| AX Code | Function Name |
|---------|---------------|
| 71A0h | Get Volume Information |
| 71A1h | Find Close |

# Cooperative Multitasking versus Preemptive Multitasking

Multitasking is one of those nebulous words that everyone uses, but no one takes time to define. The first thing that you need to do before you can understand multitasking is to define the word *task*. A task is essentially an application that is running. When you start Windows, you may think that nothing is running, but there are already several applications getting work done on your machine. For example, Explorer (or Program Manager) is considered a task. Any network connections or print spoolers are considered tasks. A screen saver is yet another task. There are numerous system related tasks as well. For example, the Windows kernel is considered a task. Industry uses two terms to refer to a running application or thread: process and task. I prefer *task* since it is a little less nebulous in connotation than *process* is. However, you will probably see a mixture of both in the documentation that you read.

When talking about Windows 3.1, you can associate every task with a single application. The definition of task doesn't really stop here for Windows 95 and Windows NT. Some 32-bit applications use a technique called multithreading that enables them to perform more than one task at a time. For example, you could recalculate your spreadsheet and print at the same time if the application supports multithreading. What happens is the spreadsheet starts another task (called a thread) to take care of printing. It may even start a second thread to do the recalculation so that you can continue to enter data. One way to look at threads is as a subtask under the application that is running.

Now that you understand what a task is, it's time to look at the definition of multitasking. Everyone assumes multitasking is just that; several tasks (or processes) running simultaneously on one machine. That is a good start for a definition, but it just doesn't end there. An important consideration is how the operating system allocates time between tasks. When talking about Windows, it becomes very important to actually define the method used to manage tasks and to differentiate between different kinds of multitasking. There are two kinds of multitasking supported by Windows 95: cooperative and preemptive.

Windows 3.0 introduced a feature called cooperative multitasking. This is the way it was supposed to work: Application A would run for a little while, just long enough to get one component of a task finished. It would then turn control of the system back over to Windows so that Windows could take care of any housekeeping chores and allow application B to run for a while. This cycle continued in a round-robin fashion between all the tasks running at any given time.

What really happened is that some applications followed the rules, but others didn't. Under cooperative multitasking the operating system gave up too much control; an application could hog all the system resources if it wanted to. Some applications do just that. The result is that cooperative multitasking really doesn't work all that well. Most of the time the user spends looking at the hourglass is really time in which Windows has temporarily lost control of the system to an application that doesn't want to share with anyone else.

All the legacy applications that run under Windows 95—the 16-bit applications that you moved from Windows 3.x—still have to run in a cooperative multitasking mode. However, Windows 95 minimizes the impact of these applications by running them in one shared address space. All of the 16-bit applications have to cooperate with each other, but they don't affect any 32-bit applications running on your machine. This includes Explorer and any other Windows 95-specific tools. (And, of course, you will upgrade most of your commonly used 16-bit applications, like your Word Processor and Spreadsheet, to Windows 95 versions.)

When Microsoft designed Windows NT, it wanted something better than cooperative multitasking, so it designed an operating system that uses preemptive multitasking. Windows 95 supports preemptive multitasking for any 32-bit applications you may run. Think of it this way: Preemptive multitasking works like a traffic light. Traffic gets to go for a while one way, then the light changes color and traffic gets to go for a while the other way. Sure, the actual amount of time that each task gets is weighted by the user and the operating system to meet some criteria, but this access is supposed to be fair. Every application is supposed to get its fair share of processor time and preemptive multitasking enforces this principle. Windows 95 monitors each application and interrupts it when its time is up. It doesn't matter if the application wants to give up control over the system or not; Windows 95 doesn't give it a choice.

There is another, more important, difference in the way the system reacts under preemptive multitasking. Under Windows 3.1 an hourglass means that the system is tied up. You can't do anything else until that hourglass goes away. On the other hand, an hourglass under Windows 95 only means that the current task is tied up. You can always start another task or switch to another existing task. If that task isn't busy, then you can perform some work with it while you wait for the initial task to complete its work. You know when the original application has finished because the hourglass will go away when you place your cursor over the task's window. The bottom line? Preemptive multitasking means that the user doesn't have to wait for the system.

Finally, cooperative multitasking has a serious flaw. Since Windows lost control when some applications took over, there was no way to clear that application if the machine froze. Since Windows 95 maintains constant control over the machine, you'll no longer need to worry about the machine freezing in the middle of a task. Even if one application does hang, you only need to end that task, not reboot the entire machine. Just like Windows 3.1, pressing Ctrl-Alt-Del does not automatically reboot the machine. However, unlike Windows 3.1, Windows 95 displays a list of applications and you get to choose which one to terminate. (See Figure 23.6.)

**Figure 23.6.**

*Preemptive multitasking means that Windows 95 never loses control over the machine. It also means that you can recover from an application error with ease. Simply choose the errant application (usually the top application in the list); Windows 95 will resume normal operations after it terminates the application you select.*

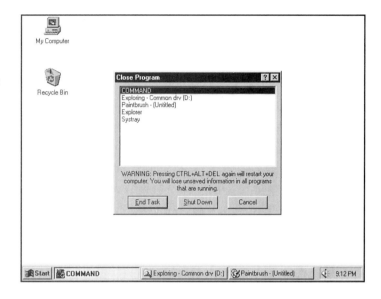

You may wonder why Microsoft (or any other vendor) would use cooperative multitasking if preemptive multitasking is so much better. There are a few good reasons. First, DOS is nonre-entrant. This means that you have to allow DOS to complete one task before you give it another one. If you disturb DOS in the middle of a task, the entire system could (and will) freeze. Since Windows 3.x runs on top of DOS, it cannot use preemptive multitasking for any services that interact with DOS. Unfortunately, one of those services is the disk subsystem. See now why it would be fairly tough to use preemptive multitasking on any system that runs on top of DOS?

The second problem with preemptive multitasking is really a two-part scenario. Both relate to ease of designing the operating system. When an operating system provides preemptive multitasking, it also has to include some kind of method for monitoring devices. What if two applications decided they needed to use the COM port at the same time? With cooperative multitasking, the application that started to use the COM port would gain control of it and lock the other application out. In a preemptive multitasking situation, the first application could get halfway through the allocation process, get stopped, then the second application could start the allocation process. Now, what happens if the first application is reactivated by the system? You have two applications who think they have access to one device. In reality, both applications have access and you have a mess. Windows 95 handles this problem by using a programming construct called a critical section. (I discuss this feature a little later in the chapter.)

Preemptive multitasking also needs some type of priority system to ensure that critical tasks get a larger share of the processor's time than noncritical tasks. Remember that a task can no longer dictate how long it needs system resources—that's all in the hands of the operating system. Theoretically, you should be able to rely on the users to tell the operating system how they want their applications prioritized, then allow the operating system to take care of the rest. What really happens is that a low-priority task could run into a fault situation and need system resources immediately to resolve it. A static priority system can't handle that situation. In addition, that low-priority task could end up getting little or no system resources when a group of high-priority tasks start to run. The priority system that Windows 95 uses provides a dynamic means for changing a task's priority. When a high-priority task runs, Windows 95 lowers its priority. When a low-priority task gets passed over in favor of a high-priority task, Windows 95 increases its priority. As you can see, the dynamic priority system enforces the idea that some tasks should get more system resources than others, yet ensures that every task gets at least some of the system resources.

There is a final consideration when looking at preemptive multitasking. Even if you use the best dynamic priority system in the world and every piece of the operating system works just the way it should, you will run into situations where a task has to complete a sequence of events without being disturbed. For example, the application may need to make certain that a database transaction is written to disk before it hands control of the system back to the operating system. If another task tried to do something related to that transaction before the first task completed, you could end up with invalid or damaged data in the database. Programmers refer to a piece of code that performs this task as a critical section. Normally a critical section occurs with system-related tasks like memory allocation, but it can happen with application-related tasks like writing information to a file as well. Cooperative multitasking systems don't have to worry as much about critical sections because the task decides when the operating system regains control of the system. On the other hand, a preemptive multitasking system needs some way for a task to communicate the need to complete a critical section of code. Under Windows 95, a task tells the operating system that it needs to perform a critical section of code using a semaphore (a flag). Now, if a hardware interrupt or some other application were to ask to perform a task that did not interfere with any part of the critical section, it could proceed. All a critical section guarantees is that the task and its environment will remain undisturbed until the task completes its work.

# What Can the Registry Do For You?

Any discussion on the evolution of Windows has to include something about the registry. Anyone who has spent time working with Windows 3.1 knows about the fun of working with the SYSTEM.INI and WIN.INI files. The WIN.INI file holds Windows environment settings; it changes the way that Windows interacts with the user. The SYSTEM.INI file contains hardware and device driver configuration information; it changes the way that Windows configures itself during startup. Of course, the exact distinction between these two files is somewhat blurred. For example, WIN.INI holds the serial port and printer configuration information.

These are the two poorly organized, cryptic files that hold the vast majority of the configuration information for the Windows 3.1 system. Every time the user adds an application to Windows 3.1, the application adds yet another heading or two and some additional entries to both files. On the other hand, when the user gets rid of that application, the entries don't go with it. They just sort of hang around and slow the performance of the system. Some of the entries can even cause error messages or perhaps, in extreme circumstances, cause a system crash.

Windows 95 still supports these rather archaic and difficult-to-understand files, but it prefers that applications use the new registry. Under Windows 3.1, the registry contained some file association information and that's about it. Under Windows 95, the registry contains file association information, user configuration and setup, hardware configuration and setup, network, and even some performance data. This all-inclusive approach to managing the Windows environment has some definite advantages.

You use the RegEdit utility to view and change the contents of the registry. It displays the registry in the format shown in Figure 23.7. Windows 95 uses two hidden files USER.DAT and SYSTEM.DAT to store the registry information, but RegEdit displays them as one contiguous file. Even though the RegEdit display may look a bit difficult to understand at first, it's really not. The big difference between the registry and the Windows 3.1 alternative of SYSTEM.INI and WIN.INI is that the registry uses a hierarchical organization and plain English descriptions that you will find easy to edit and maintain. Yes, every application the user adds will also add entries to this file, but the organization of the file makes it easy for an application to remove those entries when the user uninstalls it. Even if the user installs a legacy application that doesn't understand the registry, he or she can still remove its entries with ease.

*Figure 23.7.*
*This screen shows a typical RegEdit opening screen. Each HKEY key controls a different part of the Windows setup.*

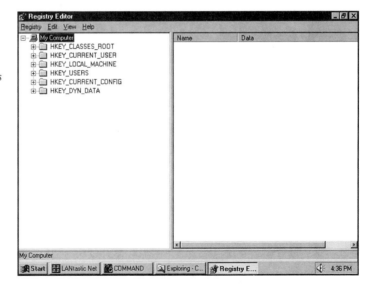

The Windows 95 registry uses two types of entries to maintain its organization: keys and values. *Keys* are a RegEdit topic. Think of a key as the heading that tells you what a particular section will contain. Looking at all the keys provides an outline for a particular topic. The topics could range from the setup of each drive in the system to the file associations needed to configure the machine. The key at the top of the hierarchy usually contains generic information. Each subkey provides a little more detail about that particular topic. The keys always appear on the left side of the RegEdit window.

*Values* are the definition of a RegEdit topic; they describe the key in some way. Think of a value as the text that fills out the heading provided by a key. Values are like the text in this book while keys are the headings that organize the text. A value can contain just about anything. For example, the value for a file association key can tell you what application Windows 95 will start when you double-click on a file with that extension in Explore. A value could tell you what interrupt and I/O port settings a piece of hardware uses as well. Suffice it to say that you will find the value you need using the keys, but the actual information by reading the values. There are three types of values: binary, string, and DWORD. There are very few cases where anything but applications use the binary and DWORD value types. The values usually store configuration data in a format not in human readable form. Some applications will use DWORD or binary values to store data as well. For example, you might find the score from your last game of Solitaire here. The string values provide a lot of information about the application and how it is configured. Hardware usually uses string values as well for interrupt and port information. Values always appear on the right side of the RegEdit window.

There is also a superset of the key entry. I differentiate these particular keys from the rest because they are the major headings in the registry. During the rest of this discussion I refer to these special keys as *categories*. Think of categories as the chapter titles in a book. You need to go to the right chapter before you will find the right type of information. In fact, information in one category may appear in the same order and at the same level in another category. The difference between the two is when Windows 95 uses the entries in one category versus another.

The categories include one of the six main keys under the "My Computer" key. Categories divide the registry into six main areas: HKEY_CLASSES_ROOT, HKEY_CURRENT_USER, HKEY_LOCAL_MACHINE, HKEY_USERS, HKEY_CURRENT_CONFIG, and HKEY_DYN_DATA. Each category contains a specific type of information. The following paragraphs provide an overview of the registry categories.

There are two types of entry in the HKEY_CLASSES_ROOT category. The first key type (remember a key is a RegEdit topic) is a file extension. Think of all the three-character extensions that you used in the past, like DOC and TXT. Windows 95 still uses them to differentiate one file type from another. It also uses them to associate that file type with a specific action. For example, even though you can't do anything with a file that uses the DLL extension, it appears in this list because Windows 95 needs to associate DLLs with an executable file type. The second entry type is the association itself; the file extension entries normally associate a data file with an application or an executable file with a specific Windows 95 function. Below the association key are entries for the menus that you see when you right-click an entry in the Explorer. This section also contains keys that determine what type of icon to display and other parameters associated with a particular file type. Figure 23.8 shows the typical HKEY_CLASSES_ROOT organization.

**Figure 23.8.**

*This is a typical HKEY_CLASSES_ROOT display. Notice the distinct difference between file extension and file association keys.*

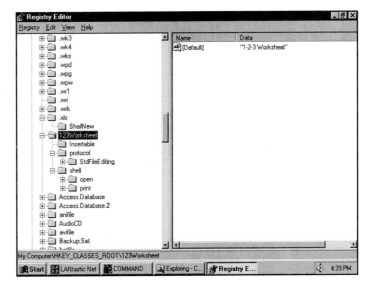

The HKEY_CURRENT_USER category contains a lot of "soft" settings for your machine. These soft settings tell how to configure the desktop and the keyboard. It also contains color settings and the configuration of the Start menu. All the user-specific settings appear in this category.

The HKEY_CURRENT_USER category is slaved to the settings for the current user, the one who is logged into the machine at the time. This is differentiated from all the user configuration entries in other parts of the registry. This is a dynamic setting category; the other user-related categories contain static information. The registry copies the contents of one of the user entries in the HKEY_USERS category into this category, then updates HKEY_USERS when you shut down.

This is the area where Windows 95 obtains new setting information and places any changes you make. As you can see from Figure 23.9, the keys within the HKEY_CURRENT_USER category are pretty self-explanatory in most cases. All of the entries adjust some type of user-specific setting, nothing that affects a global element like a device driver.

The HKEY_LOCAL_MACHINE category centers its attention on the machine hardware. This includes the drivers and configuration information required to run the hardware. Every piece of hardware appears somewhere in this section of the registry, even if that hardware uses real mode drivers. If the hardware doesn't appear here, then Windows 95 can't use it.

There is a lot of subtle information about your hardware stored under this category. For example, this category contains all the Plug and Play information about your machine. It also provides a complete listing of the device drivers and their revision level. This section may even contain the revision information for the hardware itself. For example, there is a distinct difference between a Pro Audio Spectrum 16+ Revision C sound board and the Revision D version of that same board. Windows 95 stores that difference in the registry.

**Figure 23.9.**
*The*
*HKEY_CURRENT_USER*
*category contains all the*
*user-specific settings.*

This category does contain some software-specific information of a global nature. For example, a 32-bit application will store the location of its Setup and Format Table (SFT) here. This is a file that the application uses during installation. Some applications also use it during a setup modification. Applications like Word for Windows NT store all their setup information in SFT tables. The only application information that does appear here is global configuration-specific like the SFT. Figure 23.10 shows a typical HKEY_LOCAL_MACHINE category setup.

**Figure 23.10.**
*The*
*HKEY_LOCAL_MACHINE*
*category contains all the*
*hardware- and device-driver-*
*specific information about*
*your machine. It also*
*contains the global applica-*
*tion setup information.*

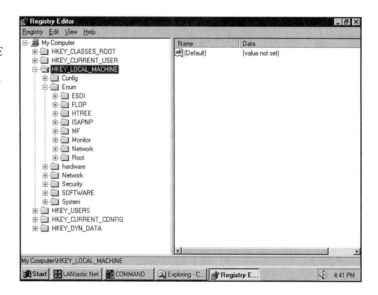

The HKEY_USERS category contains a static listing of all the users of this particular registry file. It never pays to edit any of the information you find in this category. You can, however, use this category for reference purposes. The reason for this hands-off policy is simple: None of the entries here will take effect until the next time the user logs in to Windows 95, so you really don't know what effect they will have until you reboot the machine. In addition, changing the settings for the current user is a waste of time since Windows 95 will overwrite the new data with the data contained in HKEY_CURRENT_USER during logout or shutdown.

There is one other problem associated with using this category as your sole source of information. Windows 95 actually maintains multiple registries in a multiuser configuration—one for each user that logs into the system in some cases. Because of this, you never quite know where you'll find the information for a particular user. Windows 95 tracks this information, but it really is a pain for the administrator to have to do it as well. Besides, Microsoft thoughtfully provided a utility that helps the network administrator maintain the various registries. The Policy Editor utility enables the network administrator to maintain the static user information with ease. Using the Policy Editor will enable the network administrator to bridge the various registry files on the system when each user provides his or her own desktop configuration.

Figure 23.11 shows a setup that includes the default key. If this system were set up for multiple desktops, then each user would have a separate entry in this section. Each entry would contain precisely the same keys, but the values might differ from user to user. When a user logs into the network, Windows 95 copies all the information in their profile to the HKEY_CURRENT_USER area of the registry. When they log out or shut down, Windows 95 updates the information in their specific section from the HKEY_CURRENT_USER category.

*Figure 23.11.*
*Windows 95 creates one entry in the HKEY_USERS category for each user that logs in to the machine.*

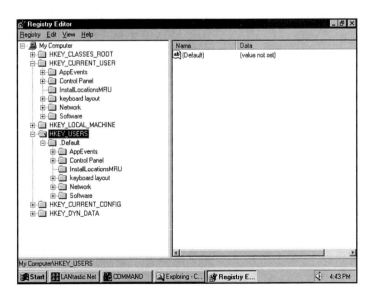

The HKEY_CURRENT_CONFIG category is the simplest part of the registry. It contains two major keys: Display and System. Essentially, these entries are used by the GDI API (described later) to configure the display and printer.

The Display key provides two subkeys: Fonts and Settings. The Fonts subkey determines which fonts Windows 95 uses for general display purposes. These are the raster (non-TrueType) fonts that it displays when you get a choice of which font to use for icons or other purposes.

The Settings subkey contains the current display resolution and number of bits per pixel. The bits per pixel value determines the number of colors available. For example, 4 bits per pixel provides 16 colors and 8 bits per pixel provides 256 colors. The three fonts listed as values under this key are the default fonts used for icons and application menus. You can change all the settings under this key using the Settings tab of the Properties for Display dialog found in the Control Panel.

The System key looks like a convoluted mess. However, only one of the subkeys under this key has any meaning for the user. The Printers subkey contains a list of the printers attached to the machine. It does not include printers accessed through a network connection. Figure 23.12 shows the major keys in this category.

**Figure 23.12.**
*The HKEY_CURRENT_CONFIG category echoes the settings under the Config key of the HKEY_LOCAL_MACHINE category.*

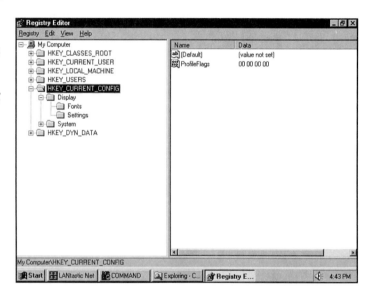

The final category, HKEY_DYN_DATA, contains two subkeys: Config Manager and PerfStats. You can monitor the status of the Dynamic key using the Device Manager. The PerfStats key values appear as statistics in the System Monitor utility display. Figure 23.13 shows these two main keys and their subkeys.

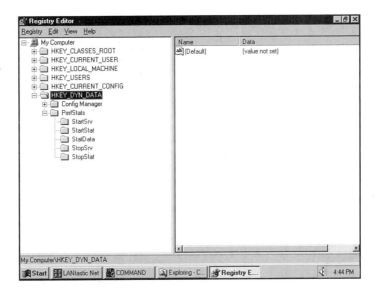

*Figure 23.13.*
*HKEY_DYN_DATA*
*contains registry entries for*
*current events. The values in*
*these keys reflect the current,*
*or dynamic, state of the*
*computer.*

As you can see, the Windows 95 registry is much enhanced from its Windows 3.1 counterpart. Even though Windows 95 still has to use the infamous SYSTEM.INI and WIN.INI files for antiquated applications, the use of the registry for all other purposes does reduce the user's workload. Eventually all applications will use the registry to store their configuration data.

# The Windows 95 Interface

Now that the history lesson is over, I want to take a look at the new interface that Windows 95 provides. I'm not talking about the tattered Program Manager interface used by older versions of Windows; I'm talking about the new Explorer interface. You choose to install the old shell with Windows 95 if you want to—and it works just like it always has—but to get the most out of this new operating system you really should use the new shell. Figure 23.2 on page 477 shows what the Windows 95 Explorer interface looks like.

The first thing you'll notice is that this display looks a lot cleaner than the old one. Don't let that fool you—there is a lot more here than meets the eye. There are six main objects in the new interface. Two of them are optional additions. All of them are folders in one way or another as well. The following paragraphs give you an overview of what to expect. I cover each item in detail later.

- Desktop—Just like your physical desktop, the Explorer Desktop holds everything you need to work on. You can keep your Desktop as messy—or as clean—as you like. Adding items to the Desktop is easy; just drag them there. Likewise, you can remove items from the Desktop by moving them somewhere else, or simply throwing them in the Recycle Bin.

- Taskbar—This is one of the neatest features provided by Explorer. One of the things that I really hated about Program Manager was having to completely rearrange my desktop every time I needed to find a particular application. Windows 95 gets rid of this organizational problem with the Taskbar. Instead of looking for that application, all you need to do is click on its button to bring it up.

- My Computer—This is a folder that contains the physical description of your computer. Think of it as a hardware inventory and configuration program, and you'll have a pretty good idea of what the My Computer folder can do for you.

- Recycle Bin—Every office, even an electronic office, needs a trash can. The Recycle Bin is an important feature for Windows 95. Older versions of Windows didn't provide any way to get that file you needed back—unless of course you had a third-party unerase program like my Norton Utilities handy. The Recycle Bin enables you to put stuff in and take it out again, just like the trash can in your office. Of course, you still have to take the trash out once in a while or your hard drive will overflow with the refuse of previous sessions.

- Network Neighborhood (optional)—Computers don't sit on people's desks as lone islands of computing power anymore. The best way to make your computing environment better is to share those resources with someone else. The Network Neighborhood tells you who is logged on to the network and what resources you can borrow from them as needed.

- Briefcase (optional)—Taking work home used to be a chore—it still is—but the least Windows can do is make it easier for you to gather everything up. This briefcase works just like the physical briefcase you use to store papers. It makes a handy place to stick your electronic paperwork. When you want to move to another computer, just pick up your briefcase and go.

# The Desktop—Where Everything Else Congregates

Trying to describe everything the Desktop could contain is like trying to put a lid on Pandora's box—you just can't do it. A Windows 95 desktop can contain the electronic version of just about anything your physical desktop could contain. I prefer a neat desk myself, but that's a personal preference. Windows 95 will allow you to keep you desk in whatever shape you think best.

Before I discuss the Desktop itself, you need to know the definition of two terms. First, a *folder* is the graphic equivalent of a directory. That's not precisely true, but it does get the idea across. A folder is also a Windows object—that's the big difference between a folder and a directory.

The second term is *object*. This term can mean a lot of things depending on your perspective. From a Windows user point of view, an object is anything you can interact with. For example, a folder is an object. The desktop is an object. Even applications, files, and icons are objects. In most cases, if your mouse pointer can touch it, it's an object. I explain what the implications of being an object are a little later. Right now, all you need to remember is that objects are a lot more flexible than the icons you got in Windows 3.*xx* and Windows NT.

Now that you know that the Desktop is both a folder and an object, let's take a look at what that means. Every object in Windows provides at least two different mouse contexts. The first is the left mouse click you used under Windows 3.*xx* and Windows NT. It enables you to select the object, move it around, resize it, and perform a variety of other tasks. The right mouse click is new. Figure 23.14 shows what happens when you right-click on the Desktop.

*Figure 23.14.*
*The Windows 95 Desktop*
*provides more than meets the*
*eye when you right-click on it*
*with the mouse. This simple*
*menuing system can move*
*you around quickly and*
*reduce the amount of work*
*required to modify your*
*environment.*

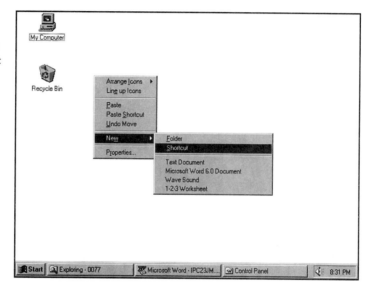

The Desktop object menu provides quick access to a few features that you may have had to spend a lot of time to find under Windows 3.*xx* (if they existed at all). This is what all the excitement about objects is about. Right-clicking on a Windows 95 object always provides a menu that lists the things you can do with that object. The Desktop object menu contains some similarities, and some differences, with the other object menus that you'll use. The important thing to remember is that many of those menu items that you had to search through under Program Manager are now available through a simple right click. The following paragraphs describe these options in detail.

- Arrange Icons—Ever want to reorganize your display quickly? This option sorts the Desktop icons into whatever order you select. For example, rearranging them by name will place the icons in alphabetical order. I find the "by Type" option the most useful when I need to find something fast. Windows 95 automatically groups my executables in one area, making them very easy to find. Of course, the same holds true for any data files. The "by Size" option enables me to find those big files quickly when it's time to clean up my hard drive.

- Line Up Icons—This option is the best one to select if you simply need to clean up and organize your desktop after placing the icons in the order you want. When you select this option, Windows 95 will line everything up, but it won't sort the icons into any particular order.

- Paste—Use this option to paste a copy of an application or other object onto the desktop. I find it comes in handy when I'm working on a project. I simply copy all the files that relate to the project from their directory onto the desktop. That way, all I need to do to get to a particular file is double-click on it. The copying process also means that I have a duplicate of the file in the original directory if I make a mistake and need a new copy to work on.

- Paste Shortcut—Shortcuts are one of the handiest features that Windows 95 provides. Think of a shortcut as a road sign that points to the real thing. Double-clicking on a shortcut is the same thing as double-clicking on the real object. Using shortcuts enables you to place pointers to a file or application wherever they're handy. Shortcuts also provide a measure of safety. Ever erase a file that you really needed by accident? If you erase a shortcut, the original file is still there; only the shortcut is erased. You can use this feature to setup a foolproof desktop for novice users; even if they do find the Recycle Bin, they won't be able to destroy their setup with it. Every shortcut you create consumes a meager 1KB of disk space, so they're a pretty good resource to use whenever necessary.

- Undo x—This option always begins with the word Undo followed by an action. It enables you to undo your previous action. For example, if you just copied a file to the Desktop, then this option will say Undo Copy. If you just erased a file, then it will say Undo Delete.

- New—This option is a lot more powerful than some people would expect. Whenever an application registers itself with Windows 95, it also adds the ability to create new files to the object menu. The two default selections are Folder and Shortcut. All you need to do to create a new data file of any type is select it from this menu. Of course, there are limitations. For example, a new Word document always uses the default stylesheet (NORMAL.DOT for Word 6.0).

- Properties—Every object menu has one of these entries. The Properties option usually opens a dialog box that enables you to configure the object in some way. For example, when you select this option for the Desktop, it brings up a dialog that enables you to change the display settings. The same dialog enables you to change the desktop background and even the screen saver that Windows 95 uses.

# Getting Your Tasks Organized

A major part of the new look in Windows 95 is the Taskbar. This is the gray bar at the bottom of the display in Figure 23.2. You could think of the Taskbar as Windows 95 replacement for Program Manager, but you'd be selling it short. The Taskbar can do a lot more for you than that. The Taskbar is the central control area for most of the things you will do under Windows 95. It contains three major elements: Start Menu, Task List, and a Settings Area.

Before giving you a full description of each of the major elements, I want to show you a few ways you can configure the Taskbar itself. The Taskbar starts out at the bottom of the display, but you don't have to leave it there. With Windows 95, you can always change your desktop to suit your needs. Figure 23.15 shows what happens when you grab the Taskbar with the mouse pointer and move it toward the right side of the display. You can place the Taskbar on any of the four sides.

**Figure 23.15.**
*You can move the Taskbar where it's needed by grabbing it with the mouse and moving it. The gray box shows where the Taskbar will appear when you release the left mouse button.*

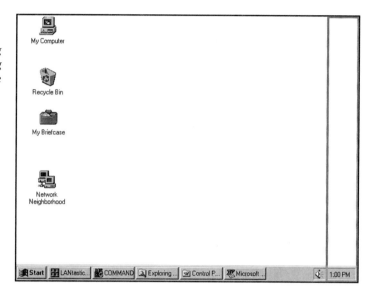

Like the other objects under Windows 95, the Taskbar also provides a Properties dialog. There are two pages in this dialog; one controls the Start Menu setup and the other controls the Taskbar itself. The four settings on the Taskbar tab enable you to change how it reacts. For example, you can remove the Taskbar from view by removing the check mark from the Always on Top field. The Show Clock field enables you to clear more space for applications on the Taskbar by removing the clock from view. My personal favorite is the Auto Hide field. Figure 23.16 shows what happens when you select this option. The Taskbar appears as a thin gray line at the bottom of the display. The second the mouse cursor approaches it, the Taskbar resumes its normal size. This enables you to get rid of the Taskbar to clear space for application windows, yet keep it handy for when you need it.

Right-clicking on the Taskbar displays a few other object specific options as well. All of them affect the way that Windows 95 organizes the applications currently displayed on the Taskbar as follows.

- Cascade—When you select this option, all the application windows are resized to the same size. Windows 95 arranges them in a diagonal, much like the display you would normally see in a spreadsheet when opening more than one file. This enables you to select any one application out of the entire list by clicking on its Title Bar (the area at the top of the application window that contains the application name).

**Figure 23.16.**
*The Auto Hide feature of the Taskbar Properties dialog makes it possible for you to remove the Taskbar from sight until needed.*

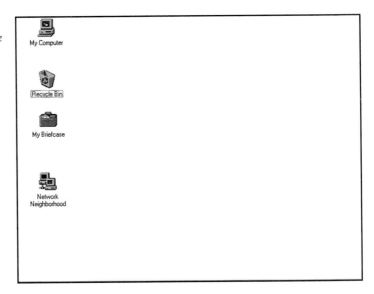

- Tile Horizontally or Tile Vertically—Use either of these options if you want to see the window areas of all your applications at once. Windows 95 uses every available inch of Desktop space to place the applications side by side. Each application receives about the same amount of space.

- Minimize All Windows—If you ever get to the point where your screen is so cluttered that you can't tell what's opened and what's not, use this option to clean up the mess. The Minimize All Windows option minimizes every application that you have running on the Desktop.

## The Start Menu

The Start Menu normally appears on the left side of the Taskbar. It contains a complete listing of all your applications, access to some system settings, and a few other things thrown in for good measure. Figure 23.17 shows how the Start Menu looks. Notice that there are actually seven main entries in the Start Menu. The following paragraphs describe each entry in detail.

- Programs—This is the list of applications installed on your machine. Unlike Windows 3.xx, the Explorer interface enables you to place folders within folders (programmers call this nesting). As Figure 23.17 shows, you can place applications several levels deep within the menu tree.

- Documents—Use this option to select a document that you previously opened using Explorer. This list does not store the names of documents that you open using the File | Open command of your application. The list can contain up to fifteen document names.

**Figure 23.17.**
*The Start Menu replaces Program Manager as the means to start applications installed on your machine.*

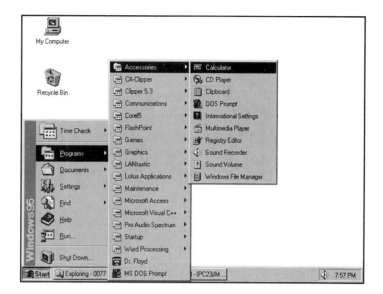

- Settings—Windows 95 provides you with a number of ways to change your environment. The Settings menu is just one centralized location for this information. It provides access to the Control Panel, Printers configuration dialog, and Taskbar configuration dialog.

- Find—This option opens the same dialog that you see when you use the Tools | Find command within Explorer. It enables you to find any file on your hard drive or a network drive using a variety of search criteria. Not only can you select a file by name and location, but by modification date as well. The Advanced tab of this dialog even enables you to look for a file based on its contents or its size.

- Help—The Help option opens the main Windows 95 help file. You can use this file to search for just about any information you need to run Windows 95. Microsoft has gone a long way in improving the help files in this version. Instead of providing you with dry facts, these files actually provide procedures you can use to get the job done. If that weren't enough, some of the help screens provide angled arrows as shown in Figure 23.18. When you click on an angled arrow, Windows 95 starts the application that the help topic relates to. For example, I opened up the Date/Time Properties dialog by clicking on the angled arrow shown in this figure.

- Run—Remember the File | Run command under Program Manager? Well, you can still use it under Windows 95. The Run option opens a dialog that enables you to start an application by typing its path and name. You can also include any appropriate parameters.

- Shut Down—Windows 95 is a lot more complex than its predecessor, Windows 3.*xx*. You saw one form of this complexity in the Registry section of this chapter. This option enables you to perform an orderly shutdown of Windows 95. This includes things like making sure all the data gets written to disk and that the registry information gets saved.

**Figure 23.18.**
*The Windows 95 help screens provide a lot more than dry facts. They also provide procedures you can use to get the job done and the ability to automatically start the applications required to do it.*

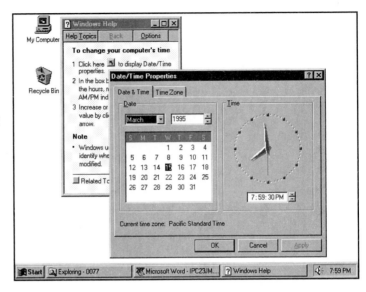

## The Taskbar Buttons

The Taskbar proper contains one icon for each application currently running on the machine. This group of buttons replaces the old task manager found in Windows 3.*xx*. Instead of using the Alt-Tab key combination to switch from application to application, you can now choose an application much as you would select a station on your television remote control. All you need to do is press the appropriate button.

There are a few features that you should be aware of. For one thing, the buttons shrink in size as needed to accommodate all the running applications. You can increase the size of the Taskbar to hold two, three, or even more rows of buttons if you so desire. Placing the mouse cursor near an edge produces the same double arrow that you use to resize other objects under Windows 95. Of course, the buttons will only get so big, then stop growing.

Another feature is the ability to obtain more information about the application by simply placing the mouse cursor over the top of its button. After a few seconds Windows 95 displays a long title for the application and the foreground data file. The same principle holds true for other items on the Taskbar. For example, holding the mouse cursor over the time indicator shows today's date. In some cases the information you receive from a button is less than awe inspiring. For example, the Volume icon displays a single word—Volume.

# The Settings Area

The Settings Area of the Taskbar usually contains two or more icons. Each icon can serve multiple purposes depending on what piece of hardware it is supposed to control. The two most common entries in this area are the Clock and Volume icons. In the preceding section, I explained how each of them reacts when you position the mouse cursor over their respective icons.

The Volume icon does a couple of things depending on what you do. A single click produces a master volume slider. You can use this to adjust the volume of all sounds produced by the sound board. Double-clicking on the same icon displays the Volume Control dialog. This dialog provide detailed control over each input to your sound board. It also includes a master volume slider. Right-clicking the icon displays an object menu. In this case it only displays two entries. The first takes you to the Volume Control dialog; the second displays the Audio Properties dialog.

The Clock icon provides similar functionality. A double click displays the Date/Time Properties dialog. A right click shows the object menu.

**Note:** There are several other interesting icons that can appear in the Settings Area. One of them enables international users to adjust their settings with ease. There is a special icon for PCMCIA-equipped machines. It displays the current bus status and type of card plugged in to the bus. Portable users will appreciate the battery indicator that appears in this area as well. With a quick click of the mouse, you can check your battery status before it becomes critical.

# The Physical Element

The My Computer folder provides a complete picture of the hardware status of your machine. This includes configuration as well as the actual device status. Figure 23.19 shows what the My Computer folder contains.

Notice that you can break the contents of this folder into three main groups: Printers, disk drives, and Control Panel. The printer icon shows a list of printers attached to the machine. This includes network as well as local printers. In all respects, the printer interface hasn't changed from Windows 3.*xx*.

The disk drive icons are new to Windows 95. Windows 95 displays a different icon for each drive type. The object menu for a disk drive is very complete as well. You can explore, format, find a particular file, and change the properties of the drive all from one menu, as shown in Figure 23.20.

**Figure 23.19.**
*My Computer is the central point for all hardware configuration and status information. This includes network as well as local devices.*

**Figure 23.20.**
*The Drive Object Menu contains everything you need to use and maintain the disk drives attached to your system.*

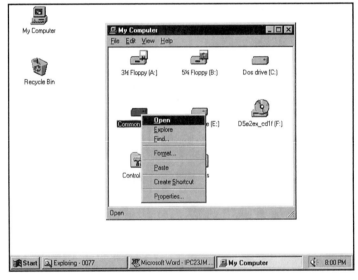

One of the more intriguing options is the Drive Properties dialog shown in Figure 23.21. The first tab provides some statistical information such as the formatted drive capacity and the amount of space the drive has left on it. The second tab gives you access to all the utilities that Windows 95 provides for the drive. This includes backup, defragmenting, and scanning tools. Lest you forget to perform these tasks from time to time, the dialog tells you when you last performed them. A simple click on the appropriate button launches a disk utility for that drive.

**Figure 23.21.**
*The Drive Properties dialog provides complete statistical information about the drive and access to the Windows 95 utilities for maintaining it.*

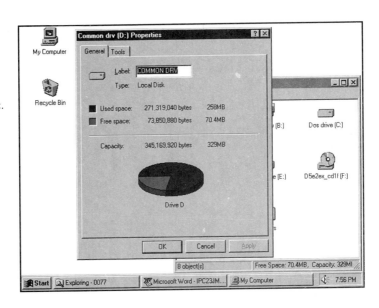

Computers contain a lot more that just drives and printers. This is where the Control Panel (Figure 23.22) comes in. Every device has its own icon in this section. Notice that there are icons for the display, mouse, joystick, sound card, and other devices. The purpose of each icon is to configure the hardware attached to your machine.

**Figure 23.22.**
*The Control Panel enables you to configure the majority of your hardware settings. It also provides icons for setting some software configuration parameters, and adding new software or hardware.*

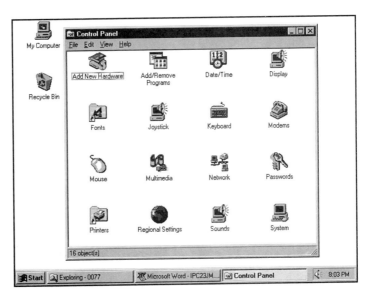

There are a few nonhardware icons here as well, and they deserve special mention. The Add/ Remove Programs icon enables you to add Windows-95 specific software to your machine. Do you remember the problems you used to have installing Windows software? Every time you wanted to remove one application and install another, it required a trip to SYSTEM.INI and WIN.INI to remove the old application's entries. The Add/Remove Programs dialog eliminates this. You can use the same dialog to add or remove software from your system. Windows makes sure all the registry entries stay up-to-date for you.

There are two other tabs in this dialog. The first enables you to add or remove parts of Windows 95 itself. For example, if you want to remove all the games that you installed, you would do it here. The third tab provides the means for creating a boot disk. The boot disk enables you to reboot from a floppy in case of a major hard disk failure. One of the problems with previous boot disk attempts is that the user could not easily update them to reflect changes in system setup. This new technique takes care of that problem.

The Fonts folder is much improved from Windows 3.xx as well. Instead of just giving you a list of fonts available on your machine, the Fonts folder provides detailed font information and a plethora of management tools. I especially like the ability to print out a sample of the font in a variety of point sizes. The fact that this folder now displays the name of the company who created the font will make it easier for system administrators to ensure that they comply with copyright laws.

The Control Panel is so important to computer operations that Microsoft provided three ways to access it in Windows 95. We've just seen one way to do it. I told you about another form of access through the Start Menu | Settings option as well. The third way is through Explorer itself. The Explorer utility is the Windows 95 version of File Manager. Unlike File Manager, though, it is not content to work only with disk drives. Explorer also provides the means to access the Control Panel and the Fonts Folder. So, what makes this method of accessing the Control Panel so special? Look at Figure 23.23. In addition to the large icon display that you saw before, Explorer provides several other views. The one that I find most helpful is the details view. Instead of the sometimes cryptic icon names displayed in the other views, this view provides a detailed name for each icon in the Control Panel.

# Moving from Place to Place

Windows 95 includes a briefcase. Like its physical counterpart, you use the Windows Briefcase to store files that you need to move from place to place. Of course, a physical briefcase uses paper as its storage media while the Windows Briefcase uses electronic media. The Briefcase sits on the desktop along with the Recycle Bin and My Computer.

Setting your briefcase up is very easy. All you need to do is install the Windows software (it's optional) and a Briefcase icon will appear on the desktop. Now, stuff the briefcase with all those files that you plan to move from place to place. What you should get is a centralized storage location for all the files you work on, even if those files appear in different areas of your hard drive. (For that matter, they could appear on a network drive.)

**Figure 23.23.**
*You can use Explorer to gain a detailed view of the Control Panel. Even though the icons are smaller in this view, the detailed explanations really help identify the purpose of each entry.*

Working with Briefcase files is no different than working with any other file. Windows 95 monitors the status of the files and presents a display of their status when you open the Briefcase icon. (See Figure 23.24.) Notice that it tells you when your Briefcase requires an update to keep it up-to-date with the files on your machine. All you need to do is select the Briefcase | Update All command if the files are out of date. Once the files are up-to-date, you can move the briefcase from your machine to a network drive or floppy.

**Figure 23.24.**
*Briefcase offers a fast and convenient method of centralizing your files. It also provides the means to move those files from work to home and back with a minimum of fuss.*

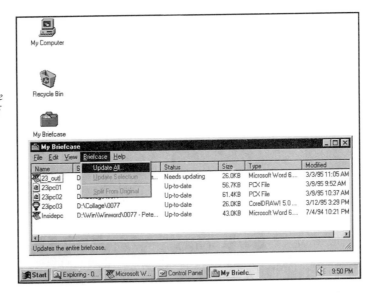

Moving your Briefcase from work to home is just as easy as using it. Just stick a floppy in one of your drives and right-click on the Briefcase icon. You should see a display similar to the one in Figure 23.25. Notice that you can update the Briefcase from here as well; you don't have to open it up if you don't want to. To move the Briefcase from your machine to a floppy, just select the Send To menu option and select a location. The Briefcase icon will disappear from the desktop and reappear on the floppy. Moving it back to your desktop the next day is just as easy. Just select the floppy drive in Explorer so you can see the Briefcase icon. Now right-click on it and drag it over to the Desktop. When Windows displays a menu asking what you want to do, click on Move. That's all there is to it!

**Figure 23.25.**
*Pop-up menu for My Briefcase.*

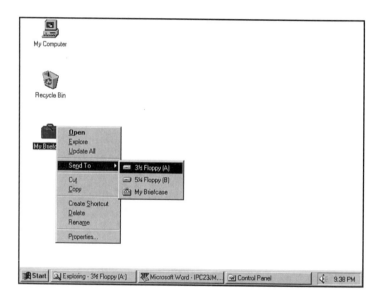

**Tip:** Here's a tip for those of you with bulging briefcases. You can compress the floppies used to transport information from one machine to another. Use the Drivespace utility to do this. Compressing the floppy will nearly double its carrying capacity, especially when you consider that most people carry data files, not the executable files required to edit them. Data files normally contain a lot of empty space that compression programs can squeeze out.

# Understanding Windows Memory Models

Just as Windows 95 gives you a completely new interface to work with, it also brings you some big advantages because of its new ways of handling memory. Before I can help you understand why

Windows 95's changes are such an improvement, I need to talk a little bit about how Windows used memory in versions 3.11 and earlier.

There are two distinct memory models in Windows. Windows 3.1 provides 16-bit application support. A 16-bit application uses 16-bit registers. A 16-bit register can only access 65,536 bytes of memory. This means that Windows can't access all of a machine's memory using one register. Because of this, Windows 3.1 uses a segmented memory model. The short definition of segmented memory is that a segmented memory model uses two registers combined to access all the memory in your machine. A segmented memory model introduces extra work because the programmer has to worry about both a segment register and an offset register. I explain exactly how this works in the next section.

Windows NT provides 32-bit application support. All of these applications use 32-bit registers. Because Windows NT can use all 32 bits of the 80386 and faster processor's registers, it doesn't have to rely on segmentation. One register can hold an entire address for up to 4,294,967,296 bytes of memory. The result is the flat memory model. Because the programmer only has to worry about one register, the flat memory model is more efficient than the segmented memory model.

Windows 95 provides support for both memory models. It uses the 16-bit segmented memory model to support older applications. Any new applications use the 32-bit flat memory model.

# Windows 3.1 Segmented Memory Model

The previous section briefly presents the two Windows memory models and how they differ. I made a statement that the segmented memory model is a lot harder for a programmer to use than the flat memory model used with Windows NT. Of course, the first question that comes to mind is why Microsoft would even bother using the segmented memory model for enhanced mode Windows 3.1. After all, enhanced mode is designed for the 80386, and we already know that it supports the flat memory model. There are two good reasons. First, the 80286 processor does not provide flat memory model support. If Microsoft had decided to use the flat memory model, they would have had to include a double set of files for every aspect of Windows 3.1. The second reason is equally simple. Windows 3.1 rides on top of DOS and DOS uses 16-bit code. Windows 3.xx already performs quite a juggling act in talking with DOS, and keeping a 32-bit ball up in the air as well would have been a little too much. So, we ended up with a 16-bit operating environment called Windows 3.1.

Now that you have some feel for why segmentation is still around, let's look at how it works. A segmented memory model uses two 16-bit registers to hold an address. In real mode the processor uses a segment and an offset. Think of the segment as the street number, and the offset as a specific house on that street. The processor combines the segment with the offset to create a 20-bit address for the 8086 or a 24-bit address for the 80286. Just how does it do this? The processor shifts the segment register's contents 4 bits to the right to make the transition. A 20-bit address yields the 1MB of address space that we have all come to know and love when using DOS. Of course, the bottom line for the application is that the application, not the operating system, has control over the memory it uses.

(Refer to Chapter 15, "The Memory Workbench," if you need more information on real mode operation.)

Windows doesn't operate in real mode; it uses protected mode. The theory behind the protected mode segmented memory model is slightly different than real mode. Take a look at Figure 23.26. This shows a simplified version of the protected mode segmented memory model. Notice that we no longer use a segment:offset pair, but a selector:offset pair. There is a big difference between a segment and a selector. A segment represents an actual location in memory, while a selector represents a position in a descriptor table. The table contains the actual location in memory. (It also contains a variety of other information that I won't cover here.)

**Figure 23.26.**
*Windows 3.xx uses the segmented memory model shown here. Windows 95 also uses this model for 16-bit applications.*

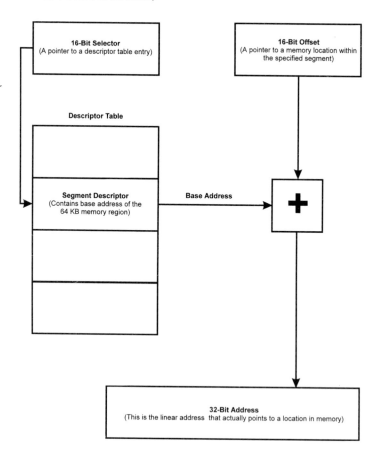

So how does this look-up table work? When Windows grants an application access to a specific range of memory, it gives that application a key to it. That key is the selector. The application sends two values to the processor when it needs to access memory. The first value is the key (selector) that the processor needs to unlock the memory. The second value is the exact location (offset) within that range. Using selectors gives the operating system control over the entire range of memory on the system. Since an application must use a key to unlock its memory and only the processor knows the physical location of that memory, the system should be fairly secure.

In fact, the selector does provide some security information to the operating system. Bits 0 and 1 of the selector tell the operating system its privilege level. This equates the rings of protection that I discuss later. Suffice it to say right now that 0 (00b) provides the most privileged access and 3 (11b) the least privileged. All applications run at privilege level 3 under Windows; only the operating system runs a privilege level 0. Bit 2 contains the number of the table that Windows should use to access the memory. There are two descriptor tables, the global descriptor table (GDT) and the local descriptor table (LDT). A value of 1 selects the LDT. Windows uses the GDT for all common data. There is only one GDT for the entire system. Each application also has its own LDT for private data. Finally, bits 3 through 15 contain the actual index into the table.

Rather than get mired in a wealth of bits at this point, let's just say that Windows verifies the application's security level is high enough to access the data it wants to see. It then takes the base address value (the protected mode version of a segment) that it finds at the specified location in the descriptor table and combines it with the offset to find the physical location of the requested data in memory.

There are several problems with the segmented memory model. The biggest one if you're a programmer is that you can only allocate memory in 64KB chunks. Remember, the address is made of a selector and an offset. Since the offset register is only 16-bits, it can only handle 64KB of memory. What this means to the programmer is that he or she has to write an application that manages a bunch of selectors, each pointing to a different 64KB chunk of memory. The chance of corrupting one of those selectors increases as the application uses more and more memory. It isn't too difficult to understand why a 16-bit Windows application could get confused and end up writing to the wrong section of memory. The results are usually catastrophic and end in a frozen machine.

Of course, there is a limitation here for the user as well. Have you ever wondered where all those "Out of Memory" messages come from? Many users have experienced the problem of Windows reporting that it has all kinds of memory available, then deciding for no reason at all that it doesn't. Well, here's one culprit. Every icon, every dialog box, every menu, and every other resource you can imagine has to go some place in memory for Windows to use it. When Microsoft originally designed Windows 3.0, they decided that all those resources had to go in what programmers call the near heap. The near heap is a 64KB chunk of global memory that Windows 3.0 sets aside for resources. Using the near heap increases execution speed, especially for time-consuming screen redraws, since the operating system isn't constantly manipulating selectors to access multiple 64KB chunks of memory. Needless to say, when you consider that just one icon is 766 bytes, it doesn't take too many of them to fill that 64KB heap.

After many user complaints about strange memory problems, Microsoft set aside two heaps in Windows 3.1. The first heap contains icons and other graphic resources. It's called the GDI heap. The other heap contains nongraphic resources like dialog boxes. It's called the USER heap. Even with two 64KB heaps, Windows 3.1 users still ran out of memory. There is an easy way to determine if you are about to run out of space in one of these two heaps. Look at the Program Manager About dialog sometime and you'll notice a percent of system resources value. This tells you the amount of that 64KB chunk of memory that's left in the smallest heap. In other words, if the GDI heap has 20 percent of its space left and the USER heap has 30 percent, Windows will report a value of 20 percent (12.8KB) for system resources.

> **Technical Note:** As did previous versions of Windows, the beta for Windows 95 uses a single USER heap for resources. At press time, it was impossible to determine whether this anachronism would be part of the final release of Windows 95—so there's no way to be certain this latest release of Windows won't bring with it the competition for resources that has so plagued its earlier versions.

# Windows NT Flat Memory Model

When Microsoft designed Windows NT, they decided to use a different memory model supported by 80386 and faster processors. This memory mode is known as the flat memory model. When the operating system places the processor in this mode, it essentially says that everything is going to use the same segment. The processor hasn't done away with segmentation, but the operating system chooses to ignore the capability. Eliminating segmentation greatly simplifies life for the programmer. No longer does the programmer need to worry about the segment registers; only the address is important.

## Finding an Address

You may wonder how the operating system maintains control over memory using the flat addressing scheme. Under the segmented scheme the processor maintained control through a table of selectors. The application used a selector as a key to open up to a 64KB chunk of memory. The flat addressing mode has a protection scheme as well. In fact, this scheme provides even more flexibility than the segmented model. Figure 23.27 shows the flat memory model.

There are three fields in each 32-bit address. Each field corresponds to one level of protection enforced by the processor under the flat memory model. Even though the programmer doesn't have to worry about these fields when writing an application, the operating system and processor do. The first field resides in bits 31 through 22 of the address. It points to an entry in the page table directory. Just like the segmented memory model, the flat model gives the application a key to specific piece of memory, not its actual location. Locating the right page table is the first step in finding the address.

**Figure 23.27.**
*The flat address model doesn't use a selector:offset pair to address memory. Each register contains a 32-bit address that is split into three fields.*

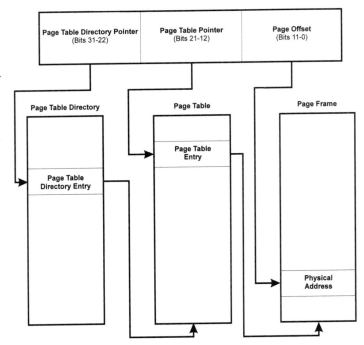

Let's take a couple of seconds to look at what a page table really is. Remember that in the segmented memory model an application would have to allocate memory in 64KB chunks. If it needed a larger allocation, then the application would have to ask for multiple chunks. A page table gets rid of this problem; the application simply asks for the total amount of memory that it needs and Windows provides it. The number of pages in this table corresponds to the number of 4KB pages that the application allocates. If an application asked for 400KB of RAM, then the table would contain 100 entries. As you can see, the flat address model is already more flexible than the segmented model.

Once Windows finds a specific page table, it uses the value in bits 21 through 12 of the address to find a specific page. Think back to what I told you about an application's memory limit before. Every application can use up to 4GB of memory. Now, look at the number of bits set aside for pages under Windows; there are 10. There are also 10 bits set aside for page table directory entries. If you take $2^{10}$ Page Table Directory Entries $\times 2^{10}$ Page Table Entries $\times$ 4KB pages, you get...4GB.

After Windows finds a specific page within a specific page table, it takes the address it finds there and adds it to the offset in bits 11 through 0 of the address. These 12 bits allow an application to select any byte within the 4KB page.

# Sleight of Hand Memory Management

Using 4KB pages provides a number of benefits when it comes to memory management. Remember in the previous section when I talked about the page table directory and the page table? Each entry in these tables contain 32 bits of data, yet the actual pointers consume a lot less than that. So, what does the processor use the additional space for? I don't want to get into a blow-by-blow description of every detail of 80386 memory management. However, it might be useful to look at what some of these extra entries do. Fortunately, both tables use the same format, so we'll cover them both at the same time.

Of course, the main purpose of using these tables in the first place is to point to something. That's what bits 31 through 12 do. In the page table directory they point to a page table. In the page table they contain the physical address that gets combined with the offset in the original address. Bit 6 contains the "D" or dirty bit. Whenever an application changes the contents of a page of memory, Windows changes the dirty bit. This is a reminder to the processor that it hasn't written the change to disk. If the processor wants to use this page of physical memory for some other purpose, then it needs to write the existing page to the Windows swap file.

Bit 5 contains the "A" or accessed bit. Whenever an application reads, writes, or executes a 4KB page of memory, Windows changes the status of this bit. Windows can use this bit to determine whether or not it should remove the page from memory to make room for something else.

Bit 2 contains the "U/S" or user/supervisor bit. This is part of the 80386 protection scheme. If the bit is set to 0, then it contains a supervisor page. Applications can never access supervisor pages because they belong to the operating system. On the other hand, setting the bit to 1 means that it's a user page. Applications can access any user pages that belong to them.

Bit 1 contains the "R/W" or read/write bit. You wouldn't want an application to overwrite the code in a page. Setting this bit to 0 prevents and application from doing so. Data pages are set to 1; code pages are set to 0.

Bit 0 contains the "P" or present bit. Windows needs to know whether a page is in physical memory or not. The application cannot use a page of memory that's sitting on disk in the swap file. The page has to reside in physical memory. If the application asks for access to a page of memory that is on disk, the processor raises an exception (basically an alarm). The exception tells Windows that it needs to retrieve the page from its swap file on disk so the application can access it.

As you can see, these table entries help Windows perform memory management sleight of hand. It can move 4KB pages from physical memory to disk as needed. Other bits protect operating system specific memory from prying application eyes. Still other bits help to protect your application from itself by preventing it from overwriting precious application code.

# Virtual 86 Mode

Up to this point you have seen how Windows manages memory for its own applications. What happens when you open a DOS box and run an application? The first thing you need to realize is that Windows takes a snapshot of your DOS environment before it completely boots. It creates a "phantom" DOS environment and holds on to it until needed. When you open a DOS box, Windows creates what is known as a virtual machine. This isn't a physical machine that you can touch, but it has all the same capabilities of a standard 8086. Once Windows creates this virtual machine, it copies the phantom DOS environment to it and you have a DOS box. This DOS box has all the same device drivers and TSRs as the DOS environment you left when booting Windows.

But what differentiates a virtual DOS machine from the rest of the Windows environment? The 80386 processor introduced a new mode called Virtual 86 mode (V86 for short) in which Windows can create multiple 8086s. Each of these virtual machines thinks that it is the only machine running. On the other hand, Windows applications run in protected mode. Windows has to switch between protected mode (to run Windows applications) and V86 mode (to run DOS applications). I won't go into the actual intricacies of how the processor switches between protected and V86 here; only a heavy-duty chip designer would enjoy that conversation. Suffice it to say that each machine is totally separate and that V86 mode is a third mode that emulates real mode, but doesn't actually run there.

# Windows Memory Types

Windows uses a variety of memory types to accomplish a variety of tasks. Some of them relate to Windows itself; others to the applications that Windows supports. The following paragraphs will help you understand these memory types.

- Conventional—This is the original 640KB of memory that IBM sets aside for DOS applications. Every DOS application needs conventional memory to run. Windows always uses a small piece of conventional memory as well, even if there is enough upper memory for it to load. Even though the processor can access that upper memory, DOS can't. For Windows to activate itself, it has to load a section of itself where DOS can call it. Remember our diagram of how Windows and DOS interact for file transfers? This is the reason why Windows has to load part of itself low. DOS calls this "stub" to get Windows' attention.

- Upper—IBM set aside 384KB of the 8086 address space for ROMs and video memory. In most cases a system never uses all that memory. A memory manager can fill this area with RAM, allowing you to load some of your device drivers high and free conventional memory for applications. Part of Windows 3.1 has to load in either conventional or upper memory as well to support the file system and other DOS-related functions. The more upper memory that Windows has to use, the more conventional memory that you'll have free to run DOS applications.

- High—This is a magic 64KB block that actually appears above the 1,024KB address limit. Special segmentation techniques make it possible for the processor to address this memory in real mode. Most users place DOS in this area to free more conventional memory.

- Extended—This is where Windows spends most of its time. A machine has to run in protected mode to access extended memory. This is the area beyond the addressing capability of the 8086.

- Expanded—Many game and some older business applications require expanded memory. At one time you needed a special EMS card to create expanded memory. Now, memory managers can convert extended memory to expanded memory on the fly. There are a number of ways to convert extended memory to expanded memory under Windows. The easiest way, of course, is to simply specify the amount of expanded memory you need in a PIF file.

# Windows 95 Architecture

Several elements make up the Windows 95 architecture, as shown in Figure 23.28. Each element takes care of one part of the Windows environment. For example, the Windows API (Application Programming Interface) layer enables applications to communicate with Windows internals like the file management system. You couldn't write a Windows application without the API layer. I describe each of these main components in detail in the following sections.

Before I begin a discussion of individual Windows architectural components, I'd like to direct your attention to the "rings" of protection that the 80386 (and above) processor provides. There are four security rings within the Intel protection scheme, but most operating systems only use two (or sometimes three) of them. The inner security ring is Ring 0. This is where the operating system proper is. The outermost ring is 3. That's where the applications reside. There are some situations in which an operating system gives device drivers better access to some operating system features than an application gets by running them at ring 1 or 2. Windows doesn't make any kind of a concession; device drivers run at Ring 0 or Ring 3, depending on their purpose.

Windows uses these protection rings to make certain that only operating system components can access the inner workings of Windows, that an application cannot change settings that might cause the entire system to crash. For example, Windows reserves the right to allocate memory from the global pool; therefore, the capabilities needed to perform this task rest at Ring 0. On the other hand, applications need to access memory assigned to them. That's why Windows assigns local memory a protection value of 3.

Think of each ring as a security perimeter. Before you can enter that perimeter, you have to know the secret password. Windows only gives the password to applications that it knows that it can trust; everyone else has to stay out. Whenever an application does try to circumvent security, the processor raises an exception. Think of an exception as a security alarm, and you'll have a pretty good idea of how Windows reacts. It sends the Windows police (better known as an exception handler) after the offending application. After its arrest and trial, Windows calmly terminates the offending application. Of course, it notifies the user before performing this task, but the user usually doesn't have much of a choice in the matter either.

*Figure 23.28.*
*Windows contains several major elements. Each element provides a different service to the user and other applications running under Windows.*

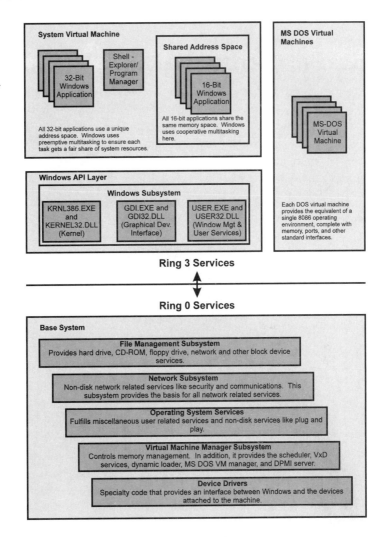

Figure 23.28 provides you with a pretty good idea of exactly whom Windows does trust. Applications and device drivers running at Ring 3 have very few capabilities outside their own resources. In fact, Windows even curtails these capabilities somewhat. Some of the activities that a DOS application could get by with, like directly manipulating video memory, aren't allowed here. The reason is simple, video memory is a shared resource. Any time another application would need to share something, you can be certain that your application will not be able to access it directly.

Now, on to the various components that actually make up Windows. The following paragraphs break the Windows components up into main areas; each of these general groups contain descriptions of the individual components and what tasks these components perform. Remember that this is only a general discussion. Windows is a lot more complex than it might first appear. The deeper you get as a programmer, the more you'll see the actual complexity of this operating system.

# System Virtual Machine

The System Virtual Machine (VM) component of Windows 95 contains three main elements: 32-bit Windows applications, the shell, and 16-bit Windows applications. Essentially, the System VM component provides most of the Windows 95 user specific functionality. Without it, you couldn't run any applications. Notice that I do not include DOS applications here. This is because Windows uses an entirely different set of capabilities to run DOS applications. It even runs them in a different processor mode.

Theoretically, the System VM also provides support for the various Windows API layer components. However, since these components provide a different sort of service, I chose to discuss them in a separate area. Even though applications use the API and users interact with applications, you really don't think about the API until it comes time to write an application. Therefore, I always think of the API as a programmer-specific service, rather than something that the user really needs to worry about. The following paragraphs describe the System VM components in detail.

- 32-bit Windows Applications—These are the new Win32 specific applications that use a subset of the Windows NT API. In fact, many Windows NT applications like Word for Windows NT will run just fine under Windows 95. A 32-bit application usually provides better multitasking capabilities than its 16-bit counterpart. In addition, many 32-bit applications support new Windows features like long filenames while most 16-bit applications do not. There are two additional features that 32-bit applications provide. The biggest one is the use of preemptive versus cooperative multitasking. This makes your work flow more smoothly and forces the system to wait for you as necessary, rather than the other way around. The second one is the use of a flat memory address space. This feature really makes a difference in how much memory an application gets and how well it uses it. In addition, an application that uses a flat address space should run slightly faster since it no longer has to spend time working with Intel's memory segmentation scheme.
- The Shell—There are two shells supplied with Windows 95, and you can choose to use either one of them. The newer shell, Explorer, provides full 32-bit capabilities. It also sports the new interface shown in Figure 23.2. Explorer combines all the features that you used to find in Program Manager, Print Manager, and File Manager. You can also use the older Program Manager (Figure 23.1) interface with Windows 95. It doesn't provide all the bells and whistles that Explorer does, but it will certainly ease the transition for some users who learned the Program Manager interface. Switching between shells is easy. All you

need to do is change the Shell= entry in the [Boot] section of SYSTEM.INI. Of course, Windows 95 also enables you to choose which shell you want to use when you install it.

- 16-bit Windows Applications—All your older applications—the ones you own right now—are 16-bit applications unless you bought them for use with Windows NT. Windows 95 runs all these applications in one shared address space. What this means is that it essentially groups all these 16-bit applications into one area and treats them all as if they were one task. You really won't notice any kind of a performance hit as a result, but it does make it easier for Windows 95 to recover from application errors. With it, Windows 95 can mix 16-bit and 32-bit applications on one system.

# Windows API Layer

There are actually two Windows APIs included with Windows 95. The first API is exactly like the old one supplied with Windows 3.1. It provides all the 16-bit services that the old Windows had to provide for applications. This is the API that a legacy application will use when it runs.

The other API is the new Win32 API used by Windows NT. It provides a subset of the features that all 32-bit applications running under Windows NT can access. The 32-bit API provides about the same feature set as the 16-bit API, but it is more robust. In addition, a 32-bit application enjoys the benefits that this environment provides. Of course, the biggest benefit that you'll hear most programmers talk about is the flat memory address space. Every application running under Windows—until now—has had to spend time working with Intel's segmented address scheme. A 32-bit application does not need to worry about segmentation any more. Every call is a near call; every call is in a single segment.

No matter which API you use, there are three basic components that your application will address. The 16-bit versions of these files are: GDI.EXE, USER.EXE, and KRNL386.EXE. The 32-bit versions of these files are: GDI32.DLL, USER32.DLL, and KERNEL32.DLL. The following paragraphs describe these three components in detail.

- Windows Kernel (KRNL386.EXE or KERNEL32.DLL)—This is the part of Windows 95 that provides support for the lower level functions that an application needs to run. For example, every time your application needs memory, it runs to the Windows Kernel to get it. This component does not deal with either the interface or devices; it only interacts with Windows itself.

- Graphical Device Interface (GDI.EXE or GDI32.DLL)—Every time an application writes to the screen, it is using a GDI service. This Windows component takes care of fonts, printer services, the display, color management, and every other artistic aspect of Windows that the user can see as they use your application.

- User (USER.EXE or USER32.DLL)—Windows is all about just that—windows. It needs a manager to keep track of all the windows that applications create to display various types of information. However, User only begins there. Every time your application displays an icon or a push-button, it is using some type of User component function. It is easier to think of the User component of the Windows API as a work manager; it helps you organize things and keep them straight.

There is actually one more piece to the Windows API, but it's a small piece that your application will never use. Windows 95 still starts out as a 16-bit application. It has to start out as a 16-bit application to implement Plug and Play. The Plug and Play BIOS contains separate sections for real mode and 16-bit protected mode calls. If Windows 95 started out in 32-bit mode, it couldn't call the Plug and Play BIOS to setup all your devices without a lot of overhead (see the section on thunking to understand why). All device configuration has to occur before Windows actually starts the GUI.

However, 16-bit mode operations end very soon after you start Windows 95. The user shell is a 32-bit application. As soon as the 16-bit kernel sees the call for the shell, it loads an application called VWIN32.386. This little program loads the three 32-bit DLLs that form the Win32 API. Once it completes this task, VWIN32.386 returns control to the 16-bit kernel, which in turn calls the 32-bit kernel. Windows runs in 32-bit mode from that point on.

## Getting 16-Bit and 32-Bit Applications to Work Together

Windows 95 consists of a combination of 16-bit and 32-bit applications. All those legacy applications and device drivers you use now have to work within the same environment as the new 32-bit drivers and applications that Windows 95 provides. You already know how Windows takes care of separating the two by using different memory schemes. The 16-bit applications work within their own virtual machine area. It would be nice if things ended there, but they can't.

There are times when 16-bit and 32-bit applications have to talk to each other. This doesn't just apply to programs the user uses to perform some work, but device drivers and other types of Windows applications as well. Most Windows applications use a memory structure called the stack to transfer information from one application to another. Think of the stack as a database of variables. Each record in this database is a fixed length so that every application knows how to grab information off it. Now here's where the problems start. The stack for 32-bit applications is 32 bits wide. That makes sense. It makes equal sense that the stack for 16-bit applications should be 16 bits wide. See the problem?

Of course, the problems are only beginning. What happens when you need to send a 32-bit value from a 16-bit application to a 32-bit application? The 32-bit application will expect to see the whole value in the EAX register. On the other hand, the 16-bit application expects to see the value in a combination of the DX and AX registers. This same problem translates to pointers as well. A 32-bit application, for example, will use the SS:ESP register pair to point the stack.

But wait, there's more! Remember that 16-bit applications use a segmented address space. An address consists of a selector and an offset. A 16-bit application combines these two pieces to form a complete address. On the other hand, 32-bit applications use a flat address space. They wouldn't know what to do with a selector if you gave them one. All they want is the actual address within the total realm of available memory. So, how do you send the address of a string from a 16-bit to a 32-bit application?

By now you are probably wondering how Windows keeps 16-bit and 32-bit applications working together. After all, there are a number of inconsistencies and incompatibilities to deal with. The stack is only the tip of the incompatibility iceberg. It is easy to envision a method for converting 16-bit data to a 32-bit format. All you really need to do is pad the front end of the variable with zeros. But, how does a 32-bit application send data to a 16-bit application? If the 32-bit application simply dumps a wide variable onto the stack, the 16-bit application will never know what do to with the information it receives. Clearly, the data needs to go through some type of conversion. Windows uses something called the "thunk" layer to allow 16-bit and 32-bit applications to communicate. Figure 23.29 shows the interaction of 16-bit and 32-bit applications through the thunk layer.

As you can see, the three components of the API layer also provide translation services in addition to the other services they perform. Each API component translates the data and addresses within its area of expertise. For example, the two GDI components translate all graphics data between 16-bit and 32-bit applications.

Most thunking is pretty straightforward. For example, Windows simply moves register data to the appropriate register. The thunk layer builds a new stack to meet the needs to the application receiving it. Address translation takes a little more work. In addition, address translation is very expensive timewise. Every time Windows has to translate an address, it has to perform several selector loads. The processor has to verify every selector load, so these translations can get cumbersome. Fortunately, you as an application programmer, won't have to worry too much about the actual thunk process. What you do need to worry about is making certain that the process actually takes place when calling a piece of code that needs it.

# Windows and DLLs

Under DOS an application has to contain every component that it needs to execute. The programmer links in library support for graphics, low-level utilities, and a variety of other needs. Of course, this whole scenario is based on the fact that the application is the only thing running under DOS.

Windows is a different kind of an environment. There is always more than one task running under Windows. Somewhere along the way someone figured out that if you have multiple applications running, there might be some duplicate code out there as well. For example, the display routines used by one application are probably the same as the display routines used by another application at some particular level. The same person probably figured out that you could reduce the overall memory requirements of a system if you allowed all the applications to share these redundant pieces of code instead of loading them from scratch for each application.

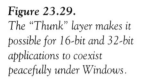

**Figure 23.29.**
*The "Thunk" layer makes it possible for 16-bit and 32-bit applications to coexist peacefully under Windows.*

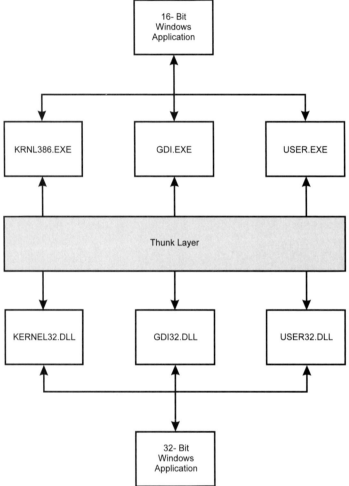

The DLL (dynamic link library) is the culmination of just such an idea. There are two forms of linking under Windows (or OS/2 or UNIX for that matter). The first link combines all the object modules required to create a unique application. That link cycle happens right after the programmer finishes compiling the code. The second link cycle happens when the user goes to load the application. This is where the DLL comes in.

There are unresolved references to functions inside every Windows application. Microsoft calls them Import Library calls. What these calls do is load a DLL containing the code required to satisfy that function call. If the DLL happens to be in memory when Windows calls it, then Windows increments the DLL's usage level to indicate that more than one application is using the DLL. When an application stops using a DLL, then Windows decrements its usage level. When the DLL's usage count goes to 0, then Windows can unload it from memory. In effect, using DLLs can save quite a bit of memory when loading multiple applications.

So, what does this have to do with the API? The Windows API starts with three files as described above. However, those three files call other files, DLLs to be exact. Rather than create three huge (or even on bigger than that) files, Microsoft chose to reduce the size of the Windows kernel by using DLLs.

This capability also provides Windows with a lot of flexibility. Consider printer support. All you need to add printer support for a new printer to Windows is copy some files to disk. At least one of those files will be a DLL. Every printer DLL contains the same entry points (function names), so Windows doesn't need to learn anything new to support the printer. The only thing it has to do is install a new DLL. Your application performs the same task when you tell it to print. It looks at the DLLs currently installed for the system. The application doesn't have to care about whether the printer is a dot matrix or a laser. All it needs to know how to do is tell the printer to print; the DLL takes care of the rest.

# Base System

The Base System component of Windows 95 contains all the operating system specific services. This is the core of Windows 95, the part that has to be in operation for Windows to perform its work. The following paragraphs describe each part of the Base System in detail.

- File Management Subsystem—This particular part of Windows 95 is examined in detail in the Windows Evolution section of this chapter. Essentially, this part of the Base System provides an interface to all the block devices connected to your machine. It doesn't matter how the connection is made—physically or though a network—all that matters is that your machine can access the device. The big thing to remember about the File Management Subsystem is that Windows 95 no longer relies on DOS to manage files.

- Network Subsystem—Windows for Workgroups was the first version of Windows to address the networking needs of the workgroup. It even incorporated networking as part of the operating system, rather than as an add-on, third-party product. Windows 95 extends this capability. Not only can you run a Microsoft peer-to-peer network, but Windows 95 provides protected mode hooks for most major LAN products as well. In fact, you can keep more than one network active at a time. Of course, the modular nature of the Network Subsystem enables other vendors to add to Windows 95 inherent capabilities through the use of VxDs.

- Operating System Services—This is the part of the operating system that deals with features like Plug and Play. It also fulfills miscellaneous user and operating system requests. For example, every time the user asks Windows 95 for the time of day, they are requesting a service from this Windows 95 component.

- Virtual Machine Manager—Ever wonder where the exact center of Windows 95 is? This is it; this is the component that holds everything else together. The Virtual Machine Manager takes care of task scheduling and it starts and stops every application on the system (including any DOS applications that you may run). This is the operating system component that manages virtual memory on your machine as well. Of course, your application uses the Windows API to make the request rather than talk with this part of the system directly. Since the Virtual Machine Manager handles all memory allocations, it also has to act as a DPMI (DOS Protected Mode Interface) server for DOS applications that run in protected mode. When a DOS application makes a memory request, it is actually calling routines in this component of Windows. As with Windows applications, DOS applications cannot directly access this component of Windows, the DOS application uses a DOS extender API to make its call. Finally, the Virtual Machine Manager is responsible for intertask communication. All this means is that all DDE and OLE requests filter through this section of the operating system.

- Device Drivers—Windows would never know what to do with your system if it weren't for the lowly device driver. This bit of specialty code acts as an interpreter. It takes Windows requests and provides them to the device in a format that it can understand. There are two forms of device driver supported by Windows 95. The first type is the real mode device driver that you used with Windows 3.1. The problem with using this type of driver is that Windows has to keep switching between real and protected mode to use it. Windows 95 provides a second type of device driver as well. The VxD or virtual device driver enables Windows to talk with the devices on your system without switching to real mode. There are three reasons to use VxDs over standard, real mode device drivers: Your system remains more stable, runs faster, and recovers from errors better.

# MS-DOS Virtual Machine

I separated the DOS virtual machine component of Windows from the other components for several reasons. DOS applications have formed the basis for using the PC for a long time. In fact, for many years there was nothing else available. Yet, most of these applications were written at a time when the standard PC ran one application and one application only. That one application had total control of the entire machine.

Windows 95 has to deal with that type of application in a different way than it deals with the Windows-specific applications on your machine. Each DOS application runs on what Intel terms as a virtual machine. Essentially the processor fools the application into thinking that it is the only application running on your machine at that moment. Each virtual machine has its own memory space and access to devices on the system. The amazing thing is that you can have many virtual machines running on your one physical machine at a time.

The word "virtual" is severely overused within the Windows environment. We have virtual memory, virtual system machines, and every other kind of virtual device that you can think of. I wanted to make sure that you understand that the DOS virtual machine is a different kind of virtual than all these other virtuals on the system. A virtual DOS machine runs in the Virtual 8086 mode of the processor, all the other virtual machines in Windows run in protected mode. Virtual 8086 mode creates multiple 1MB 8086 machines in protected memory. Each machine has its own copy of DOS, device drivers, I/O space, and everything else that an 8086 would have. About the only thing missing is the hardware itself, and that's why this machine is known as a virtual machine. It is a machine that you cannot touch, but it does exist. As far as the application is concerned, there is no difference between this machine and any real machine that it could run on.

The virtual machine hasn't changed much since the days when Quarterdeck first introduced QEMM. Except for a few new features designed to enhance the performance of applications running under the Windows virtual machine, this aspect of Windows hasn't really changed much from Version 3.1. There is, however, one exception to this rule. Some DOS applications use DPMI-compatible extenders that allow them to run in protected mode. Under Windows 3.1 these applications would still run under the processor's virtual 8086 mode. Windows 95 improves system performance by allowing these applications to run in protected mode.

# Events Drive Windows

Windows is an event-driven operating system. Just what is an event? Every time you press a key, touch the mouse, or change a setting, Windows recognizes it as an event. Applications can trigger events as well. For example, when Print Manager completes all the printing tasks in its queue, the printer icon disappears from the list of active applications. Completing all the print jobs in its queue is an event. There are timer events as well; you can program Windows to perform some task based on the ticking of a clock. Windows performs some task for every event. Either it calls the application that can handle the event, or it takes care of processing the event itself.

Unlike DOS applications, where a program follows a specific sequence of steps, a Windows application never knows what will happen next. The user could select a menu item or press a speed key sequence at any time. Other events include minimizing, maximizing, or resizing the applications' window. The user could perform any of the tasks that the application is programmed to perform in any order. The multitasking nature of Windows means that the application cannot even assume that it is supposed to handle the event. The user could use the mouse to select a menu item in another window that belongs to a different application. As a result, a Windows application contains two components: an event handler and a series of modules that actually respond to the events. Figure 23.30 shows a typical Windows application structure.

An application registers its event handler with Windows when you start it. Whenever an event happens, Windows calls each application to see if the event applies to it. The application that the event belongs to has to interpret the event and take a proper course of action. Usually this means that it calls one of the event-handling modules. Of course, it doesn't call the module directly; it goes through Windows first. This is another area where Windows and DOS differ. An application running under Windows has to coordinate all of its actions with the system as a whole.

**Figure 23.30.**

*A Windows application must provide the means for answering any type of user input at any time. Nothing happens in a set order with a Windows application.*

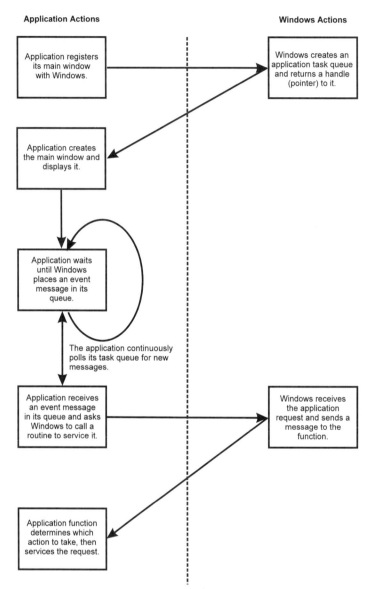

**Application Actions**

Application registers its main window with Windows.

Application creates the main window and displays it.

Application waits until Windows places an event message in its queue.

The application continuously polls its task queue for new messages.

Application receives an event message in its queue and asks Windows to call a routine to service it.

Application function determines which action to take, then services the request.

**Windows Actions**

Windows creates an application task queue and returns a handle (pointer) to it.

Windows receives the application request and sends a message to the function.

# The Programmer's View of Windows

As far as a programmer is concerned, Windows offers many of the same programming features as DOS, but with a graphic, event-driven orientation. Of course, there are vast differences in memory structure and so forth, but the basic goals and methods of reaching those goals are similar. If anything, Windows provides a level of programmer oriented tools that far exceeds what they get under DOS.

Perhaps it's not too amazing that you can draw some parallels between the services offered by the DOS interrupt 21h interface, and those offered by Win32 API supported by Windows 95 and Windows NT. (Remember that I discuss the DOS interrupt 21h services in Chapter 20, "DOS Serving Programs.") Table 23.2 shows the correlation between DOS services and similar services under Windows.

Table 23.2. Correlation Between DOS and Windows Functions.

| Int 21h Function | MS-DOS Name | Win32 API Call |
|---|---|---|
| 0Eh | Select Disk | SetCurrentDirectory |
| 19h | Get Current Disk | GetCurrentDirectory |
| 2Ah | Get Date | GetDateAndTime |
| 2Bh | Set Date | SetDateAndTime |
| 2Ch | Get Time | GetDateAndTime |
| 2Dh | Set Time | SetDateAndTime |
| 36h | Get Disk Free Space | GetDiskFreeSpace |
| 39h | Create Directory | CreateDirectory |
| 3Ah | Remove Directory | RemoveDirectory |
| 3Bh | Set Current Directory | SetCurrentDirectory |
| 3Ch | Create Handle | CreateFile |
| 3Dh | Open Handle | CreateFile |
| 3Eh | Close Handle | CloseHandle |
| 3Fh | Read Handle | ReadFile |
| 40h | Write Handle | WriteFile |
| 41h | Delete File | DeleteFile |
| 42h | Move File Pointer | SetFilePointer |
| 43h | Get File Attributes | GetAttributesFile |
| 43h | Set File Attributes | SetAttributesFile |
| 47h | Get Current Directory | GetCurrentDirectory |
| 4Eh | Find First File | FindFirstFile |
| 4Fh | File Next File | FindNextFile |
| 56h | Change Directory Entry | MoveFile |
| 57h | Get File Date and Time | GetDateAndTimeFile |
| 57h | Set File Date and Time | SetDateAndTimeFile |

*continues*

Table 23.2. continued

| Int 21h Function | MS-DOS Name | Win32 API Call |
|---|---|---|
| 59h | Get Extended Error | GetLastError |
| 5Ah | Create Unique File | GetTempFileName |
| 5Bh | Create New File | CreateFile |
| 5Ch | Unlock | UnlockFile |
| 67h | Set Handle Count | SetHandleCount |

Of course, it is very important to realize that the correlation is not precise; there are some differences that the programmer needs to consider. For example, some services may not react exactly the same way under Windows that the DOS counterpart does. Certainly getting and setting file attributes for these new operating systems is slightly different because the file system is different, but the concept is the same. In addition, some functions may be combined under Windows 95. For example, you only need one function to get the date and time, instead of the two required for DOS. Other Windows services may perform double duty. You use the CreateFile call to either create a new handle or open an existing one. DOS uses two calls to perform the same task.

There is another important point illustrated by this table. Note that you need to remember a hexadecimal number to call an interrupt 21h service under DOS. The same cannot be said of Windows. The programmer uses a plain English API (application programming interface) call instead. This makes Windows code a lot easier to document than similar DOS code. Some industry pundits (including me) call this self-documenting code.

This was one of the developer-oriented goals of the Windows development team. Even though the Windows programming environment is a lot more complex and certainly more confusing than its DOS counterpart, the code that a programmer writes is easier for someone else to read. No longer do you need to keep a book handy to translate esoteric codes, the API call name usually tells you the basics of what a function will do.

# Some Things to Think About or Try

1. Why do you think Microsoft decided to completely change the way the registry works in Windows 95? Open the Registry Editor and look under HKEY_CURRENT_CONFIG category. Can you find the key that contains your current display adapter settings? Do these settings differ from those found under the HKEY_LOCAL_MACHINE | Config key? Look at the other keys under the HKEY_LOCAL_MACHINE category. What purpose do you think that the entries under the Enum | Root key serve?

2. Windows provides a variety of protection mechanisms for the applications that run under it. For example, all 16-bit applications run in a shared memory space, while all 32-bit applications get their own memory space. What would be the effect of allowing each 16-bit application to run within its own memory space?

3. I provided a list of some Win32 calls and their DOS equivalents in Table 23.2. Why do you think that Microsoft chose not to include some of the older DOS service calls in the Windows 95 API? What is the benefit to using names, rather than numbers, to call various system services?

4. You saw how Windows uses events and messages queues to interact with each application. Can you think of any other way that Windows could more efficiently manage multiple applications without using an event driven architecture? How do you think other machines like the Macintosh handle this? Why would an event-driven architecture prove inefficient under DOS?

# 24

# Plug and Play

One of the most frustrating experiences a PC user or owner can encounter is installing an upgrade or new devices in his or her PC. Even so-called "PC experts" are often stumped by the problems encountered. Many have a real fear of anything electrical and opening up a PC can be a very intimidating experience. It is a little like opening up your VCR and playing with the circuit boards each time you wanted to play a new tape, or opening your TV to change channels. To most, the insides of a PC chassis are as foreign as the surface of the moon, so opening a PC is approached with great apprehension by the vast majority of users and owners. The exposed cables, circuit boards with strange devices, jumpers, and switches are looked upon as delicate, complex, and dangerous. In reality, a PC with its power off is generally safe and immune to normal handling, assuming a fairly static-free environment.

However, due to the historical nature of the PC's design, it is a very user-unfriendly device. This is particularly true when it comes to installing new devices or upgrades. Many times, installing an upgrade requires not only configuring the new device but reconfiguring one or more existing devices. Often a complex software installation procedure is required in addition to the hardware installation. Recent data indicates that a high percentage of installations are unsuccessful. Further, attempts to reverse an unsuccessful installation often result in the system no longer operating properly. Studies have shown that more than 25 percent of the multimedia upgrade kits (CD-ROM and Sound Card) sold are returned as a result of unsuccessful installation. Many computer stores and other retail outlets now offer installation and upgrade services to alleviate this problem. Another survey shows that the cost of maintaining and installing software and hardware upgrades in a corporate environment over the life of a PC exceeds $40,000 per system! Corporate users are typically better off than home PC users since a PC "specialist" is generally available to solve user problems on the job. The home consumer is left on his own to deal with poor documentation or constantly busy and poor customer service telephone support. Often, the home user's best alternative is to enlist the aid of a friend or relative with PC experience.

It has been estimated that nearly 30 percent of the households in the United States have some type of computer. The difficulties in maintaining, upgrading, and providing economical customer support are viewed as a key factor constraining wider acceptance of PCs in the home/consumer market segment. I am not sure this is really a barrier for first-time buyers, since most first time buyers expect PCs to be easy to use. Installation issues and problems are a major concern for providers of upgrade products and companies that have to provide end user customer-support services. Similarly, corporate PC users and managers are always interested in controlling PC costs. Another concern of the IBM PC-compatible market is how it competes with Apple and Apple Power PC products, which have traditionally been easier to install and upgrade than PCs. Many of the exciting new multimedia applications require installation of upgrade kits to operate properly. There is a fear that difficulties in supporting and installing PC upgrades will have a negative effect on the entire industry, limiting its growth and reducing profits. This fear is particularly acute in the services-sensitive large consumer/home market segment. There is a gathering consensus that PCs must become more user-friendly when it comes to maintaining and upgrading a system.

Against this backdrop, Microsoft and Intel, along with others, decided to address the upgrade nightmare. In 1994, at the Windows Hardware Conference, Microsoft and Intel proposed a comprehensive set of new standards to address this problem. These new standards are called the "Plug and Play" standards, sometimes abbreviated PnP. The goal of the standards is to promote the concept that new devices and upgrades should simply be plugged in and play, or operate properly, without the need for the PC owner or user to adjust or reconfigure the PC via jumpers, switches, special cables, or complex software installations. Simply put, new devices or upgrades would *plug in and play* without hassle. This does not mean that the system would not be reconfigured, just that configuration activities would be automatic and hidden from the user.

# Plug and Play: Not a New Idea

The idea that personal computer upgrades should be hassle-free and not require setting of jumpers or switches is not all that new. The original Apple II computer expansion slot design reserved blocks of memory space for each slot such that configuration information could be stored on each adapter board. It was possible to determine exactly what was installed in each expansion slot and, theoretically, automatically configure each of the adapters to eliminate conflicts. Most early Apple II adapters either ignored this capability or only used it to give fixed configuration information to the system's software. Very few adapters actually supported software reconfiguration. At least, the basic concepts and bus architecture features necessary to support Plug and Play were present, even though early products rarely used them fully.

The Amiga system introduced by Commodore in 1985 defined and supported a full Plug and Play capability. This "AutoConfig" feature totally eliminated jumpers and switches on the Amiga adapter boards. The specification permitted the operating system to interrogate the adapters and reconfigure them, if necessary, to eliminate conflicts and assign priority levels to meet the adapters' performance needs. Amiga's operating system enforced AutoConfig compliance and all third-party adapter suppliers complied with the specifications. This was perhaps the first system to have the hardware architecture and operating system support for true Plug and Play.

When Intel and Compaq promoted extending the ISA (PC AT) bus architecture to support 32 bits and new high-performance bus cycle types, slot-specific I/O port register space was allocated. This gave the new Extended Industry Standard (EISA) bus the necessary hardware support to enable Plug and Play. Unfortunately, the EISA specifications stopped at this hardware level and did not fully define a true Plug and Play system level (software) function.

When IBM introduced the PS/2 family of systems with the new Micro Channel Architecture (MCA), switchless, jumperless configuration was well-defined in the MCA architecture. The MCA standard required all adapters to fully participate in a well-structured protocol for identifying and configuring expansion slot adapters. Even motherboard subsystems fully complied with the MCA specification. Each third party adapter developer was assigned an ID number and was required to implement a minimum level of configuration capability. Unfortunately, the MCA architecture did not become a widespread success and has been surpassed by both VESA Local Bus systems and the newer PCI systems in popularity.

The newer VESA Local Bus and PCI busses define slot-specific addressing and reserve configuration space for each slot device. Again, this capability enables Plug and Play but does not in itself implement a full system level Plug and Play capability. Even if these expansion bus architectures fully implemented a Plug and Play specification, the system would still have to deal with the ISA slots also on these systems. All PCI and VESA systems are actually hybrid systems implementing both PCI or VESA Local Bus slots and ISA slots.

# Why Plug and Play Is Difficult on a PC

Each adapter and its associated application software and device driver software requires a certain set of PC resources to operate properly. This may include certain I/O port addresses, specific interrupt request levels, specific DMA channel, and access to specific blocks of memory address space. On the PC there are three basic problems:

1. There is a finite number of key system resources that must be shared.
2. There is no easy or standardized way to determine which resources are in use or which are available.
3. There is no easy or standardized way to determine an adapter or device's actual configuration, or to reconfigure an adapter's use of resources to eliminate conflicts.

The problems are further complicated by the fact that some adapters and applications, even if reconfigurable, may not operate properly. For example, certain applications and adapters—including most sound cards—require specific interrupt level priorities and/or DMA channel priorities to ensure proper operation. Simply assigning an unused interrupt level or DMA channel may not ensure proper operation. The new high-performance multimedia applications can be particularly sensitive to configuration settings. Many of these applications require sustained minimum data rates and are very sensitive to their interrupt level priority and DMA channel priority. The lower the DMA channel or interrupt level number, the higher its priority or importance. Higher priority numbers are serviced first over lower priority levels.

The first problem, that of finite resources, is common to all computer systems. Cost and other limitations simply do not permit unlimited resources. Even with unlimited resources, however, only part of the allocation problem would be solved. Problems can still be encountered when adapters and applications inadvertently select the same specific resource. In general, the PC's problem is not a lack of sufficient resources but of allocating resources so that conflicts of use are not encountered.

This problem exists both on the PC expansion bus slots and on other expansion ports on the PC system. The Plug and Play standards are being developed for all expansion bus architectures and interface ports on the PC. This includes ISA bus, EISA bus, PCI bus, VESA Local Bus, PCMCIA slots, serial ports, parallel ports, display monitor ports, IDE ports, and SCSI ports.

To reap the full benefit of the proposed Plug and Play standards, all levels of the system must cooperate. Busses and ports must be designed to enable extraction of device identification codes and configuration information. Adapters and devices must be designed to provide this information. Devices and adapters must be reconfigurable under software control to enable conflict resolution. A PC system's BIOS must support Plug and Play services. The PC operating system must be able to support resource allocation, provide application notification of selected resources, and report conflicts and problems that cannot be resolved. And finally, applications and device drivers must access configuration information and dynamically adjust to the environment when possible. This sounds like everything in the PC must change to enable Plug and Play. However, many benefits can be realized with only partial implementations of the full Plug and Play standards.

Before any level of Plug and Play support can be provided, it is necessary that the system's hardware and software support positive identification of device types in each slot or port and have access to the configuration information of each device. The capability to obtain this information directly from the attached device is the preferred option. Obtaining configuration information from hard disk files or nonvolatile memory not associated with the specific device carries the risk that the information is incorrect and does not correspond to the actual configuration settings on the device, or has become corrupted. For example, the information about hard disk type and configuration you might obtain from the battery-backed CMOS RAM on a PC's clock chip could even be wrong about the type of disk actually installed in the system.

In general, most expansion ports require no hardware changes to support Plug and Play capabilities. However, the devices that normally attach may require changes to support access to configuration information and support for software reconfiguration. The most stubborn problem to solve is how to provide Plug and Play support on the popular ISA bus. Even in the latest VESA Local Bus and PCI bus systems, which support slot specific configuration information, ISA bus slots are present. In fact, the majority of adapter upgrades are installed in the older ISA slots on these systems. This includes the popular upgrades such as FAX/modem boards, sound boards, CD-ROM drive adapters, and many LAN adapters. Adapters installed on the ISA bus contend for a specific set of system resources, including I/O port addressees, interrupt levels, DMA channels, and memory address blocks. All adapters installed on the ISA bus must select and use these common resources in a nonconflicting, cooperative manner.

Without the system knowing what adapters are installed and what their resource requirements are, it is impossible to automatically detect, let alone resolve, problems. If it were possible to identify the type of adapter in each slot and access information concerning its resource requirements and configuration status, at least potential problems could be detected by the system's software. Unfortunately, the ISA bus was not originally designed to support access to slot specific configuration information. Any adapter can operate anonymously in any slot, and identification of an adapter in a specific slot is not easily accomplished on the ISA bus. With all critical resources common to all ISA slots and no easy method for identifying an adapter type, its location, and its resource needs, management of resource allocation is left totally to the PC owner or user. Resource management is typically done manually by adjusting jumper and switch settings on adapter boards to avoid conflicts for the ISA bus resources. This often becomes a trial-and-error process, resulting in much frustration and often ending an unsuccessful upgrade installation.

# ISA Bus I/O Port Address Contention

Examination of the ISA bus I/O port addressing architecture illustrates the basic problems that any Plug and Play standard must deal with. The Intel X86 microprocessors all support addressing for 65,536 8-bit I/O port or registers. I/O port registers are used to communicate with I/O devices and their adapters installed on the system's expansion bus. A total of 16 address lines are used by the Intel processors to select I/O ports. In the original PC and PCXT designs, only the low order 10 bits of the I/O address field (bits A0 to A9) were used to select port addresses. This scheme allowed for a total of 1024 I/0 port addresses on both motherboard and the expansion bus slots. Even though the PC bus supported all 16 bits of the I/O port address, the PC design only decoded 10, resulting in the same 1024 addressees appearing at each 1K block boundary in the X86's I/O port address space. The PC design further divided the 1024 port addresses into two 512 address blocks. Addressees 0 to 511 were reserved for use by devices on the motherboard and addresses 512 to 1023 were available for use by adapter or devices installed on the expansion bus.

Later, the PCAT systems design changed the partitioning such that port addresses 0 to 255 were reserved for the motherboard devices and the expansion bus port range was increased by 256 addresses. I/O port addresses 256 to 1023 are valid on the PCAT or ISA bus expansion slots. Since most adapters are designed to operate on either the PCXT or ISA bus, few take advantage of the extended range available on PC AT ISA bus systems. Figure 24.1 illustrates the PC's use and partitioning of the X86 I/O port address space.

This limited I/O port address space must be shared by all expansion bus-installed adapters and devices. Some de facto standards have developed over time, and certain adapters and devices have accepted I/O port address locations. This is particularly true of motherboard devices installed on the ISA bus, such as the IDE port, and common expansion devices such as serial ports adapters, parallel port adapters, display adapters, and sound cards. Figure 24.2 illustrates usage of the I/O address by commonly installed adapter boards.

**Figure 24.1.**
*PC I/O port address partitioning.*

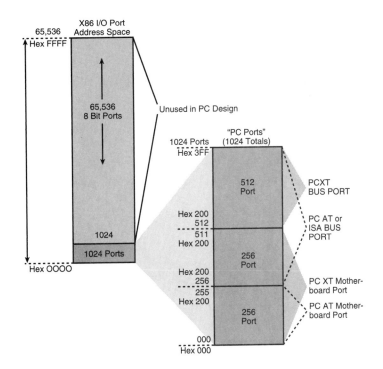

**Figure 24.2.**
*Typical usage of PC I/O port addresses.*

| Hex Range | Device |
|---|---|
| **ON THE MOTHER-BOARD** | |
| 000-01F | DMA controller 1, 8237A-5 |
| 020-03F | Interrupt controller 1, 8259A, master |
| 040-05F | Timer, 8254 |
| 060-06F | 8042 (keyboard) |
| 070-07F | Real-time clock, NMI mask |
| 080-09F | DMA page registers, 74LS612 |
| 0A0-0BF | Interrupt controller 2, 8259A |
| 0C0-0DF | DMA controller 2, 8237A-5 |
| 0F0 | Clear math coprocessor busy |
| 0F1 | Reset math coprocessor |
| 0F8-0FF | Math coprocessor |
| **ON THE ISA EXPANSION BUS\*** | |
| 1F0-1F8 | Fixed disk |
| 200-207 | Game I/O |
| 278-27F | Parallel printer port 2 |
| 2F8-2FF | Serial port 2 |
| 300-31F | Prototype card |
| 360-36F | Reserved |
| 378-37F | Parallel printer port 1 |
| 380-38F | SDLC, 2 bisychronous |
| 3A0-3AF | Bisychronous |
| 3B0-3BF | Monochrome display and printer adapter |
| 3C0-3CF | Reserved |
| 3D0-3DF | Color/graphics monitor adapter |
| 3F0-3F7 | Diskette controller |
| 3F8-3FF | Serial port 1 |

Note: These represent typical usage; there is no guarantee that these devices will actually correspond to these I/O port addresses in an actual system.

**Technical Note:** Several schemes have been developed to expand the I/O port address space to accommodate adapters that have large port address requirements. The most common scheme is to use indirect port addressing. This scheme uses an I/O port address register to hold a target I/O port address. Since each port I/O port is 8 bits in size, a total of 256 indirect port addresses can be defined for each normal I/O port address. Accessing an indirect port address requires two steps: first, the indirect address must be set and second, the actual read or write to the indirect port must be executed. Another common scheme is to use the higher order I/O port address bit (bit 10 to 15) not normally included in the port address. These 5 bits exist on the PC bus and can be used as additional register select bits. With this scheme, each PC I/O port address can be expanded to 64 additional port addresses. With these schemes, the number of I/O port addresses available on the expansion bus is generally not a problem.

The basic problem is how to avoid selecting an I/O port address block that is not already in use by some other device. A typical new upgrade often has a default setting that is selected on the basis that there is low probability that a conflict will exist. If the adapter fails, the user is often advised to select an alternate I/O port address block. If this alternate fails, the user typically needs to determine the cause of the conflict by examining all installed adapters, recording their settings, and adjusting them so that no conflicts exist. This is often just the tip of the reconfiguration iceberg. Device driver software and application software may also require reconfiguration to adjust to the new address block selected to avoid the hardware conflicts.

# ISA Bus Interrupt Request Level Contention

Interrupt request levels are another critical shared resource that must be allocated on the ISA bus. Interrupt requests are used by the adapter or device to notify the system's software that a device needs attention to either transfer data or to notify the system of a problem. The original PC design used an Intel 8259A interrupt controller chip to provide eight prioritized interrupt request inputs. Two of the inputs were used to support the motherboard's timer/counter interrupt request and the keyboard service interrupt request. The remaining six interrupt requests were available for use on the PC's expansion bus slots. Later the PCAT design expanded the number of interrupt requests by seven. This was done by the addition of a second 8259A interrupt controller chip. To input these new chip's interrupts to the system, interrupt input request level 2 was used on the first chip. Thus the PCAT and present-day PC support a total of 15 interrupt request inputs. One additional Non-Maskable Interrupt (NMI) request also exists and goes directly to the microprocessor. It is used to report high-priority error conditions. Interrupt request inputs are also defined on the VESA Local bus slots and the PCI bus slots. Typically, these interrupt request inputs are routed to one or more of the ISA bus interrupt inputs, usually under software control. Figure 24.3 illustrates the PC's interrupt request architecture and typical usage.

*Figure 24.3.*
*PC interrupt request*
*level usage.*

| Level | | Function |
|---|---|---|
| Microprocessor NMI | | Parity or I/O channel check |
| *Interrupt Controllers* | | |
| *8259A-1* | *8259A-2* | |
| | | |
| IRQ0* | | Timer 0 output |
| IRQ1* | | Keyboard interrupt input |
| IRQ2* | | Interrupt input from 8259A-2 |
| | IRQ8* | CMOS real-time clock interrupt |
| | IRQ9 | Replaces bus IRQ2 |
| | IRQ10 | Extension slot IRQ |
| | IRQ11 | Extension slot IRQ |
| | IRQ12 | Extension slot IRQ |
| | IRQ13* | Numeric coprocessor IRQ |
| | IRQ14 | Fixed disk adapter IRQ |
| | IRQ15 | Extension slot IRQ |
| IRQ3 | | Serial port 2 if installed |
| IRQ4 | | Serial port 1 |
| IRQ5 | | Parallel port 2 if installed |
| IRQ6 | | Diskette controller |
| IRQ7 | | Parallel port 1 |

PCI or VESA Local Bus Interrupt requests are mapped to one or more of these inputs

Note: IRQ 8 through 15 are cascaded through IRQ 2.
Note: IRQ 0 is the highest priority and IRQ 15 is the lowest priority.
*Used on Motherboard.

As with the I/O port addressing, there is no easy or defined way of determining which interrupt request inputs are in use, although a number of de facto standards exist, as shown in Figure 24.3. As with the I/O port addressing problem, allocation of interrupt request inputs is the PC owner or user's responsibility and is managed manually by jumpers and switches on each adapter board. Selection of interrupt input requests involves one additional problem not present in the I/O port selection process. The interrupt input requests are prioritized and certain applications need a certain priority level input to operate properly. Simply avoiding a usage conflict will not guarantee that the upgrade will operate properly. Unlike the I/O port addresses, where the number of I/O port addresses are normally not an issue, the number of interrupt input requests are often insufficient to support a system with several adapters installed. It would be highly desirable to dynamically reassign interrupt input requests. Unfortunately, this is very difficult on the PC due to the use of the edge-sensitive mode on ISA bus interrupt request inputs. In an edge-sensitive mode, an interrupt level is only recognized when it changes state—from off to on. All new busses support the level-sensitive mode, thus permitting multiple devices to simultaneously attach to and use the same interrupt request input. In a level-sensitive mode, an interrupt is considered active all the time, even after it changes state. Thus the request can be detected at any time, even after it transitions to an active state.

# ISA Bus DMA (Direct Memory Access) Channel Contention

Another scarce, shared resource on the PC ISA bus is its DMA channels. In the PC design, DMA channels are used to perform high-speed data transfers between adapters or devices and system memory. This is done without interrupting the microprocessor and is key to supporting many high-speed devices such as LAN adapters, Video Capture devices, and CD-ROM drives. The original PC design supported four 8-bit DMA channels using the Intel 8237A-5 chip. One of these channels was used to support system-wide DRAM memory refresh cycles. The remaining three channels were available on the PC and PCXT expansion bus slots. With the introduction of the PCAT, a second 8237A-5 chip was added to the system. The second DMA controller supported three 16-bit channels, the fourth channel was used to cascade DMA requests from the original 8-bit controller. In addition, channel 0 on the original controller was relieved of its memory refresh functions and made available for general use on the ISA expansion bus slots. Figure 24.4 illustrates how DMA channels are used in the PC.

**Figure 24.4.**
*PC DMA channel usage.*

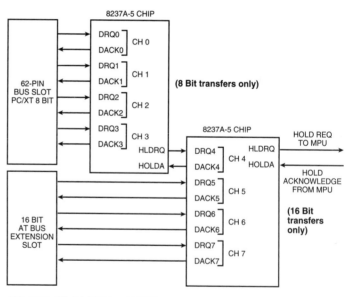

Note: 1) Highest Priority is DRQ0, Lowest is DRQ7.
      2) The System Floppy Disk Controller uses 8 Bit DMA channel 3.

Allocation of DMA channels is even more complicated than interrupt level request inputs. DMA channels are also prioritized and some applications are very sensitive to the priority assigned. Furthermore, not all of the DMA channels are the same; some are for 8-bit data transfers and others are only for 16-bit data transfers. To select a DMA channel, two jumpers or switches normally are needed: one to select the request (DRQx) and another to enable the correct acknowledge response (DACKx) signal.

# ISA Bus Memory Address Contention

Some device adapters contain BIOS code in ROM or data buffer RAM. LAN adapters are examples of upgrade adapters that typically have both BIOS ROM and a RAM data buffer. These memory devices must be allocated memory address space on the ISA bus. This problem is nearly identical to the I/O port address allocation problem. Most devices want to share memory space in the crowded area below the 1M memory boundary. Fortunately, most adapters with on-board RAM or ROM support enable and disable modes along with programmable relocation support. Installable ROM BIOS extensions are already defined using a header in each ROM device. The Plug and Play standards define extensions to this header to further assist in managing Plug and Play conflicts.

One can begin to appreciate the difficulties in managing system configurations when adapters or devices have to follow so many rules concerning configuration of I/O addresses, interrupts, DMA, and memory address blocks. Without access to device information and the ability to reconfigure devices, system software (BIOS, operating systems, device drivers, and even applications software) can be of little assistance.

# How ISA Bus Plug and Play Works

To overcome the lack of slot-specific address space supporting device identification on the ISA bus, Microsoft derived a clever algorithm that, when combined with new circuitry on each Plug and Play compliant adapter board, enables access to configuration data on Plug and Play boards installed in ISA bus slots. Unfortunately, the scheme only works on newer adapter boards that implement Plug and Play circuitry. However, the scheme gracefully allows coexistence of both older ISA adapter and new Plug and Play boards. The scheme does not allow identification of which boards are in what slots, but it does enable all installed Plug and Play boards to report their presence and configuration information in a complete and orderly manner.

After a PC is powered on, all Plug and Play adapters are initially set in an inactive mode and do not respond to any ISA bus commands. All Plug and Play adapters are set into configuration mode by the system's software issuing an *initiation key sequence*. This consists of a series of I/O port writes to special auto configuration I/O port registers on each Plug and Play adapter. All adapters simultaneously check this key sequence and, if properly received, set themselves to configuration mode. Once all Plug and Play boards are in configuration mode, each board is isolated using feedback data on the ISA data bus, which uniquely defines each board by a 72-bit serial identification code assigned to each adapter and stored on the adapter in nonvolatile memory. Once a Plug and Play board is isolated, on-board configuration data can be read and a handle assigned to that board. This process is repeated until no boards respond to the isolation protocol. The final step is for the system's software to reconfigure the Plug and Play boards to remove all conflict in resource allocation and meet the priority level needs of each board's DMA and interrupt performance requirements.

For a much more detailed explanation of the initiation key sequence and its associated hardware and the adapter isolation protocol and related hardware, please refer to the Plug and Play ISA Specification from Microsoft or Intel. Each Plug and Play adapter is required to implement a minimal set of functions, including a minimal set of Card Control Register, Logical Control Register, and Logical Device Configuration registers. The Plug and Play ISA specifications include a complete ISA Plug and Play board example design, complete with schematics. Figure 24.5 illustrates the functional flow of events for a complete Plug and Play compliant system design. Figure 24.5 also defines the Plug and Play responsibility split between BIOS and the operating system. A Plug and Play BIOS specification has also been developed by Microsoft and several prominent BIOS suppliers.

**Figure 24.5.**
*Plug and Play event sequence in a full Plug and Play system.*

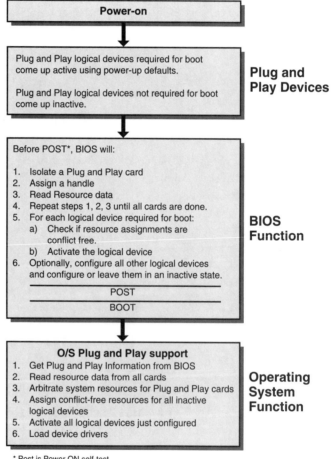

**Power-on**

Plug and Play logical devices required for boot come up active using power-up defaults.

Plug and Play logical devices not required for boot come up inactive.

**Plug and Play Devices**

Before POST*, BIOS will:

1.  Isolate a Plug and Play card
2.  Assign a handle
3.  Read Resource data
4.  Repeat steps 1, 2, 3 until all cards are done.
5.  For each logical device required for boot:
    a)  Check if resource assignments are conflict free.
    b)  Activate the logical device
6.  Optionally, configure all other logical devices and configure or leave them in an inactive state.

POST

BOOT

**BIOS Function**

**O/S Plug and Play support**
1.  Get Plug and Play Information from BIOS
2.  Read resource data from all cards
3.  Arbitrate system resources for Plug and Play cards
4.  Assign conflict-free resources for all inactive logical devices
5.  Activate all logical devices just configured
6.  Load device drivers

**Operating System Function**

\* Post is Power ON self-test

# Levels of Plug and Play Support

For a PC system to be fully Plug and Play compliant, many levels of support for Plug and Play must simultaneously exist. At the highest level, the application must be Plug and Play aware. It must be capable of automatically requesting system resources from the operating system and dynamically adjusting its needs as dictated by the operating system. The operating system must be fully capable of managing the available resources to eliminate conflicts, meet the needs of the applications requesting resources, and support the automatic installation and reconfiguration of device drivers. The system's BIOS must be able to isolate and interrogate Plug and Play devices and report conflicts or attempt to resolve them by reconfiguration. BIOS must also support reconfiguration requests from the operating system. And of course, the adapters and devices must fully support Plug and Play specifications associated with device identification, configuration reporting, and reconfiguration support. The following is a progressive list of the expanding levels of support that Plug and Play provides in a system, depending on the level of Plug and Play compliance supported.

1. Basic assistance in hardware configuration through separate installation utilities and manuals requires no Plug and Play levels.

2. Automatic configuration of Plug and Play compliant hardware elements requires Plug and Play BIOS or operating system.

3. Automatic configuration of both Plug and Play compliant hardware and its associated device drivers requires both Plug and Play BIOS and operating system.

4. Dynamic configuration and reconfiguration of Plug and Play compliant hardware and device drivers (permits changes on the fly after system boot) requires both Plug and Play BIOS and operating system.

5. Dynamic configuration and reconfiguration of Plug and Play compliant hardware, device drivers, and applications requires Plug and Play compliant BIOS, operating systems and applications.

# Limitations of Plug and Play in Partial Implementations and Mixed Systems Environments

What happens when the system is not fully Plug and Play compliant or one or more of the Plug and Play elements are missing? Also, how does Plug and Play deal with mixed systems in which some adapters or devices are Plug and Play compliant and others are not? Given the ambitious nature of the Plug and Play initiative, partially compliant and mixed systems are likely to be common over the next few years as the industry proceeds to full compliance. For example, Windows 3.1 does not support Plug and Play, so what benefit can be derived from having a Plug and Play BIOS or Plug and Play adapters or devices? Even without a Plug and Play operating system, a Plug and Play BIOS will still try to configure your system to minimize resource conflicts. If Plug and Play adapters are present, they will automatically be set up to at least their default configurations. Intel is now offering a Windows upgrade that adds Plug and Play support to Windows 3.1. What happens when the operating system supports Plug and Play but the BIOS does not? For example, how does Windows 95, a Plug and Play operating system, operate on older non-Plug and Play systems? In this case the operating system takes on much of the function of the Plug and Play BIOS and in most cases properly configures and allocates resources in spite of the BIOS. Microsoft makes no pretense concerning its dislike of PC BIOS. They would like to eliminate BIOS and absorb its function in Windows. Why buy Plug and Play compliant adapters and devices if neither the OS or BIOS supports Plug and Play? Adapters and devices that support Plug and Play often come with set-up utilities or Plug and Play drivers. The install utilities allow the user or owner to plug in the device and perform the manual configuration via a software set-up menu. This at least removes the confusion over jumpers and switches and eliminates the need to reopen the system to reconfigure the adapter or device. What about mixed systems? A Plug and Play compliant system can handle both Plug and Play adapters and non-Plug and Play devices. Due to the presence of non-Plug and Play adapters and devices, the success rate of trouble-free upgrades may be reduced. But at least the problem is not with the Plug and Play devices. Further, reconfiguration of Plug and Play devices is still easier, even in a mixed system.

# User Strategy for Plug and Play

The key point is that any level of Plug and Play compliance improves the upgrade situation. In general, Plug and Play capability can be added to any system, either through operating systems upgrades or BIOS upgrades. Selecting adapter or devices with Plug and Play compliance now, even though your system is not fully Plug and Play compliant, will ease installation problems immediately and in the future. Obviously, a fully compliant system is the best, but any level of Plug and Play will provide immediate benefit when it comes to upgrade installations.

# Plug and Play on Other Busses and Ports

Plug and Play support for the ISA bus has received most of the industry's attention. This is because it is the most popular expansion bus and has the most challenging problems to solve. Full Plug and Play specifications are being developed for other expansion bus architecture and interface ports. Generally speaking, these busses and expansion ports already support device identification and access to configuration information as part of their specification. Plug and play efforts to support these other busses and ports normally involve extending the existing specification to provide additional information and a standardized method and approach to implementing reconfiguration under software control. Plug and Play extensions are under development for VESA Local Bus Expansion slots, EISA bus expansion slots, PCI bus expansion slots, IDE and Enhanced IDE ports, parallel ports, serial ports, PCMCIA slots, and display monitor ports.

Another area that creates a significant set of problems for PC users is the upgrading of display adapters and/or display monitors. Configuring display adapter device drivers to match display monitor refresh rates, scan rates, and screen resolution sizes can be a formidable task. The Video Electronics Standards Association (VESA) has recently defined a new serial bus interface between the display adapter and display monitor that permits the system's software to interrogate the display and automatically configure the display adapter and device driver to match the display's capabilities. This VESA Plug and Play standard uses the Access.bus protocol to communicate between the display and display adapter.

# Impact of Plug and Play on System's Cost

In general, the basic system incurs no additional costs to support Plug and Play. No extra circuits or chips are required on the system to support Plug and Play. If you have an older system, you may have to purchase a new Plug and Play BIOS. If you select a system with a FLASH memory BIOS, you will be able to upgrade to Plug and Play by reprogramming the FLASH memory with a Plug and Play BIOS version.

Some expense may be incurred if you have to upgrade adapters or devices to support Plug and Play. A chip that converts a normal ISA bus adapter to Plug and Play costs about $5.00. If the function is implemented in an existing chip, the cost may be less. Plug and Play requires that certain configuration information be installed in nonvolatile memory on the adapter or device. This is normally done in an EEPROM device or FLASH memory device costing $1.00 to $2.00. The total cost increase to support Plug and Play should be less than $7.00 per device or adapter. This would translate to approximately $14.00 at the retail level.

# Plug and Play and Other Related Standards

In April of 1994 the Desktop Management Task Force, a consortium of industry leaders in hardware, software, and networking, completed the specification of a new standard called the Desktop Management Interface (DMI). The DMI standard was developed primarily to manage PC configurations on networks. DMI's intent is to not only support Microsoft Windows but most major operating systems environments and non-Intel architecture platforms. The DMI standard can be viewed as a higher level of systems software that interfaces to the Plug and Play operating systems services. DMI generates a number of small files called Management Information Format(MIF) Files. These MIF files contain detailed information on the system's resources and configuration. In general, the Plug and Play facilities of the PC system can be used to help construct these files.

Standards such as Plug and Play and DMI are key to enabling the PC to expand its markets. Difficulty of use is a major problem limiting the PC's acceptance by less technical users. One of the fastest growing markets for the PC is the home consumer market. Without PC improvements like Plug and Play, the PC will have a difficult time meeting the needs of the set of nontechnical users who expect the PC to be as simple to operate as a TV!

# 25

# Multimedia

PC "multimedia" is a term clearly open to interpretation. Ask ten people for a definition, and you are likely to get ten different answers! You can think about multimedia as applications or as technologies available to applications. Here, I take the second approach, looking at PC multimedia as a set of enabling technologies for multimedia applications. The enabling technologies that fall under the heading of multimedia are generally agreed to include PC graphics (including text), 2-D and 3-D images and animation, video (including full-motion live video and recording and playback of stored compressed video), and sound (including recording and playback of digital voice and music as well as speech recognition and synthesis). There are also a number of multimedia supporting technologies such as CD-ROM, high-performance LANs, and data compression and decompression technology.

In the purest definition of the term, practical use of any two or more of these technologies defines a multimedia application. In many of these areas, standards have been developed to enable applications across different hardware and software environments on PC platforms. I also try to point out where standards exist and how to avoid the many pitfalls in developing and using multimedia applications. Due to the high data rates and stringent real-time performance requirements of multimedia, system performance is key. Tailoring a system design to support multimedia applications can be a complex task. I will point out areas that are critical to supporting certain types of multimedia technologies and applications. This, in turn, will help you optimize your current system and make wise purchase decisions about systems you acquire in the future.

# Multimedia Applications

A good way to gain an understanding of multimedia is to cover a few basic multimedia applications and point out which multimedia technologies are used in each. Multimedia applications have always taken a long time to develop, primarily due to a lack of useable development tools. Now with better tools, Pentium-based PC performance and dramatically improved audio and video technologies, multimedia applications are coming to market at a much higher rate and with much better quality. The following summary is only a sampling of the major multimedia applications. I am sure you can think of many more!

Perhaps the most demanding multimedia applications are games. A game typically uses animation, real-time 3-D graphics, video playback, user input from game controllers, prerecorded sound, and generated sound. Many of these data types are obtained from compressed data stored on CD-ROMs. Due to the high level of fast action interactivity required by games, they are among the most demanding multimedia applications.

Education and training are other classic multimedia applications that involve a use of graphics, video, and audio, often in an interactive mode. Computer-aided education and training applications enable learning at an individual's pace while using realistic still and full-motion video images to reinforce the desired message. Training can be brought right to the job site and these applications provide independence from a classroom, instructor, or restrictive schedule.

Use of 2-D and 3-D graphics combined with text is now common in PC-generated presentations and information-display applications. Now audio and full-motion video are being added to the latest PC presentation software packages.

Video conferencing is now becoming popular across both local area networks and wide area networks. New high-speed LAN and digital wide area networks such as ISDN have enabled use of full-motion video and audio between PCs.

Virtual reality for games, complex modeling, and simulations are now possible on the latest PCs. These applications make use of real-time 3-D rendering, with compression and decompression algorithms for both video and audio. New PC display adapter technology combined with the high-performance Pentium class processor now makes applications that were once only available on mainframe computers or expensive workstations available on reasonably priced PCs.

Just like in "Star Trek," you now can speak to your computer. The latest voice synthesis and recognition software and hardware enable you to navigate through an application using voice commands. The more sophisticated technologies can recognize speaker-independent, continuous speech (speech in which the words run together as in normal talking) with better than 90 percent accuracy.

With the advent of online services such as Prodigy, America Online, and CompuServe, applications supporting advertising and home shopping are now developing. These applications need photo realistic 3-D images that are compressed and decompressed by the PC. New low-bit-rate full-motion video is also very desirable because it reduces the speed of data transfers and the amount of data needed to represent moving or still image pictures in the PC environment. Many online services offer distribution of digital compressed CD-quality audio over the service. Interactive multiplayer games are also becoming more popular.

One of the more demanding applications of multimedia technology is video production. This application requires video capture, image compression and decompression, image editing, special effects such as fades and transitions, and audio synchronization. The capability to add captioning and graphic overlays to video is also necessary. Two levels of this application exist: the professional user involved in studio video production and the home or office user who wants to edit and produce home video or presentation-quality video for personal or corporate applications.

# Multimedia Audio Technology

Due to the low cost and relatively low performance requirements of digital audio, it is one of the most widely accepted and deployed multimedia technologies on the PC. Digital audio is commonly used to support games and many PCs now come with a sound card or sound support built in on the motherboards. New Pentium class PCs are now powerful enough to perform much of the sound processing directly on the PC, further reducing the cost of sound on PCs. Sound is not only a requirement for games but many multimedia applications benefit significantly, for example, video conferencing, educational and instructional applications, and play back of full-motion movies all require sound support on the PC.

# The Basics of Digital Sound

Sound in the analog world is normally represented as a voltage or current that is continuously varying in amplitude and frequency. The amplitude of the signal can be thought of as the volume level and the rapid variations in amplitude (frequency) as the tone. The audio analog signal is amplified and applied to an electromagnet, which moves the cone of a speaker, producing the audible sound waves that your ear picks up. For the computer to handle an audio signal, it must convert this analog electrical signal to digital information. This is done with a device called an Analog to Digital Converter (ADC). The reverse process of converting a digital sound representation back to an analog signal is accomplished with a device called a Digital to Analog Converter (DAC). The ADC does the conversion of the analog signal to a digital one by sampling the amplitude of the signal at a periodic rate. This is like taking a digital snapshot of the analog signal at a very high speed. The size of the sample used and the rate at which the samples are taken determine how well the digital data represents the analog signal. For example, the human ear can generally hear audio signals in the frequency range of 20 to 20,000 KHz. Mathematically, it can be proven that to reproduce an audio signal with a maximum frequency content of 20,000 Hz (the limit of human hearing), the sample rate must be at least 40,000 times/second or greater, or twice the maximum frequency content of the audio signal.

The other key element of digital quality is the sample size. If, for example, the analog signal is sampled and assigned a maximum 8-bit value, only 256 signal levels can be used to represent the signal's amplitude at the sample time. (This is analogous to the fact that 8-bit color depth gives you only 256 colors on-screen.) When these samples are played back, they can only crudely approximate the true values of the original analog signal. Figure 25.1 illustrates how an analog audio signal is first sampled and converted to a digital data stream, and how that digital data is then used to reconstruct the original signal. The large steps between the 8-bit samples cannot properly reproduce the original smooth analog signal. These large steps in the signal, due to use of a small sample value (8 bits), actually introduce high frequency noise in the output of the DAC. All of these problems are most effectively handled by increasing the sample size to, say, 16 bits. Now, the digital signal can have more than 65,000 different levels, enabling the creation of a much smoother digital pattern, more closely representing the original signal.

So, the important thing to remember is that digital sound quality is dictated by both the sample rate and size. Other factors are also important, as I explain later, but the overriding specifications that define a sound system's maximum capabilities are governed by sample size and rate. To give you an idea of the effects of sample size and rate on audio quality, a telephone-quality audio signal is transported in the telephone's digital switching system as an 8,000 Hz sample rate signal with a sample size of 8 bits or 256 levels per sample. A CD-quality audio system uses a 44,100 Hz sample rate with 16 bits per sample or 65,536 levels! Table 25.1 lists some of the standard sampling rates and sample sizes used for audio. Also, I have calculated the amount of memory required to store one minute of stereo audio at each sample rate and size.

**Figure 25.1.**
*Converting analog audio to digital data samples and back to an analog signal.*

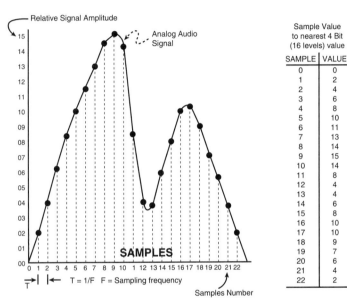

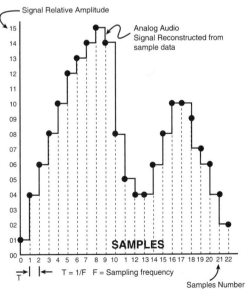

Table 25.1 Standard Digital Audio Sample Rates, Sizes, and Storage Requirements for One Minute of Stereo Audio.

| Sample Rate | Sample Size | Monaural/Stereo Data Rates of Stereo | Bytes/1 min. |
|---|---|---|---|
| 8,000/sec | 8 bits | 8/16 KB/sec | 960KB |
| 11,025/sec | 8 bits | 11.025/22.05 KB/sec | 1.324MB |
| | 12 bits | 16.54/33.07 KB/sec | 1.9845MB |
| | 16 bits | 22.05/44.1 KB/sec | 2.652MB |
| 22,050/sec | 12 bits | 33.07/66.15 KB/sec | 3.969MB |
| | 16 bits | 44.1/88.2 KB/sec | 5.292MB |
| 44,100 | 16 bits | 88.2/176.4 KB/sec | 10.584MB |

For high-quality stereo digital audio, digital data must be created at a very fast rate. If this is stored for later playback, it can use up lots of storage space. For example, referring to Table 25.1, one minute of 16-bit stereo 44.1 KHz-sampled CD-quality audio requires more than 10 MB of data to store! Nearly all of the latest 16-bit sound boards support at least the sample rates and sample sizes listed in Table 25.1 and can record and play back digitally sampled sound files at these sample rates and sizes. When the ADC and DAC functions are combined, they are some times called a CODEC, which stands for COder and DECoder. The CODECs can also implement compression and decompression of the audio digital data.

**Technical Note:** When talking about CODECs, the term "oversampling" is often used. If sampling at fast rates is good, sampling at even faster rates must be even better. Sampling at faster rates allows the sampled or generated analog signal to more closely track and recreate the actual analog signal. On DAC output of the recreated wave forms, it is possible to create additional sample points between two real samples by mathematically interpolating new intermediate samples and feeding these created samples to the DAC. The DAC then actually runs faster than the basic input's data rate. This oversampling technique creates a smoother wave form with less quantization noise. You have likely seen the marketing phrase "4 Times Oversampling" on your home or portable audio CD player; 4 times and 8 times oversampling on CODEC's is common. Since oversampled data is data created from the original input samples, the basic data rate and size of the playback files are not changed by oversampling. Oversampling can also be used on the ADC conversion. Here, the ADC is actually run at much higher sampling rates, often as high as 64 times the desired rate, (64X). The extra samples are then used to create a weight-average sample that is actually passed on by the ADC. The weight-average sample value can take into account rapid signal changes that would not have been seen by a slower sample rate.

# Audio Compression and Decompression

It is pretty obvious from Table 25.1 that enough sampled digital audio to fill up a game or a multimedia encyclopedia can create some very large data files. One solution to this problem is to compress the digital audio information. There are literally hundreds of compression/decompression schemes for audio. Audio compression and decompression algorithms use two basic concepts. First, redundant information is removed. For example, a long period in which the samples have the same value can be replaced with a code indicating that the next (n) samples have the same value. These schemes tend to be *lossless*. That is, they can completely reconstruct the exact input information from the compressed information. Another set of algorithms are *lossy*, meaning they actually remove information during the compression process. Of course, the secret is to only remove the information that has the least impact on audio quality. To talk in great detail about any compression/decompression algorithm is beyond the scope of this section, but there are several algorithms which are popular with PC applications. I'll talk about each, briefly.

## Companding

A technique used by the telephone company that minimally compresses (typically between 1.5 and 2 to 1) digital audio is called Companding. Companding is simple to implement either in software or hardware and can give the effect of having a larger sample size than actually exists. With normal sampled digital audio, the sample size—say, 8 bits—would specify 256 equal amplitude steps. With companding, the 256 steps would not be equal. By assigning different values to each step code in the sample, specific volume ranges or samples could have their importance increased or decrease. For example, low amplitude samples could contribute less and mid-value samples could contribute more to the new companded value. This can create more dynamic range in the important mid-range volume levels. The telephone industry uses two companding schemes, one called aLaw for the United States and a second called uLaw for European telephone systems. This type of compression is analogous to a technique used with graphic images called *pallettizing*, in which only 256 distinct colors are used in a final 8-bit image, but these 256 colors are, essentially, hand-picked by the computer, based on the colors that are actually present in the original, higher-bit-value image.

## ADPCM Compression

Companding is simple to implement and allows for more dynamic range (amplitude range). The most popular PC-based compression and decompression technique is ADPCM (Adaptive Differential Pulse Code Modulation). This scheme can be used on any data sample size or rate and can reduce data files by nearly a factor of 4. ADPCM is a lossy technique, so less compression gives better quality audio. ADCPM works by outputting the difference between two samples rather than the full samples. A further modification allows the variance sample values to vary (adapting the amplitude increment/code values on the fly). With quickly changing signals, the variance between samples may be very large and thus requires a large amplitude change between adjacent samples (delta values) to track the rapidly changing signal. Obviously, ADPCM works best with audio signals that have small, slowly changing amplitudes or volumes. For speech, ADPCM works well, but it can severely compromise the output quality of music. Most audio boards for the PC support at least decompression of ADPCM files. For example Sound Blaster-compatible sound boards support ADPCM decompression.

## MPEG Audio Compression

When the Motion Picture Expert Group (MPEG) standards committee developed compression/decompression standards for full-motion video, they also specified an accompanying audio compression/decompression standard. There exists audio compression standards for both MPEG-1 and MPEG-2. The MPEG-1 standard supports a very highly compressed audio data stream that provides near CD-quality stereo audio with data rates between 128 and 256 kilobits/second. The standard supports multiple levels of audio compression and allows the product producer to select the best for their application. The MPEG-2 Standard is not fully specified at the time of this writing, but will support CD quality with Quad channel (surround) sound at data rates slightly higher than MPEG-1.

## True Speech

The DSP Group, a manufacturer of audio technologies and Digital Signal Processors (DSPs), has developed a compression/decompression algorithm called True Speech. This algorithm will be supported in the new Windows 95 operating system from Microsoft and is proposed for use in the new low-bit-rate video compression/decompression MPEG-4 standard. This standard provides telephone quality audio with bit rates between 4 and 8 kilobits/second. True Speech is ideal for business audio applications requiring low to medium audio quality levels with reasonable data rates and storage requirements. True Speech is likely to be used extensively in future video conferencing applications.

## Special Effects and DSPs

Once audio information has been converted to digital information, it can be processed to create all types of effects, such as reverberation, surround sound, chorus, and other distortion effects. The computation necessary to produce these types of effects is best performed by a special-purpose, dedicated processor called a Digital Signal Processor (DSP). DSPs have a special architecture and instruction set designed to handle analog information that has been converted to digital. The Intel X86 architecture is not well-suited for performing these types of calculations, but with the brute force power of the new Pentium-class PC processors, significant signal processing can actually be done on the PC without a DSP. Many of the latest sound boards use a DSP to perform both special effects (such as Simulated Surround Sound) and the compression and decompression functions. DSPs are also very capable in sound and music synthesis, as you will see later.

# Audio Synthesis

Another way of overcoming the data rate and storage requirements of digital audio is to create the audio as it is needed in real-time. There are many applications in which a sound can be generated. For example, in a game, the firing of a gun or explosion need not be stored as sampled data and replayed each time the sound effect is needed. In this section I cover two of the most popular audio synthesis techniques used today on PCs for multimedia applications: FM synthesis and Wave Table Synthesis.

## FM Synthesis

You may know from a calculus class that any amplitude- and time-varying signal can be converted from the time domain to the frequency domain and represented as a summation of sine waves of harmonic frequencies. In other words, any arbitrary time- and amplitude-varying signal can be broken down into a set of sine waves of varying amplitude. Since this is true, the reverse is also true—any signal can be synthesized by summing a set of harmonic sine waves.

This is exactly the theory behind FM or Frequency Modulation sound synthesis. By generating a number of sine waves at different frequencies and amplitudes and summing them together (modulating one sine wave with another), it is possible to synthesize a desired audio signal. This scheme was developed by John Chowning at Stanford University in 1971 and licensed to Yamaha, which held the rights to this technology until the patent expired recently. This technology is easy to implement in PC chips or DSPs. Summing of a very few sine waves can actually create a large family of sounds containing the original summed frequencies and new frequencies created by the summation process. To even further enhance the richness of possible sounds, partial summation results can be fed back as additional inputs, creating even more complex wave forms.

FM synthesis chips contain functions called Operators. *Operators* are functions in the synthesis chips that combine two input frequency sources and add other special effects such as envelope control and feedback. Operator functions can be combined to create even more complex and rich sounds. The original Sound Blaster boards used a Yamaha chip called the OPL2 device. It supported two operator functions with 12 operator cells available. These two operators could then be combined two at a time in two connection modes to create six FM-synthesized sounds. Five other sound channels using custom built-in sound effects could create effects simulating percussion instruments. Pure FM synthesis techniques do not work well for percussion instrument synthesis. The Yamaha OPL2 chip was thus capable of 11 simultaneous sounds (instruments or other effects). Some sound boards used two OPL2 chips to create stereo sounds, but today most PC sound boards use the newer OPL3 chips which has four operators that can be combined in four ways with 15 operator cells for 15 FM melodies and five percussion effect sources. The OPL3 thus supports 10 voices or simultaneous stereo instruments. Today most sound generated on the PC uses the FM synthesis techniques to simulate instruments and special sound effects. FM synthesis requires very little processing power or data storage, but the actual quality of the synthesized music is simply not equal to fully sampled 16-bit, 44.1 KHz stereo digital data available from sample files or CDs.

## Sound Blaster

When the digital record and playback CODEC feature is combined with the FM synthesis functions provided by the Yamaha chip set, you have the basic definition of the "Sound Blaster" audio boards for the PC. This board and its functions have become a de facto standard in the industry for supporting multimedia sound on the PC. Creative Labs developed and manufactured the Sound Blaster brand of boards, but many others now produce Sound Blaster-compatible products. Figure 25.2 is a block diagram of a typical Sound Blaster-compatible audio board. From the block diagram you can see that these boards are designed for the ISA or PC AT bus. Audio data rates can easily be supported on the older ISA bus, so moving this function to a higher speed VL-bus or PCI bus slot is not driven by any performance requirements.

**Figure 25.2.**

*Basic Sound Blaster-compatible PC audio board block diagram.*

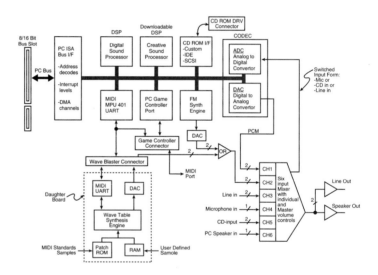

From the block diagram in Figure 25.2, one can see that two other basic functions have been added to the CODEC and FM synthesis blocks. The first is the block called the audio processor function. The audio processor is an embedded microprocessor that accepts commands from the ISA bus and controls the basic functions on the sound board, such as command and data routing, decompression of compressed data, and control of the audio mixer function. The second major added functional block is the audio mixer. As indicated in the block diagram, the audio mixer can accept analog audio inputs from several sources and individually control their volume and mix them to create a single stereo output with a master volume control for each stereo channel. On the block diagram of the sound card, there are two places where additional features can be added. One of the expansion capabilities is provided by an open chip socket that can accept an Advanced Signal Processor (ASP)

or sometimes also called the CSP (Creative Sound Processor) chip. In reality, the device is a DSP used to add new capabilities to the sound board. The second upgrade connection supports a MIDI Wave Table synthesizer feature. I cover this topic in more detail a little later.

## Sound Blaster Special Effects Processsors (ASP or CSP)

The CSP is a downloadable DSP that can support all types of audio enhancement to the sound board. For example, most sound boards do not support compression of incoming audio data in real-time. The CSP can be programmed to perform this function. Other special effects such as 3-D or Q Sound are supported by the CSP with downloaded software. Some of the latest sound boards use DSPs to perform all of the sound functions typically found on a Sound Blaster-compatible PC board. A good example of a full DSP sound implementation is a product from IBM called Mwave. With downloadable DSPs, it is possible to change and add new capabilities to your sound card as new software algorithms are developed. Downloadable DSPs are more expensive than fixed function sound boards but offer much more flexibility. In the long run, DSPs will take over much of the audio market.

## Wave Table Synthesis

Wave table synthesis is rapidly gaining in popularity as an alternative way to generate very high quality, natural-sounding musical instrument audio. The basic concept is quite simple. For each musical instrument to be synthesized, a small segment of actual instrument audio is recorded and converted to sampled digital data. When the instrument is to be played or synthesized, the small sampled data segment is accessed and processed by a wave table synthesizer; in most cases the synthesizer is a DSP. By processing the small sampled data segment and then playing back the processed data samples, realistic audio simulating the actual instrument can be generated. The sampled instrument data segments are called a patch set and are typically stored in a special ROM (Read Only Memory) chip. Some implementations of wave table synthesis allow the patch set to be moved to system memory and changed or added to. Often, the patch set ROM or sampled instrument data is compressed to save memory space. Patch set memory sizes vary depending on the number of instruments supported and the level of compression implemented. Patch memory sizes from 512KB to 4MB are common. The wave table synthesizers are capable of playing multiple instruments simultaneously and mixing the results, creating an orchestra effect. With many sound boards that support both FM synthesis and wave table synthesis, the two can be mixed so that background music comes from wave tables and special effects come from the FM synthesis output.

# MIDI

For audio applications to be portable across sound boards and different synthesizer technologies, a standard way of controlling the synthesizers was needed. MIDI (Musical Instrument Digital

Interface) provides a mechanism for controlling both synthesizers and musical instruments. The MIDI interface protocol supports 16 channels or different synthesizers. On each channel, commands can be sent to control a number of voices. The commands sent are actually codes that invoke a specific synthesizer program which, in turn, synthesizes an instrument or audio effect. Unfortunately, the same program codes will produce different sounds on different synthesizers. To overcome this problem and to ensure that the same MIDI control files produce the same results across a family of instruments and synthesizers, the instrument and synthesizer makers have defined a standard set of 128 program codes. This set is called the General MIDI standard. Applications that use the General MIDI program command set will produce similar sound on different synthesizers. Most PC sound cards have a MIDI serial port interface enabling PC control of external MIDI instruments and synthesizers.

# Game Ports

As discussed earlier, games are a primary PC multimedia application, thus many sound boards also support attachment of game controllers. Most of the Sound Blaster-compatible sound boards support the PC's four-switch, two joystick controller interface defined on the original PC. Since connector space is in short supply on audio boards, the MIDI interface signals are typically placed in the game port connector on unused pins. See Chapter 2, "Hardware: The Parts of the PC," for information on the game port connectors and MIDI interface signal pin assignments.

# CD-ROM Interface

Many newer 16-bit PC sound boards also include support for attaching CD-ROM drives. This is accomplished in three different ways. Some boards support direct attachment of CD-ROM drives through proprietary serial interfaces defined by the CD-ROM drive manufacturers. Some sound boards provide a SCSI interface allowing attachment of CD-ROM drives with SCSI interface ports. Now that the PC IDE hard disk port has been extended under the new EIDE standard, many sound boards support IDE interfaces for attachment of IDE interface CD-ROM drives.

# Speech Synthesis

Many interesting applications make use of speech synthesis, or the ability for your computer to speak to you. The simplest way to do audio responses is to digitally sample the full set of audio responses the application will use and when the desired audio response is required, simply play back the sample data through the DAC on the CODEC. Of course, if a lot of different responses are needed, the data files, even when compressed, can be large. Another more flexible scheme is to be able to convert arbitrary text to speech. Numerous software and hardware products are available that do a reasonable job of text to speech conversion using the basic CODEC's DAC on sound boards. A speech synthesizer software package is often included when you purchase a sound board. Most text-to-speech synthesizers use phonemes to construct an audio response from a word. Phonemes are a set of basic building blocks of speech that, when strung together, can approximate human speech. A phoneme is similar to a wave table instrument sound sample; instead of being a digital sample of a musical instrument, it is a digital sample of a basic human speech component (a phoneme). A text-to-speech program generates a set of phonemes for each word and the phoneme sounds are then played through the CODEC's DAC, approximating human speech for the word. By adding pitch and rate of play information to the phoneme strings, fairly realistic speech is created. Of course, one set of text-to-phonemes conversions does not work in all environments when one considers different languages, male and female voices, and other variables.

There are other sophisticated speech synthesis schemes that mathematically model the human vocal tract. In general, these schemes require significant computing power to implement, often one or more high-performance DSPs. Also, these schemes typically do not rely upon use of prerecorded phoneme sound samples because the sounds are generated dynamically as needed by the vocal track modeling algorithms.

# Speech Recognition

Now that your computer can talk to you, it would be nice if you could talk to it. Unfortunately, speech recognition is significantly more complex than speech synthesis. Consider some of the following basic problems. Each person speaks the same words differently, so how does a speech recognition program support the wide range of variations in human speech? Normal human speech is "connected." Words are run together. How does a speech recognition function determine word boundaries? Many words are pronounced identically but have totally different meanings depending on the context. Consider problems with specialized vocabularies that exist in scientific or medical speech environments. Dealing with these types of problems and supporting large vocabularies make speech recognition a very complex task. To make speech recognition manageable, limitations often are imposed. When the vocabulary is limited, connected speech is not supported, and the recognition function is speaker-dependent (training for only one person), speech recognition works well on PCs.

Most command and control applications, such as directing the computer to do a specific task using one or two word commands, can be supported with software on existing PC sound boards. For example, Microsoft's Audio for Windows package does a good job of directing the PC with verbal Windows and DOS commands, and can be used to control and perform data entry for a spreadsheet. If you require real-time conversion of speaker-independent connected text, such as in a dictation process, special sound boards and microphones are typically required. Also, the supporting software is complex, usually expensive, and needs to be run on high-performance PCs. Many of these packages do a reasonable job of converting dictated speech to text, often with more than 90 percent accuracy.

# The Windows Sound System

A few years ago Compaq began to support a basic "business audio" sound capability on some of their systems. Later, Microsoft adopted this capability and developed software and hardware to support a set of basic audio functions using hardware similar to that implemented by Compaq. This hardware and basic software became known as the Windows Sound System. The Windows Sound System hardware consisted of a 16-bit stereo CODEC supporting programmable sample sizes and rates up to 16 bits and 48 KHz. Also supported was a basic mixer function with programmable volume controls. Since the CODEC was attached directly to the PC's ISA bus, FIFO memory and DMA support were provided to increase performance with low CPU overhead. The Windows Sound System hardware is a basic CODEC and Mixer with no synthesis or compression/decompression in hardware. Support for these types of features must be implemented in the PC software.

# Native Signal Processing (NSP)

As the PC's microprocessor has become more powerful, many audio processing functions are now possible on the PC with minimal hardware. Intel recently announced what they call Native Signal Processing (NSP). The concept is to move signal processing functions, such as audio compression/decompression, sound synthesis, speech synthesis, and recognition from special purpose hardware and DSPs to the PC's native processor, the 486, or Pentium. For example, Intel now supports wave table synthesis on 486 class systems and higher, entirely in software.

# Wave Guide Technology

A new sound technology that will eventually be available on PCs is called Wave Guide Sound. This technique mathematically models an instrument and dynamically generates the correct sounds. This technique is very computation-intensive and becomes very difficult to implement if many instruments need to be simultaneously modeled. With today's DSP technology, typically four instruments can be modeled simultaneously using Wave Guide techniques.

# Video on the PC

As outlined earlier in the chapter, many multimedia applications require use of video. Video for this discussion is defined to be TV-quality still and moving images from cable, broadcast, CD-ROMs, laser disks, VCRs, and video camera sources. This chapter discusses how the PC gets access to these video sources, processes the images, and stores and displays them on the PC's display screen, alone or mixed with other PC-generated graphics. If you have not read Chapter 11, "On-Screen Video," it would probably be a good idea to review that chapter before you proceed.

# Video Capture

One of the most common uses of video is to capture video images from existing material for use in a presentation. For example, say you wanted to capture a full-color image from a video tape or laser disk, or even from a live camera or cable, and store it for use later on your PC's hard disk. To perform this capture function, you need special hardware and software on your PC. The hardware is typically called a video capture board. The video capture board takes as input either a TV composite video signal or an S-Video Signal from a camera, VCR, tuner, laser disk, or other source. These signals are analog signals containing TV raster timing, image chroma (color), and luminous (brightness detail) information that must be converted to digital data that the PC can handle and display.

## Digital Video and How It Is Represented

The conversion from an analog to digital representation is done by a device called a video decoder. The video decoder converts the composite analog video signal to a stream of digital data. Decoders sample the serial video image analog signal and convert it to a digital YUV representation. YUV digital video images are similar to the PC's RGB images used by the display adapter. Instead of defining a digital Red, Green, and Blue component, the YUV scheme contains all of the image color (chroma) content in the U and V data and the image brightness and detail in the Y or Luminous component.

It is a straightforward process to convert a YUV image to a RGB image. The conversion is called a color-space conversion and it is necessary to display TV images on the PC using the PC's RGB mode display adapter. As with audio, the quality of the converted image is dependent on the number of samples or conversion used to represent the YUV image. A TV studio broadcast-quality image is defined as a 720×484 pixel image where odd lines are scanned at 60 frames per second and, simultaneously, even lines are scanned at 60 frames per second. The entire image is thus presented at 30 frames per second. Most PC capture boards assume the image is overscanned and only capture a 640×480 area at 30 frames per second.

One of the reasons decoders use YUV color mode rather than RGB has to do with the concept of subcolor sampling. It turns out that your eye does not detect color changes well in moving images but is sensitive to detail. By separating the color and detail information as the YUV scheme does, the sampling rate for Y and UV can be different. That is, the color information is sampled at a lower resolution or slower data rate. Often video capture cards specify the YUV sampling rates as a series of three numbers (4:2:2). Each of these numbers refers to the sampling rates of the Y:U:V image components. A one value is approximately equivalent to a 3.375 MHz sampling rate.

To determine the maximum data burst rate of the YUV digital data, simply multiply each sampling rate ratio by 3.375 and add the results. For example, a broadcast-quality 640×480 image at 4:2:2 sampling is: (4×3.375)+(2×3.375)+(2×3.375)= 27 MHz. If each sample is 8 bits in size, an instantaneous data rate of 27 MB/second is generated by the image capture process! Another way to look at the problem is that each 30 frames of the image generates 27 MB of information! There are two ways to deal with the data rate and data volume problems of image capture. First, simply capture a smaller portion of the image or sample at lower speeds, reducing the image resolution and quality. Even at image sizes that are one-fourth the screen size, the data rate still exceeds the capacity of the ISA or PC AT bus to handle. The second solution is to compress the image to an acceptable data rate that the PC and its storage devices can realistically handle.

## Still Image Capture

Most low-cost PC video capture boards only capture one frame at a time and are primarily used to capture a still image from a video source. If the video image is not moving and each frame is the same, the data rate can be reduced by sampling and converting only a portion of each frame. Using this technique, the image capture board does not need to buffer any of the image and can send it directly to the PC's memory at a slow rate, a frame portion at a time. If it is important to capture a single frame in its entirety, like in a snap shot, the capture board will likely have a frame buffer memory on the board. To capture a 640×480 pixel frame using YUV (4:2:2) sampling, two bytes per pixel are required. Thus a (640×480×2) = 614,400 byte frame buffer is required. When this image is converted to RGB true color form (8:8:8), the image memory size increases by a factor of 1.5 to 921,000 bytes!

## Full Motion

Obviously, for the data rates and image sizes outlined above, capture of any significant amount of real-time full-motion video is difficult to achieve in the PC environment. Even with one-quarter-size images at 4:1:1 sampling, the instantaneous data rate is still more than 5 MB/second. Newer video capture boards now attach to the PC through the PCI or VESA local busses, which can easily support the full screen 30 frames per second YUV data rates. Unfortunately, one quickly runs out of storage with just a few frames. Storing data on the system's hard disk is the next alternative. Even if the amount of data weren't prohibitive, the data rates are still too high even for the fastest EIDE or Fast Wide SCSI disk drives. Some hard disk manufacturers are now building special Audio Video Interactive or Interleaved (AVI) hard disks that can support video data rates and very large capacities. If the actual data volume is manageable, it is possible to capture a small video clip by capturing just a few frames from each pass of a playback. By repeating this process and capturing different frames each playback, it is possible to capture all frames of a small video clip. Even with trick techniques like this, it is still obvious that some other solution is required. As you will see later, video data compression comes to the rescue.

# Live Video in Window and Video Processors

When video from a source just needs to be displayed on the PC's screen and not captured or stored, the data rate and data size are not as much of an issue because the data is used up as it is created. The key problem here is how to merge the PC's graphics with the video data stream. Consider some of the following problems. The PC's display is running at a different scan rate and probably is not interlaced. The PC's pixel screen size is probably larger than the video image size. The PC's screen may not be in a true color mode. The PC may want to shrink or expand the video image to a window on the PC's screen, and thus combine video and PC graphics on the same screen. And, of course, the video image is in the YUV format and the PC graphics in the RGB format. Special circuitry that deals with these problems is called a video processor, or video pixel processor. As it turns out, the functions of the video processor subsystem are common and more or less independent of the video source. Video processors deal with native video either from a live source composite video input, a software decompression engine, or a hardware decompression engine during playback from a CD-ROM or hard disk file.

If you wish to support video on the PC's screen, either as AVI file playback or live video in a window on the PC, you will need a video processor's functions to accelerate playback or handle live video. The video processor can be built into your display adapter, or it can be a separate card or a daughter board that attaches to your display adapter. If your primary goal is to play back compressed AVI files and support is not required for live video in a window, many of the newer display adapters have the video processor function built in and are typically called video playback accelerators. The video processor or playback accelerators perform the following functions:

1. Convert the YUV data to the PC's more familiar RGB representation. This process is called color space conversion and typically expands the data from a 16 bit per pixel mode to a 24 bit per pixel mode.

2. Scale the image to the desired size. Some systems simply throw away pixels when scaling down and duplicate pixels when scaling an image up in size. This is the least desirable scheme, as it does not support smooth scaling and creates pixelated images. The best video processors use what is called pixel interpolation. When scaling an image from its original captured size, new pixels are created that represent averages of the nearest pixels. This scheme creates a much clearer image with smooth scaling.

3. Next, the video processor places the image, which has been color space converted and scaled, in the PC's display buffer and adjusts the window position. The video window position can be specified as an $x$ and $y$ pixel coordinate or by a chroma key code in the PC's display memory. The video processor can detect a specific pixel color and replace that pixel with the video pixel at that position. Some high-function video processors can also perform alpha blending or perform the mixing of the two video sources to create a transparency effect.

## Mixing Video and Graphics

In Chapter 11, we determined that two basic architecture approaches exist to support the actual display of video images on the PC display. The highest performance and most expensive solution is to store the video image in a special scan converter memory and merge the pixel data from both the PC's graphics and video image from the scan convert memory at the input to the DAC (Digital to Analog Converter). The merging of pixel data is typically done using the VFC (VGA Feature Connector) or the newer VAFC (VESA Advance Feature Connector) on the PC's display adapter. Since the video data never passes through the PC's display memory, it does not take display memory bandwidth. Further, the display adapter controller does not have to deal with simultaneously displaying multiple pixel data types, that is, true color video images in an 8-bit pseudo-color PC screen.

A less expensive scheme for merging video and graphics is to share the PC's display memory and directly store the video processor's output into the screen memory. This scheme is most often used when the video processor is built in to the display adapter controller chip or attaches to the display controller chip. This scheme is often called the Shared Frame Buffer (SFB) approach. This SFB scheme saves memory, is very low cost, and often is built into the display adapter's display controller chip at a small additional cost. The basic problem with this scheme is that the PC's graphics updates, video processor memory references, and screen refresh cycles all have to be shared in a single memory. The shared frame buffer approach is only feasible with display adapters having 64-bit busses or VRAM implementations. (See Chapter 11 for more information on DRAM and VRAM designs and the issues associated with display memory types and widths.)

If the video processor is a separate board, it can still use the shared frame buffer approach. The data path from the video processors to the PC's display adapter memory is critical. Most video processors today use a proprietary bus, but the VESA standards group has proposed a special high-speed 32-bit bus for interconnecting video and graphics subsystems supporting pixel traffics at the uncompressed native device speeds. The pixel channel is called the VESA Media Channel (VMC) and is available on some adapter boards as a special connector. The VMC supports data transfer rates as high as 132 MB/second. For more information on merging video and graphics images, see Chapter 11.

# Video Compression/Decompression Standards

Clearly, to overcome the data rate and storage size issues created by full-motion video, image compression and decompression must be addressed. As indicated earlier, a 30 frame/second TV-quality, full-motion video image requires an instantaneous data rate of approximately 27 MB/second; if the data rate is smoothed across the entire frame rate (by using frame and scan line retrace times to also send data), the continuous data rate is approximately 18 MB/second. A standard CD-ROM drive can transfer data at 300 KB/second. This means that to use a CD-ROM drive to support full-motion video, a compression ratio of 60 to 1 is needed! Even at 1/4 screen size and frame rates of 15 frames/second, a compression ratio of at least 10 to 1 is needed!

## Symmetry

One of the key features of a compression algorithm is its symmetry. Basically this means it takes the same compute power and time to compress as to decompress. Nonsymmetric algorithms are fine for compressing images for later playback, such as from a CD-ROM. It is better to spend a lot of time and effort compressing the image and allow for a low amount of time and effort for decompression. For compression and decompression of live real-time images, such as in a video conferencing application, it is best if the algorithm is more symmetric requiring similar compression and decompression times.

## Lossy versus Lossless

One of the best and easiest ways to compress an image is to throw away some of the image content. This is called a lossy compression scheme. Of course, the trick is to throw away only the information that least affects the image quality. Lossy compression techniques often depend on the characteristics of the human vision system to not detect missing information. Nearly all of the high compression ratio algorithms use lossy compression techniques.

## Spacial and Temporal Compression

For moving images, two types of compression are possible. Spacial compression is devoted to the compression of information in a single image frame. Spacial compression tries to shrink the data associated with a single image using the fact that some of the regions of the image have the same color and can be represented by a code for that color region. The compressed code thus is a much more compressed indication of a region or the image.

Temporal compression relies on the fact that in a moving image, very little of the image changes from frame to frame. Since much of the image does not change, temporal compression would simply send the changes between frames.

### Compressing and Decompressing Video Images

A full treatment of the subject of compression and decompression algorithms for full-motion video is beyond the scope of this section, but the following is a list of techniques that are often used in combination in popular PC compression/decompression standards.

1. Run-length coding. Rather than send each pixel with the same data when a region of the same color is detected, the color is sent once along with a length field indicating how long to continue to use the color.

2. Huffman coding. When an image or data block has a limited number of repeating patterns, those data patterns that occur most often can be assigned compacted code values. Less frequently occurring data patterns are assigned larger code values. The theory is that most of the image or data can be represented using the smaller compacted code values, thus compressing the data. Huffman codes are normally used as a second stage of compression, for example, after a DCT system has been used.

3. Vector quantization. This scheme divides the image up into small blocks and looks for repeating patterns. Then a compacted table of repeating patterns is sent, followed by a coded list of vectors pointing to the patterns to be used to reconstruct the image. Again, this scheme is often used with other compression techniques.

4. Subcolor sampling. This technique is the first step in many compression schemes. As outlined earlier, since the human eye does not see color change well, the color content of the image is sampled at a lower rate, thus reducing the data need.

5. DCT. The DCT or Discrete Cosine Transform scheme produces very high compression ratios for lossy compression. The technique is to convert the time-domain-sampled data to the frequency domain. The varying time signals representing the color components are converted to a set of harmonic frequencies. (Remember Fourier transforms in school?) This transformation in itself does not compress the image, but the array of frequency coefficients representing the image blocks can easily be divided into a small set of quantized values. (This is equivalent to throwing away the very high frequencies that the eye does not see well.) By arranging the quantized coefficient values in a special array pattern, they can be Huffman or run-length coded very efficiently. DCT compression is used by MPEG-1, MPEG-2, H.320, and JPEG compression standards.

6. Delta frame change. This scheme is primarily used after frame compression and sends only the changes between frames. This scheme works well for low-color images or images with large areas of the same color or patterns between frames. AudoCad's

AutoDesk FLC file format uses a delta frame change scheme to support animation on the PC.

7. Motion estimation. Part of the MPEG (Motion Picture Expert Group) standard is a function called motion predication or estimation. This scheme divides the image into small blocks and compares the position of the small blocks of the image between frames. If the block changes mainly by position, motion vectors are sent indicating the direction and distance the small block has moved. This can dramatically reduce the data actually sent to reconstruct a new frame from earlier frame information. Motion estimation can be used to create new predicted frames of information by combining motion vector information with information from previously sent frames.

# Popular PC Compression/Decompression Standards for Full-Motion Video

The following is a summary of the most popular full-motion video standards for the PC. The compression ratios possible—symmetry, basic technology employed, and applicability to software versus hardware implementations—are covered for each standard. It should be pointed out that many applications, in particular games, use proprietary schemes that are specifically tailored to the application's performance needs.

## Cinepak

This is a popular compression/decompression scheme primarily based on the vector quantization scheme. It is asymmetric and thus difficult to use in live two-way applications. It is, however, easily implemented in PC software of 486 class systems. It works very well in low-color depth applications and achieves compression ratios as high as 40 to 1. Frame rates as high as 30 frames/second are achievable for 320×200 screens with 65,000 colors on Pentium class systems. Cinepack is one of the AVI file formats supported under Video for Windows.

## Indeo

Indeo was developed by Intel as a software alternative to their DVI (Digital Video Interactive) hardware technology. Indeo is actually a family of compression/decompression algorithms that are used separately and in combinations. Run-length coding, subcolor sampling, delta frame change, and vector quantization are all part of the Indeo standard. Depending on the frame rates, image size, and color depth desired, Indeo will automatically select a compression scheme for you. Depending on the scheme selected, Indeo can be more or less symmetric. However, it is primarily used for playback of AVI files and uses mostly nonsystemic schemes. Indeo can achieve compression ratios as high as 40 to 1 and display 30 frames per second, 320×200 images with 65,000 colors on Pentium-class systems. Indeo is also supported as an AVI file format under Microsoft's Video for Windows.

# MPEG

The MPEG standard is actually a family of standards based on the DCT and Motion Estimation techniques. MPEG-1 supports TV-quality images at a resolution of 352×240 in a noninterlaced mode. MPEG-2 is a standard for high-resolution images and is typically used to support broadcast TV images of 720×484. MPEG-2 is also the basic standard adopted for HDTV (High Definition TV) and the new digital interactive cable networks. These standards also incorporate compression and decompression of synchronized audio. Both standards produce compression ratios as high as 1 to 200 with 1 to 100 more typical. MPEG-1 encoding and decoding is very asymmetric. Real-time encoding of MPEG-1 or MPEG-2 takes a lot of expensive hardware. Today MPEG encoding adapters for PCs range from a low of several thousand dollars to more than $30,000. If the video image is available on a laser disk or video tape, software encoders are available that use existing video capture boards. It can often take several hours to encode even small video clips on PCs using software compressors. Decompression of MPEG-1 images at 30 frames/second with 352×240 resolution is possible in software on a Pentium-class system.

A special version of MPEG is also used in video conferencing applications over digital networks such as ISDN and switched 56 digital services. This standard is sometimes called the P.64 standard because it allows data transfer rates in increments of 64 kilobits/second. Of course, lower bit rates support lower frame sizes, frame rates, and color depths. The complete video conferencing standard is called H.320, and the subsection that deals with the full-motion video portion is called H.263. Also, a new full-motion video standard for very low-bit rate environments (analog phone lines) is planned called MPEG-4. This standard is still in development and will not be available for use for at least another year.

# Motion JPEG

The JPEG (Joint Photographic Expert Group) standard is very similar to MPEG without inter-frame motion estimation. The standard uses the DCT compression scheme but does not specify any specific resolution or frame sizes. It is primarily used to compress still images. JPEG is often used in motion applications in a mode called motion JPEG. Without interframe compression, the motion JPEG scheme obtains a compression ratio between 6 and 10 to 1. Motion JPEG is primarily used when the moving image needs to be edited in a frame-by-frame environment, such as in video production work. Because the MPEG standard often creates many versions of the frames, it is very difficult to edit MPEG data streams. Often video is first compressed to JPEG frames, converted to Motion JPEG, edited, and then transcoded to MPEG for distribution and playback.

## AutoCad AutoDesk FLC Files

For the playback of computer animation files with low color depth, the AutoCad AutoDesk file format called FLC (FLICK) is popular. It works well for games, and it is easy to implement in software. Obviously, it is not symmetric and is primarily used for playback of FLC files. It is based on simple run-length coding and delta frame change inter-frame compression.

# Video Processing and Playback Acceleration Support for Decompression

Earlier, I mentioned the video processor function and how it could be used to accelerate the merging of video data on to the PC's screen. The video processor's color space conversion, scaling, and window placement hardware can dramatically improve the frame rates available from both hardware and software decompression engines. Most decompression engines, software or hardware, output the decompressed image in YUV format at the same image size as was inputted to the compression engine. Analysis of the time spent decompressing an image and performing color space conversion, scaling, and window updates, indicates that over 50 percent of the entire process is spent in the latter three functions. The best way to accelerate the playback of compressed full-motion video files is to have hardware video processing built in to your system. In most instances the decompression to the native image size and color space is best done by the system processor. The video processor can then handle the more difficult tasks of color space conversion, scaling, and window updates.

# Real-Time 3-D

Playback or viewing of stored video images is fine for a number of applications. Unfortunately, this does not work well for interactive applications, such as games and virtual reality applications requiring modeling and simulations. In these applications, the PC must create realistic 3-D images in realtime. In response to different viewing positions and lighting situations, the entire image may need to be updated on a frame-by-frame basis. For a brief review of the technical challenges created by real-time 3-D, see Chapter 11. Today, most PC applications for 3-D fall into two categories: fast low-resolution real-time 3-D rendering for entertainment and virtual reality applications and high-performance, high-resolution rendering required for more traditional CAD and graphics design applications. Figure 25.3 illustrates the 3-D applications and the predominant Application Program Interfaces (APIs) supported. Hardware support for 3-D rendering is just now beginning to emerge. The existing hardware support is primarily targeted to support existing workstation applications in CAD and graphics design applications. The next generations of PC display adapter hardware will likely concentrate on much lower cost 3-D hardware supporting the entertainment applications.

**Figure 25.3.**
*3-D API standards
for the PC.*

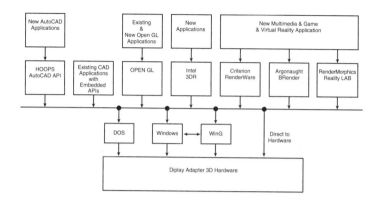

The PC graphics subsystem is not well suited to support game or entertainment graphics. Next generation PC graphics systems will likely add features such as panning on multiple virtual screens (virtual playfields), large numbers of sprites, multiple-color palettes, chroma-keyed overlays for full-motion video backgrounds, high-performance scan line 3-D rendering into playfields and sprites, and support for multiple-color depth pixels with alpha blending on the display screen. Since both video and graphics are often combined on a PC screen, hardware support for fades and transitions between video windows and graphics would also be highly desirable. These features are common in game machines such as Sega and Nintendo and account for the very high performance graphics associated with game play on these platforms. Sprites are small, quick-moving objects such as missiles and bombs in a game. Playfields simulate a multiple-layered effect for a simulated 3-D environment. Chroma-keying allows two images to overlap, with one image taking precedent over another at specified points on the screen. 3-D Rendering is a special effect that makes objects look three-dimensional on a two-dimensional display screen.

# WinG

You may have noticed that game developers have generally avoided the Windows environment and prefer to use DOS or load their own operating system environment. The primary complaint with Windows is that graphics performance suffers as the result of using the Windows Screen API. Windows just does not like to have an application writing directly to the screen buffer. Microsoft recently announced a new interface extension to Windows called WinG or Windows for Games. WinG is not a full 3-D graphics package, but allows graphics developers to create graphic images in system memory or in off-screen display memory, bypassing the Windows API. When the image is ready to be displayed, WinG moves the image to the on-screen display area in cooperation with the existing Windows API. This scheme requires more system memory, but allows WinG games under Windows to achieve nearly DOS levels of performance.

## DCI

Many of the features available in the latest generation of PC display adapters cannot easily be invoked through Windows. For example, hardware decompression engines, video capture hardware, and the video processor functions, such as color space conversion, scaling, and video window image updates, cannot be controlled through the standard Windows Screen API. To solve this problem, Microsoft, with assistance from Intel, has developed a new DCI (Display Control Interface). This interface allows applications to directly access the advanced multimedia features of the display subsystem hardware.

# CD-ROMs and Multimedia Data Types

CD-ROMs immediately come to mind in any discussion of multimedia. As you have seen, multimedia data types such as graphics, video, and audio take a lot of storage, even when highly compressed. This makes the CD-ROM the ideal distribution media for multimedia applications. With more than 600 MB of data available per CD and the drives costing less than $200 each, the CD-ROM has taken over as the preferred method for storing multimedia data types. Initially, CD-ROMs were very slow with data transfer rates of only 150 KB/second and average access times of over 800 milliseconds. Today's latest drives support transfer rates as high as 600 KB/second with access times below 200 milliseconds. Even with these speed increases, the CD-ROM is primarily a distribution media. It is still too slow for most interactive multimedia applications. In particular, games and virtual reality applications suffer from the low performance of CD-ROM drives. However, the CD works well for linear-play full-motion video applications and for background music. For high-performance interactive applications, motion video is often moved from the CD-ROM to the much faster systems hard disks.

# LANs and Multimedia

Transmission of multimedia data types such as audio and full-motion video is difficult to achieve on most existing LANs. The primary problem is the inability of the LAN to guarantee minimum sustained data rates. LANs typically transmit data in bursts at high speeds and then have long gaps where no data is being transferred, or data is being transferred to another device on the LAN. Since LANs share the transmission media's bandwidth with several others on the LAN, a specific device on the LAN cannot assume it has all of the bandwidth it needs all the time. This bursty data transfer mechanism is just fine when transferring data from a hard disk server to a client PC because speed and reliability, not smoothness of the transfer, is what matters.

Multimedia data types such as digital sound and full-motion video cannot tolerate this type of environment. For voice conversation to be coherent, it must have a sustained minimum data rate reflecting the same data rates as generated by the source or speaker. Gaps or speedups in speech are simply not tolerable. Similarly, full-motion video must have a sustained data rate or the frame rate will change from the original source video and appear to be jerky or speeded up. Another problem with LAN is the inability to easily synchronize audio and video data so that they arrive synchronized at a PC. If they are not synchronized, the PC will need to perform this function and will probably have to dedicate significant processing power and memory buffers to do so.

An additional problem occurs when audio and video traffic is two-way, such as in a video conferencing application over a LAN. Although LANs are fast, there can be significant delay time between two PCs. This can complicate the audio-video synchronization and create other problems. It is generally assumed that any delay over 250 milliseconds in an audio network makes continuous voice conversation difficult. Also, the audio subsystems now have to deal not only with speaker phone problems, but with echo cancellation in high-delay networks. If a voice transmission path has a long delay, voice signals that are echo back (speaker output picked up at the microphone) will interfere with and distort the incoming audio signal creating an echo effect. Special techniques called echo cancellation are often used to reduce this echo effect in networks with long delays. LAN used to transport voice channels will experience additional problems when they are routed over the traditional public-switched networks. The public-switched voice networks assumes that the voice traffic entering the network has less than 100 microseconds of delay and expects to be able to add significant additional delay without impairing the voice call's quality. If the voice traffic already has significant delay before entering the public-switched network, the call quality may be degraded to an unacceptable level.

If you consider a full-motion video and audio digital data rate of 1.5 megabits/second (MPEG-1), it's not difficult to see how problems can develop on a 10-megabit/second Ethernet LAN. Even a few users will quickly use up all the LAN's bandwidth. One simple solution to this problem has been to introduce the concept of Hubs in the LAN. Hubs not only make it easier to wire and locate faults on a LAN, they also keep traffic isolated to local segments of the LAN. Using LAN Hubs combined with new higher speed LANs, such as Fast 100 megabits/second Ethernet, significantly improves the conditions for multimedia. However, the LAN still exhibits a bursty data transfer mode. A further enhancement to LAN called LAN-switching can eliminate this problem. With LAN-switching, each LAN-attached device has a dedicated LAN connection that is not shared with any other device or PC, and the full bandwidth of the LAN connection is available. This scheme emulates the point-to-point (not shared) connection environment of the public-switched telephone network, but with much higher speed connections. Another approach is to add a special isochronous data channel to the LAN that is available simultaneously with the normal LAN data channel. In the Ethernet environment, this is called Isochronous Ethernet. The idea is to provide a fixed bandwidth (data rate) channel synchronous to a network clock that always provides a stable fixed bandwidth channel that is not shared. Thus, on each transition of the network clock, a specific data block or bit is transmitted. In an isochronous network, data is sent and received at a very predictable data rate directly proportional to the network clock speed.

Most would agree that the just-described approaches to enabling multimedia data types on existing LANs are at best Band-Aid approaches. What is needed is a LAN that provides very high data rates, sustained data rates, and low network delay. It would also be nice if it were compatible with wide area networks and the public-switched networks. Believe it or not, such a LAN/WAN technology actually exists. The technology is called Asynchronous Transfer Mode (ATM). The telephone switching industry has been developing this technology to support digital voice traffic in the public-switched telephone networks. ATM supports data rates of 50, 155, and 620 bits/second, primarily over fiber optic networks. New standards being developed by the ATM Forum will support lower data rates and transmission over coax and twisted-pair copper wire. The ATM Forum is a group of computer industry users and manufacturers that are applying ATM to LAN and WAN applications. ATM sends data in small 53-byte packets, thus allowing fast, low-delay switching. Data integrity is the network's responsibility, thus extensive data checking and recovery software protocols are normally not needed (low delay once the data gets to a PC). ATM service is a switched service with a guaranteed data rate and quality level. ATM is perfect for multimedia LAN applications. Since ATM is also used in the public-switched networks, it is very easy to bridge remote LAN, since ATM LANs and WANs have a seamless compatible interface. ATMs LAN and WANs also reduce the network delays caused by LAN bridges, routers, and gateways. Unfortunately, ATM LANs and PC adapters are still much more expensive than existing LANs and adapters, so it will be awhile before ATM LANs will be pervasive. ATM is exactly what LAN multimedia applications need.

# Fast Modems and Digital Networks for Multimedia

To many home and small business PC users, the only remote communications access available is the public-switched telephone system, (the telephone line). Modems are used to interface the PC's serial COM ports to the telephone line and the public-switched network. This network has two attributes favorable to multimedia data types, point-to-point connections with sustained data transfer rates and low network delays. Unfortunately, the data transfer rates are limited to around 28.8 kilobits/second with the latest modem technologies. This slow data transfer rate is a severe limitation to many multimedia applications. Consider transmission of full-motion video with a data rate of more than 27 MB/second for a TV-quality image in uncompressed mode! Even with the best video compression technologies supporting 200 to 1 compression ratio and data rates as low as 1.5 million bits/second, modems are still more than 50 times too slow!

Audio data fares better in this environment, but not much better. Again, consider a stereo CD-quality audio signal with 16-bit digital audio sampled at 44 KHz. Simple arithmetic shows that this quality of audio requires a data rate of 176 kilobits/second, or more than 6 times the data rate available on the best modems. Also consider one of the most popular multimedia applications over networks, video conferencing. In this application, two-way video and audio is needed, doubling the needed transfer rates. To support full-motion video and audio over fast modems, some compromises need to be made. The first is to sacrifice video and audio quality. Sending video images that are smaller with fewer colors at slower frame rates can significantly reduce the data transfer rate. For example, a full-motion video, TV-quality image with full color at 30 frames/second with a pixel resolution of 352×240 and fully compressed takes about 1.2 megabits/second (MPEG-1 Compression). If the frame rate is reduced to 7 frames/second and the image reduced to approximately 160×100 pixels, the data rate is approximately 40 kilobits/second, still too fast for fast 28.8 kilobit/second modems. At present, images of 160×100 pixels with only 256 colors and frame rates of 3 to 5 frames/second are possible over existing analog telephone lines using the best modems.

If the application requires audio, like the video conferencing applications, the audio data must share the available bandwidth of the connection. By using monaural 8-bit sampled audio at low sampling rates and compression techniques, telephone grade audio is possible with bit rates as low as 2400 to 4800 bits/second. Both AT&T and Intel have proposed new modem standards that support simultaneous voice and data over analog phone lines and modem. It's pretty obvious that modems severely limit multimedia applications, causing limited capabilities with respect to video and audio quality. There are two courses available for improving the existing wide area network's ability to carry multimedia data types: better compression technology and faster modems. Advances are likely in both areas, but dramatic improvements are not anticipated quickly.

# High-Speed Digital Networks

The quickest way to improve multimedia capabilities on wide area networks is to improve the data transfer rate and reliability. Several alternatives are under development with some actually available to PC users. For several years the telephone companies have offered user access to their digital backbone networks. Unfortunately, these high-speed digital services required special conditioned wiring and special "modems" that are very expensive and only available in limited service areas.

# Switched 56/64 Digital Services

Switched 56 service is perhaps the oldest high-speed digital service available. Using special modems called CSUs/DSUs(Customer Service Units/Data Service units) and specially conditioned phone lines, data rates are available in increments of 56 kilobits/second. Newer networks also offer data rates in 64 kilobits/second units. Since this service is expensive and limited to major metropolitan areas, it is primarily used by larger business customers for LAN interconnections and video conferencing. In general, use of switched 56 technology for the masses is not practical or cost effective.

# T1 Services

For years the telephone companies have transmitted multiple voice calls digitally on what is called a T1 carrier network. Digital network supports 24 digital voice channels; each voice channel is either 56 or 64 kilobits/second. The T1 carrier system thus can carry any capacity from 56 to 1,536 kilobits/second traffic. T1 can be thought of as the next step up in digital network hierarchy in the all-digital switching systems of the public-switched network. As with switched 56 service, special lines and interface adapters are required, and this service is not pervasively available. The service is also very expensive, costing thousands of dollars per month to lease a T1 connection across the US.

# ISDN

In the early 1980s, standards were developed to bring all digital network services to the masses. The technology is called ISDN (Integrated Service Digital Network). ISDN brings 144 kilobits/second digital services to any point that the existing analog network could reach. The basic ISDN network uses the existing copper analog wiring that presently services your home. ISDN provides several levels of service:

1. Basic Rate: 144 kilobits/second service divided into 3 channels, a 16 kilobit/sec "D" channel primarily of low-speed data transmission and call control and setup and two 64 kilobits/second "B" channels. The B channels can be used for digital voice or data in any combination on a per call basis. Basic Rate ISDN is intended to be the service provided to most residential customers.

2. Primary Rate: This service is basically the old T1 1.5 megabits/second service using ISDN signaling protocols for call setup and control. Primary Rate service is intended to support business customers.

3. Broad Band ISDN: This service supports data rates of roughly 150 and 600 megabits/second and uses ATM as the underlying transport. It is intended for fiber optic networks.

ISDN has been slow to catch on, primarily due to the lack of good standards and the high cost of customer premise equipment (digital phones and modems). Today most central office switches can support ISDN and the service is becoming more widely available. The service is still slightly more expensive than a standard analog line, and the modems (called terminal adapters) are very expensive compared to analog modems. Remember, if you want to use ISDN for data transfer applications, it must be available at both ends of the connection!

# ADSL

Recently, the phone companies have been experimenting with much higher bandwidth connection to the home using the existing copper wiring. One of the technologies now being tested is called

ADSL (Asymmetric Digital Subscriber Loop). This technology is an attempt by the phone companies to compete with the cable companies for distribution of full-motion video movies. Transmission speeds of between 1.5 and 6 megabits/second are being proposed and tested. The technology supports the existing analog telephone with a primarily one-way digital data stream from the central office to the home. A low bit rate back channel is support for interactive applications. This technology is ideal for PC wide area networks supporting multimedia data types. Unfortunately, this technology is just now being used in trial applications, and it will be a while before it is widely available.

## Cable TV

Whereas the phone company has switched point-to-point service (each party thinks they are attached directly together) with low bandwidth, the cable companies have high bandwidth multidrop (all parties are attached to listen to the same signals)and one-way connections. Adding switching (ability to address an individual user) and two-way data transfer to the existing cable networks would provide an instant high bandwidth multimedia-ready network. Again, several trials are underway to test the feasibility of converting a cable network to a high-speed wide area LAN. As with ADSL, conversion of existing cable networks is a long way off due to the high cost of network conversion. Also, the cable companies are primarily interested in distribution of entertainment and interactive TV applications and have generally ignored the PC as a possible cable-connected device.

# MPC Standards and System Performance Requirements for Multimedia

MPC or Multimedia Personal Computer is a standard for the configuration of a PC that is capable of supporting multimedia applications. The standard was developed by the Multimedia Marketing Council, a group of PC hardware and software suppliers attempting to promote multimedia on PCs. This standard has gone through several updates, the latest being the MPC-2 standard. The idea is that if you have an MPC-compliant system, you can use the MPC logo and run applications that are MPC-compliant. The basics of the MPC-2 standard are as follows:

1. 486 class processor

2. Minimum of 4MB of system memory

3. Minimum of 160MB of hard disk

4. A 16-bit sound card

5. A 2X speed (300 KB/second) CD-ROM drive with a minimum access time of 400 milliseconds

6. A VGA-compatible graphics card and monitor

Given today's multimedia applications and their appetite for performance, the MPC-2 standard is probably already out of date for many interesting multimedia applications.

# Shopping Tips for a Multimedia PC

As we have seen, multimedia applications have a very large appetite for PC performance. If you are going to be running multimedia applications, I would highly recommend starting with a Pentium class PC with no less than 16MB of main memory and a 500MB hard disk. For a small additional cost premium, you should select one of the newer 4X or 600 MB/second CD-ROM drives. In the display adapter area, a 64-bit DRAM or VRAM design with a minimum of 2MB of display memory would be wise. If you plan on playing full-motion video files, you should also consider a display adapter that has a built-in video processor that can accelerate video file playback. Given the new lower costs of 17-inch displays, I would high recommend the small additional cost.

If you intend to capture video images or view live video sources at full-screen sizes, you may want to consider a VRAM-designed display adapter that can accept an independent video processor through the new VAFC or VMC connectors designed for high-performance video subsystem attachment.

In the audio area, a 16-bit Sound Blaster-compatible audio board with a wave table synthesis add-on feature would be a good bet.

It's hard to have too much performance when it comes to multimedia applications. This is particularly true if you intend to do multimedia application development.

# 26

# Exploring and Tinkering

On the surface of things there is only so much that you can discover, but when you dig down just a little, you can unearth wonders. That's pretty much what this chapter is about: how you can dig into the PC and explore and tinker with it. In this chapter, I cover the good reasons why it's not just interesting but truly valuable to know how to dig below the surface of the PC, and you learn about two of the tools that can be used to do this exploring.

# Why Explore and Tinker?

There are more reasons than you might imagine why it's beneficial to know how to explore, examine, change, and tinker with the PC. The best reason of all is one that doesn't have a direct, immediate benefit: Exploring widens and deepens your knowledge of the PC family, and that makes you a more proficient PC user—better able to use the full range of the PC's powers, better able to avoid problems with your PC, and better able to deal with problems when they do occur.

Among the things that you can learn by tinkering with the PC is how data is organized on the disk, both the structure of the disk itself and the internal structure of the data files with which programs work. Similarly, you can learn a great deal about how programs work, how they manage data, and how they use memory and other parts of the computer's resources. There often are hidden wonders in programs (particularly some very interesting messages) that you can unveil.

There are direct benefits to tinkering, as well. If a disk is damaged or the data in a file is corrupted so that the program working with that data rejects it, you sometimes can use your tinkering skills to repair the damage. This isn't always possible, of course, but sometimes you can hammer things back into shape and carry on.

So whether it's to expand your knowledge, satisfy your curiosity, or attempt emergency repairs, exploring and tinkering can be quite worthwhile. You can use many program tools to do your exploring and tinkering, but this chapter focuses on the two that are most widely available and that provide a good spectrum of features: DOS's DEBUG program and the Disk Editor program from the Norton Utilities. (If you have a version of the Norton Utilities earlier than 5.0, use the NU program.)

DEBUG is in some ways the more powerful and also the more difficult to use. To a certain extent, of course, those two properties go hand in hand; powerful features are almost necessarily accompanied by complex commands. But that isn't the only reason DEBUG is more demanding.

Any program tool, from a spreadsheet to the tinkering tools discussed here, is designed to serve a particular need. In the case of DEBUG, the technical needs of advanced programmers were the target. As a free program included with every copy of DOS, DEBUG wasn't intended to be the ultimate programmer's tool, just a good basic tool for programmers. DEBUG's features are technical, and its command structure and user interface are crude, but it gets the job done.

Together, DEBUG, the Disk Editor, and NU give you a good example of the range of utility program features that enable you to tinker and explore.

# Working with DEBUG

This section discusses the things you can do with DEBUG. And, because DEBUG is included with every version of DOS, everyone who has a PC has a copy.

You can find instructions for using DEBUG in your DOS manual or in the *DOS Technical Reference Manual*, which is sold separately depending on the version of DOS that you have. However, because this manual is interesting and useful, you may want to buy it regardless of what version of DOS you are using. Another source for DEBUG information is my book, *Peter Norton's Complete Guide to DOS 6.22*, published by Sams. In that book, I discuss all the commands and how to use them.

As already explained, DEBUG is a technically oriented tool designed to serve the needs of programmers and others who have no difficulty working with the microprocessor and are comfortable using hexadecimal numbers and segmented addresses. Almost everything you can do with DEBUG requires that you specify your commands in hex and that you enter and interpret segmented addresses (also given in hex). If you are not familiar with these things, you may want to forget about using DEBUG. If so, skip this section and move on to the next, where you learn about a more civilized tool, the editing functions in the Norton Utilities.

DEBUG.EXE (which is usually found in your DOS directory) is a powerful tool with many features, and a great deal more power than I can explore here. You already have had a taste of some of that power with the DEBUG U (Unassemble) command, which can be used to decode the hexadecimal of absolute machine language instructions into the more intelligible assembly language format. You learned about that DEBUG feature in the discussion of interrupt drivers in Chapter 4, "Microprocessor Traffic Control." DEBUG also has an A (Assemble) command, which acts as a crude assembler turning assembly language statements into machine language and features that enable you to follow the steps a program takes by watching it execute and seeing the results of each step. Those commands and others like them are fascinatingly powerful, but they're more than I can deal with here. These details belong in a book on advanced programming techniques.

This chapter discusses some of the DEBUG commands that enable you to snoop and explore. First, some background on DEBUG. DEBUG works with a minimum of fuss (and a minimum of online help), which takes a little getting used to. You start the program with this simple command:

DEBUG

DEBUG then displays its command prompt, which is a hyphen. Whenever you see that DEBUG command prompt, DEBUG is ready to receive a command. All of DEBUG's commands (except for a few of the newer expanded memory commands added with DOS 4.0) are abbreviated as a single letter. You might as well start by learning the command to finish using DEBUG and return to DOS. It's the Q (Quit) command.

For snooping around with DEBUG, one of the main commands to use is the D (Display) command. D tells DEBUG to display some of the contents of the computer's memory in a form that combines hexadecimal and character format. Following is an example of what the D command might show you:

```
24B4:0600  00 00 00 00 00 00 00 00-00 00 00 00 00 00 00 00   ................
24B4:0610  00 00 00 00 00 00 00 00-00 00 00 00 00 00 00 00   ................
24B4:0620  00 00 00 00 00 00 00 00-00 00 00 00 00 00 00 00   ................
24B4:0630  00 00 00 00 00 00 00 00-00 00 00 00 00 00 00 00   ................
24B4:0640  00 00 00 00 41 52 49 46-59 4E 05 41 62 6F 72 74   ....ARIFYN.Abort
24B4:0650  07 2C 20 52 65 74 72 79-08 2C 20 49 67 6E 6F 72   ., Retry., Ignor
24B4:0660  65 06 2C 20 46 61 69 6C-01 3F 08 72 65 61 64 69   e., Fail.?.readi
24B4:0670  6E 67 00 08 77 72 69 74-69 6E 67 00 0E 20 25 31   ng..writing.. %1
```

This display information appears in three parts. On the left is the memory address of the data being displayed; in the middle is the data in hex format; and on the right are the characters that correspond to the hex information shown. DEBUG censors the character data, showing only ordinary text characters. This censoring has its good and bad aspects. It doesn't show all the interesting characters that lurk in the data, but it does ensure that you can copy the data to a printer without accidentally sending a control code that might make the printer act up. (By contrast, the data displays generated by the Norton Utilities show every character so that you can see it all, but you may not necessarily be able to print it.)

DEBUG displays any data it has in memory, which can be just about anything. As you saw in Chapter 4, DEBUG can look at the beginning of the computer's memory (say, to look at the interrupt vectors) or at the higher reaches of memory where the ROM BIOS routines are stored. You look at some of those shortly. From the middle part of memory, you can display DEBUG's ordinary program data area. This is where you have DEBUG load a program or data file you want to inspect.

If, for example, you want to use DEBUG to browse around in DOS's command interpreter COMMAND.COM, you can tell DEBUG to load COMMAND.COM into memory when it starts and then display the beginning of the contents of COMMAND.COM, like this:

```
DEBUG COMMAND.COM
-D
```

When you do that, you get a display like the following (I've skipped from the beginning of COMMAND.COM to a part that you can recognize):

```
24B4:2280  70 61 63 65 0D 0A 5E 0D-0A 0D 0A 4D 69 63 72 6F   pace..^....Micro
24B4:2290  73 6F 66 74 28 52 29 20-4D 53 2D 44 4F 53 28 52   soft(R) MS-DOS(R
24B4:22A0  29 20 56 65 72 73 69 6F-6E 20 36 2E 32 32 0D 0A   ) Version 6.22..
24B4:22B0  20 20 20 20 20 20 20 20-20 20 20 20 20 20 43 29            (C)
24B4:22C0  43 6F 70 79 72 69 67 68-74 20 4D 69 63 72 6F 73   Copyright Micros
24B4:22D0  6F 66 74 20 43 6F 72 70-20 31 39 38 31 2D 31 39   oft Corp 1981-19
24B4:22E0  39 34 2E 0D 0A 28 53 70-65 63 69 66 69 65 64 20   94...(Specified
24B4:22F0  43 4F 4D 4D 41 4E 44 20-73 65 61 72 63 68 20 64   COMMAND search d
```

The DEBUG D (Display) command by itself shows just 128 bytes from its current work area. If you want the command to show another area, you can give it the address you want it to show, such as D 2280 (which is what I used to display the part of COMMAND.COM that you see above) or D 0:0 (which is what you would do to get the very beginning of memory). To have the D command show more than 128 bytes at a time, you just add the letter L (for length) and indicate in hex the number of bytes you want shown. The command D F800:0 L 300, for example, shows hex 300 (768) bytes, starting high in memory in the ROM-BIOS area.

All by itself, the D command can be used to explore much of the PC's memory and disk data, but other DEBUG commands help you find even more.

The S (Search) command enables you to search through data, which can be very helpful in finding messages that you know are stored in a program. If you know the text of one message and use DE-BUG to find it, you're likely to find the area where other messages are stored, and studying these messages can tell you a lot.

Like the D command, you enter the search command with the initial letter S followed by whatever memory address and length you want the search to act on. Following that, you tell DEBUG what you want it to search for, either as a number in hex or, if you're looking for characters, a string of characters enclosed in quotation marks. The following is an example:

```
S F000:0 L FFFF "1790"
```

I used this command once when an old PC AT that belonged to a neighbor of mine acted up. It started displaying error message number 1790, but he didn't know exactly what that meant. Because the message appeared when his machine was first turned on, I knew that the message was part of the power on self-test routines that are stored in the computer's ROM BIOS. To find out more about this message, I used DEBUG to find this message, searching through the ROM BIOS area (from address F000:0 for a length of hex FFFF, the full 64KB of the ROM BIOS area) for the text 1790. (With the PS/2s, as discussed in Chapter 17, "BIOS: Digging In," the ROM BIOS area starts at E000:0 and is 128KB long.) DEBUG located the message and told me where it was by displaying the following message:

```
F000:E3DB
```

Then I used the D command to display the full message and anything around it. I gave DEBUG a starting address just ahead of where it found the 1790, so that I could see more of the surrounding messages. I entered D F000:E390, and DEBUG showed me the following:

```
F000:E390  72 0D 0A 31 37 38 30 2D-44 69 73 6B 20 30 20 46   r..1780-Disk 0 F
F000:E3A0  61 69 6C 75 72 65 0D 0A-31 37 38 31 2D 44 69 73   ailure..1781-Dis
F000:E3B0  6B 20 31 20 46 61 69 6C-75 72 65 0D 0A 31 37 38   k 1 Failure..178
F000:E3C0  32 2D 44 69 73 6B 20 43-6F 6E 74 72 6F 6C 6C 65   2-Disk Controlle
F000:E3D0  72 20 46 61 69 6C 75 72-65 0D 0A 31 37 39 30 2D   r Failure..1790-
F000:E3E0  44 69 73 6B 20 30 20 45-72 72 6F 72 0D 0A 31 37   Disk 0 Error..17
F000:E3F0  39 31 2D 44 69 73 6B 20-31 20 45 72 72 6F 72 0D   91-Disk 1 Error.
```

```
F000:E400   0A 32 01 04 00 00 80 00-00 00 00 00 00 31 01 11   .2...........1..
```

Given the full text of those messages, my friend was able to get a clearer idea of what had gone wrong with his machine. This is just one real-life example of the variety of things that DEBUG can do for you.

If you want to learn more about what DEBUG can do for you, you must be prepared to cope with some messy technical details, but DEBUG can reward your efforts with a wealth of information. Although I don't have space here to explain all the wonders of DEBUG, I can list the DEBUG commands that are most important for exploring and tinkering. You already have learned about the D and S commands. To make changes to data, you need to learn about the E (Enter) and F (Fill) commands. To read and write data stored on a disk, you need to learn about the L (Load) and W (Write) commands. If you learn the basics of these DEBUG commands, you can inspect and change any data in your computer.

Next, you learn about another tool, one whose powers have a different dimension than DEBUG's and one that can be quite a bit easier to learn and use.

**Note:** You should be aware that if you attempt to use DEBUG under protected mode (for example, while Windows is running) you will be working under the restrictions inherent in protected mode. Specifically, you are likely to receive the DOS error:

```
Sharing Violation
Abort, Retry, Fail?
```

if you attempt to debug either a file or an area of memory that is being used at the same time by Windows or a Windows application. Having received the error, the only logical step for you to take is to Abort. In this situation, Retry will never succeed so long as Windows is running, and the Fail code generated by Fail will not provide you with any additional error sense. Once you leave protected mode, of course, you can explore Windows files and the memory used by Windows at will.

# Working with the Disk Editor

The Norton Utilities' Disk Editor, like DEBUG, is a program that can teach you many things about your PC's disks and memory. The Disk Editor cannot do everything that DEBUG can; in particular, the Disk Editor does not concern itself with the PC's machine language instruction set the way DEBUG's U (Unassemble) and A (Assemble) commands do. The Disk Editor does, however, enable you to examine and edit any floppy or hard disk, even those that for some reason cannot be read by DOS. Moreover, you can use the Disk Editor to examine any area of memory.

Using the Disk Editor is easy. All you have to do is press either the Alt or the F10 key to access the pull-down menus after the editor is running. Move to any menu and make a selection. If you have a mouse, you can click a menu name and then click the option of your choice.

After you choose a disk, you can use the Info menu to display information. You see an outline of all the basic information about your disk. You see absolute information, such as the size of the disk, the number of sides and tracks, the number of sectors per track, and the hexadecimal drive ID number. And, you see such DOS-related information as the size of a sector, the size of a cluster, the number of clusters, and the size of a FAT entry.

This information provides a small gold mine of information about the dimensions and setup of any disk, including virtual disks (RAM disks). By using the information in this screen, you can learn how each disk is structured.

Even more fascinating than the technical disk information is the disk space map, which provides a representative drawing of how the space on the disk is being used. Each position on the map represents a small portion of the disk storage space. You can see which areas are in use and which areas are free. If the disk has any bad track areas, they also are shown. Finally, you can see exactly which clusters are occupied by the file you have selected.

You also can select a particular file and ask to see its characteristics. You then are shown information about the file's directory entry, including the filename and extension, the size, the date and time stamp, and file attributes. You also can see information that usually is unavailable, such as the number of clusters used by the file, the starting cluster number, and how fragmented the file is. (This refers to how many contiguous sets of clusters are being used.)

In addition to finding out about a part of a disk, you can look inside it. The Disk Editor displays the information in the format that makes the most sense, in hexadecimal or as ASCII text. The Disk Editor also formats information for viewing special areas, such as directories, the file allocation table (FAT), the partition table, and the boot record.

One of the things you can do with the Disk Editor is make direct changes to the data you are displaying. To guard against catastrophes, however, the Disk Editor defaults to read-only mode, in which you cannot make changes. If you do want to modify something, you can select the Configuration option from the Tools menu and turn off the read-only setting.

To make changes, all you have to do is move to what you want to change and type right over it. You can do this not only with files but with directories, partition tables, and so on. Be careful though; unless you know exactly what you are doing, you may cause irreparable damage. Before you make changes, you might want to read the *Disk Editor* section of the manual that comes with the Norton Utilities, Version 8. You'll find complete instructions for the disk editor there.

Using the features of the Disk Editor, you can get into any part of the disk, see what's there, and, if you know how, tinker with and modify the data (either change it or repair damage). The manual that comes with the Norton Utilities explains how all manner of repairs can be made.

Following are some examples, from my own experience, of situations in which this capability came in handy. DOS contains two programs, BACKUP and RESTORE, that are used to back up hard disk data onto floppy disks. In an early version of DOS, the BACKUP program sometimes recorded one of the backup disks incorrectly, with a hex 0 in place of part of one of the filenames. This tiny error made it impossible to restore data that had been copied to the floppy disk—a disaster.

Fortunately, when this happened to me, I was able to use Disk Editor to browse around on the bad disk until I discovered what the problem was. After I figured it out, all I had to do was replace the erroneous hex 0 with a proper character for a filename. It was an easy repair job, which would have been impossible without an exploring and patching tool. In that case, the Disk Editor saved an entire hard disk full of data.

Another example is the time that a computer belonging to one of my associates had been used for DOS and UNIX. He decided he wanted to devote his entire hard disk to DOS, but there was still an old UNIX partition on it. The then-current version of DOS (this was back before Version 5.0) would not delete the unwanted partition. Using the Disk Editor, he was able to modify the partition table and delete the partition. (Of course, this is not the type of thing you would do unless you knew exactly what you were doing.)

These examples offer powerful demonstrations of why it can be worthwhile to have a tool like the Disk Editor and to know how to use it.

# Some Things to Think About or Try

1. Using DEBUG, search through your computer's ROM to find the copyright notice on the ROM-BIOS. Give DEBUG the command D F800:0 and then follow that with the command D until you see what you're looking for. If you don't find the message starting at F800:0, try again at F000:0. If you have a PS/2, try a search starting at E000:0. (Remember, PS/2s use both the E and F blocks for the ROM-BIOS.)

2. If you have the Norton Utilities, use the Disk Editor (or NU) to look at the dimensions of each disk you have. What do the figures tell you?

3. Again, if you have the Norton Utilities, make a copy of one of your floppy disks and experiment with making changes to it. Find the root directory and change one of the filenames by typing over the name. Test to see whether the name was properly changed.

4. Using the Disk Editor's capability to show the same data in directory and hex format, display part of your disk's directory and then try to find just where each part of the directory (name, extension, date, and size) is recorded in the hex part. Changing the hex data and seeing what changed in the directory display can help you tell what's what.

# A

# How IBM Developed the Personal Computer

There were many activities within IBM that preceded the start of the PC project, including the development of several early small systems marketed by IBM with very limited success. Many believe that the PC was IBM's first small computer system and the first IBM product to use Intel microprocessors. In fact, the IBM PC was preceded by no fewer than five earlier small system designs!

IBM's first small computer system was a product called the 5100. Designed as a small scientific machine, the system executed a powerful math-intensive language called APL (Algorithmic Programming Language). The 5100 was packaged as a portable system, similar to the early Osborn portable or the original Compaq transportable PC, and it had a small built-in CRT display and used tape cartridges for mass storage. This system was based on an IBM-developed microprocessor that actually interpreted IBM 370 mainframe instructions. By interpreting the 370 instruction set, it was possible to easily move the APL interpreter program from the mainframe to the 5100 without having to rewrite the program. Of course, this double level of interpretation made the system very slow. The development of the 5100 was a joint project between a small IBM laboratory in Los Gatos, California and the Rochester Minnesota development laboratory.

This system had one additional distinction: It was the first IBM product to use an Intel microprocessor! The Intel processor was not the main processor but served as a communication controller in the 5100 product. The first Intel microprocessor used by IBM was the 8080, an eight-bit predecessor to the 8085 and 8086. An enhanced version of the 5100, called the 5110, supported 8-inch floppy disk drives and added an IBM Basic language interpreter. The Basic interpreter was moved from the IBM System 3 computer and, like APL, was implemented by interpreting the System 3 instruction set on the 5110's main processor. The last of the 5100 family was the 5120, developed in Boca Raton in 1980. This product was a 5110 in a new mechanical package designed to be a nonportable desktop system. The 5100 family of computers were never as successful as IBM wished, primarily due to the high cost, very low performance, and lack of compatibility with any industry software. Although not a success, the 5100 laid the groundwork for the next generation of small computers from IBM.

# The Way Is Paved for the PC

As IBM developed the 5100 family of products, many at IBM felt the basic technology being used to support low-end products was not competitive with new microprocessor technology being developed by Intel, Motorola, Zilog, and others. It was felt that IBM was trying to apply its mainframe technologies to small system designs and was incurring a significant cost disadvantage. This was reinforced by the rapid deployment of very low-cost and powerful mini-computers that threatened IBM low-end mainframe systems and by the loss of IBM terminal sales to a number of small startup companies using industry technologies and microprocessors. As a result of this concern, a small laboratory was informally started in Atlanta, Georgia, to investigate the use of non-IBM technologies to develop low-end IBM products. This small lab built several early prototype PCs using Intel 8085, Motorola 6800, and Zilog Z80 microprocessors. This activity managed to encourage IBM to develop a number of small systems using Intel microprocessors. As a result of pioneering work done by this small lab, the IBM Displaywriter(8086), IBM 5250 Terminal(8085), and the IBM Datamaster/System 23(8085) products were developed using Intel microprocessors. IBM also selected the Intel 8048 micro controller for use in their keyboards. Contrary to popular belief, IBM had a long relationship with Intel prior to the PC project.

# The IBM Datamaster/System 23: IBM's First Attempt at a PC

In 1979, IBM was planning its next move into the small computer arena. They could continue to develop the 5100 family or develop a new system based on the latest industry microprocessor technology. In typical IBM fashion, they decided to do both. The small group of engineers in the Atlanta lab moved south to Boca Raton, Florida, with the clear intent of building IBM's first PC. The plan was to establish an independent business unit for the purpose of developing a new small desktop system that used Intel microprocessors, an industry standard operating system, and a Basic language interpreter compatible with the industry software. The project would be done in record time and would bypass all IBM development procedures. This was the beginning of the Datamaster/System 23 project. As the project progressed, IBM got cold feet and slowly reimposed IBM's overly conservative and slow development methodology based on exclusive use of internal technology; for example, they began to develop its own operating system and Basic interpreter language. The project schedules slipped and the costs increased, and in the end the Datamaster was just another 5100 class system with high cost, low performance, and no software. The first attempt at an IBM PC had failed! Although this was very discouraging for the Datamaster engineers, they continued to work under the table on the true PC, developing new graphic adapters and support for 5.25-inch non-IBM disk drives. Figure A.1 shows the family of small systems that preceded the PC.

**Figure A.1.**
*The IBM PC Lineage.*

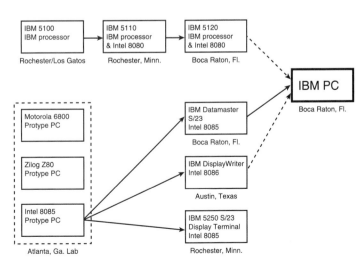

# The Group of Thirteen

In 1980, the PC project got a boost from the top at IBM. Small systems from Apple, Tandy, and others were beginning to sell in large volumes beyond the hobbyist markets. These systems were actually being used in business to perform applications that IBM felt were encroaching on their turf. IBM never viewed the new PCs as much of a direct threat to mainframes and saw no large revenue opportunity in this market. Their major concern was that "new users" were using non-IBM products, and when the need to do "real" work arose, they would not be familiar with IBM products and would select a non-IBM system in the future. IBM had seen this trend occur in the mini-computer market, where Digital Equipment had given systems to universities, and when students graduated to the business world, they selected DEC computers over IBM systems.

In May of 1980, IBM Chairman Frank Cary and President John Opel concluded that IBM must have a PC offering that competed with Apple and Tandy and established the IBM name at the lowest entry point in the computer market. Bill Lowe, the systems manager for the Datamaster project and now laboratory director for the Boca Raton site, was asked to formulate a plan to develop a PC. After several weeks of study, he reported back to Frank Cary and John Opel that IBM's best strategy was to purchase an existing design from Atari and manufacture it with IBM's name. This proposal was rejected and Bill Lowe was asked to return to Boca Raton and develop a plan for an "IBM" PC design. Bill formed a small task force of marketing and manufacturing people and included several of the engineers on the Datamaster project, including those that worked on the original PC prototypes in Atlanta. This task force included many of the group of 13 who eventually worked together at the beginning of the PC project. The Datamaster engineers already had a good idea of the PC system that they wanted to build and had secretly built many of the components in the lab. Within two weeks the task force had agreed on a system design using the Intel 8088 microprocessor, a simple metal enclosure, a keyboard from the IBM S/34 terminals, and industry 5.25" floppy disk drives. The plan was to use Digital Research's CP/M operating system and the BASIC 80 interpreter from Microsoft. The plan called for a total development cycle of 9 months, from start to product shipments.

As word spread inside IBM that a PC project was likely to be approved at the highest levels, several competing proposals came forward. Most of these proposals involved using IBM developed microprocessors, technology, software, and development methodology. They simply could not meet the aggressive costs and schedules defined by the group of 13. Even as additional progress meetings with IBM top management were being held, the group of 13 began working on the PC design, although the project had not been formally approved. The PC project was officially approved on September 6, 1980 as the result of a meeting between Bill Lowe, key members of development team, Frank Cary, and John Opel at the IBM headquarters in New York. At this meeting a "prototype PC" was demonstrated. The prototype was actually a Datamaster/System 23 mother board with an 8085 microprocessor, a new graphics display adapter and a new 5.25-inch floppy disk controller. It was packaged in a wedge-shaped keyboard style enclosure made of wood and painted a glossy black. The demo prototype ran a public domain Tiny Basic from Lawrence Livermore Labs on top of a modified monitor program originally designed for the Motorola 6800 microprocessor. This was the same software that was developed and demonstrated in the small lab in Atlanta nearly two years earlier! At the meeting a game called "Lunar Lander" was demonstrated, along with several high-resolution graphic images. It actually bore no resemblance to the PC defined by the task force!

As a result of this key meeting, the PC project was approved as a totally independent business unit that reported directly to the chairman and president, bypassing all IBM middle management. The old Datamaster engineers finally got their wish, a new system totally free from IBM's design methodology and technology constraints. They had their second chance to produce the IBM PC they had planned more than two years earlier. Looking back, it is ironic that IBM's decision to enter the PC market was based on the premise of protecting its present mainframe business rather than on creating a whole new industry—an industry that now threatens this very mainframe business!

# Why the 8088?

The 16-bit 8086 processor was introduced in June of 1978, more than three years before the introduction of the IBM PC. The IBM PC development group selected the less powerful 8088 microprocessor in a attempt to keep the PC's costs down. The 8088 was similar to the 8086, since it supported an internal 16-bit bus, but its external bus was only 8 bits wide. This made it easier to attach the standard 8-bit peripheral chips and enabled a smaller entry memory size in the PC design. This feature of the 8088 enabled the IBM PC to compete with popular less costly 8-bit systems, yet have the performance advantage of a large address space and 16-bit internal processor. The 8088 selection also guaranteed compatible performance in the migration path to the 8086 and the 286 processors. The PC development team was aware of the 286 in development at Intel; in fact, it was announced by Intel only six months after the announcement of the PC, and yet was not used by IBM for three years!

The most important reason for selecting the Intel processor family had nothing to do with its performance or cost compared to other alternatives. The Intel processor family had a set of native development tools. This meant that a software developer could actually write software and develop applications on the PC. The other 16-bit processors from IBM or others still required a cross system environment, or the use of a mini-computer or mainframe system to develop software. Most competitive microprocessors did not have development tools that ran on their own microprocessors. This was considered a major obstacle to wide acceptance of the PC and the development of new PC applications. Intel also provided a conversion tool that would semiautomatically convert existing 8080 code to 8086/8088 code. Many of the original applications were 8080 applications converted using this code translator.

The 8088's major distinguishing features over the existing family of 8-bit processors was its internal 16-bit data paths and 1M address space. The increase in address space was accomplished using a scheme called segmentation. Program instructions could not address any memory location in the 1M address space directly. A two-step process was used. First, a segment register was loaded that pointed to a 64 KB block of data or instructions; this could be on any 4-byte boundary in the 1M address space. Next, the normal X86 instructions could access any data or instructions in the 64 kilobytes. To access data outside the 64 KB block, the segment registers needed to be reloaded with new pointers. Four 16-bit segment registers were provided: one each for instruction accesses, data accesses, and stack accesses, and a special extra segment register. Programmers hated this scheme, since it meant that the programmer had to be constantly aware of values of the segment registers and adjust them when spanning a segment boundary. It was not until the introduction of the 80386 processor that new addressing modes permitted full linear addressing in the X86 architecture. The 8088 was implemented with 29,000 transistors and was housed in a 40-pin package. The latest Pentium processors are implemented with 3.1 million transistors and require a 296-pin package.

# The PC's Datamaster S/23 Heritage

Many features of the earlier Intel 8085 microprocessor-based Datamaster design were quickly adopted for use in the PC. The adapter-card-on-motherboard packaging approach was adopted from the Datamaster. The PC's card size and right angle connector bracket mounting was adopted. Even the expansion bus connector and the bus signals were adapted. The 8085 microprocessor's bus was very similar to the newer Intel 8088 microprocessor's interface and only minor changes were made in the Datamaster's expansion bus architecture for use in the PC. It is a little-known fact that the adapter boards designed for the PC would actually fit into and work in an older IBM Datamaster system! The adoption of the earlier Datamaster's key architectural and packaging features and its prior history of rigorous testing greatly enhanced the PC's development schedule and chances of success. Even after the official formation of the PC development group, many of the Datamaster engineers who were not transferred quietly continued to work on the PC project.

# The PC Development Project

As part of the assumptions for meeting cost and schedule targets, Frank Cary and John Opel agreed that the PC development group would have total freedom from IBM's rigid development process. Bill Lowe had seen how the Datamaster project had started with the same assumption and was slowly forced back into the rigid IBM mold. This was attributed to the massive middle management reporting structure in IBM. As each decision moved up the chain, the conclusion was eventually reached to take the safe course and do things the IBM way. To avoid a repeat of this process, the PC project reported directly to IBM's top management, bypassing the middle management bureaucracy entirely.

The PC development group started the project with some very basic assumptions that were totally counter to IBM's product development procedures:

1. The group would not use any IBM computer-aided design systems; all schematic, timing verification, and circuit board layout would be done manually according to industry standards.

2. Qualification of vendors' components would be dramatically reduced or eliminated. Standard IBM qualification procedures could typically take several months, requiring the vendor to build special higher cost versions for IBM.

3. The product testing procedures would be dramatically reduced to a two-stage process testing only preproduction and production level units. The standard IBM product test procedure had four or more phases of testing and typically lasted over two years.

4. Case packaging and style did not have to meet IBM guidelines. The PC was the first IBM small system to use a metal case. Plastic cases required tooling of complex molds often requiring a year to develop.

5. The PC did not have to maintain compatibility with any existing IBM systems. The earlier Datamaster was forced to use IBM's character set and codes, which precluded any possible use of industry standard software.

6. The PC group could ignore requests by internal IBM groups to justify selection of non-IBM technology for use in the PC. The Datamaster project had become bogged down in endless meetings that challenged the use of outside technologies.

7. All PC system software was to be purchased from third party sources. The PC group's software activities were to be limited to developing diagnostic and BIOS routines and testing the procured software.

With the project's goals now well defined, the project needed to be staffed and a home selected. Several IBM sites were candidates for the PC project. Rochester, Minnesota was considered since all low-end business systems were developed there; Atlanta, Georgia was given brief consideration since the original PC work was done there; Boulder, Colorado was given highest priority due to the lack of an existing product mission and a pool of available engineers. In the end, the PC project stayed in Boca Raton. Rochester was too cold, Atlanta meant moving everyone, and Boulder turned down the PC project because it was too risky. However, a number of engineers were recruited from the Boulder site and joined the PC project in Boca Raton.

# The PC Project Schedule

Due to the covert work performed by the Datamaster engineers prior to the project start, the PC development got off to a running start. Shortly after the official start of the project in September, 1980, the first true PC prototypes were running, and a few weeks later they were delivered to Microsoft. It quickly became obvious that the development group would have a product and that a more complete organization needed to be put in place to market, service, and manufacture the PC. The search was started for a PC Systems manager to organize and run the project as a fully independent business unit. Phillip Don Estridge, the former software development manager for the IBM Series 1 mini computer, was selected to run the PC business unit.

With the basic PC system unit design completed, the PC group turned to procurement and design of the other system components. The monochrome and color CRT monitors were procured from the Far East, the PC printer was procured from Epson in Japan, and the floppy disk drives from U.S. vendors. The PC group also designed a number of PC expansion boards, including the Color Graphic Display Adapter, Monochrome Display Adapter, Floppy Disk Drive Adapter, Printer Port Adapter, Asynchronous Communication Port Adapter, Bi-snyc Communications Adapter, and Game Port Adapter. By late spring of 1981, most of the PC product family was ready to be released to manufacturing. It would take approximately three additional months to gear up manufacturing and to build a small stockpile of systems ready to be shipped on announcement day.

# The PC Operating System

The Datamaster development team had initially wanted to use Digital Research's CP/M operating system and Microsoft's Basic 80 Basic language interpreter in the Datamaster/System 23; they were very familiar with these products, even though the System 23 eventually used an all-IBM software solution. It was only natural for the PC to follow the path abandoned by the Datamaster. At the time, Bill Gates and Paul Allen, partners in Microsoft, had built a reputation in the microcomputer industry by porting their BASIC language to more than 20 different systems. IBM met with Bill Gates and presented the PC product and project plans. Gates offered his criticisms and suggestions concerning the PC's designs. He recommended adding a small color palette to the CGA display adapter and graphics characters to the PC character set, and recommended a keyboard layout. All of these suggestions were incorporated into the PC design. Of course, like all software people, he wanted a faster, more powerful processor with more memory, but in the end agreed to the PC's design.

While one IBM group was working with Microsoft on the languages to be supported on the PC, a second group attempted a meeting with Digital Research to explore porting CP/M to the PC. The initial meeting between IBM and Digital Research went poorly when Digital Research refused to sign an IBM nondisclosure agreement. It looked like working with Digital Research would be difficult and could possibly delay the PC schedule. When Bill Gates was asked his advice, he recommended the use of an alternate operating system from Seattle Computer Products, a maker of an 8086 S-100 board product that had an operating system similar to CP/M called QDOS. Microsoft obtained rights to QDOS and began porting it to the PC, thus PC DOS was born. It was agreed that while Microsoft would port QDOS to the PC and modify BASIC for PC, IBM would write the BIOS ROM software. The BIOS was the software that served as the interface between the operating system and the PC's hardware.

When the PC was announced in August 1981, PC DOS was its primary operating system. Although it lacked many of the features that users take for granted today, such as subdirectories and hard disk support, PC DOS 1.0 was very successful. Comparing PC DOS 1.0 to today's Windows 95 and Windows NT 3.5, one would have to say Microsoft has come a long way!

# The Father of the PC

When Don Estridge took over the PC project, most of the PC architecture and product definition had been completed. Still, the PC was a long way from being a sure success. Estridge quickly embraced the maverick spirit of the group and became a strong protector and leader of the PC project, fending off attacks from rival groups within IBM and securing IBM top-level management support. What Estridge did was to lay out a step-by-step plan that took the PC from a prototype development to a real product that could be manufactured, serviced, and marketed through nontraditional IBM sales channels. He added just enough organization to the project to ensure its success without stifling its creative energy.

Perhaps Estridge's most enduring contribution was his support of the PC as an open system. This was a concept totally foreign to most people at IBM; why invite competition? The idea that third parties would be allowed to design add-in cards, peripheral devices, and even compatible systems was simply unheard of! The development group wanted an open system; they knew that it would be impossible for IBM to provide all of the technology, peripherals, and expansion features needed to make the PC a success. They pointed to the Apple II and the large third party products market that existed. Taking the Apple II manuals as a model, IBM finally relented and published the IBM technical reference manuals containing full BIOS listings and system schematics. It is interesting to note how IBM and Apple have swapped positions: IBM used the Apple example to justify an open system and Apple used the IBM example to justify becoming a closed system. IBM actually had taken some steps that provided a measure of protection against manufacturers of clone systems. First, the BIOS was copyrighted and, secondly, the PC hardware design was protected by a number of patents. These initial precautions offered little protection against off-shore clone manufacturers, however. IBM now licenses the patents to clone developers and receives a significant stream of royalties.

Looking back, one would have to say that the PC had many fathers: the small group in Atlanta that built the first PC prototypes and paved the way for the PC; the 5100 development group in Rochester, Minnesota and Los Gatos, California that pioneered small system development in IBM; the Datamaster engineers who tried to build the first PC and kept the idea alive by covertly developing PC technology; Bill Lowe, the PC task force chairman who proposed the PC project; Frank Cary and John Opel, IBM's top management who demanded a PC product; and of course, Phillip Don Estridge, who managed the PC project to success.

# The PC Announcement

In August 1981, IBM officially announced the PC and began volume shipments in October. Many in IBM considered the project to be doomed. Marketing computers through Sears, J.C. Penney, and IBM store-front outlets was crazy! Who would buy a computer that was not attached to a mainframe? One executive even predicted that IBM would have to make a massive recall, making the recall announcement during the half-time of the Super Bowl game. This was predicated on the fact that the PC's design was shabby and unreliable, since it had bypassed all of the IBM quality tests and design procedures. Of course this dire prediction did not come true and the PC established a totally new market and revenue stream for IBM. Today, nearly 50 million PCs are produced annually world-wide by IBM and a host of other manufacturers.

# B

QBasic
Program
Listings

# MAZE: Start-to-Finish Maze (Introduction)

```
'Define default alphanumeric variables to be integers
DEFINT A-Z
 'Declare program functions
   DECLARE FUNCTION ChooseDistance (Direction, CurrentRow, CurrentCol)
   DECLARE FUNCTION NotYetDone (CurrentRow, CurrentCol)
 'Declare program subroutines
   DECLARE SUB ChooseDirection (Direction, MovingChar, CurrentRow, CurrentCol)
   DECLARE SUB DrawMessageBox (Msg$, Foreground, Background, CurrentRow, CurrentCol)
   DECLARE SUB Move (Distance, Direction, MovingChar, CurrentRow, CurrentCol)
   DECLARE SUB NextLocation (Direction, CurrentRow, CurrentCol)
   DECLARE SUB SoundTone (SoundCancel, SoundBase, SoundTime)
 'Do setup work
   CLS
   RANDOMIZE TIMER
   SoundCancel = 1: SoundBase = 50: SoundTime = 100
   CurrentRow = 2: CurrentCol = 10: Direction = 1
   PLAY "MB"
   DrawMessageBox " Start ", 0, 7, 1, 1
   DrawMessageBox " Finish! ", 0, 7, 22, 68
   LOCATE 2, 9, 0: PRINT CHR$(204)
   COLOR 7, 0: MovingChar = 205
 'Main program loop
   WHILE NotYetDone(CurrentRow, CurrentCol)
     SoundTone SoundCancel, SoundBase, SoundTime
     Distance = ChooseDistance(Direction, CurrentRow, CurrentCol)
     Move Distance, Direction, MovingChar, CurrentRow, CurrentCol
     ChooseDirection Direction, MovingChar, CurrentRow, CurrentCol
   WEND
 'Report triumph and finish
   SOUND 100, 0
   FOR I = 1 TO 10
     DrawMessageBox " Finished! ", 7, 0, 22, 66
     SoundTone SoundCancel, SoundBase, SoundTime
     DrawMessageBox " Finished! ", 0, 7, 22, 66
     SoundTone SoundCancel, SoundBase, SoundTime
   NEXT I
   DrawMessageBox " Finished! ", 28, 15, 22, 66
   LOCATE 12, 25: COLOR 7, 0: SOUND 100, 0
   PRINT "Press a key to return to DOS... ";
   WHILE INKEY$ = "": WEND
SUB ChooseDirection (Direction, MovingChar, CurrentRow, CurrentCol)
 'Subprogram to choose direction and turn corner
   RightTurn = INT(RND * 2)
   DO
     RightTurn = 1 - RightTurn
     SELECT CASE Direction
     CASE 1
       NewDirection = 3 + RightTurn
     CASE 2
       NewDirection = 4 - RightTurn
     CASE 3
       NewDirection = 2 - RightTurn
     CASE 4
```

```
        NewDirection = 1 + RightTurn
      END SELECT
      TryAgain = 0
      SELECT CASE NewDirection
      CASE 1
        IF CurrentCol > 75 THEN TryAgain = 1
      CASE 2
        IF CurrentCol < 5 THEN TryAgain = 1
      CASE 3
        IF CurrentRow < 5 THEN TryAgain = 1
      CASE 4
        IF CurrentRow > 20 THEN TryAgain = 1
      END SELECT
    LOOP WHILE TryAgain
    SELECT CASE Direction
      CASE 1
        IF RightTurn THEN TurnChar = 187 ELSE TurnChar = 188
      CASE 2
        IF RightTurn THEN TurnChar = 200 ELSE TurnChar = 201
      CASE 3
        IF RightTurn THEN TurnChar = 201 ELSE TurnChar = 187
      CASE 4
        IF RightTurn THEN TurnChar = 188 ELSE TurnChar = 200
    END SELECT
    PRINT CHR$(TurnChar);
    Direction = NewDirection
    IF Direction < 3 THEN MovingChar = 205
    IF Direction > 2 THEN MovingChar = 186
    NextLocation Direction, CurrentRow, CurrentCol
END SUB
FUNCTION ChooseDistance (Direction, CurrentRow, CurrentCol)
' Function to choose distance
  SELECT CASE Direction
    CASE 1
      Limit = 78 - CurrentCol
    CASE 2
      Limit = CurrentCol - 2
    CASE 3
      Limit = CurrentRow - 2
    CASE 4
      Limit = 23 - CurrentRow
  END SELECT
  IF Limit < 1 THEN Limit = 1
  ChooseDistance = INT(RND * (Limit + 1))
END FUNCTION
SUB DrawMessageBox (Msg$, Foreground, Background, CurrentRow, CurrentCol)
' Subprogram to draw a message box
  COLOR Foreground, Background
  LOCATE CurrentRow, CurrentCol
  PRINT CHR$(201); STRING$(LEN(Msg$), 205); CHR$(187)
  LOCATE CurrentRow + 1, CurrentCol
  PRINT CHR$(186); Msg$; CHR$(186)
  LOCATE CurrentRow + 2, CurrentCol
  PRINT CHR$(200); STRING$(LEN(Msg$), 205); CHR$(188);
END SUB
SUB Move (Distance, Direction, MovingChar, CurrentRow, CurrentCol)
' Subprogram to move
  LOCATE CurrentRow, CurrentCol
  FOR I = 1 TO Distance
```

```
      PRINT CHR$(MovingChar);
      NextLocation Direction, CurrentRow, CurrentCol
   NEXT I
END SUB
SUB NextLocation (Direction, CurrentRow, CurrentCol)
' Subprogram to change to next location
   SELECT CASE Direction
     CASE 1
       CurrentCol = CurrentCol + 1
     CASE 2
       CurrentCol = CurrentCol - 1
     CASE 3
       2CurrentRow = CurrentRow - 1
     CASE 4
       CurrentRow = CurrentRow + 1
   END SELECT
   LOCATE CurrentRow, CurrentCol
END SUB
FUNCTION NotYetDone (CurrentRow, CurrentCol)
' Function to check for end
   IF (CurrentRow < 22) OR (CurrentCol < 68) THEN
     NotYetDone = 1
   ELSE
     NotYetDone = 0
   END IF
END FUNCTION
SUB SoundTone (SoundCancel, SoundBase, SoundTime)
' Subprogram to sound tones
   IF SoundCancel THEN SOUND 100, 0          ' cancel previous
   SOUND SoundBase + 750 * RND, SoundTime    ' generate random tone
END SUB
```

# ALL-CHAR: Show All PC Characters (Chapters 12, 15)

```
' Main Program
  DEFINT A-Z
  DECLARE SUB DoSetup ()
  DECLARE SUB ShowChar (CharValue)
  COMMON SHARED VideoSegment
  DoSetup
  FOR CharValue = 0 TO 255
  ShowChar (CharValue)
  NEXT CharValue
  LOCATE 23, 24: COLOR 1
SUB DoSetup
' Subroutine to do set-up work
  SCREEN 0: WIDTH 80: CLS
  LOCATE 3, 25: COLOR 1
  PRINT "The Complete PC Character Set";
  VideoSegment = 0
  DEF SEG = &H40: VideoMode = PEEK(&H49)
  IF VideoMode = 7 THEN VideoSegment = &HB000
```

```
  IF VideoMode < 4 THEN VideoSegment = &HB800
  IF VideoSegment = 0 THEN
    LOCATE 12, 25
    PRINT "Error: unfamiliar video mode!"
    END
  END IF
END SUB
SUB ShowChar (CharValue)
' Subroutine to show each character
  Row = CharValue MOD 16 + 5
  Col = (CharValue \ 16) * 3 + 16
  ScreenOffset = Row * 160 + Col * 2
  DEF SEG = VideoSegment
  POKE ScreenOffset, CharValue
END SUB
```

# REF-CHAR: Characters with Reference Numbers (Chapter 12)

```
' Main Program
  DEFINT A-Z
  DECLARE SUB DoSetup ()
  DECLARE SUB PressAnyKey ()
  DECLARE SUB ShowChar (CharValue)
  COMMON SHARED VideoSegment
  DoSetup
  FOR CharValue = 0 TO 255
    ShowChar (CharValue)
  NEXT CharValue
SUB DoSetup
' Subroutine to do set-up work
  DEFINT A-Z
  SCREEN 0: WIDTH 80
  VideoSegment = 0
  DEF SEG = &H40: VideoMode = PEEK(&H49)
  IF VideoMode = 7 THEN VideoSegment = &HB000
  IF VideoMode < 4 THEN VideoSegment = &HB800
  IF VideoSegment = 0 THEN
    LOCATE 12, 25
    PRINT "Error: unfamiliar video mode!"
    END
  END IF
END SUB
SUB PressAnyKey
' Pause
  PRINT
  PRINT "Press a key to continue... ";
  WHILE INKEY$ = "": WEND
END SUB
SUB ShowChar (CharValue)
' Subroutine to show each character
  DEFINT A-Z
  IF CharValue MOD 128 = 0 THEN
```

```
      COLOR 7: CLS : COLOR 1
      LOCATE 3, 25: PRINT "Reference Character Set ";
      IF CharValue = 0 THEN PRINT "1st";  ELSE PRINT "2nd";
      PRINT " Half";
   END IF
   COLOR 7
   RelativeChar = CharValue MOD 128
   Row = RelativeChar MOD 16
   Col = (RelativeChar \ 16) * 10
   ScreenOffset = Row * 160 + Col * 2 + 814
   DEF SEG = VideoSegment
   POKE ScreenOffset, CharValue
   LOCATE Row + 6, Col + 1
   PRINT USING "###"; CharValue;
   PRINT " ";
   IF CharValue < 16 THEN PRINT "0";
   PRINT HEX$(CharValue);
   IF CharValue MOD 128 = 127 THEN PressAnyKey
END SUB
```

# BOXES: Box-Drawing Characters (Chapter 12)

```
' Main Program
  DEFINT A-Z
  DECLARE SUB PrintTitle (BoxType, Title$, BaseRow, BaseCol)
  DECLARE SUB DrawBox (Codes(), BaseRow, BaseCol)
  DECLARE SUB DrawBoxExpanded (Codes(), BaseRow, BaseCol)
  DIM Codes(6, 6)
  CLS
  FOR Expanded = 0 TO 1
    RESTORE
    FOR BoxType = 1 TO 4
      READ Title$
      FOR Row = 1 TO 5
        FOR Col = 1 TO 5
          READ Codes(Row, Col)
        NEXT Col
      NEXT Row
      PrintTitle BoxType, Title$, BaseRow, BaseCol
      IF Expanded THEN
        DrawBoxExpanded Codes(), BaseRow, BaseCol
      ELSE
        DrawBox Codes(), BaseRow, BaseCol
      END IF
    NEXT BoxType
    LOCATE 25, 1: PRINT "Press a key to continue... ";
    WHILE INKEY$ = "": WEND
  NEXT Expanded
  END
DATA "All Double Line:"
DATA 201, 205, 203, 205, 187
DATA 186,  32, 186,  32, 186
```

```
DATA 204, 205, 206, 205, 185
DATA 186,  32, 186,  32, 186
DATA 200, 205, 202, 205, 188
DATA "All Single Line:"
DATA 218, 196, 194, 196, 191
DATA 179,  32, 179,  32, 179
DATA 195, 196, 197, 196, 180
DATA 179,  32, 179,  32, 179
DATA 192, 196, 193, 196, 217
DATA "Double-Vertical:"
DATA 214, 196, 210, 196, 183
DATA 186,  32, 186,  32, 186
DATA 199, 196, 215, 196, 182
DATA 186,  32, 186,  32, 186
DATA 211, 196, 208, 196, 189
DATA "Double-Horizontal:"
DATA 213, 205, 209, 205, 184
DATA 179,  32, 179,  32, 179
DATA 198, 205, 216, 205, 181
DATA 179,  32, 179,  32, 179
DATA 212, 205, 207, 205, 190

SUB DrawBox (Codes(), BaseRow, BaseCol)
  ShowRow = BaseRow
  FOR Row = 1 TO 5
    Times = 1
    IF Row = 2 OR Row = 4 THEN Times = 3
  FOR I = 1 TO Times
    ShowRow = ShowRow + 1
    LOCATE ShowRow, BaseCol + 4
    PRINT CHR$(Codes(Row, 1));
    FOR J = 1 TO 9
      PRINT CHR$(Codes(Row, 2));
    NEXT J
    PRINT CHR$(Codes(Row, 3));
    FOR J = 1 TO 9
      PRINT CHR$(Codes(Row, 4));
    NEXT J
    PRINT CHR$(Codes(Row, 5));
    NEXT I
  NEXT Row
END SUB

SUB DrawBoxExpanded (Codes(), BaseRow, BaseCol)
  ShowRow = BaseRow
  FOR Row = 1 TO 5
    FOR Times = 1 TO 2
    ShowRow = ShowRow + 1
    LOCATE ShowRow, BaseCol + 3
    IF Times = 1 THEN
      PRINT " ";
      PRINT CHR$(Codes(Row, 1));
      PRINT "    ";
      PRINT CHR$(Codes(Row, 2));
      PRINT "      ";
      PRINT CHR$(Codes(Row, 3));
      PRINT "    ";
      PRINT CHR$(Codes(Row, 4));
      PRINT "      ";
```

```
          PRINT CHR$(Codes(Row, 5));
        END IF
        IF Times = 2 THEN
        FOR Col = 1 TO 5
        X = Codes(Row, Col)
        IF X = 32 THEN PRINT "     ";
        IF X <> 32 THEN PRINT USING "###  "; X;
        NEXT Col
        END IF
        NEXT Times
      NEXT Row
END SUB

SUB PrintTitle (BoxType, Title$, BaseRow, BaseCol)
  SELECT CASE BoxType
    CASE 1
      BaseRow = 1: BaseCol = 5
    CASE 2
      BaseRow = 1: BaseCol = 45
    CASE 3
      BaseRow = 13: BaseCol = 5
    CASE 4
      BaseRow = 13: BaseCol = 45
  END SELECT
  LOCATE BaseRow, BaseCol
  COLOR 9
  PRINT Title$;
  COLOR 7
END SUB
```

# KEYBITS: Display the Keyboard Control Bits (Chapters 13, 17)

```
' Main Program
  DEFINT A-Z
  DECLARE SUB DoSetup ()
  DECLARE SUB ShowData ()
  DIM SHARED Msg$(16)
  COMMON SHARED Continuing
  DoSetup
  WHILE Continuing
    ShowData
  WEND
SUB DoSetup
' Subroutine to do set-up work
  DEFINT A-Z
  SCREEN 0, 1: WIDTH 80
  Continuing = 1: LOCATE , , 0
  Msg$(1) = "Insert state"
  Msg$(2) = "CapsLock state"
  Msg$(3) = "NumLock state"
  Msg$(4) = "ScrollLock state"
  Msg$(5) = "Alt pressed"
```

```
      Msg$(6) = "Ctrl pressed"
      Msg$(7) = "Left Shift pressed"
      Msg$(8) = "Right Shift pressed"
      Msg$(9) = "Ins pressed"
      Msg$(10) = "CapsLock pressed"
      Msg$(11) = "NumLock pressed"
      Msg$(12) = "ScrollLock pressed"
      Msg$(13) = "Hold state active"
      Msg$(14) = "PCjr click state"
      Msg$(15) = "(not used)"
      Msg$(16) = "(not used)"
      CLS
      LOCATE 1, 5
      PRINT "Displaying the keyboard control bits; press Enter to stop"
      LOCATE 3, 5
      PRINT "To see the changes in action, press these keys:";
      LOCATE 4, 7
      PRINT "Both shift keys, Ctrl, Alt, ";
      PRINT "CapsLock, NumLock, ScrollLock, Ins";
      FOR I = 1 TO 16
        FOR J = 1 TO I
          LOCATE 24 - I - I \ 9, 5 + J * 2 + J \ 9
          PRINT CHR$(179);
        NEXT J
      NEXT I
      FOR J = 1 TO 8
        LOCATE 15, 5 + J * 2
        PRINT CHR$(179)
      NEXT J
  END SUB

  SUB ShowData
  ' Subroutine to show the data state
    DEFINT A-Z
    DEF SEG = 0
    Bits& = PEEK(&H417) * 256& + PEEK(&H418)
    FOR Bit = 1 TO 16
      STATE$ = "0"
      IF Bits& >= 32768 THEN STATE$ = "1": Bits& = Bits& - 32768
      Bits& = Bits& * 2
      LOCATE 6, 5 + Bit * 2 + Bit \ 9
      PRINT STATE$;
      LOCATE 24 - Bit - Bit \ 9, 5 + Bit * 2 + Bit \ 9
      PRINT CHR$(192); "> "; Msg$(Bit);
      IF STATE$ = "0" THEN
    PRINT " off";
      ELSE
    PRINT " ON ";
      END IF
    NEXT Bit
    WHILE Continuing
      EndTest$ = INKEY$
      IF EndTest$ = CHR$(13) THEN END
      IF EndTest$ = "" THEN EXIT SUB
    WEND
  END SUB
```

# HEXTABLE: Generate Hex Arithmetic Tables (Chapter 14)

```
' Main Program
  DEFINT A-Z
  DECLARE SUB PressAnyKey ()
  DECLARE SUB ShowTitle (Operation)
  DECLARE SUB ShowValue (Operation, I, J)
  FOR Operation = 1 TO 2
  ShowTitle (Operation)
    FOR I = 0 TO 15
      FOR J = 0 TO 15
        ShowValue Operation, I, J
      NEXT J
    NEXT I
    PressAnyKey
  NEXT Operation

SUB PressAnyKey
' Pause
  PRINT
  PRINT "Press a key to continue... ";
  WHILE INKEY$ = "": WEND
END SUB

SUB ShowTitle (Operation)
' Titles
  SCREEN 0: WIDTH 80: CLS
  LOCATE 3, 20: COLOR 1 + 8
  PRINT "Hex ";
  IF Operation = 1 THEN PRINT "Addition";
  IF Operation = 2 THEN PRINT "Multiplication";
  PRINT " Table";
  COLOR 7 + 8
  LOCATE 5, 20
  FOR I = 0 TO 15
    PRINT HEX$(I); "  ";
  NEXT I
  FOR I = 0 TO 15
    LOCATE 7 + I, 16
  PRINT HEX$(I);
  NEXT I
  COLOR 7
END SUB

SUB ShowValue (Operation, I, J)
' Show the value
  IF Operation = 1 THEN X = I + J
  IF Operation = 2 THEN X = I * J
  Show$ = HEX$(X)
  ROW = I + 7
  COL = J * 3 + 18 + (3 - LEN(Show$))
  LOCATE ROW, COL
  PRINT Show$;
END SUB
```

# MSG-HUNT: Hunt for ROM-BIOS Messages (Chapters 15, 16)

```
' Main Program
 DEFINT A-Z
 DECLARE SUB DoSetup ()
 DECLARE SUB PrintMessage (Msg$)
 DECLARE SUB TestForMessage ()
 COMMON SHARED offset&
 DoSetup
 WHILE offset& <= 65535
   TestForMessage
   offset& = offset& + 1
 WEND

SUB DoSetup
' Subroutine to do set-up work
 SCREEN 0: WIDTH 80: CLS
 LOCATE 2, 1: COLOR 7
 PRINT "Searching the BIOS for apparent messages"
 PRINT
 offset& = 0
 DEF SEG = &HF000
END SUB

SUB PrintMessage (Msg$)
' Print the message found
 COLOR 7
 PRINT "At F000:";
 PRINT HEX$(offset&);
 PRINT " this was found: ";
 COLOR 1
 PRINT Msg$;
 COLOR 7
 PRINT
END SUB
SUB TestForMessage
' Subroutine to test for a message
 DEFINT A-Z
 Msg$ = ""
 COLOR 7
 PRINT "Searching at F000:";
 PRINT HEX$(offset&);
 LOCATE , 1
 Byte = PEEK(offset&)
 WHILE ((Byte >= ASC(" ")) AND (Byte <= ASC("z") AND (offset& < 65535)))
   Msg$ = Msg$ + CHR$(Byte)
   offset& = offset& + 1
   Byte = PEEK(offset&)
   IF LEN(Msg$) > 100 THEN EXIT SUB
 WEND
 IF LEN(Msg$) > 4 THEN PrintMessage (Msg$)
END SUB
```

# Index

**617**

# Add to Your Sams Library Today with the Best Books for Programming, Operating Systems, and New Technologies

## The easiest way to order is to pick up the phone and call

# 1-800-428-5331

### between 9:00 a.m. and 5:00 p.m. EST.

## For faster service please have your credit card available.

| ISBN | Quantity | Description of Item | Unit Cost | Total Cost |
|---|---|---|---|---|
| 0-672-30614-X | | Peter Norton's Complete Guide to DOS 6.22, Premier Edition | $29.99 | |
| 1-56686-127-6 | | The Winn L. Rosch Hardware Bible | $35.00 | |
| 0-672-30529-1 | | Teach Yourself REXX in 21 Days | $29.99 | |
| 1-56686-094-6 | | Peter Norton's PC Problem Solver | $29.95 | |
| 0-672-30291-8 | | DOS 6 Developer's Guide | $39.95 | |
| 1-56686-080-6 | | The Data Recovery Bible (Book/Disk) | $49.95 | |
| 0-672-30524-0 | | Absolute Beginner's Guide to Multimedia (Book/CD-ROM) | $29.99 | |
| 0-672-30413-9 | | Multimedia Madness!, Deluxe Edition (Book/Disk/CD-ROM) | $55.00 | |
| 0-672-30269-1 | | Absolute Beginner's Guide to Programming | $19.95 | |
| 0-672-30342-6 | | Absolute Beginner's Guide to QBasic | $16.95 | |
| 0-672-30545-3 | | OS/2 Warp Unleashed, Deluxe Edition (Book/CD-ROM) | $39.99 | |
| 0-672-30464-3 | | Teach Yourself UNIX in a Week | $28.00 | |
| 0-672-30519-4 | | Teach Yourself the Internet | $25.00 | |
| 0-672-30382-5 | | Understanding Local Area Networks, 4th Edition | $26.95 | |
| 0-672-30501-1 | | Understanding Data Communications, 4th Edition | $29.99 | |
| ❏ 3 ½" Disk | | Shipping and Handling: See information below. | | |
| ❏ 5 ¼" Disk | | TOTAL | | |

Shipping and Handling: $4.00 for the first book, and $1.75 for each additional book. Floppy disk: add $1.75 for shipping and handling. If you need to have it NOW, we can ship product to you in 24 hours for an additional charge of approximately $18.00, and you will receive your item overnight or in two days. Overseas shipping and handling adds $2.00 per book and $8.00 for up to three disks. Prices subject to change. Call for availability and pricing information on latest editions.

### 201 W. 103rd Street, Indianapolis, Indiana 46290

**1-800-428-5331 — Orders     1-800-835-3202 — FAX     1-800-858-7674 — Customer Service**

Book ISBN 0-672-30624-7